LEGAL ORDER IN A VIOLENT WORLD

PUBLISHED FOR THE
CENTER OF INTERNATIONAL STUDIES,
PRINCETON UNIVERSITY

A list of other Center publications
appears at the back of the book.

LEGAL ORDER IN A VIOLENT WORLD

BY RICHARD A. FALK

PRINCETON UNIVERSITY PRESS

PRINCETON, NEW JERSEY

1968

for Florence

Yes, it's all easy when you know why,
a mere matter of magic.

Samuel Beckett, *Molloy*

Introduction

THE CHAPTERS included in this volume describe and appraise the relevance of international law to the management of international violence. The principal point of intellectual departure is to consider the impact of the extralegal setting of international society upon the tasks of and prospects for international legal order. This extralegal setting emphasizes, above all, the persisting strength of the sovereign state as the repository of military strength and human loyalty. A part of this emphasis is to underscore the relative inability of international institutions to cope adequately with the dominant patterns of international violence.

The centrality of the sovereign state in international affairs is conditioned to some extent by some significant developments that have taken place since World War II. These developments shape the patterns of international conflict and give concrete form to the problems of maintaining a tolerable degree of legal order in a world beset by conflict and instability. Among the developments relevant to international violence that set the stage for contemporary international law, the following appear to be the most significant:

(1) The development of a long-range nuclear weapons technology, its inhibiting effect on military risk-taking, its implications for general war, and its tendency to divide states into categories of nuclear and nonnuclear;

(2) The collapse of the colonial system in Asia and Africa leading to the emergence of a large number of newly independent, relatively nonmodernized and poor states that aspire to become modern and viable as rapidly as possible;

(3) The widespread occurrence and international importance of political violence carried on within the borders of a single state, soliciting outside intervention and tending to blur the distinction between civil war and international war, and resulting in the virtual suspension of legal doctrines associated with nonintervention and territorial sovereignty;

(4) The accelerating drive on the part of the poor states to revise the international legal order by increasing its welfare and wealth-distributing activities and by mobilizing the political support needed to eliminate racism and colonialism in Southern Africa;

(5) The spread of Communist influence to the Afro-Asian world, generating a Western reaction, especially on the part of the United States, that has led to an ideological struggle for preeminence waged on global dimensions;

(6) The emergence of regional and subregional supranational actors of varying degrees of cohesion and formality who play an increasing role in managing and terminating conflict within their relevant area, as well as in determining the legitimacy or not of a contested use of violence;

(7) The slow, but discernible, growth of a community-centered idea of consensus as the basis of legal authority in international society, thereby supplanting the sovereignty-centered idea of consent that has served as the basis of authority in international law since the Peace of Westphalia in 1648;

(8) The embryonic stages of acknowledgment that individuals are entitled to access to domestic legal institutions, especially courts, to test whether the acts of a government on behalf of the state (even in the area of war and peace) conform to international law, and if not, to enjoin these acts or receive compensation for any damage sustained by governmental acts in violation of international law;

(9) The increasing emphasis on strengthening the procedural norms that regulate recourse to international violence and that provide for regional and global assessments of legally controversial uses of force in international relations. Offsetting this emphasis has been a relative decline of interest in strengthening substantive norms purporting to identify authoritatively what constitutes permissible and impermissible international violence; this decline is evidenced, for instance, in the loss of interest in negotiating an agreed treaty definition of the concept of aggression, or, for that matter, of such related concepts as "self-defense" and "armed attack."

What are some of the consequences of these developments for approaching the study of the relevance of international law to the management of international conflict? First of all, the definite prohibitions upon recourse to international violence that are contained in the Charter of the United Nations and in the rules of positive international law offer limited guidance as to the character of permissible recourse to international violence.[1] The Charter allows sovereign states to use force *only* in self-defense against an armed attack across an international boundary. Such a spatial concept of action and reaction is not easily adapted to the most serious contemporary situations of

[1] It is also possible to maintain that the prohibitions on the Charter are not definite and that states retain considerable discretion to act in individual and collective self-defense as they deem circumstances warrant. The modest role of the Charter exists, therefore, whether one concludes that state practice has departed from the *definite* rules embodied therein or one concludes that state practice is compatible because the Charter rules are *indefinite*. In either event, the Charter abridgements of state sovereignty do not appear to be significant alteration of pre-Charter patterns of legal expectation.

international violence—namely, nuclear warfare and civil war intensified by one or more foreign intervention. In the case of nuclear war there is no real confidence, even in this period of relatively invulnerable missile systems located underwater and underground, that a state anticipating a nuclear attack can be reasonably expected to wait until it occurs before responding; perhaps it is more accurate to suggest that the intricate logic of nuclear strategy is neither explicitly nor implicitly coordinated with Charter conceptions, and that the limits on using nuclear weapons derive more from prudence and inhibition than from any reasonable acceptance of the limiting character of notions of armed attack and self-defense.

Similarly, with respect to the kind of large-scale civil war that generates the military participation of third states, the ideas of restraint embodied in the Charter are of declining significance. The ideological conflict among leading states usually prevents the formation of a political consensus as to whether participation in civil strife is legal or illegal. Without the functioning of these procedures it is impossible to identify authoritatively permissible and impermissible responses to civil strife merely by reading the Charter. The result is legal indeterminacy that accords provisional legitimacy to whatever a particular government of a given state regards as being in its national interest. The result of this indeterminacy has been to encourage high and low minded critics and apologists of controversial behavior to invoke law to applaud or condemn the respective government. International law functions in such circumstances primarily as an aspect of international communication and contributes to the conduct of international diplomacy. Rules of international law are invoked by diplomatic adversaries largely for hortatory purposes.

Besides comprehending the limited role of international law in the existing international system, it is also relevant to consider whether or not changes in the structure of international society might be desirable, and if so, of what sort, and under what conditions they might become feasible. In addition to incremental changes at the margin, it is important to consider whether drastic changes in the structure of international society might not become feasible and desirable, as well as the role that law might play in bringing such changes about and maintaining their existence afterwards in a beneficial form.

The objective of these studies is to establish an intellectual and moral climate appropriate for the study of international violence from the perspective of international law. As such, the primary concern is with the depiction of the problems themselves. Only by penetrating the concrete circumstances in which the ordering capabilities of international society are challenged by the actuality or immanence of international violence can we begin to understand what international law can and cannot do in the existing international environment. Perhaps the development of an appropriate understanding will encourage a more serious peacetime effort to appraise our arrangements for national and international security than has taken place in the past; it appears willfully self-destructive to postpone critical evaluations of international order until after nuclear warfare.

A first normative premise of these legal studies is that those who are appointed to arrange the peace after World War III, should it occur, will introduce fundamental changes in the structure of international society in an effort to prevent World War IV. Implicit in such a premise is a belief that we have no reasonable assurance that we can avoid World War III given present security arrangements and that such assurance might exist if an alternate structure of ordering the relationship between political authority and the instruments of human violence could be brought into being. As the nation-state overcame the anarchy of latter-day feudal society, so today the danger of large-scale war summons us to the task of creating new political forms that might remove the main tasks of establishing military security from the control of the sovereign state. Also implicit in my premise is the belief that human inertia, bureaucratic rigidity, and vested interests are so powerful that only after the convulsive experience of World War III would there exist, to judge from past international history, enough fluidity of will to enable changes in the international power structure to be seriously entertained, much less enacted. Perhaps by the processes of insight and education, even perhaps by simulation, it might be possible to bypass the traumatic reassessment of the means at our disposal for the management of international violence.

A second normative premise is that the need for a new, more centralized international system exists independent of the risk of nuclear war. For one thing, World Wars I and II caused sufficiently widespread death and destruction to create a need for a new system for managing military power in international affairs. For another, the interventionary pattern of Great Power diplomacy in the affairs of the Afro-Asian countries has produced and threatens to continue to produce havoc on a unit basis that is equivalent for the society in question to the havoc of nuclear war on a system basis. Furthermore, one need not accept the tenets of Theilhard de Chardin's evolutionary spiritualism to acknowledge that there has been a gradual strengthening of moral consciousness and human compassion so as to make the reorganization of the political basis of human existence on a global scale a meaningful goal. And finally, it is worth taking note of what Kenneth Boulding has called "a 'macro-learning' process" at work in the international system that has led "within the last 200 years" to the emergence of "stable peace in segments of the international system." Boulding is suggesting that it may be possible to enlarge and generalize such segments—such as the relations of the United States and Canada or of the Scandinavian countries *inter se*—until the entire international system is affected.[2] The positive ideal of the unity of mankind is available for use in the service of a movement that is vivid and universal enough to enlist the energies of peoples with widely divergent cultural, national, ideological, and economic perspectives in the work of building a more solid foundation for world peace than now exists. The essence of this enterprise is to work toward the drastic disarmament of states at the national level and toward the evolution of security substitutes for national military power at the supranational level, whether of regional or global scope, or both.

The organization of this volume seeks to carry out these analytic and normative intentions. The initial group of legal studies in Part I develops the basic jurisprudential orientation and sets forth an argument in favor of strengthening the ordering capacities of the international system by working simultaneously for its reform and revolution. Part II examines the efforts of international law to regulate foreign intervention in civil strife. It is the practice of interventionary diplomacy that has produced the most destructive forms of international violence in the nuclear age and represents the most severe challenge to world order in the existing international system. Part III examines the distinctive world order issues raised by the existence of nuclear weapons, presupposing thereby that the prospect of nuclear war is itself a distinctive challenge of the present period. Finally, Part IV examines the extent to which drastic disarmament can proceed without endangering the security of national societies, especially those weaker societies that are the main targets of covert and indirect forms of aggression.

2 Kenneth E. Boulding, "The Learning and Reality-Testing Process in the International System," *Journal of International Affairs*, xxi (1967), 1-15, at 14.

Acknowledgments

THIS volume seeks to delineate an approach to the role of law in regulating international violence through a series of inter-connected, but quite separable, studies. Early versions of several chapters have been previously published, mostly in scholarly journals. All of these chapters have been revised with a view toward their integration in a single volume and to allow the author to take some advantage of intellectual hindsight.

In deference to the integrity of the original analysis, however, I have refrained from tampering with the policy context within which the chapters were originally written. As my views have changed over the period there results some unevenness in outlook. In particular, I find myself progressively alienated from that mainstream of American foreign policy which has culminated in the United States involvement in the Vietnam War. I have, however, not wanted to subordinate my sense of conceptual sequence to make more manifest my own intellectual history through a chronological arrangement of chapters. I have instead merely noted at the end of each chapter the date of its principal composition.

Many people, often unwittingly, have helped me to produce this book by their encouragement or their criticism, or best of all, by both. In particular, my large intellectual debt to Professor Myres S. McDougal has grown to unmanageable proportions as a result of his careful reading of the entire manuscript leading to many suggestions for revision. It is hardly necessary, I suppose, to say that my gratitude is greater, not less, because Professor McDougal has taken such an interest in a manuscript with which he disagrees in many essential respects. I have also been very fortunate to have received the benefit of very extensive criticisms from Professor Quincy Wright, who combines to startling effect an erudite command of that which is past with an acute receptivity to that which is to come. Such an intellectual marriage is bound to be a happy one and I am glad to have been rewarded with a share of its bounty.

Nelson Rosenbaum, who has worked as my Research Assistant while still an undergraduate at Princeton during these past two years, has helped in many ways; especially, as affable adversary, Mr. Rosenbaum has served me well.

Work on this book has been carried on under the auspices of the Center of International Studies of Princeton University, an association immensely enhanced by the sympathetic backing of its Director, Klaus Knorr. I have also had the benefit of much-valued assistance in many forms from Elsbeth Lewin. Thanks to the sprightly intelligence of Jean McDowall, head of the Center secretarial staff, a tight ship has borne an untidy manuscript through troubled waters on schedule. Priscilla

Bryan has been so persistently and pervasively valuable, from typing to turtles, that I am at a loss to find words enthusiastic enough. June Traube and Mary Merrick helped, particularly with the typing, and always with skill, patience, and sympathy.

I am grateful to William McClung, the Social Science Editor of the Princeton University Press, for the interest he has taken in my work, and to Marjorie Putney for being such a helpfully scrupulous editor.

My wife, Florence, deserves far more than a dedication; in a genuine sense, the outcome is partly her consequence, through acute suggestion and support.

It is also my pleasure to acknowledge the permission of the following journals and publishers, thereby enabling me to reprint here in revised form the following chapters: Chapter III in the *Natural Law Forum*; Chapter V in the *Howard Law Journal*; Chapter VI in the *Ohio State Law Journal*; Chapters VII and VIII in the *Yale Law Journal*; Chapter IX in *The Correspondent*; Chapter XI in *Law and Contemporary Problems*; Chapter XII in the *American Journal of International Law*. Chapter IV is a revised version of my chapter in James N. Rosenau, ed., *International Aspects of Civil Strife*, published by Princeton University Press, in 1964 and Chapter X is a revised version of my chapter in Roland J. Stanger, ed., *Essays on Intervention*, published by the Ohio State University Press in 1964. Chapters I, XIII, and XIV were given limited circulation in the memoranda series of the Center of International Studies, Princeton University.

Finally, I claim all errors and infelicities as my own.

Contents

LEGAL ORDER IN A VIOLENT WORLD

PART ONE

A STATEMENT OF OUTLOOK

Introduction

THE task of Part I is to describe the relevance of international law to the management of international violence in the world of today. In the course of describing this relevance certain appraisals are made about whether the present system of safeguarding national security is tolerable. The outcome of these appraisals is a normative position that consists of three assertions: first, that international law discharges certain very important functions that enhance security in the present international system; second, that the development and diffusion of a nuclear weapons technology severely challenges the rationality of concentrating control over military power in the governments of the principal sovereign states; and third, that it is essential to consider whether international law can contribute to the improvement of national and international security by playing a role in bringing into being alternative systems of world order.

The emphasis on the negative appraisal of security in the existing international system does not imply optimism about the prospects for a new, improved system. On the contrary, one function of these opening chapters is to suggest that there is not much capacity for change evident in the overall structure of international society, especially in connection with problems of war and peace. It is the inertia of the international system as much as the new weapons of mass destruction that makes it so difficult to project any basic improvements in the quality of international order. This inertia has been periodically eliminated to some extent in the past by a breakdown of international order through the outbreak of general warfare. All of the past efforts to provide the international system with improved security have been in the form of postwar peace settlements. At present there is no serious evidence that any revisions in the structure of international society are being contemplated with sufficient seriousness to make them in any sense politically relevant, at least so long as peace is maintained at the strategic level.

Several conclusions emerge. First, it is important to persevere in the search for ways by which the procedures and processes of international law might contribute to the emergence of a more satisfactory regime of order in international society, despite the poor prospects for peacetime realization. Second, because the search for new forms of international order is not likely to enjoy success, it is essential to clarify the contributions to security that can arise from the growth of more law-oriented behavior within the existing structure of international society. Third, to achieve more law-oriented behavior by principal states in the war-peace area it is necessary to examine the connection between the pursuit of national interests and habitual adherence to the rules and procedures of international law. We need, then, to consider simultaneously the prospects for improving the quality of international order by changing the *structure* of international society and by changing the *behavior* of the principal actors within the existing structure, as well as the possible interplay between structural and behavioral revisions.

The problem of making international law work more effectively in international society is multifaceted. First of all, it requires a formulation of the national interests that is persuasive to governments of powerful states. Second, it requires a clear distinction between the impartial application of international law and its adversary use by governments. Third, it requires new procedures whereby the requirements of international law can be interpreted rapidly, impartially, and authoritatively. Fourth, it requires the regular use of these procedures by principal states.

Such a reorientation of foreign policy does not imply necessarily any greatly expanded role for international institutions. It may become possible to make increased use of domestic legal institutions as sources of relatively impartial guidance in the war-peace area. In this respect some attention is given in these chapters to evidence that individuals, at least in democratic societies, are beginning to demand recourse to domestic courts to enforce international law against their own governments in times of war. Such evidence, although still fragmentary, may yet be the first stage in the evolution of a new political consciousness that will redress the balance between national patriotism and international solidarity. It is also worth noting this evidence to encourage a new direction of thinking on the part of those devoted to promoting the role of international law—namely, that infranational developments within the sovereign state may do more to regulate national control over military power than supranational developments. Of course, the growth of security in international society can proceed on both the infranational and supranational level, but the intellectual history of efforts at international reform betrays an unwarranted obsession with the prospects for supranationalism.

The particular attention given in Chapter III to the work of Myres S. McDougal warrants explanation. In my view Professor McDougal has made the most significant statement of our time about the relevance of international law to the management of international violence. It is a statement that shapes my own intellectual orientation. At the same time, I wish to make clear the extent of my disagreement with what I understand to be McDougal's ideological orientation, as this disagreement cuts to the core of the entire attempt to strengthen the role of international law through the adoption of more law-oriented patterns of behavior by principal sovereign states. McDougal, in my judgment, confirms the auto-interpretative role of national elites so as virtually to nullify the distinction I deem crucial between the impartial application of international law and its adversary use. In any event, both my praise and criticism of McDougal's work helps to clarify the orientation that guides the more specific legal studies in the remainder of the volume.

I. The Future of World Order: A Comparison of Reformist and Revolutionary Perspectives

A CONSENSUS of states and statesmen seems to support a foreign policy aimed at the avoidance of nuclear war. At the same time states have not felt so intimidated by the prospect of nuclear war as to re-define their interests in cooperative terms or to change drastically the structure of international society. Nuclear weapons are retained and developed by the superpowers, and additional states are coming to the conclusion that their interests are better served with nuclear weapons than without them. And those states that possess nuclear weapons have made it clear and credible that their policy to avoid nuclear war is not an absolute one, that certain provocations might be perceived as unacceptable threats to their well-being of so grave a nature that it would seem preferable to initiate nuclear war rather than to sacrifice some other policies, and to take such risks as the loss of territorial integrity or political independence, or perhaps even the defeat of allies or the loss of foreign markets and assured sources of raw materials.

This chapter conceives the problem of minimizing the use of nuclear weapons from the central perspectives of revolutionary change and reform in the international system. The revolutionary perspective argues that minimizing the use of nuclear weapons requires the substitution of a supranationally organized international system for the present decentralized international system.[1] In effect, the position adopted asserts that the national control over military power is intolerable in the nuclear age and that nothing less than a drastic structural revision of international society can render it tolerable. At the same time, the analysis is conditioned by skepticism. This skepticism arises from an interpretation of international history that suggests that drastic changes in the structure of international society, to the extent that they occur at all, are feasible only after a great war has taken place. Therefore, the attainable goals seem to fall decisively short of what are postulated as the alterations of the international system needed to render it capable of fulfilling the policy of minimizing the use of nuclear weapons. An aspect of the argument favoring system-change (as well as of those arguments opposing it as unnecessary and undesirable) is the contention that the outcome of one's reasoning on these issues is far more reflective of a particular life-style (in the sense of

[1] I have tried to develop the idea of revolution in relation to changes in international society in an essay "Revolution and International Order" appearing in the NOMOS volume *Revolution*, New York, Atherton, 1966.

Weltanschauung) than it is susceptible to rational and objective analysis, and that, in fact, the final determination of the adequacy of the present international system relative to models of alternative systems is crucially dependent upon the processes of human judgment, processes that arrive at outcomes not susceptible to scientific sorts of proof.[2]

The second central perspective of reform considers what can be done within the existing international system to minimize the use of nuclear weapons. To take seriously a reformist perspective is one outcome of being skeptical about the prospects for a nontraumatic realization of the system-change predicated by the revolutionary perspective. The two perspectives are not entirely dissociated since the achievement of reform might create an atmosphere more conducive to the drastic changes advocated from the revolutionary perspective.

I. The Revolutionary Orientation Toward Minimizing
the Use of Nuclear Weapons

There is a form of sophistication that tends to be quite reassuring about the prospects for indefinitely maintaining nuclear peace. Such reassurance arises, in part, from the failure of states to use nuclear weapons during the period since World War II despite very considerable provocations taking place in an international atmosphere beset by conflict, hostility, and distrust. The nuclear superpowers in particular have exhibited, it is pointed out, a joint interest in keeping the magnitude of conflict well below nuclear thresholds and have displayed a growing mastery of the techniques of pursuing adversary goals within apparently "safe" boundaries. There is unquestionably a sense in which international rivals have learned to bargain toward mutually tolerable solutions of international crises. The process of provocation and response is a more studied one, and the promotion of national objectives is constantly conditioned by an awareness of the need to defuse dangerous confrontations. Perhaps the Cuban missile crisis of 1962 or the Middle Eastern War of 1967 illustrate this distinctive pattern emerging in international politics: the United States and

---

[2] Hedley Bull has argued persuasively against the attempt to exclude the role of human judgment from the analysis of international political issues in the article, "International Theory: The Case for a Classical Approach," *World Politics*, xviii, No. 3 (April 1966), 361-77. Mr. Bull suggests in his opening paragraph, "If we confine ourselves to strict verification and proof there is very little of significance that can be said about international relations." He goes on to affirm the dependence of judgment upon "a scientifically imperfect process of perception and intuition." In this essay I am contending not only that the orientation of perception and intuition is scientifically imperfect, but that it is decisively conditioned by the life-style of the observer, by the values and beliefs and fears developed out of the personal and community experiences of living.

the Soviet Union, despite intense rivalry, each taking precautionary steps to avoid a breakdown of international order. There is no question that foreign-policy elites in the principal states are undergoing a "learning" process adaptive to the dramatic vulnerabilities of all states, however powerful, in the nuclear age. The special policy-making task is to find ways to carry on through traditional modes of foreign policy without taking the traditional risks of an all-out challenge in the form of war posed by a principal rival state.

But to acknowledge that nation-states are consciously adapting the style of their statecraft to the avoidance of World War III is not to be reassured, or at any rate not sufficiently so. Although past international crises have all been "managed" in the sense of achieving an avoidance of catastrophe, they have been accompanied by a severe sense of anxiety extending even to those responsible for making policy. That is, the prospects for avoidance did not appear nearly so favorable in the setting of the crisis itself as its accomplishment now does in retrospect.[3]

The anatomy of international crisis behavior supports the assumption that some finite risk of catastrophe in the Cuban crisis was an almost inevitable ingredient of the situation.[4] In fact, it is this risk of catastrophe that is manipulated by the nuclear superpowers to support their diplomatic position in the face of opposition. Without such a risk neither the Soviet nor the American bargaining contentions would have produced a crisis or could have persuaded one power to back down in face of the claims of the other. The sense of crisis engendered

[3] As reported by Sorensen, for instance, President Kennedy considered that the policy adopted by the United States in the Cuban missile crisis involved a risk of general world war somewhere between the odds 1:3 and 1:1. Theodore C. Sorensen, *Kennedy*, New York, Harper and Row, 1965, p. 705. It does not appear farfetched that a more militant or more frightened Soviet leadership might have felt it was as important to Soviet security to get the missiles into Cuba as it was important to us to keep them out. It is true that the local area superiority put the burden of escalation on the Soviet side, but as the role of the United States in Viet Nam since 1954 suggests, a Great Power will sometimes find itself drawn almost irreversibly into a violent conflict in which it can maintain the *status quo*, if at all, only by escalating the scale and dimensions of violence.

See also Daniel Bell's discussion of the RAND study of the future by Olaf Helmer and Theodore Gordon in which, among other items of projection, assessments were made of the prospects for "large-scale war." Bell reports that "the mean estimates of the experts on this panel were a 10 per cent probability of large-scale war within the next ten years and a 20 per cent probability within the next 25 years." Daniel Bell, "The Study of the Future," *The Public Interest*, i (1965), 119-30, at 128.

[4] Among the six definitions of catastrophe that Webster's New International Dictionary, 2nd edn., gives, three are relevant to my usage: "a final event, usually of a calamitous or disastrous nature"; "an event overturning the order or system of things"; "a sudden calamity; a great misfortune." An event that is perceived to shake the foundations of the existing international system for the upholding of security and the management of military power is the sort of catastrophe relevant to the argument in this chapter.

by a confrontation of the superpowers bears witness to the reality, or at the very least to the perceived reality, of the risk of catastrophe. The use of a bluff or threat is relevant to the conduct of international diplomacy only if the intention to carry it out under specified conditions is maintained as credible. It is well understood by both sides that *use* as distinct from *the credible threat to use* would be self-destructive; hence, there is a tendency to make it increasingly hard to achieve a posture of credibility without being prepared actually to carry the threat out.[5] If the other side analyzes a threat of this sort as a mere bluff, then there is created a potential for miscalculation that appreciably increases the risk of catastrophe in the context. How will a state act when its bluff is called? Why not call the bluff if it is highly unlikely that the threat will be carried out? Might not the attempt to deter certain forms of behavior (for instance, the deployment of missiles in a neighboring country) require interacting response patterns in which the initiation of a nuclear war would become an inevitable link in the logic of credibility? It is not necessary to predict any dire consequences as a matter of probability. But the logical and existential presence of a risk of catastrophe does, to some extent at least, undermine the persuasiveness of those who argue that the international system is operating rather safely, and who support such an inference by reference to the nonuse of nuclear weapons since 1945 and by an emphasis upon the growing skill and technique of crisis management.[6]

Another aspect of the confident intellectual demeanor of many specialists in the nuclear age is the assurance that even if a nuclear war takes place it is highly likely to be of a noncatastrophic sort comparable to wars of the past.[7] There is a widespread appreciation of the

[5] That is, participants in international diplomacy are now sensitive to the precarious dynamics of positing credible bluffs. This sensitivity makes it very difficult, however, for the side relying on bluffing to do so without taking very serious risks of miscalculation. Since to carry out the threat is self-destructive, the threatened side is aware that if it remains adamant the threatening side will probably search for ways to back down gracefully. But it is very hard to back down even if it is self-destructive to carry out a threat. Such self-destructive conduct is characteristic of political behavior of nation-states that pursue policies the success of which is tied up with the prestige and ego of the nation; the drive to uphold a self-image may generate a variety of actions that cannot be accounted for by a purely rational calculation of risks, costs, and benefits.

[6] Aside from the profound difficulty in

specifying what "safety" means in the context of world order, there is the additional difficulty of considering relative safety in alternative international systems. Furthermore, there are dimensions of world order other than the maintenance of peace that must be introduced into any assessment of the overall adequacy of an international political system.

[7] It is worth noting that from the subsystemic viewpoint of Korea or Viet Nam the wars in their societies have produced a level of devastation and dislocation comparable to that which might result in a Great Power as the consequence of a nuclear war of "moderate" proportions (e.g. a war that produces from forty to eighty million casualties in the superpowers).

For a series of essays that analyze strategic uses of nuclear weapons other than in the course of a general nuclear war see

need to confine uses of nuclear weapons to minimum targets and minimum magnitudes and to keep open lines of communication that will enable negotiations to take place in the midst of even the worst imaginable devastation. The conclusion implied is that the kinds of nuclear violence reasonable to contemplate as adjuncts to international conflict are not nearly so bad as the conjurings of apocalyptic minds would have us suppose. It is suggested that only a crazed leader liberated from the moderating influence of his bureaucratic environment would initiate all-out nuclear war. Such a possibility is considered to be in the nature of a limiting human condition—as remote from the circumstances of political reality as an attack launched on the earth by some kind of extragalactic enemy of mankind.

This sophisticated stereotype of the sensibility that is content with the degree of international stability now available is encountered in implicit form in the suppression of any inquiry into changes in the system by asserting either the inevitability of the *status quo* or its acceptability or both.[8] Those who point to the danger of World War III, to the unacceptability of the international society as it now is constituted, and to the need for the drastic action of a system-change are usually regarded by practicing statesmen and leaders as alarmist or utopian, and in either case as irrelevant to the processes of rational analysis by which a prudent government should guide its conduct.[9] Often underlying a critique of the existing arrangements for the maintenance of security is the assumption that everything in the way of warfare that preceded the nuclear age is more or less compatible with a tolerable form of international society. To some extent it is the tendency of radical critics of the existing order to base their positions too exclusively upon the horror of nuclear war that accounts for the wide-

---

Klaus Knorr and Thornton Read, eds., *Limited Strategic War*, New York, Praeger, 1962.

[8] There are many variations on the pervading theme that the *status quo* must provide "the given" for policy analysis and that proposed revisions must be modest lest their consideration be deemed "utopian" or "unrealistic." This kind of outlook is summarized in a maxim popular among the conservative temperaments found in all governments—"The best is often the enemy of the good."

[9] A most convincing account of this sort of gradualistic decision-making characteristic of government operation is to be found in David Braybrooke and Charles E. Lindblom, *A Strategy of Decision*, New York, Free Press, 1963. See also Thornton

Read, "Military Policy in a Changing Political Context," Policy Memorandum No. 31, Center of International Studies, Princeton University, December 11, 1964, especially the section aptly, if unconvincingly, entitled "On Being Realistic," pp. 68-73. See further Robert A. Levine's misleading and uninformed identification of antiwar systematists as favoring either pacifism or unilateral disarmament, in *The Arms Debate*, Cambridge, Harvard University Press, 1963, pp. 282-305. Levine by this characterization excludes even from consideration the sort of systemic antiwar outlook adopted in this volume. For a critique of Levine on these grounds, see, among others, Philip Green, "Method and Substance in the Arms Debate," *World Politics*, xvi (July 1964), 642-67.

spread acceptance of this assumption. The conservative and so-phisticated response to world order radicals, then, is that if one analyzes carefully the prospects for catastrophe in the present age they are not worse than in earlier ages—and perhaps they are not even as bad—because the large nation-states are today more conscious of the mutually destructive consequences of warfare and are taking elaborate steps to prevent war; in fact, it is argued, governments are now so aware of the need to avoid a general nuclear war that it is almost certain never to take place even if restricted uses of nuclear weapons should occur.[10] At this point advocates of system-change, rather than questioning the adoption of a 1945 baseline, are inclined to reply simply that nuclear warfare really is worse than earlier forms of war-fare and to commend that their adversaries dip into the Cassandra literature on the subject, and there confront a world of shambles that entails the permanent death of civilization.

The preceding paragraph caricatures the kinds of arguments that pro-ponents and defenders of a system-change in international society typ-ically make. I should like now to state a somewhat different, more broadly formulated argument for seeking drastically new arrange-ments for managing the role of military power in international life. It is my view that a repudiation of the present international system which rests upon the peculiar dangers of nuclear war is neither fully convincing nor radical enough. It is not convincing because the exist-ence of nuclear weapons have had certain beneficial effects upon international relations, such as improving the processes of crisis man-agement and dispute settlement, generating a new seriousness about the elimination of war as a social institution in the international arena, and, in the present period, inhibiting aggressive states to some extent from recourse to certain subnuclear uses of force because of the un-certainty connected with escalation across the nuclear threshold.[11] It seems plausible that in the absence of nuclear weapons the two al-liances led by the United States and the Soviet Union would have already confronted one another in a third World War fought with improved conventional weaponry, and possibly causing unprece-

10 This viewpoint can be found in Ed-ward Teller (with Allen Brown), *The Leg-acy of Hiroshima*, Garden City, Doubleday, 1962.

11 The causal impacts of nuclear weapons upon the foreign-policy process are com-plex and differential. Aggressive states are not necessarily inhibited. In fact, the in-hibition of the nuclear powers as a conse-quence of their concern about escalation may restrain them from taking steps to curtail the aggressive moves of nonnuclear

powers. A country such as Indonesia may have greater freedom of action in the use of military power for aggressive purposes precisely because other states are inhibited by the danger of nuclear war. To advance our understanding of this issue we need comparative studies of factors influencing the formation of foreign policy in the nuclear age, especially studies focusing upon decisions to use or to refrain from using force to promote national interest.

dented devastation and loss of life. To have reduced the risks of major conventional warfare is itself an enormous improvement in the quality of international order, an improvement that cannot be dissociated from the awesome threat of catastrophe posed by the possibility of a nuclear war. Thus the case for a system-change in the structure of international society is more convincingly stated by going back at least to the experience of World Wars I and II, and thereby generalizing the need to find a better way to control international violence than the offsetting threats and capabilities of alliances formed among territorially organized nation-states.[12] The dramatic facts associated with nuclear technology are then perceived more as a symbolic event that carries to a sort of extreme the technology of mass destruction which for decades men and nations have been introducing as necessary for the protection of their security or as useful to the promotion of their ambitions. Such an anti-mass-war position need not retreat logically to pacifism as the proper ethical posture—it is reasonable to maintain an intermediate view that looks with qualified, if reluctant, favor upon violence as a legislative energy in international life, capable of reaching either beneficial or detrimental ends.[13] At some point, however, the costs associated with this mode of legislating in the international system grow too high to be tolerable and a search for new legislative modes begins. My contention is that these costs, as measured by almost any yardstick of human fulfillment, whether it be ethical or economic, grew too high in the experience of World War I. If any doubt of this remained, it should have disappeared after the experience of World War II, culminating at Hiroshima and Nagasaki with a foretaste of World War III.[14]

Such an analysis of the inadequate structuring of international so-

[12] For a conservative but acute perspective on these issues see Raymond Aron, *The Century of Total War*, Boston, Beacon Press, 1955; and Aron, *On War*, Garden City, Doubleday, 1959.

[13] To avoid freezing the *status quo* some means is needed to achieve social and political change. If violence is eliminated, then a substitute must be found either in endowing existing international organs with a legislative competence or in establishing an international legislature. I have attempted a preliminary statement of these issues in the setting of a disarming world: "Provision for Peaceful Change in a Disarming World," in Richard J. Barnet and Falk, eds., *Security in Disarmament*, Princeton, Princeton University Press, 1965, pp. 347-60.

[14] As has been frequently mentioned in commentary on World War II, the raids with conventional weapons on Dresden and Tokyo did greater damage on single occasions than did the atomic bombs at Hiroshima and Nagasaki. However, even aside from the lingering quality of radiation sickness and the uncertainties of genetic transmission to future generations, the psychological impact of the atomic bombings marked off the event in human history in a way that can neither be explained, nor be explained away, by the size of the casualties. Insight into the relevance of the atomic experience to the Japanese personality of today is very eloquently stated in a talk given at Harvard in the fall of 1965 by the novelist Kenzaburo Oē under the title "Japanese Literature in the Age of Tension."

ciety also implies a more radical line of solution than would be required if the problem could be confined to eliminating or drastically reducing the threat of nuclear war. It becomes clearly insufficient (although quite probably necessary) to achieve nuclear disarmament, or even general and complete disarmament. Violence normally plays a role in coercing domestic social change as it has in the civil rights movement taking shape in the United States. In the international system, because of its lack of governmental institutions, actual and threatened violence has played a peculiarly central role as legislative agent.[15] Therefore, to avoid freezing the *status quo* (and thus making it both unjust and vulnerable to upsetting challenges posed by those seeking change) it is essential to couple the elimination of war with the creation of governmental alternatives. Thus the task of disarming nations includes within itself the need to design a new international system that in turn creates governmental substitutes for war, although such a design for world order need not take the form of a world government in any conventional sense.[16]

Having broadened the context within which the issue of minimizing nuclear weapons is appropriately understood it is now possible to consider more fully the argument that the present international system is rather safe because nuclear weapons have not been used during the period of the last two decades. Part of the difficulty in dealing with this fundamental issue arises from the inherent limits of our knowledge and from the inability to find ways to appraise alternative risks in an objective fashion. Such a demand for objectivity is, in fact, part of what traps mankind within the *status quo*, however dangerous the existing situation may be to eventual survival and however detrimentally it may affect the growth of desirable forms of human personality and beneficial varieties of political activity.

It seems obvious that no foreign policy of restraint can promise perfection or even durable success. As an analytical proposition it seems plain, given a finite risk of failure, that however much the level of risk may alter with time, eventually a policy of restraint will fail; a risk of failure, however small, is bound to be realized if only the time interval is long enough, just as a number is bound eventually to turn up however many more numbers are added to a roulette wheel.[17]

---

[15] See Harold L. Nieburg, "Uses of Violence," *Journal of Conflict Resolution*, VII (March 1963), 43-54, for an argument on the dependence of societal progress upon violence and its threat.

[16] There is an array of alternative international systems based on imperial, federalist, and governmental ideas of political integration. We need fully articulated models in addition to the form of limited world government projected by Louis B. Sohn and Grenville Clark in *World Peace Through World Law*, 3rd rev. edn., Cambridge, Harvard University Press, 1966.

[17] But see the caveat on this reasoning in Albert Wohlstetter, "Technology, Pre-

Therefore, the fact that no use of nuclear weapons has been made since the end of World War II does not tell us anything very encouraging about the structure of international conflict or about the reliability of the nuclear peace that has so far prevailed.[18] It is true that we have no way to assess the relative risks of catastrophe in alternative international systems, including even a disarming one, and that as some finite risk of war remains present, the same kind of analytical pessimism applies. Dangerous driving does not necessarily, nor even usually, lead to a car accident, and may not lead to one even over a very long period of time—and yet it may remain entirely appropriate to counsel or coerce a dangerous driver so far spared a disaster to give up driving. The relevance of this reasoning to the current practice of international politics suggests itself in several respects.[19] First, the nonuse of nuclear weapons does not demonstrate that the danger of their future use is slight or tolerable, nor that the restraint so far manifested with respect to these weapons is compatible with reasonable expectations of a peaceful world in future years and decades. Second, the risk of future use can therefore be appraised as sufficiently great to make it rational to advocate stronger measures of restraint. And third, there is available to resolve such an issue only a calculus of probabilities, of more or less danger being made more or less tol-

---

diction, and Disorder," in Falk and Saul H. Mendlovitz, eds., *The Strategy of World Order: Toward a Theory of War Prevention*, New York, World Law Fund, 1966, I, pp. 92-107. Wohlstetter dismisses these demonstrations as "impeccable but empty statistical arguments," pointing out that a similar chain of reasoning from finite risk might be used just as validly to show "the outbreak of the rule of law and eternal peace . . . 'sooner or later,'" p. 103. I find Wohlstetter's analysis here somewhat misleading because the occurrence of a war is a finite *event*, whereas the maintenance of peace and the rule of law is a novel set of social and political circumstances, implying a systemic transformation. To revert to the example of roulette, it is as if one tried to assess the prospects for the red color never appearing at all on successive turns of the wheel—such a prospect being statistically possible, but practically impossible, unless the wheel were first redesigned to alternate thenceforth between, say, blue and brown.

18 Nor, in contrast, would the use of nuclear weapons necessarily suggest that the international system is unsafe. It might only represent the occasion on which an exceedingly unlikely event took place. That is, the use or nonuse of nuclear weapons over a rather short historical period is but one of several variables relevant to assessing the risks of nuclear war in the present international system. It is in this sense that the simplistic illustrations of the accident rate of a dangerous driver or the pattern of numbers in roulette appear instructive. The conclusion sought is simply that the actual record of experience is not to be confused with an analysis of risks vis-à-vis that record of experience.

19 The noniterative character of international events is significant here. There is a process of adaptation going on in international society by which risks are reduced (or increased) as a consequence of prior experience. Therefore, the assessment of risk is constantly in flux, and the quantitative assessment of risk level is hardly more than a way of expressing degrees of concern about the adequacy of existing arrangements. How, for instance, can we make sense of an argument between two "experts," one of whom feels the risk of nuclear war in the next ten years is 1:10, the other 1:2? And if we cannot make sense of such a discussion is there any way to determine a rational course of conduct?

erable, and not any kind of unqualified assurance that a given course of action will remove the danger altogether, or even under evolving circumstances necessarily reduce it.

Part of the difficulty of analysis encountered here is the inability to demonstrate the validity of one's intuition about the degree of safety or danger of the existing international system, or its character vis-à-vis alternative systems. So long as no nuclear weapons are used, the formidable reality of inertia and national egocentrism makes unlikely the adoption of drastic steps designed to reduce or remove the danger in any significant respect.[20] If nuclear weapons were used in significant intensity against heavily populated targets, then it would be much more probable that a future nuclear peace would be put upon a more reliable basis through the combination of drastic disarmament and stronger international institutions, especially in the peacekeeping field. And yet the occurrence of a nuclear tragedy would not by itself make the adoption of such an approach any more rational—perhaps it might be less so—than would its adoption before such an occurrence. The odds at roulette for the next roll are not altered by the appearance of a given number nor is the dangerous driver any more dangerous because he has finally had an accident.[21]

In international society major political reconstructions have always followed a breakdown in the form of a major war, and represent a part of the reaction to catastrophe, a reaction that includes a commitment to avoid its repetition. In fact, it is reasonable to generalize from international history by concluding that the structure of international relations is rather rigid during interwar periods. This quality of rigidity has certainly been exhibited on both the national and supranational levels since the end of World War II and expressed in such diverse ways as the disappointing results of the disarmament talks at Geneva, the shortcomings of the United Nations in peacekeeping, and the slowness of nations, even of such a judicially oriented nation as the United States, to accept unconditionally the compulsory jurisdiction of the International Court of Justice.[22] If one accepts this rigidity as descrip-

[20] One of the best accounts of the relevance of national egocentrism to international order is to be found in Charles De Visscher, *Theory and Reality in Public International Law*, Princeton, Princeton University Press, 1957, pp. 71-129.

[21] See note 19. The risk of war in international society is obviously not a constant in the sense of the odds on a particular number turning up at the next roll of the wheel in roulette. But so long as the risk exists and is in some sense a finite term, then the reasoning seems to hold—namely, that the danger of war persists despite its nonoccurrence for a period of time.

[22] Article 36(2) of the Statute of the International Court of Justice allows states to accept compulsory jurisdiction by filing a declaration with the Court. The United States filed such a declaration in 1946 but attached to it the so-called Connally Reservation, the most important provision of which is that disputes falling within the domestic jurisdiction of the United States *as determined by the United States* shall be withheld from the International Court

tive of prevailing attitudes toward world order it follows that only very modest modifications of the *status quo* are presently feasible, that it is necessary to wait until World War III to discover an opportunity for drastic changes, and that the prospects for a policy of minimizing nuclear weapons to the extent of avoiding their use altogether are not especially bright.[23]

The catastrophic event, assuming it to take the form of a global war, is not by itself sufficient to assure the drastic revision of the structure of international society. Among other preparatory factors in the prewar or interwar period is the development of cogent and disseminated lines of advocacy directed at the avoidance of war through the revision of the system for the management of military power in international affairs. As the experience following World Wars I and II discloses, these lines of prewar advocacy become the starting-point for efforts to reconstruct international society—tacitly, albeit unconvincingly, acknowledging that the occurrence of the catastrophe established, at least provisionally, both the inadequacy of the existing structure and the plausibility of the rejected proposals for change put forward at earlier times.

These proposals are usually generated with the principal intention of avoiding the catastrophe that has already taken place rather than taking precautions to prevent the next one. As well, the revision of world order in the postwar period is generally deflected by the efforts of the victorious powers in the war just ended to assure themselves a favorable relative position in the new international order (thereby sowing the seeds of discontent in those national societies whose interests are sacrificed—especially, that is, in the states that lost the war; such a process was more evident after World War I than after World War II). The spirit of reordering international society is also dampened by the revival of national ambitions in the postwar period, a revival accentuated, in general, by the absence of any perceived immediate dangers to international security. In the world wars of this century the victorious coalition emerged from the fighting with no serious international rivals except former allies. The conse-

of Justice. It is the self-interpreting nature of the reservation that has made it into a symbolic issue in the national debate between those jealous of sovereign prerogative and those insistent on the transfer of sovereignty to international institutions. For text of the Connally Reservation see Louis B. Sohn, ed., *Basic Documents of the United Nations*, Brooklyn, Foundation Press, 1956, pp. 217-18.

[23] The general point made here has been profoundly analyzed in the context of re-

ligious thought by Paul Tillich. Tillich makes use of the concept of *kairos* to suggest those intervals in human history when the breakdown of the existing order creates an opportunity for a radical renewal of all dimensions of experience, including the renewal of the political order. See Paul Tillich, *The Protestant Era*, Chicago, University of Chicago Press, 1948; *id.*, *The Religious Situation*, New York, Meridian Books, 1966; *id.*, *The Shaking of the Foundations*, New York, Scribners, 1948.

quence of this temporary sense of international security has been to reduce the willingness of powerful states to transfer their authority and capability to international institutions, and to cut down whatever enthusiasm supports rebuilding the system along safer lines. In fact, it is difficult to convince national elites and their populations that there is yet anything very dangerous about the national management of military power. When the awareness of a new serious danger of global war emerges, as it did in the early 1930's, then the interwar rigidity of international relations inhibits anything more ambitious than marginal alterations. Before the sense of danger is made concrete in the form of "an enemy," the abstractness of the danger arising from the mere apparatus of war—the weapons and armed forces —does not seem capable of shifting the balance of political thought to support radical change. Once the "enemy" is present, then national security is mostly associated with the superiority of national military power, the conditions for international negotiation are poor in view of rivalry and hostility, and preparations for conflict take precedence over preparations for accommodation and control.

These observations are offered to underline the point that the occurrence of a catastrophe in the form of World War III does not assure the emergence in the postwar period of a new world order structured along the lines proposed herein. The conclusion drawn is merely that without World War III such an opportunity for conscious restructuring is far less likely, and that, furthermore, present criticism of the existing international system as war-prone may lead to a greater receptivity to such criticism in the tragic event that a major war does take place.

There appears to be a dominant form of political consciousness that guides the policy of major governments. An attribute of this consciousness is the close association of power with security, the maximization of the one enhancing the other. Especially, it is assumed that the maintenance of military superiority, or at least the avoidance of perceived inferiority, vis-à-vis political rivals is beneficial in a period of tension and conflict. The dynamics of this set of beliefs is to generate arms races and to inhibit any significant effort at competitive disarming, as well as to reinforce the security patterns that have been relied upon to the ultimate doom of every past human civilization. The culminating doom does not prove anything by itself as the disastrous end might have come sooner and in a worse way if the political consciousness had been conditioned away from an association of strength and security.[24] Again neither the tendency to despair

[24] In fact, it is plausible to argue that the failure of the liberal democracies to establish in Europe a security system based on military strength facilitated the expansion of Germany under Hitler and led to the outbreak of World War II. Such "a lesson of Munich" has, perhaps, induced in the period following World War II an

over nor the tendency to affirm the existing order of things in international life is susceptible to any very important kinds of proof. Essentially, to choose a salient instance, one's view of the impact of nuclear weapons upon the future of mankind is an outgrowth of an entire world view that arises from an overall interpretation of life experience, including such apparently remote judgments about the hostile or complaint quality of the environment as are formed in infancy, as well as attitudes shaped by the restless insistences of subconscious and unconscious psychic energies.[25] It is a judgment passed on the nature of human reality that extends beyond the grasp of reason, necessarily beyond it, and has to do with the assessment of the relevance of human aggressiveness and of psychic forces such as the death wish or will to self-destruction, as well as with a kaleidoscopic mixture of undiscovered motives, fears, hopes, desires. Rational analysis, although useful for the depiction of the relevant issues, is incapable of exhausting this subject. It is even incapable of fully grasping it, as we are dealing with questions for which the mind cannot assemble adequate answers. Such questions can be resolved in the form of commitments, although the direction and intensity of the commitment may be appreciably influenced by various sorts of knowledge.

The existing life-style of system-maintenance that prevails in matters of foreign policy and world order at the present time can be criticized from another valid standpoint: its bearing upon the development of human personality and upon the quality of social relations. In this regard the *present* impotence of the *status quo* is disclosed, as is the high actual toll exacted in moral terms to keep an uncertain nuclear peace. The debate some years ago over civil defense serves as an illustration. It may be recalled that one prominent issue that arose in various communities was whether or not it was desirable and moral to equip a private shelter with firearms so as to be in a position, in the event of an actual emergency, to prevent the entry of unauthorized persons, such as neighbors without shelters. Obviously a shelter cannot function if too many people come into it, and since a matter of life and death is involved for both those who seek entry and those who act to refuse it, the purchase of guns seems a reasonable step for shelter owners (and perhaps also for those without shelters, in order to give themselves the possibility of shooting their way in or threatening to do so). It is this kind of fragmentation of the most naïve acceptance

---

overreaction—every kind of negotiating initiative needs to proceed from "strength."

[25] For an attempt to give a full exposition of the impact of the atomic bomb on all dimensions of human experience see Karl Jaspers, *The Future of Mankind*, trans. E. B. Ashton, Chicago, University of Chicago Press, 1958.

of a sense of local community that epitomizes the inability of nuclear weapons to give "security" even in periods of peace. For security is by implication reduced to the rudest form of physical survival, and the awareness of this causes a dehumanizing denial of even modest forms of beliefs in the reality of a human community extending beyond one's immediate family. The prevailing life-style is led to find protection in ways that are so inconsistent with professed belief-systems that most citizens resist the full concrete enactment. Only a few, very logical subscribers to the prevailing view did go so far as to equip their shelters with guns and learn to use them. It was more common, it seems, for people to shrink from building a shelter altogether because of what it would imply about the conditions of security in the situation where the shelter would be used.

This illustration is not fully worked out. One could counterargue to some extent that since the illustration applies only to shelters provided by private initiative and not to community shelter programs, it tells us nothing fundamental about life-style. But is it not accurate to suggest that the protection of shelters from intrusion is a model of the security system devised by nations in relation to one another, a system disclosing all of its horror in the nuclear age where nations expend huge resources to have at their disposal the means to devastate foreign societies? The notion of community, if it is to have any reality, has to be extended to the whole of mankind and not be restricted to the caprice of propinquity and nationality. It makes very little more ethical sense to be willing to blow up foreign hospitals, families of women and children, and centers of culture than to guard the sanctity of one's fallout shelter from neighbors. The contention being made is that there is a revealing, although partial, analogy between the moral dilemma posed by the need to safeguard a fallout shelter against unauthorized entry in times of emergency and the need to protect a national society or a group of national societies against the dangers of massive armed attack.[26] The concreteness of the choice in the setting of familial security clarifies the nature of the commitments made by strategies of mutual deterrence in the setting of national security. The inadequacy of any security system that rests upon a fragmentation of the unity of mankind seems to arise from the same

[26] The threat to use nuclear weapons is not, of course, restricted to responses to nuclear attack. The implications of our European strategy are ambiguous about what circumstances of nonnuclear military provocation would prompt the use of nuclear weapons by the United States. The character of this ambiguity has been responsible for our European allies' seeking greater independence of the United States in matters of military affairs, as well as, apparently, for arousing Soviet anxieties about the rung on the escalation ladder at which nuclear weaponry is introduced into conflict.

ethical premise, and the local and the universal system stand or fall together.

Such a formulation may cause some confusion. This is not a purist conception, one unwilling to acknowledge the reality of conflict and violence as endemic in the human condition. I intend only the more modest conclusion that a security system that rests upon the mass and direct threat to kill innocent human beings and upon the need to make preparations to carry out that threat is a denial of the unity of mankind so fundamental as to make prevailing modes of national security unacceptable on ethical grounds (as well as upon the prudential grounds that international society is too dangerous as it is now constituted). It is this great emphasis on preparations to carry out the threat —working out a supporting ideology and communicating the credibility of intentions to the other side by instilling them within oneself— that entails a present sacrifice of human values of incalculable proportions.[27]

It is, of course, true that modern warfare has always demanded such preparations, but somehow the implications were more muted. The ethical support for the use of nuclear weapons, especially to the extent that it is based on a countercity strategy, makes the implications of mass warfare far more explicit and thereby requires a numbing of ethical sensibilities in order to undertake the preparations needed to sustain security in this sort of world.[28] But such a numbing of sensibilities is bound to reinforce other modern trends, including especially the growing depersonalization of modern industrial society, which together are responsible for reducing the spiritual significance of modern life for so many.[29]

[27] The moral issues are admirably identified by Paul Ramsey in *War and the Christian Conscience*, Durham, Duke University Press, 1961.

[28] Although animated by a somewhat different perception of the character of international conflict in the present world, Paul Ramsey is unusually sensitive to the moral implications of a countercity strategy. Paul Ramsey, *The Limits of Nuclear War —Thinking About the Do-able and the Un-do-able*, New York, Council on Religion and International Affairs, 1963. Judged from my perspective, Professor Ramsey resolves these moral issues to conform too closely to the national interests of the United States. By advocating the adoption of a strategy that maintains, perhaps enhances, the United States deterrent while it reduces the value of the Soviet deterrent, there is created some impression that moral principles are being made to serve the needs of U.S. foreign policy. Asymmetries in the relative numbers of long-range deliverable missiles account for the conclusion that a counterforce deterrent posture is much more favorable to United States security interests than to those of the Soviet Union. On the extent of present asymmetries see *The Military Balance: 1965-1966*, London, Institute for Strategic Studies, 1965. For an explanation of the Soviet adoption of and adherence to a countercity strategy, see P.M.S. Blackett, "Steps Toward Disarmament," in Morton Berkowitz and Peter Bock, eds., *American National Security*, New York, Free Press, 1964, pp. 209-21.

[29] For an elaborate presentation along these lines, including the bearing of military policies upon the development of personality in a modern industrial society, see Herbert Marcuse, *One-Dimensional Man*, Boston, Beacon Press, 1964.

Tolerating violence as a means of coercing change is quite different from accepting the need to threaten mass destruction as a means of maintaining a system of security. It is the regularizing and routinizing of this threat in the process of organizing "the defense effort" of the major states that make it so detrimental to the prospects for the progressive development of man. To offer an analogy, it is the *systemic* nature of apartheid that makes the racial discrimination found in South Africa so especially corrosive of the moral dignity of the assenting white citizen in that society; when "evil" is institutionalized it takes on a bureaucratic and impersonal quality that relieves individuals of responsibility for their acts and their choices. We have come to admit this conclusion with regard to certain forms of coercive terror used to maintain order in domestic society, but we have tended to resist the ethical consequences of relying upon terror to maintain order in international society. "The balance of terror," a phrase apparently so responsive to the realities of perceived security in the nuclear age that it has become a platitude, is accepted as the *systemic* requirement for world order. The rejection of the life-style that prevails, then, can be amply and assuredly justified by the *present costs* of tolerating the system as well as by reference to the *uncertain risks* that it may fail to provide the order it promises. An advantage of a rejection in this form is that it is based on the *reality* of its present impact rather than on *speculation*, and reflects an ethical viewpoint rather than a prudential concern with maximizing safety, and that thereby the contingency of one's choice of life-style is somewhat reduced, while at the same time its premises are more clearly posited.

From this argument based on ethics, several conclusions emerge. First, principal nation-states uphold their security through large-scale preparations to inflict terror on foreign societies. Second, this security system has developed out of the interaction of nation-states operating as units of conflict and cooperation and has operated as long as wars have been fought among the units. Third, modern weaponry, but especially nuclear weapons, have made explicit this postulate of terror and have pushed the threat to carry it out to almost unimaginable extremes. Fourth, this new explicitness compels either a blunting of man's ethical sensibility or a radical rejection of the existing international security system. And fifth, any new international security system proposed as a substitute should include, as a minimum ethical constituent, an affirmation of the solidarity of mankind.[30]

[30] The adoption of an ethical basis for world order compatible with professed beliefs is not without deep difficulties. For one thing, professed beliefs—in this case, the solidarity of mankind—do not take account of the various instinctual drives associated with aggressive and hostile behavior. For another, the fulfillment of

It seems desirable now to summarize the entire argument up to this point so as to clarify the remainder of the discussion. First, the dominant form of political consciousness seems committed to the maximization of national security by the achievement of the appropriate level of national strength and opposed to the achievement of comparable levels of security through the reduction of strength. Second, this crystallization of viewpoint cannot be either fully demonstrated or refuted by an examination of evidence. Third, such a viewpoint is an outgrowth of an orientation that is so deeply rooted in the political culture and so intertwined with structures of vested interest that it is likely to alter, if at all, only in response to trauma. Fourth, induced trauma may indirectly and by an invisible process of psychic regeneration reshape political consciousness. Such an induced trauma is not possible to achieve by argument, but it may be related to the arts. This phenomenon of recreating consciousness is what Shelley had in mind when referring to poets as "the unknown legislators of the world." Fifth, therefore, the reformer committed to drastic change should pay attention to the techniques for bringing nonrational forces to bear, as well as discussing and analyzing the advantages that follow a new system of political order. Political science, if it is to concern itself with this kind of issue, requires methods to grasp various types of nonrational reality.

The nature of this reorientation of political science is beyond the scope of this study. However, so as to make the proposal somewhat less abstract and facile, a brief statement seems appropriate. I would, first of all, stress a distinction between *diagnostic* and *therapeutic* perspectives.[31] The diagnostic perspective would try to diagnose the present international system to clarify the nature of "the political given." The therapeutic perspective on the basis of a reasonable range of diagnostic interpretations of what exists (that is, allowing for a measure of disagreement among interpreters) would attempt to develop a reasonable range of responses designed to substitute a new interna-

---

professed beliefs involves more than achieving a peaceful world; it requires, as well, the realization of the ideals of human solidarity in matters of economic and social well-being. In short, it proposes a utopia of the most idealistic sort, something that seems unrelated to either individual or group consciousness at their present stages of development. For a perceptive inquiry into these questions see Ranyard West, *Conscience and Society: A Study of the Psychological Prerequisites of Law and Order*, New York, Emerson

Books, 1945.

[31] This distinction parallels certain more familiar dichotomies used in social analysis: empirical observation and policy prescription, fact and value, "is" and "ought." The new nomenclature is introduced to suggest the systematic nature of the disorder in international society—the idea of a pattern of symptoms amounting to a syndrome and the further notion that "the body politic" can be restored to health only by treating the underlying causes, and not by "curing" the symptoms.

tional system for the one that currently exists. This therapeutic phase presupposes the elaboration of models of alternative international systems that seeks to remove the disabilities of the existing one without creating new, more serious disabilities. In effect, these models of relevant utopias would specify a set of goals for the present international system useful for the guidance of thought and action. In addition, the therapeutic perspective must deal with the problems of transformation and transition, with how a political system can be transformed and how its transition to a preferred alternative can be guided. These abstract concerns are to be conceived, especially, as an aspect of studying war-peace issues and the connected inquiry into the nature of world order.

A further central distinction needed for this undertaking is between *thought* and *action*. We need, first of all, to develop a conceptual framework that allows us to think about these issues with maximum clarity. We also need a set of strategies to mobilize action of the appropriate sort. Clarity of thought and effectiveness of action interact in many ways, especially in this area of international affairs. Too often the advocates of drastic change in the international system have drawn up their blueprints for grand solutions without any sense of mitigating the pressures of system-maintenance or solving the problems of transition. Their proposals have been put forward as if it were possible to choose between the existing political system and an alternative one in the ways in which one might make any kind of rational choice. Such a style of proposing has created a utopian literature put in glass cases for library exhibits devoted to the cause of world peace but rarely taken out to be read by those concerned with action.[32]

We find in the Marxist tradition one model for an effective merger of thought and action, combining a devastating critique of an existing social order (including a critique of its ethical implications) with a strategy for organizing a seizure of power so as to bring a new social order into being. It is the technique for seizing power on behalf of another set of values, to promote another life-style, that is the central desideratum of a therapeutic perspective. Such speculation about

[32] The most convincing critique of the tradition of thought favoring drastic revision of international order is Walter Schiffer, *The Legal Community of Mankind*, New York, Columbia University Press, 1954. Schiffer effectively demonstrates that this style of thought presupposes that nations and their governments will accept any reasonable system of world order, whereas, as he argues, a study of the management of power throughout international history discloses a pervasive unwillingness to govern behavior by what is reasonable or by what is in the common interest. See also F. H. Hinsley, *Power and the Pursuit of Peace*, Cambridge, Cambridge University Press, 1963; Roland N. Stromberg, *Collective Security and American Foreign Policy*, New York, Praeger, 1963; and Bart Landheer, "The Image of World Society and the Function of Armaments," *Proceedings, Ghent Conference of the Peace Research Society*, 1964, pp. 232-41.

how to translate thought into action must also take specific account of the relevant historical circumstances. In addition to the Marxist orientation, there is need for a Leninist identification of specific revolutionary opportunities.

Such a reference to Marxism-Leninism is not, of course, meant in a literal way, but only to suggest the character of the intellectual endeavor that is being called for. It may be, for instance, that nonviolent movements by citizens against the system-maintaining policies of their governments offer the main revolutionary opportunity at the present time. But the point here is only that political scientists as scholars and as human beings have an obligation to promote this kind of inquiry.

Such an obligation can be discharged only by combining traditional with modern methods of research and data collection.[33] For instance, it would be very helpful to get a better sense of the values and interests held by political elites in the leading national societies, as well as to acquire a better understanding of patterns of elite recruitment and elite training that takes place in various types of national political systems.[34] Such an endeavor would help document the inertia that exists, if it does, in government circles, as well as test whether the extent of inertia can be correlated to any significant degree with the characteristics of the national political system, or whether it functions more like a constant on the national level. This kind of inquiry can use both the traditional and modern methods familiar to political scientists, including those quantitative methods associated with behavioral approaches (ranging from interviews and questionnaires to computer simulation).

But, as well, there is an apparent need to gain access to facts by less conventional data. In some respects it is the literary sensibility, rather than a direct scrutiny of political phenomena themselves, that penetrates more convincingly and certainly more daringly, especially by disclosing the connections between the personal modes of living and the public modes of acting, into the structure of values and interests that upholds a political order. As illustrations, Camus' *The Plague*, Broch's *The Sleepwalkers*, and Doris Lessing's *The Golden Notebook* suggest the kind of coherent awareness of the nature of the political

[33] In this respect I disagree with the implication of Hedley Bull's article cited here in note 2, that it is necessary to choose between the classical and the scientific approaches to the study of political behavior. It would seem to me that the more constructive concern is with how they might be combined to preserve the strengths of each in relation to whatever specific problem is engaging the attention of a student of international relations. A similar position is developed by David Vital, "On Approaches to the Study of International Relations, Or, Back to Machiavelli," *World Politics*, XIX, No. 4 (July 1967), 551-62.

[34] For an important study along these lines see Samuel P. Huntington and Zbigniew Brzezinski, *Political Power: USA/USSR*, New York, Viking Press, 1964.

"given" that eludes the analyst who looks only at the epiphenomenal level of political issues. What is needed, of course, is for the sophisticated political scientist to adapt with due caution these literary statements—taken as data—to the sensitive development of a better understanding of the international system, in both a diagnostic and a therapeutic sense.[35]

As well, the work of psychoanalysis is certainly relevant to a depiction of political behavior that involves violence. Patterns of belief lodged in the collective unconscious of a civilization, irrational drives to destroy embedded in the unconscious part of the psyche of individuals acting on behalf of the group, or even group psychosis seem to bear in an important way on the role of violence in human affairs and upon the attempt to shift control over the principal instruments of violence from one social structure to another.[36] The transition from feudal Europe to modern Europe gives a historical example of the violent patterns of resistance that arise during a period of transition between one political system and another.[37] Understanding this psychological dimension certainly should improve our grasp of the "reality" connected with altering the structure of the present international system, but it may eventually also open up new possibilities for therapeutic responses, that is, possibilities additional to those presented in the event of the convulsion and catastrophe that we might expect to accompany World War III.

Among the issues at stake here is the viability of the nation-state as the prime organizing and value-realizing unit in world politics. For those who covertly and overtly maintain its viability in the nuclear age there is an acceptance of the continuity of political process in prenuclear and postnuclear times; for those who deny the viability of the nation-state there is usually an assumption that the advent of nuclear weapons created the objective social basis upon which to build a new political order for world affairs.[38] The retention of na-

[35] Among recent writing that develops the relationship between literature and politics see William Wasserstrom, "The Strange Case of F. Scott Fitzgerald and A. Hyd (Hid)ell," *The Columbia University Forum*, VIII (Fall 1965), 5-11; Robert A. Nisbet, "Sociology as an Art Form," in Maurice Stein and Arthur Vidich, eds., *Sociology on Trial*, Englewood Cliffs, Prentice-Hall, 1963, pp. 148-61; Erich Fromm, "Science, Art, and Peace," *Co-Existence*, III-IV, 1964.

[36] This viewpoint is set down by Sigmund Freud in *Civilization and Its Discontents*, trans. James Strachey, New York, W. W. Norton, 1961; also in Freud's

long letter of September 1932 to Albert Einstein on the preconditions for the elimination of war, reprinted in Arthur and Lila Weinberg, eds., *Instead of Violence*, New York, Grossman Publishers, 1963, pp. 201-11.

[37] For a broad conception of the relationship between the adequacy of the international structure for the management of power and the course of history see William H. McNeill, *The Rise of the West*, Chicago, University of Chicago Press, 1963.

[38] See, for instance, John H. Herz, *International Politics in the Atomic Age*, New York, Columbia University Press, 1959;

tionalism, then, as an ideology of action and belief, is to endorse an anachronism and to indulge a belief-system responsive to one set of needs in a situation in which a series of incompatible needs is to be found—but such an assessment constitutes, because of the unavailability of sufficient evidence, an appeal rather than an argument.

The entire enterprise of advocating and opposing particular systems of world order rests for the foreseeable future upon the unreliable foundations of intuition, ethics, and life-style. Furthermore, there is no accumulation of data that will objectify our choices, operationalize our crucial speculative perspectives, or rescue us from the essential contingency of our judgments. Certain systematic procedures may clarify the issues in dispute, may upgrade or discredit evidence (e.g. about the behavior of our adversaries) relevant to policy, and may bring certain undertakings into domains of feasibility (e.g. the modeling of a world police force, its patterns of recruitment, command, and mission). But no matter how rational our approach and rhetoric, the decisions and policies themselves arise from a substratum of contingency and indeterminacy. This constraint upon the validity of thought applies as much to reformist critics as to establishment strategists. We have no satisfactory way to assess the relative risks and costs of any position in foreign policy, or of any change in that position. The reality of these constraints upon rational choice achieves a certain vividness in the setting of conflict in the nuclear age. The consequences of a single erroneous calculation seem so grave—indeed, decisive. The calculus of risks and costs seems so dependent on a pre-World War III conditioning and so likely to undergo drastic revision in the event of World War III. How can we assess the relative risks, costs, benefits of alternative systems of world order? And if we cannot make such assessments, are we completely trapped in the indeterminacy of our situation, trapped, that is, until possibly coerced by disaster into a reaction hoped to be corrective?

The background of the problem of minimizing the use of nuclear weapons is crucially affected by several considerations. First, the virtual impotence of thought, argument, and appeal to achieve any drastic reform of existing policies.[39] Second, the anticipated potency of collective trauma to achieve some sort of drastic reform. Third, the nonobjective quality of choice with respect to relevant policies whether prior

---

for a more sophisticated approach to viability in terms of *degrees* rather than *alternatives* see the discussion of "conditional viability" in Kenneth E. Boulding, *Conflict and Defense: A General Theory*, New York, Harper and Brothers, 1962,

pp. 58-79.

[39] On the impotence of argument in the context of choosing between policies for the avoidance of World War III, see Herbert Read's comments in A. and L. Weinberg, *op.cit. supra*, note 36, pp. 49-51.

or subsequent to the traumatic events. Fourth, objectivist and scientistic fashions of rhetoric and styles of thinking that obscure the mythic and elitist basis of our entire national orientation toward the question of "security." And fifth, underneath the whole tormenting situation, the paucity of relevant experience—we propose to test the viability of the entire international system by its capacity to avoid a single instance of dramatic failure.

Given such an acceptance of the shortcomings of political self-awareness is there any valid way to approach our subject? I would argue that there is, although the approach is not consistent with most conceptions of the ways in which knowledge can normally be used to solve human problems. The first step is to face the radical consequences of indeterminacy and contingency. An encounter with these consequences is part of the purpose of this introductory section. A second step is to acknowledge the relevance of life-style to "the solution," that is, to the exposition of a coherent viewpoint. It is not a matter of ethics, as contradictory life-styles may each give priority to the avoidance of war, one by a strategy of belligerence and the other by a strategy of altruism. A third step is to formulate the implications of a particular life-style for the problems that are being produced by the political situation so that those responsive to the outlook can begin to mobilize support and catalyze the latent sympathies of others presently inattentive to these issues. In effect, it is a contribution to work out an ideology expressive of an alternative life-style with revolutionary or system-changing propensities. In this way political analysis is reconnected to its real roots in human consciousness, sham is eliminated, and the responsibility to translate thought into favored action is fully acknowledged.[40] Part of this acknowledgment is to confront the reality of political inertia and the other immense obstacles (vested interests, habit, suppression of dissent, and so on) facing those who challenge the entrenched ideology. One consequence is to compel a consideration if not an acceptance of the dependence of the challenge upon trauma induced by revolution or awaited in the form of catastrophe or as the outcome of the interaction between revolution, reform, and catastrophe.

One part of a response to this type of analysis is to suggest that those with a life-style incompatible with the operative ideology can seek to infiltrate the existing order in more modest ways. The issue is then not all-or-nothing, but more-or-less, and energies are assembled to induce minor shifts, to accent the virtues of the challenge, to work to-

[40] For one comprehensive statement of the connection between political thought and political action see Jean-Paul Sartre, *Critique de la raison dialectique*, Paris, Librairie Gallimard, 1960.

ward a consensus based on a hybrid life-style, and to hope that political behavior comes to achieve a closer harmony with one's values and ideal images. This is still to reason almost in the void, but contemporary political structures are the occasion and subject of the response and there is some prospect for exerting an actual influence. Of course, even these prospects for modest reform are bleak because the prevailing life-style is self-protective and hostile to alien demands. In the context of international affairs, the strategy of arms control, the growth of world law, the expansion of the United Nations are a very weak undercurrent in the main river of political reality, swept aside by the logic of deterrence, the interventionary bias of foreign policy, and the enchantment of the arms race with its interactive and mutually reinforcing promises and fears of decisive breakthroughs in military research and development.[41] A life-style committed to achieving something so far-reaching as a transition to, say, a Sohn-Clark world must either get a divorce from this political reality or accept the hardships and torments of an exceedingly unhappy marriage.[42]

II. Foreign Policy Preconditions for a Transition to a New International System

Reasoning toward a process of nuclear restraint requires a framework, but the framework itself is necessarily posited. The most politically relevant form of reasoning is the framework evolved to suit the values and interests of the prevailing elite.[43] This framework, however, does not conform in certain crucial respects to the life-style that expresses my own outlook. For one thing it tends to examine the problems of world order from the perspective of foreign policy at the na-

---

[41] Of course, there are various roles played by different nation-states in the present international system. The generalization in the text is a comment on the tone of political life, a tone set especially by the behavior and priorities of the dominant nation-states, especially in recent years by the United States and the Soviet Union. Many factors influence the international role played by a nation-state, "power" (despite its vagueness) being generally regarded as in some sense the most formative factor. But the present posture of Japan is suggestive of the importance of such additional factors as history, culture, economics, domestic politics, and so on, in the role-playing process. On the general issues of "bipolarity" and "multipolarity," see Robert Ducci, "The World Order in the Sixties," and Kenneth N. Waltz, "The Stability of a Bi-Polar World," in Falk

and Mendlovitz, *op.cit. supra*, note 17, I, pp. 174-214.

[42] See Sohn and Clark, *op.cit. supra*, note 16. For an attempt to connect the pursuit of the ideal of limited world government with a realistic appreciation of the obstacles and of political environment see Falk and Mendlovitz, *op.cit. supra*, note 17. On the general relevance of life-style to the outlook on world order see Anatol Rapoport, *Strategy and Conscience*, New York, Harper and Row, 1964. On the dependence of utopian thought upon social context see Karl Mannheim, *Ideology and Utopia*, trans. Louis Wirth and Edward Shils, New York, Harcourt, 1951.

[43] This assumption is borne out by all those approaches to decision-making by way of marginal analysis. See sources cited in note 9.

tional level, and endorses a foreign policy that maximizes the very immediate national interests of the United States.

For another, the inhibitions upon violence that operate effectively are mostly of a prudential variety, being neither conditioned by a strong sense of revulsion with warfare nor growing out of a firm acceptance of restraining rules of international conduct. A part of this prevailing attitude toward the utility of military power is a refusal to forego military advantages that appear to arise from a superiority in nuclear weapons despite the fact that this superiority can usually be translated into political influence only by *credible threats* of devastation.[44] The promotion of national objectives through unilateral uses of violence to resolve international disputes is part of the operative code of behavior accepted by foreign policy-making elites, entailing a high degree of unresponsiveness to world public opinion outside of the acting nations and an unwillingness to rely upon collective procedures at the disposal of regional and universal international institutions to satisfy national security interests.

In dissent from such an endorsement of the continuing role of military power and of national control over its exercise this study stresses several distinct characteristics. First, the relevant time interval for foreign-policy decision-making is expanded to the concerns of twenty to forty years hence, giving greater relevance to such emerging issues as overpopulation, proliferation of nuclear and other weapons of mass destruction, thwarted modernization, automation, and an increase in the transnational interdependence of thought, action, and welfare.[45] A consequence of adopting this outlook is to reduce the attention given to adjusting national policy to the particular phases of contemporary political conflict, especially the cold war, which already seems to have changed its character so basically that the old images of hostility and saliency seem deceptively superseded by events. Such a middle-range perspective is chosen mainly to relax the grip of transitory and *ad hoc* political perceptions upon the reasoning process used to articulate national policy, and to seek a shift from a conflict-oriented foreign policy to a control-oriented foreign policy.

Second, the nation-state as the primary political focus of human loyalty and welfare is put into serious question. The result is to encourage new forms of political order that might acquire from the nation-state certain of its functions, especially functions relating to decision-making

[44] Such a point of view dominates the outlook of a recent article opposing acceptance by the United States of a proposal to prohibit the first use of nuclear weapons. Mason Willrich, "No First Use of Nuclear Weapons: An Assessment," *Orbis*, IX (1965), 299-315.

[45] For a perceptive discussion of some of these issues see Kenneth N. Waltz, "Contention and Management in International Relations," *World Politics*, XVII (July 1965), 720-44.

concerned with the use and regulation of force, with legislative procedures for redistributing wealth and income, and with the attainment and maintenance of minimum human rights. One way to summarize the outlook is to distinguish levels of analysis, proclaiming a wider policy-forming relevance for the conclusions reached at the levels of regional and global outlook and a reduced relevance for those of a national outlook, at least so far as the latter proceed on various war-peace issues from a zero-sum perspective.[46] Human welfare becomes more closely associated with regional welfare, and even global welfare, and is less clearly the crystallization of national welfare.[47] Another approach to this matter would be to work toward a national perception of international relations as a network of interaction, one far less dominated by conflict than by the potentialities for collaborative conduct, and including especially a potential for the resolution of conflict.[48]

And third, a far more constrained sense of national discretion with respect to the use of violence in world affairs is displayed, especially with respect to the threatened or actual use of nuclear weapons. This constrained sense could be manifested in several ways worthy of concise enumeration:

(1) A more visible and intense commitment to existing legal rules prohibiting recourse to force except as a response to an armed attack by one country upon another.[49]

(2) An acceptance of the need for community review at the regional and global level in the event that a use of force under (1) is challenged as impermissible.

[46] The "zero-sum" notion is here used in a metaphorical sense to highlight the contrast between cooperation and conflict in various contexts of foreign policy-making. In each actual case there is, of course, "a mix"—we know that "our gain" is not mechanically equivalent to "their loss," but the dominant idiom shaping thought and action is one of a rivalry for coveted "goods" in which the outcomes are measured in terms of the relative adjustment of rival claims. The major arenas of cold war struggle are understood in this fashion, especially by the nations leading respective alliances. Deference to regional and global perspectives in these contexts might lead to a more mediational, less adversary, approach to the adjustment of conflict.

[47] This generalization has less relevance, perhaps, to the rather newly formed states of Asia and Africa, states in which the search for dignity and self-respect may be best fulfilled by an emphasis upon na-tional identity and by the pride of nationalism.

[48] Among other approaches to this conclusion see Vincent Rock, *The Strategy of Interdependence*, New York, Scribners, 1964; and Roger Fisher, "Fractionating Conflict," in Roger Fisher, ed., *International Conflict and Behavioral Science*, New York, Basic Books, 1964.

[49] Rules most authoritatively found in the Charter of the United Nations, especially in Articles 2(4) and 51; for a conflicting assessment of these rules see Louis Henkin, "Force, Intervention, and Neutrality in Contemporary International Law" and Myres S. McDougal's critical comments thereon in *Proceedings, the American Society of International Law, 1963*, pp. 147-69. McDougal's view also seems to underlie the thinking of Julius Stone in *Quest for Survival: The Role of Law and Foreign Policy*, Cambridge, Harvard University Press, 1961.

(3) Some serious attempt to posit in advance criteria for the identification of "aggression" and "self-defense" so that the processes of national decision under (1) and the procedures of community review under (2) can approximate principled decision rather than reflect *ad hoc* political majorities.

(4) An increased willingness to subordinate national policy to regional and global policy in the peacekeeping area, thereby fostering the growth and perception of international institutions as autonomous actors in international life.

(5) An effort to clarify the rules of the game regulating participation in internal wars, bringing influence and resources to bear so that the internal warfare is insulated from outside interference and is not allowed to become an arena of competing interventions, and seeking settlements for internal wars in a manner consistent with the manifest general will of the world community.[50]

(6) A deference to the international consensus evolving in favor of a complete prohibition of nuclear weapons, involving a classification of these weapons as possessing the same proscribed status as poison gas and bacteriological weapons.[51]

(7) A show of primary ethical allegiance to the unity of mankind as transcending national boundaries and as constituting an indispensable ingredient of the policy-forming process at the national level.

III. The Role of Nuclear Weapons in the Formation of a Transition Strategy

The outlook partially depicted is an aspect of a transition strategy to promote a system-change in international society, a change that may be summarized as the shift from an internationally organized world to a supranationally organized world.[52] The effort at preventing war concentrates upon the structural revision of international society and the ethical transformation of political man. The supranationalizing of world politics would involve the reduction of national power and influence through drastic disarmament and the expansion of international

50 For some thoughts as to how this task might proceed see Chapter IV.

51 Among the recent manifestations of this consensus the following might be mentioned: General Assembly Resolution 1653, XVI; Schema XIII adopted at the Ecumenical Council ending in 1965; Shimoda and others v. Japan, decided on December 7, 1963, by the Tokyo District Court and reprinted in English in *1964 Japanese Annual of International Law*, VIII, pp. 212-252. See Chapter XII for detailed discussion.

52 For some of the values at stake in the choice between an internationally organized and a supranationally organized world see Klaus Knorr, "Supranational versus International Models for General and Complete Disarmament," in Barnet and Falk, eds., *Security in Disarmament*, pp. 384-410. The idea of transition as a focus of system-changing analysis is treated in Falk and Saul H. Mendlovitz, "Toward a Warless World: One Legal Formula to Achieve Transition," 73 *Yale Law Journal* 399-424 (1964).

institutions by the creation of a world police force, an independent taxing authority, and a limited supranational legislative competence.[53] The ethical transformation of political man involves a maximum realization of the significance of the unity of mankind in the processes of thought and action operative at every level and center of political organization. Especially in the formation of foreign policy and in the entry into the life of world politics, the new ethical emphasis would accept the need to act so that the nation's conduct is productive of global welfare.

The appeal in the transition period is mainly for a revision of national perspectives in the dominant nation-states. This appeal will not be persuasive until its explication is widely disseminated and developed in terms of values widely shared and goals deeply held. Only after such a period of domestic dissemination can a coherent life-style emerge as alternative to the prevailing one and act to challenge the existing rationale for national conduct in the war-peace area. Only after this educational phase is completed is there hope—aside from the vision of a phoenix arising from a heap of ashes—of adapting the pattern of policies to a system-changing perspective. To allude briefly to the analysis in Section I, the prevailing framework is committed consciously and unconsciously—by interests, education, and values— to system-maintenance. Such a framework is inhospitable to any drastic revision in the allocation of authority, power, and wealth in the international system. Only a combination of an actively perceived threat of collapse and education in the feasible reality of alternatives might permit the serious redefinition from within of the existing life-style relevant to the conduct of world politics.

In the unlikely event that this educational process should meet with some considerable success both in conveying an alternative life-style and in causing the modification of the prevailing life-style, then its level of influence would depend upon the extent to which it received positive and negative reinforcement in its initial experimental and controversial undertakings. Of course, it would be almost essential that

[53] This kind of future system of world order is vigorously opposed in Soviet juridical thought as "Mondialism." See Edward McWhinney, "Soviet and Western International Law and the Cold War in the Era of Bipolarity: Inter-Bloc Law in a Nuclear Age," *Canadian Yearbook of International Law, 1963*, pp. 40-81, esp. pp. 52-63. Cf. also Appendix, "The Russian Idea of a World Without Arms," in Arthur Larson, ed., *A Warless World*, New York, McGraw-Hill, 1963, pp. 175-209.

Such a future system is opposed by some thinkers on the ground that drastic disarmament and war prevention can proceed without other alterations in the structure of international society. See Walter Millis and James Real, *The Abolition of War*, New York, Macmillan, 1963; see also Arthur I. Waskow's pamphlet, *Keeping the World Disarmed*, Santa Barbara, Center for the Study of Democratic Institutions, 1965; Amitai Etzioni, *The Hard Way to Peace*, New York, Collier Books, 1962; and Etzioni, *Winning Without War*, New York, Doubleday, 1964.

the educational preparation proceeded at a congruent rate and with a converging content in rival national societies and achieved equivalent impacts.[54] This may be an unrealistic expectation to indulge in to any significant degree so long as there exist among national rivals political systems of such totalitarian and ideological austerity that the espousal of a life-style other than the prevailing one is *ipso facto* a punishable heresy. In this sense the domestic suppression of political liberty may thwart altogether even the small prospect that might otherwise exist of achieving a nontraumatic transition to a new world order. Even if we can assume parallel educational experience in national societies it is still necessary to be extremely skeptical. The self-conscious experimental indulgence of the supranationalist life-style would not generate new modes of behavior unless the rationality of the new outlook were substantiated by the governmental responses of other actors, and not just by the presence of sympathetic foreign minority factions.[55]

The constraint of nuclear weapons is a symbolic and dramatic issue in the wider educational setting.[56] The shock tactics of films like *The War Game* and *Dr. Strangelove*, even though based upon somewhat misleading presentations of the risks of war in the existing system, suggest the power of the nuclear symbolism to penetrate human consciousness. But if we seek to educate, as well as to shock, through national techniques of persuasion then additional modes of approach are obviously needed; such modes may be able to make constructive use of the attitude of fear and revulsion that is connected with nuclear war.

It is in this respect that a proposal for the "no-first-use" of nuclear weapons makes a profound appeal by providing an opportunity to disseminate and vindicate a supranational life-style. The proposal itself, even if one hypothesizes its adoption, augurs no big change in the structure of world society, but the process of political adherence would presuppose a widespread and radical encounter with traditional internationalist conceptions of national security. This encounter provides in my view a useful focus for the educational transvaluation that must pre-

54 The point here is that it is not enough to achieve a disposition favorable to system-change in the principal centers of national societies; the various parallel dispositions must be compatible with one another. Thus if the United States favors a centralized world order of the sort projected by Clark and Sohn, the Soviet Union favors a highly decentralized disarmed model, and the Chinese favor a highly centralized, imperial model under the custodial direction of militant Maoist ideology, the result is not an encouraging one.

55 It is possible to envision a series of mutually reinforcing steps in the direction of system-change building confidence and gathering momentum. Such a prospect underlies Charles E. Osgood's *An Alternative to War or Surrender*, Urbana, University of Illinois Press, 1962.

56 See Robert Jay Lifton, "On Death and Death Symbolism: The Hiroshima Disaster," *American Scholar*, xxxiv (Spring 1965), 257-72.

cede what I would consider a minimum policy of minimizing nuclear weapons.

The risk of nuclear war cannot be detached from coercive processes at work in international life nor from the overall structure of international relations nor even from the general problems of managing and settling international conflict of all types. Nuclear weapons are not a discrete issue—especially not now after the enormous costs incurred by the principal states in the world to perfect nuclear technology for military purposes. The role of nuclear weapons is too crucial to the existing security system to be changed in any fundamental way without a simultaneous change of comparable and offsetting magnitude in the security system—its structure and assumptions—itself. Therefore, this elaborate formulation of what is at most an approach leads to the modest conclusion that we cannot hope to resolve the nuclear issue as an independent one.

IV. Conclusion

The simultaneous acceptance of revolutionary and reformist modes of reasoning about the state of international society may seem to involve an inconsistency. Can it not be said, for instance, that if the international situation warrants a revolutionary transformation, then reasoning about system-maintaining reform *has* a distracting effect? It is logically possible to give an affirmative answer to this question, but it is not my answer, at least not yet. The contingency of our knowledge about the degree of danger in the existing international system and in proposed alternatives to it induces intellectual humility. A consequence of this humility is to recognize that one cannot be sure about what is to be done, and for this reason different possibilities for constructive action exist.

In terms of preventing a third world war, then, this chapter has argued that a radical transformation of the international system in the direction of limited world government seems necessary, but that at the same time its creation seems impossible given the inertia and values of governing elites. And also, considered quite apart from the question of instituting drastic change, its creation might also be at this stage of human history the wrong sort of revision to contemplate, leading to heightened risks of breakdown or tyranny.

Given this uncertainty about what should be done and observing the strong restrictions upon what is likely to be done, there is reason to consider how the existing international system might be improved, including even how it might develop capabilities to assure its maintenance under such severe stress as various forms of nuclear warfare. It is true that the success of reform may diminish the prospect of revolution, but such diminution is neither necessarily certain nor is it even correlated with international affairs with sufficient definiteness to warrant opposition to reform on the assumption that if the existing order can be perceived as bad enough, a newer, better one is more likely to be brought into being. Since the connection between the advocacy of reform and revolution is so conjectural, it seems responsible, as well as consistent, to advocate both at once.

In addition, if the underlying commitment is to a revolutionary change in international society, then measures of reform can be approached in the spirit of transition, as steps taken to create the confidence and shape the attitudes that will support the acceptance of more far-reaching changes later on. Reform then becomes an adjunct of the revolutionist's strategy, especially insofar as the revolution is sought to be induced by nontraumatic means—that is, without the experience of a great war. It may also be the case that revolutionary transformations can be brought about by a gradual process consisting of steps perceived as "reform" because each was understood in isolation from the others. The process of decolonization in the period since 1945 gives some support to this way of putting the issue of how to go about drastically improving the quality of world order without seeming to do anything very fundamental.

The involvement by the United States in Viet Nam during the past decade may create some kind of potential for revolutionary action in international society. In response to the difficulties of ending the war in Viet Nam, there is a widespread questioning here and abroad about the methods by which military power is brought to bear to influence the outcome of international conflicts. Part of this questioning concerns the legitimacy of using military power without some sort of authorization by community procedures broader than the foreign policy-making of the nation-state. The questioning extends to whether such traditional control by sovereign states can reach beneficial results in the nuclear age. For the United States this questioning means reexamining the unilateral responsibility for defending governments with force against real or alleged indirect aggression initially undertaken in the Truman Doctrine, and carried forward in the Eisenhower Doctrine and recently extended in the so-called Rusk Doctrine.[57] Such

[57] For the Truman Doctrine, see Message of the President to the Congress: Recommendations on Greece and Turkey, *U.S. State Department Bulletin*, XVI, March 23, 1947, pp. 534-37. For the Eisenhower Doctrine, see Joint Resolution to Promote Peace and Security in the Middle East, March 9, 1957, *U.S. State Department Bulletin*, XXXVI, March 25, 1957, p. 481. For the Rusk Doctrine, see testimony by Secretary Rusk to the Senate Foreign Relations Committee, February 18, 1966

a questioning goes to the very essence of the subject matter of this volume as it suggests some disposition in a principal state (a disposition that may, however, amount to nothing more than weak nerves during the costly phases of the war in Viet Nam) to question the way in which military power is used to influence political behavior in world affairs. To restructure the use of military power by increasing the role of collective procedures (whether regional or global) might be a structural change of such proportions that in retrospect it would appear revolutionary. At least, this possibility is worth pondering as we grope toward a settlement in Viet Nam and beyond.

There are, then, two intertwined conclusions. First, reform and revolution in the international system are not mutually exclusive perspectives on the issues presented by the need to minimize the use of nuclear weapons. And second, the prospects for revolutionary transformation may be improved by disguising the revolutionary potential with a reformist ideology.

1965

Hearings on S. 2793 (Supplemental Foreign Assistance Fiscal Year 1966—Viet-Nam) before the Senate Committee on Foreign Relations, 89th Cong., 2nd Sess., Part 1, pp. 563-684; and James Reston, "The Rusk Doctrine," *New York Times,* Section IV, February 20, 1966, p. 12.

II. The Regulation of International Conflict by Means of Law

"The observance of law and the establishment of a stable international legal order are a necessary preliminary to universal peace. . . ."[1] Y. Korovin, a leading Soviet international law expert, expressed this conclusion in an article published by *International Affairs* (Moscow). President Kennedy's Law Day, U.S.A.—1963 Proclamation similarly suggests that "In a time when all men are properly concerned lest nations, forgetting law, reason and moral existence, turn to mutual destruction, we have all the more need to work for a day when law may govern nations as it does men within nations."[2] This convergent reliance by the leaders of rival states upon law as the means to attain the common goal of enduring peace is a significant, if ambiguous, indication of converging perspectives in this era of immanent danger and global antagonism. Perhaps the legal order as a neutral common denominator, more neutral than either morality or alliance systems, will gradually, and through time, evolve the norms and procedures by which to safeguard the existing international order and transform it into something both more durable and beneficial.

Of course, it is not realistic to rely upon law as an *independent* instrument of order and change. For law provides only the method and ritual by which deeply held values and policies can be preserved and promoted. Law is an integral aspect of a functioning social system. It is not an autonomous force able to overlook the dominant expectations that guide action in the relevant community. Thus so long as the effective elites of major states are conflict-oriented and deferential to the habits of sovereignty, the prospects for the qualitative growth of a world legal order are not favorable.[3]

An assessment of the role of world law in the future of mankind is a problematic subject. In one sense, a unified legal order represents the common dream of men of goodwill otherwise separated by morality, culture, and ideology. In quite another sense, world law is a de-

[1] Y. Korovin, "International Law Through the Pentagon's Prism," *International Affairs*, VIII (December 1962), 7.

[2] President John F. Kennedy, *Law Day, U.S.A.—1963*, No. 3515, Federal Register, XXVIII (January 1963), 817.

[3] Growth becomes qualitative only when it alters the basic pattern of interaction in the social system; it is quantitative when the role of law is extended to new situations. To some extent the identification of a qualitative change is an act of judgment and an occasion for persuasion. For instance, an observer may identify World War I as a phenomenon that led to a qualitative change in the character of international law, either because belligerents pursued unlimited objectives with almost unlimited means or because it became evident that war was no longer an instrument of policy that could be entrusted to the discretionary use of sovereign states.

lusive expectation, leading us to ignore the extent to which we are trapped by the social and moral variables of a political heritage of ardent nationalism that resists any effort, even such largely symbolic ones as the acceptance of the compulsory jurisdiction of the International Court of Justice or ratification of the Genocide Convention, that promises to bring a stronger world legal order into being. This dual reality poses a formidable challenge: the discovery of intellectual tools adequate to depict the positive mission of law in world affairs without succumbing to the deceptions of a facile and false optimism; we need a vision of the goal to guide our actions toward the kind of future that we seek, but we also require an accurate account of the obstacles that impede its attainment.

There is a second delicate balance to be maintained in this kind of analysis. Law can serve either to promote conflict or cooperation. Law can serve to provide a self-justifying explanation for a conflict position, and hence provide a respectable explanation for aggressive and destabilizing behavior; Hitler advanced legal arguments to support various aggressive uses of military power by Germany in the 1930's. But law can also provide a series of techniques to overcome conflict. For instance, the Antarctica Treaty established a cooperative regime that clarifies the rights and duties of those twelve states concerned with the use of Antarctica. Therefore, it is necessary to examine the status of law and conflict in a series of specific settings. To describe the role of law requires an appreciation of its variable impact upon human behavior as well as an understanding of its different uses as an instrument of change and order. Law is available in conjunction with the relevant index of capability to implement whatever policies achieve dominance for decision-makers, including the increase of national power, prestige, and wealth at the expense of others or the gradual conversion of a system based on conflicting sovereign states into a global peace and welfare system. There is, of course, a spectrum of law possibilities, not just a choice between the sectors of pure conflict or pure cooperation; in fact, the mix of various proportions in various settings is the most significant sector. These comments about the role of law are applicable to its operation in any social system, and are not meant to pertain only to the way law functions in world affairs.

Every legal order is assessed to some extent by its capacity to exert control over violent conflict. Every legal order seeks to minimize recourse to unauthorized violence by those subject to its norms and to monopolize for itself the effective right to use violence when necessary.[4] This general proposition points to the special problems of developing legal control over international conflict, namely, the continuing dominance of national decision-making in the realm of international conflict combined with a virtual monopoly by nations of the instruments of violence. The national locus of power raises a difficult question for world affairs: Under what conditions can law contribute to the regulation of human conflict in a social system that is decentralized in the manner of the present international system? A response to this question is the central, if deferred, undertaking of this chapter. International law promotes stability even in situations of crisis and violence by moderating, or at least by providing actors with a way, if they so wish it, to moderate conflict before it generates devastation. International society, as a primitive social system that contains dangerous and powerful rivalries, imposes upon law a primary task—to prohibit, or at least to contain effectively violence and threats of violence within tolerable limits. Nonviolent and less violent means must be developed as feasible alternatives for the resolution of international conflict. The promotion of human rights and economic welfare are also increasingly germane to the reduction and avoidance of violent conflict and these traditionally domestic matters must become increasingly susceptible to supranational regulation if law is to succeed in keeping the peace.

This introductory focus on violence ignores the complexity of the overall connection between law and conflict. To acquire a more complete appreciation of this connection we propose to examine first some general relations that have developed in domestic society between law and conflict. This discussion will be followed by an account of the special task of developing effective legal control of international conflict. With this background, the relevance of law to the regulation of international conflict will then be considered in terms of the existing world, a postulated warless world, and the transition between the two.[5] Such analysis presupposes the projection of an ideal system of world legal order the attainment of which must be gradually conceived of as an instrumental question of social engineering; if we

---

[4] However, violence and its threat also functions as a positive instrument, inducing major reforms in social policy to avoid the costs of prolonged and intensified violence and conflict (cf. H. L. Nieburg, "The Threat of Violence and Social Change," *American Political Science Review*, LVI [December 1962], 865-73). This situation today prompts the federal government, for instance, to promote the cause of racial equality in the United States. The prospect of violence may generate reactionary pressures, as has been the case, for example, in the Republic of South Africa, or in totalitarian social systems.

[5] Falk, "Historical Tendencies, Modernizing and Revolutionary Nations, and the International Legal Order," 8 *Howard Law Journal* 128-51 (Spring 1962).

want to achieve certain goals, we need to invent and propose the facilitative means. Otherwise, our aspirations are utopian in the bad sense of being cut off from both political and intellectual reality. It is not enough to project an ideal. Responsible advocacy must also set forth the relevant processes by which the realization of such an ideal may be achieved, not, to be sure, with certitude or all at once or immediately, but through an interconnected sequence of phases that amount to a strategy for coordinated system-change on the international level.

Law provides a disciplined interpretation of social phenomena that is capable of taking significant account of the totality of social reality, including political, moral, and historical variables. But law, unlike the other social sciences, is a functioning part of social reality to be understood, as well as a specialized way to present and interpret social reality. Thus the relevance of law to conflict is a matter to be settled by systematic empirical inquiry, and so far as the claim to consider a warless world is accepted as a legitimate part of the task, then the future-oriented aspect of such inquiry is necessarily speculative, although it need not be irresponsibly so. It is useful to begin by describing how legal rules, procedures, and institutions have responded to various forms of human conflict; it is also clarifying to examine the distinctive methods developed by jurists to comprehend legal phenomena, for these methods help to disclose the strengths and weaknesses of a legal approach to the resolution of human conflict.

I. Law and Human Conflict: Some General Issues

The relationship between legal order and human conflict depends upon social, political, economic, moral, psychological, scientific, and cultural variables. In general, the legal process, through its institutions, works to clarify the shifting boundary between permissible and impermissible modes and ends of conflict. As the governmental center of a society grows in power and prestige, recourse to violence or its threat by a citizen tends to become an increasingly forbidden method for resolving private conflict; law communicates the prohibition authoritatively, establishes procedures to interpret alleged violations, punishes violations, and organizes public dominance over the instruments of violence. The example of totalitarian societies discloses the extent to which law can become the servant of arbitrary rulers to oppress and abuse a population. The Nazi extermination of the Jews, South African debasement of the blacks, Communist purges, and Portugal's colonial pretensions have called, with varying degrees of sanctimoniousness, upon law to do the back-alley work of constituted power, to carry out the mandate of the rulers to sustain a scheme of domination, and to "legitimate" the entire enterprise of government by surrounding it with the scaffolding of law. It is well that those who conceive international salvation to be synonymous with the effective establishment of "the rule of law" remember that the authority of law has been used through the course of human history to carry out prevailing policies of government, no matter how arbitrary and brutal. The triumph of law does not assure the triumph of justice. The relation of law to justice in any social system depends on the extent to which the governing values of the elite in control of the instruments of power accord with whatever is regarded as the prevailing conception of justice.

On occasion, law is expected to engender conflict. This is especially true in a capitalist society committed to the overall efficacy of economic conflict, called "competition." Antitrust laws and regulatory patterns are designed precisely to prevent the attainment of harmony among firms producing the same kinds of products; the legal order thus strives to provide society with the putative benefits of economic conflict. Even with respect to economic competition, however, the social mandate is not delivered in pure form. No general welcome is given to the natural play of the forces of competition. In many areas of activity the regulation of competition is found essential for the protection of the consumer. There is little disposition, even in an ardently capitalist society, to distribute contaminated food or to establish several postal systems and military establishments. Legal order seeks to stimulate socially beneficial conflict and to prevent socially destructive conflict, and legal institutions are expected to identify which is which.

Human conflict may or may not be perceived as beneficial, depending upon an elaborate appraisal of the relevant context in light of both the anticipated effects of the activity and of prevailing community values. It is also a matter of restricting the extent of conflict. Unions are generally given the right to go out on strike against their employer, but denied the right to use violence in order to promote the success of the strike. A limited tolerance for conflict has often established an equilibrium of forces, balancing the rights and interests of different social groups, and thereby reducing the need and disposition to have recourse to either more intense expression of conflict or to more forceful government regulation. This reconcilation of group interests conveys a sense of the fundamental fairness of the social system, thereby encouraging the acceptance of adverse results by the losing side in a particular controversy. Law contributes to this equilibrating process of social sublimation by authorizing, inventing, and protecting certain procedures for the expression of conflict and for the promotion of peaceful change. Once conflict reaches certain levels of intensity, law frequently insists or allows the parties to a conflict to make use of a variety of rules, procedures, and institutions that enable settlement, at least temporarily. Law also provides the enforcement machinery to assure compliance with the terms of legal settlement, and gives to discontented parties an opportunity to challenge an adverse decision of law. Appellate review qualifies the finality of legal settlement, especially if the notion of appeal is broadly understood in a functional sense to extend beyond the judicial context to such diverse matters as executive and administrative discretion, legislative competence to repeal and amend, the capacity of the polity to revise its constitution, electoral procedures, and ultimately, as including rebellion and revolution. That is, the dynamic substratum of the social system suggests that every legal resolution of conflict must in some sense be understood as provisional, its permanence depending on its acceptability.

The coordinates of what constitutes acceptable conflict reflect the distribution of power and values within a social system. An indiscriminate enthusiasm for the apparatus of legal order often leads to unrealistic refusals to connect the claims of law with the facts of power and value. This is a familiar but deceptive ground for skepticism about the role of law in world affairs. It is deceptive because it is true for any legal order, not just the international one. The shape of legal order is also a product of cultural heritage. It is now familiar to suggest the similarities between czarist and Soviet patterns of rule in Russia, to commend England for its democratic tradition, or to condemn Germany for its bellicose disposition. One would not expect law in the United States to protect the interests of capitalists if a domestic political system changed over to socialism. Law generally helps prevailing groups to realize their interests. Thus it often resolves conflicts by putting the authority and power of the state to work for the interests and values of elites. In a democratic society, depending on electoral ratification and the delicate balance struck among interest groups, the performance of service for dominant elites is subtly achieved by the legal order. The structure of preferences woven into the United States tax system illustrates this subtlety. Often, too, there are social conflicts between central legal institutions and more local institutions; this is a familiar attribute of democratic federal states. Usually there is some allocation of legal competence between the federal structure and the state structure. A direct clash, as between the South and the federal government on the issue of Negro rights in the United States is subject to legal resolution by judicial interpretation and executive implementation. Such conflicts can be resolved also by the development of a national consensus expressed in legislation that refuses to tolerate the expression of deviant values in subunits of the system; the civil rights movement of the 1950's and the 1960's illustrates an attempt to establish the supremacy of federal elite values.

Law provides a convenient way to register a moral or cultural abhorrence of certain forms of social conflict. Prohibitions upon dueling or gambling indicate the use of the legal system to enforce prevailing social judgments about the limits of permissible conflict. The tolerance or intolerance of religious and political diversity is often a fundamental indication of where a given society sets its limits upon what constitutes permissible conflict.

It also is a task of law to formalize social membership attitudes. This task, too, is heavily value-laden. Minorities are characteristically denied full participation in the privileges of, even if they are formally eligible for, citizenship. Law can be used to challenge discriminatory structures of authority as it has done increasingly on the national level in the United States, or it can be the means by which to assure the imposition of unequal standards as in the legal system evolved by South Africa. Often a social conflict is fought out as a battle between different orders of normative authority. For instance, to what extent is Congress able to restrain activities of the United States Communist party? The answers to this question depend upon how the courts interpret the relationship between legislative action and constitutional provision; the Attorney General (through his use or nonuse of prosecutor initiative), Congress, the Constitution, and the Supreme Court are all functional parts of the legal order, and "the law" on a given point represents a dynamic adjustment between those separate rules and institutions, constantly subject to readjustment. What we call "the law" is often a process developed for the reconciliation of "laws" or claims to establish a particular normative conclusion that is provisional, subject to repeal or reversal later on.

Law helps to standardize behavior, thereby making it possible for people to plan their conduct in the light of reliable expectations. It is not so important whether cars drive on the left or right, but it is obviously important that they do one or the other. Safety and health regulations respond to the complicated reliance needs of a modern industrial society. Similarly, public regulation of corporate security issues gives a certain minimum protection to investor activities. This is partly a matter of achieving certain substantive results—the prevention of cheating—but it is also an endeavor to give people confidence to rely upon the offer of a bargain. This confidence is essential for the health of a credit economy resting upon a high level of private investment.

When the organized legal community takes over certain activities vital to human security it must provide adequate substitutes. The elimination of self-help remedies in the Wild West was not consistently successful until an effective constabulary could protect victims of abuse; many individuals were unwilling to change their habits and surrender their instruments of violence to the authority of the state until they could clearly perceive that governmental control was a superior alternative.[6] Such a transition from private to public responsibility often requires a vivid appreciation of the deficiencies of the existing security system; blood feuds were often replaced by the apparatus of social justice in the midst of tragedy. International disarmament awaits both the emergence of substitutes for national security systems and a widespread understanding of the tragic shortcomings of the existing pattern of defense. Law cannot autonomously generate the arrangements needed for the control of certain forms of human conflict. Law must await a favorable social disposition, although the advance blueprinting of suitable arrangements may influence the social climate by adducing evidence, perhaps decisively, on the issue of whether it is feasible to change reliance patterns. For the transfer of power often depends upon confidence that the transferee can perform as anticipated. This lack of confidence is more responsible than any other factor for the disappointingly slow growth of world legal order.

It is necessarily the case that certain actors will find that law imposes obligations or makes determinations that frustrate their vital interests or are incompatible with their ethical conscience. A man steals from the rich to feed the poor, one state intervenes in the affairs of another to prevent persecution or genocide, or an official in a totalitarian regime commits some form of treason. It is both logically and existentially possible to reject the particular ways in which law chooses to regulate conflict, especially if the law is the instrument of a social order that is itself considered to be unjust. There is an important distinction between denying the claims of an entire *legal system* and the claims of a *particular rule* in that system that parallels the distinction between a revolutionary and a mere lawbreaker or reformer. The U-2 overflights of the Soviet Union and other foreign states indicates a repudiation by the United States of the *particular rule* establishing the exclusive authority of the subjacent state over manned aircraft, whereas participation in a scheme to seize the power of the state to establish

---

[6] It should be remembered that such a right of self-help is to some degree preserved in the Third Amendment to the United States Constitution: "A well regulated Militia, being necessary to the security of a free State, the right of the people to keep and bear Arms, shall not be infringed."

a new social order is a denial of the *entire system* of authority. It is inappropriate to make an uncritical connection between the claims of law and duties of obedience. However, if there is general approval of a social order, especially a weak one, then it may be important to comply with particular rules, however objectionable, to promote the growth and strength of the system as a whole. Violations of particular rules of international law should be understood as entailing the serious consequence of further weakening a weak fabric of law-obedience.

It is evident that domestic law establishes many postures toward particular conflicts: it may reinforce the claims of one side (civil rights), it may mediate between the ground rules for conflict by specifying permissible limits and procedures (strikes, mass demonstrations), it may provide arrangements for the resolution of conflict (courts), it may prohibit certain means (violence) or interdict certain ends (racial discrimination). In general, law tries to implement the values of those in control of the governmental machinery. These values usually include stability and order which may require some deference to community expectations that dissent from elite values, and the values of the elite may genuinely represent the interests of the community that they control. The response of law to conflict is just one aspect of the complex commitment of government to the achievement of prevailing values.

II. The Quest for Legal Control over International Violence[7]

Legal order has enjoyed reasonable success in its efforts to manage conflict arising out of the relations between social units other than states. The legal control of international conflict is hampered by the weakness of centralized sources of authority and by the concentration of the instruments of violence on the national level. Therefore, unauthorized violence as a means to resolve crucial conflicts has been rather frequent and of spectacular magnitude in the history of international affairs. The absence of an international legislature has often allowed unauthorized coercion to play a constructive role in bringing about desirable social changes in the history of international relations. Just as the opportunity for, and threat of, revolution are available to challenge domestic oppression, so the possibility of international

[7] Accompanying efforts to establish a legislative process in world affairs must parallel the attempt to eliminate violence from international relations. Perhaps the notion of "elimination" is misleading; for it is more a matter of removing certain especially destructive instruments of violence (weapons of mass destruction) and centralizing in international institutions the authority and capability to threaten or use violence to reach certain community goals.

war has created the opportunity for the more exuberant and progressive nations to expand their beneficial influence in international society; at least this rationalization has been widely accepted and can be supported with considerable evidence.

The special crisis of the contemporary world arises because the costs and dangers of unauthorized national violence, always high and occasionally intolerable, must be understood in terms of the existence of long-range thermonuclear weaponry. Thus the traditional willingness to allow violence to serve as a means to resolve international conflict, a tolerance that has long been tormenting to many of those familiar with the brutality and suffering occasioned by warfare, is now challenged by the dismal prospect of an eventual catastrophe of global proportions. This objective situation, accented by radical changes in the status and outlook of the less industrialized states, prompts a search for new ways to gain control over national capabilities to use violence for conflict resolution. There is a much smaller margin of tolerance for violence in international affairs than in domestic society. We read of unsolved homicides in daily newspapers without losing confidence in the viability of the domestic legal order. Not so with an international delinquency. For single instances of international delinquency tend to be perceived as decisive enough to undermine the credibility of the regulative authority claimed on behalf of international law as a whole. And especially with nuclear warfare as a serious possibility, a legal system that cannot give virtually perfect assurance that it can prevent unauthorized violence will be perceived, and quite prudently so, as almost worthless, providing inadequate protection against potential dangers. Thus the devastating consequence of inadequately controlled international conflict imposes a requirement upon international order that no domestic society has been yet able to satisfy. It is well to appreciate that it is the impact of weapons technology upon the conduct of international conflict more than the deficiencies of international law that account for the current anxiety about the dangers of general warfare. Our conception of peace on the international level is much purer than it is for domestic affairs for there is less capacity to withstand the impact of a single diligent violator if it happens to be a major state that is pursuing a major program of expansion.

Skepticism about the reality of international law also emanates from the divisive tendency of nations and national jurists to use law as a rationalization for national policy no matter how evident the illegality of conduct might appear to an impartial observer. The availability of legal explanations for contradictory courses of action underlies the adversary nature of law and is a well-understood attribute of domestic legal process. Thus the United States may claim that principles of self-defense or collective security legitimize its insistence in October 1962 that the Soviet Union remove missiles from Cuba, whereas the USSR and Cuba can invoke their interpretation of self-defense (against an American invasion) or assert that bilateral military arrangements are matters within the domestic jurisdiction of the transacting states to support their allegation that the U. S. claim of removal underlying the quarantine was illegal. It is not the availability of these opposed legal arguments, each rather plausible, that helps to disclose a deficiency of international legal order; for this is the characteristic mode of adversary contention in any legal system.[8] It is rather the absence of any acceptable means for an *authoritative* resolution of adversary debate about the requirements of international law that provokes confusion. There is no regularly available and respected neutral decision-maker that will provide the community with a principled and reasoned determination of which side is "correct" about its claim of what it is that the law permits.[9] This situation is aggravated by the patriotic habits of jurists, who in the rhetoric of scientific objectivity, provide their governments with legal apologia,[10] a process aptly described as the nationalization of truth.[11] Scholars, detached from an exclusive identification with national welfare, might contribute a rather authoritative interpretation of legal requirements if they were not drawn into the political process as experts in the instrumental manipulation of legal doctrine. One's nation becomes a client that expects a brief; international law, especially when it is invoked in crisis situations, functions more as a self-righteous rhetoric to describe national policy than as a constraining set of limits. It is true that even if nationalism continues to dominate the juristic imagination, international law facilitates routine or noncrisis transactions; as part of the bureaucratic apparatus of the modern state, international law is mechanically ap-

8 Cf. Benjamin H. Cardozo, *The Nature of the Judicial Process*, New Haven, Yale University Press, 1921; and Myres S. McDougal, "The Ethics of Applying Systems of Authority: The Balanced Opposites of a Legal System," in Harold D. Lasswell and Harlan Cleveland, eds., *The Ethic of Power*, New York, Harper and Brothers, 1962, pp. 221-40.

9 The International Court of Justice is potentially available, but at this stage of international development there is no willingness on the part of states to entrust vital determination to judicial institutions. On the other hand, it is important to appreciate the role of the Court in providing authoritative legal analyses on a variety of issues; the small number of cases is no guide to the contribution that has been made by the Court to the growth of world law. See Sir Hersch Lauterpacht, *The Development of International Law by the International Court*, London, Stevens and Sons, 1958.

10 Compare W. T. Mallison, Jr., "Limited Naval Blockade or Quarantine Interdiction: National and Collective Defense Claims Valid under International Law," 31 *George Washington Law Review* 335-98 (December 1962), with Korovin, *op.cit. supra*, note 1.

11 Julius Stone, *Legal Controls of International Conflict*, Sydney, Australia, Maitland Publications, 1954, pp. xli-xliii.

plied and scrupulously adhered to so long as legality is not perceived to impair the defense of vital national interests.[12] Therefore, acceptance of this point does not imply a rejection of international law in toto, although it does confine its operations to rather trivial subject matter, subject matter that is quite remote from the problems of war and peace.

The character of a legal order is a consequence, first of all, of the way in which power and values are distributed in the social system. Despite the reality of supranational institutions, especially the United Nations and regional security organizations like NATO and the OAS, law in world politics continues to be most characteristically applied and violated as a result of a series of decisions made by national officials. That is, nations are both the chief actors in world affairs and the main agents of the world legal order; this contrasts with domestic law systems in which a hierarchy of institutions and officials apply law in a relationship of superordination and subordination. This contrast can be highlighted by regarding international law as a predominantly horizontal legal order and domestic law as a predominantly vertical legal order.[13] Note that this distinction is analytic in character. There is no sharp separation of types in an empiric sense, but the use of these analytic categories enables us to describe briefly the distinctive attributes of international law as a legal system in the following tables.

TABLE 1

THE STRUCTURE OF WORLD LEGAL AUTHORITY

Traditional System	Predominantly Horizontal (Law developed and applied by nations in multistate environment)
Transitional Phase	Mixed Progressive (Fluctuating allocation of legal competence between national and supranational actors)
Limited World Government	Predominantly Vertical (Law developed and applied primarily by supranational actors)

[12] Roger Fisher, "Bringing Law to Bear on Governments," 74 *Harvard Law Review* 1130-40 (April 1961).

[13] Falk, "International Jurisdiction: Horizontal and Vertical Conceptions of Legal Order," 32 *Temple Law Quarterly* 295-320 (Spring 1959).

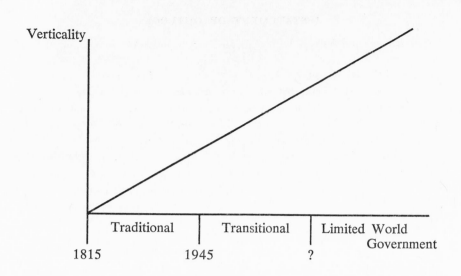

Verticality

| Traditional | Transitional | Limited World Government |

1815   1945   ?

TABLE 2

THE PLURALITY OF LEGAL ORDERS CONSTITUTING
INTERNATIONAL LAW

Type	Illustration
International Law	Diplomatic Immunity
Regional Law	OAS Claims against Castro's Cuba
United Nations Law	Peacekeeping Operations
Common Law of Mankind	Human Rights
Supranational Law	UN refusal to interfere with OAS action against Cuba

TABLE 3

PERSPECTIVES OF NATIONAL ACTORS TOWARD THE
EXISTING INTERNATIONAL LEGAL ORDER

Outlook	Objective
Revolutionary Nations	System Change or System Dominance
Modernizing Nations	Radical System Reform
Status Quo Nations	Minimum System Change

TABLE 4

THE RELEVANCE OF LEGAL RESTRAINT TO NATIONAL
DECISION-MAKING IN THE CONTEMPORARY WORLD

Nature of Decision	Role of Law
Routine or Noncrisis Decisions	bureaucratic direction expectations of reciprocity habit of respect for law general preference for order sense of fundamental fairness
Crisis Decisions	formulation of claim reduction of provocation communication of limited claim and response restrains domestic decision-making processes

TABLE 5

VIABILITY OF TRADITIONAL INTERNATIONAL LAW AT THE
LEVEL OF NATIONAL INSTITUTIONS

Classification of Activity	Category of Issue	Role of National Institution
Legitimate Diversity	Expropriation of Private Property	Deference to Supra-national or Territorial Decision-Makers
Universal Consensus	Equality of Races Colonialism War Crimes against Humanity	National Application of World Community Policy

This analytic distinction between horizontal and vertical legal orders emphasizes the degree of centralized authority and enforcement as decisive for the classification of any particular legal system; decentralization, as in a horizontal legal system has its own ordering logic resting heavily upon notions of reciprocity, estoppel, waiver, precedent,

TABLE 6

THE FORM OF APPROPRIATE LEGAL CONTROL OVER POLITICAL
VIOLENCE THREATENING TO INTERNATIONAL PEACE

Arena	Form
Interstate Violence	Stable Vertical Limits
Intrastate Violence	Unstable Horizontal Limits

symmetry, and self-help. The basic conception can be expressed by
some simple propositions:

1. State A is inclined to fulfill its duty to State B to encourage B
to fulfill its duties to A and to acquire a general reputation for norm-
oriented behavior;

2. State A may refrain from making claim Y so as to be in a position to prevent or protest a claim equivalent to Y being asserted by
State B, C . . . n (e.g. deployment of bombs in orbit);

3. State B can normally assert claim X without receiving objections
from other states that have already asserted claims similar to X (e.g.
French nuclear testing on the high seas);

4. Once State A has successfully carried out claim Z it can no longer
protest if claim Z is asserted by State B, C . . . n (e.g. U.S. response
to nuclear testing by China);

5. If State B violates the reasonable expectations of A, then A, if
it possesses the capability, will normally undertake proportionate hostile countermeasures (e.g. U.S. response to Cuban expropriation of
property owned by U.S. nationals).

The United States claim in 1962 to interdict the deployment of Soviet missiles in Cuba can be interpreted in terms of its implication for
world legal order. The American claim appears to have been a direct
challenge to the principle of symmetry that underlies a horizontal legal
order. For the bilateral agreement between Cuba and the Soviet Union
that led up to the intended deployment of Soviet missiles in Cuba
appeared to be functionally equivalent to similar arrangements previously carried out by which the United States deployed its missiles
in Turkey and Italy. The United States, supported by a regional organization eager to keep nuclear weapons out of the Western Hemisphere, effectively demanded that the Soviet Union refrain from claiming X even though the United States had done what amounted to
X, over Soviet protest, on previous occasions. This denies the validating role of precedent, avoids estoppel and waiver, and seems to assert

that considerations of security, even if self-determined, take precedence over reciprocity; such a claim of security, which was regionally endorsed and globally tolerated, established in this prominent instance an asymmetrical pattern of rights and duties. Asymmetry is very threatening to the concept of justice that underlies the development of horizontal law in a divided world, for it undermines the parity of rights and duties enjoyed by participants who would otherwise adhere to common rules; unless restricted by future behavior, an asymmetrical claiming procedure encourages states to insist that their relative rights are simply reflections of power differentials; if such material inequality becomes a principal basis for order, then power, rather than common standards, is accepted as a legitimate organizing principle of international affairs.[14] Such a relegitimation of power seems entirely inconsistent with the prohibition of force in the Charter, and far exceeds the prudent understanding of relative power advantage as an instrument of ultimate resort.

A second feature of decentralization is the extent to which it confers upon actors the formal discretion to specify their own rights and duties. This feature was dramatically illustrated by the legal discretion of a state up until World War I to wage war virtually whenever and for whatever it saw fit; the UN Charter prohibition of force except for self-defense is a significant centralizing transfer of authority. However, significant areas of discretion remain, including, of course, the initial determination of the conditions under which it is appropriate to act in self-defense, and the specific quantum of force that can be used in a situation in which a right of self-defense does exist. National control over military force and the rapidity of nuclear destruction mean that decisions about defense and security, at least at the nuclear level, remain a matter of sovereign prerogative. In other areas of international activity, national discretion is preserved in a more formal way. Such familiar subjects as recognition of states and governments, immigration and naturalization, and foreign exchange rates are controlled almost exclusively by national determinations that are not subject to supranational review. National officials in courts and foreign offices also interpret applicable rules from a position that ranges from impartiality to one that is an explicit application of national foreign policy, as when a domestic court defers to executive policy if called upon to determine the validity of a claim of sovereign immunity put forth by a defendant political entity.

[14] Cf. Oliver J. Lissitzyn, "International Law in a Divided World," *International Conciliation*, No. 542 (March 1963), 1-69, and Quincy Wright, *The Role of International Law in the Elimination of War*, Dobbs Ferry, N.Y., Oceana Publications, 1961.

There is a third consequence of decentralization that affects the behavior of law. This effect may be unfamiliar to those acquainted primarily with advanced domestic law systems. In domestic law a violation of a particular rule of the system normally creates an enforcement job for the machinery of state, although a government may decide tacitly or covertly to forego enforcement in any given specific instance. However, the violation by A does not affect the duty of other actors to obey even if A's violation was contrary to their interests; A's illegal, but profitable, price-fixing does not authorize B to undertake corresponding action. However, in international law the situation is different in certain crucial respects. For instance, the persistent violation of nonintervention duties by State X cannot be dealt with ordinarily by the enforcement machinery of the organized community of states (either regional or global). Therefore, a violation of rule A by X tends to create a legal basis for states Y, Z . . . n to violate in similar proportionate fashion. This is part of the thoroughgoing reciprocity that characterizes decentralized systems of legal order, a reciprocity that is to some extent offset by the capability of powerful states to deny reciprocity to weaker ones in exceptional circumstances. Thus the obligatory character of those rules of international law that have a strong connection to political conflict depends upon mutuality of adherence; the option of states to reciprocate noncompliance creates a marginal incentive to comply, especially as the noncomplying response is often not readily predictable. A violation of international law may itself become the efficient cause of an escalation of tensions and conduct, bringing an underlying conflict closer to the threshold of violence. A counterviolation may then have a status that ranges from a second violation to that of a sanction applied to penalize the first violation.

There are three perspectives from which it is useful to think about the actual and potential contribution of law to the regulation of international conflict. First, there is the conflict-restraining role played by legal rules and processes in the existing system of international relations. Law helps international actors to confine conflict within manageable boundaries. Second, there is the conflict-restraining role that might be played by law in an international system in which a limited world government has emerged; that is, substantial disarmament has taken place simultaneously with the buildup of international institutions and welfare activities. Third, there is the conflict-restraining role of law as a transformative agent in the movement from the existing decentralized order to a more centralized system.[15] This third per-

---

[15] The dependence of phased disarmament upon legal structure and process illustrates this role. Law enables states to envision their risks and burdens with a

spective is the least familiar. It can be identified with the contribution that law is able to make to the solution of the transition problem.[16] If an objective of foreign policy is to construct a stable peace system, does this fact influence the role of law in the contemporary world? For example, does this pursuit encourage a self-denying respect for legal rules by powerful states that is intended to raise the confidence of nations in the reliability of the international system? One way to envision the system-changing perspective is in terms of transfers of sovereign prerogative to the organs of the United Nations, transfers that are themselves designed to accelerate the global acceptance of a phased process of general and complete disarmament. Sensitivity to this focus on transition highlights such political preconditions of limited world government as the need to make elites and publics sympathetic to a world community orientation as an emerging substitute for the predominantly national orientations and loyalties that continue to dominate political attitudes relevant to the conduct of international affairs.[17]

Scholarly emphasis upon a world community orientation is itself a political and normative act, affirming certain supranationalizing tendencies in the existing legal order and looking forward to a world in which the nation as a social unit occupies a greatly diminished status. A consequence of national control over the major instruments of force is that significant recourses to violence, whether of an offensive or defensive character, are largely determined on the national level even if these decisions are subject to a formal right of review by the United Nations or a regional security organization. At the same time, it is possible to apprehend the growing importance of supranational, infranational, and transitional actors in world politics. These actors generate norms, procedures, and institutions that fall within the enterprise of international law. International law is an umbrella conception despite its literal reference to inter-nation transactions that expresses the totality of legal phenomena germane to the control of international conflict. The following subcategories suggest the major components of

---

precision that is not otherwise obtainable in social and political affairs. This allows alternative risks to be appraised and encourages a rational style of political action. The terminal goals of the transition can also be clarified by the construction of futuristic legal models. The detailed Clark-Sohn model admirably serves this function. Cf. Grenville Clark and Louis Sohn, *World Peace Through World Law*, 3rd rev. edn., Cambridge, Harvard University Press, 1966.

[16] Cf. Falk, *op.cit. supra*, note 5; Falk, *Law, Morality, and War in the Contemporary World*, New York, Praeger, 1963.

[17] Cf. John H. Herz, *International Politics in the Atomic Age*, New York, Columbia University Press, 1959; C. Wilfred Jenks, *The Common Law of Mankind*, London, Stevens and Sons, 1958; and Harold D. Lasswell, "A Brief Discourse about Method in the Current Madness," *Proceedings, the American Society of International Law, 1963*.

the world law concept.[18] First, there is the traditional system of international law concerned with the development of rules and processes that pertain to direct relationships among sovereign states. Second, there is United Nations Law that grows out of the claims and activities of the various organs and agencies that comprise the Organization. A conception of United Nations Law is needed to govern the peacemaking operations of the Organization. Such a legal order also serves to establish a constitutional structure of "United Nations." This structure is needed to legitimate claims by the United Nations to use its authority to prevent or moderate violence that threatens international peace. Thus the role of the United Nations in Suez in 1956, in Lebanon during 1958, or in the Congo after 1960 generates standards and precedents about the allocation of authority between the host state government and the Organization. Third, there is the network of legal rights and duties that results from the activities of regional organizations. The Organization of American States makes claims to act as a collective unit that possesses a different legal status than if made either by a single state or by the United Nations. The various efforts by the United States to get OAS support for its undertakings against Castro's Cuba can be understood in part as an effort to legitimate national policy by placing it within a regional setting.[19]

Fourth, there is a consistent, if vague, trend toward the effective realization of a universalistic legal consciousness.[20] The regulatory basis is the unity of the human community and the object is the promotion of the human dignity of the individual person. This trend has been identified by one author as "the common law of mankind,"[21] a phrase placing stress upon the directness of the contact between the legal claim and the human conduct, and disregarding the interposition of national governments. The Charter, by providing for the promotion of human rights, gives the United Nations some authority, as yet undeveloped, to apply the rules of the common law of mankind regardless of objections made by the government of the nation within whose territory the activity takes place. Civil strife and human rights are the principal areas where the connection between human conflict and this new basis of claim is most evident. These matters

[18] For similar typology, cf. Quincy Wright, "Toward a Universal Law for Mankind," 63 *Columbia Law Review* 435-58 (1963).

[19] Abram Chayes, "Law and the Quarantine of Cuba," *Foreign Affairs*, XLI (No. 3, 1963), 550-57, and Covey Oliver, "The Inter-American Security System and the Cuban Crisis," The Hammarskjöld Forums, Association of the Bar of the City of New York, working papers, November 1962.

[20] Jenks, *op.cit. supra*, note 17, but cf. McDougal and Harold D. Lasswell, "The Identification and Appraisal of Diverse Systems of Public Order," in McDougal and Associates, *Studies in World Public Order*, New Haven, Yale University Press, 1960, pp. 3-41.

[21] Jenks, *op.cit. supra*, note 17, pp. 62-172.

would, by traditional notions, be considered to fall within the domestic jurisdiction of a sovereign state, the constituent acts being performed mainly by nationals subject to the paramount authority of their territorial government. A universal legal order denies the "domesticness" of the activity by claiming the competence to prevent human abuse and political violence wherever it takes place and regardless of the character and status of the combatants.

And fifth, there is the complex set of rules and procedures that concern the interaction among regions, blocs, nations, international organizations, and individuals in their relations with one another, identified here, with some reluctance, as supranational law. The relations between the Congo and the United Nations, between Cuba and the Organization of American States, between a corporation and a foreign government that are parties to a concession agreement, between the Warsaw Pact and NATO illustrate this complex legal network.

The heritage of the past deepens one's understanding of the growth and deficiencies of law in world affairs. The Catholic Church in medieval Europe provided an institutional and normative center for the resolution of conflict among the leading international actors, all purporting to be obedient to the will of Rome.[22] On several occasions the Church performed peacekeeping roles; for example, the papal bull *Inter coetesa* served as the basis for allocating colonizing claims between Spain and Portugal in the treaties of Tordesillas (1494) and Saragossa (1529). With the Reformation, the secularizing spirit of the Renaissance, and the rise of strong nation-states, a heroic attempt was made to combine the Roman Law heritage of Europe with the natural law tradition to form a common normative framework for international activities.[23] This law tried to regulate national recourse to violence by positing a doctrine of just war. Such a doctrine specified standards of justice that were assumed to be acceptable to every reasoning man and to every Christian sovereign, standards which, if adhered to, would preclude war. But the absence of an authoritative decision-maker allowed each sovereign to claim the presence of a just cause whenever *raison d'état* dictated war.[24] Normative authority proved insufficient to restrain an ambitious nation possessing the capability for and will toward aggression. Legal doctrine was invoked

[22] Arthur Nussbaum, *A Concise History of the Law of Nations*, rev. edn., New York, Macmillan, 1954, pp. 17-23.

[23] Cf. Paul Ramsey, *War and the Christian Conscience*, Durham, Duke University Press, 1961; and Lynn H. Miller, "The Contemporary Significance of the Doctrine of Just War," *World Politics*, XVI (January 1964), 254-86.

[24] Third states also showed no willingness to identify an aggressor and come to the defense of its victim. There was no disposition to create a decentralized collective security system based on a consensus among states to resist aggressive or unjust uses of force.

to rationalize national policy rather than to constrain it. The maintenance of peace, so far as maintained, depended on alliances that confronted the potential aggressor with the prospect of defeat if he made the costly recourse to forcible forms of conflict. Law did not contribute to this process. Sovereignty counted far more than did universal norms embodied in the natural law tradition.

This led international jurists in the eighteenth and nineteenth centuries to identify law with the manifestations of sovereign *consent*. Thus treaties (express consent) and custom (implied consent) replaced *reason* as the foundation of authority in international affairs. State governments would not agree, however, to qualify their discretion to use force to promote national ends. From a legal point of view recourse to warfare was treated as legal as a proper matter for sovereign discretion. A peace treaty legitimated the fruits of conquest. Law did help restrict the *scope* of violent conflict by defining the rights and duties of neutrals and belligerents toward one another, thereby compromising the interest of nonparticipants in maintaining normal commercial intercourse despite the war with the interest of the belligerent in achieving a maximum negative impact upon its enemy. Rights of blockade, notions of contraband, rules for the visit and search of merchant ships on the high seas were designed, in elaborate detail, to allow the war to go on without drawing neutrals into the fray. As well, law tried to provide rules designed to eliminate *unnecessary suffering* from the belligerent experience. Rules concerning the treatment of prisoners, the care of the sick and wounded, the obligations of belligerent occupation were aspects of this effort to humanize war. These efforts culminated in the conferences at The Hague prior to World War I and were partly renovated in the Geneva Conventions of 1949 after World War II. This compatibility of war with law during the early centuries of the state system was partly a consequence of the limited objectives pursued by major states in warfare between themselves. There was a general recognition that international stability depended upon the continuing existence of the major national actors.[25]

World War I signified the end of the aloofness of law from national determinations to use force. The hardening of alliance patterns in the pre-1914 period led to a struggle for dominance that typically takes place whenever two adverse power centers aspire to increase their power, prestige, and wealth at each other's expense. This polarity encouraged one side to work toward attaining a superior military capability to eliminate the only other competitor for world dominance, as

[25] Morton A. Kaplan, *System and Process in International Politics*, New York, John Wiley, 1957, pp. 22-36.

well as to avoid being eliminated. Moreover, military technology (submarine, aircraft, mass armies) and the absoluteness of belligerent objectives (unconditional surrender) undercut the restraining limits developed through several centuries by the earlier variety of international law. Almost all trade became contraband, submarines and aircraft could not visit and search neutral ships, and the reliance on the distinction between civilian and soldier and between military and non-military targets was seriously challenged by bombing expeditions and strategies designed to weaken the enemy's industrial base and will to defend. The higher stakes of war—national impotence or ascendancy —and the greater destructiveness of the new technology led nations after World War I to plan for the elimination of war from international life.[26] The League of Nations might be considered as a search for a new balancing mechanism that would confront a potential aggressor with overwhelming force—that is, the unified capability of the League membership brought to bear to frustrate the objectives of the warmaker—just as the possibilities for realignment in nineteenth century Europe had been used to discourage aggression by redressing the power relationships in favor of the defense. Legal technique and institutions were expected to implement this attempt to achieve a new kind of security: organized collective security.[27] This new reliance on the collective strength of the overall world community, a return to the expectation of the early natural law theory that nations would aggregate their own strength to defeat an unjust user of force, was reinforced by the Kellogg-Briand Peace Pact of 1928 prohibiting national recourse to force in international affairs except for purposes of self-defense.[28] Despite the formal assertion of these radical legal claims to control conflict, the primacy of national sovereignty over collective restraint produced a new polarization of political power that exploded in the form of World War II. The trends toward belligerent absolutism present in World War I were carried much further by the

[26] Stanley Hoffmann, "International Systems and International Law," *World Politics*, XIV (October 1961), 205-37; for a thorough study of the various perspectives toward the reconstruction of world order after World War I see Hans F. Petersson, *Power and International Order*, Lund, Sweden, Gleerups, 1964.

[27] But the system was too voluntaristic to solicit the cooperation of states dedicated to the pursuit of egocentric goals (national interests). In this respect it resembled the post-medieval attempt to control force by the just war doctrine.

Implementation was not forthcoming in either system and for the same reasons. Despite the League machinery, states were not committed to effective participation in a community system of law enforcement. Cf. Walter Schiffer, *The Legal Community of Mankind*, New York, Columbia University Press, 1954. See also Hedley Bull, "The Grotian Conception of International Society," in Herbert Butterfield and Martin Wight, *Diplomatic Investigations*, London, Allen and Unwin, 1966, pp. 51-73.

[28] See Wright, *op.cit. supra*, note 14.

acceptance of the concept of total war, by the development of modern air power and radar, and by the use of rockets and atomic bombs. The role of law in restraining the nature of belligerent confrontation seemed trivial indeed. Traditional limiting notions were subordinated to belligerent strategy, including the sustained bombardment of cities without even a consistent restriction to military or industrial objectives.

Post-World War II gave rise to the United Nations, an increased effort to prohibit recourse by states to violence by proposing to deal collectively with the state that violated the peace. The will of the community was formalized by the unanimous endorsement of the General Assembly of the Principles of the Nuremberg Judgment, chief principle among which was the conclusion that planning and preparing for or engaging in an aggressive war is the most serious of all crimes against mankind. Whereas the League failed to thwart Italy's flagrant aggression against Ethiopia, the United Nations has succeeded in mobilizing sufficient defensive forces to frustrate aggressors in Korea and Suez, the two major instances of overt recourse to force across a boundary. However, the basic decentralization of power and authority persists, baffling every realistic prospect for effective long-term control. Once more a destabilizing repolarization of power has taken place in international society, this time augmented by nuclear technology and rigidified by ideological fervor. The place of law in this contemporary system is examined in the remainder of this chapter.

III. Some Contributions of Law to the Control of World Conflict

The reality of conflict is pervasive and multifaceted. However, in world affairs, the urgency of concern about the prevention of war encourages a concentration upon the relevance of conflict to the control of political violence in interstate relations. This orientation conditions thought about law. It leads law to be conceived frequently, albeit simplistically, as the one alternative to force in the resolution of international disputes; this dichotomy is much too sharp as it overlooks the dependence of law upon force and fails to appreciate the moderating effects that law can have even when violence has been introduced into social relations by threat or use. Nevertheless, this chapter accepts the premise that the regulation of violence is the proper focus for a study of the relevance of law to international conflict, an acceptance predicated upon the paramount importance of maintaining nuclear peace.

There has been a tendency on the part of those who view law and force as mutually exclusive alternatives to devote their attention to the description of existing, and the invention of new, procedures and institutions for the pacific settlement of disputes.[29] Pacific settlement provides a significant series of opportunities for international actors locked in conflict to resolve their differences in a nondestructive manner. As such, these procedures and institutions are important, especially as either anticipations or ingredients of a more ordered world; but a present emphasis on methods of pacific settlement distracts one from an appreciation of the role that law can presently play in world affairs. Although the renunciation of force must be accompanied eventually by reliable substitutes, there is not yet in sight a significant disposition on the part of nations to entrust vital disputes to legal tribunals and procedures for third-party settlement. And, in fact, much misunderstanding is caused by "rule of law" movements that act as if the truly urgent obstacle to the growth of world law is the Connally Amendment, and the like. Diplomacy, rather than law—although the divorce is not a separation (law affects the course of diplomatic negotiation)—is the realm for fruitful pacific settlement.[30]

A major criticism of the approach taken by specialists in international relations to the contribution law makes to the control of international conflict arises from their tendency to overstress formal apparatus: the World Court and treaty-making procedure.[31] If this apparatus is extolled as even potentially adequate to guard the peace, it encourages a naïvely optimistic outlook. If law is categorically dismissed because the apparatus is unable to regulate reliably the more fundamental aspirations of states for power, wealth, and security, then an equally naïve cynicism emerges that is quite misleading.[32] Legal process and order have contributed, and continue to contribute significantly to the avoidance of destructive conflict and to the reduction of its destructiveness, but *not* by providing the kind of institutional structure or law-making procedure that has led us to rely so heavily upon the judiciary and legislature in our domestic life. The character of law in world affairs is shaped by the decentralized distribution of power, producing a horizontal legal system that, by its very nature, emphasizes substitutes for central or vertical institutions.

It is the aim of this section to outline some of these contributions

29 E.g. Arthur Larsen, *When Nations Disagree*, Baton Rouge, Louisiana State University Press, 1961; Charles S. Rhyne, "World Peace Through Law," 44 *American Bar Association Journal* 937-40, 997-1001 (1958).

30 Percy E. Corbett, *Law in Diplomacy*, Princeton, Princeton University Press, 1959.

31 E.g. Frederick H. Hartmann, *The Re-* *lation of Nations*, 3rd edn., New York, Macmillan, 1962, pp. 103-22; John G. Stoessinger, *The Might of Nations*, New York, Random House, 1961, pp. 240-56.

32 Most notably, Hans Morgenthau, *The Decline of Democratic Politics*, Chicago, University of Chicago Press, 1962, pp. 282-307.

that law presently makes to the control of conflict. The first task is to discuss how the classical concerns of international law must be updated to take recent developments into account. This discussion will, secondly, be supplemented by a description of law as a process for the communication of national claims to act; this is a characteristic of classical international law, but it has not been appreciated to be so until recently.[33] Third, it is necessary to deal with the special importance of nuclear weaponry for the operation of law in world affairs. Fourth, it is useful to consider the role of the United Nations—a significant focus for the centralizing tendencies of the existing world order system. Fifth, a short description will be given of certain unfamiliar functions fulfilled by international law in the contemporary world. And sixth, some comments will be made about those developing areas of international law that pertain to the control of international conflict in the decades to come.

(1) On the Continuing Relevance of Classical International Law

There are several relevant categories to be distinguished: recourse to violence, rules of conduct, instruments of violence, belligerent objectives, and responsibility (national and individual).

Recourse to Violence. It should be recalled that until after World War I a state was regarded as entitled to have recourse to force and war whenever it saw fit. Now, of course, law attempts to regulate *recourse* to force in international relations, restricting its legitimate role to situations of individual and collective self-defense or to security operations that have been authorized by the United Nations.[34] The prohibition of force produced a search for precise limiting standards, explaining the frequent attempts to persuade nations to agree upon an authoritative definition of aggression.[35] The complex reasons that explain the failure to reach an agreement about a definition of aggression cautions against a reliance upon the present capacities of law to excr-

[33] Cf. the principal writings of Myres S. McDougal; for discussion with appropriate citation see Chapter III.

[34] Certain provisions of the UN Charter indicate the extent to which national claims to use force have been prohibited. Article 2(4): "All Members shall refrain in their international relations from the threat or use of force against the territorial integrity or political independence of any state, or in any other manner inconsistent with the Purposes of the United Nations." Article 51: "Nothing in the present Charter shall impair the inherent right of individual or collective self-defense if an armed attack occurs against a Member of the United Nations, until the Security Council has taken the measures necessary to maintain international peace and security . . ."

[35] Report of the Secretary General, "Question of Defining Aggression," A/2211, October 3, 1952; Quincy Wright, "The Prevention of Aggression," 50 *American Journal of International Law* 514-32 (1956); Julius Stone, *Aggression and World Order*, Berkeley, University of California Press, 1958.

cise control over national decisions to make use of force in world affairs.[36]

This failure of implementation encourages a skeptical attitude toward the significance of the Charter claims to prohibit national uses of force. Nevertheless, the willingness of nations to subscribe, even in principle, to the renunciation of their rights to use (except in self-defense) force, is a significant step, an expression of willingness to move in one direction rather than another, and a disclosure of consensus on the most important aspect of political order in world affairs. And there is more to this consensus than a mere gesture of goodwill. However, a prohibition of force is not even a guide to behavior if its scope is not uniformly understood by those entrusted with decision on behalf of sovereign states. Each state remains free to adopt a broad definition of self-defense that is capable of rendering the Charter renunciation of force almost meaningless. Even if an acceptable definition could be agreed upon by major states, it would not inspire confidence, unless it is accompanied by procedures to enable reliable and effective implementation. If international law is to control behavior, then it is necessary to provide an assured way to translate legal standards into action, and thereby construct a sturdy bridge between the realms of authoritative utterance and national behavior. Nevertheless, the record of United Nations control over national dispositions to violence is encouraging. This record is especially impressive if one takes into account the absence of centralized power in the United Nations, that is, of a regular police force and a reliable basis for fiscal support; nevertheless, the Organization has been successful in frustrating significant attempts (Korea, Suez) to commit outright aggression that have taken place since it came into existence. Contrariwise, failure of the United Nations to curtail the Vietnam War is the most dramatic indication of the limited role of the Organization in the maintenance of world peace.

Rules of Conduct. A second area of legal activity involves the establishment of rules and procedures for the conduct of war, the traditional "laws of war." Such matters as treatment of prisoners, care for the sick and wounded, and the rights and duties of belligerent occupation are governed by fairly clear and widely accepted rules, many of which are contained in international agreements and are included in national field manuals for the guidance of military personnel.[37] These rules were developed primarily to govern international wars, and it

[36] For a full discussion of these issues see Chapter XV.
[37] See generally, Morris Greenspan, *The* *Modern Law of Land Warfare*, Berkeley, University of California Press, 1959.

is now important to extend their application more fully to the conduct of civil or internal wars.

Instruments of Violence. There is also evidence of concern on the part of lawyers with the legal status of particular instruments of violence, especially with the status of nuclear weapons.[38] This kind of concern goes back at least as far as 1868, when the Declaration of St. Petersburg required the parties "to renounce, in case of war . . . the employment . . . of any projectile of less weight than four hundred grammes, which is explosive, or is charged with fulminating or inflammable substances."[39] There is disagreement about whether it is legitimate to use nuclear weapons in the pursuit of traditional military objectives; as well, there is some disagreement about a demographic military strategy that proposes cities as targets. Legal controversy has also involved the right to use the high seas and atmosphere to test nuclear weapons, despite uncertainties about the effect of fallout and the entry of objections by nonnuclear states.[40] The historic debate about the legal status of poison gas as a military weapon indicates that international law has long sought to regulate those instruments of violence responsible for indiscriminate suffering and permanent destruction.

Belligerent Objectives. The subject of belligerent objectives has also always been on the borderland of law. If it is permissible to use force, it remains necessary to specify whether limits condition the objectives that can be sought. Under existing conceptions, this involves, primarily, a definition of the scope of self-defense; other national uses of force are assumed to be illegal. But is the state that properly claims self-defense entitled to compel its attacker to surrender? Or is there a norm of proportionate response that limits the defender's objectives to a restoration of the *status quo ante*?[41] What limits apply when a regional organization undertakes collective security measures or applies sanctions for wrongful behavior? Or when the Security Council, General Assembly, or Secretary General employ force? Or when the use of force is in the nature of intervention or counter-intervention in an internal war? These questions are just beginning to

---

[38] Cf. William V. O'Brien, "Nuclear Warfare and the Law of Nations," in W. J. Nagle, ed., *Morality and Modern Warfare*, Baltimore, Helicon Press, 1960, pp. 126-49; Georg Schwarzenberger, *The Legality of Nuclear Weapons*, London, Stevens and Sons, 1958; and Nagendra Singh, *Nuclear Weapons and International Law*, New York, Praeger, 1959.

[39] James B. Scott, ed., *Texts of the Peace Conferences at The Hague, 1899 and 1907*, Boston and London, Ginn and Co., 1908, pp. 381-82.

[40] Cf. M. H. Margolis, "The Hydrogen Bomb Experiments and International Law," 64 *Yale Law Journal* 629-47 (March 1955); and Myres S. McDougal, "Hydrogen Bomb Tests in Perspective; Lawful Measures for Security," 64 *Yale Law Journal* 648-710 (March 1955).

[41] Robert W. Tucker, *The Just War: A Study in Contemporary American Doctrine*, Baltimore, Johns Hopkins University Press, 1960, pp. 97-162; Falk, *op.cit. supra*, note 16.

be seriously raised. There is no consistent response provided by law at this stage; the formulation of these issues, however, suggests a new source for limits upon the competence of all international actors, not just states, when force has been used in the course of conflict. This further suggests that an attempt to control force by even a perfectly defined and implemented definition of aggression and a coordinate concept of self-defense is insufficient. We need, as well, to know more precisely about the relations between a nation acting in self-defense and an international organization acting within the scope of its authority. This area of international action is badly in need of normative clarification.

Responsibility: National and Individual. The victorious side after World Wars I and II attempted to emphasize the responsibility of the losers for the war. A peace treaty, no matter how much a product of duress, represents a valid legal instrument; therefore, "victor's justice" is law, in the international system. There was a considerable shift in the attitude of the victors toward the vanquished after the two great wars, a shift dramatized by a comparison of the Versailles Treaty with the Nuremberg Judgment.

The prevailing idea after World War I was to make Germany suffer as a nation for the destruction and suffering caused by the war. Reparations were claimed and restrictions imposed upon Germany's freedom to reestablish its military prowess. There was some attempt to prosecute the Kaiser as a war criminal, but it was thwarted by his unavailability for prosecution. The causal relationship that many people believe connects the austerity of Versailles to the emergence of Hitler prompted a virtual abandonment, especially by the West, of any attempt to punish Germany as a nation after World War II. Instead, the responsibility for the war was attributed to the evil apparatus of government as administered by its leaders. This produced the Nuremberg and Tokyo judgments, and in Germany, a multitude of lesser military and civilian trials imposing responsibility upon individuals who carried out the inhumane or aggressive designs of the Axis governments. Despite the deficiencies of these trials from the perspective of domestic due process, there is a growing willingness to make individuals responsible for carrying out government policies that are in flagrant disregard of world community values. It is significant that no member of the Security Council questioned Israel's authority to prosecute Eichmann, even though the allegedly criminal acts committed by Eichmann were committed abroad in accord with German territorial law at a point in time prior to the existence of Israel, the prosecuting state and, of course, before the statutes defining the offenses upon which the prosecution rested were enacted. National courts in the existing system act as agents of the world community, deriving part of their mandate and authority from the presence of a supranational consensus that acts to supplement the assertion of national authority.[42]

The effectiveness of symbolic retribution against national officials is certainly undemonstrated as a deterrent. Nevertheless, from the standpoint of the possibilities for international law, these developments are encouraging. For there is disclosed a willingness to accord significance to world community perspectives in the appraisal of human conduct. The growth of a transnational consciousness is an essential preparation for further transfers of power and authority to supranational institutions, especially if it is our intention to prevent violent resolutions of international conflict.

(2) LAW AS A CLAIMING PROCESS

There is a frequent tendency to understand law statically as a system or corpus of rules. A major divide between the positivist and sociological approaches concerns whether or not processive elements of legal order are properly included within the jurist's province.[43] It is strongly urged here that one of the major contributions of law in conflict situations is to provide a regular and highly articulated procedure for the assertion and refutation of national claims. The claiming procedure enables precise communication to take place in a horizontal authority structure. The failure to assert such claims and justify them with reasons gives action an arbitrary appearance that undermines the reliance of international law upon a regime of self-imposed restraints. Myres McDougal emphasizes this point by noting that the application of authoritative policies in particular instances inevitably requires a determination of reasonableness in context.[44] Thus a United States claim to develop a communication system based on copper needles in the atmosphere (Project West Ford) acquires some legal status if the United States gives its reasons for doing this and attempts to meet Soviet and British objections, but not otherwise. The entire pattern of behavior surrounding the assertion and withdrawal of claims appears to be critical for the maintenance of present stability

---

[42] Falk, "Toward a Theory of the Participation of Domestic Courts in the International Legal Order: A Critique of Banco Nacional de Cuba v. Sabbatino," 16 *Rutgers Law Review* 1-41 (Fall 1961).

[43] Myres S. McDougal, "International Law, Power, and Policy: A Contemporary Conception," 82 *Recueil des Cours* 137-259

(1953); McDougal, "Some Basic Theoretical Concepts About International Law: A Policy-Oriented Framework of Inquiry," *Journal of Conflict Resolution,* IV (1960), 407-31.

[44] For discussion and criticism of this aspect of Professor McDougal's approach see Chapter III.

and the encouragement of future changes. In no other setting can one perceive quite so clearly the reality or delusiveness of national intentions to give up or insist upon short-term advantages in exchange for the improvement or sacrifice of the intermediate and long-term prospects for world order. The acceptance of this obligation to demonstrate the reasonableness of controverted national claims is a development of legal accountability that extends beyond the classical notion that a sovereign state is entitled to do whatever it is not forbidden from doing.[45]

In crisis confrontations the communication of claims acts to prevent overreaction by making evident the limits of the claimant's objectives. The communication of claims discourages miscalculation and tends to produce a reconciliation of opposing interests by compromise and non-violent means; as well, it avoids putting a nation in the situation of choosing between surrender and forcible resistance. The installation of a "hot line" between Washington and Moscow is a further recognition of the connection between authoritative communication and the regulation of international conflict.

Why is this claiming-procedure drawn into the province of law? An answer to this question requires a brief reconsideration of the distinctive needs of a horizontal legal order. Without the availability of normal legislative procedures for the reform and extension of existing rights, reasonable claims by nations to act are themselves equivalent to legislative facts. An excellent way to demonstrate the reasonableness or unreasonableness of a controverted novel claim—that is, a claim that is not provided for by precedents—is to show that it is authorized or prohibited by policies embraced in legal doctrines acceptable to contesting parties. Law provides rhetoric, analogies, and some standards to help with the determination of whether a particular claim is reasonable. This serves to civilize the process of conflict by revealing a concern with community approval. It is a legal proceeding partly because its outcome is precedential, greatly affecting future appraisals of reasonableness, and, thereby, helping to establish boundary lines between permissible and forbidden behavior.

(3) NUCLEAR WEAPONS AND THE DOCTRINE OF NONINTERVENTION

The development of nuclear and rocket technology has such an important influence upon the tasks set for international law that it deserves separate mention in this setting. For one thing, this new military technology acts to reinforce legal norms prohibiting the use of force by one

---

[45] Case of the S.S. "Lotus," Permanent Court of International Justice, Ser. A., No. 10, 1927.

nation against another in open warfare between states. The organized response of the world community to the use of force in Korea and the Suez has further strengthened the status of this prohibition, although Goa, Tibet, and the Sino-Indian border dispute suggest that violence remains a relevant means to settle certain kinds of international disputes, especially if the victim of the coercion does not possess international personality or the stakes of conflict are relatively remote from the mainstream of strategic controversy. The mutual disadvantage of warfare on the nuclear level also discourages lesser forms of warfare and provocation that contain a significant perceived danger of escalation. This danger suggests that one effect of nuclear weapons has been to encourage sensitivity on the part of decision-makers in important nations to the need to avoid significant levels of violence in the major international arenas of conflict. Legal technique can reinforce this political disposition by clarifying the content of the prohibition, perhaps by developing an authoritative definition of aggression, which will thereafter be available for the guidance of officials in national and supranational institutions.

A related consequence of nuclear weaponry has been to shift aggressive political energies into modes of conflict that are relatively unlikely to initiate an escalation process. The cold war struggle for dominance in the underdeveloped portions of the world is far enough removed—although the Chinese and Russians disagree about how far removed—from vital centers of power to make a nuclear response, even on the level of threat, presently implausible. Modernization, the vestiges of decolonialization, and a miscellany of domestic strifes create many revolutionary opportunities in the Afro-Asian countries. These opportunities are well adapted to Sino-Soviet capability, ambition, and ideology. The attempts to extend the orbit of Communist influence has induced strong Western countermoves, and has especially encouraged military and economic aid to incumbent regimes. The result has been to produce a series of internal wars fought between rival domestic factions, supported and directed to varying degrees by either the United States or the Soviet Union. The participation of external rivals in internal war has not been effectively regulated by traditional international law. Civil strife had been regarded by international law as a matter within the domestic jurisdiction of the state and not as an appropriate subject for international concern, except to the extent of fixing certain standards for the relationships between the insurgent faction and external states. The traditional system allowed foreign states to help the incumbent suppress minor or short-term challenges to its governmental supremacy (rebellion, insurgency) favoring, to this extent, the stability of the *status quo*, whereas it prescribed neutrality toward the warring factions if the challenge was protracted and substantially sustained in scope and duration (belligerency). Such a scheme, never overly persuasive nor conspicuously observed, has collapsed under the pressure of the cold war conflict.[46, 47]

(4) THE UNITED NATIONS AND REGIONAL ORGANIZATIONS

The growth of supranational institutions is, like the advent of nuclear missiles, so important for the shape and prospect of international law that it, too, warrants some separate consideration. The evaluation of the role of these institutions cannot be isolated from the significant fact that major wars *between* nations are now most characteristically fought *within* a single nation. This new pattern is facilitated and sustained by the many revolutionary situations created by the modernization process that is going on and will continue to go on for decades to come throughout the ex-colonial world. The recurrence of protracted political violence has become a threat to *international* peace even if the fighting is confined to the territory of one nation, and as such, has been increasingly treated as a matter of supranational concern that legitimates the assumption of jurisdiction by regional and global institutions.

It is artificial to separate the study of international norms from a consideration of the role of supranational institutions. This is especially true with respect to the regulation of conflict in the contemporary world. The character of world legal order is partly created by the expectation that the United Nations has a considerable capability to regulate violent conflict, whether in the traditional form of a war between states or in its more modern form of rival sponsorship of factions in a war within a third state. United Nations contributions are usefully divided into three categories: First, the United Nations can organize the community against an aggressor, authorizing or undertaking countermeasures, for example, Korea or Suez. If the realities of power prevent an effective response, it can, provided the political support is forthcoming, at least censure an aggression: Hungary (1956). Second, the United Nations is available to intervene in a situation of civil strife to restore peace if foreign participation is present or threatened; the alternative to United Nations intervention is often a competition between national interventions on the side of rival domestic factions. The Congo was a setting in which United Nations in-

---

[46] See Chapter IV.
[47] Manfred Halpern, "The Morality and Politics of Intervention," in James N. Rosenau, ed., *International Aspects of Civil Strife*, Princeton, Princeton University Press, 1964, pp. 249-88.

tervention was chosen as the preferable, if problematic, alternative to the danger of interventions by the Great Powers. Third, and as yet untried, the United Nations can use its authority and the support of its members to prevent national interventions, thereby insulating a domestic conflict enough to allow it to reach a "natural" outcome. A policy of insulation was the original idea of a policy of nonintervention with respect to foreign civil strife: the role of the United Nations would be to assure mutual compliance with duties to refrain from intervention. A successful discharge of this role might reestablish contact between the principle of self-determination and the doctrine of nonintervention that has been broken by the tendency of aggressors since the Spanish Civil War, especially Hitler and the Soviet bloc, to expand the domain of national influence by helping a sympathetic elite to win control of a foreign government.[48] As yet, except in exhortatory fashion, the United Nations has not yet tried to make itself an effective instrument of noninterventionism. These same three functions can be performed by regional organizations, subject only to overall United Nations supervision to prevent the commission of "regional aggression" in the guise of a regional security operation. The growth of an improved system of international law will depend heavily, it is felt, upon how effectively and justly the security organs of the United Nations and regional organizations are able to carry out these three functions.

(5) THE FUNCTIONS OF LAW IN THE CONTEMPORARY WORLD

This section tries to identify some of the less evident functions performed by international law in situations of acute international conflict. As this undertaking is not within the repertory of the traditional concerns of lawyers, it will be set forth in a most tentative way.

If we conclude that the persistent violation of nonintervention norms has temporarily suspended their application in international relations, law, as rule and as technique, nevertheless provides or emphasizes certain limiting rules for participation in internal war. The basic character of law is to make a common standard of behavior explicit and to establish certain expectations on the part of international actors, the disappointment of which will produce destabilizing escalation. Two kinds of limits illustrate this conception of law: first, the failure to use or threaten nuclear weapons to influence the outcome of an internal war; second, the failure to expand the arena of violence across bound-

---

[48] Samuel P. Huntington, "Patterns of Violence in World Politics," in Huntington, ed., *Changing Patterns of Military* *Politics,* New York, Free Press, 1962, pp. 17-50.

aries except perhaps to provide or attack sanctuary for insurgent groups. These two horizontal norms serve to limit the conflict in method and space. A legal character can be attributed to these norms because a departure from them would be discernible and it would be viewed as a wrongful act contrary to community expectations that justifies censure and retaliatory action. The widespread opposition to the decision by the United States Government to bomb North Viet Nam, beginning in February of 1965, in response to its role in assisting the Vietcong's war effort in South Viet Nam illustrates the reality of this legal expectation, even as it also illustrates the relative impotence of international law to prevent altogether, although it may be effective in curtailing the extent of the violation, a determined Great Power from violating applicable legal restraints. It is the provision of common standards for conduct and not the method by which these standards are generated, that establishes the horizontal content of international law. Thus, despite the failure of rules of nonintervention to govern the behavior of nations, law continues to be relevant to national participation in the internal affairs of foreign states by contributing minimum stability to the prevailing patterns of interventionary politics. It is the task of the jurist to make this function of law more operative by clarifying the role of these norms in the maintenance of minimum international stability. A failure of national officials to adopt policy that conforms with these limits could precipitate dangerous breakdowns of order, imperiling seriously the state of nuclear peace. Cold war participation in internal struggles for power, as a relatively safe but effective way to promote expansionist politics, has limited ends, the attainment of which is worth only limited risks. Just as the dangers of pursuing unlimited political objectives in Europe shifted the main arenas of conflict to overseas colonial wars in the eighteenth and nineteenth centuries, now after nuclear technology and the devastation of two world wars, there again seems to be an increasing disposition to avoid a violent encounter at the European center of conflict; this disposition is difficult to implement, however, because each side seeks to assure stability within its own domain, an end that can be gained only by giving Berlin, a symbol in the overall struggle for world dominance, completely to one side or the other. The main control functions of law in relation to international conflict in the existing world are to reinforce the renunciation of force across international boundaries expressed in the phrase of the strategists—"nuclear stalemate"—and to identify the limits of permissible participation in intrastate conflict. These two endeavors are linked because a refusal to abide by intrastate limits endangers the stability of the interstate prohibition.

[72]

There are additional roles played by law in contemporary conflict patterns. For one thing, if one nation violates clear norms of international law, then it strengthens the appeal of the victim to the organized community for protection of its rights; if this protection is not forthcoming, then recourse to self-help, even of a violent variety, is perceived as less unreasonable. For example, in the first paragraph of its note of protest to Haiti charging a violation of the immunity of its embassy, the Dominican Republic typically characterized the events as "glaring violations of the rules of international law, universally consecrated and especially recognized by the inter-American system."[49] The Soviet Defense Minister, Marshal Malinowski, invokes international law as one basis upon which to castigate United States policy toward Castro's Cuba and to urge adoption of a militant Soviet counterpolicy. This is partly self-justifying rhetoric, but it is also an appeal to that portion of the conscience of the world community that expects states to abide by the common standards set by international law. Furthermore, evidence of a serious violation of law by one state helps to vindicate a neutralizing coercive response by another state. This consequence, which is especially prominent when the violation of a generally accepted norm is patent—as when Haitian police violated the Dominican Embassy—acts by itself to deter conduct that is readily demonstrated to be illegal. Most nations seem sensitive about their reputations and eschew illegal conduct except when acting under great pressure. It is this determination to behave in accord with community expectations, as specified in part by the acknowledged content of international law, that also acts to discourage nations from adopting extreme positions. In the context of domestic decision-making there is some pressure that can be created to bring national conduct into as close conformity with international law as the pursuit of policy deemed necessary permits. The illegality of an act is itself a provocative challenge directed at another state stimulating it to make a major response, if only to uphold its pride and prestige. The effort of the United States, in 1962, even if not entirely persuasive, to assert its demand that the Soviet Union remove nuclear-capable missiles from Cuba without unnecessary interference with the freedom of the seas and with the authorization and participation of the regional security organ, the Organization of American States, may have not only restrained United States behavior (precluding invasion or bombardment of the missile bases) but, as well, restrained the Soviet and Cuban responses. Law permitted the claim to be conveyed in narrow terms, guarding against the possibility of a Soviet interpretation of United States conduct as a demand for unacceptable

[49] *New York Times,* April 29, 1963, p. 1.

action and limiting the affront to Soviet and Cuban dignity. Thus in a crisis situation there are several considerations that may allow international law to perform moderating functions, even though some applicable legal rules may be extended sufficiently beyond their normal meaning or accepted usage to make the conduct appear as a "violation" from the perspective of a third-party; first, there is a motive to avoid a clear violation of law so as to discourage community responses in favor of the victim; second, censure of the lawbreaker at home and in international forums encourages the domestic adoption of those policy alternatives that are in accord, or at least adhere as closely as possible to, applicable norms of law; and third, there is a greater likelihood of eliciting an accommodating response to hostile demands if these demands are restrained by the display of a general acceptance of legal boundaries. These restraining functions of law are peculiarly applicable in crisis confrontations, that is, at just those times when it is popularly supposed that international law has nothing to contribute, nothing at least until it has developed a regular police force capable of instantaneous and nonpolitical responses to illegal behavior. In noncrisis or precrisis situations, there is, of course, even more pressure to behave within the limits of law; the pressure is generated partly by the bureaucratic administration of the modern state that assures a basic disposition toward rule-oriented behavior.[50] A bureaucracy does not depart from applicable rules, even if international rules, unless it has been authorized to do so by the top political leadership; and as leaders do not participate in the formulation of noncrisis policy, such departure is administratively difficult to arrange. This induces a basic pattern of automatic compliance that often appears to elude those who offer cynical assessments of the importance of international law.

(6) NOTES ON THE FRONTIERS OF INTERNATIONAL LAW

There is also an emerging role for law with respect to the participation of organs of the United Nations or regional institutions in the control of domestic conflict that threatens the peace. Authorization for action is based upon the UN Charter, an international agreement that serves as the basic constitutional document of the institution. The right to resist aggression has been claimed as a basis to legitimate, by reference to principles of collective security and self-defense, claims by regional organizations to resolve conflicts in accordance with the will and capability of the consensus. The indeterminate extent to which regional discretion is subject to United Nations control is an inevitable,

---

[50] Fisher, "Bringing Law to Bear on Governments," *op.cit. supra*, note 12.

but troublesome consequence of the development of law on several levels without adequate coordination among them. In general, Article 53(1) of the UN Charter claims that ". . . no enforcement action shall be taken without the authorization of the Security Council." However, no content has been given, as yet, to this custodial responsibility over regional action that has apparently been entrusted to the United Nations; if we shift the focus from Cuba versus the OAS to Israel versus an Arab regional organization, or Formosa versus an Asian one, a clearer sense of the potential dangers implicit in the subjection of a nation to regional consensus may emerge.[51]

The relation between the domestic suppression of human rights and the use of international intervention as a technique of liberation is also a matter that lies along the frontier of a developing world law system. If a consensus transcending the cold war can be developed in support of a consistent interventionary policy based on fixed objectives and restraints, then it is quite probable that the United Nations will be increasingly entrusted with a role in the promotion of human rights regardless of whether or not the incumbent government gives its consent; the Republic of South Africa is likely to provide the first important test of the limits and effectiveness of this form of community intervention under United Nations auspices.[52] Such an interventionary claim is a radical denial of traditional notions of territorial sovereignty and domestic jurisdiction; these norms that hallowed the doctrine of sovereignty allowed, despite occasional instances of so-called humanitarian interventions (Turks persecuting Christian minorities in the nineteenth century), a government to determine conclusively the rights of its nationals, even if national administration resulted in shocking suppression. The notion of "crimes against humanity" was expressed, although not made the basis for criminal responsibility in the Nuremberg Judgment. This development creates some limit upon the extent of supranational deference to the sanctity of the social policies promoted by national elites. The expression of public opinion on the world level and the relative openness of most of the non-Communist world generate powerful political pressures that curtail national discretion in the area of human rights. Increasingly, national boundaries are being subordinated to the claims of racial affinity in the human rights area. This is not an altogether progressive development, but it does undermine the reactionary dogma of sovereign prerogative with respect to human rights, and establishes the basis for the imposition of certain minimum community standards. This development is linked to the central concern here: the management of international violence. For

[51] For amplification see Chapter IV.   [52] For amplification see Chapter X.

the prolonged suppression of human rights in secondary states will produce in the contemporary world an eventual protest movement, often abetted by interventionary support from abroad. This support, given the pervasity of the bipolar struggle, is likely to acquire a cold war tone, perhaps inducing competing interventions, generating crises, increasing tensions, and enlarging the scale and costs of conflict. An effective prophylactic intervention by community institutions emphasizes an axiological, rather than a political (or cold war) mode of conflict resolution. International law is just beginning to devise procedures and norms by which to carry out such stabilizing operations, although no formal legal commitments have been made as yet.

IV. A Policy Orientation

Should nations be expected to obey the "law" under all circumstances? It is difficult to find out just what this question means. For if legal rules are necessarily susceptible to interpretation in light of the policy they serve, and if a legal system provides complementary rules and policies,[53] then there is always available a legal argument to justify a course of national behavior. But if law is to be *guide* to behavior, rather than a mere *rationalization* of it, then to obey the law must mean something more than finding a legal argument to support a particular national position. There is a difference between invoking law to justify action already taken and invoking law to identify in advance the limits of permissible action.

In the context of conflict, the predominant directive of international law is to require states to refrain from the threat or use of force except in situations of self-defense. This limiting principle, so vital if we seek to guard against the outbreak of war, is corroded if major nations remain free to interpret self-defense. There is a need for objective limits, discernible by all actors, upon the concept of self-defense. Article 51 of the UN Charter could provide these limits, but only if the requirement of a prior armed attack is taken quite literally; that is, a nation is not entitled to resort to self-defense unless it has been the victim of an armed attack across an international frontier.[54] But can

[53] McDougal, "The Ethics of Applying Systems of Authority," *op.cit. supra,* note 8.

[54] The conditions surrounding the start of the Middle Eastern War of 1967 suggest certain qualifications of the position taken here in the text. The encirclement of Israel, the insistence by the United Arab Republic, Jordan, and Syria on proclaiming their intention to destroy Israel, the vulnerability of Israel to surprise attack,

the removal of the insulating presence of United Nations troops, the provocative closure of the Straits of Tiran to Israeli shipping, and the mobilization of Arab armed forces are among the factors that militate against regarding Israel's recourse to force as "an armed attack" rather than as "self-defense." This entire setting creates the need for a reinterpretation of the argument for a literal reading of Article 51. Unfortunately, these events occurred

a nation anticipating a nuclear surprise attack be expected to wait until the enemy missiles have been delivered? I think that the answer even here is properly given in the affirmative; such an assertion is based upon the availability of an invulnerable second strike capability and its consequence of making a nuclear surprise attack an act of suicide.

But limited force may be used to prevent the risks of major uses of force thereafter. Does a region have the legal discretion to use force to maintain regional security? To keep nuclear weapons out? Do regional organizations possess a broader competence to use force than does a single state? No authoritative answers are contained in the current law. However, the dangers of escalation require the effort of law to prevent, to the extent possible, international force, even if backed up by a supranational claim. Assuredly interregional force should not be employed more readily than international force. The more difficult questions are raised by the need to limit intraregional force. Here there is an ill-defined analogy to the status of intrastate force, the regional organization possessing some of the attributes of the incumbent government in relation to civil strife. Regardless of the context, reliance on force should be minimized. This is the central effort of law. But it is not the only effort. Otherwise there would be no right of self-defense whatsoever. Therefore, there is an attempt by law to balance interests in peace and survival. Particular rules are developed: for example, the norms of nonintervention in the internal affairs of sovereign states. Intervention, especially if in the form of coercive force, would appear to be an illegal use of force. But is not a military intervention an "armed attack" within the meaning of Article 51? Is there anything in law that corresponds to self-defense that can protect a state from minor coercion, perhaps applied in the form of support for or suppression of an insurgency? These questions are rarely analyzed from a legal point of view. A brief response is to suggest that norms of law in a horizontal legal order are valid only so long as there is a pattern of mutual adherence. The intervention by X in Y entitles Z to counterintervene to a proportional extent; or the facts of intervention justify the counterintervention of a regional or global international institution.

In addition to the avoidance of force, obedience to world law requires deference to community procedures and decisions. How much deference? Suppose the General Assembly passes a resolution that recommends a prohibition on underground nuclear testing. What is the legal status of the resolution? What conditions should prompt the United

---

too recently to be taken into account in my presentation other than by way of   mention in this footnote.

States to disregard the resolution? Here, the role of reasonableness in the assessment of legality is crucial. If a state disregards the resolution without giving an adequate account of its reasons for doing so, then it sets a precedent for self-reliance that is most damaging to the status and future of law. The minimum demand of horizontal law is that a nation, when its action is seriously challenged by other significant actors in the system, provide reasons. This notion of minimum reasonableness, the giving of reasons, is less burdensome than is optimal reasonableness: an impartial balancing of the reasons for and against the contested conduct in argument and in behavior. A refusal to satisfy the demands of minimum reasonableness discloses the unwillingness of a nation to acknowledge that the will and welfare of the world community is an important determinant of national policy.

Suppose, however, that an unambiguous decision adverse to national interests is rendered by an international institution. At this stage some flexibility of national response must be retained in form because it will be manifest in fact. Therefore, a rigid commitment to deference or submission is unrealistic. A legal claim is just one of several sources of guidance. But the significance of respecting international law may be lost in the effort to avoid the burdens of total acquiescence. A state that refuses to accept the adverseness of a *particular* supranational determination, especially if it is a state that is exercising the kind of leadership that sets the precedents that evolve authoritative patterns of practice, damages the role of law in world affairs. By its refusal to abide, such a state creates a *general* atmosphere of response to adverse judgments, thereby conditioning the expectations of other members and of the community as a whole, as well as restricting the support that can be mobilized to coerce compliance. Therefore, the acceptance, even if awkward and frustrating, of an adverse international judgment or adherence to a legal rule that interferes with immediate national aspiration, may often serve the national interest of the state to a greater extent than would lawless behavior. It seems reasonable to accord some weight at this point to the longer term interests of states in transforming the world to achieve more reliably national interests measured out over decades and centuries of security and survival rather than months or years of temporary advantage; the transformation of the world must gradually come to be an instrumental element in present behavior. Otherwise the gap between facts and goals is necessarily made permanent. Realism for the nuclear age resembles idealism in early centuries, but this remark is encouraging only to the extent that governing elites and publics can be made to perceive and behave accordingly. To make this reorientation operational—that is, to strengthen the law orientation of major actors in world affairs—requires a convinced sense of the relevance of the goal of a warless world to the conception and execution of present policy, and this enlivened awareness encourages, in turn, a new and essential juridical concern with the "transition problem"—to inventory the means available to transform the existing system for regulating international conduct from a threat system into a genuine peace system.

1962

III. McDougal and Feliciano on Law and Minimum World Public Order

THE CONTEMPORARY situation of mankind gives an acknowledged prominence to two intertwined challenges: the prospect of thermonuclear catastrophe and the spread of totalitarianism. These dangers seem so overwhelming that many choose paths of despair or evasion, thereby renouncing the freedom of responsibility to use human energy to shape human destiny. The crisis of our age requires moral courage to defend a way of life and yet the spiritual wisdom to avoid a means of defense that is itself the occasion of unprecedented suffering and destruction. This dangerous and inevitably ambiguous moral imperative, supported now by a slowly forming consensus, solicits every resource of will and mind available in a nontotalitarian society.

Myres S. McDougal consciously responds to this contemporary situation with extraordinary insight and industry. McDougal has joined with Harold D. Lasswell to develop techniques that bolster the prospects for the peaceful preservation of our way of life at this historic time of awesome danger.

One of McDougal's distinctive achievements is to transform the *critical* tools sharpened by the legal realist movement into tools of *construction* for the development of a new vision of a value-oriented legal order.[1] The critical perspective of the realists allows law to remain liberated from myths of logical and doctrinal restraint. These myths had embodied a falsely mechanical image of the legal process that conceived of law as a method for achieving the objective application of the single rule that alone properly governs the outcome of a legal controversy. McDougal has proceeded from the destruction of this myth to a primary emphasis on ways to assure the subordination of law to the moral and social service of the community. McDougal's concern with values and community policies, as ascertained objectively by the techniques of social science (not, as he is so often misunderstood as advocating, by the arbitrarily relevant values and policies of the authorized decision-maker), reintroduces into the legal process a pervasive and nonexpedient source of restraint historically associated with the rise of natural law in Western moral philosophy. However, McDougal substitutes the empirical generalizations of social science for the metaphysically based propositions of reason and religion. On top of this foundation for his moral universe McDougal erects, somewhat

---

[1] I have tried to outline an interpretation of McDougal's general jurisprudence elsewhere: Falk (Book Review), 10 *American Journal of Comparative Law* 297 (1961).

disarmingly, a set of community goals called "the values of a public order of human dignity" that are *postulated* as a preferred orientation. McDougal's typically modern distrust of authoritative epistemologies is forthrightly indicated: "Any derivations by others which support our postulated goals are regarded as acceptable."[2] In a world of diverse cultures, religions, and races McDougal pleads for an effective use of the moral convergencies that exist, discarding as irrelevant luxuries of earlier ages the classical inquiries into the grounds as well as the content of moral commitments. Whether such a postulation transcends the currently prevailing moral ideals of Western liberal democracies is of vital concern to the philosopher who seeks to evaluate the claim made by McDougal to resolve contemporary legal conflicts by a value- and policy-oriented jurisprudence.[3]

McDougal perceives the phenomena of international affairs in light of the distinctive structural and processive characteristics of international law. Adequate account is taken of the special ordering characteristics of a decentralized legal system that must depend heavily upon patterns of voluntary compliance by national officials who have been entrusted with a primary responsibility for maximizing the exclusive interests of their particular nation. McDougal, building upon the work of George Scelle, brilliantly demonstrates the wide and significant compatibility between national and international interests that allows a national official to serve simultaneously his own society and the interests of the world community. Lasswell vividly praises McDougal in his Introduction for recognizing "the role that scholars, and particularly legal scholars, can play in perceiving the realities of the inclusive interests of mankind, and showing how the traditional instruments of legal order can be flexibly adapted to the urgencies of the age."[4] This comment highlights the importance that McDougal attributes to exercising influence upon those responsible for making decisions. The decision-maker is the appropriate target for any policy approach that hopes to influence behavior and, hence, improve the capacities of men and nations to fulfill the conditions of human welfare. Thus the reform of the international legal order depends not only upon "the invention and establishment of institutionalized sanctioning practices—the authority structures and procedures" but also on the creation and foster-

---

[2] McDougal, "Some Basic Theoretical Concepts about International Law: A Policy-Oriented Framework of Inquiry," *Journal of Conflict Resolution*, IV (1960), 337, 343.

[3] We seek also to know whether morality can contribute something more authoritative than a statement of social preferences.

This possibility depends upon the epistemological basis for moral judgments.

[4] Myres S. McDougal and Florentino P. Feliciano, *Law and Minimum World Public Order: The Legal Regulation of International Coercion*, New Haven, Yale University Press, 1961, p. xxvi.

ing of the necessary predispositions in effective decision-makers to put some structures and procedures into operation.[5]

This orientation profoundly suggests that the task of highest scholastic priority is to influence the patterns of awareness held by elite actors. The goal is to gain acceptance for views that more fully reflect the needs of legal order in the contemporary world. Continuing demands of sovereign prerogative, for instance, should be overcome by reorientation of loyalty. Such shifts might partially arise from an acceptance of the insight that mutual security is now often promoted more by supranational than by national agencies of control; it does not advance the cause of world order to manufacture blueprints, however ingenious, that would distribute international power differently until dominant groups are persuaded of the necessity for a new power structure. For once the appropriate supranationalizing disposition emerges, the development of implementing techniques would be easily achieved; and without it, nothing else matters much. However, the *existence* of a persuasive blueprint itself acts to convince skeptical people of its feasibility.

The primary work of the legal scholar is the presentation of reality to encourage the perception of significant contradictions between preferred values and existing behavioral patterns. For as the field of awareness alters, an assurance is born that obsolete patterns of response will be correspondingly changed. Accordingly, McDougal and Feliciano implore "every one genuinely committed to the goal values of a world public order of human dignity" to take on the job "of creating in all peoples of the world the perspectives necessary both to their realistic understanding of this common interest and to their acceptance and initiation of the detailed measures in sanctioning process appropriately designed to secure such interest."[6] This recommended reorientation of perspective is critical for the future of world order in view of the continuing decentralization of power and authority in the international system. For international restraints relating to the use of force become effective only when reinforced by voluntary compliance, a reinforcement that cannot come about until the major national actors realize that their self-interest is served by conforming national policy to the common interests of the world community. This emphasis by McDougal upon the importance of actor perception—so novel for international jurists habitually concerned with the intricacies of doctrine, or at best, with the interplay of legal rules and social facts—helps to distinguish sharply between the existence and the perception of common interests.

[5] *Ibid.*, p. 263. See also pp. 260, 375.   [6] *Ibid.*, p. 376.

With respect to the development of international law it is the policy function of the scholar to overcome the perceptual lag that arises from the failure of leaders and their peoples to understand the impact of the interdependent and nuclear modern world upon the character of national self-interest.[7] McDougal and Feliciano readjust traditional calculations about the balance between (exclusive) and international (inclusive) interests. This readjustment is achieved by a demonstration of the radical relevance of such developments as nuclear technology and ideological conflict. Too little attention is given by the authors to the importance of the new nations and their distinctive perspectives.

In the context of coercion it is asserted, "From an objective vantage point, certainly the most conspicuous fact about the contemporary world social process must be the common interest of all peoples, whatever the comprehensive public order to which they adhere, in the maintenance of minimum order."[8] This is a complicated way of saying that there are no political objectives in the world today, however justifiable they may appear to be, that are worth major recourse to the instruments of war. The basic principle of minimum order is "that force and intense coercion are not to be used for the expansion of values"; it is defended as basic to goals of the proponents of human dignity and considered to be "perhaps even the price of survival."[9] Such advocacy certainly seems persuasive when the risks of nuclear conflict are great; for example, if the threatening expansion of values involves international violence undertaken by a cold war rival. It is less clear when use of "intense coercion" to expand values is made outside the main cold war confrontations, as when India absorbs Goa, or Indonesia proceeds against West Irian, or the African states prepare to coerce the Republic of South Africa. Thus the principle of minimum order appears presently to operate as a special principle applicable to the bilateral confrontation of the United States and the Soviet Union; it does not yet serve as an adequate statement of required conduct for every actor in the contemporary international system. Even the superpowers seem able to make selective use of intense instruments of violence to promote political expansion if the arena of conflict is within rather than between national societies.[10] In this regard, McDougal and Feliciano do not give enough attention to the distinction between in-

[7] Lasswell in his Introduction, *ibid.*, p. xxv, suggests that the facts of interdependence may actually inhibit centralizations of loyalty by accentuating the concern of system units with their own particular identity and interests.

[8] *Ibid.*, p. 375.

[9] *Ibid.*, p. 377.

[10] This capability of the two superpowers is well developed by Samuel P. Huntington, "Patterns of Violence in World Politics," in Huntington, ed., *Changing Patterns of Military Politics*, New York, Free Press, 1962, pp. 17-50.

ternal and international wars in their formulation of the principle of minimum order.[11]

The authors reveal a deep realization that the decentralization of the international legal order "has infected with formidable ambiguity both the characterization of unlawful coercion and the detailed prescriptions of the fundamental policy of minimum destruction of values."[12] The tendencies to self-interpret the content of and occasions for self-defense and military necessity jeopardize the community policies expressed in the restraining norms of behavior. For the perspective of the actor outweighs his sense of just proportion between potentially antagonistic claims of national aspiration and world peace. Here, as elsewhere, McDougal accepts the pervasive reality of legal indeterminacy that is a consequence of the logical applicability of complementary structures of norms to any set of facts in contention.[13] And here, as elsewhere, reliance must accordingly be placed upon the governing norm of "reasonableness" that is supposed to mediate between the conflicting policies expressed by contradictory rules of law that are simultaneously applicable. When intermediate range missiles are stationed in Cuba, their removal by a coercive claim challenges every national perspective to choose between the principles of minimum destruction and self-defense; a reasonable unilateral claim must, at least, threaten to use as little force as is essential to achieve its security goal. Thus McDougal and Feliciano stress this inevitable reliance upon rational choice and the nonarbitrary character of the test of reasonableness:

> Reasonableness in particular context does not mean arbitrariness in decision but in fact its exact opposite, the disciplined ascription of policy import to varying factors in appraising their operational and functional significance for community goals in given instances of coercion.[14]

This characterization of decision-making is accurate only to the extent that "policy" is specified by the objective methods of the social sciences rather than by the preferences and particular aims of the individuals entrusted with the power of decision. In international affairs the decision-maker is often acting in a role in which the paramount commitment is to serve the exclusive and perhaps antagonistic interests

[11] Some attempt to carry through this line of analysis is made in Falk, *Law, Morality and War in the Contemporary World,* New York, Praeger, 1963.

[12] McDougal and Feliciano, *op.cit. supra,* note 4, p. 59.

[13] For a more jurisprudential statement see McDougal, "The Ethics of Applying Systems of Authority: The Balanced Opposites of a Legal System," in Harold D. Lasswell and Harlan Cleveland, eds., *The Ethic of Power,* New York, Praeger, 1962, pp. 221-40.

[14] McDougal and Feliciano, *op.cit. supra,* note 4, p. 218.

of the national community, and this commitment is understood by everyone in the system. Even the International Court of Justice, perhaps the most objective decision-making authority in international affairs, makes statutory provision for the appointment of a national judge in the event that a litigant's nationality is not already represented on the bench. This approach contrasts interestingly with domestic adjudication in which an assumed similarity of outlook that joins a judge to a litigant —say, the outlook shared by members of the same family—would lead to the immediate disqualification of the judge.

McDougal has been fairly and unfairly criticized for his appreciations of the role of the committed decision-maker in international law. Quincy Wright takes issue with McDougal:

> It is difficult to conceive how a game could proceed unless its rules are distinguished from the strategies of the players. . . . It is no less difficult to conceive of a stable society in which the laws defining its basic order are not distinguished from the policy and strategy of parties and people.[15]

Roger Fisher offers similar criticism:

> It is one thing to urge an organized national community, in which the common values are widely shared, to construe its rules in the light of those values. It is another thing to tell the world community, a community whose members hold sharply conflicting views, that their conduct should not be governed by rules, that each nation should pursue its ends by whatever means seem reasonable to it. Such advice seems ill suited to the task of persuading governments that their enlightened self-interest lies in exercising restraint along lines which other governments may also be prepared to respect.[16]

Such criticisms, often made in crude forms,[17] are unfair whenever they imply that McDougal is trying to instruct states to substitute the perspectives of national policy for those of international order. McDougal's argument arises from his understanding of the nature of law, regardless of the character of the social order. It is not that McDougal desires judges to substitute policy for rules, but rather he is arguing for explicit policy-making instead of implicit policy-making. The existence of complementary sets of norms with equal relevance necessarily throws the real basis of legal decision onto some nonobjective level of preference. If the preference is obscured by the mystique of tradi-

15 Quincy Wright (Book Review), 39 *University of Detroit Law Journal* 145, 148 (1961).

16 Roger Fisher, *Science*, 135 (1962),

658, 660.

17 E.g. Anthony D'Amato (Book Review), 75 *Harvard Law Review* 458 (1961).

tional legal dogmatics then it is hard, according to the McDougal canon, to hold the decision-maker accountable. For such a tradition persuades the community to receive the decision as a technical matter in which the decision-maker had no appreciable range of discretion. Furthermore, unless the decision-maker is made aware of the policy basis of law, rational decision-making is frustrated; for there is no consideration given to the relative merits of the policies promoted by the alternative normative directions of decision. Thus an inquiry into the policies at stake is essential both to the *discovery* of the most rational decision and for its *justification* to other actors and to the community.[18] In this respect Fisher seems to miss McDougal's point when he argues that, "to accept his policy-science is all but to ignore the policy of having law."[19] McDougal presupposes that it is a policy that we promote whenever we apply law, whether it is realized or not, whether it is liked or not. McDougal does not mean to assume an attitude toward law; he purports to describe the real demythologized nature of law.

There is, however, a crucial matter of political self-interest involved in McDougal's argument about international legal order; for McDougal considers that the failure to perceive law as an instrument of policy produces defeat for the policies favored by one's own value system. Therefore, the very conflict in policy mentioned by Fisher as characteristic of contemporary international politics makes it especially necessary for McDougal to disclose, rather than to disguise, the policy consequences of alternative interpretations of law. In domestic society the presence of a comparative harmony of values makes it somewhat less dangerous to obscure a particular policy choice.

This general point is made specific by McDougal's perception of the cold war. First of all, for McDougal, the cold war represents a value conflict between Communist totalitarian myths and the Western defense of human dignity and liberal democracy; thus the outcome of the struggle has a crucial significance for all that we cherish as nontotalitarians.[20] Second, the Communist strategists are fully aware that law is really a process for the promotion of policies and are adept at manipulating legal doctrine to serve Communist policies.[21] Third, a mechanical sub-

[18] The separation of these two modes of endeavor is suggested in general terms by Hans Reichenbach. It makes particular sense in a legal context where it is one discipline to determine the appropriate decision and another to communicate to the relevant community a decision that has been reached.

[19] Fisher, *op.cit. supra*, note 9, p. 660.

[20] E.g. pp. 43, 60, 70ff., 75, 88ff., 91, 262, 279, 356, 377 of the book under

review.

[21] McDougal and Feliciano apparently accept without question (at least they do not disclose any questioning) the image of the cold war put forward by Robert Strausz-Hupé and others in *Protracted Conflict*, New York, Harper and Brothers, 1959; see, e.g. p. 279, passim. I find this image to be an unacceptably self-serving interpretation of the cold war that over-rigidifies "the enemy" and is *too clear*

servience to legal restraint by Western nations, independent of policy implications, handicaps our side in the cold war and gives the Sino-Soviet group of states a pervasive and unnecessary advantage that may prove to be decisive. In view of this situation it is a matter of moral and political survival, as well as jurisprudential integrity, to acknowledge that a public official properly applies the law only when he promotes the policies of the moral community that he serves. There is no existing universal moral order. Without such universality the world exhibits contending systems as its primary characteristic and it is up to those on our side to help it prevail. Thus Quincy Wright is naïve to assume, as he does, that

> . . . the prime function of law must be to maintain a basic order among members of a society who differ in values, goals, and interests except that they share a common interest in order, permitting all to formulate and pursue policies and strategies within the limitations of the law, secure in reliance that the basic order will be observed by others.[22]

McDougal dissents on both jurisprudential and sociological grounds. Rational actors use every means at their disposal, including law, to maximize their values. The quality of human rationality depends upon the extent to which an actor perceives opportunities for the maximization of values. Normative indeterminacy prevents a choice of "basic order" as the means to maximize values; there is no neutral decision, for every decision chooses among relevant rules that reflect relevant dominant policies. Furthermore, the Communists behave in an extremely policy-oriented fashion, disregarding rules whenever they conflict seriously with policies that permit pursuit by behavior that violates the rules. For example, Communist states place stress on conservative norms of national sovereignty, territorial jurisdiction, and nonintervention, whereas elsewhere in the world, practice and doctrine are mobilized to support just wars of national liberation.[23] The apparent contradiction on the level of norms is resolved on the level of policy where both claims, confined to their proper context, help the Communist system to maximize its goals in the present world.

---

about his objectives. Such a perception of the main patterns of international conflict influences the relative roles of law and force in world affairs. For if a major actor is identified unambiguously as an aggressor, then the premise of mutuality that underlies the validity of rules of legal restraint is undercut. I would agree that such a premise is lacking for rules governing participation in internal wars, thereby sus-pending nonintervention norms, but that it is emphatically present for military conflict across boundaries. This argument is spelled out in Chapter IV. This note should also be read as applicable to the text accompanying note 14.

22 Wright, *op.cit. supra,* note 8, p. 148.
23 Cf. Leon Lipson, "Outer Space and International Law," RAND Paper P-1434, 1958.

McDougal's philosophical premises are kept too implicit for a direct jurisprudential appreciation. If I understand his work correctly he is making an authoritative judgment that legality depends upon the extent to which decisions by officials (wherever situated in the social order)[24] implement the policies that promote "human dignity" as it has been interpreted by Western moral and political tradition, and including evidently the welfare of Western democratic states.[25] It is important to recall that this orientation is "postulated" without any argument for its validity as measured against other conceptions of welfare that could easily be articulated, with sincerity, in the rhetoric of human dignity. Certainly a convinced Marxist could promise to deliver man from the purportedly frightful alienation of capitalist society by ushering in the classless community; this vision remains the dream of certain socialists.[26] But is it proper to base a social order of diverse normative systems upon the presumed superiority of one's own system? Is not such self-validating assurance itself a defection from one of the prime discoveries of those seeking to promote the values of human dignity in the West? We have come a long way from the lethal certitude that provided a moral underpinning for the Inquisition and the Crusades. Or have we?

It is one thing to commit oneself to the preservation of a moral position, even risking death and destruction to maintain spiritual integrity. Such resolve is essential to the vitality of any morality of significance. It is quite another to transform this commitment into a holy mission that claims for itself a privileged position from the perspective of law. It should be apparent that very practical consequences follow from McDougal's formulation if it is accepted as a serious jurisprudential appeal. Actors that accept McDougal's concept of human dignity are entitled to contaminate the atmosphere by nuclear testing, propose "defensive" invasions of Cuba, and station attack missiles around the borders of a potential enemy—and thereby *fulfill* the law. For the law turns out to be what helps a certain set of policies to prevail in the struggle for power. Identical claims to act by the enemies of McDougal's version of human dignity are, by the same reasoning, illegal, as their objectives deny the values of human dignity upon which

24 That is, whether the decision-maker is a national official in foreign office, an international civil servant, or a judge of (say) the International Court of Justice.
25 For a sympathetic review emphasizing McDougal's choice of human dignity as an axiological base, see Enrique M. Fernando, "An International Law of Human Dignity," 1 *Philippine International Law Journal* 178 (1962).
26 See, e.g. precisely this insistence upon human dignity by a socialist in Martin Buber, *Paths in Utopia*, London, Routledge and K. Paul, 1949. Marx's critique of capitalism emphasizes the alienation of man in a class society and the reacquisition of human dignity in a classless society.

law rests. This suggests an all-pervasive asymmetry between the United States and the Soviet Union with respect to the use of force. For instance, as of 1962 one must contend that United States missiles in Turkey are permissible, whereas Soviet missiles in Cuba are illegal. Are Soviet missiles in Russia also illegal? Why not? Does an opponent of "human dignity" have the right of self-defense under international law? Is it a narrower right than that granted by the same Charter norm (Article 51) to the proponents of "human dignity?" Is this something that should be decided by the actor claiming the privileged position, or is it more appropriately assessed by the portion of the world community that has sought to withdraw from the normative conflict by the pursuit of nonalignment policies?

Some of these questions can only be answered by making a decision about how to interpret applicable legal objections. It is perhaps useful to suggest that the quality of complementariness of legal norms is itself a matter of degree that can be emphasized or diminished. Thus nations can find a norm to support their preferred policy by stretching language and expectations—we can identify a United States invasion of a hostile Cuba as "self-defense." But nations can also try to fit their policies within the boundaries set by the common understanding of applicable legal obligations—a nation does not act in self-defense when it initiates an armed attack designed to overthrow the incumbent government in a weak neighbor like Cuba. The point is that the extent of policy and normative flexibility represents less a jurisprudential "fact" (as it appears to be in McDougal's work) than a policy chosen because it promotes other policies (here: the successful prosecution of the cold war). In this regard, I feel that McDougal sacrifices too many of the stabilizing benefits of a rule-oriented approach to international law by stressing policy flexibility. This sacrifice is especially great in international affairs where, as Fisher suggests, policy conflict and insufficient institutions make the reality of restraining norms depend on the comparative autonomy of rules symmetrically perceived and applied. I think an orientation toward rules in this sense serves the United States better today even if the hypothesis is correct that Communist states accept international law only to the extent that it conforms to their political policies.

McDougal's policy orientation also presupposes a certain kind of epistemological confidence which he never sustains with solid evidence. How do we achieve knowledge about the content of human dignity? Can there be diverse conceptions of human dignity several of which have an equivalent epistemological status? Can human reason ever invoke the methods of the social sciences to assure unambiguous access to truth? Can decision-makers find a rational vindication for recourse to nuclear warfare? Can a decision for which no adequate comparison exists ever satisfy McDougal's quest for reasonableness? Must not the preparation for and the resolve to use nuclear weapons rest instead upon either some spiritual commitment to defend the moral integrity of a particular social order or upon some commitment to express a biological adherence to a way of life? A decision that involves a potential willingness to inflict death and suffering upon millions of helpless and innocent people and to reduce to ashes the great centers of human civilization does not appear susceptible of rational justification.[27]

In fact, the customary self-restraining humility that arises from rational analysis forbids such a high risk to achieve a contingent secular

---

[27] Perhaps it is appropriate to note here that a rational contemplation of the connections between law and war in the nuclear age needs desperately to fuse the analyses produced by legal consciousness and the illuminations made possible by literary consciousness. A sense for the law governing coercion can no longer be exclusively entrusted to the guidance of the "rational technologist" who "simply places his knowledge and skill at the disposal of others" after he has uncovered the possibilities for legitimate action. Alf Ross, *On Law and Justice,* Berkeley, University of California Press, 1958, p. 377. We need, as well, to take account of the culminating insight achieved by the heroine of a recent remarkable novel by Doris Lessing: ". . . I had known, finally, that the truth for our time was war, the immanence of war." *The Golden Notebook,* New York, Simon and Schuster, 1962, p. 505. This is not just a dramatic part of the tableau, it is central to the very possibility of personality: ". . . I was experiencing the fear of war as one does in nightmares, not the intellectual balancing of probabilities, possibilities, but knowing, with my nerves and imagination, the fear of war." *Id.,* p. 503. This absolute awareness is reached during a routine London life far from battlefields. Lessing provides us with an incongruous cultural complement to the calm and influential calculations of RAND specialists. It is not that we can dispense with these specialists, but we must come to recognize that they are not able by themselves to form a just response to all that imperils our moral and physical existence.

McDougal, despite assuming the costume and gesture of a rational technologist, provides an intellectual foundation for closing this gap that separates these two orders of analytic and intuitive awareness. He insists that a legal decision always should promote the values that sustain the dignity of the individual person. Thus he is committed, in principle at least, to the acceptance of Doris Lessing's form of awareness, although not necessarily its method or its content. It is somewhat odd, I suppose, that I praise McDougal for doing something that he apparently denigrates; witness, for instance, the irony in this respect of a wry comment directed at Lon Fuller: "If I have mistaken for a serious essay, what was intended as poetry . . ." McDougal, "Fuller v. The American Realists," 50 *Yale Law Review* 827, 840, note 41 (1940-41). My contention is that it is almost no longer possible to write a serious essay on war that does not also include the world of poetry—poetry conceived of as a way of knowing, not as a metrical arrangement of words. We can no longer afford to compartmentalize our approaches to reality. They must enrich one another or they each exist as an abstraction, too partial to serve well this urgent quest for awareness. Such an intellectual program awaits fulfillment. In the meantime, it is essential to explicate as fully as possible the meanings of our commitments to use force to promote political objectives and to reaffirm the restraints of law and morality that are able to survive nuclear technology. McDougal and Feliciano deserve our deep gratitude for disclosing just how much law continues to be usefully relevant to decisions about the application of coercion.

objective. It is the nonnuclear states, fearing their agonizing witness to the folly of nuclear conflict, that express more clearly the demands of reason. And so one finds a Resolution of the General Assembly, supported by a large majority of members, that states the case for the advocates of rational restraint; it sets the stage with a countdown:

> Recalling that the use of weapons of mass destruction, causing unnecessary human suffering, was in the past prohibited as being contrary to the laws of humanity and to the principles of international law, by international declarations and binding agreements, such as the Declaration of St. Petersburg of 1868, the Declaration of the Brussels Convention of 1874, the Conventions of The Hague Peace Conferences of 1899 and 1907, and the Geneva Protocol of 1925, to which the majority of nations are still parties.[28]

The Resolution goes on to declare that the use of nuclear weapons "is contrary to the spirit, letter and aims of the United Nations and, as such, a direct violation of the Charter," that such use "would exceed even the cause of war and cause indiscriminate suffering . . . and . . . is contrary to the rules of international law and to the laws of humanity"; that any employment of nuclear weapons "is a war directed not against an enemy or enemies alone but also against mankind in general"; and that, as such, the state making such a use "is to be considered as violating the Charter . . . as acting contrary to the laws of humanity and as committing a crime against mankind and civilization."

McDougal's position starts from a premise developed in an earlier study with Norbert Schlei: "It is not the physical modality of destruction that is relevant to law and policy but rather the purposes and the effects of the destruction and the relation of these purposes and effects to the values of a free world society."[29] Thus the combatant state is authorized to use nuclear weapons if use is otherwise consistent with the broad restraining norms of international law: proportionality of response and a minimum destruction of values consistent with the successful attainment of the military objective. The development and destructiveness of nuclear weapons lead McDougal and Feliciano to state that "a very strong case would have to be made to establish that no possible use of nuclear and thermonuclear weapons could conceivably be within the scope of military necessity for objectives legitimate

---

[28] Declaration on the Prohibition of Nuclear Weapons, G.A. 1653, p. xvi; and see Ninčić, "Nuclear Weapons and the Charter of the United Nations," 2 *Jugoslovenska Revija za Medunarodno Pravo* 197 (1962).

[29] Myres S. McDougal and Associates, *Studies in World Public Order,* New Haven, Yale University Press, 1960, p. 817; cf. McDougal and Feliciano, *op.cit. supra,* note 4, p. 79: ". . . the purpose and level of destruction obtained are of prime import to legal policy."

by standards making reference to human dignity." Indeed, the presence of nuclear weapons and the difficulties of agreeing about their effective control "must suggest expectations of their military effectiveness and the perils of relying upon any *alleged limitations* derived from analogies" (e.g. prohibition of poison gas). But what of the perils of refusing any limitations? And why, after the sentence about human dignity, should the prospect of military effectiveness reassimilate decisions about the use of nuclear weapons into the usual framework for decisions about the use of force in international affairs? McDougal and Feliciano end at precisely this position:

> The *rational position* would appear to be that the lawfulness of any particular use or type of use of nuclear or thermonuclear weapons must be judged, *like the use of any weapon or technique of warfare,* by the level of destruction effected—in other words, by its *reasonableness in the total context of a particular use.*[30]

But whose version of reasonableness? Are we once more to retreat to the bloody terrain of subjective appreciation? So often in the past national leaders have plunged their society into bloody turmoil that appears fruitless in retrospect. Now the backward glance may be all but denied if we do not invent restraints upon the use of force that satisfy the inclusive interests of mankind in the maintenance of peace.

This issue has been developed in detail because it bears so crucially upon the moral foundations of the theory of coercion developed by McDougal and Feliciano as the appropriate basis for the examination of all traditional problems in the area. The same style of analysis leads them to reject a strict interpretation of the right of self-defense and not to attempt stable definition of aggression across an international frontier. Even in an inflamed world of distrust McDougal and Feliciano prefer to entrust the guidance of behavior to self-determining decisions of reasonableness by the participants in a conflict situation rather than to impose common restraining limits upon human discretion; this preference seems to hold regardless of the temptations that may exist in some instances to coerce a favorable outcome by recourse to nuclear warfare.

The McDougal-Feliciano approach to decisions involving the use of nuclear weapons appears to me deficient in several respects:

First, it places excessive trust in the capacity of national officials to determine the nature of reasonableness in situations where the outcome of conflict is perceived as a matter of vital national interests. In

---

[30] All quotations in this paragraph are taken from *ibid.,* p. 78 (emphasis supplied); cf. also pp. 244, 659-68 for further exposition of the McDougal-Feliciano position on nuclear weapons.

addition, once the basic reasonableness of the claim to act in self-defense is granted then there exists a wide range of discretion to implement that claim in accordance with national policy. Of course, broad humanitarian considerations may operate as constraints, as may deference to such general limiting notions as are derived from the rule of proportionality and from the laws of war, but the overriding deference is to self-determined perceptions of "military necessity," an all-purpose solvent of legal restraint in the application of violence that results in giving almost full control over the content of reasonableness to the states acting against each other. Therefore, not only is the basic decision to use force made in self-serving fashion, but the extent of use and the character of "defensive" objectives are also determined by officials of the acting state. Given the misperceptions of "aggression" that arise from a biased interpretation of the facts by a state that feels its interests threatened by another state, it is quite misleading to identify the outcome of its governmental decision-making processes with "reasonableness," regardless of the range of facts considered. National decision-making with respect to the use of force is likely to be "unreasonable" because of the partisan and impassioned *interpretation* of the facts rather than because of any lack of *comprehensiveness*.

Second, it fails to differentiate between present decisions to use military force and prenuclear decisions. As a result, it is overly pessimistic about the failure of past efforts of law to discourage the use of weapons with military importance. It seems to overlook the widespread perception that before nuclear weapons some international actors could always expect to gain by the major use of force in an aggressive manner, whereas today it is implausible for anyone to contemplate such gain. The new situation reinforces any scheme of prohibition, as there is so much less incentive to violate.

Third, it purports to classify authorizations of nuclear warfare as potentially reasonable, thereby neglecting their radical and problematical relevance to the human situation.

Fourth, it makes no attempt to indicate in illustrative detail how the proponents of human dignity would rationalize recourse to nuclear weapons or provide certain limiting conditions (e.g. targeting restrictions or a restriction to second use or a restriction to use in response to massive conventional armed attack for which no other defense exists).

Fifth, it does not rely upon the values of human dignity to alter the character of military objectives in light of the unprecedented risks of contemporary warfare. If human dignity does not give a distinctive operational direction to decision-makers in the context of nuclear weapons, then it hardly serves as a moral orientation toward life. For if it fails to guide our response to this challenge to the cultural and biological survival of mankind, then it merely offers a new ideological rhetoric that helps with the creation of a rationalizing myth. This myth might produce a higher vindication of self-interested behavior. It does not, however, as it implies, provide rational guidance based either upon empirical inferences or upon the application of *a priori* principles of minimum public order.

The McDougal-Feliciano position also neglects the special hazards and the peculiar ordering potentialities of the international system as a decentralized system. The difficulties of achieving explicit agreement between hostile actors urge us to consider far greater reliance upon tacit restraints that are adopted to promote universal interest in the avoidance of nuclear war.[31] Such a regime of tacit restraint depends upon the development of limitations of national discretion that are based upon relatively objective boundaries. These boundaries should be easily discernible regardless of moral or cultural perspective. The dividing line between nuclear and nonnuclear weapons, the requirement that an armed attack precede a claim of self-defense, and the distinction between initiating force *across* boundaries (direct aggression) and using force *within* boundaries, appear crucial in this respect.

Such a regime also depends upon symmetry as an essential ordering characteristic. What is claimed by one state must, by this logic, be permitted to all other states. United States missiles in Turkey do legitimize an equivalent claim by the Soviet Union. An aggressor must be restrained, but not by our asymmetrical interpretation of rights of self-defense and other governing norms. Such unilateral interpretation would undermine the basis of respect for law. It also would jeopardize adherence to common restraints, the effectiveness of which might increase the prospects for maintaining peace in the decades ahead. Symmetry would, moreover, guard against the distorting determinations of world community welfare that are made by national officials when they are subject to intense domestic pressures.[32] These pressures make the advocacy of noncoercive methods for the resolution of conflicts tantamount to treason during certain periods of crisis. We in the United States need the protection of these fixed restraints on our use of

---

[31] Cf. Thomas C. Schelling, *The Strategy of Conflict,* Cambridge, Harvard University Press, 1960, pp. 83-118.

[32] E.g. Robert C. North, "Decision-Making in Crisis: An Introduction," *Journal of Conflict Resolution,* VI (1962), 197:

"During these investigations it became apparent that the high stress that is almost universally characteristic of international crisis situations tends to have a crucial effect upon the decision-making of the leaderships involved."

coercion, especially if the American public and its legislative leadership do not adapt their expectations somewhat to the staggering dangers and costs of warfare in the contemporary world.

Unfortunately, McDougal and Feliciano do not use their formidable talents to advance an understanding of the desiderata of world order. Little light is shed upon the legal relevance of choosing an invulnerable second strike military posture as opposed to Secretary McNamara's "no cities" strategy or the Air Force's advocacy of counterforce capabilities. No attempt is made to examine the potentialities for arms control and disarmament through various modes of negotiation and mutual self-restraint, nor is the quest for disarmament or the curtailment of the arms race made an explicit concern of these advocates of human dignity. Furthermore, there is no attempt made to balance the claims by supranational actors (for example, the organs of the United Nations) to serve as authoritative decision-makers against the claims of national actors. If the General Assembly prohibits further nuclear testing, should the United States consider itself free to test anyway if its prevailing experts deem it to be militarily necessary? How do we distinguish authoritative decision-making from conscientious determinations of national interests? Is it not precisely the gradual willingness to sacrifice the caprices of national will to the emerging vividness of world community consensus that provides the one solid foundation for the growth of a stable and just world order? McDougal and Feliciano are themselves led to comment, albeit in a footnote, that ". . . whatever the specific type of decision and whatever the degree of involvement of the general community, continuous and purposeful focus upon long-term goals and policies may help in promoting rationality in decision."[33] Nevertheless the authors, despite their definitive account of law governing coercion within the traditional framework of war, accord very little attention to the ways in which national decision-makers should take legal account of the significance of such new developments as the growth of the United Nations or the destructive potential of the new generation of nuclear weapons. There is, that is, no attempt made to revise the framework for decision in a manner that is operationally relevant. This failure seems to neglect the radical developments of the age to which the authors attribute their own primary motivation. Thus rationality of decision, the prime objective of a jurist with McDougal's orientation, seems to suffer from insufficient attention as the longer term needs of world order are not adequately assimilated into the framework of analysis.

Beyond this, the prospect for rationality is itself conceived somewhat

[33] McDougal and Feliciano, *op.cit. supra*, note 4, p. 156, note 93.

uncritically. McDougal and Feliciano do not acknowledge the problems that arise from the limits of rational analysis. Choices between competing policies can often not be resolved by the methods of policy science. How reasonable is it to kill? Such a question transcends my comprehension of the outer limits of reason and yet states the abiding issue for officials responsible for making decisions about violence. No matter how much we flee from the soft center of human resolve it remains to torment us with the ambiguity of every human resolve. One cannot permanently ignore the wisdom of Nicholas Berdyaev, who suggests that "The inconsistencies and contradictions which are to be found in my thought are expressions of spiritual conflict, of contradictions which lie at the very heart of existence itself, and are not to be disguised by a facade of logical unity."[34] The existentialist critique of rationality deserves a most serious response from jurists who propose to rely upon reasonableness as the basis of a progressive system of world order.

[34] Nicholas Berdyaev, *Slavery and Freedom*, New York, Scribners, 1943, p. 8.

1962

PART TWO

CIVIL STRIFE, INTERVENTION, AND

MINOR COERCION

Introduction

MUCH OF the conventional wisdom about regulating international violence is misleading. It is misleading because it falsifies the nature of violence in international life and, consequently, the nature of the regulatory regime required to control it. Emile Benoit, the noted economist, has written a passage that summarizes the conventional wisdom with which I propose to disagree:

> Warfare has been endemic in most human societies except where repressed by the rule of law supported by a legitimate authority with preponderant force. Warfare has gradually been eliminated *within* most nation-states, but not in the relations *between* nation-states, where the requisite rule of law, legitimate authority, and preponderant force are lacking.[1]

The initial objection to this formulation arises from Professor Benoit's implication that the problem of better ordering international relations consists of making wars between states as infrequent as are wars within states. Such an assertion strikes me as a misunderstanding on at least two levels: first, it inaccurately presupposes the relative frequency of international wars and the relative infrequency of internal wars; second, it inappropriately homogenizes the requirements for adequate order in national and international society.

It is not the incidence of warfare *between* nations that is so threatening, it is the seriousness of certain particular instances, however infrequent or improbable. There is no doubt that nuclear deterrence discourages frequent recourse to interstate violence; this is the empirical justification for the use of such terms as "the balance of terror" or "the nuclear stalemate"—however delicate. It is a fundamental misunderstanding of the dangers implicit in contemporary international relations to suppose that these dangers could be overcome if the "rule of law, legitimate authority, and preponderant force" of international society could be made to approximate what exists in domestic societies. It is considerably more probable, one would suppose and hope, that a serious civil or internal war will occur in Spain or India within the next five years, than that an international war will be fought during this period between the Soviet Union and the United States. And yet I should suppose that it would be difficult to find a responsible person willing to allege that Spain or India is vulnerable to civil strife because they possess deficient domestic law systems. Or, to put it

[1] Emile Benoit, "Economic Adjustments to Arms Control," *Journal of Arms Control*, I (1963), 105-111.

even more remotely, that a highly developed legal system backed by a strong constabulary would be able to guarantee the state against the outbreak of civil war. But such a position seems to be the unambiguous implication of Benoit's language. And it is an implication often reflected in the work of the rule of law movement. The possession of "preponderant force" by domestic enforcement institutions has never been able to remove permanently the specter of civil strife from domestic life, nor is there reason to suppose that the acquisition of preponderant force by international institutions would eliminate the prospect of war from international life.

The confusion, then, concerns the kind of expectations that it is appropriate to associate with the improvement of international law as a system for regulating the behavior of sovereign states. There is confusion both about the kinds of tasks that law (rules, procedures for their interpretation, and institutions for their enforcement) can and cannot be expected to perform successfully and about the significance of the differing requirements of minimum order in domestic and in international affairs. No legal order, however perfected, can by itself guarantee absolute compliance with a norm, no matter how crucial it may be for the survival of the social fabric to prevent even a single violation if a society is to survive. The role of law is first to increase the incentives to comply and then to control as fully as possible those who remain unresponsive to these incentives, either by punishing, reforming, or removing them from the social system. But the development of a complementary capacity for response to noncompliance is an assumed ingredient of every operating legal system.[2] No matter how much legal structure and process in world affairs can be improved, it is unreasonable to expect absolute compliance with critical norms of social control. But nuclear technology has been prudently interpreted to require the development of a system of order that makes the use or threat of force in international affairs virtually impossible. To make something "impossible" requires, if it is ever a realistic goal, more than law; it requires, at least, the effective removal of the principal instruments of violation. It may also require basic shifts in attitudes toward the role of violence in human affairs and, perhaps, as well a modification of the aggressive element in human nature. It is for this reason that reliable and complete disarmament becomes a minimum social pre-condition for the emergence of a warless world.

This conclusion leads us to consider further the distinction between

---

[2] Ideas concerning responses to violations of international agreements have been most fully developed in the area of arms control and disarmament. For representative thinking see the chapters by R. J. Barnet and Louis B. Sohn in Barnet and Falk, eds., *Security in Disarmament*, Princeton, Princeton University Press, 1965, pp. 157-203.

minimum order in domestic and international affairs. We read daily about unsolved homicides in newspapers or gradually grow aware that even in a country as advanced and prosperous as the United States, considerably over one million serious crimes (felonies) are reported each year. We know about the persistence and pervasiveness of communal behavior and yet we do not lose faith in the viability of a domestic legal and political order. Why not? The minimum order of domestic society is not ordinarily imperiled by violations of its particular rules, even if these violations are widespread. The social need to uphold the principle of respect for law appears to be quite compatible with a rather high, but not unrestrictedly so, degree of lawlessness. A refusal to obey a particular rule of domestic law, however, if supported by citizens of wealth, prestige, and power, may undermine the integrity of the legal order if successfully sustained over a period of time. This vulnerability of the legal order was vividly illustrated in the United States after World War I by the legal prohibition on the sale of alcoholic beverages; not only was the particular rule violated with pride by law-abiding citizens, but the social processes generated by widespread violations produced a whole series of collateral lawless activities, as well as tending to blur the distinction between agencies of law enforcement and crime. The police were themselves often widely implicated in the endeavors to circumvent the prohibition laws.

A generalized adherence to governing rules will not do in world affairs, at least if the rules in question involve the duty of principal sovereign states to refrain from the use of force in their relations with one another. For in world affairs, especially given the existence of weapons of mass destruction, the prospect of a single violation is so terrifying that we would deem any legal order to be a failure that did not insure us against the outbreak of war. But this is similar to expecting a design of a domestic legal system in which we could be sure that a homicide would never be committed. Such an objective requires "a new man"; no societal mechanism, no matter how it is improved, can be expected to satisfy such a demand for perfection.

The failure of law in world affairs is frequently misunderstood at this point. International law is not a weak system because it is frequently violated; it is a weak system because it cannot accommodate certain kinds of violation, however infrequent (especially, recourse to war). The way to strengthen the system is not primarily to find ways to raise the rate of compliance, but rather to deprive the national actors in the system of the capacity for destructive noncompliance and to change basic patterns of behavior. A domestic legal system is normally judged stable to the extent that it has been able to monopolize for itself the capability to commit very destructive violations. A formula to achieve comparable control in the international legal order over the capability to commit destructive violations is the chief desideratum of our time.

Posing the problem in this form, however, suggests a further difficulty implicit in the disarmament approach to world order. Domestic societies have not, in fact, been particularly successful, as is so often supposed, in their efforts to eliminate the capability of their members to commit destructive violations. Revolution amounts to a violation of domestic order that is often as threatening to it as war is for the international order. This is especially disturbing if we are aware of the frequency of domestic or internal "wars" in the modern world. George Modelski reports on 100 internal wars for the period between 1960 and 1962, covering a wide range of countries at different stages of political and legal development.[3] The suggestion is sometimes made that totalitarian systems of government have solved the problem of the destructive violation. But the 1956 uprisings in East Germany and Hungary challenge such a conclusion, as have the convulsions in China a decade later. It is important to appreciate the magnitude of our international objective, especially if we assume that it is unacceptable to guard against the possibility of a destructive violation by instituting a global social and legal system that claims and maintains its authority in a manner similar to the more stable totalitarian societies. Certainly the American Civil War and the Spanish Civil War suggest that liberal democratic societies have not found a way to protect themselves against the commission of a destructive violation.

The domestic endeavor to regulate violence is certainly worthy of close attention in our efforts to study a comparable endeavor on the international level, but this attention can distort, rather than deepen, our understanding if it is apprehended in a mechanical or literal fashion. The creation of adequate international order cannot proceed by imitating what we have come to accept as adequate legal order on the domestic level. Thus it is essential to grasp the interconnection between political violence and legal control when trying to transfer the experience of domestic societies to the international environment. For one thing, the logic of extrapolation is complicated. For another, it is easy to be misled by an interpretation of domestic experience, especially if it is factually wrong. We need to determine more clearly than we have been able to do in the past the *nature* of realistic ex-

<hr>

[3] George Modelski, "International Aspects of Internal War," in James N. Rosenau, ed., *International Aspects of Civil* *Strife*, Princeton, Princeton University Press, 1964, pp. 122-53.

pectations about the control of violence in various kinds of social systems. Once this has been done, we will then be in a position to appreciate the distinctive character of the effort to restrict, to the extent possible, the capacity of international actors to commit destructive violations. If we can establish this context with some precision, then, and only then, can we discuss meaningfully "the rule of law supported by legitimate authority with preponderant force."

Earlier chapters have already stressed the extent to which the rivalries of the Great Powers are productive of opposing interventions in the internal affairs of sovereign states. In fact, it is the violence carried on within the boundaries of a single state that represents the most prevalent form of international violence in the present period of international relations. Partly the prominence of internal warfare is a prudential adjustment to the hazards of direct encounter between the two superpowers, given the existence of arsenals filled with nuclear weapons. Partly this prominence reflects the substitution by the Great Powers of a quest for influence and ideological sympathy for the territorial ambitions that operated in earlier periods of international history. The issues that dominate the internal arenas of struggle are often ideological cleavages that parallel the cleavages that caused the Great Powers to align in opposition to one another in the period following World War II, an ideological bipolarity that appears in recent years to have somewhat diminished in significance. Finally, the prominence of internal warfare is a direct consequence of the nation-building process going on in the Afro-Asian world, a process that can proceed according either to Western or Communist models, or by a mixture, and a process in which the Great Powers have both the temptation and the opportunity to intervene. The vulnerability of the Afro-Asian world to outside intervention is aggravated by the absence of traditions of peaceful change and by the susceptibility of these national societies to manipulation by covert action.

The problems posed for world order as a consequence of this interventionary pattern of diplomacy are considerable. It is essential to rethink the relevance of international law to these forms of intrastate violence. This effort at rethinking is hampered by an assumption that the task of international law has been to regulate conduct *among* states but not *within* a state. Certain ideas of nonintervention were a natural doctrinal consequence of state sovereignty and territorial supremacy, but such ideas have always served more as an ideological basis of international legal theory than as an operative code of conduct. In addition to the basic deference of international law to the idea of domestic jurisdiction, there exist special issues of ascertaining what is permitted and what is forbidden in relation to intrastate violence. First of all, it is exceedingly difficult to obtain a clear account of the facts; it is easy to fabricate a pretext for intervention by alleging prior covert intervention on the other side. Second, even if the facts of outside participation are clear, there is a considerable uncertainty as to whether and under what conditions outside states may discriminate in favor of an incumbent government being challenged by an insurgent group; this uncertainty is complicated by the contemporary contention that certain incumbent governments are "illegitimate" either because they are "puppets" or "colonial" or "racist" or "neo-colonial," and that, therefore, outside discrimination in favor of the insurgent faction is legally warranted. For instance, the Organization of African Unity had received contributions from Yugoslavia and Indonesia for a "special fund" created to support rebel organizations in Angola and Mozambique.[4] Therefore, there are no clear legal standards to govern outside participation in internal warfare.

International law confers on a state considerable discretion to manipulate legal symbols of legitimacy and thereby govern its relations with the factions contending for power in a foreign society in accord with its policy preferences. The most characteristic mode of manipulation is by means of discretion to accord or deny formal status to the revolutionary faction through the process of recognition and non-recognition, graduated in terms of "rebel," "insurgent," and "belligerent." These symbols are not used in recent practice, although it has been frequently suggested that recognition of the belligerent status of the National Liberation Front might be a significant step in the direction of negotiating a settlement of the war in Viet Nam.[5]

Contemporary practice of states inclines toward either a just war rationale of their relations with the two factions, identifying the one as just and the other as unjust and thereby vindicating discrimination in favor of the just side, or toward a highly political explanation that action on behalf of one side has been rendered necessary and legal as a consequence of prior intervention on the other side. In the context of decolonialization, the just war approach prevails, whereas in the context of "cold war" struggles action tends to draw on both arguments based on just war and on counterintervention.

We find considerable confusion in the writing of international lawyers about the proper attitude of third powers toward an ongoing civil war. There are three main views: (1) third powers have an obligation to treat both sides equally by displaying an attitude of impartiality

[4] *New York Times*, March 1, 1967.
[5] See, e.g. *Report of the Ad Hoc Con-* *gressional Conference on Viet-Nam*, February 15, 1966.

toward the outcome of the civil war; (2) third powers are entitled to discriminate in favor of the incumbent faction; (3) third powers are entitled to discriminate in favor of the faction deemed just, whether it be the incumbent or the revolutionary faction. I will illustrate these three positions by reference to the writings of Hall, Garner, and Vattel. It might be instructive to consider which position is most descriptive of United States foreign policy, of Soviet and Chinese foreign policy at various stages and in the varying setting. And it might also be useful to consider which of these positions accords most closely with the interests of the developing countries. One might want to maintain that it is useful for national government to retain the legal discretion to choose from among several inconsistent approaches so as to be able to adapt a response to the distinctive character of given civil wars on an *ad hoc* basis.

One might also question the entire discussion by taking very seriously the implication of President Johnson's speech at Baylor University (May 28, 1965) in which he said "the old distinction between civil war and international war has lost much of its meaning." According to President Johnson this loss of meaning has arisen because "the enemies of freedom" are "talking about wars of national liberation"; the speech made shortly after the American intervention in the civil strife going on in the Dominican Republic implies that "the friends of freedom" are entitled to use military power to influence the course of a civil war because the revolutionary input is a consequence of Communist agitation amounting to aggression. It is against this general background that we turn to examine the views of Hall, Garner, and Vattel.

The view of Hall is that international law requires third powers to be neutral toward the factions in contention. Hall's main reasoning is contained in the following passage:

> Supposing that intervention is to be directed against the existing government, independence is violated by an attempt to prevent the regular organ of the state from managing its affairs in its own way. Supposing it on the other hand to be directed against the rebels, the fact that it has been necessary to call in foreign help is enough to show that the issue of the conflict would without it be uncertain, and consequently there is doubt as to which side would ultimately establish itself as the legal representative of the state.[6]

[6] A. Pearce Higgins, *Hall's International Law*, 8th edn., London, Oxford University Press, 1924, p. 347; this is the apparent conclusion reached by Ann Van Wynen Thomas and A. J. Thomas, Jr., in their comprehensive survey of the relevant doctrine of international law: *Non-Intervention—The Law and Its Import in the Americas*, Dallas, Southern Methodist University Press, 1956, pp. 215-21.

Garner, in the setting of the Spanish Civil War, argues that Soviet aid to the incumbent Loyalist regime was legal, whereas German and Italian aid to the insurgency of Franco was illegal.[7] The underlying conception in Garner's view is that international law permits third states to discriminate in favor of the constituted government beset by civil war. The Garner view, in my judgment, offers the best available, although least invoked, legal justification for United States policies in Viet Nam during the period since 1954.

There is also a view going back at least as far as Vattel that third states have the option to intervene on the side that in their view is pursuing the juster cause. The relevant passage in Vattel is surprisingly pertinent:

But if a prince, by violating the fundamental laws, gives his subjects a lawful cause for resisting him; if, by his insupportable tyranny, he brings on a national revolt against him, any foreign power may rightfully give assistance to an oppressed people who ask for its aid. The English justly complained of James II. The nobility and patriotic leaders resolved to put a check upon his policy, which clearly tended to overthrow the Constitution and to destroy the liberties and the religion of the people, and they obtained the help of the United Provinces.

. . . To give help to a brave people who are defending their liberties against an oppressor by force of arms is only the part of justice and generosity. Hence, whenever such dissension reaches the state of civil war, foreign Nations may assist that one of the two parties which seems to have justice on its side.[8]

This Vattelian conception most closely resembles current proclaimed patterns of state practice in the Afro-Asian portion of the world. As has been already indicated, the current variants of just war uphold the right of a nation to assist the side that it favors to win a civil war, and, since international relations are now dominated by ideological issues, the side favored is identified as the side pursuing a just cause.

The United States has recently seemed to adopt the Garner notion that help to the incumbent is always legal, whereas help to the insurgent is always illegal regardless of the relative merits of the conflict. Such a doctrinal bias in favor of constitutional legitimacy, if it were to be universally accepted, would seem to freeze the *status quo* in favor of abhorrent as well as beneficial governments, as well as posit

---

[7] James W. Garner, "Questions of International Law in the Spanish Civil War," 31 *American Journal of International Law* 66 (1937).

[8] Emmerich de Vattel, *The Law of Nations* (1758), Bk. II, §56, p. 131 (Vol. III, *Classics of International Law*, Washington, Carnegie Institution of Washington, 1916).

as "law" a position that neither the Communist states nor the non-aligned states are prepared to accept. Hall's conception of an unqualified duty of nonintervention on either side is equally out of keeping with either prevailing doctrine or practice, although its converse —a right of intervention on either side—is somewhat descriptive of the inability of international law to regulate interventionary activity in the Afro-Asian world.

In such a situation of factual and legal indeterminacy the decentralization of international society becomes an important factor militating against the development of uniform international standards of behavior. Decision-makers in third states "self-determine" their response and invoke a legal explanation that accords with their foreign policy preferences. There are no legal criteria or central decision-makers regularly available to override decisions taken at the national level. In contrast to the use of force by the armies of one country against the territory of another, it is very difficult to mobilize a consensus on any basis other than political preference, which in the world of today is closely related to ideological sympathies. In the event that an internal conflict does not directly replicate the ideological struggle between East and West, then, as in the instance of the strife on Cyprus, a supranational consensus may be both mobilized and sustained to permit concerted action by international institutions at the global level. At the regional level, assuming a degree either of regional hegemony by a Great Power or ideological homogeneity, it may be possible to take concerted action despite the ideological character of the internal conflict; as has been the case of the Organization of American States' role in relation to Cuba since 1960 and the Dominican Republic in 1965.

The chapters in Part II are all concerned with aspects of the problem posed by intervention and intranational violence. Chapter IV attempts to place the subject matter of internal war into the overall framework of the international legal order. Chapters V, VI, apply these general considerations to the history of American interventionary practice in Latin America since the Monroe Doctrine and in the global context since the enunciation of the Truman Doctrine. Chapters VII, VIII, IX, and X examine some of the arguments for and against entrusting an interventionary role to regional and global institutions either as an alternative to third-party intervention or as a way to give effect to the will of the international community, as in the countries of southern Africa. Finally, Chapter XI is an attempt to explore the outer limits of intervention in the difficult setting of proposals to regulate the flow of international propaganda. The setting is difficult because propaganda can be such a manipulative force in internal affairs and, at the same time, the insulation of domestic societies from these forms of outside interference helps to stabilize the most retrograde forms of domestic governance.

In the likely event that the structure of international society does not change radically in the next few decades, the most crucial area wherein international law can be strengthened has to do with developing common standards of fact-finding and rule-determining with regard to third-party intervention in domestic affairs, as well as with specifying roles for and constitutional restraints upon international institutions that undertake interventionary roles in relation to events physically confined within foreign sovereign states. It is questionable whether, given the growth of global consciousness, events such as the 1965-66 massacres within Indonesia will be perceived in the future as matters of domestic concern just because their occurrence was internal to Indonesia and did not arise from or prompt any third-party intervention.

IV. The International Law of Internal War: Problems and Prospects

1. The Reconciliation of Legal Restraint and Cold War Strategy

Violent encounter of major rivals in world affairs has always been primarily a matter of warfare *between* states; now suddenly it is participation in warfare *within* states. It is easy to appreciate this as an objective fact by making a survey of international affairs during the period after World War II. It is much more difficult to do something about, even to the extent of adapting our thinking to these altered circumstances. Recently a writer has given the international significance of internal phenomena a usefully wide formulation: "International affairs are affected at least as much by events which are not international as by events which are; by events, that is, which proceed within a state without proceeding or primarily impinging upon the relations between two or more states."[1]

The literature of international law has been slow to respond to this aspect of the altered condition of the contemporary world. At this stage, then, an inquiry into the international legal status of intrastate violence seems dramatically appropriate.[2] The drama is partly a consequence of the cold war: is there much doubt that the struggle for world dominance will be resolved by internal wars between armies of composite nationality and diverse ideology? Aside from the possibilities of accident and miscalculation, a major international war seems unlikely to take place, unless it is chosen as a suicidal gesture, initiated by the losing side to make political defeat mutual. However, the implausibility of a calculated initiation of major warfare does not dissolve the problems that face the foreign policy-makers of principal states. It is still necessary to deal with subtle forms of coercion throughout the world that tend to undermine particular patterns of political

---

[1] Peter Calvocoressi, *World Order and New States*, New York, Praeger, 1962, p. 101.

[2] International lawyers have shown some interest in the significance of international law for the conduct of civil war for a surprisingly long time.

Two important studies indicate a flourish of interest in the importance of civil strife for international law at the turn of the century: Carlos Wiesse, *Le droit international appliqué aux guerres civiles*, Lausanne, 1898; Antoine Rougier, *Les guerres civiles et le droit des gens*, Paris, Larose, 1903. See also L. Stéfanesco, *La guerre civile et les rapports des belligérants*, Paris,

Arthur Rousseau, 1903; P. Sadoul, *De la guerre civile en droit des gens*, Nancy, 1905. A resurgence of interest in the subject was occasioned by the Spanish Civil War: Norman J. Padelford, *International Law and Diplomacy in the Spanish Civil Strife*, New York, Macmillan, 1939; Charles Rousseau, *La nonintervention en Espagne*, Paris, Pedone, 1939. A recent general treatment is Erik Castren, *Civil War*, Helsinki, Suomalainen Tiedeakatemia, 1966; see also Roger Pinto, "Les Règles de Droit International Concernant la Guerre Civile," 114 *Recueil des cours* 451-553 (1965).

equilibrium that it is deemed desirable to maintain. It is still necessary to implement policies that propose to build up the power and authority of institutions that might usher in a reign of world law at some future date. This dual challenge signifies an orientation towards the problems of international violence in an age of nuclear politics. This introductory section serves to depict the political confrontation that alters the legal environment and to disclose my own bias about the desiderata of world order.

Perhaps a question helps to identify the primary nexus of law and politics: can the United States defend its interests in the contemporary world without continuing to compromise its tradition of respect for international law? American interventionary participation in the internal wars of Southeast Asia and sponsorship of the illegal 1961 invasion of Cuba suggest the character of the problem. We find embarrassed attempts by national officials to reconcile American foreign policy with pledges to continue our adherence to the norms of nonintervention.[3] This satisfies neither the cold warrior who would have us discard every restraint upon behavior that is not a product of strategic thinking nor the ultra-legalist who would paralyze our response to Communist patterns of expansion by a pedantic insistence upon asymmetrical adherences by the West to the restraints of law. It is hard to find a foothold on such slippery terrain—to sustain the relevance of law without making the victim's compliance an asset to the aggressor. A foothold requires, first of all, some modernization of the international legal system to take account of recent changes in the character of world politics.

It is illuminating to put in preliminary focus substantive problems that arise from attempts to achieve increasing international control of contemporary political violence. It is taken for granted that attitudes of unrestraint about international violence tend toward the employment of thermonuclear weapons. It is further assumed that the eventuality of nuclear war is perceived by dominant national actors, regardless of ideology or culture, as a mutual disaster of such extent that it significantly inhibits recourse to nuclear weapons. Such a perception tends also to discourage reasoned recourse to nonnuclear forms of international violence that contain serious risks of nuclear war. This risk accompanies aggression carried on by any major armed attack across an international frontier. Therefore, the common interest in the avoidance of nuclear war discourages recourse to explicit forms of international violence that possess a high escalation potential and serves to reinforce those existing legal rules that prohibit the use of force to re-

---

[3] For a sophisticated argument, see, e.g. Abram Chayes, "The Legal Case for U.S. Action on Cuba," *U.S. State Depart-* *ment Bulletin,* XLVII, November 19, 1962, pp. 763-65.

solve international disputes or to promote national objectives.[4] Legal techniques and institutions helpfully clarify and implement this common interest, guarding especially against instances of myopic disregard which, if not systematically suppressed by community action (Suez, Korea), might lead to an abandonment of this fundamental basis of universal restraint. It is generally the case that the effectiveness of law is enhanced by a convergence of the legal rule with the conscience and welfare of those subject to its claim, especially when this convergence is vividly perceived and rigorously implemented, as well as objectively present.[5]

This healthy situation, however, does not exist for lesser forms of aggression that do not depend upon border-crossing military attacks by the armed forces of one nation upon another. In fact, intrastate violence is governed by diametrically opposed considerations, whether approached from the perspective of law, morality, or national interest. It remains quite rational in the contemporary world to pursue national and ideological objectives by a selective use of the instruments of intrastate violence.

Internal wars present expanding nations and blocs with opportunities for strategic expansion that do not involve the high risks of reaching those self-destructive levels of conflict that are likely to attend major armed attacks across international boundaries. This political characteristic places heavy pressure upon nonintervention norms that are designed to restrain partisan foreign participation in domestic strife. This pressure is accentuated by the moral commitments that are held currently by many important international actors. Both the Communist and the Afro-Asian states endorse, with missionary zeal, the importance of achieving certain radical changes in some domestic societies—such as the elimination of colonialism or constitutional racism. Ordinarily the governing elites of these target societies will not permit radical change to come about by peaceful means. This breeds recourse to illegal protest movements and insurgent violence, stimulated and supported by friendly nations abroad.

This congeries of capability, risk, goal, and necessity places great emphasis upon the strategic manipulation of intrastate violence by groupings of nations contending for dominance in the world today.

[4] Cf., e.g. the language of Articles 2(4) and 51 of the United Nations Charter. Of course, the extent of renunciation and the scope of the persisting right of self-defense are subject to serious debate. Nevertheless, the legal claim seems to have a clear intention: to eliminate national discretion to employ force except in situations of self-defense.

[5] For a discussion that highlights the destructive gap that often separates the perception of self-interest from the facts of self-interest, cf. Myres S. McDougal and William T. Burke, "Crisis in the Law of the Sea: Community Perspectives versus National Egoism," in McDougal and Associates, Studies in World Public Order, New Haven, Yale University Press, 1960, pp. 844-911. The argument in the context of the use of the seas is transferable to any assertion of a national competence that infringes the welfare of other nations.

If empire once depended primarily upon the extent of colonial occupation, it now increasingly depends upon the capacity to influence the outcome of important internal wars.

Thus the Afro-Asian and Communist states appear pledged to repudiate the norms of nonintervention as a general principle of restraint. In such an international atmosphere, the continuing existence of formal commitments based on the doctrine of nonintervention seem to give the West, and especially the United States, the debilitating alternatives of cold-war frustration and international lawlessness.

Can there be any relevance of international law to internal war in such a situation? This question cannot be answered without considering the dynamic and normative relevance of preferred policy goals. Law becomes relevant, then, to an assessment of where we want to go as well as what we want done with events as things now stand. This requires policy preferences as well as a confrontation of the apparent dilemma posed by the need to choose between law-complying political defeat and law-violating political effectiveness. To build a safer international system we should take advantage of the potentialities for improving the present system of world order. Prospects for this improvement are almost always seriously diminished when leading national actors, especially those possessing revered domestic traditions of compliance with law, behave as if their duty to obey international law were confined to matters of postal regulation and maritime safety. Our challenge to these patterns of conduct requires a persuasive demonstration that national sovereignty will be best served by the progressive submission of states to common norms of restraint even in those situations involving risks to vital national interests. This demonstration can no longer be dismissed as a utopian project; it is a matter of immediate self-interest for all major nations. This is especially obvious with regard to all violent conflict. Peace exists only when the world is free from unauthorized patterns of sustained violence everywhere. A crucial variable is increasingly the magnitude of the violence; and this expands the traditional concern with whether or not the violence constitutes a military struggle between nations that brings to bear the law of war. It is thus necessary to examine the maintenance of peace in the light of the legal status of various foreign involvements in internal wars.

This concern leads to undertaking a critique of prevailing interpretations of rules of international law. In this respect, also, it seems useful to blur deliberately the line that is supposed, according to hallowed juristic tradition, to separate commentary on the state of the *lex lata* from speculations *de lege ferenda*. In an age of system transition on the international level,[6] it is necessary to identify the expanding competencies of new institutions and to accord provisional legal status to emerging patterns of stable restraint.[7] Otherwise one misses the main contribution of law to the rational control of behavior and neglects the capacity of global and regional organizations to act in legislative and constabulary roles. This period of transition and legal creativity is especially relevant to an understanding of the role of intrastate violence as the main instrument of coercion in the cold war. The characterization of a pattern of restraint as "law" itself adds obligatory force, since respect for law is itself a factor in the growth and effectiveness of a restraint. The scholar's perception and his supporting rationale operate in a primitive legal order as a subsidiary way to specify the province of law, and thereby to curtail the dangerous tendency to deny that there exists a national self-interest in world order, a tendency that unfortunately reflects popular attitudes about the national pursuit of power, wealth, and respect.

Although the traditional system of international law is seriously inadequate, many of the traditional rules remain helpfully relevant in setting reciprocal standards of behavior. This is true, for instance, of the rules that give individual combatants in major internal wars some protection from humanitarian rules of warfare, mainly as they have been incorporated into the Geneva Conventions of 1949. In our haste to reform the major prescriptions that govern national participation in internal wars, we should not be oblivious to the achievement of an earlier international law, especially at the margins of the subject. It is not our desire to promote an abandonment of older rules until we find the basis either for agreement or for tacit coordination that will support the reliable formation of more adequate new rules. In this interim it is often better to abide by unsatisfactory norms of guidance than to be without any guidance at all.

It seems useful to begin with a brief account of the conception of international law that will be used to analyze the problems of internal war. This is followed by a description of the basic approach taken by the traditional system. The descriptive account is then criticized for its failure to deal adequately with some extralegal developments: cold war, nuclear weapons, Communist strategy, the United Nations, regional

6 This view of system transition pervades the recent literature of international relations. It has been most comprehensively developed by Morton A. Kaplan in *System and Process in International Politics*, New York, John Wiley, 1957.

7 This has been done in a creative fashion from a legal perspective by C. Wilfred Jenks in the series of essays that comprise *The Common Law of Mankind*, New York, Praeger, 1958; cf. also Falk and Saul H. Mendlovitz, "Some Criticisms of C. Wilfred Jenks' Approach to International Law," 14 *Rutgers Law Review* 1-36 (Fall 1959).

organizations. After this critique, a final section argues in favor of certain shifts of competence from national to supranational decision-makers. Perhaps, here, an early warning will reduce confusion and misunderstanding. The criticisms directed at national policies of intervention and the argument for supranational legislative competence are not considered to provide a *solution* to the problems posed by internal war, but are presented as an optimum response in *certain circumstances* to a dangerous and difficult situation, however handled. For so long as domestic instability is widespread and intense, so long as there is an international Communist movement that participates in national politics with the benefit of external guidance, so long as there is a cold war and an arms race, the problems of responding to intrastate violence will remain serious and controversial both for United States policy-makers and for architects of an improving world order. This discussion tries only to shorten the distance between these two perspectives and to make suggestions for improvement. Such a purpose falls far short of claiming that one's ideas, if accepted, could overcome the torments of the day.

There are many current and obvious restrictions upon the capacities of supranational institutions to act effectively or justly. Some of these restrictions will be discussed at the end of this chapter after the argument for their strengthening has been strongly stated, perhaps overstated; to favor a gradual substitution of supranational for national participation in internal wars involves creating difficulties not present heretofore. Perhaps a few salient caveats will serve to qualify, at the outset, my own endorsement of the position urged.

First of all, there is little hope that dominant nations are presently prepared to transfer increased authority and power now and forever to emerging international institutions. Second, this chapter adopts an instrumental perspective—how should we act to maximize the world order values at stake?—which is quite disconnected from patterns of national behavior that are formed, as might be expected, by the irrationalities of imperial competition.

In a sense, one seeks for an unavailable prince in an age when events have rendered Machiavelli's cynical prescription obsolete.[8] There is a need, that is, for a new cynicism that turns out to look curiously like idealism. The egoist and the altruist share an increasingly common interest. To proclaim this is not to demonstrate it and to demonstrate it is not to change settled habits of thought. Part of the resistance to this

---

[8] It is intriguing to note, as Lucian Pye has pointed out, "Lessons from the Malayan Struggle Against Communism," M.I.T. Center of International Studies, C/57-15, that Machiavelli was also trying to formulate a strategy that would enable nation-building to overcome insurrectionary harassment.

style of argument arises from hardened habits of "political intelligence" that have assimilated too deeply the willingness to trust only egocentric pursuits of power in world affairs. It is itself an occasion for lament that, should he present himself, a contemporary Machiavelli, perceiving this novel necessity for a community of mankind, might be dismissed by the best minds as recklessly utopian. One danger arises from precisely this inability and unwillingness to reform our perception of what is practical politics. I hope that this reform will come about by the evolution of a new awareness forced upon us by a perspicuous response to the gathering facts, rather than by awaiting that other kind of compulsion—the corpse-littered rubble of our cities.

Mankind solicits the destiny of the dinosaur if it responds to these urgencies with complacent trust in present patterns of thought and conduct.

II. A Framework for a Contemporary System of International Law

Three series of distinctions help to identify the conception of international law that is used here to clarify the relations between law and internal war: the functions of international law, the actors in the international legal system, and the types of norms and processes that claim to assert legal control. It is necessary also to appreciate that this presentation accepts implicitly a controversial interpretation of the province of law in international affairs that is considerably more fluid than the one authorized by the Austin-Kelsen tradition.

First, then, let us describe the *functions* assigned to the international legal system at the current stage of its development. We are interested only in the performance of functions that influence the extent and quality of the legal control of the international impacts of internal war:

(1) International law provides a process for designating the degree of formal *acknowledgment* by third states of the claims made on behalf of the antigovernment faction; this allows the internal war to remain fully domesticated ("rebellion"), partially internationalized on an *ad hoc* basis ("insurgency"), and fully internationalized on an *a priori* basis ("belligerency").

(2) International law contributes a rhetoric for claiming and contesting various forms of external *participation* in internal wars; legal arguments, "just wars of national liberation," or "national self-determination" can thus confront various allegations of "intervention" or "indirect aggression and subversion."

(3) International law establishes a system for regulating the *scope* of hostilities by the application of the rules of war to the conflicting

factions, provided that the internal war attains sufficient magnitude to receive international status.

(4) International law facilitates the exercise of limited control over the *outcome* of internal wars whenever the community consensus can be effectively mobilized in support of one faction; this control arises especially in response to internal violence that is deemed to threaten external peace and security.

Second, there are various kinds of actors, the identity of which is an important ingredient of the legal status of claims to assert control over internal wars:

(1) Nations. The classical level of national interaction remains paramount; there is, then, in international law a primary emphasis upon the rights and duties of a nation vis-à-vis the factions involved in an internal war.

(2) Individuals, corporations, political parties. There is an increasing significance given to infranational participation. Individuals, private groups, transnational political associations instigate, participate in, and use intrastate violence to achieve political objectives abroad; this emphasizes the extent of the legal duty assumed by a domestic government to forbid the use of its territory to carry out hostile expeditions abroad.

(3) Regional organizations. Regional actors are beginning to claim and assert competence with respect to internal wars and threats to the peace within the region.

(4) The United Nations Organization. Universal actors, the principal organs of the United Nations, claim and assert an increasing competence to control the dimensions of and to influence the outcome of internal wars that constitute a threat to the maintenance of international peace.[9]

Third, there are various types of norms that have relevance to the legal control of internal war:

(1) There are norms that express decentralized grants of semi-discretionary authority; for example, each nation has discretion, within broad limits, to confer on or withhold provisional legitimacy from an insurgent by its control over the recognition ceremony; the discretion

---

[9] It is also exceedingly important to clarify the various spheres of competence given to each set of actors, especially in view of the likelihood of overlapping, incompatible claims to assert control. The hierarchy of actors is not necessarily a guide to their relative competence. For instance, nations have retained some vague claim to supremacy by virtue of the domestic jurisdiction concept, at least with respect to some subject matter. Regional actors may operate on the basis of very restricted grants of competence from their membership in relation to universal actors. Article 53(1) of the Charter seems to require a regional actor to await Security Council approval for any undertaking that is properly classified as an "enforcement action."

is restricted, since a nation that recognizes an insufficient insurgent is guilty of a form of illegal intervention that is often described as "premature recognition."

(2) There are norms that involve decentralized grants of fully discretionary authority; for example, a state is at liberty to grant or refuse asylum to foreign political fugitives.

(3) There are centralized norms of restraint; these concern the various international codifications of the rules of war, including especially the rights and duties of belligerents and third states on the high seas and the so-called humanitarian rules of warfare (care for the sick and wounded, treatment of prisoners).

(4) There are norms that involve centralized claims of authority and control; as when, for instance, the United Nations invokes its authority to manage an internal war (the Congo operation).

(5) There are decentralized tacit norms of restraint; for example, the nonuse of nuclear weapons as a mode of external participation in internal wars; nonparticipation in internal wars carried on within a cold war bloc: Hungary (1956), Cuba (1958-1959).

(6) There are decentralized norms arising from the effective assertion of novel claims to act; for example, the prudent use of the high seas or the atmosphere to test nuclear weapons or the use of outer space to orbit intelligence-gathering satellites over other nations.

(7) There are intermediate norms arising from the claims of regional actors; for example, the determination at the Punta del Este Conference of 1962 to exclude Castro's Cuba from the Inter-American System because of the incompatibility of Marxism-Leninism with hemispheric ideals.

This differentiation of perspective based on functions, actors, and norms underlies the description of the traditional system that follows. This system arose in a simpler international environment in which most interaction was between nations, and especially between a few dominant nations centered in a rather small part of the world.

III. The Old International Law of Internal War

The rights and duties of nations are governed, first of all, by the status accorded to the factions in conflict. Traditional international law provides three relevant statuses: (1) rebellion, (2) insurgency, (3) belligerency. These characterizations of a challenge to the authority of an incumbent regime are designed to distinguish among conflicts along a continuum of ascending intensity.[10] Rebellion is sup-

[10] This standard view is expressed in relation to grants of recognition: ". . . it is believed to be the nature and extent of the insurrectionary achievement, rather than any other consideration, that afford the test of the propriety of recognition." Charles Cheney Hyde, *International Law Chiefly as Interpreted and Applied by the United States*, I, 2nd rev. edn., Boston, Little, Brown, 1945, p. 202.

posed to be invoked in response to a sporadic challenge to the legitimate government, whereas insurgency and belligerency are intended to apply to situations of sustained conflict, a serious challenge carried on through a considerable period of time over a wide space and involving large numbers of people within the society.

If the faction seeking to seize the power of the state seems susceptible to rapid suppression by normal procedures of internal security, then it is supposed to be treated as a "rebellion." For instance, Kotzsch indicates that "domestic violence is called rebellion or upheaval so long as there is sufficient evidence that the police force of the parent state will reduce [sic; induce] the seditious party to respect the municipal legal order."[11] If the status of rebellion is given to an occasion of "internal war," then external help to the rebels constitutes illegal[12] intervention.[13] Furthermore, the incumbent government can demand that foreign states accept the inconvenience of domestic regulations designed to suppress the rebellion, such as the closing of ports or interference with normal commerce. Foreign states have no duty to remain aloof (as nonparticipants) or neutral, and therefore are free to render affirmative assistance to the incumbent as requested. There is also a general duty to prevent domestic territory from being used as an organizing base for hostile activities overseas.[14] This duty is imposed upon foreign states regardless of the scope of the internal war, but it seems to be especially applicable in a situation that precedes recourse by rebels to the instruments of violence. Thus if an internal war is a "rebellion," foreign states are forbidden to help the rebels and are permitted to help the incumbent, whereas the incumbent is entitled to impose domestic restrictions upon commerce and normal alien activity in order to suppress the rebellion.

International law thus purports to give no protection to participants

11 Lothar Kotzsch, *The Concept of War in Contemporary History and International Law*, Geneva, Librairie E. Droz, 1956, p. 230.

12 The United States tends to avoid challenging a particular rule of restraint. Instead it bases noncompliance upon special political circumstances that overcome the relevance of law. This makes legal restraint avoidable whenever it turns out to be inconvenient. The U-2 incident and the Bay of Pigs invasion of Cuba both suggest this kind of denigration of the legal order in situations in which more candid challenges of particular rules would have been both more convincing as an explanation and less destabilizing as "illegal" conduct.

13 The basic norms of noninvolvement were adopted by the Institute of International Law in 1900. For texts, see James Brown Scott, ed., *Resolutions of the Institute of International Law Dealing with the Law of Nations*, New York, Oxford University Press, 1916, pp. 157-61.

14 Cf. note 48 *infra*. See generally Hersch Lauterpacht, "Revolutionary Activities by Private Persons Against Foreign States," 22 *American Journal of International Law* 105-30 (January 1928); Manuel R. Garcia-Mora, *International Responsibility for Hostile Acts of Private Persons Against Foreign States*, The Hague, Nijhoff, 1962.

in a rebellion.[15] Rebellion usefully covers minor instances of internal war of a wide variety: violent protest involving a single issue (Indian language riots, Soviet food riots) or an uprising that is so rapidly suppressed as to warrant no acknowledgment of its existence on an extranational level (East European rebellions against Soviet dominion in 1953 and 1956). These norms of identification are, however, debatable and seldom serve *expressis verbis* to adjust the relation between the rebellion as a state of affairs and international actors affected in various ways by its existence.

It is even more significant, however, to suggest the separation between the *facts* of strife and the *decisional* process by which national officials invoke norms to explain and justify a national response. The self-determination of norms identifying the legal status of civil strife severely restricts any role of law connected with the establishment of an objective status binding on all actors uniformly through the system. A decree of marriage or divorce usually generates a status for the parties that is given universal respect. International law is not generally able to fulfill this role of status creation for internal strife on a system level, although it does so bilaterally, and occasionally on a regional or bloc basis. The existence of international institutions provides a structural basis for further centralization of procedures of status creation in this sensitive area.

"Insurgency" is a catch-all designation provided by international law to allow states to determine the quantum of legal relations to be established with the insurgents. It is an international acknowledgment of the existence of an internal war but it leaves each state substantially free to control the consequences of this acknowledgment. This contrasts with "belligerency," which establishes a common regime of rights and duties that exist independent of the will of a particular state. On a factual level, almost all that can be said about insurgency is that it is supposed to constitute more sustained and substantial intrastate violence than is encountered if the internal war is treated as a "rebellion." It also serves as a partial internationalization of the conflict, without bringing the state of belligerency into being. This permits third states to participate in an internal war without finding themselves "at war," which would be the consequence of intervention on either side once the internal war had been identified as a state of belligerency. Interven-

---

15 Kotzsch, *op.cit. supra,* note 11, p. 230. See also Ambrose Light Case 25 F. 408, 1855; Emmerich de Vattel, *The Law of Nations, or the Principles of Natural Law Applied to the Conduct and to the Affairs of Nations and Sovereigns,* trans. of 1758 edn. by Charles G. Fenwick, Washington, Carnegie Institution of Washington, 1916.

tionary participation in an insurgency may arouse protest and hostile response, but it does not involve the hazards and inconveniences that arise if a state of war is established with one or the other factions.

Hersch Lauterpacht suggests the relative vagueness of the legal concept of insurgency by observing that "the difference between the status of belligerency and that of insurgency in relation to foreign states may best be expressed in the form of the proposition that belligerency is a relation giving rise to definite rights and obligations, while insurgency is not."[16] The unreliability of the factual test becomes evident if one realizes that such major internal wars as the Cuban independence wars in the late nineteenth century and the Spanish Civil War of 1936–1939 were both treated by many principal nations as instances of insurgency. The insurgent is often given extensive rights by foreign states and is usually assumed to have the duty to conform to applicable rules of international law. Thus, for instance, British courts respected, as valid, Falangist legislation enacted to apply to territory under the control of the insurgency and accepted an insurgent claim of immunity for a public vessel under insurgent control.[17] These decisions had the consequence of treating the Franco faction as equivalent to a foreign sovereign state with respect to activity carried on within its orbit of effective administration. Such deferential treatment is a flagrant disregard of the incumbent government's normal claim to be the exclusive agent of the state for all matters within *national* jurisdiction. However, it represents a characteristic attempt by international law and national actors to use law to reconcile the claims of formal right with the facts of effective control; to maintain trade with a port under insurgent control it is essential to heed the administration of it by insurgent institutions even if this requires a disregard of the regime of law created by the government acknowledged in world affairs as the sole and legitimate seat of national authority. Actually, foreign states are rather free, given limitations of capability, to determine their own relations with insurgent and incumbent. Ordinarily insurgents are permitted to use the high seas for naval and air operations against the incumbent, provided that there is no interference with the shipping of third states. Thus, although third states have no duty to respect insurgent rights and no duty to subject themselves to the obligations of neutrality, there is a characteristic tendency to regard insurgent operations on the high seas as nonpiratical and to give some domestic deference to the governmental nature of an insurgent regime for territory under its control (for

---

[16] H. Lauterpacht, *Recognition in International Law*, Cambridge, Cambridge University Press, 1947, p. 270 (hereinafter cited as *Recognition*).

[17] The leading case came before the House of Lords in Great Britain: The Arantzazu Mendi, 1939, A.C. 256; cf. also Banco de Bilbao v. Rey, 1938, 2 K. B. 176.

example, insurgent legislation and official acts are often validated to the extent relevant to the outcome of a domestic legal controversy).[18]

For humanitarian reasons, there is an increasing willingness to regard the laws of war as applicable to protracted conflict if it is carried on in a form that entitles it to the status of an insurgency. The acceptance of this viewpoint by the incumbent is conclusive. Third states cannot treat an internal war as a "rebellion" once it has been identified as an "insurgency" by the parent government.

In general, the status of insurgency is a flexible instrument for the formulation of claims and tolerances by third states. If it is used to protect the economic and private interests of nationals and to acknowledge political facts arising from partial successes by the insurgents in an internal war, then it can adjust relative rights and duties without amounting to a mode of illegal intervention in internal affairs. Trouble arises, however, when third states use the status of insurgency to influence the outcome of an internal war. Political objectives distort the connection between the status of insurgency and the existence of the facts warranting it; such a distortion is often disguised, however, by the decentralized grant of competence that authorizes the third state to characterize an internal war and to proceed as it sees fit.

A special application of insurgent status involves the occasional claim of third states to treat certain actions on the high seas as piratical. Thus, for instance, the Nyon Agreement concluded by several states during the Spanish Civil War provided for collective measures to destroy submarines that attacked third-power shipping on the high seas if they attacked in a manner forbidden by Part IV of the London Treaty of 1930, governing submarine attacks on merchant shipping.[19] The characterization of insurgents as "pirates" by the incumbent is not binding on third states.[20] Nevertheless, it is generally conceded that unrecognized insurgent operations on the high seas can be treated by third parties as piratical, provided that the factual conditions of belligerency do not exist.[21] Even when this is done, it is, as Lauterpacht observes,

[18] See Kotzsch, op.cit. supra, note 11, pp. 232f. However, in the context of intense political conflict, the presence of executive hostility to the insurgent faction may determine the judicial outcome. Cf. Salimoff and Co. v. Standard Oil of New York, 262 N.Y. 220, 186 N.E. 679, 1933, and Bank of China v. Wells Fargo Bank & Union Trust Co., 104 F. Supp. 59, N.D. Cal., 1952.

[19] Lauterpacht, Recognition, pp. 295-96.

[20] For a discussion of the relation between piracy and claims of governmental status in the contemporary world, see Ferenc A. Vali, "The Santa Maria Case,"

56 Northwestern University Law Review 168 (1961).

[21] States retain a general discretion to characterize the facts according to their subjective appreciation; therefore, it may be questioned whether a third state is ever under an objective obligation (that is, an obligation that is not self-imposed) to respect a nonconstituted regime's claim to enjoy belligerent status, unless a condition of belligerency has been already established for the conflict through a proper claim of belligerent rights by the constituted regime.

infrequent that the notion of piracy is extended to the officers and crews of insurgent ships seized for piratical operations.[22]

Belligerency, as distinct from insurgency, is a formalization of the relative rights and duties of all actors vis-à-vis an internal war. Kotzsch puts it simply: ". . . the recognition of belligerency gives rise to definite rights and obligations under international law, insurgency does not."[23] Usually the conferral of belligerent status is achieved by indirect means rather than by explicit statement. Commonly, acknowledgment of belligerent rights on the high seas to either faction establishes a state of belligerency. International law treats an internal war with the status of belligerency as essentially identical to a war between sovereign states. This also means that an interventionary participation on behalf of either the incumbent or the insurgent is an act of war against the other. That is, in a truly international war in which neither side has been identified authoritatively as an aggressor, a state is given the formal option of joining with one of the belligerents against the other or of remaining impartial.[24] Of course, the sharpness of the choice is belied by the history of international relations, which abounds in instances of partiality and participation that are treated as fully compatible with neutral status.

Belligerent status, if objectively determined by the community, would enable supranational actors to have a technique to justify treatment of serious internal wars as international wars. That is, rebellions and insurgencies could be treated as remaining within the scope of domestic jurisdiction, subject to the traditional distribution of claims and duties between internal factions and external actors. But belligerencies should be internationalized, thereby vindicating the claims of regional or global institutions to restore internal peace either by reference to constitutional (incumbent) or normative (insurgent; human rights) legitimacy. This new notion of belligerency requires an explicit assumption of competence by the relevant institutions first to confer the status, then to act in view of it. Traditions of sovereignty and the split associated with the cold war are formidable obstacles to this recommended centraliza-

---

[22] Lauterpacht, *Recognition*, p. 304.

[23] Kotzsch, *op.cit. supra*, note 11, p. 233.

[24] The compatibility of this option with the United Nations system is open to serious question, even for nonmembers, see Article 2(6). Certainly, once a determination of aggression has been made authoritatively by a principal organ of the Organization, then other states are not "at liberty" to help the state or states characterized as the aggressor nor are states free to remain neutral, see Article 2(5). The formal claims of the Charter must, however, be regarded as no more than *potential* norms of restraint in view of *actual* patterns of practice. Practice continues to affirm the option of states to decide for themselves, and so the textual statement possesses a continuing validity, despite the presence of a formal agreement, Charter, pledging members of the United Nations to renounce discretion in this area of national behavior.

tion of supranational authority over *serious* internal wars. The status of belligerency would be equivalent to a determination of the seriousness of the internal war; that is, it would be a flexible and formal way for the regional or global organization to convey its claim of competence to the actors in the community. Criteria of seriousness could be formulated to restrict somewhat the judgment of belligerency by the organization, or at least to give the judgment a greater appearance of restriction.[25]

The degree to which incumbent and third states have discretion over the decision to recognize belligerent status is virtually unrestricted; diplomatic practice also seems to waver between the duty of third states to allow insurgents to claim belligerent rights if certain factual conditions are present and the discretionary nature of the insurgent claim. If the incumbent claims belligerent rights on the high seas, then it operates to confer the status of belligerency upon the entire conflict. Third states are expected thereafter to regulate their relations in a way that accords each faction formal parity; partiality shown to either faction is regarded as an act of war, or at least as a violation of neutral rights. The insurgent faction, for instance, must then also be able to assert belligerent rights on the high seas. The humanitarian laws of warfare become fully applicable to all hostilities.[26] Among the specific claims authorized by acquiring belligerent status, the following are quite prominent: the right to obtain credit abroad, to enter foreign ports, to maintain blockades, to engage in visit and search procedures, and to confiscate contraband.[27]

The incumbent government cannot oblige third states to accept its claim to exercise belligerent rights unless certain factual conditions

[25] Appearances of principled behavior are especially needed in an emerging legal order. The early success of English common law can be attributed, in part, to its clever insistence upon pomp, ritual, and technicalities. These attributes of law, now degraded as "mystique," help to gain habitual respect for law by members of the community. The development of such a habit continues to be a desideratum in international affairs.

[26] It is significant that Article 3 of the Geneva Conventions of 1949, regulating aspects of the conduct of international war, makes the humanitarian norms applicable "in the case of armed conflict not of an international character occurring in the territory of one of the High Contracting Parties." Also Article 4 of the Prisoners of War Convention and Article 13 of the Wounded and Sick Convention extend coverage to "members of regular armed forces who profess allegiance to a Government of an authority not recognized by the Detaining Power"; this presumably applied to any factual *or* legal state of prolonged insurgency. However, if the insurgency is conducted by unconventional military techniques, then it is unclear under what conditions the personnel qualify as members of "regular armed forces." For a discussion of when various rules of the law of war, especially the Geneva Conventions of 1949, apply to guerrilla warfare, see Morris Greenspan, "International Law and Its Protection for Participants in Unconventional Warfare," *The Annals,* Vol. 341, 1962, pp. 30-41.

[27] Cf. Ann Van Wynen Thomas and A. J. Thomas, Jr., *Non-Intervention: The Law and Its Import in the Americas,* Dallas, Southern Methodist University Press, 1956, p. 219.

are satisfied.[28] Hersch Lauterpacht summarizes these conditions in the following way: ". . . first, there must exist within the State an armed conflict of a general (as distinguished from a purely local) character; second, the insurgents must occupy and administer a substantial portion of national territory; third, they must conduct the hostilities in accordance with the rules of war and through organized armed forces acting under a responsible authority; fourthly, there must exist circumstances which make it necessary for outside States to define their attitude by means of recognition of belligerency."[29] These conditions are supposed to govern the propriety of attaching the status of belligerency. If these conditions are not satisfied, then it is premature to grant belligerent rights to either warring faction. Once they are met, however, then it is arguable that it is intervention to refuse recognition of the insurgency as belligerency. As there is no objective way to meet the test of belligerency, attention is often given to the conduct of the incumbent that discloses a willingness to negotiate with the insurgent elite on the level of equality. Such a demonstration often forms part of an argument that there can arise a duty for third nations to treat a given internal war as an instance of belligerency.[30]

The status accorded to an internal war is designed primarily to reconcile its character as violent conflict with the orderly maintenance of the interests of third states. A presumption in favor of stability in the world allows foreign states to intervene on behalf of the incumbent in the situation of mere rebellion. However, if the intrastate conflict is sustained in time and place, it becomes interventionary, according to the traditional theory, to help either faction. Therefore, the notions of insurgency and belligerency are designed to allow third states to remain neutral and yet to have some control over interferences with their normal activities that result from strife between internal factions.

There are several difficulties with this form of response by international law to the phenomenon of internal war. First, the tendency of nations to avoid express bestowals of status makes it hard to establish the precise nature of claims by third states; the functional role attributed to the distinctions between rebellion, insurgency, and belligerency is more an invention of commentators than a description of state behavior. Second, the decentralized assertion of claims to treat an internal war as rebellion, insurgency, or belligerency makes it impossible to stand-

---

[28] This is important with regard to the right of internal war factions to subject neutral shipping on the high seas to various interferences.

[29] Lauterpacht, *Recognition*, p. 176.

[30] This argument was applied to the Algerian War of Independence by Mohammed Bedjaoui, *Law and the Algerian Revolution*, Brussels, Publications of the International Association of Democratic Lawyers, 1961.

ardize what is permitted and what is forbidden with sufficient clarity to enable a protesting party to identify a violation; thus international law cannot do much to promote community policies favoring nonintervention, self-determination, and the rights of peoples to resort to revolution by distinguishing among various types of internal wars.[31] The basic duty of third states to maintain impartiality is difficult to implement. Third, the goals of noninterference are incompatible with the revolutionary ideology of China and the Soviet bloc and the anticolonial commitments of the Afro-Asian nations. Notions of support for wars of national liberation and anticolonial wars are direct repudiations of the duty to refrain from evaluating the contending claims of the factions in an internal war. The old international law based its regime upon the factual character of the conflict and not upon the justice of certain insurgent causes. If major national actors reject in practice and doctrine the policies of impartiality in the traditional system, then adherence to the rules becomes self-destructive for the remainder of the community.[32] Although it sounds paradoxical, offsetting participation by nations in internal wars may often be more compatible with the notions of nonintervention than is an asymmetrical refusal to participate.[33] Therefore, the decline of mutuality makes the idea of nonintervention obsolete, even dangerous, if mechanically applied by the non-Communist and nonmodernizing nations in the world.[34]

As a consequence, several desiderata exist. First, objective tests and centralized interpretations of the factual character of an internal war are necessary. Second, a rule of mutuality is needed to act as a basis for applying policies of nonparticipation in sustained instances of civil conflict. Third, it would be helpful to have procedures to enable an expression of community approval, most probably through the agency of supranational institutions, for certain instances of insurgency; approval would thereby serve to authorize some forms of outside participation. The Congo Operation suggests the growth of a community will-

[31] At best, *norms of relationship* are established by the *specific* responses of individual states. The status distinctions may help to clarify and identify the character of a specific response, thereby fulfilling the role of international law to provide national actors with a medium of communication. There are no norms generated that set system-wide standards of response. Participation by the United Nations or a regional organization may qualify this assertion somewhat.

[32] And yet the violation of clear norms by law-oriented societies leads to confused behavior that disappoints the conscience of the community, both within the society and without. The response of the United States to Castro's Marxism-Leninism illustrates the difficulties of either ignoring or adhering to applicable legal restraints.

[33] Such a conclusion is a central tenet of Manfred Halpern's stimulating essay, "The Morality and Politics of Intervention," in James N. Rosenau, ed., *International Aspects of Civil Strife*, Princeton, Princeton University Press, 1964, pp. 249-88.

[34] Cf. also George Modelski's "International Settlement of Internal War," in *ibid.*, pp. 122-53.

ingness to remove internal wars from the sanctuary of "domestic jurisdiction," especially if the magnitude of the conflict is considerable and
if the alternative is likely to be interventionary participation by the big
powers.

Traditional international law bases its response to civil war upon the
factual characteristics of the conflict and its material effect upon externally situated international actors. Thus a third state with shipping
interests subject to harassment on the high seas was regarded as more
entitled to accord recognition of rights to an insurgent faction than was
a state unaffected by the internal war.[35] Today, however, the interdependence of domestic and international conflict, the special attitude
of Communists and newly independent states toward the outcome of
internal wars fought for political objectives, and the dangers of nuclear
war escalating from internal war create new requirements of minimum
order.[36] The rules and processes of law must be revised to take appropriate account of these extralegal developments. We need, first of
all, to discriminate between internal wars that it is acceptable to treat
as domestic so as to proscribe participation by outside nations or supranational institutions, and those that it is not possible to insulate legally
either because the internal arena of conflict is the scene of serious intervention or because the war involves a struggle for certain minimum
domestic rights that the world as an emerging and limited community
is coming to recognize as mandatory.[37] Once this discrimination seems
to have been made, then, as has been indicated, it is important to develop processes for regional and universal management of internal wars
with an important strategic impact on patterns of international conflict
or upon firm and overwhelming crystallizations of international morality. If community institutions fail to perform in a situation where an
internal war is an arena within which third powers seek to extend their
national domain of political influence, then it is essential to authorize
neutralizing participation by others. The rules of nonparticipation
would thus be made subject to suspension whenever any major international actor violates them; this premise of mutuality must be intro-

[35] "The right of a state to recognize the
belligerent character of insurgent subjects
of another state must then, for the purposes of international law, be based solely
upon a possibility that its interests may be
so affected by the existence of hostilities in
which one party is not in the enjoyment of
belligerent privileges as to make recognition
a reasonable measure of self-protection."
William E. Hall, *A Treatise on International Law*, 8th edn., ed., A. Pearce Higgins, Oxford, Clarendon Press, 1924, p. 39.
[36] For an exciting exposition of the relations between legal order and the maintenance of peace in the contemporary
world, see Myres S. McDougal and Florentino P. Feliciano, *Law and Minimum
World Public Order: The Legal Regulation
of International Coercion*, New Haven,
Yale University Press, 1961, esp. Chapters
1-4.
[37] For a fuller development of this
theme, see Falk, *Law, Morality, and War
in the Contemporary World*, New York,
Praeger, 1963.

duced into the legal process so as to reconcile interests of collective self-defense with notions of respect for applicable legal rules.[38]

IV. Toward a New International Law of Internal War

It is essential to approach this exposition with an awareness of the significance of the decentralized quality of the international system, for this encourages an appreciation of the broad discretion that exists on a national level. This discretion is complicated by the presence of complementary patterns of norms and explicit grants of competence that allow nations to confer authoritative legal status by their own characterization of the contested facts. Recognition practice serves as a paradigm instance of the formation of legal status by reliance upon decentralized processes. Each state is free to accord or withhold recognition from a new state or government as it sees fit.[39]

Acknowledgment of this decentralized pattern underlying the establishment of legal rules should make one somewhat skeptical about the value of international legal restraints; it is quite proper to be dubious about the degree to which the rules described as regulative do, in fact, restrain the behavior of national and other international actors. But such a caveat is not, as is so often supposed, reason to denigrate the role of international law in relation to the control of internal war. It is an oddly shared mistake of idealists and cynics to evaluate the success or failure of a legal system by examining the extent to which national behavior conforms to international rules. The restraint of behavior is only one of several functions performed by law in any social order. It is a function in international affairs that can be best appraised by reference to the characteristic of a horizontal legal order.[40] A central

---

38 Cf. the opening pages of this chapter and note 32. It is essential to find a way to act that avoids embarrassment or opportunism. To be compelled to choose between such alternatives disowns our heritage and violates the fundamental basis of international order. See I. C. MacGibbon, "Some Observations on the Part of Protest in International Law," 30 *British Year Book of International Law* (1953), pp. 293-319.

39 For an explanation of the rule against premature recognition, see Lauterpacht, *Recognition*, pp. 94-96, 283-84. Cf. the argument of Mohammed Bedjaoui in favor of early recognition of the anti-French Algerian insurgency as a matter of policy *and* duty, *op.cit. supra,* note 30, pp. 110-38.

40 The character of rules for a legal order must reflect the functions assignable to law by a given social order. The horizontality of the international legal order

implies a range of interpretative discretion by nations that impedes the growth of highly specific rules of restraint. This is simply an attribute of the system. It is not an occasion for lament. It does not inform us at all about the success or failure of various rules of international law as measured in terms of their distinctive ordering functions. There is an ironic tendency for people to expect law in international affairs to do more for the order and welfare of the community than it does in domestic affairs. Perhaps law is given special duties in world affairs to compensate for the weak international social structure; when these extravagant expectations are disappointed, the contributions actually made by law to world order are extravagantly neglected. Neither extremes of expectation nor extremes of disappointment are conducive to an awareness of reality.

function of international law, especially with regard to the use of force, is to provide participants with an orderly process for identifying, asserting, and communicating claims to engage in controverted conduct.[41] That is, legal discourse operates to clarify communication between international actors. This is itself an indirect restraining influence. It expresses the basic nature of horizontal law: a process of claim and counterclaim that can be vindicated or repudiated in any particular instance, depending upon (1) the extent to which it can be established as reasonable or unreasonable in the context of assertion, (2) the degree to which its application is accompanied by community approval and participation, and (3) the degree of effectiveness achieved in the assertion of the claim.[42] Such a medium of communication inhibits the tendency of nations to overrespond to perceived crises, and it establishes a matrix and rhetoric that facilitate diplomatic negotiation. This puts international law in a position to contribute significantly to the supranational management of the dangers to international peace that arise from those patterns of intrastate violence that highlight the conflict between cold war rivals in a nuclear age. It is in this spirit that the limits and opportunities of legal order should be conceived for the contemporary world.

However, the reality of normative indeterminacy[43] requires a sharp

41 The relation between national assertions of claims to engage in controversial conduct and the development of world order is examined in Falk, "Space Espionage and the World Order: A Consideration of the Samos-Midas Program," in R. J. Stanger, ed., *Essays on Espionage and International Law*, Columbus, Ohio State University Press, 1962, pp. 45-82.

42 This approach to the validation of a unilateral claim permits a sophisticated legal argument to be made in support of the imposition by the United States of its 1962 "quarantine" upon shipping bound for Cuba that was carrying as cargo components of "offensive" military equipment. Reference should be made to the narrowness of the claim, to the minimum threat of force consistent with the attainment of the security objective, to regional support and participation, to the degree of acquiescence to the claim by shippers subject to its interference, to the willingness of the United States to negotiate, and to the Soviet compliance with the demand. As an adversary process is implicit in the legal system of settlement, a contrary set of considerations can be advanced to oppose the legality of the claim: a failure to attempt prior negotiations, an unwarranted threat to use force in violation of Charter norms, an impermissible interference with shipping on the high seas, an intervention in the domestic affairs of Cuba, an asymmetrical claim to defend national security in view of United States "offensive" missile bases along the Soviet periphery, an unreasonable assertion of competence vis-à-vis the shipping of third states, and so on.

International law often comes into being through the gradual acceptance of behavior first perceived and condemned by casual observers as "illegal." The doctrine of pacific blockade was itself established by the effective assertion of limited unilateral claims by dominant national actors. This poses difficult problems concerning the distinction between a violation of an existing rule and a claim to establish a new or revised rule and between illegality and legislative enactment. For stimulating discussion, see Lauterpacht, *Recognition*, pp. 426-30.

43 That is, the same set of facts is capable of two or more plausible contradictory legal characterizations. This is a characteristic of all law, not just international law. However, the absence of centralized and objective international decision-making often makes it impossible to eliminate indeterminacy. Cf. note 60 *infra*.

sense of the distinction between the facts *as impartially perceived* and *as characterized by national officials* holding heavy stakes in the outcome of a particular internal war.[44] A state eager for a successful overthrow of an incumbent government is much more inclined to characterize the facts in a manner that is favorable to the insurgent cause.[45] A proper awareness of the success of international law in its role as a restrainer of national conduct depends upon measuring the distance between the facts and the doctrinal response.

It is very important to maintain the distinction between the rights and duties of international actors and their implementation by domestic societies. For example, the discretionary nature of recognition permits the executive, by virtue of his primary responsibility for foreign affairs, to influence the way in which the judiciary treats the legal claims of an insurgent faction either during or after an internal war.[46] This may have an important influence on the fiscal position of a revolutionary society, affecting its access to foreign assets and exchange. It is often very important to obtain respect abroad for controversial economic acts at home; it influences the international capital position of a government, especially if it is a newcomer to the international stage, as is the case after a successful revolution. Very often dramatic controversies surround the international validity of expropriation laws and decrees. There is a connection here with foreign policy, for a refusal to recognize a new government or its radical economic program alienates it and tends to encourage it to adopt the orientation of those nations that acknowledge the validity of its existence and show respect for its governmental undertakings.[47] This is a very crucial aspect of the

---

[44] This distinction is made sharply by William T. Burke in "The Legal Regulation of Minor Coercion: A Framework of Inquiry," in R. J. Stanger, ed., *Essays on Intervention and International Law*, Columbus, Ohio State University Press, 1964, pp. 87-125. Cf. also McDougal and Feliciano, *op.cit. supra*, note 36, p. 10.

[45] The divergent images of reality held by participants with varying perspectives constitute one of the most profound themes in human experience; this insight achieved consummation in the evocative Japanese tale, *Rashomon*. For a more pertinent illustration, one might compare a standard positivistic international law text—say, that of Lauterpacht and Oppenheim—with representative writing from the newly independent or socialist states—say, J. J. G. Syatauw, *Some Newly Established Asian States and the Development of International Law*, The Hague, Nijhoff, 1961, or Bedjaoui, *op.cit. supra*, note 30.

[46] A British case acknowledges this influence: A. M. Luther v. James Sagor & Co., 1921, 3 K.B. 532; cf. also 1 K.B. 456. American practice is very complicated. Cf. the affirmative internal effect that is supposed to be achieved by recognition, United States v. Pink, 315 U.S. 203, 1942, with the negative effects of nonrecognition, Latvian State Cargo & Passenger S.S. Line v. McGrath, 188 F. 2d 1000, D.C. Cir., 1951. For discussions of executive-judicial relations with respect to the influence of the foreign policy of the forum upon the outcome of a legal controversy, cf. Bernstein v. N.V. Nederlandsche-Amerikaansche, 173 F. 2d 71, 2d Cir., 1949, with Banco Nacional de Cuba v. Sabbatino, 193 F. Supp. 375, S.D.N.Y., 1961, aff'd 307 F. 2d 845, 2d Cir., 1962, rev'd 376 U.S. 398, 1964 and Rich v. Naviera Vacuba, S.A., 295 F. 2d 24, 4th Cir., 1961.

[47] For instance, an expropriating state cannot compete in international commer-

way in which the international system reacts to internal war, as it subtly accentuates the discretion of national actors to regulate their participation or nonparticipation without contradicting the formal obligation to treat an internal war as if it were a matter within domestic jurisdiction of the strife-torn state. The difficulty of conceiving of international law as a common regulative regime is also disclosed. For if each nation is free to determine the internal effects of "nonrecognition" and is free to refuse recognition, then it is clear that there is no common set of duties that arises from the *factual* circumstances in the course of or at the end of an internal war. The techniques used by judicial institutions of third states to adjudge the competing claims of insurgent and incumbent are beyond the scope of this study, although they are relevant to full appreciation of the limits of traditional notions such as nonintervention and the duty of impartiality. For it is obvious that the court must be able to identify the legal interests of the state in the midst of an internal war in order to settle disputes about ownership, immunity, and obligation that come before it.

Somewhat related to the impact of internal war on the operation of domestic courts is the degree to which nations are permitted to tolerate or encourage activity within their territory that is related to the pursuit of an internal war abroad.[48] Here the range of activity includes hostile propaganda, asylum, governments-in-exile, and the financing, training, equipping, and transporting of insurgent expeditions. To what extent are these activities essentially within the domestic jurisdiction of the state in which the constituent acts take place? If the concern is with political stability, then it is desirable to assert some supranational control over conduct taking place in A that is designed to

---

cial markets without reasonable assurance that it can pass secure title. In fact, even the prospect of litigation would dissuade most purchasers unless the offering price was a real bargain. This means that often socialist states are alone available as traders willing to pay fair value for expropriated property. Apart from possible unfairness to investors, it is clear that asymmetrical responses by third states to nationalization has an important influence on the capacity of a state to benefit from its program of capital centralization.

[48] See, e.g. Draft Code of Offenses Against the Peace and Security of Mankind, Adopted by the International Law Commission, 28 July 1954, GAOR, IX, Supp. 9, A/2693, pp. 11-12, Article 2, which designates "offenses against the peace and security of mankind" in paragraph (4): "The organization, or the encouragement of the organization, by the authorities of a State, of armed bands within its territory or any other territory for incursions into the territory of another State, or the toleration of the organization of such bands in its own territory . . . as well as direct participation in or support of such incursions," and paragraphs (5) encouragement of civil strife by acts or their toleration, and (6) *ibid.*, use of terror. To like effect, see Convention on the Rights and Duties of States in the Event of Civil Strife, to which the United States is a ratifying party; 22 *American Journal of International Law*, Documents Supplement 159 (July 1928). The United States has not been implementing domestic legislation that makes it a crime to plan, organize, or participate in a hostile expedition against a state with which the United States is at peace. Cf. 18 U.S.C.A. § 960, 1948.

change the political *status quo* in B. The willingness of the Republic of the Congo to advertise its support of training bases for Angolese rebels on its territory is an illustration of flagrant disregard for the traditional assumption that one state has a duty to prevent its territory from being used to endanger the political independence of another state. Tolerance by the United States of anti-Castro exiles and the Soviet training programs for insurrection, guerrilla warfare, and subversion further illustrates a tendency to immunize aggressive designs by acting behind the walls of territorial sovereignty. Does the target state have any recourse in the absence of express treaty commitments? And even if target states can invoke obligations to enforce neutrality abroad, is there any way to enforce compliance? Behavior in states other than the state that is the scene of the internal war may be highly interventionary; yet given the fundamental territorial distribution of authority that persists in the world, it may be difficult to stigmatize or control. Thus the policies of nonparticipation inherited from the traditional image of the posture of international law toward internal war give way to the realities of participation. These realities are dramatically important in the modern world in which mass communication, rapid transportation, economic interdependence, ideological fervor, and transnational revolutionary parties are significant characteristics. The traditional system shields activity by spatial criteria (jurisdictional formulae) although function and space increasingly diverge; that is, the policies of nonparticipation cannot be protected by rules against explicit participation in the internal war itself. For instance, it would be strained to contend that the overt participation of the United States in the internal wars throughout Southeast Asia was more interventionary up until the American escalation of the Vietnam War in 1964 than was the covert participation of the Soviet Union in the People's Republic of China. We witness, then, the inadequacy of traditional norms of territorial allocation of authority to uphold the world community policy—the insulation of internal war from external participation. To overcome this inadequacy requires either centralized procedures to assure the domestic suppression of insurrectional activities or a candid abandonment of nonintervention obligations on the grounds of nonmutuality of adherence and of the failure of self-restraint to serve as a sufficient ordering technique. It is better explicitly to discard particular rules of international law that have become obsolete than to make the entire legal system appear obsolete by disregard of rules in practice.

It is today properly commonplace for experts to criticize the traditional system of international law as inadequate to meet certain specific needs of modern life. The problematic relevance of the traditional norms of international law to the various contemporary phenomena of sustained intrastate violence, collectively identified throughout this chapter as "internal war,"[49] is as yet strangely exempt from this line of criticism, perhaps because the subject has been inexplicably absent from recent scholarly concern.[50]

The term "internal war" is consciously selected as a substitute for the usual designation: civil war. This is done to facilitate an accurate perception of the modern phenomena of intrastate political violence. It is especially important to appreciate the extent to which external actors participate in internal wars so as to distract the mind from a predisposition to view internal war as a domestic matter. The spatial matrix of conflict does not always adequately reveal the necessary boundaries of significance. It is certainly true that instances of internal war such as the 1962 food riots in the Soviet Union or the Bombay language riots are accurately considered afflictions of a single society. But the dominant examples of internal war in the post World War II era possess a different character. In fact, warfare *between* states now most frequently takes place *within* a single national society. The emergence of the shift in the role of intrastate violence in world political processes first became evident in the Spanish Civil War, although there had been a much earlier emphasis on internal war during the period of struggle between democratic liberalism and monarchial legitimacy, in the decades follow-

---

[49] Cf. James N. Rosenau's "Internal War as an International Event," in James N. Rosenau, ed., *International Aspects of Civil Strife,* Princeton, Princeton University Press, 1964, pp. 45-91, for a useful differentiation of internal wars based on struggles concerning personnel, authority, and structure. Recent definitions of internal war have been based upon the identification of different kinds of violent struggles carried on within national territory. For example, Harry Eckstein defines internal war as "any resort to violence within a political order to change its constitution, government, or policies" (mimeographed report on "Internal War: The Problem of Anticipation," p. 1, submitted to the Research Group in Psychology and the Social Sciences at the Smithsonian Institution on January 15, 1962). To emphasize the disparateness of internal war raises the important question of whether variables other than the extent of internal violence and of external participation (intervention) and impact (e.g. threat to international peace) should be taken into account in recommending an adequate international legal response to contemporary phenomena of internal war. To fail to add such variables is to neglect the objective of an insurgency in the study of the relevance of supranational legal norms to the control of internal wars. This corresponds more closely to the definitional emphasis suggested by Andrew C. Janos: "For purposes of systematic inquiry, internal war has been defined as a violent conflict between the parties subject to a common authority, and of such dimensions that its incidence will affect the exercise or structure of authority in society," in "Unconventional Warfare: Framework and Analysis," *World Politics,* xv (July 1963), 636-46. The issue is quite significant. For if one treats the objective of a particular insurgency as crucial to its status as an internal war, then it is probably important to develop a parallel series of normative responses. This chapter raises this fundamental question only implicitly. The explicit focus adheres to the traditional concerns of international law with the coercive impact within and without the afflicted society. It might be very illuminating to develop the international law of internal war on the basis of Rosenau's three types of internal wars.

[50] See note 2 *supra.*

ing the French Revolution and then in the period following the Congress of Vienna (1815). It is important to distinguish between the extranational consequences of civil strife that arise as an inevitable result of social, economic, and political *interdependence* and the distinctively modern *participation* of rival nations in domestic arenas of violence. Significant multinational participation transforms an internal war into a species of international war.[51] And, in fact, as a result of the inhibiting impact of nuclear weaponry upon recourse to direct forms of aggression, it becomes increasingly evident that the politics of expansion are now mainly concerned with the struggle to help sympathetic elites gain control of the apparatus of government in foreign societies.[52] This concern is coincidental with and reinforced by the mounting pressures for radical social change throughout the portions of the world engaged in the modernization process. For these pressures produce a climate hospitable to revolution and domestic violence.[53] Thus the external ambitions of imperial dynamism combine with domestic conditions of instability to give an unprecedented prominence to internal wars in contemporary patterns of world politics.

Such an extralegal environment places new strains upon the traditional system of international law. In the course of examining international law in the light of these developments, we discover the need for reinterpreting part of the traditional approach, discarding another part, and retaining, almost unaltered, a third part. We are led at the outset to question the adequacy of the *apparently rigid* separation of civil strife and international war, itself derivative from the overarching dis-

---

[51] Even without multinational participation, the outcome of an internal war may have an unsettling impact upon international affairs. This is illustrated by the Batista-Castro struggle, which seemed to be as domestic as we can expect conflict to remain in the modern world. The course taken by Castroism subsequent to its victory would suggest to many Western observers that an early intervention would have improved the quality of world order; that is, even with mutual adherence to the norms of nonparticipation, occasions may arise where considerations of world order or the maintenance of human rights might prompt intervention on either side. Who would look back critically upon a successful insurgency in Nazi Germany that had depended heavily for success upon the interventionary participation of third powers? Our search is for more than the discovery of norms and institutions that establish an effective formula of nonparticipation, and thereby allow the balance of domestic forces to decide the political destiny of each society. We seek, as well, a process for facilitating the elimination of intolerable domestic social orders, because they are intolerable and because their existence threatens world peace.

[52] This line of analysis is strongly developed by Samuel P. Huntington in two essays: "Instability at the Non-strategic Level of Conflict," Study Memorandum No. 2, Special Studies Group, Washington, Institute for Defense Analyses, October 6, 1961, and "Patterns of Violence in World Politics," in *Changing Patterns of Military Politics*, New York, Free Press, 1962, pp. 17-50. This pattern is studied from the perspectives of law and morality in Falk, *op.cit. supra*, note 37.

[53] This domestic receptivity to social and political violence results from a combination of factors: rising expectations, inadequacy of constitutional methods of achieving domestic change, absence of democratic capability or tradition, oppressive and privileged governing elites.

tinction between war and peace.[54] Standard legal commentary regards recourse to intrastate violence as a normal process of domestic political life; such an insulation of civil strife from international legal concern has as its normative justification the attempt to reconcile the rights of revolution with the authority of an incumbent government to establish order within its territory. Thus tolerance of revolutionary activity expresses the traditional reliance upon the territorial ordering capacity of governments as a principle designed to stabilize international transactions and to promote a climate hospitable to the activity of nationals abroad. From the exclusive perspective of protecting the political *status quo*, it would make more sense to use the power of third states, on a mutual basis, to secure the stability of governments in the face of domestic protest and rebellion. It is rather surprising that the incumbent regimes of sovereign states did not perceive a common interest and react in concert to the threat of international revolution. For in an international society lacking ideological levels of conflict, there was less tendency to appraise foreign governments as good or bad. Nevertheless, despite this mutuality of interest in the security of governmental tenure, international law developed a stronger emphasis upon anti-intervention doctrine than upon doctrine favoring constitutional legitimacy. This produced a tradition of deference to the natural outcome of a violent struggle between hostile factions for domestic control as the fundamental response of international law to internal war.

This deferential pattern rested upon a factual assumption: that an internal war possessed a truly domestic character. But, as we have tried to indicate, many instances of internal war now operate primarily as a restricted arena of international conflict. It seems inappropriate for international law to refuse a response to internal wars that attain major magnitude or that include the substantial participation of third powers. This is especially true whenever an internal war grows out of or into the cold-war rivalry, as was the case in the violent conflicts taking place since World War II in Greece, Malaya, Laos, and South Viet Nam. This variety of civil strife is more realistically characterized as a form of "international war" despite the confinement of military operations to the territory of a single nation and despite the absence of an armed attack across an international boundary.[55] Internal wars of this dimen-

[54] See Philip C. Jessup, "Should International Law Recognize an Intermediate Status Between Peace and War?" 48 *American Journal of International Law* 98 (January 1954); McDougal and Feliciano, *op.cit. supra*, note 36, pp. 97-120; Fritz Grob, *The Relativity of War and Peace*, New Haven, Yale University Press, 1949.

[55] Despite this "recognition," it is crucial to retain the distinction for *military* purposes between intrastate and interstate violence. This distinction is quite consistent with the hypothesis of this chapter that internal war provides the main arena for contemporary forms of violent inter-

sion increase the risks of escalation into nuclear war and intrinsically disrupt international peace and security.

But international law, even in its traditional formulation, is capable of a more complicated relationship to internal war than is indicated by the basic policy of noninterference. In fact, much of the superficial inadequacy of traditional international law arising from this apparent unconcern gives way upon closer scrutiny to residual concern that supports a perception of potential adequacy. For the ascription of belligerent status to the insurgent group by word or deed can lead to the treatment of the factions of an internal war almost as separate states. This, in turn, subjects the conflict to the regulatory claims of international law.[56] Over a century ago, Emmerich de Vattel made the authoritative observation that "Civil war breaks the bonds of society and government . . . it gives rise, within the Nation, to two independent parties, who regard each other as enemies and acknowledge no common judge. Of necessity, therefore, these two parties must be regarded as forming, for a time at least, two distinct Nations."[57] This allowed nations to assimilate an internal war into the normative framework applicable to international war even before the League Covenant or the United Nations Charter came into existence.[58] It is not without interest to observe that leading treatises of international law discuss problems of belligerent status for insurgents under the rubric of "War"

---

national conflict. But the facts of political, social, and economic interdependence that tend increasingly to ignore national boundaries and thus to depreciate their objective significance do not lessen the usefulness of national boundaries as conflict-retaining limits in intrastate military campaigns. The antagonistic perspectives of General MacArthur and President Truman in the Korean War illustrate the nature of the problem. Within their respective roles both men seem to have been correct, but fortunately the principles of military necessity gave way to the principles of minimum international order. A decentralized legal order must seek to preserve respect for the few objective limits that exist; a limit is objective if its nature is easily discerned independent of the perspective of the actor —for example, a well-defined boundary or recourse to nuclear weaponry. This reliance upon limits to restrain conflict is especially important for international affairs as the hostility and distrust prevailing between principal actors inhibit explicit agreement and direct communication of mutually acceptable self-restraining standards of behavior. The role of tacit limits upon international actors is sharply

perceived by Thomas C. Schelling in *The Strategy of Conflict,* Cambridge, Harvard University Press, 1960, pp. 81-118.

56 The concept of "belligerency" as a transforming norm is discussed later in detail. To the extent that actors have discretion (a type 1 norm, cf. p. 116), nations have authority to change the status of an internal war from a matter of domestic jurisdiction to one of international concern.

57 Emmerich de Vattel, *op.cit. supra,* note 15.

58 This has importance in refuting the argument that participation by the United Nations in an internal war is an unwarranted intrusion upon domestic jurisdiction. For it is evident that an internal war, if sustained, is from a functional point of view a breach of international peace. This does not, however, lessen the need to emphasize the factual internalness of violence in order to assure the applicability of the restraining rules associated with intrastate warfare—a need that goes back to the stabilizing relevance of objective limits in a decentralized order, cf. note 55 above.

rather than "Peace." A more accurate description of the traditional system, then, includes acknowledgment of a basic normative disposition to defer to intrastate strife as a domestic matter, but couples this with reference to residual norms that enable other nations to internationalize its legal significance if this should be found necessary.

Even this initial vindication of the traditional system must be qualified by four serious criticisms. First, the law of war never made extensive claims to restrain the significant elements of national discretion with regard to war. In fact, with the collapse of the just-war doctrine in the nineteenth century, international law allowed states to decide for themselves, as a matter of sovereign prerogative, when to wage war. The role of law was restricted to the avoidance of unnecessary suffering and inconvenience arising from the pursuit of belligerent objectives. Such matters as neutral rights, the protection of civilians, the treatment of prisoners, and the rules of belligerent occupation were developed to reduce the impact of evil side effects (to counter tendencies toward brutality) and to confine the scope of belligerency (to avoid the involvement of neutrals). Thus the traditional law of war must be considered as an essentially modest attempt to impose legal restraints upon national discretion to use force, and even if applicable to an internal war it does not contribute much regulation.

Second, the traditional criteria used to support the recognition of belligerent status are insufficient for modern needs. The old rules allowed belligerency to be proclaimed when the insurgents controlled territory, established an administering government that appeared effective, displayed a willingness to be bound by the laws of war, and impinged upon maritime or other interests of worldwide concern.[59] Today, however, it is essential that substantial participation in the internal war by private or public groups external to the society experiencing violence serve as a basis for internationalizing civil strife. The facts of external participation are more important than the extent or character of insurgent aspirations as the basis for invoking transformation rules designed to swing control from the normative matrix of "domestic jurisdiction" to the normative matrix of "international concern."[60] There

---

[59] From a legal perspective, many complications arise from the decision to treat an insurgent as a belligerent. Among other consequences, it changes rights and duties on the high seas and influences the treatment of domestic controversies involving property of the state that is the scene of the war. For a general survey of problems, see Lauterpacht, *Recognition*, pp. 175-328.

[60] A legal system provides contradictory and complementary norms that permit antagonistic actors to express their preferred outcome in the rhetoric of a legal claim. This facilitates the use of the adversary process and expresses the non-mechanical quality of legal decision-making. The legality of behavior, then, is not a logical exercise of finding the rule that fits the facts. It is rather a balancing of a variety of considerations, including past treatment (precedent) community expectations, the promotion of community

is a need, therefore, to develop criteria for the recognition of belligerency that takes account of internal war as the most prevalent and threatening form of international violence, involving both the principal pathway of aggression and a dangerous breeding ground for a provocative initiation of an escalatory spiral that has a thermonuclear catastrophe as its upper limit.

A third flaw in the traditional system is its allocation of authority on the basis of a world composed of sovereign states. International law arose to permit rising nation-states to accommodate their relations by the acceptance of common standards to serve the bilateral or multilateral convenience and interests of the states concerned. Throughout this period of growth between the Reformation and World War I, the notion of national sovereignty played a dominant ordering role in international relations and law, expressing its importance by the rule that required national consent to act as a basis of all international obligations and by the tendency to confer maximum discretion upon states to specify unilaterally their attitude toward new political developments in the world. This discretion is most familiarly present with respect to the recognition of new states and governments, but pervades the relevance of law to the response of a nation to an internal war elsewhere in the world. Thus, for instance, the recognition of belligerency is itself a discretionary act by a foreign state.[61] Hall states the prevailing view as follows: "As a belligerent community is not itself a legal person, a society claiming to be belligerent, and not to have permanently established its independence, can have no rights under that law. It cannot therefore demand to be recognized, and recognition, when it takes place . . . is from the legal point of view a concession of pure grace."[62]

In a world of intense rivalry for political influence, it is not surprising that decisions granting and refusing recognition are dominated by political considerations.[63] If the transformation rules of international law

---

policies, acquiescence of the state subject to the claim. See Myres S. McDougal, "The Ethics of Applying Systems of Authority: The Balanced Opposites of a Legal System," in Harold D. Lasswell and Harlan Cleveland, eds., *The Ethic of Power,* New York, Harper and Brothers, 1962, pp. 221-40. The classic statement of this characteristic complementarity of the legal order is found in Benjamin N. Cardozo, *The Paradoxes of Legal Science,* New York, Columbia University Press, 1928.

[61] That is, there is no duty to recognize once a certain set of facts exists. This

tolerance of decentralized authority-processes allows status to depart radically from role. This is most obvious in the post-internal war situation in which recognition is withheld; for instance, United States recognition of the Soviet Union was deferred until 1933 and the People's Republic of China remains unrecognized today.

[62] Hall, *op.cit. supra,* n. 35, p. 39.

[63] Even in 1947, Lauterpacht wrote in his Preface that ". . . there is probably no other subject in the field of international relations in which law and politics appear to be more closely interwoven [than recognition]. As a result, there has grown up a

remain politicalized, then the flexibility of the traditional system is almost without value for the problems of today. It brings neither stability nor control to the phenomenon of internal war if nations of the world are free to manipulate the legal status of intrastate violence to express their preferences with regard to the outcome of the particular conflict.[64] National discretion is formally restricted by certain minimal duties owed by foreign states to established governments; thus there are norms that prohibit "premature recognition" of an insurgent elite. However, it is difficult to apply any norms consistently once behavior becomes as conditioned to political manipulation as recognition practice has become. The dangers of unregulated internal wars are great in a world community that is increasingly riven; this makes it imperative to discover an objective method to transfer an internal war into the realm of official international concern. Preliminary to this, however, is the need for a reformed doctrine of recognition, imposing upon foreign states a duty to recognize, once certain uniform criteria set down in advance as ground rules are satisfied. Ideally, this would lead to the development of a nonpolitical procedure of collective recognition in which the more impartial judgment of the community was used to answer certain factual questions about the conditions of governmental tenure in the society in question.[65] The legal status of an internal war is thus objectified and centralized. This would produce a more uniform treatment of an instance of insurgency; the traditional system allows various states to overindividualize their relationship to an internal war. One consequence of this is to allow the same set of facts to give rise to several inconsistent patterns of rights and duties.[66]

A fourth difficulty with traditional international law results from the changed dimensions of internal war. The old types of civil strife normally involved either a spasm of insurgent activity that succeeded or failed in a

---

tendency to maintain that the crucial question of granting or refusing recognition is not one of international law," *Recognition*, p. v.

[64] The result is that the same constitutive acts possess a different legal character depending upon the national setting in which the determination is made. Thus, title to property conveyed by insurgents may give good title in some places, but not in others. It is an expression of the totalness of modern political conflict that there is an increasing tendency to govern private transactions involving a society undergoing internal war by reference to national policy about the preferred outcome. Cf. especially Bank of China v.

Wells Fargo Bank & Union Trust Co., 104 F. Supp. 59, N.D. Cal., 1952; Latvian State Cargo & Passenger SS Line v. McGrath, 188 F. 2d 1000, D.C. Cir., 1951, cert. denied, 342 U.S. 816, 1951; Stanley Lubman, "The Unrecognized Government in American Courts: Upright v. Mercury Business Machines," 62 *Columbia Law Review* 275 (February 1962).

[65] Lauterpacht, *Recognition*, pp. 165-69; Thomas and Thomas, *op.cit. supra*, note 27, pp. 250-72.

[66] John Fisher Williams, *Aspects of Modern International Law*, London, Oxford University Press, 1939, pp. 109-10. See also note 58 *supra*.

very short time or a protracted war between regular military forces using conventional tactics. In recent decades, however, several varieties of irregular warfare have developed that enable an insurgency to continue for a considerable period without establishing a clear belligerent or political identity. This new phenomenon of prolonged insurgency requires a special international status that enables third states to adjust their relations, but there is no assured way to achieve this on a noninterventionary basis. Nations can neither deal with the insurgent and incumbent elites on the basis of impartiality nor can they ignore the existence of insurgency. The range of contemporary options tends to eliminate neutrality and to polarize participation in internal wars in the factional manner that dominates international politics. United States neutrality in the Castro-Batista struggle for control of Cuba illustrates the kind of difficulty, for intervention on either side at some early stage would have reached more stable results, requiring less internal polarization to attain or to renounce the proclaimed goals of the revolution.

The emergence of supranational institutions on a regional and quasi-universal basis provides the apparatus to permit the recommended changes in the locus of competence. However, hostility and distrust militate against the acceptance of mandatory political responses by the leading cold war antagonists. The political atmosphere and the state of national consciousness in powerful nations lag seriously behind existing institutional growth and even further behind the minimum needs of world order. And yet few would doubt that any serious move to create a warless world by implementing a disarmament arrangement must include a grant of comprehensive authority to supranational actors to exercise decisive control over internal wars that threaten the strategic stability of the system. Already there is some movement toward the supranational management of internal violence when the situation is acknowledged by major states to threaten international peace. In the Congo Operation, the United Nations shifted its justification for action from the duty to repel Belgian aggression to the duty to restore and maintain internal order; to a lesser extent, the earlier presence of the United Nations in Lebanon and Jordan also rested upon the competence of the Organization to preserve internal order in a situation where the consequences of civil strife are perceived by dominant actors as a serious threat to international peace.[67] To some extent this development was anticipated, or—more accurately—not foreclosed, by the language of the Charter, which qualified the deference in Article 2(7) to "matters which are essentially within domestic juris-

---

[67] For a thorough narrative, see Arthur Lee Burns and Nina Heathcote, *Peace-* *Keeping by U.N. Forces from Suez to the Congo,* New York, Praeger, 1963.

diction" by a clear assertion that "this principle shall not prejudice the application of enforcement measures under Chapter VII."[68]

This centralization of authority might come to jeopardize ideals of national self-determination, especially as they are dependent upon revolutionary activity. The need for peace overrides an optimal preference to allow the natural outcome[69] of a violent domestic clash to resolve questions of challenged national destiny. Quincy Wright attempts to balance the competing claims in the following way: "Since international law recognizes the right of revolution, it cannot permit other states to intervene to prevent it. The United Nations itself cannot intervene to stop civil strife, unless it concludes that such strife threatens international peace and security or violates an internationally recognized cease-fire line."[70] This way of perceiving traditional international law suffers from its tendency to repress a recognition of the possible contradictions between rigid adherence to ideals of self-determination, self-defense, domestic jurisdiction, nonintervention, and the maintenance of peace. A particular phenomenon—say, internal war—must be perceived in relation to the overall normative climate; the traditional system, relying on the dominance of national power and authority perspectives, does not indicate a univocal normative response. It permits nations wide discretion and generates a spectrum of norms that enables nations to form a clear statement of national response. Without central institutions and assurances of enforcement, international law, in relation to coercion, was more concerned with the development of a rhetoric for the self-respecting resolution of disputes by diplomacy than with the imposition of common standards of re-

---

[68] The architects of the design for the United Nations evidently did not understand that the central peace-keeping tasks of the post-World War II world would require gradually expanding competence to restrain the scale and scope of intrastate violence.

[69] Earlier views of national self-determination assumed the hermetic reality of the national unit. This expresses the spatial approach to international relations that underlies the traditional conception of international law and gives rise to such fundamental doctrines as territorial jurisdiction, nonintervention, domestic jurisdiction, and sovereign equality. It is no longer possible to speak rigorously of a natural outcome for the domestic clash of forces, as extranational influence has necessarily been decisive in so many of the recent instances of internal war. It is now very dangerous for major states to remain aloof from civil strife by adhering to a doctrinaire faith in the acceptability of outcomes generated by the supposedly free play of internal processes of self-determination. Participation or nonparticipation by third states has become a crucial part of policies of aggression and collective self-defense pursued by expanding and containing states. We need a new vocabulary that can justify the legal competence that is developing to take the action needed to prevent internal wars from becoming the domestic scene of major international violence.

[70] Quincy Wright, "Subversive Intervention," 54 *American Journal of International Law* 521-29 (July 1960). Wright's approach assumed a more legalistic deference of supranational actors toward the domesticity of internal war than does this chapter. See, generally, Quincy Wright, *The Role of International Law in the Elimination of War*, Dobbs Ferry, New York, Oceana Publications, 1961.

straint. This discussion accepts a conception of international law that is wide enough to include the processes of claim and counterclaim that make use of normative rhetoric; it seems imperative to liberate the understanding of international law from a habitual perception of its role in domestic life.[71] The form of every legal order depends upon the distinctive structural and cultural characteristics of the social order within which it performs.[72] This assertion, which may seem like a digression, applies to the relevance of international law to internal war. For the diverse perspectives of national actors lead to a wide variety of behavioral postures and to considerable disagreement as to the character of relevant legal expectations. This does not mean that there is no legal order, but it does require us to comprehend legal order as something other than the effective establishment of behavioral regularities.[73] This "something other" is mainly the formulation of claims to

[71] This should enable nonlawyers to perceive the relevance of international law to matters of vital national interest and convince lawyers that international law cannot be understood when it is torn from its socio-political context. In a sense, both kinds of audience often share a provincialism about the nature and function of international law. Of course, this position assumes a basic jurisprudential stance for the purpose of deepening the comprehension of a single substantive problem: law and internal war.

[72] Law does not operate as an autonomous force. Its rules on crucial matters gain effectiveness as their claims overlay perceptions of self-interest. The convergence of law and self-interest is not, as is so frequently suggested, a weakness of a legal system; it is a central constituent of law's effectiveness in any social order. However, until the actor perceives the convergence, even if it should exist in the objective situation, the restraining impact of law is likely to remain minimal, especially in planning crisis responses. Thus the growth of effective law depends greatly upon a reorientation of the perceptions of self-interest by officials acting on behalf of nations. International law, especially, would benefit from an improved perception of the role of processes of spontaneous adherence. In like manner, instances of violation do not reveal lawlessness, but suggest the identity of the limit transcended. The dominance of patterns of conformity permits us to take note of the nonconforming instance. Perfect compliance suggests the triviality of a rule, for significant rules are those designed to restrain or suppress tendencies to act in a manner that has been forbidden by the rule. If there is no pressure on the rule, there would be no social function for it. Thus one would expect every significant rule of law to be subject to violations and to be challenged by conduct that has an ambiguous legal status. The legal process only gradually crystallizes a consensus in order to identify with assurance instances of illegality through the development of procedures of authoritative decision-making. These characteristics are now taken for granted in domestic affairs. One would not challenge the validity of domestic law after reading about unsolved homicides in the newspaper or even after discovering the disappointing ratio that exists between crime and enforcement in the United States. Why, then, does a successful violation of international law tend to put the whole system in doubt? It is a totally false expectation to expect national governments to comply 100 per cent with legal restraints that seem to forbid the satisfaction of their interests on certain occasions. A compliance rate of 97 per cent may not be enough to prevent a system breakdown—for instance, if the 3 per cent sector includes a nuclear war—but it remains an achievement of law to secure that level of compliance. At least, one should realize what one is denying when one denies the contribution of international law to world order, as well as appreciate the loss of stability that would follow from its non-existence.

[73] I have attempted a depiction of the special character of international law in a series of articles: Falk, "International Jurisdiction: Horizontal and Vertical Conceptions of Legal Order," 32 *Temple Law*

engage in controversial action in such a manner as to convey behavioral intentions to other concerned international actors and, thereby, to create a basis for further claims, counterclaims, explanations, and, possibly, an eventual resolution by way of compromise. This function of international law closely resembles a very loosely structured process of international negotiation, the main feature of which is sustaining communication.

It is important also to consider the special role of legitimacy in the application of international law to internal war. The term "legitimacy" itself was first used by international law to express the propriety of claims to dynastic succession in monarchial systems of government throughout Europe until after the French Revolution. The legitimate government was not, then, necessarily the government in effective or constitutional control of the national community. However, the rise of nonmonarchial societies to international prominence and the desirability of conferring legal status upon the operative governments of national societies led to an identification of legitimacy with the incumbent government, especially if its power was stabilized and constitutionalized over time and its authority acknowledged by widespread diplomatic recognition. The frequency of revolutionary challenges to established government in Latin America led to the Tobar Doctrine, which expressed a policy of refusing recognition to any government that had attained power by unconstitutional means.[74] This policy seeks permanently to deprive insurgents of the means to achieve legitimacy in the international legal order. The Tobar Doctrine never did attract much of a

Quarterly 295-320 (Spring 1959); Falk, "Jurisdiction, Immunities, and Act of State: Suggestions for a Modified Approach," in Falk et al., *Essays on International Jurisdiction*, Columbus, Ohio State University Press, 1961, pp. 1-20; Falk, "Toward a Theory of Participation of Domestic Courts in the International Legal Order: A Critique of Banco Nacional de Cuba v. Sabbatino," 16 *Rutgers Law Review* 1-41 (Fall 1961). It is important to appreciate that horizontal law implies decentralized decision-making. This entails tolerance for a range of discretion exercised by those charged with the application of common standards in international law. Such discretionary latitude would disturb us in domestic law. Thus, for instance, there is wide agreement about the status of activity that takes place in "territorial waters," but considerable disagreement persists on matters affecting their width, effective claims varying from 3 to 12 miles.

Again, states are free to fix the diverse conditions attaching their nationality to ships, but this freedom can be exercised only if a "genuine link" connects the ship to the flag. Cf. Art. 5 of the Geneva Convention on the High Seas (1958).

74 The Tobar Doctrine was incorporated into Central American treaties in 1907 and 1923 and followed in practice by the United States on several occasions. (See Lauterpacht, *Recognition*, p. 129.) It is interesting that subsequent Latin American concern with the interventionary impacts of nonrecognition produced the Estrada Doctrine, which stood for the opposite principle: recognition is automatically conferred upon the government in control, regardless of whether it attained power by constitutional means. Cf. *The Foreign Relations Law of the United States*, Philadelphia, American Law Institute, 1962, pp. 361-62.

following, although it illustrates a recurring temptation to identify legitimacy with the established social order and to repudiate the right of revolution. It also tries to develop as a role of law the expression of national policy in a form that helps the world community to render judgment and make a response. For the rejection of the Tobar Doctrine requires an explicit appreciation of the dependence of legal status in international affairs upon the effective facts of political control. It is generally inadvisable for a decentralized legal order to use criteria other than effective control to qualify a status as "legitimate." For this reason, practices of prolonged nonrecognition violate the integrity of the international legal system. Only a strongly hierarchical legal order can shape the facts to express the commitments to justice that prevail in the community.

In recent decades, however, legitimacy has been tied to a policy of justifiable intervention by powerful states. Notable illustrations include Western counterrevolutionary intervention in Russia after World War I, Fascist and Communist interventions in the Spanish Civil War, and successful resistance of the Western Hemisphere to Fascist encroachment in South America—especially in Bolivia, where collective and consultative nonrecognition led to the fall of a pro-Fascist government.[75] That is, legitimacy has reacquired a normative quality in contemporary world politics. There is less interest in stability *per se* than in a stability that extends and defends the sphere of influence of one of the major groupings of nations that exist: Afro-Asians oppose stability for South Africa, favor it for the Congo; the Soviet Union opposes stability for most of Asia and Latin America, favors it for East Europe; the United States opposes stability throughout the Sino-Soviet sphere of influence, favors it elsewhere.[76] We are concerned here with the quality of the connection between certain dominant attitudes toward normative legitimacy and the pursuit of a policy of active participation in intrastate violence by nations acting individually or in concert.

It is thus relevant to mention the pledge to support "wars of national liberation" that has been taken by Communist states.[77] The official Soviet textbook on international law revives the classical distinc-

[75] Thomas and Thomas, *op.cit. supra,* note 27.

[76] This analysis is developed in Falk, "Historical Tendencies, Modernizing and Revolutionary Nations, and the International Legal Order," 8 *Howard Law Review* 128-51 (Spring 1962).

[77] It is important to distinguish among various Communist interpretations of the "pledge." A main difference among Soviet, Chinese, and Yugoslav foreign policies arises from the extent of support that is appropriate. For to give sympathy, guidance, and asylum to the supporters of a foreign insurgency is probably an illustration of permissible coercion that does not violate the duty of nonintervention. This contrasts with clandestine shipments of arms and ammunition, the establishment of rebel training bases, or the direction of a revolutionary movement.

tion between just and unjust wars, explicitly including wars of national liberation in the category of just wars.[78] If the idea of "liberation" extends eventually to any movement directed against a nonsocialist order, as it apparently does,[79] then this is a far-reaching justification for active participation in internal wars. The Yugoslav theorist, Edvard Kardelj, denounces international warfare as being destructive and as acting as "a brake on internal progressive social processes"; nevertheless, with evident pride he writes that "socialist Yugoslavia has within the limits of her capabilities always offered the oppressed peoples consistent all-round support in their struggle for liberation."[80] Kardelj —following the Soviet doctrinal lead—considers defensive war and "people's liberation and internal revolutionary wars" as the only types of "progressive, justified war."[81] From a legal and political viewpoint, the most discouraging aspect of this policy of giving support to certain forms of insurgency is the apparent autonomy of the claim. For there is no willingness to entrust supranational institutions with competence to implement wars of national liberation on behalf of the community of nations. So long as participation in internal wars is left a matter of national policy, it is profoundly inconsistent with a serious quest for workable and acceptable disarmament.[82] The only apparent way to balance social progress with enduring peace is to entrust regional and universal institutions with a gradually increasing competence and responsibility for social change.[83] From this perspective the Congo operation and the resolutions of the General Assembly concerning Rhodesia, South Africa, and Angola are encouraging. It is also well to appreciate the significance of the distinction between United States sponsorship of the invasion of the Bay of Pigs in 1961 and United States leadership at the Foreign Ministers' Conference at Punta del Este in 1962, which excluded Castro's government from participation in the inter-American system because its Marxism-Leninism was considered incompatible

[78] *International Law: A Textbook for Use in Law Schools,* Moscow, Foreign Languages Publishing House, n.d., p. 402.

[79] Cf., e.g. "Declaration of Representatives of the Eighty-one Communist Parties Meeting in Moscow, November-December 1960," in Dan N. Jacobs, ed., *The New Communist Manifesto,* 2nd edn., New York, Harper Torchbooks, 1962, pp. 27-29.

[80] Edvard Kardelj, *Socialism and War: A Survey of Chinese Criticism of the Policy of Coexistence,* London, Methuen, 1960, pp. 32, 99, 107; cf. generally pp. 30-109, 178-94.

[81] *Id.,* p. 194.

[82] Disarmament cannot proceed safely or significantly without an accompanying assurance that a political rival is unable to use force to achieve aggressive political objectives. This requires the development of techniques to prevent third powers from the pursuit of policies based on the exploitation of domestic instability. In view of Soviet and Chinese doctrines, capabilities, and practice with respect to the exploitation of domestic discontent, this assumes a peculiar urgency as an essential input in current disarmament thinking. These issues are the central concern of Chapter XV.

[83] For further discussion see Chapter X.

with the objectives and principles of the Organization of American States.[84] The point is that the future of international legal order depends upon the emergence of effective supranational management on a regional and universal basis of external participation in internal wars. Normative legitimacy, if codified, objectified, and centralized, would provide a suitable basis for guiding the conduct of supranational agencies of social change. However, so long as participation in internal wars is left to national discretion and capability, the rhetoric of normative legitimacy merely confers a semblance of respectability upon policies fraught with danger and instability. It should be stressed, perhaps, that there is a need to promote certain social changes by organizing and encouraging external participation in antigovernmental insurgencies, but that this participation must itself be legitimized by a centralized process of decision and implementation. So far as this problem is a consequence of the broad discretion given to nations by traditional law, it suggests the need for, but hardly the probability of, a fundamental reallocation of authority between national and supranational communities. Ideological rivalry, nuclear weapons, pressures for rapid social change bid us heed with new seriousness T. A. Walker's comment in 1893: "Men do not always distinguish easily between the impelling power of conscience and the attractive force of interest."[85] Dependence upon self-restraint and a regime of self-construed reasonableness do not produce a reliable legal order, especially when the atmosphere is made tense by fear, hostility, and a sense of vital concern. These conditions curtail the ordering potentiality of decentralized systems of law.

The facts of participation contradict the norms of nonintervention. Behavior does not conform to the claims of the traditional legal order. Major nations identify their vital interests with the outcome of internal wars. This identification stimulates substantial participation in internal wars that is moderated only by dangers of escalation, cost-benefit analyses, and considerations of resource utilization. Restraining rules are undercut by notions of normative legitimacy that are available to vindicate participation by characterizations of "anticolonial war," "war of national liberation," or "anti-Communist war." In addition to this, there is a widespread acceptance of the propriety of counterinterventions designed to neutralize a prior intervention even if the counterintervention is of disproportionate character and even if the facts of intervention

---

[84] There exists a full and provocative discussion of the general problems: A. J. Thomas, Jr., and Ann Van Wynen Thomas, "Democracy and the Organization of American States," 46 *Minnesota Law Review* 337-82 (December 1961).

[85] T. A. Walker, *The Science of International Law,* London, C. J. Clay and Sons, 1893, p. 148.

on the other side are ambiguous or doubtful. The participation of the United States in the wars in Laos and South Viet Nam[86] seems to depend primarily upon this justification.[87] Also, there is a continuing acceptance of participation in internal wars on behalf of and in response to a request for help by the established government; the entry of United States troops into Lebanon in 1958 illustrates this type of participation.[88] This discrimination in favor of constituted governments helps unpopular and oppressive regimes to suppress insurgents indefinitely; if this principle of discrimination became an operative principle in a disarming world, it might prolong indefinitely the life of a government premised upon the abuse of fundamental human rights. In contrast, societies subject to external pressure and internal subversion are quite vulnerable to skillfully exercised take-overs. The engineering of the Communist coup d'état in Czechoslovakia illustrates this method of extending political influence—as the Communist Party acted within, Soviet troops massed along the borders.[89]

Several conclusions seem to follow. First, there is the adoption of an interventionary approach to political expansion by China and the Soviet Union. Second, there is the development of a counterinterventionary approach to political containment by the West. Third, there is the vulnerability of small states to the power rifts of the great states. Despite these characteristics of contemporary international relations, there was no disposition to challenge foreign participation in an internal war by threat or recourse to an old-fashioned armed attack by one state upon another, at least until the extension of the Vietnam War to the territory of North Vietnam, Laos, and Cambodia through the principal means of aerial bombardment in the period since February 1965.

In effect, then, these several varieties of foreign participation in in-

[86] See, e.g. "A Threat of the Peace—North Viet-Nam's Effort to Conquer South Viet-Nam," Parts I and II, U.S. Department of State Publication 7308, December 1961. Cf. also Roger Hilsman, "A Report on South Viet-Nam," U.S. State Department Bulletin, XLVII, October 8, 1962, pp. 526-33.

[87] After the Spanish Civil War, prevailing United States *practice* has assumed the privilege of counterrevolution. However, no accompanying revision of *doctrine* has been attempted to diminish the validity or extent of the claims of strict nonintervention commitments. For a comprehensive critique of United States policy toward intervention, see Manfred Halpern, "The Morality and Politics of Intervention," in

James N. Rosenau, ed., *International Aspects of Civil Strife*, Princeton, Princeton University Press, 1964, pp. 249-88. Cf. also Karl Loewenstein, *Political Reconstruction*, New York, Macmillan, 1946.

[88] This occasions sharp criticism from the perspective of positive international law; it is a result of the failure of traditional rules to be responsive to the changed social function of intrastate violence in world affairs. See Quincy Wright, "United States Intervention in Lebanon," 53 *American Journal of International Law* 112-25 (January 1959).

[89] See Morton A. Kaplan, *The Communist Coup in Czechoslovakia*, Research Monograph No. 5, Center of International Studies, Princeton University, 1960.

ternal wars are more or less tolerated by the legal system, except for an occasional interposition of supranational authority as in the Congo. If substantial participation on behalf of the insurgent is identified by the incumbent, then it provokes notes of protest and perhaps a proportionate response, especially an appeal for help to third states in order to neutralize the insurgent strength that is claimed to be attributable to external sources. This continuing tolerance by the legal system of participation on the side of one's choice in an internal war gradually assumes a place in the horizontal, self-delimiting portion of international law. A horizontal norm is a rule derived from patterns of national behavior, adherence to which is widely perceived by actors as obligatory and violation of which is understood to be destabilizing.[90] A horizontal norm may be inferred that prohibits the use of nuclear weapons in the course of participating in an internal war. Another horizontal norm prohibits significant assistance to an insurgency that challenges the incumbent government in the central spheres of influence of either nuclear-bloc leader; for example, the West remained aloof from the uprisings of 1956 in East Europe and the Soviet bloc did not render support to Castro until well after he was acknowledged and formally recognized as the leader of the incumbent government of Cuba.

The argument made here is that these horizontal norms convey the impact of law upon behavior with far greater accuracy than do the norms of the traditional system of international law. First, the rigidity of nonintervention is inappropriate for a world of growing interdependence, where the welfare of nations often depends upon foreign aid, technical assistance programs, guaranteed prices, and military alliances; whatever a nation does or does not do, once it possesses the capacity to influence the outcome of an internal war, is bound to be "interventionary" unless powerful nations participate or refrain from participation on a symmetrical basis. Symmetry neutralizes external participation far more than does unilateral adherence to a policy of strict nonintervention. Second, the tactics, ideology, and organization of the Communist Party give the Sino-Soviet bloc a big comparative advantage under the traditional system. Participation, at least as a potentiality, is assured by the ability of the Communist Party to breed sturdy, indigenous Trojan horses throughout the world. The West, in contrast, must adopt explicitly interventionary policies to neutralize implicit intervention that follows from the presence of a revolutionary party trained and managed from Moscow or Peking. Third, the wide-

90 For development of this view, see references cited in note 73 *supra*; an application to the control of force is attempted in Falk, *op.cit. supra*, note 37.

spread refusal to honor norms of nonintervention tends to make Western nations appear as lawbreakers, thereby impairing the dignity of international law and adding weight to the claim that considerations of power are the only important influence upon international relations. It seems preferable to repudiate the traditional norms in the face of these challenges and to substitute instead a group of emerging horizontal norms.[91] Such a modification in legal appreciation would disclose more accurately the role of law in relation to internal war, and would at the same time refuse to qualify as "law," rules which have lost their effectiveness in the course of changed conditions and persistent violation.[92]

It could be argued that complementary norms introduce adequate flexibility in the traditional system. Thus participation on behalf of an incumbent can be justified by stressing arguments of legitimacy, whereas help to insurgents can be justified as self-defense. This strains the accepted usage of norms by insisting upon novel applications, as when the United States asserts that a Communist government in Cuba is a threat to our national security sufficient to legalize the use of force within the scope of self-defense. It also encourages reciprocal extensions of restraining norms: if Cuba is a threat to the United States, then Turkey or Pakistan is a threat to the Soviet Union. And, finally, complementary norms, self-interpreted and self-applied on a national level, lead to a weakening of the entire normative structure by generating self-serving invocations of norms to rationalize and vindicate behavior that we would expect impartial observers to assess as impermissible. The relation between national claims of self-defense and the Charter norm in Article 51 makes this plain. In the absence of exceptional justifying circumstances, Article 51 limits the right of self-defense to action taken in response to prior armed attacks across international boundaries.[93] This is quite different from invoking self-defense

---

[91] A critical world order issue involves the intersection of vertical decisions (that is, by international institutions of regional or global scope) with horizontal norms. To what extent do vertical decisions take precedence? Suppose, for instance, the vertical procedures are hampered by the manipulation of *ad hoc* and irresponsible political majorities? The most important issue involves the extent to which action in violation of a vertical consensus is "illegal." Cf. discussion, *infra*, Section V.

[92] A critical intellectual task is to conceive more fully the problems of overcoming obsolete norms in a legal order that lacks a legislature. An interesting, if oblique, treatment of the problem of transforming rules of international law is found in two articles by I. C. MacGibbon: "Some Observations on the Part of Protest in International Law," note 38 *supra*, and "The Scope of Acquiescence in International Law," 31 *British Year Book of International Law* 143-86 (1954).

[93] The complexities of international life make it impossible to expect national governments to refrain from defensive force in *all* circumstances other than the response to a sustained, overt armed attack. The burden of explanation is, however, heavily imposed on the state that claims some justification additional to armed attack. Recourse to force by Israel in 1956 and 1967 is a good setting within which to assess the limits of a literal reading of the language of Article 51.

to justify forcible intervention in another nation because it has adopted a hostile form of government.[94]

For all these reasons, there is an urgent need to reformulate the relevance of international law to internal war. This reformulation is guided by the need to centralize authority and control with respect to internal war, to substitute community management for domestic autonomy, and to entrust supranational actors with gradually increasing competence and responsibility for the regulation of an internal war.[95]

V. Problems, Self-Criticisms, and Conclusions

Considerable difficulties beset this recommended approach. To what extent is the test of participation to be self-determined on the national level? Does the international character of the Communist Party make "domestic" Communist participation in an internal war equivalent to explicit Sino-Soviet participation? Does the obligation of nonparticipation preclude large-scale external military and nonmilitary support for an incumbent regime confronted by the prospect of a radical protest movement? Or should there be a provisional tolerance for nonmilitary participation by third powers in support of the legitimate aspirant to domestic power? Is it desirable to consider alternatives to constitutional legitimacy as the basis for permissible third-state participation?

These questions touch upon fundamental issues that cannot be discussed in this chapter. Besides, satisfactory answers do not exist; these questions are troublesome because they identify attempts to fulfill contradictory policies: the maintenance of international order and the promotion of domestic social and political progress. Certain tentative directions of response can be suggested. An adequate line of response must begin by recognizing that decentralized patterns of control will continue to dominate international behavior whenever cold war issues and participation lie at the explicit center of intrastate violence. It is equally important to identify an emerging centralism in the response of the community to intrastate conflict involving colonialism and institutionalized racism.[96] Here, vertical processes and institutions for

94 The scope of self-defense continues to be subject to various interpretations. In view of the precarious condition of contemporary peace, this is especially unfortunate, as it leads actors to arrive self-righteously at contradictory interpretations of the same event. This may inflame international relations and even produce armed conflict. For instance, both the stationing of missiles in Cuba by the Soviet Union and the United States' demand for their removal could be plausibly included in the wider conception of self-defense that has been urged by Julius Stone in *Aggression*

and World Order, Berkeley, University of California Press, 1958; and McDougal and Feliciano, *op.cit. supra,* note 36, pp. 121-260.

95 This orientation is anticipated under very different international conditions by Hans Wehberg, "Civil War and International Law," in *The World Crisis,* New York, Longmans, Green, 1938, pp. 160-99.

96 That is, racist policies endorsed by the prevailing governmental elite and incorporated into the constitutional structure of public administration.

registering and implementing community consensus appear to be growing increasingly significant.[97]

These two opposing trends cast doubt upon any unified attempt to describe or prevision appropriate regulation for the treatment of internal wars by the international legal order. Thus, for instance, a treaty that attempted to centralize all participation in internal wars would overlook political realities by neglecting the doctrine and practices of revolutionary and Afro-Asian nations; this would make attempts to achieve centralized legal control futile. Even if a set of ground rules prohibiting indirect aggression and subversion could be incorporated into a mutually acceptable treaty, it would probably turn out to be ineffective in practice and neglected in controversy. This reflects the general ineffectiveness of legal claims that are extended too far beyond the disposition of powerful governing elites. Whenever there is a premature centralization of legal authority in world affairs, international law is likely to engender noncompliance and fall into disrepute as an instrument of community welfare.

At the same time, it is desirable to make explicit the centralizing tendencies that result from a consensus about the disposition of the colonial and racist issues. The establishment of community competence for the coercive settlement of domestic conflicts in a manner that opposes the prevailing government's policy is a radical contradiction of traditional notions of national sovereignty, domestic jurisdiction, and supranational authority. As such, it is an important area of developing law that needs appreciation. It bears closely upon the opportunities for international law to regulate the *outcome* of a certain class of internal wars. The assertion of a claim to affect outcome is itself a radical innovation if we remember that the guiding policy of traditional international law was nonparticipation in internal wars.

Regional claims to control the outcome of domestic conflict rest upon more problematic grounds. For example, should a nation that disappoints regional ideals but is acceptable to the universal order be made a victim of regional coercion or be the beneficiary of universal protection? This problem is posed by the current quality of relations between Castro's Cuba and the Organization of American States.[98] For the alleged "incompatibility" of Castro's Marxism-Leninism with the inter-American system contrasts with its evident compatibility with the United Nations Organization.[99] The coercive implementation of regional ideals

[97] Peter Calvocoressi, in *World Order and New States, op.cit. supra,* note 1, uses this line of analysis to emphasize the disappearing capability of major states to carry out peace-keeping and law-maintaining roles.

[98] Israel and Formosa also exist in a hostile regional atmosphere.

[99] This point was vividly raised by the decision of the Special Fund of the United

of social order does improve the quality of international stability by reducing the points of hostile contact in world politics. However, the human costs of homogeneity are high, especially if premised upon the general primacy of regional ideals over competing universal standards. It is difficult, for instance, to endorse an international system that would tolerate an Arab movement to eliminate Israel by the use of force. But the "incompatibility" of Israeli society with the rest of the Middle East is at least as persuasive as is that of Castroist Cuba with the Western Hemisphere. If one seeks international order, not *ad hoc* opportunism, then it is difficult to distinguish between the relative validity of these two regional claims.[100]

This point can be sharpened by a contrast. If African regional groupings sought to apply pressure upon Angola or the Republic of South Africa on the basis of "incompatibility," then this would be acceptable from the perspective of world order. For the conditions identified as incompatible are also unacceptable when viewed from the perspective of universal order. Therefore, the bases for regional coercion are consistent with wider ideals and the target states are not victims of regional provincialism. If the regional coercion is intense, then it would seem to require Security Council authorization under Article 53(1) of the United Nations Charter.[101] In any event, there is a basic difference between regional coercion that contradicts and that which fulfills universal conceptions of minimum conditions for an acceptable form of domestic order.

Notions of legitimacy, however, should enable a preliminary principle for orderly standards of national and supranational participation in internal wars to emerge. A guiding presumption of legitimate status might be given to the incumbent government. This presumption could be overcome if the incumbent regime premises its social order upon colonial subordination or upon principles of elite racial supremacy (a white minority ruling a black majority); that is, the legal rules about nonintervention are suspended in those instances in which the community is confronted with an "illegitimate" incumbent regime. To avoid instability, this certification of illegitimacy must be formally expressed

---

Nations in February 1963 to go ahead with the construction of an experimental center in Cuba to help increase agricultural productivity.

100 A persuasive argument for distinguishing Cuba and Israel could stress Cuba's insistence upon pursuing external ambitions, including using its territory as a base for Communist expansion in the hemisphere.

101 Article 53(1): "The Security Council shall, where appropriate, utilize such regional arrangements or agencies for enforcement action under its authority. *But no enforcement action* shall be taken under regional arrangements or by agencies without *the authorization of the Security Council* . . ." (emphasis supplied). There is need, of course, to interpret the meaning of what is an "enforcement action."

by the United Nations resolutions of censure that achieve support from the overwhelming majority of members, including leaders of both cold war blocs. If an internal war assumes the form of a major civil war between two rivals who each govern a portion of the disputed state (the factual conception of belligerency), then a situation of dual legitimacy exists with the participation of third powers governed by rules of mutuality. The most orderly disposition is to refrain from participation, but the duty of nonparticipation no longer binds if hard evidence exists of intervention by third nations.

The notion of dual legitimacy is an inappropriate basis for determining standing in supranational institutions. For as long as an internal war continues, the incumbent should be allowed to operate as the exclusive representative of the state. However, if the outcome of an internal war is clear and violence has ceased, then the results should be expressed by the accreditation of the party in control. This is a factual approach based on a conception[102] of international institutions as organizations that represent the wielders of the power that is distributed throughout the world and most prominently held by national actors.[103] It thus should make legitimacy depend upon effectiveness, not normative legitimacy. This matter of *standing* in the organization, however, is radically different from the response of an institution to an internal war. The presence of the incumbent in the institution is not compatible with participation in favor of the insurgent. If the outcome of an internal war is a permanent division of the old state into two or more separate units, then this, too, deserves institutional acknowledgment without prejudice to the refusal of the factions to accept such an outcome. Here, again, the prime consideration is to confer standing upon the effective agents of political power in a neutral manner with relatively little concern about the constitutional or moral propriety of relative claims.

Can regional institutions withdraw legitimate status from an incumbent regime in a state that is a member of the region? Does this withdrawal entitle coercive participation on the side of insurgent groups seeking to reestablish a social order that is acceptable to the regional consensus? These questions suggest the central issues raised by the de-

[102] An alternative conception would admit to international organizations only those states that satisfied certain minimum moral conditions in their administration of government and practice of foreign policy.

[103] The *statement* in Article 4(1) of qualifications for membership in the Organization is somewhat difficult to reconcile with the recommendations made here. In fact, the practice of the United Nations indicates much greater fidelity to the criteria of factual effectiveness than to normative compliance. And the *meaning* of the Charter is more reliably ascertained by an examination of practice than by a dissection of the statement. However, the refusal to admit the People's Republic of China does provide a most important pattern of practice pointing back to the relevance of criteria other than factual control.

termination at Punta del Este in 1962 that the Castro government, having identified itself with the principles of Marxism-Leninism, is thereby "incompatible with the principles and objectives of the inter-American system" and further "[t]hat this incompatibility excludes the present Government of Cuba from participation in the inter-American system."[104] It is possible to regard this action as a progressive step toward the centralization of authority since it claims for regional institutions a competence to withdraw legitimacy from states within its domain and thereby enables third powers to adopt a quasi-legal basis for participating in antigovernmental insurgencies. The contrary position would maintain that the Communist character of a domestic social order is irrelevant to its legitimacy in international affairs. The overwhelming majority of states, and especially the nonaligned nations, favor an international order based on mutual tolerance of Communist and capitalist systems of government[105] It is difficult to reconcile the contradictory claims of bloc politics in the cold war, the ordering role of regional institutions, and the overseeing competency of universal consensus vis-à-vis the status of incumbent and insurgent factions as legitimate and illegitimate.

If the resolutions of censure passed in the United Nations to condemn the incumbent regimes of the Republic of South Africa or Angola manifest a centralized abandonment of deference to constitutional legitimacy as a basis for world order, then the practice of according diplomatic recognition to governments-in-exile is a decentralized equivalent. For instance, prior to the Evian Accords of 1962, establishing the independence of Algeria, at least twenty-five states accorded *de facto* or *de jure* recognition to the Algerian Provisional Government as the legitimate political representative of the "state" of Algeria.[106] The community is placing certain restrictions upon the capacity of an incumbent government to retain exclusive legitimacy for itself.

There are several conclusions that seem supported by this analysis of the application of international law to internal war. First, traditional decentralization can be overcome to the extent that regional and universal institutions assume competence to interpret and act in relation to the factions fighting against one another in an internal war. The presence of supranational institutions provides the basis for standardizing community responses through the development of community proce-

[104] Final Act, Second Punta del Este Conference, January 1962, Eighth Meeting of Consultation of Foreign Ministers Serving as Organ of Consultation in Application of Inter-American Treaty of Reciprocal Assistance.

[105] See, e.g. Declaration of the Heads of State or Government, Belgrade Conference of Nonaligned Nations, 1961.

[106] For a table indicating states extending recognition to the insurgent faction, see Bedjaoui, *op.cit. supra,* note 30, p. 138.

dures of recognition. Second, deference to an overriding community policy to allow the internal war to reach an outcome that expresses the domestic balance of power is only adequate as a first approximation to determine proper national responses to internal war. The cold war, the politics of expansion practiced by the revolutionary nations, and the global character of the Communist Party undermines the international basis for adherence to the norms of nonparticipation, as these norms have been summarized in the doctrine and practice of nonintervention. Thus the applicability of traditional norms must be made subject to a condition of mutual adherence. Third, dangers to peace in a nuclear age make it desirable to promote the community management of those forms of intrastate violence that threaten to emphasize the cold war rivalry, even if this process of management may interfere with the "natural" outcome of an internal war. Fourth, community coercion to achieve outcomes in accord with a universally held consensus is an emerging form of legislative competence for supranational organizations. If the community actor has the support of a regional consensus, then it is important to require an expression of approval by universal institutions prior to intervention in favor of the anti-incumbent faction in an internal war. Fifth, nations can significantly participate passively in internal wars by allowing exiles the use of their territory in a variety of ways to instigate and carry on hostile activities against a foreign state. Such a pattern of activity is detrimental to peaceful relations between states and is normally inconsistent with the maintenance of order in a horizontal system of law.[107] On the other hand, support for exile activities expresses the unwillingness of states to accept the autonomy of domestic social order as an unqualified basis of restraint. Sixth, legitimacy as a prime criterion for distinguishing between justifiable and unjustifiable participation in internal wars is not usefully restricted to an identification of the incumbent regime. In fact, a supranational consensus can overcome a presumption of deference to the constitutional sovereign. Furthermore, the Communist states as a matter of doctrine and belief tend to confer effective legitimacy upon the insurgent whenever internal wars take place in nonsocialist societies.[108]

It is important to preserve the aptitude of the traditional system for

---

[107] The boundaries dividing Germany, Korea, and Viet Nam present certain special problems. In general, Germany and Korea appear to be divided into *de facto* sovereign states. Viet Nam, on the other hand, as of 1954 was temporarily divided pending elections. As of 1967 a condition of *de facto* sovereignty exists in South Viet Nam, but it is not clear that North Viet Nam was bound to treat South Viet Nam as a sovereign state in the early stages of the anti-incumbent uprising as of 1958-60. See further *infra*, pp. 265-67.

[108] However, one should not neglect the refusal of socialist states to grant any legitimacy to successful right-wing insurgencies —e.g. Franco's Spain.

drawing fine distinctions. In this sense, the threats to the policies of non-participation implicit in revolutionary ideology and the increasing significance of international actors other than nations call attention to the dominant function of international law in the context of intrastate violence: the provision of an instrument for the communication of precise claims by various actors concerned with the conduct and outcome of an internal war. Restraints upon behavior depend upon the distributions of value preferences and power potentials within the community more than upon the formulation of rules. Especially with respect to internal war, as a result of the various interpretations of the morality of participation, the notion of restraint based on formal rules of substance ignores the *actual* restraining role of law as a restrictive claiming and negotiating process. In this respect, the refinement of the traditional conceptions of piracy, rebellion, insurgency, and belligerency continue to be useful to describe national and supranational responses to internal wars, although dangers to the peace and order of the world in the nuclear age make it necessary to objectify the status of internal wars, to the extent possible, by the substitution of regional and universal recognition for the practice of unilateral recognition. Such centralization is also needed to confer the status of legitimacy and to determine by collective methods the proper quantum of coercive participation on the side of the legitimate faction. Centralized procedures offer an alternative to competitive diplomacy by third states, especially the nuclear superpowers. Thus the rhetoric and doctrine of traditional international law remain useful, especially if they can be adapted to the new roles of supranational actors and responsive to the realities of the cold war. The future of world order depends heavily upon the improvement of our capacity to use supranational community mechanisms to control the course and outcome of internal wars. It also depends upon the perception and acceptance of tacit norms of self-restraint by dominant national actors.[109]

1963

109 This is especially true for tacit rules about the instruments of participation—for example, the nonuse of nuclear weapons in internal wars. The point is more fully developed in Falk, *op.cit. supra,* note 37.

V. United States Practice and the Doctrine of Nonintervention in the Internal Affairs of Sovereign States

"INTERVENTION" is one of the most ambiguous terms in the literature of international law. Intervention is often used to pass moral and legal judgment upon the state that is alleged or is actually intervening in a foreign society. The term intervention is also used to identify any consequential impact that the actions of one state have upon events in another. Throughout this chapter intervention is used in the second factual sense, especially emphasizing situations in which policy-makers of the intervening state consciously intend to have an impact on the foreign society. Such a conception of intervention means that it is not *necessarily* an illegal or immoral relationship, although it may become such, depending upon its objectives and modalities. The quality of a given intervention depends in each circumstance upon its actual and intended compatibility with basic world order policies such as the character of relevant legal expectations, political independence of sovereign states, human rights, and the discouragement of aggression. The complementary idea of nonintervention is used here to indicate the normal legal prohibition upon coercion intentionally directed against a foreign society. Nonintervention also has a second usage when used to denote the intentional adoption of a policy designed to avoid a consequential impact upon events in a foreign society. The conscious policy choice between intervention and nonintervention has acquired a special contemporary relevance in discussions of the relationships between civil strife and states furnishing assistance to one or the other faction.

This study of the doctrine and practice of nonintervention deals with two central issues. First, it examines the bearing of the conditions and structure of international law upon our understanding of intervention and nonintervention.[1] Secondly, it reviews the development and current practice of the United States in the light of these general considerations.

Before embarking on these expositions it seems desirable to provide a short statement of the ideology of nonintervention as it relates to the structure of international society.[2] Responsible statesmen consistently

---

[1] Intervention is used to denote an intended consequential impact upon a foreign society, whereas nonintervention denotes the conscious pursuit of policies designed to avoid a consequential impact. It is, of course, possible to envisage an unintended consequential impact, but such an eventual-ity does not concern the subject of this chapter which is devoted to the world order consequences of foreign policies that are explicitly either interventionary or non-interventionary in character.

[2] For an unqualified endorsement of the ideology of nonintervention see Declaration

affirm the duty of states to refrain from interfering with the internal autonomy of other states. This duty is a logical sequel of the almost universal acceptance of the state as the fundamental political unit in the world. The duty of nonintervention, then, rests upon the postulate of national independence. Independence refers to the right of a state to determine its own destiny by the outcome of its own internal processes of choice, even if this outcome proves highly distasteful to other states and even if violent or oppressive processes are used to express "the choice." The case for nonintervention is the case for mutual tolerance in the sphere of international relations. In this regard the relationship between nonintervention and the maintenance of peace seems to be evident. A discussion of the formidable obstacles and objections to the doctrine of nonintervention and its implementation will be postponed until Section I. The argument favoring nonintervention has been put in this simple form to make clear at once its guiding morality. However, as will become evident, there is no attempt to prejudge the feasibility or the desirability of nonintervention.

To grasp the relevance of interventionary diplomacy to world legal order it is essential to examine the main characteristics of the international settings wherein intervention typically is alleged to have taken place. Generalizations torn from context do not advance our understanding of the subject, nor do purely contextual explications of the specifics of any given occurrence. We need rather to identify typical settings and classify occurrences in relation thereto, and then attempt generalizations. This method of inquiry is illustrated more concretely in Chapter VII when considering the legal status of the United States involvement in Viet Nam.

It is also important to perceive intervention as a process of relationships taking place over a period of time, changing in form, objective, and impact as the conditions internal and external to the society experiencing the intervention alter. Such a dynamic conception contrasts with the more normal way of thinking that conceives of intervention as a discrete event of definite dimensions.

I. General Analysis of Nonintervention in Relation to International Law

Perhaps the best way to begin is by considering the influential remarks of Sir W. Vernon Harcourt, penned in the nineteenth century

---

on the Inadmissibility of Intervention in the Domestic Affairs of States and the Protection of Their Independence and Sovereignty, Res. 2131 (XX), U.N. Doc. A/RES/2131(XX)/Rev. 1 (1966); Declaration adopted by a roll-call vote of 109 in favor and none against, with one abstention (United Kingdom).

under the name Historicus, and concerned with whether England should intervene in the American Civil War: "Intervention is a question rather of policy than of law. It is above and beyond the domain of law, and when wisely and equitably handled by those who have the power to give effect to it, may be the highest policy of justice and humanity."[3] This seems quite clear and yet if we examine another passage written by this distinguished author on the same subject the relation between intervention and law begins to appear in its true, though paradoxical, form: "I do not intend to disparage Intervention. It is a high and summary procedure which may sometimes snatch a remedy beyond the reach of law. Nevertheless, it must be admitted that in the case of Intervention, as that of revolution, *its essence is illegality*, and its justification is its success."[4] This second assertion expresses the unsatisfactory connection between law and power that often exists within the international domain. If a state is able to use its power to influence the internal affairs of another state there is an effective change of circumstances that international law is almost powerless to prevent. But the fundamental ideas of equality of states and their right to unlimited internal independence conflicts with the legitimacy of any one state using its power in this way, to influence the internal situation of another state.[5] These conceptions have been recently reaffirmed in the Charter of the United Nations.[6]

Until the end of World War I, law did not seriously attempt to regulate resort to war by a state. Therefore, if the maximum effort to exert influence upon another state is exemplified by war it is difficult to suppose that international law could place serious limits upon resort to lesser forms of influence as represented by the conception of intervention.[7] But the Covenant of the League of Nations, the Kellogg-Briand

---

[3] Sir W. Vernon Harcourt, *Letters by Historicus on Some Questions of International Law,* London, Macmillan, 1863, p. 14.

[4] *Id.*, p. 41 (emphasis supplied).

[5] See e.g. "Independence signifies the particular aspect of the supreme authority of the individual state which consists in the exclusion of the authority of any other state. . . . Consequently, each state is free to manage its internal and external affairs according to its discretion. . . . As independence is, in the absence of treaty stipulations to the contrary, a necessary quality of all states, so the duty to respect that independence is a rule of international law. Unless it is abrogated by treaties, this rule prohibiting intervention addresses itself to all states." Hans Morgenthau, *Politics Among Nations,* 2nd rev. edn., New York,

Knopf, 1954, p. 290. It seems doubtful whether it is useful to give so much emphasis to the treaty basis of interference as an immunizing factor, as the treaty authorizing intervention may itself be a consequence of a prior intervention; by adopting such a formalistic analysis Professor Morgenthau provides the intervening state with a bootstrap upon which to legitimatize its behavior. This is, of course, a consequence of the rule of international law accepting as valid treaties resulting from duress.

[6] United Nations Charter, Article 1(2), Article 2(1), 2(4).

[7] Alf Ross, *A Text-Book of International Law,* London, Longmans, Green, 1947, p. 185; see also James L. Brierly, *The Law of Nations,* 5th edn., Oxford, Clarendon Press, 1955, p. 309.

Pact of Paris, the Nuremberg and Tokyo judgments, the unanimous General Assembly endorsement of the Nuremberg Principles, the Preamble and the Charter of the United Nations, and the operation itself of the United Nations make it plain that the use of force is no longer a matter within the discretion of the state.[8] Therefore, it is now possible to say that the use or threat to use force is subject to central international legal control.[9] Thus it becomes possible to discuss lesser forms of influence exerted by one state upon another from a legal point of view, and the subject of nonintervention possesses greater appeal as a matter deserving legal inquiry. It is meaningful to classify types of intervention and to defend the selection of certain criteria to state the legally permissible limits of influence that one state may exert upon another.

It is at this point that one can discern the functional role of a concept of nonintervention in maintaining a desirable system of international order. Nonintervention is a doctrinal mechanism to express the outer limits of permissible influence that one state may properly exert upon another. This is a fundamental conception in a *decentralized* legal order in which outer limits cannot be adjusted by central impartial institutions. It is from this perspective that we see the function of nonintervention as equivalent to the endeavor of private international law (conflict of laws) to formulate jurisdiction in such a way as to achieve adequate outer limits of legal control. When one shifts from the orientation of relations between states to the relation of an international organization to a state one becomes aware that the concept of "domestic jurisdiction" is also functionally equivalent to nonintervention.[10] For here again the effort is to express the outer limit of the permissible influence that an international organization, say the United Nations, is entitled to exert upon a state.[11]

The task of formulating limits for complicated phenomena is never easy. Nowhere, perhaps, is it more difficult than in an attempt to discuss the legal outer limits of permissible influence. The frequent practice is

[8] United Nations Charter, Article 2(4), but see Article 51; cf. also Quincy Wright, "The Prevention of Aggression," 50 *American Journal of International Law* 514 (1956). But see difficulties of this position developed by Julius Stone, *Aggression and World Order*, Berkeley, University of California Press, 1958.

[9] The extreme position in this regard is developed by Professor Kelsen. See e.g. Hans Kelsen, *Principles of International Law*, Berkeley, University of California Press, 1952.

[10] This point is made by Paul Reuter, *International Institutions*, New York, Rinehart, 1958.

[11] This is evident from the language of the relevant provision of the United Nations Charter, Article 2(7): "Nothing contained in the present Charter shall authorize the United Nations to intervene in matters which are essentially within the domestic jurisdictions of any state or shall require the Members to submit such matters to settlement under the present Charter; but this principle shall not prejudice the application of enforcement measures under Chapter VII [Action with Respect to Threats to the Peace, Breaches of the Peace, and Acts of Aggression]."

to define intervention by reference to the use or threat to use force.[12] This is an adequate definition to reach such flagrant interventions as those of 1956 in Hungary and in the Suez.[13] However, it is not very adequate as a comprehensive definition for it ignores the modern techniques ranging from subversion to hostile propaganda that are used to undermine the internal autonomy of another state, and it is this autonomy that is at the center of the effort of nonintervention to preserve the independence of states. Professors McDougal and Lasswell ask a pertinent question that rhetorically suggests the obsolescence of a concept of intervention that is defined by exclusive reference to the use or threat of force: "Are principles of non-intervention fashioned to catch the more subtle modalities of coercion or only the cruder, physical forms?"[14]

The immediate temptation is to avoid these imputations of crudity by enlarging the concept of intervention almost indefinitely and to identify it with any technique used by one state to exert influence upon another. And this is what has been done by a number of prominent commentators.[15] However, such a purist conception of intervention that identifies it indiscriminately with the exertion of influence ignores the interdependent reality that characterizes international relations. The subject of intervention becomes so vague that it slips outside the framework within which legal technique can operate usefully.

In addition to the unmanageability of such a broad prohibition, it is highly doubtful whether it is desirable to commit international law to a maximum principle of nonintervention.[16] The history of international

[12] See e.g. Hans Kelsen, op.cit. supra, note 9, pp. 63-64, Hersch Lauterpacht, Oppenheims International Law, 8th edn., London, Longmans, Green, 1955, I, Section 134, p. 305; Ross, op.cit. supra, note 7, p. 184; P. H. Winfield, "The History of Intervention in International Law," 3 British Year Book of International Law 131 (1922-23); Winfield, "Intervention," Encyclopedia of the Social Sciences, IV (1932), p. 236. And compare the definition given by Ellery C. Stowell: "Intervention in the relations between states is, it will be seen, the rightful use of force or the reliance thereupon to constrain obedience to international law." Ellery C. Stowell, Intervention in International Law, Washington, D.C., J. Byrne, 1921, IV.

[13] For a good exposition of analysis in these terms see Quincy Wright, "Intervention 1956," 51 American Journal of International Law 257 (1957).

[14] Myres S. McDougal and Harold D. Lasswell, "The Identification and Appraisal of Diverse Systems of Public Order," 53 American Journal of International Law 1, 21 (1959).

[15] See e.g. Charles G. Fenwick, International Law, 3rd edn., New York, Appleton-Century-Crofts, 1948, p. 240; Charles Cheney Hyde, International Law Chiefly As Interpreted and Applied by the United States, 2nd rev. edn., Boston, Little, Brown, 1945, I, p. 245; James Kent, Commentaries on American Law, New York, W. Kent, 1826, I, p. 21; Robert Strausz-Hupé and Stefan T. Possony, International Relations, New York, McGraw-Hill, 1950, p. 314; Ann Van Wynen Thomas and A. J. Thomas, Jr., Non-Intervention: The Law and Its Import in the Americas, Dallas, Southern Methodist University Press, 1956, p. 67 (hereinafter cited as Thomas).

[16] It is important to keep clear the distinction between the techniques of intervention (force, threat, subversion, hostile propaganda) and the grounds or bases urged as justification (humanitarian, protection of nationals, self-defense).

relations exhibits many instances in which intervention was prompted by humanitarian considerations that one can condemn only by waving too vigorously the banners of sovereignty. It is (sadly) not necessary to go back to the European rescues of Christian minorities subject to Ottoman oppression in the nineteenth century. The treatment of the Jews by Hitler provides a recent vivid illustration of a situation in which respect for the internal autonomy seems to be less compelling than the impulses that prompt and, in the opinion expressed here, vindicate intervention. It is in this spirit that one admires the evaluation made by Judge de Visscher of humanitarian interventions of the nineteenth century "which, notwithstanding their sometimes political aims, helped to implant the idea of limitations upon sovereignty imposed by respect for man."[17] It should also be noted in this connection that traditional conceptions of state responsibility give individuals no formal protection against the excesses of their own state. Thus the alternatives in a concrete case may narrow to toleration of the abuse or intervention. It is hardly necessary to add, one supposes, that prudential considerations must also be taken into account. For example, Western intervention, on humanitarian grounds, in Eastern Europe (say Hungary) is almost inconceivable because it would create such a grave risk of a general war.

To vindicate intervention under certain circumstances raises some serious world order problems. Any authorization of intervention creates a manipulative nexus that can itself be used as a justification for an abusive intrusion upon the legitimate autonomy of another state. An intervening state may claim to protect human rights so as to hide its dominant motive which is remote from altruism. One need only recall that Hitler explained his invasions of Czechoslovakia and Poland by the need to rescue German minorities from oppression. Part of the problem arises from the unreliability of any decentralized determination of when it is appropriate to intervene and the absence of any reliable centralized procedures. The risk of manipulation of verbal symbols would

---

17 However, he goes on to say that ". . . unhappily this liberal tradition . . . never had the strong moral and spiritual foundations that alone would have enabled it to limit the authoritarian action of the centralizing State. As for international law, its doctrinal deficiencies were still more serious. Dominated by a dualistic separation of internal and international orders, it affected to take no interest in man, regarded indeed as a mere object of international relations—except insofar as his treatment abroad might influence relations between States. Thus it found itself power- less when the great commotions that shook the twentieth century shook the very moral and social foundations of the protection of man's rights and everywhere diminished his security in foreign lands." Charles de Visscher, *Theory and Reality in Public International Law,* Princeton, Princeton University Press, 1957, p. 172; see also the same fundamental criticism of the status accorded the individual by traditional international law as it is developed in Philip C. Jessup, *A Modern Law of Nations,* New York, Macmillan, 1947, pp. 1-42, 68-122.

be reduced, though not eliminated, by entrusting the interventionary decision to an entity more embracing than the intervening state itself. In this respect the creation and development of the collective machinery of the United Nations and the Organization of American States have contributed to the improvement of the quality of international order; in these international institutions the decision to intervene is tied to the maintenance of peace and security and depends upon collective authorization by the community of states concerned. There is less risk under these circumstances, it is felt, that intervention will be undertaken to further a narrow partisan interest of the intervening entity. Thus it seems possible to grant that intervention, especially if it is a consequence of a collective decision by an international organization, may be desirable to protect men against severe abuses from their own state; it is a way to subordinate the absolute claims of internal sovereignty to the commitment to sustain minimum standards of human dignity. Here at least, world community values take precedence over internal political autonomy.[18]

But an even more vexing challenge to an extreme position of non-intervention exists. It is a consequence of the character of international politics. A policy of nonintervention becomes almost meaningless, and its conscious pursuit becomes a dangerous deception, when there exists an important aggressor state in the world community. The failure to counterintervene to balance the influence exerted by the aggressor is to intervene (passively) on the side of one's enemy. It also strengthens the aggressor increasing the eventual threat to one's own security. This is the lesson taught, one supposes, from the conscientious policy of nonintervention pursued throughout most of the Spanish Civil War by the Western democracies.[19] Let us examine the United States "participation." The United States refrained from taking an "active" role, justifying its restraint as "nonintervention," but given the "active" intervention by Germany and Italy on the side of Franco, it would appear that the failure of the United States to balance foreign intervention amounted to "passive" intervention in favor of Franco. This is espe-

---

[18] A recent book that emphasizes universalism as a basis for an international legal order is C. Wilfred Jenks, *A Common Law of Mankind*, New York, Praeger, 1958; see also F.S.C. Northrop, ed., *Ideological Differences and World Order*, New Haven, Yale University Press, 1949; F.S.C. Northrop, "Contemporary Jurisprudence and International Law," 61 *Yale Law Journal* 636 (1952); a very interesting discussion is contained in Josef Kunz, "Pluralism of Legal and Value Systems and International Law," 49 *American Journal of International Law* 370 (1955).

[19] For fundamental accounts see Norman J. Padelford, *International Law and Diplomacy in the Spanish Civil Strife*, New York, Macmillan, 1939; N. J. Padelford, "International Law and the Spanish Civil War," 31 *American Journal of International Law* 226 (1937); Charles Rousseau, *La Nonintervention en Espagne*, Paris, Pedone, 1939.

cially so to the extent that nonintervention finds its principal justification in terms of promoting internal autonomy, particularly in regard to political self-determination. Strausz-Hupé and Possony justly observe: "This example [the Spanish Civil War] clearly shows that under certain conditions there is no such thing as nonintervention and what purports to be a policy of abstention is intervention favoring one side."[20] This point may be emphasized by a comparison between the American and the Spanish Civil Wars. The American Civil War, regardless of its merits or its costs, was an expression of internal autonomy. The Spanish Civil War from the moment of Axis involvement intentionally produced an alien interference with the natural outcome of violent processes of self-determination. *The interventionary context once established invites other states to counterintervene, at least to an offsetting degree.*

There is a single contemporary qualification. Given the regionalization of the world community into groupings of relatively harmonious states it appears that intervention to preserve the existing regional harmony is a special situation. This is one way to view the 1954 United States intervention in Guatemala and the 1956 Soviet Union intervention in Hungary.[21] The efforts to counterintervene were kept largely verbal on both sides despite the existence of strong feelings. This may suggest that that part of the internal autonomy of a state involving the choice of political system is subject to a *regional veto*, at least when the choice on the *national* level introduces into the region a political system that is a representative of an ideology dangerous to the region. This observation is limited to the regions committed to one side in the central struggle between Communism and the West; as, for example, Europe and Latin America. It is also only a *tacit* limitation upon internal autonomy. When it is made explicit as in the remarks of Mr. Lodge, it is unacceptable. Instead of prohibiting certain choices of governmental system, states comprising a region characterize the arrival

20 Strausz-Hupé and Possony, *op.cit. supra,* note 15, p. 312.

21 Mr. Lodge made the following remarks in the course of the Security Council debate on the Guatemala Question on June 20, 1954: "Why does the representative of the Soviet Union, a country thousands of miles away from here, undertake to veto a move like that? [the veto was directed towards a motion to allow the Organization of American States to deal with the claim of the Arbenz regime in Guatemala that it was a victim of aggression]. What is his interest in it? How can this action of his fail to make un-

biased observers throughout the world come to the conclusion that the Soviet Union has designs on the American hemisphere?" SCOR, IX, Mtg 675, 1954; reported in Louis B. Sohn, ed., *Cases on United Nations Law,* Brooklyn, Foundation Press, 1956, p. 387. Rarely has the claim of the exclusivity of regional concern been stated so candidly. The Soviet delegate, Mr. Tsarapkin was quick to take advantage of this exposure: "Wherever aggression occurs, Mr. Lodge, it must be stopped; territorial and geographical boundaries have no meaning in this connection." Sohn, p. 388.

of the hostile political system as "indirect aggression" (that is, prior intervention), which it may be. This allows subsequent intervention to be characterized as "collective self-defense." This allegedly defensive reaction may be an effective way to resist the expansion of Communism but the use of labels should not be allowed to disguise the nature of the phenomena, at least not from impartial observers.

However, it also remains valid to say that an expanding and contending political system makes a policy of nonintervention deceptive and dangerous. This helps to explain the United States' position in regard to the Soviet Union and the propagation of Communism.[22] Communism is regarded to be a hostile interventionary and highly coercive political movement that can be resisted only by using offsetting interventionary tactics.[23] The inquiry is decisively shifted. We are not concerned with *whether* the United States should intervene, it is rather a matter of *how*, *where*, and *to what extent*. That is, the idea of nonintervention presupposes a general acceptance in the world of the independence of other states; when this acceptance is lacking there no longer exists the objective conditions making possible the *raison d'être* of nonintervention— respect for internal autonomy. Does this acknowledgment then compel our acceptance of the already quoted words of Historicus that "intervention is a question rather of policy than of law"? Yes and no.

There is one other relevant consideration. Since Kant there has been a strong body of support for the idea that the quality of the internal order system predetermines the disposition of a state to maintain peace.[24] In particular, this position regards any government that is antidemocratic in the sense that it relies upon a high degree of coercion to govern individuals in its society, as a threat to world peace. The Kantian position argues that the maintenance of peace justifies intervention. The strength of this view was demonstrated by the line of argument often taken during debates in the United Nations proposing collective intervention against Franco Spain.[25] The connection between

[22] This position is developed, *infra,* more fully in Section II. For an incisive analysis see Bernard Brodie, "The Anatomy of Deterrence," *World Politics* XI (1959), 173.

[23] The general basis of this position is developed by Immanuel Kant, *Principles of Perpetual Peace,* Smith tran., Library of Liberal Arts, 1948; a very good modern statement is found in Karl Loewenstein, *Political Reconstruction,* New York, Macmillan, 1947; for an application to the Soviet-United States conflict see McDougal and Lasswell, *op.cit. supra,* note 14, pp. 1-6; for an application to the specific

material of intervention see Thomas, *op.cit. supra,* note 15.

[24] The Holy Alliance established following the Congress of Vienna in 1815 proceeded on an almost inverted principle, regarding the principle of legitimacy of succession to monarchial privilege as the basis for international peace and fearing the warlike consequences of republicanism. See also authorities cited in note 12 for development of this position.

[25] See convenient summary of debates in Sohn, *op.cit. supra,* note 21, pp. 527-61; perhaps the weakness of this position was also demonstrated as Spain in 1955 was

the internal order and the international danger was particularly emphasized by delegates from the Communist states. It appears here again that considerations influencing action by an international organization are quite different from those that should be available to a single state. The centralization of the decision to intervene is here also a protection against an arbitrary determination. The conditions here are similar to those humanitarian considerations that have prompted intervention to rescue individuals from oppression. Here, however, the motive of the rescue is not to protect the individuals but to relieve the situation which itself is productive of tensions that explode into international violence. The assumption implicit in this approach is that a state which imposes internal coercion is likely to resort to external coercion (war), as well, and that the internal system cannot be divorced from the external effect.

Given these complicated considerations, how do we approach a modern inquiry into the limits that are or should be imposed by international law upon the influence that one state may exert upon another? Such an inquiry must begin by a consideration of the adequacy of existing supranational organizations and institutions, especially the United Nations. This is because intervention satisfies two fundamental structural needs of the international community that must be alternatively satisfied if a state (with power)[26] is to be reasonably expected to adhere to a high standard of nonintervention. First, national security must not be endangered by events taking place elsewhere in the world; within an organic international order self-defense is much more than guarding one's borders from attack. Therefore, given the primary commitment of a state to its own preservation it might seek to intervene elsewhere rather than allow its international position to be seriously weakened. This, in fact, is one way to generalize much of the phenomena that comprise the cold war. The second need that must be met before a broad renunciation of intervention becomes feasible is to establish effective ways to achieve peaceful changes in the international *status quo.*[27] The independence obtained by the 700 million people

admitted to the United Nations without any change in its antidemocratic internal order taking place.

[26] Nonintervention by a state without power is a condition and not a decision. However, power is contextual; it depends upon the capacity of the state in a specific situation to exert influence effectively upon the internal order of another state.

[27] For the fundamental relevance of social change to intervention see F. S. Dunn, "Peaceful Change Today," *World Politics,* XI (1959), 278, being a thoughtful review of a fine book dedicated to analysis of one aspect of the subject, Lincoln P. Bloomfield, *Evolution or Revolution? The United Nations and the Problem of Peaceful Territorial Change,* Cambridge, Harvard University Press, 1957; for earlier general insight into the relationship between international stability and the development of adequate mechanisms of social change, see H. A. Smith, *The Crisis in the Law of Nations,* London, Stevens, 1947, pp. 1-51.

since the end of World War II has often been a result of varying degrees of intervention. When an internal change is strongly resisted by a prevailing elite, especially in a colonial situation, the prospect of inducing intervention is often the only way to promote democratic (the will of the people) goals. This has been the costly post-World War II experience of France as a consequence of her position in North Africa and Indochina.

There is a certain antinomy implicit in relationship between these two needs. The security considerations press toward maintenance of the *status quo*, the social change needs press toward its alteration in a way that itself contradicts the conception of security held by some states. One can illustrate this incompatibility of security needs and social change needs by recalling the early British attitudes toward independence for Cyprus. A further discussion of these matters is not appropriate here except to the extent of observing that supranational contributions to national security and social change and their mutual reconciliation appear to be today still at the margins of the serious problems posed by these considerations.[28] The international order, on crucial matters, continues to be highly decentralized; the preponderance of power and authority is located on the state level.[29]

Before undertaking a review of the evolution of American interventionary practice and a survey of its representative techniques of intervention, it seems useful to attempt a summary of my general position. Nonintervention is a name given to a set of considerations concerned with the protection of the internal public order system against fundamental interference; it is the intent and result and not the form used to achieve it that is critical. Therefore, it is unwise to adhere to the frequent technical limitation of intervention to dictatorial forms of interference. In certain situations in which a government imposes extreme conditions of oppression upon a significant segment of its population there takes place a sufficient affront to a postulated common international morality to make it desirable to legitimize intervention. It also appears evident that international stability, and hence world peace, is threatened by internal oppression in important states. How-

28 For general expositions that emphasize the marginality of law see Percy E. Corbett, *Law and Society in the Relations of States,* New York, Harcourt, Brace, 1952; Percy E. Corbett, *Morals, Law and Power in International Relations,* Los Angeles, John Randolph Haynes and Dora Haynes Foundation, 1956; Julius Stone, *Legal Controls of International Conflict,* New York, Rinehart, 1954; Stone, *op.cit. supra,* note 8.

29 This does not diminish the prospect for legal order, it merely requires the development of horizontal (state-to-state) modes of legal order as alone appropriate for the current state of international relations. For an attempt to develop these ideas see Falk, "International Jurisdiction: Horizontal and Vertical Conceptions of Legal Order," 32 *Temple Law Quarterly* 295 (1959).

ever, endorsement of intervention is offset by the undesirability of allowing the intervening state or states to make the decision to intervene; history has demonstrated that the announcement of lofty motives is often intended only to conceal the narrow advancement of national interest. Therefore, maximum centralization of the decision-making power in supranational institutions would provide a solution, resisting internal excess and yet reducing the risk of *ex parte* exploitation of the interventionary situation. However, this is a solution for the future, as today the dominant exercise of decision-making power remains located on the state level.

Furthermore it is evident that the existence of an important aggressor or "expanding" state(s) in the world community makes nonintervention *impossible*.

A refusal to exert influence to balance the opposing exertion of influence does not protect the internal autonomy of the third state, it merely forfeits its destiny to the expanding state. Eventually such forbearance will produce the threat of interference to one's own public order autonomy. That is, to a large degree, nonintervention must be a universally shared and practiced ideal if it is to be feasible for any state. Today the competition between the Communist and the non-Communists orbits to extend their influence to "uncommitted" states makes a unilateral determination to follow a policy of nonintervention equivalent to default. However, mutual agreement, tacit or otherwise, as to the permissible limits of influence may reduce the risk that this form of competition will result in general warfare. In this regard, it is possible to conclude that there has been a mutual renunciation of the use of external force as a means to change the *internal status quo*, at least when the locus of competition is not within the immediate regional orbit of either the United States or the Soviet Union.[30] Beyond this minimum renunciation of direct aggression it is difficult to discern any further stable limits upon the degree of influence that either of the two states will use to promote its cause in the cold war. Given the

---

[30] By "external use of force" I mean to suggest the use of force to cross borders to achieve internal changes; when external force is invited to enter by one faction in the course of civil strife a different situation is presented. Traditional norms allow entry at the invitation of the "legitimate" government to help maintain order; the difficulty arises because the intervening state is able to characterize the requesting government as legitimate. In an analysis it is important to distinguish the Spanish Civil War situation from the American Civil War situation; the Eisenhower Doctrine is an attempt to formalize the interventionary rights of the United States in a situation comparable to the Spanish Civil War, that is, where the internal strife is already the occasion of intervention by an expanding state and it is necessary to counter-intervene to preserve the *status quo*.

Also the regional orbit should not be taken in a merely spatial sense, e.g. Western Europe is as much, if not more, part of the United States "region," as is Mexico; this is formalized by the reciprocal assistance provisions of the NATO agreements.

lack of centralized ordering in the world community it is desirable to accept a *stable mutual self-delimitation* of competence as a norm-forming part of the *legal* framework of international relations. Thus it is appropriate to discuss nonintervention from a legal perspective even though its content depends so much upon state discretion. Nevertheless, it is true that in the cold war matrix law now operates only at the upper limits of interventionary conduct (force).

However, when one considers state conduct in a neutral context (where the struggle between the Soviet Union and the United States does not appear relevant) one tends to find a more comprehensive acceptance of the principles of nonintervention. This double standard of interventionary conduct is particularly characteristic of current patterns of United States practice. This will become clear from a survey of the outlines of this practice.

II. A Survey of United States Practice

"You are afraid," says Mr. Oswald today, "of being made the tool of the powers of Europe." "Indeed, I am," said I. "What powers?" said he. "All of them," said I. . . . [I] think it ought to be our rule not to meddle; and that of all the powers of Europe, not to desire us, or, perhaps, even to permit us, to interfere, if they can help it.

Mr. John Adams' Diary
November 18, 1782[31]

This section contains a brief historical outline of United States practice on the subject of intervention. Two preparatory caveats are necessary. First, the practice of nonintervention varies from place to place, and through time. Thus a noninterventionary attitude toward Europe in 1800 and a noninterventionary attitude toward Latin America in 1967 are in many respects two different attitudes. Secondly, the literature, especially in regard to recent practice, is unreliable, colored as it is by adversary attitudes. Standard scholarly treatment seems to over-stress "the official" explanations of interventionary phenomena. To get behind the verbal smokescreen of diplomats seems to take several generations, and consequently comment on current practice becomes especially suspect.

Historical Background. The heritage of the contemporary approach to nonintervention very clearly displays the relationship between doctrinal change and national assessments of the international situation. President Washington in his celebrated farewell address of 1797 expressed the cornerstone importance of nonintervention to United States

---

[31] Quoted from Francis Wharton, *International Law Digest*, 2nd rev. edn., Washington, Government Printing Office, 1887, I, p. 172.

policy by identifying national self-interest with a scrupulous avoidance of entanglement in European politics. Nonintervention expressed a commitment to isolationism. But isolationism is prompted by a desire to induce respect for the internal autonomy of the state that has "isolated" itself. Hence, it touches the core of noninterventionism as a basis of stability in a decentralized world order by making explicit a reliance upon reciprocity as the agency of stability. The United States refrains in exchange for the expectation that it will improve the prospect of securing reciprocal noninterference.

With the exception of trivial departures, the United States did not, until World War I, seek to influence the internal affairs of the European states. This European phase of nonintervention survived its greatest test in 1849 when the United States rejected the very popular appeal of Kossuth for American aid to carry on the Hungarian Revolution.[32] Contemporaneously, however, American Asian policy was highlighted by the highly interventionary "opening" of Japan for trade by Commodore Perry in 1853, who was ready to support his threats with warships.[33] It is still accurate to conclude that until the twentieth century the United States tended to focus its influence upon the Western Hemisphere. Commodore Perry's action does reveal, however, the willingness of United States diplomacy to resort, on occasion, to intervention, defined in the narrow force sense, even if only outside of Latin America.[34]

Even prior to the formal enunciation of the Monroe Doctrine in the Message of President Monroe to Congress on December 2, 1823 it was evident that the United States exhibited a special Western Hemisphere attitude towards nonintervention. The tenor of this attitude is suggested by the following words of President Monroe uttered on an occasion subsequent to the creation of the Monroe Doctrine itself:

> It is the interest of the United States to preserve the most friendly relations with every power, and on conditions fair, equal, and applicable to all. But in regard to our neighbors our situation is different. It is impossible for the European Governments to interfere in their concerns . . . without affecting us. . . . It is gratifying to know that

[32] For an account of the relevance of the Kossuth incident for an analysis of the nonintervention policy of the United States see John Bassett Moore, *The Collected Papers of John Bassett Moore*, "Nonintervention and the Monroe Doctrine," New Haven, Yale University Press, 1944, III, pp. 349, 351ff.

[33] Strausz-Hupé and Possony, *op.cit. supra*, note 15, pp. 326f.

[34] For a comprehensive analytical summary of United States resort to intervention up to 1912 see Memorandum by the Solicitor for the Department of State, *Right to Protect Citizens in Foreign Countries by Landing Forces*, rev. edn., 1912. Abundant documentation of early practice is found in Wharton, I, Chapter III, esp. pp. 299-509; John Bassett Moore, *Digest of International Law*, VI, Chapters XIX, XX, pp. 1-583 (1906).

some of the powers with whom we enjoy a very friendly inter-course, and to whom these views have been communicated, have ap-peared to acquiesce in them.[35]

The Monroe Doctrine itself took a threefold approach to noninter-vention:

(1) A reaffirmation of the United States policy of nonparticipation in European politics;

(2) An assertion that European powers should refrain from claiming sovereign title to land on the American continent; this was specifically intended to resist claims of territory in the Northwest, especially those by Russia to Alaska.

(3) An assertion that European powers should refrain from inter-fering with the internal affairs of the Latin American republics; this was specifically intended to discourage action seriously discussed at the Congresses of Leibach and Troppau to aid Spain to recover control over her successfully rebelling colonies in this hemisphere.

There was a suggestion of reciprocity; the United States stays out of European affairs in exchange for Europe staying out of Western Hem-isphere affairs. The narrow purposes of the Monroe Doctrine were ful-filled, but the United States did not resist *temporary* European inter-ventions in Latin American affairs until the end of the nineteenth century. Such European interventions were undertaken as sanctions of self-help to enforce violations of the rights of the intervening state or its nationals, such as nonpayment of public debts. However, when the interference threatened to intrude more permanently a European power into the hemisphere, as was the case when France sought to re-tain its influence in Mexico in the 1860's, then the United States took effective steps of resistance. However, protective intervention did not reflect consistent United States practice until 1905, the date of the Roosevelt Corollary that formalized the intention of the United States to intervene to forestall intervention by some other state—anticipatory intervention.

Until the Roosevelt Corollary, and on some occasions afterwards, it can be said that the United States use of the Monroe Doctrine built a breakwater against European influence, fostering meaningful self-determination within Latin America. Active intervention by the United States was usually occasioned either by a failure to maintain inner order or by nonfulfillment of external obligations on the part of a Latin Amer-ican state, and intervention made possible greater, not less, independ-

[35] President James Monroe's Eighth An- in Wharton, I, *op.cit. supra*, note 31, p. 175.
nual Message to Congress, 1824; quoted

ence on the part of the state intervened against.[36] The United States in a fairly benevolent sense could be justly characterized as providing Latin America with a police force available to keep order and to keep others, less benevolent, from otherwise assuming such police duties.

However, towards the close of the century, the principle of protective intervention, made explicit by the Roosevelt Corollary, became more and more to be a mere euphemism for a quasi-imperialistic suzerainty that the United States felt itself entitled to exercise over most of Latin America. The imposition of the Platt Amendment upon Cuba in 1903, with its formal grant to the United States of broad interventionary power, is perhaps emblematic of the period.[37] The expressive metaphors —"dollar diplomacy" and "gunboat diplomacy"—that characterized United States relations with Latin America are not at all distortions of the frequent use of force by the United States to promote the financial interests of its citizens.

With dialectical precision the pattern of interventionary practice, in this exploitive sense, reaching its peak between 1900 and 1915, generated into being strong anti-interventionary forces.[38] Latin American hostility to U.S. influence belied pretensions of benevolence, and exerted enough pressure to induce the United States to make a much-trumpeted return to noninterventionism in the 1930's.

In 1928 the Commission of Jurists recommended to the Sixth International Conference of American States the following statement of the nonintervention principle: "No state has the right to interfere in the internal affairs of another."[39] Despite vigorous debate the Sixth Conference rejected the principle, largely due to the defense of protective intervention by Charles Evans Hughes, then U.S. Secretary of State:

What are we going to do when government breaks down and American citizens are in danger of their lives? Are we to stand by and see them killed because a government in circumstances which it cannot control and for which it may not be responsible can no longer afford reasonable protection?

[36] Thomas, p. 51; cf. also the remark of United States Secretary of State Charles Evans Hughes: "The significant thing about military interventions in Latin American republics was not that the United States went in but that they came out." Quoted in Strausz-Hupé and Possony, p. 340. This remark does suggest an important differentiation in interventionary practice. The duration of the interference is an important way to distinguish interventions that are more or less genuine sanctions (self-help) from those that are mere dictatorial interferences (aggression).

[37] The central language of the Platt Amendment relating to intervention is as follows: ". . . the government of Cuba consents that the United States may exercise the right to intervene for the preservation of Cuban independence, the maintenance of a government adequate for the protection of life, property, and individual liberty."

[38] Thomas, p. 55.

[39] See *id.*, p. 59; cf. International Commission of American Jurists, 1927 Meeting, Ministry of State for Foreign Affairs, Rio de Janeiro, IV, 1927.

Now it is a principle of international law that in such case a government is fully justified in taking action—I would call it interposition of a temporary character—for the purpose of protecting the lives and property of its nationals.[40]

This language is not objectionable, as such, though it obscures the basic issue—if the United States retained power to maintain by force the economic *status quo* in Latin America, the republics would have to remain content with a semicolonial situation. More significant than this fact of economic domination was the injury to national self-respect that took place. This injury has not healed, even today, in an era of frequently proclaimed hemispheric solidarity. Its continuing presence is revealed by periodic outbursts of deep hostility toward the United States. A typical expression of this hostility were the violent demonstrations in 1958 directed against Vice President Nixon while he was visiting South America on what was advertised as a goodwill trip. However, in 1928 formal adherence by the United States to the doctrine of nonintervention would have been comparable to the Soviet pledge of nonintervention contained in the Warsaw Pact[41] as outside the Havana conference halls United States interventions in a dictatorial sense were simultaneously taking place throughout the Caribbean area.[42]

The significant signal of a change in United States hemispheric attitude came in 1933 when President Franklin Roosevelt announced that the United States would henceforth follow "a good neighbor policy" in relation to Latin America:

The maintenance of constitutional government in other nations is not a sacred obligation devolving upon the United States alone. The maintenance of law and orderly processes of government in this hemisphere is the concern of each individual nation within its borders first of all.[43]

Accordingly, at the Seventh International Conference of American States the United States supported the inclusion of the principle of nonintervention in a proposed Convention on Rights and Duties of States. Ratification followed although the United States did reserve interventionary rights, as provided by customary interventional law, which would seem to dilute to illusion the value of the supposed United States

---

40 Report of the Delegates of the United States of America to the Sixth International Conference of American States, 14, 1928.

41 In 1955 the Soviet Union in the Warsaw Pact agreed with the states of Eastern Europe that its relations with them would be governed by "the principles of mutual

respect for their independence and sovereignty and noninterference in domestic affairs." Quoted by Dwight D. Eisenhower, *Middle East Proposals*, U.S. Department of State Publication 6440, 1957, p. 7.

42 Thomas, p. 60.

43 Quoted from Hyde, I, *op.cit. supra*, note 15, p. 275.

concession.[44] However, in contrast to typical international practice, the United States deeds far exceeded their promises, and noninterference became operational policy. To illustrate, in 1933 the United States army left Nicaragua, in 1934 Cuba was freed from the Platt Amendment and troops were withdrawn from Haiti, in 1936 interventionary rights in Panama were surrendered, and in the 40's financial control was given up in several countries.[45] It was not the *formal* adherence to nonintervention, but the shift in *attitude* towards interhemispheric relations that must be regarded as critical in examining the change in United States practice. Due to the absence of effective international legal administration, it is the actual policy attitudes, far more than the formal commitments that reveal the willingness of a powerful nation to refrain from active intervention. Given the existing unlimited discretion of a nation to characterize the legal quality of its own acts, formal commitments can be manipulated to achieve policy objectives. For example, any intervention can be characterized as "self-defense" or disguised in any of a variety of ways as "nonintervention." As has already been mentioned, Hitler preceded his "interventions" in Austria and Czechoslovakia by explaining their "legal" character.

Thus the hardening of the formal commitment to the doctrine of nonintervention which took place at successive inter-American conferences is far less significant than was that nonformal declaration of new policy by Roosevelt in 1933. This is clear when one notes a corresponding shift in the behavior of the United States in events outside the hemisphere where no new formal adherence to nonintervention existed. In fact, the response to Latin America extended, as it was, to the orbit of Fascist aggression revealed the dangers of doctrinaire noninterventionism.[46]

This zenith era of noninterventionism can be symbolized by two occurrences: the steadfast United States refusal even to protest the persecution of the Jews in Germany during the 1930's, and the textual language of Article 15 of the Charter of Bogotá:

No State or group of States has the right to intervene, directly or indirectly, for any reason whatsoever, in the internal or external affairs of any other State. The foregoing principle prohibits not only armed force but also any other form of interference against the personality of the State or against its political, economic and cultural elements.

Recent events establish that the doctrine of nonintervention, as the

---

44 Thomas, pp. 61-64.
45 For further examples see Thomas, p. 62.

46 Cf. generally Loewenstein, *op.cit. supra,* note 23, pp. 2-83.

broad operating principle envisioned by the Charter of Bogotá, can only flourish in an atmosphere of relative political stability, such that a state's security is not endangered by what is going on elsewhere in the world. It is, by definition, not suitable when the international community is menaced by a serious aggressor state. This is particularly true when the state that had been adhering to the doctrine of nonintervention has sufficient power, as does the United States, to influence the character of international events. Without relevant power adherence to nonintervention is merely an inevitable reflection of a lack of power.

The United States did not assume any substantial responsibility to stem the tide of German, Italian, or Japanese aggression prior to the commencement of World War II, often invoking the doctrine of nonintervention to justify its passivity. However, while still nominally a neutral, a fundamental shift in attitude can be detected that indicated a new United States willingness to use its active influence over the course of international affairs. This shift expressed itself, first, by intervention in "external" affairs, most dramatically expressed by the transfer of destroyers to Great Britain in 1940, despite the "neutral" status of the United States.[47] As with the preceding commitment to noninterventionism, the act or declaration is far less revealing than is the adoption of a new attitude.

Two historical factors have contributed to the formulation of contemporary United States intervention policy. First, the Monroe Doctrine lesson that protective intervention, undertaken unilaterally by the United States, provokes hostility and cloaks abuse. Secondly, the preWorld War II lesson that reliance on standard rights of self-defense and indiscriminate adherence to the doctrine of nonintervention are inadequate protection against a significant aggressor. Up until the Dominican intervention of 1965 the response by United States policymakers in Latin America has been to rely as much as possible on collective intervention, and thereby avoid both the unilateralism of the Monroe Doctrine and the appeasement quality of absolute noninterventionism. The unrealized hope in the 1950's was to create collective machinery as the basis of United States defensive tactics in relation to "the free world," unilateral intervention was to be limited to situations in which contact with Communism was direct, and hence characterized by overt hostility, as for example, recognition practice or transmission of hostile propaganda. For panoramic purposes the decline of noninterventionism will be illustrated by three representative areas of United States practice: (1) collective security—cold war defensive policy, (2) recognition of governments and transmission of hostile propa-

---

47 See Hyde, I, *op.cit. supra,* note 15, p. 278.

ganda—cold war offensive policy, (3) extraterritorial antitrust enforcement—non-cold war context.

(1) THE CONCEPT OF "COLLECTIVE RESPONSIBILITY" ILLUSTRATED AT CARACAS

> The fact is that the doctrine of nonintervention never did proscribe the assumption by the organized community of a legitimate concern with any circumstances that threatened the common welfare. On the contrary, it made the possibility of such action imperative. Such a collective undertaking, so far from representing intervention, is the alternative to intervention. It is the corollary of nonintervention.[48]
>
> Edward G. Miller, Jr.
> Assistant Secretary
> of State

This statement presents very vividly the official United States attitude toward contemporary intervention. Reading backwards in time, it suggests that the Monroe Doctrine was a technique to secure international law enforcement, with the United States assuming the policeman's thankless task. Now, instead of relying upon decentralized unilateral enforcement, it becomes possible to centralize on a regional basis. Unless, however, a substitute security arrangement is created Bogotá noninterventionism would seem to invite an aggressor to one's borders, as only then would rights of self-defense exist. The United Nations, paralyzed by a conflict between major member states, was unable to carry out its anticipated dominant role in the preservation of security. In its place, the United States has come to rely upon a series of regional security systems, composed of relatively homogeneous states, united, at least, in opposition to Soviet encroachment.[49] The formal legality of this type of arrangement is made to conform to the requirements of the United Nations Charter by explicit provision.[50]

The Caracas Inter-American Conference of 1954.[51] The action taken at Caracas in March 1954, in the shadow of the pro-Communist Ar-

48 Edward G. Miller, Jr., "Nonintervention and Collective Responsibility in the Americas," *U.S. State Department Bulletin,* XXII, 1950, pp. 768, 770.

49 Ernst B. Haas, "Regional Integration and National Policy," *International Conciliation,* 513 (1957), 381.

50 See e.g. Inter-American Treaty of Reciprocal Assistance, Articles 1, 3, 4, 7, 10. Article 10: "None of the provisions of this Treaty shall be construed as impairing the rights and obligations of the High Contracting Parties under the Charter of the United Nations."

Signed at Rio de Janeiro, September 2, 1947; entered into force on December 3, 1948; 21 UN Treaty Series, 93-105; US Treaties and Other International Acts Series, 1838; to similar effect is the North Atlantic Treaty, see esp. Article 7, 34 UN Treaty Series, 244-50. And see acceptance of the principle of regional organization within the Charter framework, Articles 52-54.

51 For a comprehensive report see Tenth Inter-American Conference, U.S. Department of State Publication 5692, 1955.

benz government in Guatemala, is exemplary. Earlier, at the Bogotá Conference in 1948 and again at the Washington Foreign Ministers Meeting in 1951, "all of the American Republics had gone on record in condemning the interventionist character of the internationalist Communist movement and expressing their determination to take the necessary measures to counteract its subversive activities."[52] At Caracas the United States proposed a Declaration of Solidarity, an excerpt from which is given:

The Tenth Inter-American Conference

I

Condemns: The activities of the international communist movement as constituting intervention in American affairs;

Expresses: The determination of the American States to take the necessary measures to protect their political independence against the intervention of international communism, acting in the interests of an alien despotism;

Reiterates: The faith of the peoples of America in the effective exercise of representative democracy as the best means to promote their social and political progress; and

Declares: That the domination or control of any American State by the internationalist communist movement, extending to this hemisphere the political system of an extra-continental power, would constitute a threat to the sovereignty and political independence of the American States, endangering the peace of America, and would call for a meeting of consultation to consider the adoption of appropriate action in accordance with existing treaties.[53]

The official United States view is to regard the Caracas Resolution as a revivification of the Monroe Doctrine, shifted from a unilateral to a multilateral axis, and directed against Communism rather than colonialism.[54] There is a certain moral piety introduced into the phrasing of the Caracas Resolution that tends to obscure its *realpolitik* premise.[55] When one removes the pious veil, the purpose revealed

[52] *Id.*, p. 8; cf. also the official United States characterization of the basis of Guatemalan Communism resting upon Soviet intervention, *Intervention of International Communism in Guatemala*, U.S. Department of State Publication 5556, 1954.
[53] Documents in *American Foreign Relations 1954* (1955), p. 412.
[54] See the statement made by Dulles,

Intervention of International Communism, *op.cit. supra*, note 52, p. 1; cf. also Miller, *op.cit. supra*, note 48.
[55] One is dubious about participating in the deception involved in the then existing dictatorships subscribing to that portion of the Caracas Resolution, quoted first above, following the word "reiterates."

by the Declaration of Solidarity is to permit resort to the Rio Treaty of Reciprocal Assistance in the event of the establishment of a Communist government within the Inter-American System. This may be a realistic accommodation to the aggressive threat posed by Communism but it seems difficult to reconcile it in a technical legal sense with the doctrine of nonintervention that is incorporated in either the United Nations Charter, or more explicitly, in the Charter of Bogotá. To proceed presumptively, as does the Declaration, upon the assumption that Communism always derives from a foreign intervention involves a clear sacrifice of the principle of self-determination, and amounts to a departure from the narrowest conception of the doctrine of nonintervention. Historical evidence supports the view that Communism has, on occasion, been a genuine expression of self-determination. Despite strong practical justification, an anti-Communist Monroe Doctrine, even if collectively administered, presents the same dangers of intervention that aroused such hostility to the anticolonial Monroe Doctrine. The same ambiguity of terms and capacity for abuse cloaked in justification exists. It now makes it advantageous for an insecure Latin American dictator to hide popular dissatisfaction behind the label "Communist infiltration," thereby justifying internal suppression and the receipt of collective aid. As well as the Dulles version of the overthrow of Arbenz—"patriots arose in Guatemala to challenge the Communist leadership"[56]—there are those who regard the revolution as an interventionary joint venture between the United Fruit Company and Ambassador Peurifoy.

This discussion carries once again to the core issue. How can the doctrine of nonintervention be used to preserve rights of self-determination without being used as a vehicle to remove obstacles from the path of an aggressor? The present American answer is to make intervention a collective (or quasi-community) matter, reducing, as it were, the likelihood of abuse by removing the interventionary decision from the power and whim of a single state. The gradual centralization of this decision-making is, as has been said, a contribution to the establishment of an ordered world community.[57] Viewed in historical perspective, this is a revival of the method of approach relied upon by the Holy Alliance and the Concert of Europe to maintain European stability in the nineteenth century, based similarly on the justification for intervention arising out of a disruption of the political homogeneity in the area.

[56] Dulles, "The Guatemalan Crisis," U.S. Department of State Release 357, 1954; reprinted in documents in *American Foreign Relations 1954* (1955), p. 415.

[57] E.g. Hans Kelsen, *The Law of the United Nations,* London, Stevens, 1950, pp. 13, 207.

The Caracas Declaration of Solidarity is but an illustration of a coherent worldwide policy pursued by the United States since the close of World War II.[58] This policy, while conforming to the formal legal requirements of the doctrine of nonintervention, has attempted to exercise a maximum anti-Communist influence upon the internal affairs of other states. It has, by necessity, manifested the interventionary character inevitable in a world stalked by a potent aggressor. It is a broad policy of defensive interventionism, but, and this is the main point here, it is a departure from the kind of broad noninterventionism that existed during the 1930's when the United States exerted influence only by a refusal to exert it.

(2) RECOGNITION OF GOVERNMENTS

> We try to conduct our relations with all governments of the world on the basis of dealing with the government which is, in fact, in power, unless we have reasons, as we have in Communist China, for not recognizing it. [laughter] . . . You can talk about dictators and non-dictators but it isn't easy to classify on that basis. . . . We respond to the requests of governments which are friendly more than we do to governments that are unfriendly. But we do not take into account the particular degree to which they have our form of democracy. We deal with the Government of Yugoslavia and give it considerable amount of assistance or aid. That doesn't mean that we are in favor of the internal type of government that they have in Yugoslavia.
>
> Secretary John Foster Dulles' News
> Conference, May 20, 1958[59]

United States recognition practice has been used as a unilateral instrument of influence in the cold war. Despite a prior positivistic tradition, emphasizing *de facto* control, recent United States practice quite consciously employs recognition as an interventionary technique.[60] Secretary Dulles quite candidly explained this, in regard to Communist China, as follows:

> Any time it will serve the interests of the United States to recognize the Chinese Communist regime, we will do it. We are not controlled by dogma or anything of that sort. It's a very simple question: will it serve our interests and the interests of the free world and our allies to whom we are committed to grant recognition? If the answer to that is that it will help it, then we will recognize.

[58] See e.g. Dulles, *Statement before the House Committee on Foreign Affairs*, January 7, 1957, U.S. Department of State Publication 6440, 1957, p. 19.

[59] Press release 280 dated May 20, *U.S.*

State Department Bulletin, XXXVIII, 1958, pp. 942, 944.

[60] A good discussion of the relationship between intervention and recognition is found in Thomas, pp. 241-272.

If the answer is that it will not help it, then we will not recognize, and the answer today is no.[61]

Current nonrecognition of Red China, it is true, unless premised on the sheerest phantasy, does not envision the exertion of *direct* influence on the *internal affairs* of Red China.[62] Nevertheless, it is indirect internal intervention seeking, in part, to place pressure on the internal economy.

Recognition is now one more weapon in the arsenal of self-defense. A consistent interventionary use of recognition policy can be traced back to 1943 when a pro-Fascist coup d'état seized control of the Bolivian government. Here, through the use of the collective machinery of the Organization of American States, recognition was withheld by agreement.[63] Nonrecognition had the contemplated interventionary effect compelling the Bolivian government to purge itself of its more blatant Nazi sympathizers. Once the purge was carried out recognition was granted.

Similarly today, the aggressive character of international Communism has prompted the United States to follow an interventionary recognition policy. If manipulating the conferral of recognition is one way to stop or obstruct the advance of Communism then it must be considered as part of a comprehensive plan of self-defense, and so it has been employed, despite its incompatibility with the principle of self-determination. Despite official protestations to the contrary, it is doubtful that the United States government would confer rapid recognition on a state that really did "choose" Communism, free from Russian intervention. From available evidence it would appear that the victory of Communism in China was indigenous, Russian intervention being at least balanced by American intervention. Yet, as we have seen, United States recognition has not followed. Contrariwise, an anti-Communist coup d'état will receive an immediate interventionary grant of recognition by the United States, as in Iran and Guatemala, even though it is premature by normal *de facto* standards.

Latin America had long resented the potency of nonrecognition and premature recognition by the United States as an instrument of intervention. The most significant attempt to neutralize the internal influence of recognition policy, the Estrada Doctrine, came, as Thomas and Thomas point out as a "reaction to the use by the United States of its recognition policy as a tool of intervention in the domestic affairs of Mex-

---

61 *New York Times*, January 17, 1958, p. 4.
62 Cf. however, nonrecognition of the change of government in Cuba in 1933; see Thomas, p. 61.

63 *Id.*, p. 251; see generally Charles G. Fenwick, "Intervention—Individual and Collective," 39 *American Journal of International Law* 645 (1945).

ico."[64] Attempts to make recognition policy a collective inter-American matter, paralleling other aspects of collective responsibility, have, to date, failed to be accepted, although efforts continue.[65] Recalling that "a collective undertaking" is urged by United States policy-makers as "the corollary of nonintervention," recognition policy is, so to speak, in a state of suspension.[66] Unless the Communist issue is involved, as it was in Guatemala, the United States seems to be pursuing a self-consciously noninterventionary recognition policy, as it did in relation to the recent democratizing revolutions in Argentina and Venezuela.

In Latin America, sensitivity to attempts by the United States to intervene, give to such exertions a boomerang effect. This means that maximum United States interventionary effect can be obtained by the scrupulous adherence to a policy of "nonintervention," thus illustrating once again the subtlety of the distinction between intervention and nonintervention.

In summary, United States recognition practice tends to be as interventionary as possible whenever cold war issues are involved. If they are not, then despite strong axiological sympathies for the replacement of a totalitarian by a democratic government, United States recognition practice is noninterventionary, basing its grant upon effective control by the government seeking recognition.[67]

Hostile Propaganda. Cold war tactics, by their very coldness, depend upon techniques of intervention short of war. In fact, a cold war could almost be defined as a nonmilitary conflict of opposing interventionary forces. Among the more spectacular of the interventionary stratagems resorted to by the United States has been the transmission of hostile propaganda to Soviet bloc countries. Despite a genuine effort to promote self-determination by informing the local population of "the facts," the very *raison d'être* of hostile propaganda is intervention, at least in the sense of influence on internal affairs. A recent study has concluded that "propaganda is a form of illegal intervention."[68] This conclusion clearly seems correct if anything approaching Article 15 of the Bogotá Charter is an accurate codification of international law. But in the absence of a broad stabilization of international relations by agreement, as in the Organization of American States, there

64 Thomas, p. 50; cf. also at p. 244 where the authors conclude that had not the United States extended premature recognition to the Panamanian government in 1903 Colombia could have restored order and repressed the rebellion.

65 Cf. *id.*, p. 250.

66 Miller, *op.cit. supra*, note 48, p. 770.

67 Examples from the diplomatic practice of the 1950's are provided by the manner of extending recognition to the moderate revolutionary governments in Argentina and Venezuela for which the United States felt sympathy.

68 Thomas, p. 273.

is no practicable way to assert an objection to such interventionary practice, unless perhaps that it constitutes "a threat to the peace" under the Charter. As the cold war interventions arise between countries having minimum stabilization of relations *inter sese*, the determination of legality is concluded by self-approval on the state level. As there exists no *objective* way to determine whether hostile propaganda or other kindred interventionary techniques do constitute illegal intervention, the legal question is academic. The pattern of practice will be controlled by "political" considerations, despite a formal level of protest expressed in the language of law.[69]

(3) EXTRATERRITORIAL ANTITRUST LAW ENFORCEMENT

As is well known, the United States has resorted, in the past decade or so, to a vigorous unilateral extension of its antitrust regulation to business activity carried on largely within the territory of other states.[70] This regulation has been resisted by other states, in various ways, on the grounds that it constitutes an illegal interference with territorial control over the conduct of economic affairs. The controversy, though provocative of a voluminous literature, has not been, despite its character, carried on in the language of the doctrine of nonintervention. However, the implications of the argument opposing the regulation are an obvious invocation of the doctrine. And, insofar as the apologists for the regulation talk in terms of obstructing the cartelization of international trade, the argument amounts, at least in certain instances, to a covert defense of a form of *protective* intervention in the internal affairs of other states.[71] By "protective" is meant the insulation of our domestic economy from the introduction of noncompetitive forces that would result if United States antitrust regulation were to stop at "the water's edge."

One rather over-discussed case well illustrates the situation.[72] A United States court concluded that in order to terminate a conspiracy, in violation of the Sherman Act, between a British and an American firm, it would be necessary to require the British company to reconvey

---

[69] See development of this idea in Corbett, *Law and Society, op.cit. supra,* note 28, p. 87.

[70] For a survey of relevant judicial material see Report of the Attorney General's Committee to Study the Antitrust Laws, 1955, pp. 65-80; see also Kingman Brewster, Jr., *Antitrust and American Business Abroad,* New York, McGraw-Hill, 1958, esp. pp. 286-349.

[71] See e.g. Wendell Berge, *Cartels Chal-* *lenge to a Free World,* Washington, Public Affairs Press, 1944; George W. Stockings and Myron W. Watkins, *Cartels in Action,* New York, Twentieth Century Fund, 1946; Corwin Edwards, ed., *A Cartel Policy for the United Nations,* New York, Columbia University Press, 1946.

[72] United States v. Imperial Chemical Industries, Ltd., 100 F. Supp. 504, S.D. N.Y., 1951, decree 105 F. Supp. 215, 226, S.D.N.Y., 1952.

certain patents to the American corporation. However, the British company had licensed the use of a patented process, covered by the American decree, to another British firm, and this latter company instituted a successful legal action in a British court to enjoin the reconveyance of the patent. The British court resting its decision, in part at least, on the illegality of the attempt by an American court to interfere with the British performance of a contract between British parties to be fully carried out in Britain.[73]

To what extent does adherence to the doctrine of nonintervention condemn extraterritorial economic regulation of this type? The technical legitimacy of this regulation is quite separate from its wisdom. International law seems to authorize a claim to attach legal consequences to foreign events that have a direct and substantial impact upon the claimant state.[74] However, it cannot be denied that the widespread assertion of such claims would tend and is intended to produce an interventionary effect, making noncompetitive enterprise in those countries that favor or tolerate it, much more difficult. But alternative nonassertion would tend to interfere with the United States regulation of its own economy, as it would inevitably introduce noncompetitive practices into the United States. Here, also, the distinction between intervention and nonintervention seems to break down, leaving not an either/or decision but rather a choice of what type of intervention. That is, given economic interdependence, shall we extend our regulation in an interventionary fashion, or, shall we refrain, and suffer the intervention consequent upon the triumph of the economic policies adhered to by the nonregulating states?

This intervention controversy has taken place far outside the cold war matrix, largely limiting itself to a clash with the highly industrialized countries of capitalist Western Europe. Insofar as active interference in European economic administration does take place it amounts to a complete inversion of the Monroe Doctrine's active principle. However, its anticartel objectives accord with a consistent major United States interventionary motive—the promotion of a homogeneously democratic world community—and in this sense it is part of the larger policy underlying the revival of interventionism by the United States.

[73] British Nylon Spinners v. Imperial Chemicals Industries, Ltd., 1952, 2 *All. E.R.* 780; and final judgment holding that "plaintiff company was entitled to specific performance," 1954, 3 *All. E.R.* 88.

[74] Harvard Research in International Law, "Jurisdiction with Respect to Crime," 29 *American Journal of International Law,* Supp. pt. ii 439-651 (1935); the *Lotus* principle that a state possesses discretion to extend its law in any manner not *explicitly* forbidden by international law seems also to legitimatize this basis of legal competence, Case of the SS "Lotus," Permanent Court of International Justice, Ser. A, No. 10, 19, 1927; this is also expressed by the maxim *ce qui n'est pas defendu est permis.*

III. Conclusion

It is hoped that a sense of the complexity of the issues that underlie any intelligent approach to nonintervention has emerged from this discussion. It is evident that no simple prohibition or endorsement of various techniques of exerting influence upon other states can be made. The minimum contemporary concept of nonintervention is the renunciation of the use of force by states for all purposes except individual or collective self-defense against an "armed attack" within the meaning of Article 51 of the Charter.

Beyond this minimum, stable lines of limitation are not revealed by patterns of United States practice in cold war contexts. In neutral contexts some proliferation of limits can be discerned, especially in Western Hemisphere relations. *Their stability is what gives to such limits a legal character.* The development of law between coordinate political entities (states) offers more promise for the immediate future than does the corresponding development between noncoordinate political entities (international organizations—states). We should not define such an opportunity out of existence by a procrustean imposition of an Austinean definition of law upon the subject-matter of international relations.[75]

Accepting this analysis it becomes desirable to seek objective criteria that can be used by national decision-makers to determine the permissible limits of state influence. This requires that the present study of nonintervention (which ironically concerned itself more with patterns of intervention) be supplemented by a comprehensive analytical classification of interventionary phenomena that seek *explicit convenient outer limits of permissible influence.* Such an endeavor, if successful, would contribute to the usefulness of the legal techniques available to adjust relations between states in a mutually satisfactory manner. It is part of the general task of a decentralized legal order to sharpen its common awareness of the specific outer limits of state discretion, so that possible emergence of a mutual desire for reciprocally honored patterns of stability may have the opportunity it deserves to actually become the practice of states.

1960

[75] The position expressed in this paragraph is an extension of an argument made elsewhere, see Falk, *op.cit. supra,* note 29.

VI. United States Intervention in Cuba at the Bay of Pigs and International Law

> With regard to human affairs—not to laugh, not to cry, not to become indignant, but to understand.
>
> Benedict De Spinoza

I. The Cold War and the Rule of Law

The United States sponsorship of the unsuccessful rebel invasion of Cuba in April 1961 culminated the steady deterioration of Cuban-American relations that had taken place since the advent of Castro on January 1, 1959. This chapter interprets these events, emphasizing their significance for the future role of law in the resolution of disputes between nations in the Western Hemisphere.

The broader relevance of the rebel invasions to world order serves as an introduction to what intends to be primarily a case study. It is basic, for instance, to understand the extent to which the global conflict between the Soviet Union and the United States influences the character of national conduct in a situation in which American leaders appear to regard the imperatives of foreign policy as in conflict with legal commitments.

It is quite evident that United States hostility to Castro was premised upon the assumption that Cuba had become, for practical purposes, a Communist nation closely allied with the Soviet power bloc. As such, Cuba had switched sides in the cold war[1] and had established in the hemisphere a Communist beachhead of enormous psychological, if not political, potency.[2] This was regarded as endangering hemispheric solidarity and stability, as well as opening the way for Communist expansion in Latin America. Did the nature of the cold war (as of 1961) make it legitimate for the United States to act without legal restraint in relation to Castro's Cuba? This question underscores the critical issue raised by American interventionary conduct in the internal affairs of Cuba and, as well, highlights the dilemma created for American policy-makers.

For the urgency of the cold war must be balanced against the ad-

---

[1] Georg Schwarzenberger, "Hegemonial Intervention," 18 *Yearbook of World Affairs* (1959), pp. 236, 261-63.

[2] See e.g. C. Wright Mills, *Listen Yankee,* New York, McGraw-Hill, 1960, pp. 178-82, 187-89; Russell H. Fitzgibbon, "The Revolution Next Door: Cuba," *The Annals,* Vol. 334, 1961, pp. 113, 120-21; A. A. Berle, "The Cuban Crisis," *Foreign Affairs,* xxxix (1960), 40; Wymberley De R. Coerr, "Forces of Change in Latin America," *U.S. State Department Bulletin,* xliv, 1961, pp. 251, 253; Leo Huberman and Paul Sweezy, *Cuba, Anatomy of a Revolution,* New York, Monthly Review Press, 1960, pp. 145-57; Theodore Draper, "Cubans and Americans," *Encounter,* xciv (1961), 59.

vocacy by the United States of the rule of law in world affairs.[3] Senator
Warren Magnuson expressed our national sense of mission when he
said that "I have long felt that the United States . . . should stimulate
among all nations a dependence upon the rule of law in international
dealings."[4] And almost without exception our national leaders have
urged that law represents the one alternative to force in international
relations.[5] For example, in 1947 Senator Robert Taft observed that,
"I do not see how we can hope to secure permanent peace in the
world except by establishing law between nations and equal justice under law."[6] And former President Eisenhower in an important address
on the rule of law given in 1959 at New Delhi suggested that, ". . . the
time has come for mankind to make the rule of law in international
affairs as normal as it is now in domestic affairs."[7] There is a widespread awareness that international uses of force gravely heighten the
risks of nuclear catastrophe. This awareness gives sentiments expressing a plea for adherence to law in world affairs a relevance to the
politics of survival and national interest that was not present earlier in
our history.[8] The rule of law in world affairs has today become a serious
objective of "practical men." The Cuban crisis arose from a situation
in which the demands of the cold war were perceived as conflicting
with conduct in accord with the rule of law. The United States, it would
seem, resorted to indirect intervention which was explicitly prohibited
by several applicable treaties.[9] The strategy of resisting Soviet expansion was accorded precedence over legal obligations by leading American policy-makers in both major political parties. Such a course of
national action is part of a more general trend away from a law-oriented
approach to international affairs by the United States when cold war
issues are presented. Notable examples are provided by the overthrow
of the allegedly pro-Communist Arbenz government in Guatemala

[3] Two interesting recent statements are found in William W. Bishop, Jr., "The International Rule of Law," 59 *Michigan Law Review* 553 (1961), and in William O. Douglas, "The Rule of Law in World Affairs," Santa Barbara, Center for the Study of Democratic Institutions, 1961.

[4] Quoted in ABA, Special Committee on World Peace Through Law, Compilation of Quotations 11, January 1960.

[5] For representative examples see Compilation, *op.cit. supra*, note 4.

[6] *Id.*, p. 11.

[7] Dwight D. Eisenhower, *Peace With Justice*, New York, Columbia University Press, 1961, p. 193.

[8] This point is the central point of a paper presented at September 1961 An-

nual Meeting of the American Political Science Association: Falk, "Impacts of Revolutionary Nations Upon the Growth of International Law." See also Philip C. Jessup, *The Use of International Law*, Ann Arbor, University of Michigan Law School, 1959, pp. 8-29; Harrison Brown and James Real, *Community of Fear*, Santa Barbara, Center for the Study of Democratic Institutions, 1960; Walter Millis, *A World Without War*, Santa Barbara, California Center for the Study of Democratic Institutions, 1960; Walter Millis, *Permanent Peace*, Santa Barbara, California Center for the Study of Democratic Institutions, 1961.

[9] See *infra*, Section IV, for a detailed argument in support of this conclusion.

in 1954[10] and the U-2 incident in 1960.[11] Additional conduct by the United States indicates a reluctance to implement our frequent pledges to promote the growth of world law: retention of the Connally Amendment, a *political* approach to the recognition of new governments (e.g. Peking-China),[12] and an unwillingness to seek legal standards in advance of behavior in connection with the use of espionage satellites in outer space.[13] This national trend is alarming in view of the choice that exists between force and law in the conduct of foreign affairs. The Cuban dispute imposed upon our leaders the burden of choosing between legal norms and the apparent promotion of the American position in the cold war. It is possible, in view of the political failure of the interventionary tactics, that strict compliance with law might have maximized the United States' position in the cold war; nonintervention in other words, might have been the most effective way to cut our losses in Latin America as a consequence of Castro's defection from the West.

The following factors, then, seem central to an understanding of the official United States response to Castro: the use of force is the alternative to the rule of law; nonnuclear uses of illegal force increase the risk of nuclear war; legal restraint hampers the United States' effort to resist the expansion of Soviet power in international society; national leaders seem influenced more by assessments of superpower rivalry than by the struggle to extend the rule of law in international society.

Part of the purpose of this chapter is to show that this is a very dangerous and unnecessary way to comprehend most contemporary international situations. It is essential that the United States Government discover the *practical* value of legal self-restraint and that we find lawful ways to promote our political interests. For instance, it is essential that we help, rather than hinder, social revolutions in Latin America so that radical elites will not be led to the Soviet bloc as the only available source of support; specifically, Castro *might* have been allowed to develop his internal social program in such a way that Cuba would not have been led to identify with the Communist cause in world affairs, and this might have avoided the pressures that led the United States to

10 See Doris A. Graber, *Crisis Diplomacy,* Washington, Public Affairs Press, 1959, pp. 243-45 (hereinafter cited as Graber); Ann Van Wynen Thomas and A. J. Thomas, Jr., *Non-Intervention: The Law and Its Import in the Americas,* Dallas, Southern Methodist University Press, 1956, pp. 297-99 (hereinafter cited as Thomas.

11 Quincy Wright, "Legal Aspects of the U-2 Incident," 54 *American Journal of International Law* 836 (1960).

12 Cf. Hersch Lauterpacht, *Recognition in International Law,* Cambridge, Cambridge University Press, 1947.

13 See report of U.S. position on Samos (espionage satellite) in *New York Times,* October 11, 1960, p. 12, col. 1.

follow a course of dubious legality. A clear distinction between radical socialism and Communism might help us to make a more rational balance between the politics of global conflict and the rule of law.[14]

The development of supranational institutions was expected to restrain the conduct of states in the world. However, a further negative lesson of the Cuban experience is the evidence that the Organization of American States is of only marginal importance if it interferes with the United States policy of keeping Communist elites from gaining control of governments in the hemisphere. Although all Latin American countries are willing to condemn the international Communist movement as interventionary when it extends its activities to the Western Hemisphere, the stronger OAS nations of South America are unwilling to take collective action to overthrow such a government by coercion. This unwillingness was expressed first at Caracas in relation to Guatemala, and more significantly, throughout the Cuban crisis. Most South American states have been so far more concerned with defending the concept of nonintervention than with acting jointly to root out Communist control. The United States is strongly disposed to view the need to act against the Communist menace as more pressing than to guard states against intervention. In fact, the United States has consistently urged at OAS meetings that collective responsibility is a necessary complement to the renunciation of unilateral intervention as it had been practiced by the United States during the latter decades of diplomacy under the Monroe Doctrine.[15] One way, then, to view the Cuban crisis is to regard it as the American reaction to the failure of the OAS to carry out its duties of collective action. Such thinking appears to have been dominant in President Kennedy's mind when he said in an important address to the American Society of Newspaper Editors:

> ... Let the record show that our restraint is not inexhaustible. Should it ever appear that the inter-American doctrine of non-interference merely conceals or excuses a policy of nonaction—if the nations of this hemisphere should fail to meet their commitments against outside Communist penetration—then I want it clearly understood that this Government will not hesitate in meeting its primary obligations, which are to the security of our Nation.[16]

[14] That is, a program of radical social change in the direction of "socialism" should not necessarily threaten the United States' position in the cold war. This is illustrated by the political affiliations of such "socialist" nations as Israel, Uruguay, and Yugoslavia. In fact, it is felt, that socialism is a stabilizing, Communist-resisting tendency in the newly developing parts of the world, and should therefore be actively encouraged by the United States.

[15] Edward G. Miller, Jr., "Nonintervention and Collective Responsibility in the Americas," *U.S. State Department Bulletin*, xxii, 1950, p. 768.

[16] President John F. Kennedy, "The Lesson of Cuba," *U.S. State Department Bulletin*, xliv, 1961, p. 659.

The significance of this assertion of policy by President Kennedy can hardly be stressed enough. In effect, President Kennedy posits a residual claim by the United States to act unilaterally in the event that the OAS fails to act collectively. This new expression of American foreign policy (identified here as "The Kennedy Doctrine") in the Western Hemisphere may not endure, but it is part of the background against which the more blatant intervention of 1965 in the Dominican Republic took place.[17] It is evident that the United States does not feel that its hemispheric security interests are currently protected by the collective machinery of the OAS. This political conclusion must be considered in light of the American legal pledge to use the OAS in the event that coercive action is needed to overcome Communist control in a Latin American country. This revival of a unilateral diplomacy by the United States represents, then, a second dimension of the perception by American leaders of the conflict between legal and political considerations in the cold war.

The instability created by the Cuban events is further revealed by the Soviet response. Premier Khrushchev and the Soviet press emphasized generally the United States role in the violation of Cuban sovereignty that resulted from the interventionary attempt to overthrow Castro. But more significant is the stress upon reciprocity in Premier Khrushchev's Message to President Kennedy on April 22, 1961:

> Mr. President, you are taking a very dangerous path. Think about it. You speak about your rights and obligations. Certainly, everyone can have pretensions to these rights or those rights, but then you must also permit other states to base their acts in analogous instances on the same kind of reasons and considerations.[18]

If the United States can intervene to counteract the danger of Soviet domination in Cuban affairs, certainly then, the United States is foreclosed from objecting if the Soviet Union intervenes in Turkish or Pakistani affairs to thwart American domination. Khrushchev put it this way:

> You declare that Cuba is allegedly able to use its territory for acts

17 The changing international setting makes it difficult to assess the extent to which the thinking that prompted the formulation of the Kennedy Doctrine has become embedded in American foreign policy. The Dominican intervention even more clearly than the Bay of Pigs disclosed an American commitment to use its military power to prevent the emergence of a Communist or Communist-oriented government in the Western Hemisphere. This American commitment has been subjected to considerable domestic criticism and the course of American policy in the future remains uncertain.

18 "Mr. Khrushchev to President Kennedy," (unofficial translation of message dated April 22, 1961), reprinted in *U.S. State Department Bulletin*, XLIV, 1961, pp. 664-65.

against the United States. This is your assumption, and it is not based on any facts. We, however . . . are able now to refer to concrete facts and not to assumptions: In some countries bordering directly on the Soviet Union . . . there are governments which have put their territory at its [the United States] disposal to accommodate American military bases there.

The conclusion is then deftly drawn:

If you consider yourself to be in the right to implement such measures against Cuba which have been lately taken by the United States of America, you must admit that other countries, also, do not have lesser reason to act in a similar manner in relation to states on whose territories preparations are actually being made which represent a threat against the security of the Soviet Union. If you do not wish to sin against elementary logic, you evidently must admit such a right to other states.[19]

I have quoted from Khrushchev's response at this length because it seems to touch so directly upon the role of law in the context of global political rivalry—namely, to specify mutual limits upon national behavior so as to prevent outbreaks of international violence. Khrushchev's argument is based upon the idea that minimum world order arises from reciprocal self-restraint on the part of states in the world, and that this order depends upon mutuality of compliance. If one nation exceeds the prevailing limit, then it licenses other nations to do the same thing. This is a distinctive quality of the law-behavior of a decentralized political order in which power is horizontally[20] distributed. Contrast the domestic vertical order in which a violation of a legal standard by one citizen leads the state to impose direct, coercive sanctions upon the violator. There is no general notion in domestic society that because others violate the law, say against homicide or rape, I am entitled to do the same; however, a vertical order occasionally may resemble a horizontal order, as when it enacts widely unpopular laws. Reciprocity undermined the usual fidelity of Americans to law during the prohibition era. In contrast, a horizontal order will behave like a vertical legal order if an overwhelming consensus favors the enforcement of a legal rule against a violator; this is one way to examine the effective response by the United Nations to the Suez invasion initiated by France, Great Britain, and Israel in 1956.[21] Generally, however, the

---

[19] Ibid.
[20] Falk, "International Jurisdiction: Horizontal and Vertical Conceptions of Legal Order," 32 Temple Law Quarterly 295 (1959).

[21] Falk, "Jurisdiction, Immunities and Act of State: Suggestions for a Modified Approach," in Essays on International Jurisdiction, Columbus, Ohio State University Press, 1961, pp. 1-20.

international legal order depends on the horizontal restraints imposed by considerations of reciprocity if it is to be effective.

President Kennedy seemed to hint that the Soviet intervention of 1956 in Hungary was a horizontal precedent for prospective American intervention in Cuba when he said: "Should that time come [for an American intervention] we do not *intend* to be lectured on 'intervention' by those whose character was stamped for all time on the bloody streets of Budapest."[22] This accords with the logic of reciprocity, but it should be noted that the Soviet action in Hungary, bloody as it was, did not involve border-crossing (Soviet forces were lawfully present in Hungary), nor did it involve an effort to overthrow a legitimate and functioning government.

It should be observed, furthermore, that the United Nations did not provide very strong vertical direction in the Cuban crisis. Premier Khrushchev in his April 22nd Message to President Kennedy said: "I wish to stress that if the United Nations is destined to attain true strength and fulfill the functions for which it was created . . . then the United Nations must resolutely condemn the warlike actions against Cuba."[23] Regardless of how one interprets the Cuban invasion, it is clear that a member of the Organization was subject to an armed attack across its borders, which was facilitated by the willingness of other countries to give their support to enemies of the legitimate government. In the face of such coercive violation of Cuban sovereignty the United Nations did no more than to pass a Seven-Power Resolution that expressed deep concern and "exhorted all Member States to take such peaceful action as is open to them to remove existing tension."[24] A somewhat stronger Mexican Draft Resolution which obtained a 41-35 majority, failed of adoption because it did not obtain a necessary two-thirds majority in the General Assembly. It called upon all states "to seek the pacific settlement of disputes" and went on as follows:

1. Makes *an urgent* appeal to all States to ensure that their territories and resources are not used to promote a civil war in Cuba;
2. *Urges* them to put an immediate end to any activity that might result in further bloodshed;
3. *Requests* them to cooperate, in keeping with the spirit of the Charter, in the search for a peaceful solution to the present situation.[25]

22 Kennedy, *op.cit. supra,* note 16, p. 659.

23 Khrushchev, *op.cit. supra,* note 18, p. 665.

24 U.N. Doc. A/C.1/L275; adopted in plenary session April 21, 1961 by a vote of 59 (including U.S.) to 13, with 24 abstentions.

25 U.N. Doc. A/C.1/L275; the vote in plenary session was 41 to 35 (including the U.S.), with 20 abstentions; the resolution failed of adoption as it lacked the necessary two-thirds majority.

The refusal of many nations to vote for the Mexican Resolution indicates the inadequacy of the protection that will be given to an unpopular small state that is the target of aggression; this kind of inadequacy further underscores the dependence of nations upon the horizontal controls over force in international relations, especially when border-crossing (as distinct from internal civil strife) is involved.

II. Pre-Castro Cuban-American Relations

A. UNITED STATES AND COLONIAL CUBA (1498-1898)

The modern history of Cuba commences with its discovery by Columbus in 1492, and its subsequent colonization by Spain.[26] Until the nineteenth century Cuba was valuable to Spain mainly as a strategic naval base. Throughout this period it was a source of concern to the leading maritime powers in the Caribbean as its natural harbors served so well the needs of pirates and corsairs. In addition, periodic raids upon Cuban territory were staged by French, English, and Dutch buccaneers. However, with the exception of a brief period of English occupation in 1762-1763, Spanish rule in Cuba was uninterrupted. From the very beginning, the Spanish *conquistadores* cruelly exploited the inhabitants of the island, exterminating many of the native Indians and importing large numbers of slaves. Native resistance was led by an Indian named Hatüey, who when led to the stake by the Spanish, was offered Christian baptism and absolution. He asked, "are there white men in heaven?" When told that there were, Hatüey is reported to have said—"then I do not want to become a Christian, for I would not go to a place where I must find men so cruel."[27] Oppression continued to characterize Spanish rule in Cuba until its end in 1898.[28]

The earliest American interest in Cuba was part of the expansionist spirit that arose in the United States early in the nineteenth century. The primary energy of this drive was devoted to the establishment of a continental republic stretching from ocean to ocean. It was this movement—later colorfully identified as the Manifest Destiny of the United States[29]—that led to the Louisiana Purchase and the annexations of Florida, California, and Texas, but failed in its effort to incorporate Canada. Cuba, considered vital to the protection of Florida and the

[26] My historical survey relies heavily upon Graham H. Stuart's conservative interpretation of the early relations between Cuba and the United States. See Stuart, *Latin America and the United States,* 4th edn., New York, Appleton-Century, 1943, pp. 195-223 (hereinafter cited as Stuart).

[27] As told by Carleton Beals, *The Crime of Cuba,* Philadelphia, Lippincott, 1933,

p. 26 (hereinafter cited as Beals).

[28] This is developed vividly by Beals and in Leland H. Jenks, *Our Cuban Colony,* New York, Vanguard Press, 1928, (hereinafter cited as Jenks).

[29] See excellent study by Samuel Flagg Bemis, *Latin American Policy of the U.S.,* New York, Harcourt, Brace, 1943, pp. 47, 73-97.

Gulf coast was a natural object of American ambition. John Quincy Adams, writing as Secretary of State in 1823, formulated the official American expectation as follows:

These islands [Cuba and Puerto Rico] from their local position are natural appendages to the North American continent, and one of them [Cuba] almost in sight of our shores, from a multitude of considerations has become an object of transcendent importance to the commercial and political interests of our Union. . . . In looking forward to the probable course of events for the short period of half a century it is scarcely possible to resist the conviction that the annexation of Cuba to our Federal Republic will be indispensable to the continuance and integrity of the Union itself.[30]

This expectation of eventual annexation was accompanied by an overriding diplomatic policy designed to avoid the transfer by Spain of its Cuban colony to England or France. The United States did not regard Spain as much of a threat. Spain had suffered a serious decline in power and its colonial administration of Cuba was so inefficient that it did not take advantage of the island's strategic position as a natural center of trade and commerce: but English or French occupancy would have been far more threatening to American development. As early as 1810 President Madison wrote in an official letter that the United States could not be "a satisfied spectator" if Cuba were to fall "under any European government, which might make a fulcrum of that position against the commerce and security of the United States."[31] The United States, in a manner curiously analogous to its present hemispheric policy, was more disturbed about new extra-hemispheric intrusions by European nations than by an undesirable *status quo* (Spanish rule in Cuba). In 1823 this priority was even made an explicit part of the Monroe Doctrine: "With the existing colonies and dependencies of any European power we have not interfered and shall not interfere."[32] The basic United States position in this early period combined a respectful deference to Spanish claims in Cuba with the conviction that the weak Spanish administration would be overthrown from within, and that then an independent Cuba would automatically gravitate towards the United States' sphere of influence, perhaps even seeking annexation. Thus the United States interest in Cuba was adequately protected so long as no third power capable of taking full advantage of Cuba, especially England, succeeded Spain as administrator of Cuba.

---

[30] Moore, *Digest of International Law*, vi, p. 380 (1906).
[31] Quoted by Stuart, p. 17.

[32] President Monroe's Seventh Annual Message to Congress, December 2, 1823.

However, the inhumanities of Spanish colonial administration, the growing commercial importance of Cuba, and the strong pressure in the South to expand the slave-owning territory of the United States generated increasing pressures to make Cuba part of our country after the annexation of Texas in 1845. Efforts to negotiate the purchase of Cuba from Spain failed, and this induced American expansionists to propose more coercive measures to reach their end. Here again the historical antecedent recalls the contemporary situation. Cuban patriots seeking independence came to the United States to organize an expedition against Cuba. Their leader was a dedicated revolutionary named Narciso López. His cause evoked sympathy, especially in the South, and it was not surprising that his attempt "to recruit an expedition on American soil to free Cuba . . . found much assistance in high quarters."[33] However, after easily collecting "the nucleus of a force," a proclamation in 1849 by President Taylor, "warning all citizens against participation in such enterprises, had a deterrent effect. The two vessels in which the expedition planned to leave New York were seized by the authorities, though the filibusters themselves were not held."[34] López, however, was not dissuaded. In 1850 he organized a second expedition which made a landing in Cuba. This attempt also failed when López did not "receive the assistance expected from the natives" and was then "faced with an openly mutinous crew."[35] A third López expedition was defeated in 1851. The López expeditions are a curious anticipation of the exile invasions of 1961, and displayed analogous participation by the United States. Interestingly, the diplomatic competitors of the United States formally disapproved of the American failure to prevent its territory from being used by dissident Cuban exiles to overthrow Spanish rule. A treaty guaranteeing Cuba to Spain was rumored to have been signed in 1851 by Great Britain, France, and Spain, and in 1852 the United States was invited to join England and France in an agreement "disclaiming all intention of obtaining possession of Cuba."[36] The United States declined the invitation although it did assure the European nations that it not only had "no design upon Cuba itself, but it was willing to assist Spain in preserving it."[37]

United States policy wavered. In 1853, however, President Pierce appointed Pierre Soulé to Spain. Soulé was an avowed supporter of López and revived the idea that the future of Cuba must be assimilated into the Manifest Destiny of the United States even if this required the use of force. Soulé was instructed to negotiate the purchase of Cuba. The militancy of Soulé's policy was revealed in the "Ostend Manifesto"

33 Stuart, p. 208.
34 *Id.*, p. 205.
35 *Ibid.*

36 *Id.*, p. 206.
37 *Ibid.*

which entreated Spain to benefit Cuba and herself by selling Cuba to the United States. It added, "but if Spain, dead to the voice of her own interests, and actuated by stubborn pride and a false sense of honor, should refuse to sell Cuba to the United States . . . then by every law, human and divine, we shall be justified in wresting it from Spain, if we possess the power."[38] President Pierce, unwilling to apply such explicit pressure, disavowed the Ostend Manifesto, and Spain ignored it. The slavery issue gradually came to dominate American politics, and the position of the North precluded the incorporation of any additional slave territory into the Union. Cuba did not again figure prominently in American concerns until after the Civil War.

In the closing decades of the century Cuba was in a state of almost continual internal unrest, highlighted by an internal uprising in 1868 that lingered on until its final suppression in 1878. Spanish oppressive rule was slightly liberalized by concessions achieved as a result of these internal rebellions, but the situation remained intolerable. The governmental revenues, gained by burdensome taxes placed on basic items like flour and salt, were used to fill the Madrid treasury and to pay exorbitant salaries to the corrupt and inefficient Spanish colonial elite composed mainly of uneducated, petty bureaucrats. This situation infuriated the cultured upper classes in Cuba, and kept alive the passion for national independence. Reforms were illusory, disease and chaos were rampant, and a new major revolution broke out in 1895 which seems to have received important financial support in the United States.[39] The United States took an official position of aloofness, but public opinion ardently supported the Cuban independence movement. American economic interests in Cuba had grown to a point where civil strife was very costly. In addition, the United States appeared eager now to have a war so as to display its military prowess as a great power in the world.[40] Tension in Spanish-American relations mounted to a climax when the United States warship *Maine* was exploded in Havana harbor on January 25, 1898. Congress soon passed a joint resolution proclaiming Cuban independence, authorizing President McKinley to use the American army and navy to compel the withdrawal of Spanish forces from Cuba, and disclaiming any intention to impose American sovereignty upon Cuba beyond that needed to establish peace and order. Historians feel that the sinking of the *Maine* was a pretext for war rather than a cause of war. As Jenks points out, 1896 was the rational moment to intervene on behalf of the oppressed Cubans or to defend American property from plunder. By 1898

---

[38] *Id.*, pp. 208-09.
[39] *Id.*, p. 216.

[40] See Jenks, pp. 48-57.

Spain was on its way to reforming the grossest evils of its colonial administration as a result of internal and external pressure. War fever in the United States, then, is viewed as the major explanation for the decision to wage war against Spain in 1898. It was never clear, for instance, that Spain was even responsible for blowing up the *Maine*. War followed, ending quickly in a complete victory for the United States. In the peace treaty signed on December 10, 1898, Spain relinquished all sovereignty over Cuba and agreed to evacuate at once.

This first phase of Cuban history bears significantly upon the current state of Cuban-American relations. First, the nineteenth century revealed an American concern that alternated between a minimum policy of keeping political rivals from taking over Cuba and a maximum policy of annexation. This pattern of alternation between a policy of protection and one of domination has pervaded United States action in Latin America from the beginning. Second, American concern with Cuban welfare was never sufficient to lead us to intervene to establish an independent Cuba or to resist the frightful barbarism of Spanish policy. This reluctance to promote the domestic welfare of Cuba foreshadows our policy of tolerance, if not support, until very recent years, of oppressive dictatorships throughout Latin America. United States interests—whether slavery or sugar—and not altruism or hemispheric solidarity accounted for our conduct toward Cuba. It was only when the failures of Spanish rule led to internal disorders that hurt American private investments in Cuba that we were led to act against Spain, and the final coercive action was not even prompted by such rational considerations as national self-interest. The Spanish-American War was the culmination of an aggressive foreign policy that had been building up for several decades.

The dominant United States concern in the nineteenth century was to keep extra-continental political rivals out of Cuba and to protect the interests of American investors within Cuba. Many would say that the twentieth century is heir to the nineteenth.[41] One can interestingly substitute England or France for the Soviet Union, Spanish colonialism for Castroism, and López for Cardona to perceive the sturdy strands of continuity.

Contemporary Cuba inherits from colonial Cuba a tradition of authoritarian leadership and internal discontent. Fidel Castro knows how to exercise the leadership by exploiting the discontent. The dramatization of the United States as the demonic enemy of Cuba, however, depends upon developments that took place during the second

[41] This is emphasized by Beals, Jenks, Huberman and Sweezy, and Mills. For latter two books see citation *supra,* note 2.

phase of Cuban history. Even here, however, hatred of the Spaniards was a psychological preparation for hatred of the United States; in each instance it was plausible for national leaders to explain the ills of Cuba by reference to the domineering role of a foreign nation.

B. 1898-1959

The United States occupied Cuba as an administering power after the defeat of Spain in 1898. Despite some internal discontent, American administration was welcomed by the Cubans. It performed beneficently, improving health and sanitation throughout the island, and encouraging the formation of institutions of local government. The colonial legacy of disease, anarchy, and starvation was overcome by the able American Governor-General Leonard Wood.[42] Having restored order the United States acted to end its military trusteeship of Cuba, thereby honoring its pledge to respect Cuban independence and to refrain from annexation. A Cuban constitutional convention was convened to prepare the island for self-government. However, as is well-known, the United States did compel Cuba to accept, over hostile objection, the humiliating subordination decreed by the Platt Amendment.[43] The most controversial provisions restricted Cuba's power to contract foreign debts (Article II), gave to the United States a unilateral right to intervene in the internal affairs of Cuba under broad circumstances (Article III),[44] bound Cuba not to diminish her sovereignty by treaty with a foreign power nor to permit another nation to exercise military power on the island (Article I), and gave to the United States coaling and naval bases (Guantanamo) (Article VI). Cuba was particularly upset about the interventionary right claimed by the United States. Elihu Root in a dispatch to General Wood tried to relieve the Cuban fears that Article III would deprive them of their independence by saying that "it does not give the United States any right she does not already possess and she has not exercised." The treaty provision is, however, "of immense value in qualifying the United States to protect the independence of Cuba."[45] That is, American intervention is legitimated in advance, thereby overcoming the objection of third

---

[42] See able exposition in Jenks, pp. 58-84.

[43] Cf. Jenks, pp. 78-84, Graber, pp. 141-42.

[44] Article III is so important that its text will be given in full: "The Government of Cuba consents that the United States may exercise the right to intervene for the preservation of Cuban independence, the maintenance of a government adequate for the protection of life, property, and individual liberty, and for discharging the obligations with respect to Cuba imposed by the Treaty of Paris on the United States, now to be assumed and undertaken by the Government of Cuba." The entire international agreement known as the Platt Amendment may be found in *Treaties and Conventions, 1776-1909,* I, pp. 363-64.

[45] Quoted in Jenks, p. 81.

states to intervention. This was thought especially useful to meet growing criticism in Latin America of protective interventions by the United States in the internal affairs of its hemispheric neighbors during the later applications of the Monroe Doctrine.[46] The Platt Amendment adds legitimacy to the operative diplomatic policy that arose when the Roosevelt Corollary was added to the Monroe Doctrine.

The United States did intervene with armed force in 1906 to restore internal order after a protracted period of civil strife. American administration lasted until 1909, and on this second occasion was evidently oppressive, corrupt, and partial to American interests.[47] A brief intervention to protect the sugar crop from destruction during a rebellion in 1917 also took place. And in 1924 and 1934 the United States controlled the outcome of civil strife by supplying arms to the government and placing an embargo on the sale of arms to the insurgents. Beyond the actual resort to intervention, the threat of intervention exercised a potent influence on Cuban internal affairs; it has been observed that "the specter of armed action, which hovered over Cuban-American relations, undoubtedly deserves a large share of the credit for making Cubans tractable."[48] Resentment against the hegemonial role of the United States increased. American economic domination of Cuba—its sugar industry and its international trade—and the interventionary prerogative claimed under the Platt Amendment were the principal bases of the unpopularity of the United States.[49] However, as Graber has pointed out, the Platt Amendment did not actually expand the interventionary practices of the United States.[50] It merely gave a semblance of bilateralism and legality to the interventionary patterns of practice that developed in relation to the later applications of the Monroe Doctrine to protect business interests of American citizens in Latin America, and especially Central America. Proximity to the United States accounts for the particularly heavy influence, more than did the Platt Amendment. The lament attributed to the Mexican President Porfirio Diaz, "Poor Mexico—so far from God, so near to the United States," seems equally pertinent to Cuba's situation.

A permanent handicap to the image of the United States in Cuba has resulted from our apparent support of ruthless dictators of the right. American economic interests wanted internal political order and the social *status quo*. For these purposes a dictator was ideal. He could

[46] Cf. Graber, p. 141: "Judging from the use made of such treaties, they were not intended to convey rights of interference beyond those inherent in the right of intervention."
[47] See Jenks, pp. 87-103.

[48] Graber, p. 145.
[49] This is the main emphasis in the full-length studies made by Jenks and Huberman and Sweezy.
[50] See also Fitzgibbon, *op.cit. supra*, note 2, p. 114.

also be persuaded by graft to accord favorable treatment to business interests. Such dictatorships often lack internal popular support, and actually invite external intervention to suppress a popular protest movement. Thus an invitation to intervene by a reactionary dictator, although significant for purposes of legal evaluation, makes an intervention less, rather than more, acceptable to Cuban society. It is in this light that one must understand the hatred of the United States aroused by our support of the reviled Cuban dictator, Machado, from 1925-1931; this man was a bloody tyrant "crushing all his opposition to the extent of imprisoning and assassinating his adversaries."[51] In 1928 the United States sent Harry F. Guggenheim, a prominent Latin American businessman, as our Ambassador to Cuba; ". . . he stood consistently behind President Machado and the maintenance of a strong, stable government."[52] It was quite literally like supporting Al Capone as the head of state of a foreign nation, and tolerating his gangster methods.[53] Machado was eventually overthrown because a drop in the world sugar price threatened the Cuban government with bankruptcy.[54] The interweaving of the fortunes of the sugar industry and political change tell an interesting part of the Cuban story.[55]

In 1934, fearing a failure to maintain stability, the United States withheld recognition from Grau San Martín who was the first reformist figure to emerge as a Cuban leader. Our opposition to this liberal president led to the downfall of his government, and its replacement in 1934 by a dictatorship in which Batista was the decisive force. The United States thus gave its powerful backing to repressive dictatorships, opposed reformist elements, and proclaimed at Pan American Congresses its commitment to the principles of liberal democracy. The gap between the word and the deed exacerbated the wound caused by our support of reactionary governments that left the mass of Cubans in a condition of grave poverty, disease, and illiteracy.

As is well known President Franklin Roosevelt was eager to improve American relations with Latin America. He acknowledged the widespread opposition aroused by interventionary practices and claims. Thus the United States was led to renounce its interventionary privilege, whether based on the unilateralism of the Monroe Doctrine or the spurious bilateralism of the Platt Amendment.[56] Thus the United States followed its general nonintervention pledge of 1933 with a formal renunciation in 1934 of the right of Cuban intervention that had been

[51] Stuart, p. 238.
[52] *Ibid.*
[53] Stuart, pp. 237-41; Beals, pp. 235-399.
[54] Stuart, pp. 238-39.
[55] See especially books by Jenks and Huberman and Sweezy for comprehensive account.
[56] The full development is outlined further in this chapter.

conferred by the Platt Amendment. However, the United States continued to dominate Cuban affairs by exerting economic and psychological pressure. A recent commentator suggests the term "Plattism" to describe this less structured hegemony that characterized the role of the United States in Cuban affairs until the fall of Batista in 1959.[57] This American role was perceived hostily by Cubans concerned with the achievement of internal social and economic progress. As such, it must be regarded as a significant part of the background favorable to the emergence of Fidel Castro.

This survey of Cuban-American relations contains many gross simplifications. However, it is intended to help one to understand the general character of Castroism and, especially the use by Castro of anti-American sentiment to mobilize public opinion. Castro has brought to Cuba its first program of radical social change. He responds thus to the need to overcome the pitiful state of the impoverished masses, especially those living in rural Cuba.[58] His economic measures of land reform and nationalization must be viewed against this background of inequality and foreign domination. His political hostility to our country must be understood in the light of sixty years of humiliating Cuban subordination to the United States, especially drawing sustenance from our role in keeping men like Machado and Batista in power.

The early colonial history of Cuba suggests the deep roots of authoritarian political rule and foreign economic exploitation in Cuban tradition. It reveals, also, our expansionist interest in Cuba and our unwillingness to act against Spain to achieve Cuban national independence until we were ready for selfish purposes to fight the Spanish-American War in 1898. The settlement of that war led to a prolonged American military occupation and a formalized acceptance of United States hegemony in the Platt Amendment.

From the Civil War onwards the United States exercised an important role in the economic life of the island. The crippling dependence of Cuba upon her sugar industry[59] gave the United States, as dominant consumer, an enormous control lever over Cuban affairs. In addition, quota preferences and subsidies to the sugar trade helped the Americans who owned the large plantations to earn huge profits, but the profits did not filter significantly downwards to help raise the standard of living of the average Cuban. Thus American generosity to Cuba in

[57] Fitzgibbon, op.cit. supra, note 2, p. 114.
[58] Huberman and Sweezy; op.cit. supra, note 2, pp. 1-10; Lowry Nelson, Rural Cuba, Minneapolis, University of Minne-sota Press, 1950.
[59] Persuasively described with supporting statistics id., pp. 11-22; see full account in Jenks.

trade relations was usually beneficial only to a small economic elite, composed largely of Americans and a few wealthy Cuban families.

Such a negative characterization of the American role in Cuba is not the full story, but it does account for the way in which we are perceived by reformist and radical Cuban social and political groups. It would be easy to show, for instance, that without the participation of the United States in pre-Castro times Cuba would have been in an even worse condition with greater socioeconomic disparities, a less developed economy, and a political atmosphere alternating between bloody strife and bloody tyranny, but a subordinated population is not often willing to acknowledge the alleged benefits of its condition.

III. Interferences and Provocations, 1959-1961

A factual account of the deterioration of United States relations with Cuba between the period of January 1, 1959 and April 17, 1961 is enormously complex[60] and inessential to the purposes of this chapter. Some of the implications of this deterioration will be suggested in a concluding assessment. Three measures by the United States seem central to the task of legal evaluation:

(1) The elimination by the United States on July 6, 1960, of the import quota assigned to Cuban sugar at guaranteed prices; the dependence of Cuba upon revenue and foreign exchange from sales of sugar to the United States gave to this conduct a highly coercive tendency designed to impose the will of the United States upon Cuban internal affairs. Such an effort to bring Cuba to its knees will be characterized for purposes of later discussion as "indirect economic intervention."

(2) On October 19, 1960, the United States placed an embargo on all exports to Cuba "except for non-subsidized foodstuffs, machines, and medical supplies";[61] such an embargo was an explicit retaliation for Cuban confiscation of American property in Cuba and alleged fiscal discrimination against American products and business; however, such pressure brought to bear by a relatively more powerful state upon a weak state seems also to constitute "indirect, economic intervention."

[60] It can be traced by use of the *New York Times* for the period; for a convenient summary of the highlights up to November 1960 see A. G. Mezerik, ed., *Cuba and the United States,* New York, International Review Service, 1960; a full account of the U.S. position is given by the Department of State in its white paper released on April 3, 1961: Cuba, U.S. Department of State Publication 7171, 1961. An excellent analysis of the significance of this period can be found in George Blanksten, "Fidel Castro and Latin America" (paper prepared for delivery at 1961 Annual Meeting of the American Political Science Association); see also Theodore Draper, "Castro's Cuba," *Encounter* XC (1961), 6.

[61] For text of U.S. announcement of the embargo see *New York Times,* October 20, 1961, p. 8.

(3) The United States used its facilities and its territory to train, advise, finance, equip, and transport the Cuban rebels who took part in the anti-Castro invasion of April 1961; as was observed a week after the invasion: "The government [of the United States] no longer denies that the CIA, acting upon Presidential authority, did organize and direct last week's attempted invasion of Cuba."[62] Such sponsorship of an armed attack upon a nation with which we are at peace can be regarded either as an "act of aggression" or as "indirect armed intervention."

These three efforts by the United States to interfere with Cuba's independence sufficiently depict the background facts to enable a discussion of the legal doctrine of nonintervention.

The legal status of these interferences must not be viewed in isolation. It is crucial to have an awareness of the character of provocations that led the United States to pursue an interventionary course in conflict with its legal commitment to nonintervention. In fact, the apparent absence of United States alternatives to intervention is part of the reason why it is so important to attain a calm understanding of these events. To do this, however, one must realize that a provocation short of an armed attack, entitling a state to have recourse to self-defense, is virtually *irrelevant* to an appraisal of the illegality of interventionary conduct.[63] Having said this, let me enumerate now the provocations or alleged provocations[64] that led the United States to seek an illegal interventionary solution to our difficulties with Cuba:[65]

(1) Extra-hemispheric interference in Cuban affairs by members of the Sino-Soviet bloc;

(2) Characterization of the Castro government as subject to the control of the international Communist movement;

(3) Anti-American animus of Castro's leadership, arousing hostility and hatred;

(4) Castro's internal totalitarianism which was said to betray the liberal democratic ideals of the revolution as he had proclaimed them in the 1957 Declaration from Sierra Maestra;

[62] Richard Rovere, "Letter from Washington," *New Yorker* (May 6, 1961), 139.

[63] The phrasing of Article 51 of the United Nations Charter appears unambiguous on this point. "Nothing in the present Charter shall impair the inherent right of individual or collective self-defense *if an armed attack occurs against a Member of the United Nations . . .*" (emphasis supplied); but see, Julius Stone, *Aggression and World Order*, Berkeley, University of California Press, 1958.

[64] The concept of "alleged provocation" intends to highlight the absence of convincing evidence that the Soviet Union has intervened in Cuban internal affairs or that Cuba has aligned itself with the Soviet bloc or even that the Cuban government was Communist-controlled as of July 1960.

[65] See the Department of State white paper on Cuba, *op.cit. supra*, note 60; A. A. Berle, *op.cit. supra*, note 2.

(5) Confiscation of property owned by American nationals and discriminatory enforcement of taxing laws and foreign exchange regulations;

(6) Refusal by Castro to seek peaceful settlement of differences with the United States through mediation of the OAS;[66]

(7) Generation of subversion and intervention throughout Latin America by efforts of Castro to export his brand of revolution;

(8) Refusal of the OAS to take collective action of an effective variety against Castro;

(9) Fear that the success of Castro in Cuba would lead to new Castros throughout Latin America, thereby imperiling hemispheric solidarity as well as the private investments of United States citizens.

With these grievances in mind it is possible to initiate a discussion of the relevant legal norms. One question should be kept in mind. It arises from the pressure exerted by these provocations upon the absolute commitment to refrain from intervention. This pressure is underscored when the potential target of intervention is a recalcitrant debtor state that has violated legal obligations designed to protect the position of the intervening creditor state. What alternatives to intervention were available to the United States to protect the legal rights of nationals in Cuba, given the unwillingness of Castro to submit disputes to settlement and given the unwillingness of the OAS to act? This is an issue quite separate from the overriding tendency of the United States to ignore certain legal restraints under the pressure of waging the cold war.

IV. Legal Doctrines Pertaining to Nonintervention

An exposition of relevant legal doctrine reveals why the anti-Castro conduct of the United States is regarded here as illegal. An acknowledgment of illegality seems to be a necessary starting point for a useful evaluation of the United States' response to the Castro challenge. Artificial attempts to classify American conduct as legal obscure the real issue: can we adhere to the *legal* principle of nonintervention in the light of the general political character of the cold war?[67] That is, given the cold war and the tendency of the Communist movement to extend to the hemisphere its antidemocratic social order is it tolerable for the liberal democratic states to be bound by legal rules prohibiting

[66] For text of U.S. Note to OAS on Cuba see *New York Times,* October 29, 1960, p. 2.
[67] This general question was asked and answered negatively in a provocative book —Karl Loewenstein, *Political Reconstruction,* New York, Macmillan, 1946.

intervention? To date our leaders have not been willing to put the question in this way. Instead we have been given a very strained account of the facts of American participation[68] and a remarkably narrow interpretation of the relevance of the nonintervention commitment.[69]

In view of this it would seem helpful to indicate the reasons why our legal commitments have been violated by our participation in the battle against the Castro regime. We are provided, in addition, an apt occasion, first, for revaluing the adequacy of these particular legal standards in the kind of world that exists at present. Second, the failure of the interventionary course in Cuba allows us to rediscern the political strength of the nonintervention principle; that is, our concern with the politics of the cold war may have led us to fail to perceive the law-reinforcing higher relevance of the politics of nationalism. Hence, the cold war rivals, intent on keeping their conflict safely short of nuclear war, may come to discover that it is *mutually* advantageous to adhere, on a reciprocal basis, to a strict interpretation of the rules of nonintervention. But to perceive this possibility it is necessary to understand clearly the breadth of the nonintervention requirement, especially as it has developed in the Western Hemisphere. To reach this result we must carefully avoid construing nonintervention in a political manner (that is, to legitimate national conduct). This approach suggests that national policy may not always be consistent with national interest. Such a discovery might itself help to avoid the kind of tactical miscalculation that prompted us to help the rebels invade Cuba. It might even restrengthen the belief that the rule of law retains political vitality despite the tensions of the cold war.[70]

A. GENERAL CONSIDERATIONS

The legal status of the prohibition upon intervention is a vague, confusing, and complex matter. For while there is general agreement that the duty to refrain from intervention is an implied correlate of the right of national independence and sovereignty, there is considerable controversy as to the nature of this duty. It is clear that no nation may use or threaten to use armed force to impose its will upon another nation except when acting in self-defense against an armed attack.[71]

[68] E.g. the defensive position taken by U.S. officials in the United Nations and elsewhere with the unchallenged accounts in the U.S. press.

[69] President Kennedy suggested in his address "The Lesson of Cuba" that we would not attack Cuba with military force because it would have been "contrary to our traditions and to our international obligations," thereby implying that what we had done was, in contrast, consistent with our traditions and legal obligations. But, as will be shown, this cannot fairly be said to be the case.

[70] See Letter of Professor John P. Roche, *New York Times*, May 9, 1961, p. 36; letter signed by 43 Princeton professors, *New York Times*, June 1, 1961, p. 34.

[71] *Supra*, note 63.

But the criteria available to identify conduct as a prohibited use of force are far less evident, as is the identity of authoritative decision-makers capable of assessing compliance when intervention is alleged. Coercive interference by means other than armed attack—hostile propaganda, economic boycott, subversion, aid to counterrevolutionaries—appear to be equally embraced within the implied right of a nation to have its independence respected by other nations. The concept of nonintervention also seeks to implement the doctrine in international law that acknowledges the equality of states. Nonintervention is the way in which strong states fulfill the obligation to accept the equality of weak states. Therefore, in general, it is interpreted to impose a duty upon strong states to refrain from manipulating, by the use of coercion, the affairs of weak states. The legality of specific conduct would depend less upon the means used than the ends sought, provided only that the allegedly intervening state possessed superior strength; that is, it would not be intelligible to talk of Cuba intervening in the internal affairs of the United States; yet, Cuba might be guilty of intervention in the affairs of the Dominican Republic.[72]

The seriousness of intervention depends partly on the extent of its objective in relation to the independence of the target state. For instance, the early coercive objectives of the United States (e.g. the cut in the sugar quota and the economic embargo) sought only to influence internal Cuban policy (e.g. to discourage expropriations of property and involvement in the Soviet bloc); whereas, the support for the rebel exiles evidently sought to replace the Castro government with one more in accord with American interests.

We must also look at the intensity of coercion to determine the seriousness of an intervention. It is one thing to express sympathy for a revolutionary movement, as we did for Castro when he was on the verge of victory in 1958 and quite another to supply revolutionaries with arms, training, and transportation as we did for Artime, Ray, and Cardona in 1961.

Finally, the seriousness of intervention also depends upon the character of the provoking motive. The spectrum contains self-defense at one end and the gratuitous extension of national power at the other. Interventions to restore internal order, to prevent the persecution of minority groups, to overthrow an oppressive or colonial government, to enforce by self-help the legal duties of the target state with respect to private investment or public debt, to reinstate a governing elite friendly to a cold war bloc leader, to discourage the use of territory as

[72] It is, in general, the *relative power advantage* that makes intervention possible.

a base for terrorist activities[73] are typical illustrations of conduct that is more difficult to classify. Some of the difficulty arises because there is no adequate vertical institution with compulsory jurisdiction to determine whether contested acts constitute "interventions."[74] Furthermore, the instability introduced by the cold war induces double interventions by the bloc leaders, each intervening on behalf of its preferred elite; this makes a failure to intervene an acquiescence to intervention; whereas, an equivalent intervention leads to a neutralization of the first intervention. Thus, the second intervention may be non-interventionary in effect—leaving the target state about where it would have been without *either* intervention.[75]

Additional difficulty arises because the legal principles forbidding intervention are so frequently confused with moral and political considerations which favor a policy of selective intervention.[76] The problem of classification is further enhanced by the reliance of customary international law upon patterns of practice to change legal rules[77] and by the tendency for complementary opposed legal norms to be available to national actors for contrary descriptions of their conduct.[78]

Despite these difficulties of classification, two rather clear conclusions are possible: first, nations may not use armed force to carry out an interventionary policy unless they have been the victims of an armed attack and are acting in self-defense; second, recourses to interventionary coercion, other than by armed force, are incompatible with the fundamental doctrines of international law relating to sovereignty, territorial jurisdiction, equality of states, and national independence.

The United Nations Charter as the organic law of the world community, bears significantly upon the status of interventionary conduct. Article 2(4) incorporates the legal commitment to renounce the use of force in international relations; Article 2(7) withholds from the Organization the right to intervene in domestic affairs unless essential to the paramount duty to maintain world peace;[79] Article 1(4) endorses the principle of equal rights and self-determination; Article 33 pledges states to seek a pacific solution to any dispute that is likely to endanger

[73] This was part of Israel's claim of justification in the 1956 Sinai campaign.

[74] The use of the United Nations to determine issues of this sort manifests the slow growth of vertical control over the use of force, especially outside the cold war.

[75] Falk, *op.cit. supra*, note 10, p. 169.

[76] Letter of Professor Wolfgang Friedman, *New York Times*, May 1, 1961, p. 28.

[77] I. C. MacGibbon, "Customary International Law and Acquiescence," 35 *British*

Year Book of International Law (1959), pp. 115, 195.

[78] Myres S. McDougal and Florentino P. Feliciano, "Legal Regulation of Resort to International Coercion: Aggression and Self-Defense in Policy Perspective," 68 *Yale Law Journal* 1057, 1059-63 (1959).

[79] That is, the United Nations is made subject to a limited doctrine of nonintervention by the terms of the Charter. This is a complicated question that can only be raised here in general terms.

peace; Article 52(3) instructs the Security Council to seek pacific settlement of disputes through the utilization of available regional organizations; and, in addition, of course, the entire machinery of the United Nations is designed to promote the maintenance of peace. Much of the Charter as well as the Uniting for Peace Resolution are relevant in this respect. The United Nations Charter is very unspecific in its reference to prohibitions against coercion other than armed force. The entire apparatus of the Charter is aimed to reinforce the traditional view of the sovereign equality of states, which rests upon the entailed principle that no state is permitted to interfere in the internal affairs of other states. The legality of American use of coercion against Cuba must be viewed in relation to this Charter background.

B. Specific Legal Commitments

United States participation in the armed invasion of Cuba on April 17, 1961 clearly violated legal obligations contained in binding international agreements defining the international relations of states in the Western Hemisphere (other than Canada). In addition, American efforts to apply pressure by recourse to earlier coercive economic measures, especially the embargo on trade and the cut in the sugar quota, constituted illegal indirect intervention. The development of law pertaining to nonintervention in this hemisphere is an expression of protest against the extensive practice by the United States of intervention in the internal affairs of Latin American countries. The Monroe Doctrine was proclaimed in 1823 to discourage the efforts of the Holy Alliance to recover for Spain sovereign control over her Latin American colonies that had declared their independence early in the nineteenth century.[80] It was largely designed to discourage European intervention in Latin American internal affairs. When this danger receded, the Monroe Doctrine was retained and expanded to serve as a multipronged rationalization for American intervention in the internal affairs of Latin American countries on whatever occasion it seemed to serve the national interests of the United States to do so. President Theodore Roosevelt's explanation of the United States intervention in Panama in 1903 to protect the construction of the Canal expressed well the spirit of American interventionary practice:

> We, in effect, policed the Isthmus in the interests of its habitants and of our own national needs, and for the good of the entire civilized world. Under such circumstances the Government of the United States would have been guilty of folly and weakness, amount-

[80] Thomas, pp. 10-20.

ing in their sum to a crime against the nation, had it acted otherwise than it did.[81]

Our later Monroe Doctrine practice was a curious blend of imperialism and paternalism. We intervened to protect American investments and, at the same time, we kept the Latin American penchant for revolutionary politics from leading nations into a condition of chaos, and eventual bankruptcy. Our object was to maintain the social *status quo* in an atmosphere of maximum political stability—this being the most favorable situation for the promotion of our economic interests. We did not use our interventionary domination, however, as a pretext for permanent occupation. Nevertheless, opposition groups in Latin America resented the interventionary claims and practices of the United States. The Latin American view prevailed that the Monroe Doctrine should be regarded as a unilateral declaration of policy by the United States rather than as a regional understanding governing international relations in the hemisphere.[82] Pressure mounted after World War I, and the United States was gradually persuaded to join in legal pledges to refrain from intervention, thereby abandoning its role under the Monroe Doctrine.[83]

The last explicit defense of the American right to intervene was made by Charles Evans Hughes, as Secretary of State, at the Sixth Pan American Conference held at Havana in 1928. He put the United States position candidly:

> Let us face facts. The difficulty, if there is any, in any one of the American Republics, is not of any external aggression. It is an internal difficulty, if it exists at all. . . . What are we going to do when the government breaks down and American citizens are in danger of their lives? . . . Now it is a principle of international law—I would call it interposition of a temporary character—for the purpose of protecting of lives and property of its nationals.[84]

Despite the ability of the United States in 1928 to block the incorporation of nonintervention into a treaty at Havana, several important legal steps were taken to curtail, indirectly, the scope of the interven-

[81] Quoted by Graber, p. 138.

[82] A quasi-legitimation of the Monroe Doctrine was given by Article 21 of the Covenant of the League of Nations: "Nothing in this Covenant shall be deemed to affect the validity of international engagements, such as treaties of arbitration or regional understandings like the Monroe Doctrine, for securing the maintenance of the peace." Louis B. Sohn, ed., *Basic Documents of the United Nations*, Brooklyn, Foundation Press, 1956, pp. 277, 283 (hereinafter cited as Sohn).

[83] The process is described by Bemis, *op.cit. supra*, note 29, pp. 226-94.

[84] Report of the Delegates of the United States of America to the Sixth International Conference of American States held at Havana, Cuba, January 16 to February 20, 1928, p. 14, 1928.

tionary claim. For purposes of evaluating the Cuban situation, the most significant of these steps was the Convention on the Rights and Duties of States in the Event of Civil Strife, Article 1 of which seems directly to establish the illegality of American support for the Castro exiles:

The contracting states bind themselves to observe the following rules with regard to civil strife in another one of them:

1. To use all means at their disposal to prevent the inhabitants of their territory, nationals or aliens, from participating in, gathering elements, crossing the boundary or sailing from their territory for purpose of starting or promoting civil strife.

2. To disarm and intern every rebel force crossing their boundaries, the expense of internment to be borne by the state where public order may have been disrupted. The arms found in the hands of the country granting asylum, to be returned, once the struggle has ended, to the state in civil strife.

3. To forbid the traffic in arms and war matériel, except when intended for the government, while the belligerency of the rebels has not been recognized, in which latter case the rules of neutrality shall be applied.

4. To prevent that within their jurisdiction there be equipped, armed or adapted for warlike purposes any vessel intended to operate in favor of the rebellion.[85]

At the same time a Convention on Asylum was adopted to authorize signatories to grant asylum to political fugitives from other countries in the interests of "humanitarian toleration."[86] Both legal commitments have obvious relevance to the duties of the United States with respect to the Castro exiles. It is acceptable to give sanctuary, but it is certainly illegal to help exiles form a revolutionary movement on our territory, and illegal to tolerate even passively the use of our territory to foment civil strife in another country.[87]

There is a horizontal implementation of such a legal standard expressed generally in domestic legal provisions applicable to neutrality,[88] and, more particularly, in a federal provision of the United States Code making it a crime to use our territory as a base for hostile military operations against a state with which we are at peace:

[85] Convention on the Rights and Duties of States in the Event of Civil Strife, 22 *American Journal of International Law Supplement* 159 (1928).

[86] Convention on Asylum, *ibid.*, 158; but see Ambassador Stevenson's defense of U.S. grants of asylum in the UN: Adlai E. Stevenson, "Statement of April 20," *U.S. State Department Bulletin,* XLIV, 1961, pp. 681, 684.

[87] This much of the doctrine of nonintervention seems to be solidly accepted on the Western Hemisphere.

[88] 22 U.S.C.A. §§ 441-57, 1939.

§ 960 Expedition against friendly nations

Whoever, within the United States, knowingly begins or sets on foot or provides or prepares a means for or furnishes the money for, or takes part in, any military or naval expedition or enterprise to be carried on from thence against the territory or dominion of any foreign prince or state, or of any colony, district or people with whom the United States is at peace, shall be fined not more than $3,000 or imprisoned not more than three years, or both.[89]

This seems to apply clearly to Cubans or Americans that participated in the direction and execution of the April 1961 invasion, so far as their action took place "within the United States."[90] The United States was, of course, "at peace" with Cuba, despite the fact that diplomatic relations were broken in January 1961. In any event activity in the United States forbidden by § 960 long antedated the termination of diplomatic relations.

This aspect of the Cuban invasion has also received an important vertical expression in the form of the Draft Code of Offenses Against the Peace and Security of Mankind which was adopted by the International Law Commission of the United Nations in 1954. The Draft Code imposes criminal responsibility upon individuals who commit specified acts. Included among the provisions of Article 2 one finds:

(4) The organization, or the encouragement of the organization, by the authorities of a State, of armed bands within its territory or any other territory for incursions into the territory of another State, or the toleration of the organization of such bands in its own territory, or the toleration of the use by such armed bands of its territory as a base of operations or as a point of departure for incursions into the territory of another State, as well as direct participation in or support of such incursions.

(5) The undertaking or encouragement by the authorities of a State of activities calculated to foment civil strife in another State, or the toleration by the authorities of a State of organized activities calculated to foment civil strife in another State.

(6) The undertaking or encouragement by the authorities of a State of terrorist activities in another State, or the toleration by the authorities of a State of organized activities calculated to carry out terrorist acts in another State.

[89] 18 U.S.C.A. § 960, 1948.
[90] Ambassador Stevenson in the course of a United Nations debate granted the force of this legal restraint when he said, "I wish to make clear also that we would be opposed to the use of our territory for mounting an offensive against any foreign government." "Statement of April 17," *U.S. State Department Bulletin*, XLIV, 1961, p. 668.

(9) The intervention by the authorities of a State in the internal or external affairs of another State, by means of coercive measures of an economic or political character in order to force its will and thereby obtain advantages of any kind.[91]

Article 3 extends the responsibility of the Code to a head of state or to the responsible governmental official, and Article 4 excludes the defense of superior orders provided the individual charged retained the possibility to refuse the orders. Such a Draft Code is not a binding international agreement, but its endorsement by the International Law Commission may be taken as expressive of standards accepted by the international community. Given the distinctive processes for lawmaking on a global basis such an endorsement may be considered as a stage in the enunciation of a new legal doctrine. In fact, the rationale of the Nuremberg and Tokyo Judgments in the war crimes trials after World War II is illustrative of the way in which a global commitment to a standard of civilized behavior can be transformed on an *ad hoc* basis into an applicable legal obligation.

The willingness of the United States to commit itself directly and explicitly to nonintervention resulted from the view taken of Latin American relations by Franklin D. Roosevelt. As early as 1928 Roosevelt wrote an article foreshadowing the later legal-diplomatic shift of the United States:

It is possible that in the days to come one of our sister nations may fall upon evil days; disorder and bad government may require a helping hand be given her citizens as a matter of temporary necessity to bring back order and stability. In that event it is not the right or the duty of the United States to intervene alone.

"Rather," he adds, significantly, it is "the duty of the United States to give intelligent joint study to the problem, and, if the conditions warrant, to offer the helping hand or hands in the name of the Americas. Single-handed intervention by us in the internal affairs of other nations must end; with the cooperation of others we shall have more order in this hemisphere and less dislike."[92] This later matured into the Good Neighbor Policy with its stress upon common interest and cooperative action. Accordingly, in 1933 at Montevideo a Convention on the Rights and Duties of States specified in Article 8 that "No state had the right to intervene in the internal or external affairs of another."[93] This Con-

[91] Sohn, pp. 99-100.
[92] F. Roosevelt, "Our Foreign Policy," *Foreign Affairs*, vi (1928), 573.
[93] International Conferences of American States, First Supplement, 1933-1940, Convention on Rights and Duties of States, pp. 121, 122, 1940 (hereinafter cited as International Conferences).

vention was subject to a reservation by the United States which advised
that the principle of nonintervention, in the absence of a common standard of definition, would be construed in the light of "the doctrines and
policies . . . embodied in the different addresses of President Roosevelt . . . and in the law of nations as generally recognized and accepted."[94]

It is significant to observe that the United States refused to accept
the broad definition of intervention that had been included in the draft
formulation of Article 8 that was proposed at Montevideo: "Any act
of a State, through diplomatic representation, by armed force, or by
any other means involving effective force, with a view to making the
State's will dominate the will of another State, and, in general, any
maneuver, interference or interposition[95] of any sort, employing such
means, either directly or indirectly in matters of obligation of State,
whatever its motive, shall be considered as Intervention, and likewise
a violation of International Law."[96] This proposed definition and its rejection by the United States is very suggestive with respect to what
was the scope of nonintervention sought by the Latin American countries as contrasted with the legal obligation the United States was ready
to accept. A perceptive student of Latin American diplomacy has well
summarized the significance of this first legal pledge to refrain from intervention by the United States: "The Montevideo pledge meant that
the United States had abjured *armed* intervention in the *internal* affairs
of other countries. By implication, intervention through means other
than armed force could continue."[97]

Because of broader legal commitments that came later it is of no
practical importance to determine whether the United States sponsorship of the invasion by the Castro exiles constituted a violation of Article 8 of the Montevideo Convention on the Rights and Duties of
States.[98] Certainly, such sponsorship comes within the prohibition of
the Additional Protocol Relative to Non-Intervention that was concluded at Buenos Aires in 1936 and later ratified by the United States,
with neither a reservation nor a dissenting vote in the Senate. The Preamble of the Additional Protocol recalled the Montevideo nonterven-
tion pledge, and can be appropriately regarded as a full acceptance

[94] International Conferences, p. 124.
[95] This recalls Secretary Hughes' distinction between intervention and interposition
made at Havana in 1928, see *op.cit. supra*,
note 84.
[96] Seventh International Conference of
American States. First, Second and Eighth
Committees, Minutes and Antecedents, p.
165, Montevideo, 1933.
[97] Graber, p. 205.

[98] President Kennedy's interpretation of
the nonintervention doctrine amounts to
reaffirming the Montevideo pledge as the
measure of the U.S. obligation. From the
viewpoint of law, however, this neglects
the broader commitments subsequent to
1933 subscribed to by the United States.
For the Kennedy position see *supra* pp.
187-90.

by the United States of the Latin American insistence upon a doctrine of absolute nonintervention.[99] Articles 1 and 2 contain the substance of the legal obligation accepted by the United States:

Article 1.—The High Contracting Parties declare inadmissible the intervention of any one of them, directly or indirectly, and for whatever reason, in the internal or external affairs of any other of the Parties.

The violation of the provisions of this Article shall give rise to mutual consultation, with the object of exchanging views and seeking methods of peaceful adjustment.

Article 2.—It is agreed that every question concerning the interpretation of the present Additional Protocol, which it has not been possible to settle through diplomatic channels, shall be submitted to the procedure of conciliation provided for in the agreements in force, or to arbitration, or to judicial settlement.[100]

The United States accepted the obligation to refrain from interventions other than by armed force and to submit a dispute as to what constituted intervention to a supranational body of resolution. This would, as well, imply a commitment to abide by the results of such a third-party determination.

The failure of the nonintervention system to protect the national independence of Spain during its civil war[101] together with the aggressive extension of Nazi influence to some of the South American nations led to an effort to assure collective resistance to an extrahemispheric intrusion. The threat of a concerted European intervention in the Western Hemisphere was present for the first time since the Triple Alliance at Troppau in 1820 had proposed to win back Spain's lost colonies in Latin America; this was the situation, it will be recalled, that prompted the Monroe Doctrine. There was no prospect of legitimating a revival of a unilateral right of protective intervention to be exercised on behalf of hemispheric welfare by the United States. Latin American states had no inclination to give up the doctrine of nonintervention. Instead an idea of collective intervention to prevent extrahemispheric intrusion began to take definite shape in the Declaration of the Principles of the Solidarity of America approved at Lima in 1938. The Preamble of the Declaration of Lima recalled the Protocol of Non-Intervention, while the operative portions of the declaration stated the importance of "continental solidarity" so as to defend each American

[99] Charles G. Fenwick, "Intervention; Individual and Collective," 39 *American Journal of International Law* 645, 656 (1945).

[100] International Conferences, p. 191.
[101] Cf. Norman J. Padelford, *International Law and Diplomacy in the Spanish Civil Strife*, New York, Macmillan, 1939.

state "against all foreign intervention or activity that may threaten them" by recourse to effective collective action.[102] The doctrine of absolute nonintervention supplemented by a declaration of solidarity to resist extrahemispheric intrusions of influence by *collective* action continue as the explicit foundation of the legal relations between the United States and Latin America.[103]

The Declaration of Lima was supplemented in 1940 by the Act of Havana which declared that "any attempt on the part of a non-American State against the integrity or inviolability of the territory, the sovereignty or the political independence of an American State shall be considered an act of aggression"[104] and that cooperative action should then be taken in the spirit of collective self-defense.[105] The concern was to defend against the emergence in South America, by subversion or otherwise, of a government sympathetic to the Axis powers. In 1942 as a result of the threats posed by World War II the inter-American system created the Emergency Advisory Committee for Political Defense of the Continent which was quite successful in using collective nonrecognition as a means to resist the emergence of pro-Axis governments.[106] Hemispheric consensus gave strong political backing to the shift from the unilateral to multilateral resistance against extrahemispheric interference.[107] In 1945 the Act of Chapultepec, adopted at an Inter-American Conference on War and Peace, reaffirmed the commitment to hemispheric solidarity and reciprocal assistance.[108] Such sentiments were given effective implementation in the Inter-American Treaty of Reciprocal Assistance concluded at Rio de Janeiro in 1947.[109]

The most comprehensive effort to establish a legal order for the Americas is contained in the Charter of Bogotá that was signed in 1948.[110] Particularly relevant is its reformulation of the absolute nonintervention obligation to cover collective intervention in Article 15:

No State or group of States has the right to intervene directly or indirectly, for any reason whatever, in the internal or external affairs of any other State. The foregoing principle prohibits not only armed attack but also any other form of interference or attempted threat against the personalty of the State or against its political, economic and cultural elements.

[102] International Conferences, pp. 308-09.
[103] This position was taken by Christian Herter, Secretary of State, at the inter-American meeting held in Santiago in 1959.
[104] International Conferences, p. 360.
[105] *Id.,* p. 373.
[106] Thomas, p. 251.
[107] Suppose that a society chooses to become "Communist" by democratic processes and without external interference?
[108] Full account and analysis found in Manuel S. Canyes, "The Inter-American System and The Conference of Chapultepec," 39 *American Journal of International Law* 504 (1945).
[109] Sohn, p. 110.
[110] *Id.,* p. 117.

We must use this broad prohibition of intervention in order to appraise the legality of the anti-Castro course of United States policy. Such a legal obligation cannot be satisfied merely by refraining from the use of armed force in an invasion, as was implied when President Kennedy said:

> While we could not be expected to hide our sympathies, we made it repeatedly clear that the armed forces of this country would not intervene in any way.
>   Any unilateral American intervention, in the absence of an external attack upon ourselves or an ally, would have been contrary to our traditions and to our international obligations.[111]

This is true, but it is not responsive to the charge of indirect intervention brought against the United States by Cuba and others. It suggests a scope of nonintervention that is arguably in accord with Article 8 of the Montevideo Convention and the Charter of the United Nations, but it does not acknowledge the scope of the legal duty imposed upon the United States by Article 15 of the Charter of Bogotá. The conduct of the United States also seems to violate Article 16 of the same Convention: "No State may use or encourage the use of coercive measures of an economic or political character in order to force the sovereign will of another State and obtain from it advantages of any kind." Such governing standards seem to compel a conclusion of illegality.

Article 6 of the Rio Treaty of Reciprocal Assistance provides:

> If the inviolability or the integrity of the territory or the sovereignty or political independence of any American State should be affected by an aggression which is not an armed attack . . . the Organ of Consultation shall meet immediately in order to agree on the measures which must be taken in case of aggression to assist the victims of the aggression or, in any case, the measures which should be taken for the common defense and for the maintenance of the peace and security of the Continent.[112]

The Cuban Revolutionary Council has urged Article 6 as a basis for collective action by the OAS against Castro. This seems somewhat strained. It presumably makes reference to the influence exerted by the Soviet Union, and possibly Communist China, upon Cuban internal affairs. But the evidence presently available indicates that the

---

[111] Kennedy, *op.cit. supra,* note 16, p. 659.   [112] Sohn, p. 111.

Sino-Soviet interference extends only to offers of military support in the event of an armed attack by the United States upon Cuba[113] and widespread cooperation with the support for Castro in the area of trade and commerce. But if this is characterized as "aggression" it makes a mockery of the concept in a world in which bloc leaders on both sides of the cold war consistently act to ingratiate themselves with unaligned nations. Would any one contend that United States aid to Tito in Yugoslavia or even to Poland constitutes aggression?

However, the special status of the international Communist movement in inter-American relations may give some legal basis to those who urge collective action by the OAS. At the Bogotá Conference in 1948 and again at the Foreign Ministers Meeting of American States held at Washington in 1951 all the American republics went on record as "condemning the interventionist character of the internationalist Communist movement and expressing their determination to take the necessary measures to counteract its subversive activities."[114] In 1954 at the Tenth Inter-American Conference a Declaration of Solidarity was adopted which condemned "the activities of the international communist movement as constituting intervention in American affairs" and declared that "the domination or control of any American State by the internationalist communist movement, extending to this hemisphere the political system of an extra-continental power . . . would call for a meeting of consultation to consider the adoption of appropriate action in accord with existing treaties."[115]

Regardless of the desirability of making a determination in advance that the emergence of a Communist oriented government in the hemisphere has been achieved by extracontinental intervention,[116] it nevertheless abridges the principle of nonintervention only to the extent of authorizing collective action by the OAS.[117] It is a Monroe Doctrine for the Americas that shifts the responsibility from the United States to the republics acting together in joint protective action. Thus the legal discretion of the United States to act on its own is not enlarged by the formal hemispheric action condemning the international Communist movement as interventionary. Such condemnation has been reiterated under the impact of developments in Cuba at Inter-American conferences by the Declaration of Santiago at Chile in 1959 and by the Declaration of San José at Puerto Rico in 1960.[118] However, the

113 For validity of collective defense concept see Article 51 of the UN Charter quote, *op.cit. supra,* note 63.

114 Tenth Inter-American Conference, U.S. Department of State Publication 5692, 1955, p. 8.

115 Text reprinted in documents in *American Foreign Relations 1954* (1955), p. 412.

116 See text on the Lima Declaration directed against Germany and Italy in the World War II period.

117 See *supra,* pp. 175-78.

118 Note relevance of these Declarations to Article 7 of the Rio Treaty calling for

Latin American republics have not been disposed to do more than to join in a collective condemnation of the Communist movement. There has been no willingness to change the legal status of the doctrine of nonintervention or even to join in collective sanctions against governments that have been alleged to be Communist dominated.

The perception of these limits to the willingness of the Latin American republics to act against expansions of Communist influence in the hemisphere has increasingly motivated the United States to resume its role as unilateral actor. Thus the United States is widely assumed to have taken a decisive interventionary role in the organization of the revolution that succeeded in overthrowing the pro-Arbenz government in Guatemala in 1954.[119] American participation, although provoking widespread criticism, was handled subtly enough so that the issue of intervention in violation of treaty obligations was never sufficiently clear. However, the overtness of the American role in the fight against Castro makes quite clear the interventionary character of United States conduct. The absence of collective authorization by the OAS is decisive for an evaluation of the legality of the unilateral help and comfort given the plan of the Cuban Revolutionary Council to invade Cuban territory to overthrow Castro and of the economic coercive measures. Regardless of the correctness of the characterization of the Castro government as "Communist" and as a virtual member of the Soviet bloc, such coercive conduct by the United States amounts clearly to intervention forbidden by Article 15 of the Charter of Bogotá (as well as such earlier instruments as the Additional Protocol of Non-Intervention).[120]

One is led, then, to the inescapable conclusion that the United States has violated its legal obligations to refrain from intervention in the internal affairs of Cuba by its use of coercive economic sanctions (especially the export embargo) and by its support for the hostile military venture of the exiles carried out in April 1961. In addition, the United States would seem to be flagrantly guilty of violating its obligation under the Civil Strife Convention to remain aloof in the face of an internal struggle for power in Latin America. Although less evident, the United States would seem to have abused the legal right to confer asylum upon political refugees by allowing the exiles to form a counterrevolutionary plot on its territory. Furthermore, the status of United States conduct seems legally dubious in relation to the United Nations Charter provisions requiring pacific settlement of disputes and respect

the peaceful settlement of conflicts between states in the hemisphere.
[119] See generally Charles G. Fenwick, "Jurisdictional Questions Involved in the Guatemalan Revolution," 48 *American Journal of International Law* 597 (1954).
[120] See text above, p. 213.

for national independence, and quite contradictory to the aspirational Draft Code of Offenses against the Peace and Security of Mankind that was adopted, with the concurring vote of the United States member, by the International Law Commission. And finally, the conduct of Americans who helped to finance, organize, and execute the April invasion plan appears to constitute a crime under the domestic laws of the United States.

V. A Provisional Assessment

What do these events portend for the future of inter-American relations? It is too early to attempt a real assessment. Even the future shape of Cuban-American relations remains highly uncertain. An exchange of tractors for prisoners may not reestablish harmony, but it provides some hope for a mutual willingness to relax tensions. By acting as a sponsor for the Cuban rebels the United States received a political and moral defeat that is not unlike the miscalculation and setback experienced by England and France in the 1956 Suez Campaign. But the experience can also be of enormous instructive value. In this regard, I should like to conclude by identifying some of the problems and challenges illuminated by the relations of the United States with Cuba since Castro took over in 1959.

(1) There appears, in one sense, to be manifest a remarkable degree of historical continuity both within Cuba itself and in the response of the United States to a situation prevailing in a Latin American neighbor that was destructive of private investment and antagonistic to our desire to maintain hemispheric political supremacy. The pattern of Castro's authoritarian government basing itself upon the strength of his personality is consistent with a tradition of charismatic leadership deeply embedded in Cuban history since colonial times.[121] It is nothing new for Cuba to be dominated by a dictator who suppresses cruelly the political opposition, eliminates civil liberties, and controls mass media of communication for propagandistic purposes. The difference, from the viewpoint of a free press, between newspapers run by a reactionary elite friendly to Batista and run by the Castro government is not very great. It is quite true that Castro has betrayed the democratic principles proclaimed as his program in Sierra Maestra in 1957,[122] but, in so doing, he has *continued* rather than *varied* the internal Cuban atmosphere. Castro has brought into power a dictatorship from the left. This has destroyed the former middle class, perhaps

---

[121] See generally Fitzgibbon, *op.cit. supra,* note 2; Frank Tannenbaum, "The Political Dilemma in Latin America," *Foreign Affairs,* xxxviii (1960), 497.

[122] This argument is made fully in the State Department white paper on Cuba, see *op.cit. supra,* note 60.

irreparably damaging Cuban development, and certainly antagonizing the moderate group that supported him during his struggle for power. One does not find many peasants or workers among the Castro exiles, nor is there much evidence of their disenchantment with Castro. The element of continuity in the internal political life of Cuba is important if we are to assess accurately the expectations of the Cuban population. It is improbable that they will miss liberties that were never possessed.

The hostile action of the Castro government has totally destroyed the value of the huge private investment by Americans in Cuba and has brought to an end profitable international trade relations between the two countries. In addition, Cuba has turned for support increasingly to the extrahemispheric political enemies of the United States. The result has been to intrude Communist influence in the affairs of a Latin American state, threatening our relative power position in the cold war. Cuba's success serves as an example to other ambitious elites throughout Latin America. In addition, Castro was eagerly willing to export his revolution, thus disrupting internal stability throughout the Caribbean,[123] displaying a cavalier disregard in his early months of power for the principle of nonintervention. These developments illustrate extreme instances of the reasons accounting for United States intervention in Latin American affairs: (a) political conditions hostile to American investor interests; (b) the apparent extension to the hemisphere of the influence of a powerful extracontinental nation. The United States has responded, except for its failure to resort to dictatorial interference by force of arms, by recourse to a policy of "protective intervention." This suggests continuity with the hegemonial claims asserted by the United States during the later stages of the Monroe Doctrine. Interposed legal commitments to the absolute doctrine of nonintervention precluded us, however, from a revival of the Monroe Doctrine to meet the Sino-Soviet threat without embarking on a dubious path of explicit law breaking. We are no longer free to act unilaterally.[124]

(2) The United States concern with the protection of private investment seems to induce our leadership to confuse socialism with international Communism. The effort of Castro to reconstruct Cuban society by recourse to a radical and socialist program should be kept rigidly separate from considerations relevant to the distribution of power in the cold war. Otherwise we dangerously foreclose political cooperation with socialist societies, undesirably limiting our flexibility in

---

[123] Cf. Richard P. Stebbins, *The United States in World Affairs 1959*, New York, Vintage Books, 1960, pp. 353-57.

[124] See Louis Halle, "Lessons of the Cuban Blunder," *The New Republic* (June 5, 1961), 13, 15.

foreign affairs. It is my opinion that a socialist response is needed in the less developed parts of the world to hasten a higher standard of living, a rapid rate of industrialization, and an equitable distribution of wealth and services to the lower classes. The United States should encourage such developments so as to promote healthy, progressive, and stable societies in Latin America. Hence, the apparent willingness to brand Castro as a "Communist" partly because he expropriated American property is a particularly regressive aspect of the United States response to Castro.[125] It almost certainly contributed pressure upon Castro to seek external support from the Sino-Soviet bloc.[126] For if the United States withdraws support from a radical social program,[127] the national leaders will almost certainly turn for help to the Communist bloc countries. This lesson was first taught the West by Nasser's reaction to the withdrawal of United States support for Egypt's Aswan Dam project; Castro has re-instructed us in this respect. A stable socialist society unaffiliated with either power bloc is in the interests of the United States in most parts of the world.

(3) The defeat of the rebel invasion, the reaction of public opinion throughout Latin America, and the domestic criticism of United States intervention suggest the political vitality of the legal commitment to a policy of nonintervention. The sentiment of the community in Latin America strongly backs the legal norm. This support is a strong argument for adherence to nonintervention by the United States. It may indicate that our energy should be given over to the development of effective, compulsory remedies that allow creditor states some opportunity to pursue their claims against debtor states. The absence of pacific remedies against Cuba certainly contributed pressure in the direction of intervention. Also considerations of reciprocity suggest the mutual benefit of regional stability that may result for both cold war rivals if standards of nonintervention become operational. Khrushchev's message to President Kennedy[128] indicated the destabilizing effect upon East-West relations that is likely to flow from an interventionary policy reciprocally pursued against neighboring hostile states.

(4) Correlated to the vitality of the nonintervention pledge is the relative insufficiency of the OAS as an organ for the exercise of collec-

---

125 It is "regressive" because it tends to confuse internal questions of social change (socialism) with an external power affiliation (Communism).

126 In addition, the relative internal strength of the Communist party was enhanced thereby. Fitzgibbon, *op.cit. supra*, note 2, pp. 117-18.

127 A "radical social program" is a basic reordering of the society along new lines. It is not a matter of stabilizing the existing social order by external capital grants. The United States has used its influence to support *reformist* rather than *radical* social change in Latin America. This policy tends to perpetuate the basic inequities of the prevailing social orders, especially inequalities in income.

128 Quoted, pp. 188-89.

tive responsibility. The member states from Latin America are extremely reluctant to cooperate with the United States in the use of coercive measures to resist the extension of Communist or alleged Communist influence to the hemisphere. Pledges of sentiment can be elicited at inter-American conferences (Caracas, Santiago, and San José), but implementing action is not forthcoming. This failure to implement is another source of pressure upon the United States to resort to intervention, despite conflicting legal obligations. The expectation of solidarity—as a substitute for the Monroe Doctrine—has not materialized as yet in response to Communism. This lack of solidarity contrasts with the relative success of collective action, implementing the Declaration of Lima (1938) and designed to resist Fascist infiltration. What alternatives to unilateral intervention are open to the United States, given its perception that Communist control of a Latin American country imperils significantly its national security?

(5) The United Nations did not seem able to make a legal determination that objectively reflected Cuba's complaints about United States intervention. The General Assembly passed a mild resolution urging peaceful settlement of the U.S.-Cuba dispute by recourse to regional mechanisms of adjustment. The force of world condemnation of interventionary conduct, as potentially expressed in the UN, probably did restrain the United States from further or more flagrant coercive action. The formal action taken by the General Assembly did not exhaust its influence over the outcome of the U.S.-Cuban dispute. It is difficult to assess this, but it is important not to neglect it.

(6) A Latin American leader can mobilize intense public support by concentrating internal hostility upon the United States. Castro has had great mass response in his campaign to explain all the defects of Cuban society by pointing to the great dragon in the north. And his charismatic following throughout Latin America stems from his ability to show that the dragon breathes fire but is perhaps not so lethal. Other ambitious Latin American leaders can be expected to use latent mass hostility to the United States as a lever of political power.

(7) The emergence of Castro has led the United States to begin taking seriously the needs of its hemispheric neighbors. The new relevance of the cold war to Latin America will probably benefit many nations through increased participation in foreign aid and loan programs. The moderate leaders of beneficiary countries must realize that Castro has made this possible. This may help to account for their reluctance to use coercion to eliminate Castroism from the hemisphere. So long as Castro remains, the United States will do a lot to keep its friends in the hemisphere satisfied.

(8) There are certain implications of our conduct toward Castro which, although central to calm understanding, are very difficult to evaluate. First, the uniform hypocrisy of our highest leaders in their defense against Cuba's charges that we were contemplating direct or indirect intervention. The extreme hypocritical gesture was made in the United Nations by Ambassador Wadsworth when he said that the United States welcomed information that would enable a strict enforcement of our neutrality laws at a time when it was evidently governmental policy to prepare the Castro exiles for the military expedition that took place in April 1961.[129] Such blatant falsification in solemn diplomatic situations sets a very bad example, especially in view of the American tendency to speak of action taken to promote national interests in the self-righteous rhetoric of morality. President Kennedy's suggestion that our newspapers accept voluntary censorship is occasion for further alarm in this regard. How can an uninformed or misinformed society remain democratic? How can we trust our own leaders? How can other countries trust us? This is a very serious consequence of the Cuban affair, for the slow development of trust is indispensable to the growth of all international order, especially in the crucial area of arms control. Trust is the horizontal alternative to effective vertical controls.

Second, cold war pressure has led the United States to act in disregard of its legal obligations. This is very damaging to our campaign to extend further the relevance of law to international relations. More specifically, it reveals the political limits of our treaty commitment to the doctrine of absolute nonintervention. This seems likely to reactivate Latin American suspicions about our willingness to act as a good neighbor under current world conditions. It may further threaten hemispheric solidarity.

Third, the Kennedy Doctrine enumerated a unilateral assumption by the United States of a power that is inconsistent with our legal obligations. It narrowed our nonintervention pledge down in unwarranted fashion to apply only to direct armed intervention by United States military forces even though the applicable treaty provisions are carefully formulated in language broad enough to reach indirect and nonmilitary forms of intervention. Furthermore, President Kennedy announced a possibility of direct armed intervention in the event that

[129] E.g. consider this statement made in a UN debate by Ambassador Wadsworth: "It is natural and readily understandable that some Cubans on our shores should want to engage in activities against the government which has done them so much harm. *But the United States has been in no way associated with such activities. On the contrary, we have made unusual and special efforts to prevent violations of our laws.*" (emphasis supplied) "Second Statement of January 4," *U.S. State Department Bulletin*, XLIV, 1961, p. 103.

the OAS fails to discharge its responsibility to implement effectively the various Declarations of Solidarity designed to keep the Communist movement from extending its influence to our hemisphere. Finally, President Kennedy and others have suggested that the exercise of Communist influence in the hemisphere is not "negotiable"; this seems to suggest a policy of force which directly conflicts with our commitments to seek peaceful settlement of *all* international disputes. Perhaps this is necessary for national security, but we should at least be clear about the broad destabilizing effect of such a claim. It is, of course, reciprocally available to our rivals in the cold war.

Fourth, the role of the CIA raises a number of independently disturbing problems. It is not reassuring to have our international intelligence organ act with such ineptitude. The CIA badly directed the exiles and it disastrously miscalculated the chances of a spontaneous uprising within Cuba. "It used to be said that you would not need an enemy if you had a Hungarian for a friend, and Senor Castro has by now concluded that you will never need a friend if you have the CIA for an enemy."[130] Unfortunately this is more than a sardonic aside. The CIA's failure destroys one's confidence in our capacity to assess military threats that exist or are supposed to exist. This is most serious today when military security is critically dependent on knowing when *not* to push the strike buttons. Additionally, CIA's evident backing of Batista-oriented exiles is shocking. It is inconsistent with our frequently reiterated preference for the emergence of liberal democracy in Latin America, and must make our speeches against dictatorship sound rather hollow. The CIA seems to have acted without a clear Presidential mandate; it acted without even a clear internal policy as is suggested by its own split over which exile faction deserved major support. The CIA, virtually on its own, seemed to be committing the United States to a very unpopular, dubiously conceived, and disastrously executed policy of counterrevolution in a foreign nation.

VI. Conclusion

The United States response to the challenge of Castro has been awkward and lawless. It has disclosed a number of dubious assumptions that our policy-makers have used as the basis of our international conduct. It provides, therefore, an excellent opportunity for a reformulation of the relevance of law to politics, and a recommitment by the United States to the rule of law in hemispheric affairs. The pressure of the cold war need not cripple our capacity to act as a nation in accord with our traditional fidelity to law. But we must come to under-

130 "Talk of the Town," *New Yorker* (May 13, 1961), 31-32.

stand that the restraints of law often serve our national interest, even when they protect a government as hostile to our welfare as is Castro's Cuba. The world may not have much time left in which to establish an effective system of world law. To appreciate, at last, this uncertain hazard is the deepest teaching of the failure of the response to the troublesome challenge thrown at the United States by Castro's Cuba. Perhaps we can learn some respect for restraints on interventionary diplomacy by pondering the cry of impassioned Havana mobs: "Patria o muerte." This assessment of the United States conduct toward Cuba stops short at the Bay of Pigs Campaign of April 1961. No account is taken of subsequent chapters in the tormented course of Cuban-American relations. The progressive shift of attention by American policy-makers to Asian affairs since 1962 has gradually, if temporarily, eroded the anxiety associated with the persistence, against all kinds of pressure, of Castro's regime as the government of Cuba.

1961

VII. The Legal Status of the United States Involvement in the Viet Nam War

I

No contemporary problem of world order is more troublesome for an international lawyer than the analysis of the international law of "internal war."[1] A war is usefully classified as internal when violence takes place primarily within a single political entity, regardless of foreign support for the contending factions.[2] The insurgents who won the American Revolution were heavily supported by French arms. Wars of national liberation are not new, nor is external support for an incumbent regime. But considerable historical experience with foreign intervention in internal wars has not been adequately incorporated into prevailing doctrines of international law. In an age of civil turbulence and nuclear risk, the requirements of world order make imperative the effort to overcome the consequent confusion.[3]

The central issue is whether an externally abetted internal war belongs in either traditional legal category of war—"civil" or "international." Four subinquiries are relevant. What are the legal restraints, if any, upon national discretion to treat a particular internal war as an international war? What rules and procedures are available to determine whether foreign participation in an internal war constitutes "military assistance," "intervention," "aggression," or "an armed attack"? What responses are permissible by the victim of "aggression" or "an armed attack"? Finally, what should be the roles of national, regional, and global actors in interpreting and applying the relevant rules?

If the internal war is regarded as a "civil" war, then the legally permitted response to intervention is restricted to counterintervention;[4] an

1 See generally Harry Eckstein, ed., *Internal War*, New York, Free Press, 1964; James N. Rosenau, ed., *International Aspects of Civil Strife*, Princeton, Princeton University Press, 1964 (hereinafter cited as Rosenau).

2 The "internalness" of an internal war is a consequence of the objectives and arena of the violence. There are, of course, a range of different types of internal war. See Rosenau, "Internal War as an International Event," in *id.*, pp. 63-64. Rosenau usefully differentiates between internal wars, in terms of whether they are fought primarily to achieve changes in the personnel of the leadership, the nature of political authority, or the sociopolitical

structure of the society.

3 For helpful exposition see Samuel P. Huntington, "Patterns of Violence in World Politics," in Samuel P. Huntington, ed., *Changing Patterns of Military Politics*, New York, Free Press, 1962, p. 17; see also Lincoln P. Bloomfield, *International Military Forces*, Boston, Little, Brown, 1964, pp. 24-46. See the table classifying examples of internal war in terms of "basically internal," "externally abetted internal instability," and "externally created or controlled internal instability." *Id.*, pp. 28-30. Incidentally, Professor Bloomfield located the war in Viet Nam in the middle category as of 1964.

4 See "The International Regulation of

intervening nation whose own territory is not the scene of conflict may not attack the territory of a state intervening on the other side.[5] If foreign intervention were held to convert an "internal" war into an "international" war, the intervention could be regarded as an armed attack that would justify action in self-defense proportionate to the aggression. The victim of aggression is entitled, if necessary, to attack the territory of the aggressor, expanding the arena of violence to more than a single political entity.[6] Given the commitment of international law to limiting the scope, duration, and intensity of warfare, it would appear desirable to restrict severely or perhaps to deny altogether, the discretion of nations to convert an internal war into an international war by characterizing external participation as "aggression" rather than as "intervention."[7]

The American outlook on these issues has dramatically changed in recent years. John Foster Dulles is properly associated with the expansion of American undertakings to defend foreign nations everywhere against Communist takeovers by either direct or indirect aggression. But even Dulles did not propose treating indirect aggression as the equivalent of an armed attack by one country on another. In fact, during the Congressional hearings on the Eisenhower Doctrine in 1957[8] Dulles declared ". . . if you open the door to saying that any country which feels it is being threatened by subversive activities in another country is free to use armed force against that country, you are opening the door to a series of wars over the world, and I am confident

---

Internal Violence in the Developing Countries" in *Proceedings, the American Society of International Law, 1966,* pp. 57-67.

[5] The assertion in the text must be qualified to the extent that the United States decision to bomb North Viet Nam is treated as a law-creating precedent (rather than as a violation).

[6] If the conceptions of "aggression" and "armed attack" are so vague that nations can themselves determine their content, a self-serving legal description of the desired course of state action can be given and is not subject to criticism in a strict sense. A critic would be required to stress that an expansive definition of "armed attack," although not forbidden by prior rules of law, was an unwise legal claim because of its status as a precedent available to others and because of its tendency to expand the scope and magnify the scale of a particular conflict.

[7] It is important to distinguish between the factual processes of coercion and the legal labels used to justify or protest various positions taken by the participants. Aggression is a legal conclusion about the nature of a particular pattern of coercion.

[8] The critical section in *The Eisenhower Doctrine* (1957) is Section 2: "The President is authorized to undertake, in the general area of the Middle East, military assistance programs with any nation or group of nations of that area desiring such assistance. Furthermore, the United States regards as vital to the national interest and world peace the preservation of the independence and integrity of the nations of the Middle East. To this end, if the President determines the necessity thereof, the United States is prepared to use armed force to assist any such nation or group of nations requesting assistance against armed aggression from any country controlled by international communism: *Provided,* that such employment shall be consonant with the treaty obligations of the United States and with the Constitution of the United States." *U.S. State Department Bulletin,* XXXVI, 1957, p. 481.

that it would lead to a third world war."[9] In my judgment, by bombing North Viet Nam the United States is opening such a door and is setting a dramatic precedent of precisely the sort that Dulles had in mind. Our pride as a nation is now so deeply dependent upon a successful outcome in Viet Nam that our government seems insufficiently sensitive to the serious negative consequences of the Viet Nam precedent for the future of world order.[10]

The appraisal of a claim by a national government that an act of intervention is "aggression" is a complex task even if performed with utter impartiality. It depends on assessing very confused facts as to the extent and phasing of external participation, as well as upon interpreting the intentions of the participating nations. For instance, one must distinguish in the behavior of an international rival between a program of unlimited expansion through violence and intervention to assure the fair play of political forces in a particular domestic society. In the context of contemporary international politics, a crucial assessment is whether Communism or specific Communist states propose unlimited expansion by using unlawful force or whether they rely upon persuasion and permissible levels of coercion.[11] It is difficult to obtain adequate evidence on the limits of permissible political and paramilitary coercion.[12] Arguably, even a program of maximum expansion should be countered by self-limiting responses aimed at neutralizing Communist influence on internal wars and at building a world order that minimizes the role of military force.[13] We must also not overlook the welfare of the society torn by internal war. The Great Powers tend to wage their struggles for global dominance largely at the expense of the ex-colonial peoples.[14] These considerations support a conservative ap-

9 *The President's Proposal on the Middle East*, Hearings before Senate Committees on Foreign Relations and Armed Services, 85th Cong., 1st Sess., Part 1, p. 28 (1957).

10 The role of national claims of a unilateral nature in the development of international law is examined in Falk, "Toward a Responsible Procedure for the National Assertion of Protested Claims to Use Space," in Howard J. Taubenfeld, ed., *Space and Society*, New York, Oceana Publications, 1964, p. 91.

11 This is the main theme of a speech by the Secretary of State. See Rusk, Address, *Proceedings, the American Society of International Law, 1965*, pp. 247, 249-51.

12 I have discussed these issues in Falk, "On Minimizing the Use of Nuclear Weapons: A Comparison of Revolutionary and Reformist Perspectives," in Falk, Robert C. Tucker, and Oran R. Young, *On Minimizing the Use of Nuclear Weapons*, Research Monograph No. 23, Center of International Studies, Princeton University, March 1, 1966.

13 Everyone would agree in the abstract that it is important to reconcile policies directed at limiting the expansion of adversaries with those aimed at avoiding warfare, particularly nuclear warfare. See Falk, *Law, Morality, and War*, New York, Praeger, 1963, pp. 32-65.

14 Relative peace is obtained through mutual deterrence at "the center" of the international system. Struggles for expansion are confined to "the periphery" where the risks of nuclear war can be minimized and where the costs of conflict can be shifted from the great powers to the ex-colonial nations.

proach to internal wars, an approach treating them as civil wars, and permitting a neutralizing response as a maximum counteraction. And, specifically, if efforts to neutralize Communist expansion[15] in Viet Nam can be justified at all, the appropriate role of the United States is to counter "intervention" rather than to respond to an "armed attack."

The issue of self-determination is also relevant in the setting of internal war. If Communists or Communist-oriented elites can obtain political control without significant external support, it becomes difficult to vindicate Western intervention in terms of neutralizing Communist expansion. Castro's revolution represents a Communist success that was achieved without significant external support until after political control of Cuba was fully established. Part of the objection to American intervention in the Dominican Republic in 1965 arises from the absence of prior foreign intervention. The policies of preventing war, minimizing violence, and localizing conflict seem in these contexts to outweigh the objectives of anti-Communism; the United States serves both its own interests and those of the world community by respecting the outcome of internal political struggles. Unless we respect domestic political autonomy, our adversaries have no incentive to refrain from participating on the side of their faction. The primary objective in relation to internal warfare is to establish rules of the game that allow domestic processes of political conflict to proceed without creating undue risks of a major war. In addition, human welfare and democratic ideals are best served by allowing the struggle between Communist and Western approaches to development to be waged by domestic factions. Recent events in Indonesia, Algeria, and Ghana demonstrate that these internal struggles for ascendancy are not inevitably won by Communists.

Civil strife can be analyzed in terms of three different types of violent conflict.[16] A Type I conflict involves the direct and massive use of military force by one political entity across a frontier of another—Korea, or Suez.[17] To neutralize the invasion it may be necessary to act promptly

15 My own judgment, based on the analysis of the Geneva settlement in 1954, is that the war in South Viet Nam represents more an American attempt at "rollback" than a Communist attempt at "expansion." The Geneva Conference looked toward the reunification of the whole of Viet Nam under the leadership of Ho Chi Minh. The introduction into South Viet Nam of an American military presence thus appears as an effort to reverse these expectations and to deny Hanoi the full extent of its victory against the French. Cf. also Jean Lacouture, *Vietnam: Between Two Truces,* New York, Random

House, 1966, pp. 17-68 (hereinafter cited as Lacouture).

16 These "types" are analytical rather than empirical in character. In actual experience a particular occasion of violence is a mixture of types, although the nature of the mixture is what makes one classification more appropriate than another.

17 Border disputes generating limited, but overt, violence by one entity against another are a special subtype under Type I that may or may not support a finding of "armed attack" or a defensive claim of "self-defense."

and unilaterally, and it is appropriate either to use force in self-defense or to organize collective action under the auspices of a regional or global institution. A Type II conflict involves substantial military participation by one or more foreign nations in an internal struggle for control, e.g. the Spanish Civil War. To neutralize this use of military power it may be necessary, and it is appropriate to take offsetting military action confined to the internal arena, although only after seeking unsuccessful recourse to available procedures for peaceful settlement and machinery for collective security. A third type of conflict, Type III, is an internal struggle for control of a national society, the outcome of which is virtually independent of external participation. Of course, the outcome of a Type III conflict may affect the relative power of many other countries. Hungary, prior to Soviet intervention, Cuba (1958-59), and the Dominican Republic, prior to United States intervention, typify this class of struggle. It is inappropriate for a foreign nation to use military power to influence the outcome. The degree of inappropriateness will vary with the extent and duration of the military power used, and also with the explicitness of the foreign nation's role.[18] Thus, the reliance on Cuban exiles to carry out the anti-Castro mission at the Bay of Pigs (1961) is somewhat less inappropriate than the use of United States Marines. Perhaps appreciating this distinction, North Viet Nam relied almost exclusively on South Vietnamese exiles during the early years of the anti-Diem war.[19]

These three models are analytical tools designed to clarify the nature and consequences of policy choices. Reasonable men may disagree on the proper classification of a particular war, especially if they cannot agree on the facts. An understanding of the controversy over the legality of United States participation in the war in Viet Nam seems aided by keeping in mind these distinct models.

The United States is treating the war as a Type I conflict. I would argue, for reasons set out in the next section, that the war belongs in Type III. But if this position entailing nonparticipation is rejected, then the maximum American response is counterintervention as is permissible in a Type II situation.

Two general issues bear on an interpretation of the rights and duties

18 See the emphasis on the *covertness* of the United States role in sponsoring the Bay of Pigs invasion of 1961 as an influential factor in the decision to proceed in Arthur M. Schlesinger, Jr., *A Thousand Days*, Boston, Houghton Mifflin, 1965, pp. 233-97. And note that Schlesinger's opposition to the invasion was based in large part on his belief that it would be impossible to disguise the United States role. *Id.*, pp. 253-54.

19 See e.g. Denis A. Warner, *The Last Confucian*, New York, Macmillan, 1963, p. 155 (hereinafter cited as Warner); Bernard Fall, *The Two Viet-Nams*, rev. edn., New York, Praeger, 1964, pp. 316-84 (hereinafter cited as *The Two Viet-Nams*).

of states in regard to internal wars of either Type II or III. First, to what extent does the constituted elite—the incumbent regime—enjoy a privileged position to request outside help in suppressing internal challenges directed at its control?"[20] Traditional international law permits military assistance to the incumbent regime during early stages of an internal challenge. However, once the challenging faction demonstrates its capacity to gain control and administer a substantial portion of the society, most authorities hold that a duty of neutrality or nondiscrimination governs the relations of both factions to outside states.[21] A state may act in favor of the incumbent to neutralize a Type III conflict only until the challenge is validated as substantial. A crucial question is whether outside states can themselves determine the point at which the challenge is validated, or whether validation is controlled, or at least influenced, by international procedures and by objective criteria of validation. The United States legal position stresses its continuing right to discriminate in favor of the incumbent regime and to deny even the political existence of the National Liberation Front (N.L.F.), despite the *de facto* existence of the N.L.F. over a long period and its effective control of a large portion of the disputed territory.[22]

A second question partially applicable to Viet Nam is whether it is ever permissible to discriminate in favor of the counter-elite. The Communist states and the ex-colonial states of Asia and Africa assume that there are occasions warranting external participation in support of the insurgent faction. The Afro-Asian states argue that political legitimacy is established by an international consensus expressed through the formal acts of international institutions, rather than by the mere control of the constituted government.[23] This theory of legitimacy sanctions foreign military assistance to an "anticolonialist" struggle. The extent to which this new attitude alters traditional international law is at present unclear, as is its full relevance to the conflict in Viet Nam. The argument for applicability to Viet Nam would emphasize the continuity

[20] See, e.g. James L. Garner, "Questions of International Law in the Spanish Civil War," 31 *American Journal of International Law* 66 (1937).

[21] See generally Ann Van Wynen Thomas and A. J. Thomas, Jr., *Non-Intervention: The Law and Its Impact in the Americas,* Dallas, Southern Methodist University Press, 1956, pp. 215-21; see also Hersch Lauterpacht, *Recognition in International Law*, Cambridge, Cambridge University Press, 1957, pp. 199-201, 227-33; Chapter VIII, pp. 301-304.

[22] For a description of the extent of the N.L.F.'s governmental control see

Wilfred Graham Burchett, *Vietnam: Inside Story of the Guerilla War*, New York, International Publishers, 1965, pp. 223-26; for legal argument see Lauterpacht, *op.cit. supra,* note 21, pp. 175-238.

[23] The legal status of a counter-elite in a colony is certainly improved by the repeated condemnations of colonialism in the United Nations and the recent passage of formal resolutions calling for decolonialization. Factors other than claims to be the constituted government are regularly taken into account in assessing claims of legitimacy in international relations.

between the 1946 to 1954 anticolonial war in Viet Nam and the present conflict. It would presuppose that the diplomatic recognition of South Viet Nam by some sixty countries conferred only nominal sovereignty, and that the Saigon regime is a client government of the United States, which has succeeded to the imperialistic role of the French. This approach implies that external states such as North Viet Nam, China, and the Soviet Union have "the right" to render support to the N.L.F.

These notions of permissible discrimination in favor of the constituted elite or the challenging counter-elite complicate considerably the legal analysis of participation in a Type III conflict and blur the boundaries between Types II and III. Any adequate statement of the international law of internal war, must acknowledge this complexity, and admit along with it a certain degree of legal indeterminacy.[24]

II

The vast and competent literature on the war in South Viet Nam provides an essential factual background for an impartial approach to the legal issues presented in the Memorandum of Law (see Appendix A) prepared by the State Department.[25] It is impossible to summarize all of the relevant facts, but it may be useful to indicate certain lines of reasoning that account for part of my disagreement with the official legal analysis. This disagreement reflects my interpretation of the internal war as primarily a consequence of indigenous forces. Even more, it stems from my concern for taking into account certain facts entirely excluded from the Memorandum, such as the pre-1954 war against the French and the repression of political opposition by the Diem regime.

It must be kept in mind that the present conflict in Viet Nam originated in the war fought between the French and the Vietminh for control of *the whole* of Viet Nam, which was "settled" at Geneva in 1954.[26] Although the intentions of the participants at Geneva were

24 For the theoretical background on legal indeterminacy in international law see Sir Hersch Lauterpacht, "Some Observations on the Prohibition of 'Non-Liquet' and the Completeness of the Law," in *Symbolae Verzijl* 196-221 (1958); Julius Stone, "Non Liquet and the Function of Law in the International Community," 35 *British Year Book of International Law* (1959), p. 124.

25 Among those most helpful see Lacouture; *The Two Viet-Nams*; Bernard Fall, *Viet-Nam Witness, 1953-66*, New York, Praeger, 1966 (hereinafter cited as *Viet-Nam Witness*); Robert Shaplen, *The*

Lost Revolution, rev. edn., New York, Harper and Row, 1966 (hereinafter cited as Shaplen); Donald Lancaster, *The Emancipation of French Indo-China*, New York, Oxford University Press, 1961 (hereinafter cited as Lancaster); Warner.

26 The settlement was not very realistic. It failed to take into account Saigon's exclusion or the American opposition to the Geneva solution. No responsibility was imposed upon the French to assure compliance with the terms of settlement prior to their withdrawal. See Warner, pp. 142-43.

somewhat ambiguous, the general view at the time was that the Geneva agreements anticipated reunification under the leadership of Ho Chi Minh by 1956 to coincide with the French departure. France came to Geneva a defeated nation; the Vietminh held two-thirds or more of the country.[27] Had elections been held, it is generally agreed that reunification under Ho Chi Minh would have resulted, however one interprets the suppression of political opposition in the North or intimidation in the South.[28] Independent observers also agree that the anticipation of the prospect of peaceful reunification led Hanoi to observe the Geneva arrangements during the two years immediately following 1954. The undoubted disappointment caused by the refusal of the French and the Americans to make Saigon go through with the elections helps explain the resumption of insurrectionary violence after 1956.[29]

The Vietminh apparently left a cadre of 5,000 or so elite guerrillas in the South, withdrawing others, as agreed, north of the 17th parallel.[30] Those left in the South apparently went "underground," hiding weapons for possible future use. This action seems no more than a reasonable precaution on the part of Hanoi in light of Saigon's continuing objection to the Geneva terms, and in view of Washington's evident willingness from 1954 onward to give Saigon political and military support. Given the terms of conflict and the balance of forces in Viet Nam prior to the Geneva Conference, French acceptance of a Viet Nam-wide defeat, American reluctance to affirm the results of Geneva, and Saigon's repudiation of the settlement, it seems quite reasonable for Hanoi to regard a resumption of the civil war as a distinct contingency. Although a decade of *de facto* independence (affirmed by diplomatic recognition) now gives South Viet Nam a strong claim to existence as a political entity, Hanoi certainly had no obligation in 1954 to respect claims of an independent political status for Saigon.[31] To clarify the diplomatic context in Geneva, it is well to recall that the Vietminh was the sole negotiator on behalf of Vietnamese interests at Geneva in 1954.

[27] For a general account see Lancaster, pp. 290-358; *Viet-Nam Witness*, pp. 69-83; for the fullest account of the Geneva negotiations see Jean Lacouture and Philippe Devillers, *La Fin d'une guerre Indochine, 1954*, Paris, Editions du Seuil, 1960. And see Dwight D. Eisenhower, *Mandate for Change*, Garden City, Doubleday, 1963, pp. 332-75 for official American thinking during this period.

[28] There is agreement that an election held within the prescribed period would have been won by Ho Chi Minh. See, e.g. Shaplen, p. xi, Warner, pp. 142-43; Lacouture, p. 32: "The final declaration of the Geneva Conference foresaw, of course, that general election would permit the reunification of Vietnam two years later. And none doubted at the time that this would be to the benefit of the North."

[29] See Lacouture, pp. 32-50.

[30] *Id.*, p. 32-68; cf. *Viet-Nam Witness*, pp. 169-89.

[31] Hanoi was "entitled" to prevent Saigon from establishing itself as a political entity with independent claims to diplomatic status as a sovereign state. A separation of Viet Nam into two states was not contemplated by the participants at Geneva, at least not overtly.

Later in 1954 the Saigon regime under Premier Diem ruthlessly suppressed all political opposition.[32] Observers agree that organization of an underground was an inevitable reaction to this suppression, and that the N.L.F. at its inception included many non-Communist elements.[33] It also appears that Saigon was unwilling to negotiate, or even consult, on questions affecting reunification, and was unwilling to normalize economic relations with Hanoi. The refusal of South Viet Nam to sell its food surplus to North Viet Nam imposed a great economic strain on the North in the years after 1954. North Viet Nam was forced to use scarce foreign exchange to obtain part of its food supply from other countries.[34]

Furthermore, the French military presence soon was replaced by an American military presence prior to the scheduled elections on reunification.[35] The evolution of an American "commitment" to Saigon's permanence and legitimacy contrasts radically with both the expectations created at Geneva in 1954 and the subsequent attitudes of the French. United States involvement in the politics of South Viet Nam increased constantly; it was no secret that the Diem government largely was constituted and sustained in its early months by the United States.[36]

Despite the escalating American political, military, and economic assistance, the Saigon regime proved incapable of achieving political stability. Numerous regimes have come and gone since the fall of Premier Ngo Dinh Diem on November 1, 1963. None has commanded the respect and allegiance of any significant segment of the population. Often in situations of civil war diverse factions are able to establish an expedient working unity during the period of common national emergency. The N.L.F. seems to maintain substantial control over its heterogeneous followers while one Saigon regime after another collapses or totters on the brink. The United States recognized at an early stage that the Saigon regime had to transform its own feudal social

---

[32] See Warner, pp. 107-24; Lacouture, pp. 17-31.

[33] Bernard Fall, "Viet-Cong—The Unseen Enemy in Viet-Nam," in Marcus G. Raskin and Bernard Fall, eds., *The Viet-Nam Reader*, New York, Random House, 1965 (hereinafter cited as *Viet-Nam Reader*).

[34] Lacouture, pp. 34-35, 68.

[35] This is the major thesis of Lacouture, "Vietnam: The Lessons of War," reprinted from the *New York Review of Books*. March 3, 1966, p. 1, in Hearings on S. 2793 before the Senate Committee on Foreign Relations, 89th Cong., 2nd Sess., pp. 655-61 (1966), (hereinafter cited as *Vietnam Hearings*).

[36] For an account of the *covert* dimension of the United States role in the domestic affairs of South Viet Nam see David Wise and Thomas Ross, *The Invisible Government*, New York, Random House, 1964, pp. 155-64. There are also references to the exercise of covert influence by the United States in Lacouture, Shaplen, and Warner. American strategies of covert influence in foreign countries are analyzed and described in Paul W. Blackstock, *The Strategy of Subversion*, Chicago, Quadrangle Books, 1964.

structure before it could provide the basis for viable government in South Viet Nam.[37] This is a most unusual demand by an external ally; it bears witness to the fragile and dubious claim of each successive Saigon regime to govern even the parts of South Viet Nam not held by the Vietcong.

In addition, Saigon and the United States seem to have neglected repeated opportunities for negotiations with Hanoi during earlier stages of the war.[38] As late as February 1965, the United States Government rebuked U Thant for engaging in unauthorized negotiations. Until the prospects for a military solution favorable to Saigon diminished to the vanishing point, the United States made no attempt to negotiate a peaceful settlement or to entrust responsibility for settlement to either the Security Council or the Co-Chairmen of the Geneva Conference.[39] This reluctance, when added to the political losses suffered by Hanoi at Geneva in 1954, makes it easier to comprehend Hanoi's reluctance to negotiate after 1965.[40]

All of these considerations lead me to regard the war in South Viet Nam primarily as a Type III conflict, in which the United States ought not to have participated. Because of Hanoi's increasing participation on behalf of the Vietcong, it is arguable, although rather unpersuasive,

[37] Cf. letter of President Eisenhower to Premier Diem on October 23, 1954, Senate Committee on Foreign Relations, 89th Cong., 1st Sess., *Background Information Relating to Southeast Asia and Vietnam* (Committee Print, 1965) (hereinafter cited as *Background Information*). For a recent reiteration, see "U.S. and South Vietnamese Leaders Meet at Honolulu," *U.S. State Department Bulletin* LIV, February 28, 1966, pp. 302-07.

[38] The American approach to a negotiated settlement is recounted and criticized in American Friends Service Committee, *Peace in Viet Nam*, 1966, pp. 50-67. Among other observations, this report points out that "a careful reading of the *New York Times* shows that the United States has rejected no fewer than seven efforts to negotiate an end to the war." *Id.*, p. 51. See also the article by Flora Lewis, in *Vietnam Hearings*, pp. 323-34.

[39] For predictions of an American victory in South Viet Nam, see Marcus G. Raskin and Bernard B. Fall, "Chronology of Events in Viet-Nam and Southeast Asia," *Background Information*, pp. 377, 388-89, 390-92. As late as October 2, 1963, Secretary McNamara and General Taylor issued an official statement reporting their conclusion that "the major part of the United States military task can be completed by the end of 1965"; and on

November 1, 1963 General Paul D. Harkins, U.S. military commander wrote in *Stars & Stripes* (Tokyo) that "Victory in the sense it would apply to this kind of war is just months away and the reduction of American advisers can begin any time now." The point of quoting these statements is to suggest that as long as a favorable military solution seemed forthcoming at a tolerable cost the United States was not interested in a negotiated settlement.

[40] An important element in the background of Vietnamese history was the successful resistance movement led by Ho Chi Minh against the Japanese in the closing years of World War II. When the Japanese left French Indochina, Ho Chi Minh was in control of the entire territory, and was induced to accept the return to power of the French colonial administration in exchange for promises of political independence that were never fulfilled. The recollection of this first phase of the Vietnamese war, when added to the post-1954 experience may deepen Hanoi's impression that its political success depends upon military effort. On negotiating with Hanoi, see also the *Report of the Ad Hoc Congressional Conference on Vietnam*, 89th Cong., 2nd Sess., pp. 4-5 (Committee Print, 1966), (hereinafter cited as *Ad Hoc Congressional Conference*).

that this war is properly categorized as an example of Type II, so that the United States could legitimately give military assistance to Saigon, but is obligated to limit the arena of violence to the territory of South Viet Nam. The weakness of the Saigon regime compared to the N.L.F. renders necessary a disproportionately large military commitment by the United States to neutralize the indigenous advantages of the Vietcong and the support of Hanoi.[41] Our disproportionate commitment makes it appear that the United States rather than Hanoi is escalating the war. And this appearance undercuts any defense of our participation as necessary to offset participation on the other side, and thereby give "the true" balance of domestic forces a chance to control the outcome.[42] The State Department Memorandum assumes that the war is a Type I conflict, and argues that American participation is really collective self-defense in response to an armed attack by North Viet Nam upon South Viet Nam. But to characterize North Viet Nam's participation in the struggle in the South as "an armed attack" is unwise as well as incorrect. Such a contention, if accepted as an authoritative precedent, goes a long way toward abolishing the distinction between international and civil war. The war in South Viet Nam should be viewed as primarily between factions contending for control of the southern zone, whether or not the zone is considered a nation.[43] A claim of self-defense by Saigon seems misplaced, and the exercise of rights of self-defense by committing violent acts against the territory of North Viet Nam tends toward the establishment of an unfortunate precedent.[44]

[41] Bernard Fall, writing on the sort of military superiority that is required to achieve victory over an insurgency, says: ". . . in the past it [victory] has required a ratio of pacification forces versus insurgents that is simply not available in Viet-Nam today [Jan. 1965]. In Malaya, British and Malayan forces have achieved a ratio of 50 to 1; in Cyprus, British forces had achieved a 110 to 1 ratio, and in Algeria the French had reached 10 to 1. The present ratio in South Viet-Nam is 4.5 to 1, and the French ratio in the First Indochina War was an incredibly low 1.2 to 1, which (all other matters being equal) would suffice to explain France's ultimate defeat." *Viet-Nam Witness*, p. 291.

[42] Official United States Government statements frequently imply that the United States must render help to the Saigon regime equivalent to the help given by Hanoi to the N.L.F. If "equivalent" is measured by the needs of the ratio, then it may be as much as 110 times as great as the aid given to the insurgents, whereas if equivalent means arithmetically equal, it will be completely ineffectual.

[43] Hanoi itself takes a conflict-confining position that the war in Viet Nam is a civil war being waged to determine control of South Viet Nam rather than a civil or international war to determine control of the whole of Viet Nam. See, e.g. "Policy Declaration of Premier Pham Van Dong of North Viet-Nam, April 14, 1965," in *Viet-Nam Reader*, pp. 342-43 ("Hanoi's Four Points"). See also "Program of the National Liberation Front of South Viet-Nam," *id.*, pp. 216-21 (on December 20, 1960).

[44] As of August 1967, the United States has attacked North Vietnamese centers of population and has made large-scale air attacks on many industrial targets. The unjustified claim of self-defense has been noted, but it is well to appreciate the progressively weaker constraints imposed on the exercise of the claim.

III

The Memorandum of the State Department was submitted by the Legal Adviser to the Senate Committee on Foreign Relations on March 9, 1966.[45] In assessing it, we should keep in mind several considerations. First, the United States Government is the client of the Legal Adviser, and the Memorandum, as is entirely appropriate, is an adversary document. A legal adviser in Hanoi could prepare a comparable document. Adversary discourse in legal analysis should be sharply distinguished from an impartial determination of the merits of opposed positions.[46]

Second, the Legal Memorandum was evidently framed as a response to the Memorandum of Law prepared by the Lawyers Committee on American Policy Toward Viet Nam.[47] The argument of the Lawyers Committee fails to raise sharply the crucial issue—namely, the discretion of the United States to delimit its legal rights and duties by treating the conflict in South Viet Nam as an international war of aggression rather than as a civil war.[48]

Third, the Legal Adviser's Memorandum implies that both the facts of aggression and the legal rules governing self-defense are clear. This is misleading. Except in instances of overt, massive aggression across an international frontier, international law offers very *indefinite* guidance about the permissible occasions for or extent of recourse to force in self-defense. Doctrinal ambiguity is greatest with respect to internal wars with significant external participation.[49] International law offers very little authoritative guidance on the central issue of permissible assistance to the contending factions.[50] To conclude that international

---

[45] An earlier, somewhat skimpy, memorandum, "The Legal Basis for U.S. Actions against North Vietnam," was issued by the Department of State on March 8, 1965; for the text see *Background Information*, pp. 191-94.

[46] I have tried to urge a nonadversary role for the international lawyer on several occasions: see Falk, "The Adequacy of Contemporary Theories of International Law—Gaps in Legal Thinking," 50 *Virginia Law Review* 231, 233-43 (1964); and a paper delivered at the Harris Conference on New Approaches to International Relations, at the University of Chicago, June 1966, published under the title, "New Approaches to the Study of International Law," 61 *American Journal of International Law* 477-80 (1967).

[47] See Lawyers Committee on American Policy Toward Vietnam, "American Policy vis-à-vis Vietnam, Memorandum of Law,"

in *Vietnam Hearings*, pp. 687-713.

[48] The Spanish Civil War is a useful historical precedent for the legal treatment of large-scale foreign interventions on both sides of an internal war. For a full analysis see, Norman J. Padelford, *International Law and Diplomacy in the Spanish Civil Strife*, New York, Macmillan, 1939. Another way of posing the issue would be to ask whether Cuba, after the Bay of Pigs invasion, might have been entitled to ask the Soviet Union for military assistance, including air strikes against staging areas in the United States. For a critical account of the legal status of American participation in the Bay of Pigs invasion see Chapter VI.

[49] For an elaboration of this position see Chapter IV.

[50] By "authoritative guidance" I mean guidance of action by clear, applicable rules of international law that are con-

law is indefinite is not to suggest that it is irrelevant. On the contrary, if rules are indefinite and procedures for their interpretation unavailable, prevailing national practice sets precedents for the future. In this light, American activity in Viet Nam is particularly unfortunate for the future of doctrines aimed at limiting international violence.[51]

In this section I propose to criticize the legal argument of the Memorandum, taking some issue with both inferences of fact and conclusions of law. I will analyze the consequences of characterizing international participation in Viet Nam as intervention and counterintervention in an ongoing civil war. Although I will call attention to the shortcomings in the legal position of the United States, my main intention is to approach this inquiry in the spirit of scholarly detachment rather than as an adversary critic.[52] Such detachment is not value-free. I try to appraise the claims of national actors in light of the requirements of world order. My appraisal presupposes the desirability of narrowing the discretion of nations to determine for themselves the occasions on which violence is permissible or that an increase of the scale and scope of ongoing violence is appropriate. I am convinced that it is important for *any* country (including my own) to reconcile its foreign policy with the rules regulating the use of force in international affairs, and that, therefore, it does not serve *even* the national interest to accept a legal justification for our own recourse to violence that we would not be prepared to have invoked against us by other states similarly situated.[53] The international legal order, predominantly decentralized, depends for effectiveness on the acceptance by principal states of the fundamental ordering notions of symmetry, reciprocity, and national precedent-setting.[54]

In analyzing the Memorandum I will adhere to its outline of issues, concentrating on the most significant.

gruent with community expectations about permissible behavior; the rules must be clear enough to permit identification of a violation without independent fact-finding procedures.

[51] International customary law evolves as a consequence of national claims and counterclaims acquiring through time an authoritative status. States assert these claims and counterclaims to maximize policy considerations in various contexts. For a major exposition of this process, see Myres S. McDougal and William T. Burke, *The Public Order of the Oceans*, New Haven, Yale University Press, 1962.

[52] An adversary debate may be useful to clarify the legal issues, but an impartial perspective is also needed to help in the

process of choosing among the adversary presentations.

[53] America's relative inability to make effective legal protests against further nuclear testing on the high seas and in the atmosphere is partly a result of America's earlier legal defense of its own similar behavior. A legal precedent is created by the effective assertion of a claim to act, and this precedent may be difficult to repudiate, even if the precedent-setter has greater power than does the actor relying upon the precedent.

[54] See Falk, *The Role of Domestic Courts in the International Legal Order*, Syracuse, Syracuse University Press, 1964, pp. 21-52.

Collective Self-Defense. The Memorandum argues that the United States may, at Saigon's request, participate in the collective self-defense of South Viet Nam because North Viet Nam has made a prior armed attack. But may indirect aggression be treated as an armed attack without the approval of an appropriate international institution? The United States rests its case on the role of Hanoi in the period between 1954 and 1959 in setting up "a covert political-military organization" and by its infiltration of "over 40,000 armed and unarmed guerrillas in South Viet Nam" during the subsequent five years. The Memorandum concludes that "the external aggression from the North is the critical military element of the insurgency," that "the infiltration of thousands of armed men clearly constitutes an 'armed attack' under any reasonable definition," and that although there may be doubt as to "the exact date at which North Viet Nam's aggression grew into an 'armed attack,' [it certainly] had occurred before Feburary 1965."

This argument is questionable on its face, that is, without even criticizing its most selective presentation of the facts. Consider first the highly ideological character of prevailing attitudes toward the just use of force. The Communist countries favor support for wars of national liberation; the West—in particular, the United States—favors support for anti-Communist wars; and the Afro-Asian states favor support for anticolonialist and antiracist wars.[55] Consider also the importance, acknowledged by the United States in other settings,[56] of circumscribing the right of self-defense. The use of force on some other basis—for example, defensive intervention or regional security—moderates rather than escalates a conflict. But the invocation of self-defense as a rationale during a conflict previously contained within a single state tends to enlarge the arena of conflict to include states that are claiming and counterclaiming that each other's intervention in the civil strife is an armed attack. If the infiltration constitutes an armed attack, the bombing of North Viet Nam may be justified. But if North Viet Nam had operative collective defense arrangements with China and the Soviet Union it is easy to project a scenario of escalation ending in global catastrophe. If, on the other hand, infiltration is merely intervention, and appropriate responses are limited to counterintervention, the area of violence

[55] Compare with these claims the prohibitions upon the use of force expressed in absolute terms in Article 2(4) of the United Nations Charter. Self-defense against a prior armed attack appears to be the only permissible national basis for the use of force (without authorization from the United Nations).

[56] See, e.g. avoidance of a self-defense rationale by government officials offering legal justification for the United States claims to interdict on the high seas Soviet intermediate range ballistics bound for Cuba in 1962. Leonard C. Meeker, "Defensive Quarantine and the Law," 57 *American Journal of International Law* 515 (1963); Abram Chayes, "The Legal Case for U.S. Action on Cuba," *U.S. State Department Bulletin,* XLVII, 1962, p. 763.

is restricted to the territory of South Viet Nam and its magnitude is kept within more manageable limits.[57]

The argument in the Memorandum also assumes that armed help to the insurgent faction is under all circumstances a violation of international law. As mentioned earlier, at some stage in civil strife it is permissible for outside states to regard the insurgent elite the equal of the incumbent regime and to render it equivalent assistance.[58] Since no collective procedures are available to determine when an insurgency has proceeded far enough to warrant this status, outside states enjoy virtually unlimited discretion to determine the comparative legitimacy of competing elites.[59] In effect, then, no rules of international law exist to distinguish clearly between permissible and impermissible intervention in civil strife.[60] To call hostile intervention not only impermissible but an instance of the most serious illegality—an armed attack— seems very unfortunate. In addition to a tendency to escalate any particular conflict, the position that interventions are armed attacks so broadens the notion of armed attack that all nations will be able to make plausible claims of self-defense in almost every situation of protracted internal war. It therefore seems desirable to confine the armed attack/self-defense rationale to the Korea-type conflict (Type I) and to deny its applicability in Viet Nam, whether the war in Viet Nam is denominated Type II or Type III. The Memorandum's argument on self-defense is also deficient in that it relies upon a very selective presentation of the facts. It ignores Saigon's consistent opposition to the terms of the Geneva settlement, thereby casting in very different light Hanoi's motives for the steps it took in South Viet Nam to assert its claims.[61] It is essential to recall that the pre-1954 conflict was waged for control of *all* of Viet Nam and that the settlement at Geneva was no more than "a cease-fire." President Diem's ruthless suppression of political opposition in South Viet Nam from 1954 onward, in violation of the ban on political reprisals included in the Geneva agreements, is also relevant.[62]

---

[57] For a fuller rationale see Falk, *op.cit. supra,* note 4.

[58] Cf. the study of the international relations of the insurgent groups during the Algerian war of independence by M. Bedjaoui, *Law and the Algerian Revolution,* Brussels, Publication of the International Association of Democratic Lawyers, 1961.

[59] If "the will of the international community" operates as the true basis of international law, the criteria of legitimacy shift to correspond to the values of the expanded membership in international society.

[60] See Lauterpacht, *op.cit. supra,* note

21, pp. 253-55.

[61] If mutuality is the basic condition for the existence of a legal obligation, it is essential that both disputants accept the terms of settlement. If there is nonacceptance on one side, the other side is in a position to protect its position *as if* the settlement did not exist. In the setting of Viet Nam this would suggest that Hanoi was free to pursue its war aims on a pre-1954 basis and ignore the division of the country into two zones. It is ironic that South Viet Nam owes its original political identity entirely to the Geneva agreements.

[62] Cf. Article 15, Agreement on the Ces-

Furthermore, the injection of an American political and military presence was, from the perspective of Hanoi, inconsistent with the whole spirit of Geneva.[63] The United States decision to commit itself to maintaining a Western-oriented regime in South Viet Nam upset the expectations regarding the Southeast Asian balance of power; in that respect, it was similar to the Soviet attempt to upset the Caribbean balance of power by installing intermediate-range missiles in Cuba in 1962.[64]

The Memorandum seems to concede that until 1964 the bulk of infiltrated men were South Vietnamese who had gone north after the cease-fire in 1954. The use of exiles to bolster an insurgent cause appears to be on the borderline between permissible and impermissible behavior in contemporary international politics. The role of the United States Government in sponsoring the unsuccessful invasion at the Bay of Pigs in 1961 was a far more flagrant example of the use of exiles to overthrow a constituted government in a neighboring country than the early role of Hanoi in fostering an uprising in the South.[65] The claim by the United States to control political events in Cuba is far more tenuous than the claim by North Viet Nam to exercise control (or at least remove the influence of a hostile superpower) over political life in the South.[66] And Castro's regime was domestically viable in a manner that Saigon regimes have never been—suggesting that South Viet Nam presents a more genuine revolutionary situation than does contemporary Cuba. It seems more destructive of world order to help overthrow a firmly established government than to assist an ongoing revolution against a regime incapable of governing.

---

sation of Hostilities: "Each party undertakes to refrain from any reprisals or discrimination against persons or organizations for their activities during the hostilities and also undertakes to guarantee their democratic freedoms." *Background Information*, pp. 50, 53. See Lacouture, pp. 28-31; Wilfred G. Burchett, *Vietnam: Inside Story of the Guerilla War*, New York, International Publishers, 1965, pp. 109-28.

[63] The operative Great Power in the area was France. It was not in Hanoi's interest to give up a favorable battle position so that the United States could replace the French military presence. The worsening of their position in the area as a result of the negotiations at Geneva may explain, in part, their reluctance to negotiate a "settlement" and give up a favorable military position once again.

[64] One influential view of the basis of international order stresses maintaining current balances and expectations. Any attempt to rely upon military means to upset these balances and expectations is

perceived and treated as "aggression." The intrusion of Soviet military influence into the Western Hemisphere by attempting to emplace missiles constituted the provocative element. The same military result could have been achieved by increasing the Atlantic deployment of missile-carrying submarines. This sense of "provocative" might also describe the perception of the escalating American military commitment in Southeast Asia.

[65] For an authoritative account of the United States role see Arthur M. Schlesinger, Jr., *A Thousand Days*, Boston, Houghton Mifflin, 1965, pp. 206-97.

[66] The strength of Hanoi's claim arises from the prior struggle to control the entire country, the military victory by the Vietminh in that struggle, the expectations created at Geneva that the elections would confirm that military victory, the delimitation of South Viet Nam as "a temporary zone," and, finally, the refusal by South Viet Nam to consult on elections or to refrain from reprisals.

African countries admit helping exiles overthrow governments under white control.[67] American support for Captive Nations Week is still another form of support outside of the Communist bloc for exile aspirations.[68] In short, international law neither attempts nor is able to regulate support given exile groups. The activities of Hanoi between 1954 and 1965 conform to patterns of tolerable conflict in contemporary international politics.

The Memorandum contends that subsequent to 1964, Hanoi has increasingly infiltrated regular elements of the North Vietnamese army until at present "there is evidence that nine regiments of regular North Vietnamese forces are fighting in the South." Arguably, the N.L.F. was not eligible to receive external support in the early years of strife after 1954, as its challenge to the government amounted to no more than a "rebellion." But certainly after the Vietcong gained effective control over large portions of the countryside it was *permissible* for North Viet Nam to treat the N.L.F. as a "belligerent" with a right to conduct external relations.[69] This area of international law is exceedingly vague; states have a wide range of discretion in establishing their relations with contending factions in a foreign country.[70]

The remainder of the first section of the Memorandum responds to the Lawyers Committee Memorandum of Law, but is not relevant to the solution of the critical legal questions. It is persuasive but trivial for the State Department to demonstrate that international law recognizes the right of individual and collective self-defense against an armed attack; that nonmembers of the United Nations enjoy the same rights of self-defense as do members;[71] that South Viet Nam is a political entity entitled to claim the right of self-defense despite its origin as a "temporary zone";[72] and that the right of collective self-defense may be ex-

[67] In the Final Act of the Conference of Heads of States or Governments at Cairo in 1964 the following declaration was made by the forty-seven nonaligned powers assembled: "Colonized people may legitimately resort to arms to secure the full exercise of their right to self-determination."

[68] For a perceptive discussion of the status of "Captive Nations Week" in international law see Quincy Wright, "Subversive Intervention," 54 *American Journal of International Law* 521 (1960).

[69] See the extent of international recognition accorded the F.L.N. in Algeria during their war against the French, Bedjaoui, *op.cit. supra*, note 58, pp. 110-38.

[70] No clear rules of prohibition nor any required procedures exist which subject national discretion to international review.

National discretion consequently governs practice.

For useful discussions stressing the survival under the United Nations Charter of a wider right of self-defense than the interpretation offered here see D. W. Bowett, *Self-Defense in International Law*, New York, Praeger, 1958, pp. 182-99; Myres S. McDougal and Florentino P. Feliciano, *Law and Minimum World Public Order*, New Haven, Yale University Press, 1961, pp. 121-260; for a position similar to the one taken in the text see Louis Henkin, "Force, Intervention and Neutrality in Contemporary International Law," *Proceedings, the American Society of International Law, 1963*, pp. 147-62.

[71] For consideration of this question see Bowett, *op.cit. supra*, note 70, pp. 193-95.

[72] See the first sentence of Article 6 of

ercised independent of a regional arrangement organized under Chapter VIII of the United Nations Charter.[73] South Viet Nam would have had the right to act in self-defense *if an armed attack had occurred*, and the United States would then have had the right to act in collective self-defense.[74]

It is also important to determine whether the United States has complied with the reporting requirement contained in Article 51 of the United Nations Charter.[75] The United States did encourage a limited Security Council debate during August 1964 of the Gulf of Tonkin "incidents."[76] Furthermore, the United States submitted two reports to the Security Council during February 1965 concerning its recourse to bombing North Viet Nam and the general character of the war. And in January 1966 the United States submitted the Viet Nam question to the Security Council.[77] It seems reasonable to conclude that the Security Council (or, for that matter, the General Assembly) is unwilling and unable to intervene in any *overt* manner in the conflict in Viet Nam. This conclusion is reinforced by the hostility of the Communist states toward American proposals for a settlement.[78] On the other hand, there is no evidence of formal initiative by the members of the United Nations to question the propriety of the United States policies. The very serious *procedural* question posed is whether the

---

the Final Declaration: "The Conference recognizes that the essential purpose of the agreement relating to Viet-Nam is to settle military questions with a view to ending hostilities and that the military demarcation line is provisional and *should not in any way be interpreted as constituting a political or territorial boundary*," *Background Information*, pp. 58-59. (Emphasis supplied) For Saigon's relevant conduct see Lacouture, pp. 24-31.

[73] For a useful analysis see Bowett, *op. cit. supra*, note 70, pp. 200-48; McDougal and Feliciano, *op.cit. supra*, note 70, pp. 244-53.

[74] That is, it would conform to expectations about what constitutes a permissible claim to use force in self-defense. Despite considerable controversy about the wisdom of the United States involvement in the defense of Korea, there was no debate whatsoever (outside of Communist countries) about the legality of a defensive claim. There was some legal discussion about the propriety of United Nations involvement. For an argument in favor of legality see Myres S. McDougal and Richard N. Gardner, "The Veto and the Charter: An Interpretation for Survival," in Myres S. McDougal and Associates,

Studies in World Public Order, New Haven, Yale University Press, 1960, pp. 718-60. In retrospect, however, Korea exemplifies "an armed attack" for which force in response is appropriate, even if used on the territory of the attacking state.

[75] For communications sent by the United States to the United Nations and relied upon to show compliance with the reporting requirements of Article 51 see *Vietnam Hearings*, pp. 634-40.

[76] For a description of official United States views see "Promoting the Maintenance of International Peace and Security in Southeast Asia," H.R. Rep. No. 1708, 88th Cong., 2nd Sess. (1964); see Ambassador Stevenson's statement to the Security Council on August 5, 1964, in *Background Information*, pp. 124-28.

[77] No action was taken by the United Nations and the debate was inconclusive and insignificant.

[78] Neither China nor North Viet Nam indicate any willingness to acknowledge a role for the United Nations. Of course, the exclusion of China from representation in the United Nations may account for Chinese opposition to a UN solution. See also *Ad Hoc Congressional Conference*, p. 5.

failure of the United Nations to act relieves the United States of its burden to submit claims of self-defense to review by the organized international community.[79] A further question is whether any international legal limitations upon national discretion apply when the United Nations refrains from passing judgment on claims to use force in self-defense.[80]

The Security Council failed to endorse American claims in Viet Nam, and this failure was not merely a consequence of Soviet or Communist opposition. Therefore, if the burden of justification for recourse to self-defense is upon the claimant, inaction by the United Nations provides no legal comfort on the *substantive issue*—that is, the legality of proportional self-defense given "the facts" in Viet Nam. As to the *procedural issue*—that is, compliance with the reporting requirement of Article 51—the United States may be considered to have complied *pro forma*, but not in terms of the spirit of the Charter of the United Nations.

The overriding purpose of the Charter is to commit states to use force only as a last resort after the exhaustion of all other alternatives. In the early period after 1954 the United States relied heavily on its unilateral economic and military capability to protect the Saigon regime against the Vietcong. No *prior* attempt was made, in accordance with Article 33, to settle the dispute by peaceful means.[81] Yet the spirit of the Charter requires that a nation claiming to undertake military action in collective self-defense must first invoke the collective review and responsibility of the United Nations. The United States did not call for United Nations review until January 1966, that is, until a time when the prospects for a favorable military solution at tolerable costs seemed dismal, many months subsequent to bombing North Vietnamese territory. As long as a military victory was anticipated the United States resented any attempt to question its discretion to use force or to share its responsibility for obtaining a settlement.[82] American recourse to procedures for peaceful settlement came as a last

[79] To what extent, that is, do states have residual discretion to determine the legality of claims to use force in the event of United Nations inability to reach a clear decision?

[80] The nature of these restraints may be of two varieties: first, the considerations entering into the creation of a precedent; second, the restraints of customary international law requiring that minimum necessary force be used to attain belligerent objectives and requiring the maintenance of the distinction between military and nonmilitary targets and between combat-ants and noncombatants. One wonders whether these latter distinctions can be maintained in a guerrilla war such as that in Viet Nam.

[81] UN Charter Article 33(1): "The parties to any dispute, the continuance of which is likely to endanger the maintenance of international peace and security, shall, first of all, seek a solution by negotiation, enquiry, mediation, conciliation, arbitration, judicial settlement, resort to regional agencies or arrangements, or other peaceful means of their own choice."

[82] Cf. note 39 *supra*.

rather than a first resort. The United States had made no serious effort to complain about alleged North Vietnamese violations of the Geneva agreements, nor to recommend a reconvening of a new Geneva Conference in the decade of escalating commitment after 1954. Saigon submitted complaints to the International Control Commission, but that body was neither constituted nor intended to deal with the resumption of a war for control of South Viet Nam that was apparently provoked by Saigon's refusal to hold elections.

Further, not until 1965 did the United States welcome the independent efforts of the Secretary General to act as a negotiating intermediary between Washington and Hanoi.[83] Until it became evident that a military victory over the Vietcong was not forthcoming, the United States Government was hostile to suggestions emanating from either U Thant (or De Gaulle) that a negotiated settlement was both *appropriate* and *attainable*. The State Department's belated offer to negotiate must be discounted in light of its public relations overtones and our effort over the last decade to reverse the expectations of Geneva. The United States negotiating position is also made less credible by our failure to accord the N.L.F. diplomatic status as a party in conflict.[84] This failure is especially dramatic in light of the N.L.F.'s ability effectively to govern territory under its possession and Saigon's relative inability to do so.

The American approach to negotiations lends support to the conclusion that our sporadic attempts at a peaceful settlement are belated gestures, and that we seek "victory" at the negotiating table only when it becomes unattainable on the battlefield. The United States showed no willingness to subordinate national discretion to the collective will of the organized international community. In fact, Viet Nam exemplifies the American global strategy of using military power whenever necessary to prevent Communist expansion and to determine these necessary occasions by national decisions. This militant anti-Communism represents the essence of unilateralism.[85]

One must conclude that the United States was determined to use its military power as it saw fit in Viet Nam in the long period from 1954 to January 1966. In 1966 at last a belated, if halfhearted, attempt

[83] Cf. note 38 *supra*.
[84] See the recommendations to this effect in *Ad Hoc Congressional Conference*, p. 5.
[85] That is, it represents the claim to use force for purposes determined by the United States. The ideological quality of this unilateralism—its quality as an anti-Communist crusade—is suggested by "the understanding" attached by the United States to its ratification of the SEATO treaty limiting "its recognition of the effect of aggression and armed attack . . . to communist aggression." It is very unusual to restrict the applicability of a security arrangement in terms of the ideological identity of the aggressor, rather than in terms of national identity or with reference to the character of the aggression.

to collectivize responsibility was made by appealing to the Security Council to obtain, in the words of the Memorandum, "discussions looking toward a peaceful settlement on the basis of the Geneva accords." The Memorandum goes on to observe that "Indeed, since the United States submission on January 1966, members of the Council have been notably reluctant to proceed with any consideration of the Viet-Nam question." Should this reluctance come as a surprise? Given the timing and magnitude of the American request it was inevitable that the United Nations would find itself unable to do anything constructive at that stage. United Nations inaction has deepened the awareness of the Organization's limited ability to safeguard world peace whenever the nuclear superpowers take opposite sides of a violent conflict.[86] Disputes must be submitted *prior* to deep involvement if the United Nations is to play a significant role.[87] The war in Viet Nam presented many appropriate opportunities—the various steps up the escalation ladder—for earlier, more effective, American recourse to the United Nations. But during the entire war in Viet Nam, the United States has shown no significant disposition to limit discretionary control over its national military power by making constructive use of collective procedures of peaceful settlement.

Proportionality. Even if we grant the Memorandum's contention that North Viet Nam is guilty of aggression amounting to an armed attack and that the United States is entitled to join in the collective self-defense of South Viet Nam, important questions remain concerning the quantum, ratio, and modalities of force employed. Elementary principles both of criminal and international law require that force legitimately used must be reasonably calculated to attain the objective pursued and be somewhat proportional to the provocation. As McDougal and Feliciano observe, "Underlying the processes of coercion is a fundamental principle of economy."[88] This fundamental principle deriving from the restraints on violence found in the earliest version of the just war doctrine has two attributes: the effectiveness of the force employed and the avoidance of excessive force.[89]

[86] For a generalized approach to the problems of international conflict given the structure of international society, see Felix Gross, *World Politics and Tension Areas,* New York, New York University Press, 1966.

[87] In the Congo operation the outer limits of United Nations capacity were tested, perhaps exceeded.

[88] McDougal and Feliciano, *op.cit. supra,* note 70, p. 35.

[89] Implicit in the notion of economy of force is the idea that an unjust and illegal use of force is a futile use. The idea of futility is related to the attainability of a permissible belligerent objective and is difficult to measure. If a negotiated settlement rather than victory is the objective, the amount of force required can only be assessed in terms of the probable intentions of the other side, and these shift in response to many factors, including their assessment of intentions.

The United States effort in Viet Nam combines ineffectual with excessive force. The level of military commitment to date seems designed to avert defeat rather than to attain victory. All observers agree that if the other side persists in its commitment, the search for a favorable military solution will be exceedingly prolonged. Since the United States has far greater military resources potentially available, our use of insufficient force violates general norms of international law.[90] At the same time, however, weapons and strategy are being employed to cause destruction and incidental civilian damage without making a proportional contribution to the military effort. This is particularly true of our reliance upon strategic area bombing against dispersed targets of small military value.[91]

The United States has at each juncture also claimed the legal right to engage in disproportionate responses to specific provocations. In August 1964 the Gulf of Tonkin incidents consisted of allegations that North Vietnamese torpedo boats had "attacked" some American warships on the high seas. Although no damage was reported the United States responded by destroying several villages in which the boats were based.[92] This was the first occasion on which force was used directly against North Vietnamese territory and the justifications rested upon a reprisal theory that was largely disassociated from the war in South Viet Nam. Such a disproportionate ratio between action and reaction is typical of great power politics in which superior force is used to discipline a minor adversary. But this exaggerated response violates the legal requisites of equivalency and symmetry between the injury sustained and the response undertaken. Acceptance of mutuality and symmetry is basic to the whole conception of law in a sovereignty-centered social order.[93]

The bombing of North Viet Nam in February 1965 was also orig-

90 Here again a reinterpretation of traditional thinking on war is needed to satisfy the requirements of the nuclear age. American restraint in Viet Nam is explained in part by concern with generating a nuclear war or, at least, provoking a wider war in Southeast Asia. But what legal consequences follow if this inhibition leads to prolonged violence in Viet Nam of an indecisive but devastating form? For confirmation see Congressional testimony of Robert S. McNamara, "Air War Against North Vietnam," Hearings before the Preparedness Investigating Subcommittee, United States Senate, 90th Cong., 1st Sess., Pt. IV, April 25, 1967, pp. 273-373.

91 The expert participants at a conference held under Congressional auspices were in agreement that the bombings in the

north were of little military value, while the diplomatic disadvantages were very serious. Further escalation of the bombings, it was felt, could not be expected to improve the situation. *Ad Hoc Congressional Conference,* p. 4.

92 For a rather effective presentation of the North Vietnamese version of the Tonkin incidents see Nguyen Nghe, *Facing the Skyhawks* (pamphlet printed in Hanoi, 1964). For an attack on the legality of the United States response see I. F. Stone, "International Law and the Tonkin Bay Incidents," in *Viet-Nam Reader,* pp. 307-15. For the U.S. position see references cited, note 94 *infra.*

93 Cf. Josef Kunz, "The Distinctiveness of the International Legal System," 22 *Ohio State Law Journal* 447 (1961).

inally justified as a "reprisal" for a successful attack by the Vietcong upon two United States air bases, principally the one at Pleiku. Only in retrospect was the justification for attacking North Viet Nam generalized to collective self-defense of South Viet Nam.[94]

No clear legal guidelines exist to measure the proportionality of force used in self-defense. There is also some doubt whether proportionality applies to the belligerent objective pursued or the size and character of the aggression. If we assume that the appropriate quantum of military force is that needed to neutralize the Vietcong (the mere agent, in the American view, of Hanoi) then our military response (given our capability) appears to be disproportionately low. A guerrilla war can be won only by a minimum manpower ratio of 10: 1, whereas the present ratio is no better than 5: 1. Our present level of commitment of military forces merely prolongs the war; it does not aim to restore peace by means of victory.[95]

If on the other hand, North Viet Nam and the United States are considered as foreign nations intervening on opposite sides of an armed conflict, then in terms of money, matériel, manpower, and overtness the United States has intervened to a degree disproportionately greater than has North Viet Nam.[96] In the early period of the war the Vietcong captured most of its equipment from the Saigon regime and the level of material support from the North was low.

The objective of American military strategy is apparently to destroy enough that is important to Hanoi and the N.L.F. to bring about an eventual *de facto* reduction of belligerent action or to force Hanoi to make a satisfactory offer of negotiations. Are there any legal rules that restrict such a strategy in terms of duration, intensity, or destruction? This question seems so central to the future of international law that it is regrettable, to say the least, that the Memorandum does not discuss it. That formalistic document implies that if a state claims to use force in self-defense, and supports its claim with a legal argument, and if the United Nations does not explicitly overrule that claim, international law has nothing further to contribute.[97] I would argue, in contrast,

---

[94] Cf. the White House Statement of February 7, 1965, *Background Information*, pp. 146-47; see also *ibid.*, pp. 148-52 for the context used to justify extending the war to North Viet Nam. No charge is made that the attacks on United States military installations were ordered or performed by North Viet Nam personnel.

[95] Cf. note 41 *supra;* see also General Gavin's testimony before the Senate Foreign Relations Committee, *Vietnam Hearings,* pp. 270-71.

[96] For an account of some features of the escalation see Mansfield et al., Report to the Senate Foreign Relations Committee, 89th Cong., 2nd Sess., *The Vietnam Conflict: The Substance and the Shadow* (Committee Print, January 6, 1966). See also Shaplen, pp. xii, xxii; *Viet-Nam Witness,* pp. 307-49.

[97] A state, in effect, satisfies the requirements of international law merely by filing a brief on its own behalf.

that it is crucial to determine what limiting considerations come into play at this point. It is certainly a regressive approach to international law to assume that if a state alleges "self-defense," it may in its untrammeled discretion determine what military action is reasonably necessary and proportional. The opposing belligerent strategies in Viet Nam seem to call for legal explanation, especially in view of the inability of either side to "win" or "settle" the war; the present standoff causes great destruction of life and property without progressing toward "a resolution" of the conflict.

The Relevance of Commitments to Defend South Viet Nam. The second main section of the Legal Adviser's Memorandum is devoted to establishing that the United States "has made commitments and given assurances, in various forms and at different times, to assist in the defense of South Viet-Nam." Much confusion is generated by a very misleading play on the word commitment. In one sense, commitment means a pledge to act in a specified manner. In another sense, commitment means an obligation of law to act in a specified manner.

During 1965-66 the United States clearly came to regard itself as having made a commitment qua pledge to assist in the defense of South Viet Nam. President Johnson expressed this pledge on many occasions. Two examples are illustrative:

> We are in Viet Nam to fulfill one of the most solemn pledges of the American nation. Three Presidents—President Eisenhower, President Kennedy, and your present President—over 11 years have committed themselves and have promised to help defend this small and valiant nation.[98]

> We are there because we have a promise to keep. Since 1954 every American President has offered support to the people of South Viet Nam. We have helped to build, and we have helped to defend. Thus, over many years, we have made a national pledge to help South Viet Nam defend its independence.[99]

The present commitment entailing a major military effort is of a very different order than the early conditional offers of economic and military assistance made by President Eisenhower.[100] American involvement in Viet Nam is usually traced to a letter from President Eisenhower to Diem on October 23, 1954, in which the spirit of the undertaking was expressed in the following sentence: "The purpose of this offer is

[98] *New York Times,* July 29, 1965.
[99] *New York Times,* April 8, 1965.
[100] Don R. Larson and Arthur Larson, *Vietnam and Beyond,* Durham, N.C., Rule of Law Research Center, 1965, pp. 17-29.

to assist the Government of Viet-Nam in developing and maintaining a strong, viable state, capable of resisting attempted subversion or aggression through military means." The letter contains no hint of a pledge. In fact, the United States conditions its offer to assist with a reciprocal expectation: "The Government of the United States expects that this aid will be met by performance on the part of the Government of Viet-Nam in undertaking needed reforms."[101] It is important to note that the letter contained no reference to SEATO despite the formation of the organization a few weeks before it was written, and that the role of the United States was premised upon satisfactory domestic progress in South Viet Nam.

As late as September 1963, President Kennedy said in a TV interview: "In the final analysis, it is their war. They are the ones who have to win it or lose it. We can help them, we can give them equipment, we can send our men out there as advisers, but they have to win it—the people of Viet Nam—against the Communists. We are prepared to continue to assist them, but I don't think that the war can be won unless the people support the effort."[102] This expression of American involvement emphasizes its discretionary and reversible character, and again implies that the continuation of American assistance is conditional upon certain steps being taken by the Saigon regime. Even in 1965 Secretary Rusk, in an address to the Annual Meeting of the American Society of International Law, provided a legal defense of the United States position in Viet Nam that stopped short of averring a commitment qua legal obligation. Mr. Rusk did not once refer to SEATO in his rather complete coverage of the subject. The crucial explanation of the American presence is contained in the following passage:

> In resisting the aggression against it, the Republic of Viet-Nam is exercising its right of self-defense. It called upon us and other states for assistance. And in the exercise of the right of collective self-defense under the United Nations Charter, we and other nations are providing such assistance. The American policy of assisting South Viet-Nam to maintain its freedom was inaugurated under President Eisenhower and continued under Presidents Kennedy and Johnson.[103]

Each successive increase in the level of American military involvement has been accompanied by an intensification of rhetoric supporting our presence in Viet Nam. By 1965 President Johnson was, as we observed,

101 *Background Information*, pp. 67-68.
102 *Id.*, p. 99.
103 Rusk, Address, *Proceedings, the* *American Society of International Law, 1965*, pp. 251-52.

referring to Viet Nam as "one of the most solemn national pledges." It is disconcerting to realize that the United States has at each stage off-set a deteriorating situation in South Viet Nam by increasing both its military and rhetorical commitment. This process discloses a gathering momentum; at a certain point, policy becomes virtually irreversible. President Johnson's use of the rhetoric of commitment communicates the irreversibility of this policy and conveys a sense of the futility and irrelevance of criticism. If we have a commitment of honor, contrary considerations of prudence and cost are of no concern.[104]

But no commitment qua pledge has the capacity to generate a commitment qua legal obligation. The Administration seems to want simultaneously to invoke both senses of the notion of commitment in order to blunt and confuse criticism. A commitment qua legal obligation is, by definition, illegal to renounce. To speak of commitment in a legal memorandum is particularly misleading. To the extent that we have *any* commitment it is a *pledge of policy*.

Secretary Rusk has injected further confusion into the debate by his stress on "the SEATO commitment" in the course of his testimony before the Senate Foreign Relations Committee in the early months of 1966.[105] He said, for instance, in his prepared statement: "It is this fundamental SEATO obligation that has from the outset guided our actions in Vietnam."[106] The notion of the obligation is derived from Article IV(1) of the SEATO treaty which says that "each party recognizes that aggression by means of armed attack . . . would endanger its own peace and safety, and agrees that it will in that event act to meet the common danger in accordance with its constitutional processes." It is somewhat doubtful that Article IV(1) can be properly invoked at all in Viet Nam because of the difficulty of establishing "an armed attack."[107] Secretary Rusk contends, however, that this provision not

---

[104] For this reason the Administration is hostile to domestic criticism. It is, above all, unresponsive to this qualitative aspect of our presence in Viet Nam. Cf. President Johnson's speech at Johns Hopkins University on April 7, 1965, in *Vietnam Hearings*, pp. 640-44.

[105] *Id.*, p. 567. Secretary Rusk explained to the Senate Foreign Relations Committee that "the language of this treaty is worth careful attention. The obligation it imposes is not only joint but several. That is not only collective but individual.

"The finding that an armed attack has occurred does not have to be made by a collective determination before the obligation of each member becomes operative." Cf. the shifting views of SEATO obligation

recounted in Kenneth T. Young, Jr., "The Southeast Asia Crisis," The Hammarskjöld Forums, Association of the Bar of the City of New York, 1963, p. 54. Even Mr. Young, a staunch defender of Administration policy, notes that "Until the crisis in Laos in 1961, the United States looked upon SEATO as a collective organization which would take military action, with all eight members participating in the actions as well as the decision." *Id.*, p. 59.

[106] *Vietnam Hearings*, p. 567; note the absence of reference to SEATO in Rusk, *op.cit. supra*, note 103, and in the 1965 legal memorandum, *op.cit. supra*, note 45.

[107] See generally George Modelski, ed., *SEATO-Six Studies*, Melbourne, Australia, Cheshire, 1962, pp. 3-45, 87-163.

only *authorizes* but *obliges* the United States to act in the defense of South Viet Nam.[108]

Ambiguity again abounds. If the commitment to act in Viet Nam is incorporated in a treaty, the United States is legally bound. Such an interpretation of Article IV(1) would apply equally to other states that have ratified the SEATO treaty. None of the other SEATO signatories acknowledge such "a commitment" to fulfill a duty of collective self-defense, nor does the United States contend they have one. France and Pakistan oppose altogether any military effort on behalf of the Saigon regime undertaken by outside states.

Secretary Rusk later softened his insistence that Article IV(1) imposed a legal commitment qua obligation upon the United States. In an exchange with Senator Fulbright during Senate hearings on Viet Nam, Mr. Rusk offered the following explanation:

> The Chairman. . . . do you maintain that we had an obligation under the Southeastern Asian Treaty to come to the assistance, all-out assistance of South Vietnam? Is that very clear?
> Secretary Rusk. It seems clear to me, sir, that this was an obligation—
> The Chairman. Unilateral.
> Secretary Rusk. An obligation of policy. It is rooted in the policy of the treaty. I am not now saying if we had decided we would not lift a finger about Southeast Asia that we could be sued in a court and be convicted of breaking a treaty.[109]

It seems evident if an armed attack has been established, the treaty imposes a legal obligation to engage in collective self-defense of the victim. But in the absence of a collective determination by the SEATO membership that an armed attack has taken place, it is difficult to maintain that Article IV(1) does more than authorize discretionary action in appropriate circumstances.

The Memorandum argues that "the treaty does not require a collective determination that an armed attack has occurred in order that the obligation of Article IV(1) become operative. Nor does the provision require collective decision on actions to be taken to meet the common danger."[110] This interpretation of Article IV(1) is a blatant endorsement of extreme unilateralism, made more insidious by its pretense of "obligation" and its invocation of the multilateral or regional scaffolding of SEATO. Here the legal position of the State Department displays maximum cynicism, resorting to international law to obscure the national character of military action. In essence, the United States

---

[108] *Vietnam Hearings*, p. 567.
[109] *Ibid.*, p. 45; see also *ibid.*, pp. 7-8.
[110] *Ibid.*, p. 567.

claims that it is under an obligation to determine for itself when an armed attack has occurred, and that once this determination is made there arises a further obligation to act in response. This justification for recourse to force is reminiscent of international law on war prior to World War I, when states were free to decide for themselves when to go to war.[111] The regressive tendency of this position is further intensified by applying it in a situation where there was a background of civil war and where the alleged aggression was low-scale, extended over time, and covert. Under "the Rusk Doctrine" a country alleging "armed attack" seems free to act in self-defense whenever it wishes. The rhetoric of commitment seems connected with the effort to make the policy of support for Saigon irreversible in domestic arenas and credible in external arenas, especially in Saigon and Hanoi, but it has little to do with an appreciation of the relevance of international law to United States action in Viet Nam.

The important underlying question is whether it is permissible to construe an occurrence of "an armed attack" in the circumstances of the internal war in South Viet Nam. If an armed attack can be held to have occurred, then both self-defense and collective self-defense are permissible. The legal status of a claim of collective self-defense is not improved by embedding the claim in a collective defense arrangement. In fact, the collective nature of an arrangement such as SEATO might imply some obligation to attempt recourse to consultative and collective procedures before acting, at least to determine whether an armed attack has occurred and by whom. Under Secretary Rusk's interpretation of the treaty, SEATO members with opposing views on the issue of which side committed an armed attack could become "obligated" to act in "collective self-defense" against one another.[112] Surely this is the *reductio ad absurdum* of collective self-defense.

In terms of both world order and the original understanding of SEATO, the conflict in Viet Nam calls for action, if at all, under Article IV(2).[113] To categorize the conflict under Article IV(1) would seem to require a unanimous collective determination that the assistance given by Hanoi to the Vietcong amounted to an armed attack. Once that determination had been made, it might seem plausible to maintain that

---

[111] For a general survey of progressive attempts to regulate recourse to war see Quincy Wright, *The Role of International Law in the Elimination of War*, Dobbs Ferry, New York, Oceana Publications, 1961.

[112] E.g. suppose Laos and Thailand became involved in a conflict in which each state accused the other of being an ag-

gressor—and this is not impossible.

[113] Cf. *SEATO, op.cit. supra,* note 107, p. xiv. It is made clear both that internal conflicts abetted by subversion were to be treated under Article IV(2) and that this provision required consultation as a prerequisite to action and had become "a dead letter."

the obligation to act in collective self-defense exists on a joint and several basis, and that the United States might join in the defense of the victim of the armed attack without further collective authorization. Unlike the State Department position, the approach outlined in this paragraph requires that a multilateral determination of the facts precede acts of commitment. The United States might help build a more peaceful world by taking seriously the collective procedures governing the use of force which it has taken such an active role in creating.

The Geneva Accords of 1954. The agreements at Geneva were cast in the form of a cease-fire arrangement and a declaration of an agreed procedure for achieving a post-war settlement. The parties to the first war in Viet Nam were the French and the Vietminh, and the agreements were between their respective military commanders. The other powers at Geneva were mere sureties. At Ho Chi Minh's insistence the Saigon regime did not participate; Saigon was evidently dissatisfied from the outset with the terms of settlement.[114] The United States Government was also reluctant to regard the Geneva settlement as binding.[115]

The Final Declaration required elections to be held in July of 1956 "under the supervision of an international commission composed of representatives of the Member States of the International Supervisory Commission."[116] The Memorandum points out that South Viet Nam "did not sign the cease-fire agreement of 1954, nor did it adhere to the Final Declaration of the Geneva Conference" and adds that "the South Vietnamese Government at that time gave notice of its objection in particular to the election provisions of the accords." At the time of the Geneva proceedings, the Saigon regime exerted control over certain areas in the South, and this awkward fact made it unrealistic to suppose that the Geneva terms of settlement would ever be voluntarily carried out. When Diem came to power and the United States moved in to fill the place left vacant by the departure of the French, it became clear, especially in view of the nationwide popularity of Ho Chi Minh, that the contemplated elections would never be held.[117] In a sense it was naïve of Hanoi to accept the Geneva arrangement or to rely upon its implementation.[118]

---

114 See *Viet-Nam Witness,* pp. 74-83. Jean Lacouture has written that France bears a heavy responsibility for its failure to secure full implementation of the Geneva "solution" before withdrawing from Viet Nam; in Lacouture's view France's premature withdrawal created a political vacuum immediately filled by the United States. Lacouture, p. 657.

115 *Viet-Nam Witness,* pp. 69-83; see Lancaster, pp. 313-58 for a general account of the Geneva settlement.

116 See Article 7, "Final Declaration of Geneva Conference, July 21, 1954," *Background Information,* pp. 58, 59.

117 Lancaster, pp. 315-16.

118 *Id.,* pp. 313-37.

Saigon objected to the election provisions from the outset because it hoped for a permanent partition of Viet Nam. But permanent partition was so deeply incompatible with the objective sought by the Vietminh in the war against the French that it is hardly reasonable to expect Hanoi to acquiesce. In a sense, Hanoi's willingness to cooperate with the Geneva arrangement until 1956 is more surprising than is its later effort to revive the war in Viet Nam.

The Memorandum says that even assuming the election provisions were binding on South Viet Nam, there was no breach of obligation arising from Saigon's failure "to engage in consultations in 1955, with a view to holding elections in 1956." The justification offered for Saigon's action is that "the conditions in North Viet Nam during that period were such as to make impossible any free and meaningful expression of popular will." But the election provision in the Final Declaration stated no preconditions about the form of interim government in the two zones, and the type of governmental control existing in the North could have been and presumably was anticipated by those who drew up the Final Declaration. The meaning of "free elections" in Communist countries was well known to all countries including the United States, and the conditions prevailing in South Viet Nam were no more conducive to popular expressions of will.[119] The real objection to the elections was a simple one—namely, the assurance that Ho Chi Minh would win.[120] The Memorandum offers only a self-serving endorsement of Saigon's refusal to go along with the terms of the Geneva settlement, although these terms had been endorsed by the United States representative, Bedell Smith.[121]

The Memorandum suggests in footnote 10 that North Viet Nam's remedies, had there been "a breach of obligation by the South, lay in discussion with Saigon, perhaps in an appeal to the co-chairmen of the Geneva conference, or in a reconvening of the conference to consider the situation." In light of the failure of the United States to make use of international remedies which it argues are obligatory for Hanoi, this statement is a shocking instance of legal doubletalk. Footnote 10 ends by saying that "Under international law, North Viet Nam had no right to use force outside its own zone in order to secure its political objectives." This assertion is misleading. No authoritative rules govern the action of the parties in the event that a settlement of an internal war breaks down. Certainly if the settlement is not binding on *all* the parties,

[119] On the conduct of elections in Viet Nam see Bernard B. Fall, "Vietnam's Twelve Elections," *The New Republic* (May 14, 1966), 12-15.

[120] Warner, pp. 84-106, 142-43; cf. Marvin Gettleman, ed., *Vietnam; History,* *Documents and Opinions on a Major Crisis,* Greenwich, Conn., Fawcett, 1965, pp. 191-94, 210-35.

[121] For text of Smith's statement see *Background Information,* p. 61.

no one of them is bound by constraints. In the absence of the Geneva Accords, Saigon would not exist as a political entity. If Saigon repudiates the Accords, Hanoi would seem to be legally free to resume the pursuit of its political objectives and to ignore the creation of a temporary zone in the South. The principle of mutuality of obligation makes it inappropriate to argue that Saigon is free to ignore the Geneva machinery but that Hanoi is bound to observe it.

Furthermore, international law does not forbid the use of force within a single state. If Hanoi may regard Viet Nam as a single country between 1954 and 1956, its recourse to force in pursuit of political objectives is not prohibited even assuming that its "guidance" and "direction" of the Vietcong constitute "a use" of force by North Viet Nam.

The Memorandum misleadingly implies that the International Control Commission (ICC) endorsed the action of the United States and Saigon and condemned the action of North Viet Nam. Both sides were criticized severely by the ICC for violating provisions of the Geneva Accords.[122] It would appear that the massive military aid given to Saigon by the United States was the most overt and disrupting violation, directly contravening the prohibition on the entry of foreign military forces and new military equipment.[123] According to the reasoning of footnote 10, North Viet Nam's remedy lay in discussion and the Geneva machinery. But a quite different line of legal reasoning is taken to justify American activity:[124] action otherwise prohibited by the Geneva Accords is "justified by the international law principle that a material breach of an agreement by one party entitles the other at least to withhold compliance with an equivalent, corresponding, or related provision until the defaulting party is prepared to honor its obligations." One wonders why this "international law principle" is not equally available to North Viet Nam after Saigon's refusal even to consult about holding elections. Why is Hanoi bound by the reasoning of footnote 10 and Washington entitled to the reasoning of reciprocal breach? The self-serving argument of the Memorandum confers competence upon the United States and Saigon to find that a breach has taken place and to select a suitable remedy, but permits Hanoi only to *allege* a breach, and forbids it to take countervailing action until the breach has been impartially verified.

The Authority of the President under the Constitution. I agree with the Legal Adviser's analysis that the President possesses the constitu-

---

[122] For a representative sample see *Vietnam, op.cit. supra,* note 120, at pp. 160-90.
[123] Cf. Articles 17, 18, "Agreement on the Cessation of Hostilities in Vietnam," *Background Information,* pp. 28, 34-35.

[124] Cf. Department of State white paper, "Aggression from the North," in *Viet-Nam Reader,* pp. 143-55; for criticism see Julius Stone, "A Reply to White Paper," in *Viet-Nam Reader,* pp. 155-62.

tional authority to use American military forces in Viet Nam without a declaration of war. Past practice and present policy support this conclusion. To declare war against North Viet Nam would further rigidify our own expectations about an acceptable outcome and it would almost certainly escalate the conflict. It might activate dormant collective defense arrangements between North Viet Nam and its allies.

But the Constitution is relevant in another way not discussed by the Memorandum. The President is bound to act in accordance with governing law, including international law. The customary and treaty norms of international law enjoy the status of "the law of the land" and the President has no discretion to violate these norms in the course of pursuing objectives of foreign policy. An impartial determination of the compatibility of our action in Viet Nam with international law is highly relevant to the constitutionality of the exercise of Presidential authority in Viet Nam.

The President has the constitutional authority to commit our armed services to the defense of South Viet Nam without a declaration of war *provided* that such "a commitment" is otherwise in accord with international law. Whether all or part of the United States action violates international law is also a constitutional question. International law offers no authoritative guidance as to the use of force *within* South Viet Nam, but the bombing of North Viet Nam appears to be an unconstitutional use of Presidential authority as well as a violation of international law. As well, bombing nonmilitary targets, "search and destroy" tactics, toxic weapons, forced transfer of civilians, and "free bombing zones" appear to violate the laws of war as principally embodied in the Hague Conventions of 1899 and 1907, the Geneva Conventions of 1949, and the corpus of customary international law. These *primie facie* violations of international law, given the Judgment of Nuremberg, appear to entail potential individual criminal responsibility for American leaders during the course of the Vietnam War.

IV

It is appropriate to reflect on the role of the international lawyer in a legal controversy of the sort generated by our role in Viet Nam. The rather keen interest in this controversy about international law results mostly from intense disagreement about the overall wisdom of our foreign policy rather than curiosity about the content of the law on the subject. International law has therefore been used as an instrument of persuasion by those who oppose or favor our Viet Nam policy on political grounds. In such a debate we assume that the United States strives to be law abiding and that, therefore, it is important for partisans of existing policy to demonstrate the compatibility between law and policy and for opponents of the policy to demonstrate the opposite.

This use of international law to bolster or bludgeon foreign policy positions is unfortunate. It creates the impression that international law serves to inflame debate rather than to guide or shape public policy— an impression fostered by the State Department Memorandum. After a decade of fighting in Viet Nam, the Memorandum was issued in response to legal criticisms made by private groups and echoed by a few dissident members of Congress. It blandly whitewashed the existing government position. The tone is self-assured, the method legalistic, and the contribution to an informed understanding of the issues, minimal. None of the difficult questions of legal analysis are considered. In this intellectual context international lawyers with an independent voice need to be heard.

An international lawyer writing about an ongoing war cannot hope to reach clear conclusions about all the legal issues involved. It is virtually impossible to unravel conflicting facts underlying conflicting legal claims. Of course, we can hope that a legal commentator will acknowledge the uncertainties about the facts and that he will offer explicit reasons for resolving ambiguities in the way and to the extent that he does.[125]

Would it not be better, one is tempted to insist, for international lawyers to avoid so controversial and indeterminate a subject as the legal status of American participation in the war in Viet Nam? I think it important openly to raise this question of propriety, but clearly to answer it in the negative. The scholar has the crucial task of demonstrating the intractability of many, although not of all, the legal issues. Such an undertaking defeats, or calls into serious question, the dogmatic overclarification of legal issues that arises in the more popular discussions of foreign policy questions. The international lawyer writing in the spirit of scholarly inquiry may have more to contribute by raising the appropriate questions than by purporting to give authoritative answers. He may enable public debate to adopt a more constructive and sophisticated approach to the legal issues.

And, finally, an international lawyer not employed by a government can help modify a distorted nationalistic perspective. An international lawyer is, of course, a citizen with strong views on national policy,

---

[125] Cf. the lines attributed to "An Old Jew of Galicia" in Czeslaw Milosz, *The Captive Mind,* New York, Knopf, 1953, p. 2: "When someone is honestly 55% right, that's very good and there's no use wrangling. And if someone is 60% right, it's wonderful, and let him thank God. But what's to be said about 75% right? Wise people say this is suspicious. Well, and what about 100% right? Whoever says he's 100% right is a fanatic, a thug, and the worst kind of rascal."

but his outlook is universalized by the realization that the function of law in world affairs is to reconcile inconsistent national goals. The international lawyer seeks a legal solution that is based upon an appreciation, although not always an acceptance, of the position of "the other side" in an international dispute. His goal is a system of world order in which all nations are constrained for the common good by rules and by procedures for their interpretation and enforcement. This implies a new kind of patriotism, one that is convinced that to succeed, the nation must act within the law in its foreign as well as its domestic undertakings.

But are there occasions upon which it would be proper for a nation to violate international law? It may be contended that the United States must act as it does in Viet Nam because the international procedures of Geneva, the United Nations, and SEATO offer no protection to a victim of aggression such as South Viet Nam. The United States is acting, in this view, to fill a vacuum created by the failures of international regulatory machinery. In fact, it is often suggested, the refusal of the United States to act would tempt potential aggressors. Those who emphasize the obligations and ambiguities of power often talk in this vein and warn of the sterility of legalism in foreign affairs.[126] In general terms, this warning is sound, but its very generality is no guide to specific action, especially in the nuclear age. It remains essential to vindicate as explicitly as possible the reasons that might justify violating legal expectations about the use of military power in each instance by documented reference to overriding policies; slogans about peace, security, and freedom are not enough. The analysis must be so conditioned by the specific circumstances that it will not always justify the use of force. I do not believe that such an argument can convincingly be made with respect to Viet Nam, and therefore I affirm the relevance of legal criteria of limitation. If an argument in favor of military intervention is offered, then it should stress the limits and weaknesses of law or the priority of national over international concerns.[127] We would then gain a better understanding of what law can and cannot do than is acquired by the manipulative straining of legal rules into contrived coincidence with national policies.[128]

---

126 See generally the writings of the critical legalists. E.g. George Kennan, *American Diplomacy 1900-1950,* Chicago, University of Chicago Press, 1951, pp. 95, 96, 100; Hans Morgenthau, *In Defense of the National Interest,* New York, Knopf, 1951.

127 Little systematic attention has been given to the rationale and logic for reject-ing the claims of law under certain circumstances in human affairs. The consequence is to lead perceptions into naïve over-assertions or cynical denials of the relevance of law to behavior.

128 There is a role for adversary presentation, but there is a more important need to seek bases upon which to appraise adversary claims.

V

The foregoing analysis points to the following set of conclusions:

(1) The United States insistence upon treating North Vietnamese assistance to the Vietcong as "an armed attack" justifying recourse to "self-defense" goes a long way toward abolishing the legal significance of the distinction between civil war and international war. Without this distinction, we weaken a principal constraint upon the scope and scale of violence in international affairs—the confinement of violence associated with internal wars to the territory of a single political unit.[129] Another adverse consequence of permitting "self-defense" in response to covert aggression is to entrust nations with very wide discretion to determine for themselves the occasions upon which recourse to *overt* violence across international boundaries is permissible.[130] An extension of the doctrine of self-defense would defeat a principal purpose of the United Nations Charter—the delineation of fixed, narrow limits upon the use of overt violence by states in dispute with one another.

(2) The United States made no serious attempt to exhaust international remedies prior to recourse to unilateral military power. The gradual unfolding of the conflict provided a long period during which attempts at negotiated settlement could have taken place. Only belatedly and in a *pro forma* fashion did the United States refer the dispute to the United Nations. The United States made no attempt to comply with "the international law principle" alleged by footnote 10 of the Memorandum to govern the action of North Viet Nam. Nor did it attempt during the early phases of the war to subordinate its discretion to the Geneva machinery. No use was made even of the consultative framework of SEATO, an organization inspired by United States initiative for the specific purpose of inhibiting Communist aggression in Southeast Asia.[131] Policies of force were unilaterally adopted and put into execution; no account was taken of the procedural devices created to give a collective quality to decisions about the use of force. Yet the prospect for controlling violence in world affairs depends upon the growth of limiting procedural rules and principles.

(3) By extending the scope of violence beyond the territory of South Viet Nam the United States has created an unfortunate precedent in international affairs. Where international institutions fail to provide clear guidance as to the character of permissible action, national ac-

---

129 One can emphasize the refusal to permit external sanctuary for actors supporting an internal war as a constructive precedent, but its reciprocal operation creates dangers of unrestrained violence. See generally Morton H. Halperin, *Limited War in the Nuclear Age*, New York, Wiley, 1963.

130 Cf. Henkin, *op.cit. supra,* note 70.

131 On the creation of SEATO see *SEATO, op.cit. supra,* note 107, Introduction, pp. xiii-xix.

tions create quasi-legislative precedents. In view of the background of the conflict in Viet Nam (including the expectation that South Viet Nam would be incorporated into a unified Viet Nam under the control of Hanoi after the French departure), the American decision to bomb North Viet Nam sets an unfortunate precedent. If North Viet Nam and its allies had the will and capability to employ equivalent military force, the precedent would even allow them to claim the right to bomb United States territory in reprisal.

(4) The widespread domestic instability in the Afro-Asian world points up the need for an approach to internal war that aims above all to insulate this class of conflict from intervention by the Great Powers. The early use of peace observation forces, border control machinery, restraints on introduction of foreign military personnel, and standby mediation appears possible and beneficial. Responses to allegations of "aggression" should be verified prior to the unilateral use of defensive force, especially when time is available. Claims of covert aggression might then be verified with sufficient authority and speed to mobilize support for community security actions.

(5) In the last analysis, powerful nations have a responsibility to use defensive force to frustrate aggression when international machinery is paralyzed. Viet Nam, however, does not provide a good illustration of the proper discharge of this responsibility. North Viet Nam's action does not seem to constitute "aggression." Available international machinery was not used in a proper fashion. The domestic conditions prevailing in South Viet Nam were themselves so inconsistent with prevailing ideals of welfare, progress, and freedom that it is difficult to claim that the society would be better off as a result of a Saigon victory. The massive American presence has proved to be a net detriment, greatly escalating the war, tearing apart the fabric of Vietnamese society, and yet not likely to alter significantly the political outcome. The balance of domestic and area forces seems so favorable to the Vietcong that it is unlikely that the N.L.F. can be kept forever from political control. The sacrifice of lives and property merely postpones what appears to be an inevitable result. The United States voluntarily assumed a political responsibility for the defense of South Viet Nam that has been gradually converted into a political commitment and a self-proclaimed test of our devotion to the concept of collective self-defense. This responsibility is inconsistent with the requirements of world order to the extent that it depends upon unilateral prerogatives to use military power. The national interest of the United States would be better served by the embrace of *cosmopolitan isolationism*—either we act in conjunction with others or we withdraw. We are the most powerful nation in

world history. It is hubris to suppose, however, that we are the policeman of the world.[132] Our wasted efforts in Viet Nam suggest the futility and frustration of the politics of overcommitment. We are not the only country in the world concerned with containing Communism. If we cannot find cooperative bases for action we will dissipate our moral and material energies in a series of Viet Nams. The tragedy of Viet Nam provides an occasion for rethinking the complex problems of use of military power in world affairs and calls for an examination of the increasingly imperial role of the United States in international society. Perhaps we will discover the relevance of international law to the *planning* and *execution* of foreign policy as well as to its *justification*. Certainly the talents of the State Department's Legal Adviser are wasted if he is to be merely an official apologist summoned long after our President has proclaimed "a solemn national commitment."

1966

[132] Even Secretary Rusk has pointed out the limitations upon American power in emphatic terms: "We do not regard ourselves as the policeman of the universe. . . . If other governments, other institutions, or other regional organizations can find solutions to the quarrels which disturb this present scene, we are anxious to have this occur." *Vietnam Hearings*, p. 563; and Secretary McNamara stated in an address to the American Society of Newspaper Editors delivered at Montreal on May 18, 1966: ". . . neither conscience nor sanity itself suggests that the United States is, should, or could be the global gendarme." *New York Times*, May 19, 1966, p. 11.

VIII. The Legal Status of the United States Involvement in the Viet Nam War: A Continuing Inquiry

IN THE BEST traditions of scholarly debate Professor John Norton Moore has taken sharp and fundamental issue with my legal analysis of the United States role in the Viet Nam War.[1] Professor Moore has not persuaded me either that my approach is "simplistic" or that its application to Viet Nam is "unsound," but he has identified weaknesses and incompleteness in my earlier formulation. In addition, he has developed an alternative legal framework for assessing foreign intervention in violent struggles for the control of a national society. My objective in responding is to clarify the contending world order positions that each of us espouses. Although Professor Moore affirms and I deny the legality of the United States military role in Viet Nam, the main center of intellectual gravity in this debate is less passing judgment on the grand legal issue of American presence (at this stage, a legalistic exercise), than it is assessing the policy implications of the Viet Nam precedent for the future of international legal order. There is also a significant methodological issue at stake: Professor Moore challenges the efficacy of the analytic categories relied upon in the previous chapter, and prefers instead a policy-oriented contextual approach directed at the particularities of each civil strife situation. I feel confirmed in my judgment that the categorization of international violence, if not done in a mechanical or rigid fashion, contributes greater insight into the policy choices confronting government officials and their consequences, as well as avoids the worst forms of self-service that arise when a context is assessed by an interested party.[2]

Professor Moore and I agree that international law can serve as a significant source of guidance to the national policy-maker in the area of war and peace. International law implies a process of decision incorporating perspectives that tend to be left out of account when government officials develop national policies solely by considering capabilities, strategies, and current foreign policy goals that are designed to maximize the short-run "national advantage." International law contains rules and standards rooted in the cosmopolitan tradition

---

[1] Assessing the relative merits of the positions taken in the legal debate would certainly benefit from a reading of Professor Moore's article. Cf. John Norton Moore, "International Law and the United States Role in Viet Nam: A Reply," 76 *Yale Law Journal* 1051 (1967).

[2] A parallel argument is effectively presented in the context of the history of scientific inquiry by J. R. Pierce, *Symbols, Signals and Noise—The Nature and Process of Communication*, New York, Harper and Brothers, 1961, pp. 19-20.

of a community of nations, whereas foreign policy tends to be rooted in the more particularistic traditions of each state. The future of world legal order may depend to a great degree on the extent to which the decision process relied upon in principal states to form foreign policy can come increasingly to incorporate the more cosmopolitan perspectives.

International law has itself evolved through a process of decision in which national policies governing the appropriate uses of military power have been clarified by the assertion and counterassertion of adverse national claims buttressed by supporting explanations and rationale. This process is especially germane whenever the relevance of the rules to the claims of states is challenged on a legal basis, as it has been since the outset of major United States involvement in Viet Nam. The claims of governments to use or resist coercion serve as precedents for future claims and imply commitments to develop a certain kind of international legal system deemed beneficial both to the countries directly concerned and to the wider community of all states. My disagreement with Professor Moore centers upon the degree of discretion that international law presently accords to states with respect to the use of force in an international conflict resembling the one that has unfolded in Viet Nam in the years since 1954 and extends to the sorts of considerations (and their relative weight) that should have been taken into account in the decisions that led to the American military involvement at the various stages of its increasing magnitude. I would contend that the American military involvement resulted from a series of geopolitical miscalculations, as well as from a process of decision insensitive to world order considerations.

The Viet Nam conflict demonstrates the harmful consequences for the control of international violence that can arise from contradictory national interpretations of what constitutes "aggression" and what constitutes permissible acts of "defense." Given the decentralized character of international society, it becomes more important than ever, in my view, to inhibit unilateral recourse to violence arising from contradictory and subjective national interpretations of a conflict situation. The war in Viet Nam illustrates a situation in which it is "reasonable" for each side to perceive its adversary as guilty of unprovoked aggression.[3] The potential for military escalation that follows from each

[3] For a persuasive account by a psychologist as to why the North Vietnamese perceive the United States role in Viet Nam as aggression see Ralph White, "Misperception of Aggression in Vietnam," *Journal of International Affairs* xxi (1967), 123; for a more fully documented presentation of the same position by the same author see White, "Misperception and the Vietnam War," *Journal of Social Issues* xxii (1967), 1. The prospect of mutually contradictory perceptions of aggression held in good faith is central to my argument against Professor Moore's approach

side doing whatever it deems necessary to uphold its vital interests is an alarming freedom to grant governments in the nuclear age. My approach to these world order issues presupposes the central importance of establishing binding quasi-objective limits upon state discretion in international situations in which such contradictory inferences of "aggression" are characteristic. I would argue, also, that the whole effort of international law in the area of war and peace since the end of World War I has been to deny sovereign states the kind of unilateral discretion to employ force in foreign affairs that the United States has exercised in Viet Nam.[4]

Professor Moore appears content to endorse virtually unfettered sovereign discretion. In the role of a disinterested observer, he purports to pass judgment on the legal status of a contested claim to use force. Professor Moore sets forth a certain conception of world order that he posits as crucial for human welfare, and then proceeds to examine whether the claim to use force in the particular situation of Viet Nam is compatible with it. Every national decision-maker is expected to engage in the same process of assessment. But no account is taken of the serious problems of auto-interpretation that arise when recourse to force is contemplated or carried out in inflamed international settings. These problems arise because each side tends toward a self-righteous vindication of its own contentions and an equally dogmatic inattention to the merits of the adversary's position. Professor Moore's approach recalls the natural law tradition in which the purported deference to the normative restraints operative upon the behavior of a Christian prince turned out in practice to be little more than a technique of *post hoc* rationalization on the part of a government and its supporters. Surely, his analysis fails to accord reciprocal empathy to the adversary's reasonable perceptions as to who is responsible for what in Viet Nam. In fact, Professor Moore's endorsement of America's military role is neither widely nor wholeheartedly shared among states normally allied with the United States.[5]

---

to world order problems. He takes no account of the reality or hazard of such misperception.

[4] For a concise history of the efforts see Quincy Wright, *The Role of International Law in the Elimination of War*, Dobbs Ferry, New York, Oceana Publications, 1961.

[5] Anthony Lewis has summarized the situation in concise and moderate terms: "To go into the reasons for West European attitudes toward Vietnam would require rehearsing all the arguments about America's role there. Suffice it to say that only the British Government has had much favorable to say about American policy in Vietnam. No Government has had much favorable to say about American policy in Vietnam. No European country has a single soldier there. Much of the public on the Continent, rightly or not, see the situation as that of a huge power overreacting." Lewis, "Why Humphrey Got That Abuse in Europe," *New York Times*, April 16, 1967, § 4, p. 4, col. 4. Even the British Government has disassociated itself through a formal statement by her Prime Minister from United States bombing in June of

It seems plain enough that Communist-oriented observers would regard the air strikes by the United States against North Viet Nam as unprovoked "aggression." Suggestions have even been made by more militant opponents of the United States war actions that the passive role of the Soviet Union amounts to "appeasement" of the United States and that it is the Soviet Union, not the United States, that should heed the lesson of Munich.[6] Professor Moore's emphasis on the discretion of the United States to furnish military assistance to Saigon needs to be supplemented by a consideration of what military assistance it would be reasonable for the Soviet Union and China to give to Hanoi; would not North Viet Nam be entitled to act in collective self-defense in response to sustained, large-scale bombing of its territory? And what limits could be legally placed on its exercise of self-defense other than those self-imposed by prudence and incapacity?

If we examine the war in Viet Nam from the perspective of North Viet Nam and with the same deference to self-determined reasonableness that Professor Moore confers upon the United States Government then it seems clear that the failure of the war to reach global proportions has been a consequence of Soviet and Chinese restraint (or incapacity): that is, Moore's world order position seems to legalize almost unlimited escalation by adversaries that perceive an ally as a victim of "aggression," even though that perception is not vindicated by any wider community determination and even though disinterested and reasonable men disagree as to who did what to whom. My earlier classification of international conflict into three broad categories is based on the need to avoid the anarchic consequences of adversary perception by fixing arbitrary but definite legal limits upon divergent interpretations of the rights and duties of national governments that find themselves involved in Viet Nam-type situations.[7]

1966 of oil installations in Hanoi and Haiphong. For text of Mr. Wilson's statement see *British Record*, No. 12, July 14, 1966, Supp.

[6] See, e.g. a passage from an editorial appearing in the French intellectual journal *Les Temps Moderne*: "The lack of clarity, the prudent policy of 'wait and see' are the tombs of the Socialist and revolutionary movement; they pave the way for other disasters just as surely as nonintervention against Spanish Fascism in 1936 set the stage for 1940 and what followed. But the parallel extends beyond the Spanish Civil War; it includes the capitulations that preceded and followed the Munich Agreements.

"The United States is convinced that the Soviet Union will desist from any test of strength until the end." The editorial goes on to call for "Socialist counter-escalation" by means of Soviet rocket strikes at United States air and naval installations in the Pacific area. "Affirmative: A Deliberate Risk," translated and reprinted in *Atlas*, XII (November 1966), 19, 20.

[7] The basic rationale is set forth in Chapter VII, pp. 227-30. E.g. the United States is reported to have criticized the United Arab Republic for its attacks on Saudi Arabian border towns in the course of the struggle waged between the rival Yemeni factions for control of the Yemen. See *New York Times*, May 17, 1967, p. 1, col. 7.

Perhaps my position can be clarified by showing in a preliminary way why I reject the analogy between Viet Nam and Korea, an analogy that Professor Moore invokes to argue that similar defensive measures are appropriate in the two settings.[8] If the facts in Viet Nam are as Professor Moore and the United States Government contend, then it might be true that North Viet Nam is guilty of a *covert* equivalent of the aggression that was attempted *overtly* in 1950 by North Korea.[9] But the assessment of the facts in Viet Nam is subject to multiple interpretations by reasonable observers in a way that the facts in Korea were not. Only the Communist states argued seriously against the conclusion that North Korea was an aggressor. Her overt military attack was sufficiently clear to permit a global consensus to form in support of defensive action by South Korea. In contrast, the obscurity of the conflict in Viet Nam generates widespread disagreement outside the

---

[8] There are other significant differences, including a war ending in 1954 for control of the entire country, election provisions to translate this military outcome into political control at a time certain (1956), and a central government in Saigon that did not offer much prospect of governing South Viet Nam in any stable fashion even apart from Communist harassment. Part of the relevant background is the demonstrated competence of Ho Chi Minh to govern Viet Nam in an effective manner, a competence evident even in the writings of those who are hostile to Communism and opposed to reunification under Hanoi's control. The capacity to govern territorial units effectively in the areas of the world most vulnerable to domestic trauma is itself a valuable constituent of the sort of international stability that the United States aspires to achieve for the Afro-Asian world. The background of Vietnamese social and cultural history also supports strongly the interference of an autonomous Vietnamese spirit, one that above all would resist any effort at domination by the Chinese. Ho Chi Minh's reasonableness was demonstrated in the period after World War II when he cooperated successfully with non-Communist factions in Viet Nam and made notable concessions to the French in exchange for an acknowledgment of his leadership of an independent Republic of Viet Nam; the French later repudiated these negotiations and the first Indochina war was born. For the sense of background see Ellen Hammer, *The Struggle for Indochina 1940-1955*, Stanford, Stanford University Press, 1956; Lucien Bodard, *The Quicksand War*, Boston, Little, Brown, 1967; Joseph Buttinger, *Vietnam: The Dragon Embattled*, 2 vols., New York,

Praeger, 1967 (hereinafter cited as Buttinger).

These points have also been made effectively recently in Tom Farer, "The Enemy—Exploring the Sources of a Foreign Policy," *Columbia University Forum* (Spring 1967), 13; see especially his quotation of the remark of Walter Robertson, Assistant Secretary of State for Far Eastern Affairs (an anti-Communist of such extreme character as to antagonize Anthony Eden because of his "emotional" approach): "If only Ho Chi Minh were on our side we could do something about the situation. But unfortunately he is the enemy." *Id.*, p. 13.

[9] It is important, however, to appreciate the degree of ambiguity that necessarily inheres in the context of *covert* coercion unless the foreign state proclaims its aggressive design, as has the United Arab Republic in relation to Israel. Without such a proclamation, one never made by North Viet Nam, the attribution of motives is speculative and unconvincing, especially if the assumed motives are relied upon to justify major responsive violence. In Korea, it was North Korea that justified its recourse to *overt* coercion by vague and unsupportable allegations that South Korea was planning to attack North Korea.

Bernard Fall commenting on the assertion "that North Vietnamese infiltration into South Viet Nam is the equivalent of the North Korean invasion of the ROK" writes that the comparison "omits the embarrassing fact that anti-Diem guerrillas were active long before infiltrated North Vietnamese elements joined the fray." Bernard B. Fall, *The Two Viet-Nams*, 2nd rev. edn., New York, Praeger, 1967, p. 345.

Communist world as to whether either side can be termed "the aggressor," and impartial observers as august as the Secretary General of the United Nations[10] and the Pope [11] have repudiated any interpretation of the war in Viet Nam that identifies North Viet Nam as the aggressor. France has openly repudiated the United States conception of the war, and neutral public opinion at home and abroad is, to say the least, sharply split.[12] This situation of dissensus sharply distinguishes Viet Nam

[10] For representative statements of U Thant's attitude toward the Vietnam War see Falk, ed., *The Vietnam War and International Law*, Princeton, Princeton University Press, 1968, pp. 344-48. A convenient review of the Secretary General's relevant efforts through 1967 is contained in A. G. Mezerik, ed., *Viet Nam and the UN—1967*, New York, International Review Services, 1967, pp. 60-99.

[11] Cf. Pope Paul's Encyclical on Peace of Sept. 19, 1966, text in *New York Times*, September 20, 1966, p. 18, col. 2. Cf. for example, taking account of the tradition of indirect rhetoric, the following passage written with obvious application to war in Viet Nam: "We cry to them in God's name to stop. Men must come together and offer concrete plans and terms in all sincerity. A settlement should be reached now, even at the expense of some inconvenience or loss, for it may have to be made later in the train of bitter slaughter and involve great loss." The following sentence also confirms the emphasis upon the noncondemnation of either side as aggressor: "Now again, therefore, we lift up our voice, 'with piercing cry and with tears' (Hebrews, v. 7), very earnestly beseeching those who have charge of the public welfare to strive with every means available to prevent the further spread of the conflagration, and even to extinguish it entirely." More recently, Pope Paul VI has specifically urged the cessation of all forms of violence throughout Viet Nam, *New York Times*, May 25, 1967, p. 4, col. 4.

[12] I regard the unprecedented intensity, range, and character of the protest movement directed at the American military involvement in Viet Nam to be significantly relevant to an appraisal of the status of United States claims under international law. The standards governing the use of force in world affairs reflect moral attitudes toward those occasions upon which it is appropriate to rely upon military power. This widespread protest phenomenon reflects the moral conviction of people throughout the world that the United States is guilty of aggressive war in Viet

Nam; such a moral conviction is not inconsistent with the democratically based support for the war given by the American public, according priority to winning a war that should not have been fought rather than to accepting the need to acknowledge error. Edwin O. Reischauer, the former American Ambassador to Japan, has well-stated this orientation toward the war taken by those who continue to give their support, however, grudgingly, to the American effort in Viet Nam:

There is not much agreement in this country about the war in Vietnam, except that it is something we should have avoided. We are paying a heavy price for it—in lives, in national wealth and unity, and in international prestige and influence. The best we can hope for from the war is sufficient peace and stability to allow that small and weak country to get painfully to its feet at last; the worst is a nuclear conflict too horrible to contemplate. Edwin O. Reischauer, "What We Should Do Next in Asia," *Look*, April 4, 1967, p. 21.

It may be well to ponder the following paragraph from the editorial columns of *The New Republic*:

Simultaneously [with other beneficial international policies of the United States] Mr. Johnson is pushing the Vietnam war —which is a disastrous thing. It is all very well to say the country backs him. Governor Romney being the latest "me too" recruit. Yes, the polls show the public supports continued bombing, 67 percent. But a second series of polls shows only 37 percent backing Mr. Johnson's handling of the war. Reconciling these two views isn't really very difficult. The public loathes the war. It doesn't want defeat, but it wants *out*. The two moods conflict. It backs the bombing on the simplistic ground that it will end the war quickly. And it is taking out its resentment for the war dilemma consciously or unconsciously by making Mr. Johnson the scapegoat. *New Republic*, April 22, 1967, p. 2.

from Korea and strongly suggests that the discretion to act "defensively" requires some source of restraint more dependable than the wisdom of the belligerent states.[13]

The presence or absence of a consensus has considerable bearing on the legal status of a contested claim to use force in international society.[14] The Charter of the United Nations purports to restrict the uni-

---

Among those aspects of the protest against participation in the war that are most legally notable have been the efforts, never made in the Korean context to nearly the same extent, to obtain a determination by domestic courts that participation in the Viet Nam War is tantamount to the commission of a war crime; the reasoning being that the German and Japanese war crimes trials conducted after World War II concluded that an individual is criminally accountable for participation in a war of aggression (i.e. an illegal war) regardless of whether or not he is carrying out the orders of his government. There are also many cases now arising for the first time of "selective conscientious objection" in which individuals subject to the draft are claiming exemption not because they are opposed to war *in general* but because they oppose the Viet Nam War in *particular* on grounds of conscience. A dramatic instance of litigation to test whether there is a legal right of conscientious objection to a particular war has been filed by Capt. Dale E. Noyd of the Air Force Academy in the Federal District Court of Colorado in Denver. *New York Times,* April 20, 1967, p. 5, col. 3; for a description of the litigation see *Civil Liberties,* No. 245, April 1967, pp. 1, 5. For a continuing description of evidence supporting the invocation of selective conscientious objection in the Viet Nam context see the responsible reporting of the weekly British newspaper *Peace News,* the bimonthly American magazine *Viet Report,* or almost any French organ of opinion, (left, right, or center). For one (among many) vivid account of the horrors inflicted on Vietnamese society see Mary McCarthy, "Report from Vietnam II: The Problems of Success," *New York Review of Books,* May 4, 1967, p. 4.

Furthermore, for the first time during a period of war a group of international lawyers have gone on record against their own government to contend that the United States military involvement in Viet Nam is "illegal," and constitutes a violation of both international law and the U.S. Constitution. *Consultative Council of the Lawyers Committee on American*

Policy Towards Vietnam, Vietnam and International Law, 1967 (hereinafter cited as *Consultative Council*). The members of the Consultative Council are R. J. Barnet, R. A. Falk (Chairman), John H. E. Fried (Rapporteur), John H. Herz, Stanley Hoffmann, Wallace McClure, Saul H. Mendlovitz, Richard S. Miller, Hans J. Morgenthau, William G. Rice, Burns H. Weston and Quincy Wright.

Also for the first time since World War II there has been proposed a war crime tribunal to pass judgment on the United States role in Viet Nam and on the criminal responsibility of its President. Of course, Bertrand Russell's tribunal is a juridical farce, but the fact that it is plausible to contemplate such a proceeding and to obtain for its tribunal several celebrated individuals bears witness to the general perception of the war. For Jean-Paul Sartre's explanation of why he agreed to serve as a judge on the Russell tribunal see Sartre, "Imperialist Morality," *New Left Review,* XLI (1967), 3.

See also the *Policy Committee, Senate Republican Blue Book on Viet Nam* (May 1, 1967); for the text of its principal conclusions questioning the entire basis of the war see excerpts from G.O.P. Paper on War, *New York Times,* May 2, 1967, p. 10, col. 3.

[13] The vagueness of the justification is accentuated in consequence by the gradual evolution of "the commitment." What started off in Viet Nam as a reluctant and indirect involvement that needed no special justification was successively widened and deepened until the involvement itself became the principal justification. With over 400,000 Americans fighting in Viet Nam and with casualties continuing to mount, there is a sense that the American effort must not be in vain; the consequence is an apparently irreversible government commitment to use military means to accomplish a political objective—namely, to defeat the Vietcong insurrection, without according any governmental legitimacy to the N.L.F.

[14] The relevance of an international consensus to the legality of contested national action is considered in Falk, "On

lateral discretion of states to use force to resolve international conflicts.[15] In cases where a claim of self-defense is made and challenged, the burden of justification is upon the claimant. It is always possible to argue that a use of force is "defensive" and that it promotes world order by inhibiting "aggression." Therefore, fairly clear community standards would be needed to ensure that what is called "defensive" is defensive; in the absence of clear community standards it becomes important to allow international institutions to determine whether recourse to "defensive force" is justified by a prior "armed attack." Where there are no generally accepted objective standards and where rivals put forward contradictory factual interpretations it becomes difficult or impossible to mobilize a consensus in the international institutions entrusted with the maintenance of peace and security.[16] Viet Nam

the Quasi-Legislative Competence of the General Assembly," 60 *American Journal of International Law* 782 (1966). And see the dissenting opinion of Judge Tanaka in the South West Africa Cases for an analysis in the setting of human rights of the shift from an emphasis upon sovereign autonomy to community solidarity in determining the character of international legal obligations. Judgment in the South West Africa Cases, July 18, 1966, [1966] International Court of Justice, 248, 292-94.

[15] For a helpful exposition of the restrictive intention of the relevant Charter provisions see Louis Henkin, "Force, Intervention, and Neutrality in Contemporary International Law," 1963 *American Society of International Law* 147; Philip C. Jessup, *A Modern Law of Nations*, New York, Macmillan, 1948, pp. 165-67; in this context it is not necessary to contend that Article 51 restricts traditional self-defense in terms of some rigid conception of "armed attack," but only that the discretion of states to have recourse to force in self-defense is subject to justification and review. See, e.g. D. W. Bowett, *Self-Defence in International Law*, New York, Praeger, 1958, pp. 216-18, 241, 244-45, 261, emphasizing the importance of restricting discretionary recourse to self-defense, especially on a collective basis, in the Viet Nam-type situation.

[16] Even a defensive alliance such as SEATO has been unable to maintain its solidarity in the face of the disputed facts and policies generated by the Viet Nam conflict. France and Pakistan, both members, refuse to give their assent to SEATO's endorsement of the American "interpretation" of the war in Viet Nam. It should be recalled that SEATO was a pact among anti-Communist states determined to resist the coercive spread of Asian Communism, including explicitly its spread to South Viet Nam; the non-Communist neutralist states of Asia are, without exception, even more dubious about the American "interpretation." The relevant point is that a claim to be acting in a "defensive" way when force is used against a foreign society has no legal status unless it is supported by some kind of international authorization that commands respect; otherwise it is merely a contention by an adversary determined to make unilateral use of military power against a foreign society.

A study of South Viet Nam attitudes toward the war in Viet Nam indicates that even as late as 1966-67 the majority of South Vietnamese reject the official United States version of "defensive" action. A poll was conducted for the Columbia Broadcasting Company by Opinion Research Corporation, a respected professional organization; 1,545 persons living in 5 major cities and 55 hamlets were interviewed. Those interviewed were limited to civilians of voting age living in "secured areas," those not under Vietcong control. The poll took place between November 24, 1966 and February 1, 1967. When asked who was responsible for continuing the war 31 per cent blamed the Vietcong and only 12 per cent blamed the Government of North Viet Nam; when asked whether bombing should be continued against villages suspected of containing the Vietcong 46 per cent favored an end to bombing while 37 per cent wanted it continued; when asked whether to stress negotiations with North Viet Nam or to extend military operations to North Viet Nam 60 per cent favored more emphasis on negotiations whereas

presents such a situation of uncertainty and institutional paralysis. What restraints upon sovereign discretion to use force remain relevant? The appraisals of disinterested international civil servants, especially the Secretary General of the United Nations, are distinctly relevant in this setting. The Secretary General contributes an impartial perspective and can, as U Thant has chosen to do with respect to Viet Nam, delineate the character of reasonable behavior by the adversary parties.[17] Normally such an official will refrain from judging the behavior of the participants in a conflict that cannot be handled by agreement in the political organs. The persistent refusal of the United States to comply with U Thant's proposals is indicative of its unilateral approach to the determination of the legitimacy of a contested use of international force.[18] The essence of a law-oriented approach to the use of force

only about 14 per cent favored increased military action; and finally when asked whether they favored reunification after the end of the war, 83 per cent were reported in favor and only 5 per cent opposed. *New York Times*, March 22, 1967, p. 10, col. 7. The remarkable thing about this poll is that among strong anti-Communist South Vietnamese (65 per cent blamed the Communist side for the continuation of the war and only 5 per cent blamed the anti-Communist side) exposed primarily to government propaganda there still appears to be a rejection of the American idea that the war is a consequence of "aggression from the North." The attitudes on reunification also sharply question the Saigon-Washington insistence on separate sovereignty for the North and the South. See the similar character of an anti-Communist, anti-American interpretation of the war by a distinguished Buddhist in South Viet Nam, T. Hanh, *Vietnam Lotus in a Sea of Fire*, New York, Hill and Wang, 1967.

[17] The essential aspect of a legal settlement is the search for impartial sources of decision. It is the impartial decision-maker that is in the best position to assess the relative merits of adversary positions. This does not assure correct or just decisions in any particular instance, but merely that there will be a legal quality for the decision. The Secretary General of the United Nations is the most authoritative impartial decision-maker in the international system, especially in relation to members of the United Nations. To deny his role or to ignore his recommendation is to subordinate the process of impartial decision to the process of unilateral decision, tending thereby to rely on power rather than law

to shape the outcome of controversy.

[18] The opposition of the United States to the efforts of U Thant to work for a settlement are summarized in American Friends Service Committee, *Peace in Viet Nam*, 1966, pp. 50-52; Franz Schurmann, Peter Dale Scott, and Reginald Zelnik, *The Politics of Escalation in Vietnam*, Boston, Beacon Press, 1966, pp. 135-318. On June 20, 1966 U Thant made a three-point proposal for ending the war in Viet Nam:

1. Unconditional cessation of bombing in North Viet Nam;
2. Scaling down of military operations in South Viet Nam;
3. Inclusion of the National Liberation Front in any negotiations.

New York Times, June 21, 1966, p. 1, col. 5. The failure of the United States to accept this proposal, consisting according to U Thant of those steps that "alone can create the conditions" leading to a peaceful settlement, is indicative of its unilateral approach to the use of military power in Viet Nam. U Thant, as Secretary General, represents the voice of the international community, a voice that deserves to be heeded especially by a Great Power using its military power to overwhelm a small state. The role of the Secretary General in identifying reasonable conduct for parties in conflict is especially great when the political organs have failed to discharge their responsibility to maintain international peace and security. As in other dealings with the United Nations during the Viet Nam War the United States has made *pro forma* gestures indicating its acceptance of the Secretary General's role. See, e.g. Arthur J. Goldberg's letter to U Thant in which it is said that "the United States is to submit claims to the best available procedures for community review and to restrict force to the levels authorized.[19]

A second kind of restraint in a situation of ambiguity is to confine violence within existing international boundaries. The decision by the United States to bomb North Viet Nam and to take military action in the territory of Laos and Cambodia is further disregard for available limits upon the self-interpretation of legal rights.[20] It is true that the

---

Government will cooperate fully with you in getting such discussion started promptly [on ending the war] and in bringing them to a successful completion." Text, *New York Times*, December 20, 1966, p. 6, col. 4. The United States will cooperate fully provided that it does not have to alter its belligerent and political posture. U Thant is setting forth his conception of reasonable preconditions for peace talks. What does our cooperation entail if it does not lead to an acceptance of these preconditions? Our noncooperation with U Thant is heightened by the fact that the preconditions he describes are those that seem calculated to bring the war to an end and to initiate negotiations on a reasonable basis that corresponds to the domestic balance of forces. Negotiations would proceed on an unnatural basis if either the suspension of bombing was conditional— it would be a club of death suspended by a powerful state over the destinies of a weak one—or the N.L.F. was not accorded some degree of legitimacy as a political force in South Viet Nam of a character equal to that of the Saigon regime. The insistence on nonrecognition is part of the effort to negotiate as if the N.L.F. is a creature of North Viet Nam rather than a political entity with a reality of its own. President Johnson has often repeated the idea that during the negotiations "the Vietcong will have no difficulty having their views heard," but this is not a very satisfactory assurance for an insurgent faction that has fought for over a decade to control South Viet Nam. Transcript of President's News Conference on the Guam Parley, *New York Times*, March 22, 1967, p. 11, col. 3. It does not make the consent of the N.L.F. an ingredient of settlement, nor does it give to the N.L.F. any of the formal prerogatives of the Saigon regime. In effect, the civil war is ended not as a stalemate, but as a victory for the government side as it remains the sole constituted political elite.

[19] We associate the intervention of law in human affairs with the role of the third-party decision-maker who is entrusted with the task of sorting out adversary contentions. International society as it is decentralized often successfully works out the content of reasonableness through action and interaction of adversary parties, provided the issues at stake are not vital to national security or national honor. In the context of force, however, the differential of power between adversaries of unequal strength influences their degree of flexibility in responding to counterclaims; the differences between the results of adversary interaction and of impartial third-party judgment are likely to be pronounced. The substitution of law for force in any social order involves, then, the gradual replacement of the ideology of self-help by that of third-party judgment. Perhaps, the clearest jurisprudential discussion of the limits of law in a decentralized political system is contained in Hans Kelsen, *Principles of International Law*, Robert W. Tucker, ed., 2nd rev. edn., New York, Rinehart, 1966, pp. 3-87.

[20] Both sides have violated "the sovereignty" of Laos and Cambodia, but the United States has frequently bombed infiltrators and supply lines within the territory of both states, thereby expanding further the extra-national scope of violence beyond South Viet Nam. See Senator Mike Mansfield, et al., Report to Senate Foreign Relations Committee, 89th Cong., 2nd Sess., *The Vietnam Conflict: The Substance and the Shadow*, pp. 8-10 (Committee Print, 1966) (hereinafter cited as *The Mansfield Report*). An equivalent action by North Viet Nam or the Soviet Union would be to attack the United States air bases in Thailand. Such an expansion of the arena of combat would move the conflict dramatically closer to the threshold of general warfare. It is important to emphasize that the limited scope of the war in Viet Nam is a consequence of the failure of the Soviet Union and China to take *equivalent action* on behalf of Hanoi; such a failure is especially important in view of the United States demand that Hanoi take equivalent action in exchange for an end to bombing. See note 27 *infra*.

United States is *not* yet using all the military power at its disposal against North Viet Nam, but such restraint is itself based on the exercise of discretion rather than upon deference to community procedures or to quasi-objective standards of limitation.[21]

In this respect, the mode of Type I conflict (Korea) allows proportionate defense responses including unilateral action against the attacking state,[22] whereas in a Type II or III conflict (Viet Nam), third-party military action is either prohibited altogether or its scope confined to the political entity wherein the struggle is going on. In either event, the tendency to escalate is curtailed. My categorization of international conflict is intended to guide decision-makers and observers toward a sense of what is reasonable in a particular situation. A strong element

[21] The United States reserves the discretion to decide for itself the degree of military force that it requires to secure North Viet Nam's acquiescence. In this David and Goliath situation, David is on a rack of death that has been slowly tightened over the years by a process we describe as "escalation." Goliath has had and continues to have the capacity at any point to kill David, but has sought instead to inflict pain and to threaten increasing pain until David gives in to the demands of Goliath. There is no reciprocity in such a situation of inequality. To claim restraint for Goliath is to ignore the rationale for this way of proceeding by stages. Among other factors to bear in mind is that Goliath knows that David has powerful, Goliath-like friends that may enter the scene more actively. See, e.g. the report of Harry Ashmore's visit to Hanoi on behalf of the Center for the Study of Democratic Institutions in which he quotes "a Colonel of the North Vietnamese General Staff" who "answered very solemnly" a question about his estimate "of North Vietnam's capacity to resist the American troops":

We've thought about this a great deal. We think we can handle up to 2,000,000 Americans. This assumes that you do not increase your bombing beyond its present level. I think your combat troops will concede that we are masters of guerrilla war. We should be—we've been at it for twenty-five years. We are far less dependent on heavy supplies than your army. We are accustomed to fighting in this terrain of jungle and mountains and this advantage offsets the undoubted superiority of your sophisticated weapons and planes. This is why we think we can handle up to 2,000,000 of your troops, and stay here the rest of

the century if necessary. Of course, if you put in more than 2,000,000 soldiers, or if you escalate the bombing to the point where you completely destroy our communications, then we have to accept volunteers from China, from Russia, and it would be a new war. It would no longer be our war. It would be World War III.

Mr. Ashmore commented that:

I have to assume an element of propaganda in this, but I also say that I believe the Colonel meant what he said, and was consciously reflecting the considered judgment of the North Vietnamese government. Harry Ashmore, "Pacem in Terris II: Mission to North Vietnam," *Center Diary,* March-April 1967, p. 17.

[22] Korea is not truly an example of Type I, but of Type IV, because the United States role was authorized by the United Nations; see *infra,* p. 273 for explanation of Type IV. Nevertheless, to point up the relationship between Korea and Viet Nam it is possible to pierce the cosmopolitan veil, emphasize Soviet opposition, and question the propriety of an authorization obtained in the Security Council during the Soviet boycott, and thereby view the response in Korea *as if* it proceeded without benefit of United Nations approval. In that case, Korea would appear to be an instance of Type I, authorizing whatever military action is needed to restore the *status quo ante* the armed attack. On this basis I believe that the defensive armies should not have proceeded beyond the 38th parallel, although it would have been permissible to commit war acts against North Korean territory so as to restore the *status quo ante.*

of national discretion remains. The limits on international violence are only quasi-objective restrictions upon sovereign prerogatives.[23] There is also some uncertainty as to whether a particular conflict belongs in one category rather than another. So long as the organized international community is unable to determine the limits on authorized violence, thereby placing the conflict within Type IV (see next paragraph) it remains necessary to rely upon national discretion. The objective of articulating Types I-III is to enable a more rational exercise of national discretion through the clarification of the relationship between fac-

[23] The Legal Adviser, Leonard Meeker, finds no difficulty in reconciling my categories of analysis with United States policy in Viet Nam: "The evidence does not allow for the conclusion that the war in Viet-Nam was ever a simple category-one situation. It was probably, for quite some period of time, a category-two situation. By the end of 1964, however, it had become very clearly a category-three situation." Leonard Meeker, "Viet-Nam and the International Law of Self-Defense," *U.S. State Department Bulletin*, LVI, 1967, pp. 54, 59. Mr. Meeker merely characterizes the facts to support the American legal position, including the shift of the war into "the third category." (Type I) By the end of 1964, mainly over a period of four years, about 40,000 are reported to have infiltrated from North Viet Nam according to official United States statistics. Most of those infiltrated during this period were ethnic Southerners that joined up with Vietcong units. There are several factors that militate against Mr. Meeker's inference of "armed attack" (that is, category three): First, the insurgency preexisted North Vietnamese infiltration; as Fall notes "there had been a fairly strong anti-Diem insurgent current of non-Communist origins even before the 1956 deadline on elections between the two zones went by. . . ." Bernard B. Fall, *The Two Viet-Nams*, 2nd rev. edn., New York, Praeger, 1967, p. 356 (cf. map showing pattern of insurgent controls as of 1962-63, p. 254); second, the Saigon regime was enabled to resist the N.L.F. in the years before 1961 only because it was given such large amounts of economic support by the United States in the years after 1954; as the first Mansfield Report observes "in matters of defense, internal stability and economic support, the Vietnamese Government has come to depend almost wholly on the United States for outside assistance. In terms of aid, the assumption of this preponderant responsibility has meant U.S. outlays of $1.4 billion

for economic assistance during the period of 1955-62. This economic aid has had some effect on Vietnamese development, but its primary purpose has been to sustain the Vietnamese economy so that it, in turn, could maintain the burden of a military establishment which has been upward of 150,000 men for the past half decade. On top of the economic aid, there have also been provided large amounts of military equipment and supplies and training for the Vietnamese Army, Navy, and Air Force and for other defense purposes. For the period 1955-62 the total aid of all kinds in Viet Nam stands at more than $2 billion." *The Mansfield Report*, Appendix II, p. 19. For tables on the degree of United States involvement since 1954, see George McTurnan Kahin and John W. Lewis, *The United States in Vietnam*, New York, Dial Press, 1967, pp. 73, 185 (hereinafter cited as Kahin and Lewis).

The point is that North Vietnamese military assistance to an ongoing insurgency was a proportionate response at all stages to the extent of United States involvement on behalf of Saigon. And when one considers that North Viet Nam had a reasonable (if not absolutely assured) expectation that the Geneva settlement would lead to unification under their control after a period of transition enabling the French to depart, then the American interposition of a powerful non-Vietnamese "presence" must also enter into an appraisal of North Viet Nam's pre-1965 role. In such a context it seems unreasonable and without legal foundation to construe North Viet Nam's military assistance to the Vietcong as becoming an attack by one country on another. Without such a premise of attack, the United States response against North Vietnamese territory would be "unprovoked aggression." Recourse to self-defense implies a prior armed attack, and that is why the United States position depends on "the armed attack" taking place before bombing the North began in February 1965.

tual patterns and legal expectations. If states would adhere in practice to these limits, *ex parte* interpretations of fact and of law on claims to use violence in international society would decline in importance.

Professor Moore's world order position, as presently stated, ignores the relevance of international institutions and of a supranational perspective to an assessment of the legal status of a controverted use of military power. To emphasize the problem of curtailing national discretion in a world of political conflict I would now add Type IV to the previous three types.[24] Type IV conflict exists whenever a competent international organization of global (IVa) or regional (IVb) dimensions authorizes the use of force.[25] Type IVa can be illustrated by reference to United Nations actions in Korea (1950), Suez (1956), Cyprus, and the Congo (1960). The authorization or prohibition of violence by the United Nations resolves the issue of legality, even though a particular decision may be arbitrary or unjust in any given set of circumstances.[26] The point here is that Type IV entails an authoritative consensus that may be absent in Types I-III.[27] Thus, the

[24] In my earlier chapter, then, Korea and Suez are not properly examples of Type I after there was authorization of defensive action by the United Nations. Type I becomes Type IV as soon as the United Nations itself acts or authorizes action. The description, then, of Type I, found on pp. 227-28, should be amended accordingly. Types II and III can also be transferred into Type IV, although the conjectural nature of the facts and the less direct connection to international peace and security makes such a transfer less likely to take place. The Indian attack upon Goa and the Chinese attack upon Tibet are examples of Type I provided the victim entities are entitled to the status of "states." Goa's defensive prerogatives are also qualified by the limited legitimacy of colonial title to territory as of 1961.

[25] The legal status of Type IVb is more problematical than that of Type IVa. For one thing regional organizations are themselves subject to regulation by the Security Council (Article 53(1) says that "no enforcement action shall be taken under regional arrangements or by regional agencies without the authorization of the Security Council"). For another, the opposition of the Arab League to Israel, of the Organization of African Unity to South Africa, and of the Organization of American States to Castro's Cuba points to the danger of "aggression" under the legitimizing aegis of supranationalism. At the same time, the existence of regional support for recourse to coercion is a factor

that alters the legal status of a controversial use of military power. It is important to distinguish a regional actor—such as the OAS—from an *ex parte* defensive alliance—such as SEATO. Authorization by SEATO would not move the conflict into Type IVb, although the absence of such authorization might cast light on claims to respond within the framework of Type I.

[26] This possibility leads Julius Stone, among others, to deny altogether the restrictive impact of the Charter system of controls upon the discretion of sovereign states. Julius Stone, *Aggression and World Order*, Berkeley, University of California Press, 1958, pp. 1-3, 78-103.

[27] In the absence of an authoritative consensus on a global level that embodies divergent perspectives, the construction of second-order constraints upon adversary perspectives is the essential task of international law. Types I-III provide quasi-objective guidelines that tend to confine an international conflict. Departures from these guidelines could be justified legally by exceptional circumstances and for specific objectives. But the second-order system of constraint depends on a fair correlation of the conflict with the system of graduated categories. The United States insistence on viewing North Viet Nam's role as warranting a Type I response is destructive of second-order constraints as the basic categorization does not command respect from many uncommitted observers. The generalized bombing of North Viet

context of the prior chapter and of this reply to Moore is provided by the conflict in Viet Nam, a conflict in which the United Nations has not been able to act collectively through its main political organs.[28] This context is in the range of Types I-III.[29]

Having set forth the factors that shape my world order position, I will turn now to Professor Moore's specific criticisms of my approach. He has three main objectives:

Nam could not be easily justified as an exception to Type II. Specific attacks upon extraterritorial guerrilla sanctuaries might be justified if the conflict was otherwise contained within Type II limits. But the objectives of bombing North Viet Nam seem primarily connected with an overall effort to secure their acquiescence to our conception of the war in South Viet Nam. President Johnson's letter of March 1, 1967 to Senator Jackson gives the Government's rationale for bombing North Viet Nam in fairly complete terms: significantly, this letter ends by saying "we shall persist with our operations in the North—until those who launched this aggression are prepared to move seriously to reinstall the agreements whose violations has brought the scourge of war to Southeast Asia." Earlier the letter says that bombing "will end when the other side is willing *to take equivalent action . . .*" (emphasis supplied). See "President Reviews U.S. Position on Bombing of North Viet-Nam," *U.S. State Department Bulletin,* LVI, 1967, pp. 514, 516. What is equivalent action if it is conceded that extraterritorial violence is, at best, an *extraordinary* incident of a Type II conflict? Supplying and sending troops to aid the N.L.F. is a *normal* incident of Type II conflict. To demand, as seems implied by the official United States position, the elimination of a normal claim by a third-party state in exchange for the termination of an extraordinary claim (and in Viet Nam the extraordinary nature of the claim is aggravated by its assertion in extravagant, unspecific, and accelerating form) by its third-party opponent seems highly unreasonable. It is worth recalling that the United States original justification for bombing North Viet Nam in February 1965 was formulated in the restrictive and exceptional sense—explaining the logic of Type II—as a reprisal for Vietcong attacks on United States airfields in South Viet Nam; it is worth noting that the legal reflex in February 1965 was in the manner of Type II, not Type I. This is worth noting because of the subsequent official explanations that Viet Nam clearly belonged to Type I by the end of 1964. Cf. note 23

supra; see also The Legality of United States Participation in the Defense of Viet-Nam, Office of the Legal Adviser, Department of State, 112 *Congressional Record* 5274 (daily edn. March 10, 1966). For original reliance on a reprisal theory see *supra,* pp. 244-45; for legal criticism of even the attempt to rely on a reprisal theory see *Consultative Council,* pp. 53-57.

[28] But the United States bears a heavy burden of responsibility for the inaction of the United Nations as a consequence of the following considerations:

(1) Noncompliance with the proposals of the Secretary General, U Thant;

(2) Nonsubmission of the claim to act in self-defense to the Security Council or General Assembly for serious community review;

(3) Refusal in early stages of conflict to seek a peaceful settlement through negotiations;

(4) Alienation of China from the United Nations by its continuing exclusion from the activities of the Organization;

(5) Ambiguity as to the sincerity of United States offers to negotiate, as a consequence of coupling peace moves with steps up the escalation ladder. For scholarly documentation see Franz Schurmann, Peter Dale Scott, and Reginald Zelnik, *The Politics of Escalation in Vietnam,* Boston, Beacon Press, 1966.

[29] The important distinction is between the sort of legal order that exists for Types I-III and for Type IV:

Types I-III are governed by second-order constraints self-imposed by sovereign states and based upon such quasi-objective sources of guidance and limitations as past practice, public opinion, recommendation of impartial third-party actors such as the Secretary General and the Pope, and well-defined international boundaries.

Type IV conflicts are governed by first-order constraints consisting of the determinations of international institutions. First-order constraints are *procedural* outcomes on a supranational level, whereas second-order constraints are *substantive* outcomes on a national level.

(1) I have construed the Viet Nam facts in a one-sided manner;

(2) My system of categorization imposes arbitrary limits on a state using force for defensive purposes;

(3) My system really declares my views as to what international law *ought to be* although it pretends to be a statement of present legal obligations binding upon a state.

Professor Moore's first principal criticism pertains primarily to my argument that it would have been appropriate to regard the conflict in Viet Nam as an example of a Type III conflict, that is, an example of civil strife internal to one country. The second and third criticisms pertain primarily to my chief argument that the conflict in Viet Nam, whatever its early history, has become an example of Type II conflict, that is, an example of civil strife in South Viet Nam with substantial intervention on behalf of the two contending factions, the Saigon regime and the National Liberation Front (N.L.F.); (these criticisms are discussed below in Section II).

I. The Rationale Restated in Support of a
Type III Classification of the Viet Nam War

Let me state clearly that when large-scale military participation by the United States in the war began to take place—say in 1963—it became appropriate to treat the conflict as Type II. North Vietnamese large-scale military participation on behalf of the N.L.F. accentuates this classification of the war. My principal contention denies that the *factual* basis exists to warrant treating the Viet Nam War as belonging in Type I (which would authorize extraterritorial defensive measures) and, as a correlate denies that there exists a *legal* basis for extraterritorial violence if the war is classified as Type II. However, it remains important to consider the conflict in Viet Nam as belonging originally in Type III so as to appreciate the principal role of the United States in converting the war into Type II, such a conversion involving conduct itself seriously at variance with my conception of the requirements of world order.[30] It is also important to acknowledge that the expectations

---

[30] The transformation from Type III to Type II is a matter of *policy* rather than *law* in any normal sense; "In sum, international law has never been equipped to intervene in civil war situations." Wolfgang Friedmann, "Intervention, Civil War and the Role of International Law," *Proceedings, the American Society of International Law, 1965*, pp. 67, 74. There are no criteria that are usefully available to identify prohibited interventions, although some efforts have been recently made to prohibit overt and direct military participation. See Tom Farer, "Intervention in Civil Wars: A Modest Proposal," 67 *Columbia Law Review* 266 (1967). The real issues of policy confronting the United States are the degree to which it reacts to revolutionary events in the Afro-Asian and Latin American countries as properly hostile to its interests. For critical accounts of this aspect of foreign policy, see Edmund Stillman and William Pfaff, *Power and Impotence*, New York, Random House, 1966, esp. pp. 151-59, 184-226; Howard Zinn, *Vietnam: The Logic of Withdrawal*, Boston,

of North Viet Nam and of the N.L.F. were likely formed prior to the overt, large-scale intervention by the United States—that is, when the conflict still belonged in the Type III category. Clarifying the factual and legal reasons for regarding the early stages of the war as Type III is very centrally related, in my view, to the North Vietnamese perception of what would constitute a reasonable outcome of the Viet Nam War (regardless of its subsequent Type II history).

In considering the war in Viet Nam as belonging in Type III, especially in its early (pre-1963) phases, I intended a two-pronged argument: first a civil war between the two factions in the South and second, a civil war between the Northern and Southern Zones. My argument was essentially that in either case such a conflict should be determined by the domestic balance of forces and, that, in the setting of Viet Nam under either interpretation the anti-Saigon "entity" would have prevailed but for American (that is, non-Vietnamese) military intervention. My reasoning is essentially as follows: South Viet Nam had evolved, despite the contrary intentions of the Geneva settlement, as a separate *de facto* political entity, and the N.L.F. emerged as a

---

Beacon Press, 1967, pp. 37-50; and see T. Hanh, *Vietnam Lotus in a Sea of Fire*, New York, Hill and Wang, 1967, pp. 60-68 for the entangling of nationalism and Communism in the Viet Nam setting. For a pro-Administration judgment of the American response to foreign revolutionary activity see Walt W. Rostow, "The Great Transition: Tasks of the First and Second Postwar Generations," *U.S. State Department Bulletin*, XLVI, 1967, p. 491.

The transformation from Type II to Type I is regulated by international law as it implies violent conflict *between* sovereign states rather than *within* a sovereign state. Initiating recourse to international violence, as distinct from interventionary violence, requires the prior occurrence of an armed attack.

The consequences of this difference between shifting from III to II and from III or II to I are to make different kinds of arguments appropriate in each context. At the same time the differences in argument can be overstated, as the specific policies guiding the assertion of a claim to act within the legal frameworks of either Types II or I (say, Viet Nam as of 1965) tends to establish a precedent for others to act in a similar manner in future situations and facilitates the accretion process that terminates in the evolution of new legal expectation as to the character of permissible conduct. The assertion that may remain obscure is that a successful claim by a state to act is itself an ingredient of what is permissible, regardless of whether prior to the claim it had been assumed to be illegal. Furthermore, other states may invoke the claim as a precedent to vindicate a controversial claim of their own and weaken the contentions of those adversary states alleging illegality. To be specific, in the future a state will be able to vindicate legally a Type I response (i.e. self-defense) in what had been assumed to be a Type II (i.e. counter-intervention) situation before the United States carried the war in Viet Nam to North Viet Nam. In a context where legal expectations have been regarded as well-fixed policy, considerations may incline an actor to posit a legislative claim which, if effectively asserted and accepted by the wider community, tends to reshape legal expectations. In both contexts, therefore, there is an unavoidable discretionary role played by the state with the capability to act in different ways, but in the interventionary axis of decision (III-II) there is less disposition to regard the decision to intervene as a weakening of legal order than in the armed-attack-self-defense axis of decision wherein legal expectation of fairly settled character had been thought to exist, especially in view of the coordinated United States-Soviet opposition to the French-British-Israeli recourse to overt violence in the Suez campaign of 1956.

sufficiently indigenous opposition movement to be deemed South Vietnamese in character rather than as an "agent" or "puppet" of North Viet Nam.[31] In this circumstance the outcome of the N.L.F.-Saigon struggle would have been an N.L.F. victory if both the United States and North Viet Nam had remained out of the conflict, and the quantum and phasing of United States and North Vietnamese aid to the contending factions was imbalanced in favor of Saigon at every stage subsequent to 1954. This interpretation of the early stages of the Vietnamese conflict seems to enjoy the support of almost all disinterested analysts.[32]

The second prong of the Type III analysis conceives of the war in Viet Nam as a civil war between South Viet Nam and North Viet Nam waged for control of the state of Viet Nam. According to Professor Moore, such a characterization of the war overlooks the separateness as of 1960 of these two political entities, as well as the essential ambiguity of the Geneva settlement, especially with regard to reunification. Professor Moore, although sensitive to the particularities of the division of Viet Nam in 1954, closely associates the status of Viet Nam with such other divided countries as Korea, Germany, and China. Force across a partition boundary is, as he properly points out, dangerous to world peace since the de facto divisions express major unresolved conflicts between the Communist and non-Communist worlds. I challenge Professor Moore's analysis on two principal grounds:

(1) The division in Viet Nam is not usefully comparable on policy grounds to that of other divided countries;

(2) The defeat of the French by the Vietminh as embodied in the Geneva settlement of 1954, the attitude of Saigon toward the Geneva Accords, the Southern locus of the uprising, the small magnitude of Northern interference as compared to the direct and indirect military contributions of the United States Government to Saigon, the non-viability of the regime in the South, and the national popularity of Ho

---

[31] To take seriously the issue of the autonomy of the N.L.F. it would be necessary to compare its dependence on Hanoi with Saigon's dependence on Washington at the various phases of the war. Cf. Jean Lacouture, *Vietnam: Between Two Truces*, New York, Vintage Books, 1966, pp. 61-119 (hereinafter cited as Lacouture); Kahin and Lewis, esp. chapter entitled "Americanization of the War," pp. 151-80. The autonomy of Saigon's discretion to terminate the war on its *own terms*, as distinct from those insisted upon by Washington, is certainly as doubtful as is the autonomy of the N.L.F. to terminate the war on conditions at variance with those insisted upon by Hanoi.
As to the extent of the American role at earlier preinsurgency stages of South Viet Nam's history see Ellen Hammer, *The Struggle for Indo-China 1940-1955*, Stanford, Stanford University Press, 1956, pp. 346-64; "However much American officials may have wished to regard southern Viet Nam as independent, the fact and the promise of substantial American aid to the Nationalist regime gave them such influence that in the fall of 1954 it was the United States, not the Vietnamese people, who decided that Ngo Dinh Diem would continue to be Prime Minister of southern Viet Nam." *Id.*, p. 356.

[32] Lacouture, pp. 186-90; Kahin and Lewis, pp. 127-206; *The Mansfield Report*, pp. 11-12.

Chi Minh are factors that when taken into joint account make it misleading to talk of "the aggression" of the North.

THE GENEVA SETTLEMENT: FACE-SAVING OR PARTITION

Sir Anthony Eden, introducing his discussion of the Geneva Accords in 1954 and his ideas for settling the present war in Viet Nam, has said that: "No agreement can be so drawn as to be proof against every malevolent intention. That is why the observance of international engagements is the first condition of any peaceful society. Once allow treaties to be torn up with impunity and the world is headed for trouble; violators soon have imitators."[33] It seems to me that Professor Moore is somewhat cavalier in explaining away United States insistence on non-implementation of the election provision in the Final Declaration by setting it off against a Western preference for "partition" that was consistently denied both by the language of the Agreement on the Cessation of Hostilities in Viet Nam and of the Final Declaration.[34]

Ignoring the relevance of formal international engagements, Professor Moore also supports the double standard whereby North Viet Nam's alleged export of coercion through the N.L.F. is viewed as a material breach of the Geneva Accords, whereas the United States provision of military aid to Saigon, even though it admittedly preceded North Vietnamese coercion, is approved of as a "permitted defensive response." Moore facilely circumvents the determination by the International Control Commission that both sides were guilty of violations of the Geneva Accords which were not weighted as to relative seriousness, by asserting that "this neutral reporting proves little."[35] In fact, for Professor Moore the determination of the I.C.C. proves less than does the unsupported balancing of these two violations by an interested party—namely, the United States Government. As elsewhere in his analysis Professor Moore seems to endorse the discretionary competence of sovereign states at the expense either of binding international arrangements or of the determinations of impartial machinery set up to implement these arrangements. If the United States was so convinced that its aid to Saigon was a permissible defensive response then

[33] Anthony Eden, *Toward Peace in Indochina,* Boston, Houghton Mifflin, 1966, p. 31.

[34] See especially Articles 1-9, 11-15, and 27 of Agreement on the Cessation of Hostilities in Viet-Nam, July 20, 1954, and Articles 6 and 7 of the Final Declaration of Geneva Conference, July 21, 1954, Senate Foreign Relations Committee, 89th Cong., 1st Sess., *Background Information Relating to Southeast Asia and Vietnam,*

rev. edn. June 16, 1965, pp. 28-42, 58-60 (hereinafter cited as *Background Information*).

[35] For example, paragraph 84 of the Sixth Interim Report of the ICC, December 11, 1955-July 10, 1956 reads as follows: "While the Commission has experienced difficulties in North Vietnam, the major part of its difficulties has arisen in South Vietnam." 33 *Parl. Sessional Papers,* Cmnd. No. 31, p. 30, 1956-57.

[278]

why did it not have this conclusion confirmed by the I.C.C. or by a reconvened Geneva Conference in the course of the years since 1954? There is little doubt that from the time when the meetings were going on in Geneva in 1954 the United States was determined to use its unilateral military power to avoid the translation of the Vietminh's military victory over the French in the first Indochina war into a corresponding political victory. Once again it is worth quoting Anthony Eden, partly because he was a principal participant at Geneva and partly because his Tory credentials are so impeccable:

> [Dulles] reiterated his fears that, in the event, France would be compelled to depart from the seven points, and the United States would then have to disassociate herself from the resulting agreement. He said that even if the settlement adhered to the seven points faithfully, the United States still could not guarantee it.[36] I had already been warned by Bedell Smith that the United States Government could not associate themselves with the final declaration. The most they could do was to issue a declaration taking note of what had been decided and undertaking not to disturb the settlement. Since Dulles had been at least as responsible as ourselves for calling the Geneva Conference, this did not seem to me reasonable.[37]

There are two points to note. First, the United States determination from the outset not to be fully associated with the Geneva settlement. Why is this so if Professor Moore's view of its essential understanding is correct? To answer this by saying that the United States wanted to avoid ratifying the Communist acquisition of North Viet Nam is hardly a sufficient explanation (even if it is a part of the story) in light of Dulles' overall insistence upon preserving a free hand for American action in the future. The second point, one that strikes me as legally pertinent, is why it matters whether the United States approved of the Geneva Accords or not. The parties to the conflict had full power to settle it by agreement. It is rather far-fetched to contend that the United States assent is needed to secure a formally binding arrangement reached to end a war in which the United States was not itself a direct participant.

Not everything complex is ambiguous. Professor Moore's argument that the Geneva settlement was ambiguous on the issue of unification is unconvincing on several grounds:

(1) The election provisions of the Geneva Accords are explicit as to date, auspices, and preconditions;[38]

---

[36] Anthony Eden, *Full Circle*, London, Cassell, 1960, p. 156.

[37] *Id.*, pp. 159-60.

[38] See *supra*, pp. 252-53 (and authorities

(2) The fact that the Geneva Declaration was unsigned does not seriously detract from its character as a binding legal instrument;[39]

(3) The refusal of the Saigon regime to accept the Geneva Accords does not relieve it of the obligation to comply as France had the capacity that it explicitly sought to exercise, to bind its "successor";[40]

(4) Experienced and impartial observers generally agree that (a) unification by means of elections was part of the Geneva settlement and (b) that elections, if held, would have resulted in the consolidation of Viet Nam under the control of Hanoi;[41]

---

cited in note 31); *Consultative Council*, pp. 43-48; Kahin and Lewis, pp. 52-55, 80-87; 2 Buttinger, pp. 839-40; the most detailed support for regarding the failure to hold the elections promised by Article 7 of the Final Declaration for July 1956 as frustrating Hanoi's sincere understanding of the Geneva settlement is contained in a well-researched monograph, Franklin B. Weinstein, "Vietnam's Unheld Elections," 1966 (Data Paper No. 60, Southeast Asia Program, Cornell University); cf. Jean Lacouture, "The 'Face' of the Viet Cong," *War/Peace Report*, May 1966, pp. 7, 8: "One cannot say . . . that the North resigned itself, with only *pro forma* protestations, to Diem's refusal to hold the elections that had been legally set for July, 1956. During his trip to New Delhi in 1955 as well as in three separate attempts at the end of 1955 and at the beginning of 1956, Pham Van Dong, the present premier of North Vietnam, attempted to implement the provisions of the Geneva agreement. He even offered to delay the elections on condition that Saigon pledge to allow them. It was the great powers—the U.S.S.R. and Peking included—who forgot the Geneva recommendations, not Hanoi, which found itself for the second time 'cheated.' " For a full account of the first time Hanoi was "cheated" see *Hammer, op.cit. supra*, note 31, pp. 148-202; a briefer account is contained in Kahin and Lewis, pp. 25-28.

[39] See Kahin and Lewis, p. 51 (and citations contained in note 7 therein), including reference to Article 3(b) of the *Draft Articles on the Law of Treaties* and commentary in U.N. Doc. A/16309 (1966). The fact that the United States withheld its oral assent from the Final Declaration and attached a Declaration somewhat at variance with Article 7 does not alter the legal expectations created among the real parties in interest—the French and the Vietminh. For text of the United States Declaration, see *Background Information*, p. 61: "In connection with the statement in the declaration concerning free elections in Viet-

Nam my Government wishes to make clear its position which it has expressed in a declaration made in Washington on June 29, 1954, as follows:

In the case of nations now divided against their will, we shall continue to seek to achieve unity through free elections supervised by the United Nations to insure that they are conducted fairly.

With respect to the statement made by the representative of the State of Viet-Nam [Bao Dai], the United States reiterates its traditional position that peoples are entitled to determine their own future and that it will not join in an arrangement which would hinder this. Nothing in its declaration just made is intended to or does indicate any departure from its traditional position."

It is obvious that the United States altered the terms of Article 7 by the conspicuous omission of a definite date upon which elections should be held in Viet Nam and by the call for United Nations supervision. It is also clear that the refusal to give oral assent to the Final Declaration and the reference in the United States statement to its refusal "to join in an arrangement" which "would hinder" its election policy indicates the serious intention of the other participants to take seriously the terms of Article 7. It is one thing for the United States and the Bao Dai regime to disassociate themselves from the Final Declaration, it is quite another to contend that the enforceability and centrality of the election provision was in any respect reduced thereby.

[40] This conclusion appears to be persuasively established in D. G. Partan, "Legal Aspects of the Vietnam Conflict," 46 *Boston University Law Review* 281, 289-92 (1966).

[41] See the authorities cited at note 38 *supra* for relevant references, especially Franklin B. Weinstein. A typical comment is in Bernard B. Fall, *The Two Viet-Nams*, 2nd rev. edn., New York, Praeger, 1967,

(5) The United States was from the beginning manifestly discontented with the Geneva solution, refused to endorse the outcome as a party, and set about almost immediately thereafter to undo the fulfillment of its terms.[42]

Moore advises analysts to consider the total context of Geneva and yet he neglects these critical factors. He is correct in pointing to a certain aura of ambiguity connected with securing the compliance of Saigon with a settlement that was expected to extinguish its sphere of influence. It is also appropriate, as Moore suggests, to acknowledge the subsequent *de facto* sovereignty of both North and South Viet Nam, regardless of the intentions at Geneva in 1954.[43]

It would consume too much space to refute Moore's interpretation of the Geneva Accords on a point-to-point basis, especially as this task has already been done effectively by other authors.[44] I would, however, suggest the weakness of Moore's position by reference to the long passage he approvingly quotes from a book by Victor Bator. In this passage Bator argues that the Geneva Accords really intended "partition" and that this position is borne out by "the detailed accounts of Bernard B. Fall, Jean Lacouture, and Philippe Devillers."[45] Here is what Devillers actually thought about the Geneva settlement:

The demarcation line was to be purely provisional; the principle of Vietnamese unity was not questioned, and the idea of partition was officially rejected with indignation by both sides. . . .

The disproportion between the monolithic power of the Vietminh, armed and with the halo of victory, and the almost derisory weakness of the so-called Nationalist Viet Nam was such that in the summer of 1954 almost no one thought that the two years' delay won

p. 231, who writes that "On the grounds of its nonsignature, South Viet-Nam refused to hold elections by July 1956, since this would have meant handing over control of the South to Ho Chi Minh."

[42] Cf. *id.*, pp. 57-63, 229-33; 2 Buttinger, pp. 834-42.

[43] The expectations created as of 1954 remain relevant to the perception by North Viet Nam of what constitutes a reasonable outcome of the second Indochina war, and influences the formulation of minimum negotiating demands.

[44] See Kahin and Lewis, pp. 43-65; also relevant on many points is Donald Lancaster, *The Emancipation of French Indochina*, London and New York, Oxford University Press, 1961, pp. 313-58.

[45] In a long and significant scholarly review article, itself not hostile to the United States role in Viet Nam, John T. McAlister

says of Bator's longer interpretation of the Geneva Conference in Victor Bator, *Viet Nam: A Diplomatic Tragedy*, Dobbs Ferry, New York, Oceana Publications, 1965, that it "is an emotional and polemical book making no claims to be scholarly work." John T. McAlister, Jr., "The Possibilities for Diplomacy in Southeast Asia," *World Politics*, XIX (1967), 258, 269; Bator's article from *The Reporter* has been reprinted along with a series of other strongly pro-Administration articles drawn from the magazine and reflecting its partisan editorial slant in Viet Nam—*Vietnam: Why— A Collection of Reports and Comments from the Reporter*, 1966. It is, hence, strange to rely upon an occasional piece by Bator, were it not the case that the more trustworthy commentators on the Geneva Conference all cast doubt upon "the partition" hypothesis.

by M. Mendès-France at Geneva could be anything but a respite in which to salvage as much as possible from the wreck. *At the end of the period, unity would certainly be restored, this time to the benefit of the Vietminh, the basic hypothesis then acknowledged by all being that the Geneva Agreements would definitely be implemented.* (emphasis supplied) [46]

Devillers' position has recently been reaffirmed by Professors Kahin and Lewis in their careful and fully documented account of the Geneva Conference. These authors describe Geneva as the event that "officially registered France's defeat by the Vietminh and provided her with a face-saving means of disengagement."[47] In this regard Kahin and Lewis aver that it was the "promise of elections that constituted an essential condition insisted upon by the Vietminh at Geneva." Their reasoning is well worth quoting:

> France was prepared to pay the political price of that condition in order to get the armistice that she so urgently wanted. Her successor [in Saigon] would be obliged to abide by that condition or face the certain resumption of hostilities. The reason for this is patent: when a military struggle for power ends on the agreed condition that the competition will be transferred to the political plane, the side that violates the agreed condition cannot legitimately expect that the military struggle will not be resumed.[48]

Professor Moore relies upon the memoirs of Anthony Eden to establish "that [the] real core of the settlement, at least from the Western standpoint, was partition of North Viet Nam." These memoirs are too imprecise to clarify legal analysis and are internally inconsistent,[49] al-

[46] Philippe Devillers, "The Struggle for Unification of Vietnam," *The China Quarterly* (January-March 1962), 2-3.

[47] Kahin and Lewis, p. 43.

[48] *Ibid.*, p. 57.

[49] Anthony Eden seems primarily concerned with obtaining a Western negotiating consensus that would enable the war in Indochina to be brought to an end. There is no detailed interpretation given by the terms of the Geneva settlement and there is every indication that Eden thought that the election provisions would be carried out, despite the intra-Allied discussion in terms of "partition." Anthony Eden, *Full Circle*, London, Cassell, 1960, pp. 158-59. It is very strange to argue that the negotiating hopes of the United States, which were not to any degree reflected in the language or terms of the Geneva Accords themselves, should be given any weight in construing treaty-type obligations that are unambiguous on their face. It is an elementary rule of treaty interpretation that one consults the context of the agreement to the extent that the provisions themselves are unclear. Even if the Accords do not qualify as treaties in the strict sense their content was affirmed in a solemn and formal manner. In any event, although the rhetoric of partition does imply a permanent separation of Viet Nam into two separate states, it is quite consistent with a temporary period of partition followed by elections seeking reunification. Only such an interpretation brings consistency into the Eden accounting. For the most persuasive skeptical view of the Geneva Accords—one that puts a curse on both houses—see 2 Buttinger, pp. 978-81.

though they do provide considerable insight into the divergence of the American position from that of the other Western powers at Geneva in 1954. Eden, who holds very intense anti-Communist views, is especially convincing in his account of the effort that he made to discourage the United States from undermining the whole project of a conference to end the first Indochina war.[50] The United States was lobbying at Geneva to organize a collective Western intervention in support of the French, support that the French no longer desired. Eden indicates that he was distressed to learn from a French diplomat about an official document in which the United States secretly proposed to the French that military intervention in Indochina occur "either after the failure of Geneva, *or earlier if the French so desired, and he emphasized that the American preference had been clearly expressed for the earlier date*" (emphasis supplied).[51] It seems to me that a fair-minded reading of the Eden memoirs would emphasize the degree to which talk of "partition" may have been designed to mollify the United States apprehensions about the Conference. In any event, if "partition" was the bargain, it was nowhere reflected in the Geneva Accords that resulted from the Conference. Why not?

The partition hypothesis also does not reconcile easily with Eden's evident feeling that the election provision in the Final Declaration was to be taken seriously: "The Communists insisted that elections should be held during 1955 in Vietnam, whereas the French maintained, I thought rightly, that it would take at least two years for the country to be restored to a condition in which elections would be possible."[52] I conclude that (1) partition was not written into the Geneva Accords and that (2) unification by elections in July 1956 was the essential political bargain struck at Geneva in exchange for a regroupment of the fighting forces into two zones and the withdrawal to the North of the Vietminh armies. This interpretation of the Geneva Accords is crucial for an interpretation of the relevance of the post-1954 events, especially of the extent to which one emphasizes or disregards the non-implementation of the election provision. My principal contention is that once it became clear that the election provision would not be carried out recourse to coercion by Hanoi was both predictable and per-

[50] Anthony Eden, *Full Circle*, London, Cassell, 1960, pp. 120-63.

[51] *Id.*, p. 134; cf. *id.*, pp. 93, 103, 117, 126-27 for a sense of Eden's perception of American attitudes toward the Geneva Conference. Buttinger's account of the American attempts to rally support for military intervention is one of the most complete and accurate, 2 Buttinger, pp. 797-844; he writes that "the moves that Radford, Dulles and Nixon made during April 1954, to stop Communism in Indochina are among the saddest chapters of U.S. diplomacy." *Id.*, p. 819.

[52] *Id.*, pp. 158, 159; see also Anthony Eden, *Toward Peace in Indochina*, Boston, Houghton Mifflin, 1966, p. 38.

missible, in either of the two Type III variants—the N.L.F. versus Saigon or North Viet Nam versus South Viet Nam. On this basis I find it highly misleading and false to analogize the evidence of North Vietnamese support for the insurgency in the South with the massive attack by North Korea on South Korea in 1950. It is false even if (which is hardly possible) one accepts the State Department's "white papers" as accurate descriptions of the North Vietnamese role in the early stage of the conflict in South Viet Nam. Among other considerations distinguishing Korea are the following: the effort of Hanoi proceeded against a quite opposite political background, it was based on much more ambiguous evidence of coercion, and the coercion was of such small scale that it could not have resulted in any substantial disturbance had not a revolutionary potential preexisted in South Viet Nam.[53]

Viet Nam cannot be regarded as relevantly similar to the other divided countries of China,[54] Korea, or Germany. Although Korea and Germany differ significantly from one another as divided countries, the political "settlement" in each case consisted of a reciprocal acceptance of partition, at least until a more satisfactory political settlement could be agreed upon as to reunification. Until such a second or new political settlement emerges, if ever, the use of coercion in any form to achieve a favorable military settlement of the reunification issue is, as Professor Moore properly indicates, a dangerous disturbance of world order, a disturbance that entitles the victim entity to claim full defensive rights, and one that entails the gravest consequences; the Korean War illustrates and vindicates the principle that frontiers within divided states enjoy at least the same sanctity as frontiers between undivided states. The Saigon regime cannot invoke the sanctity of the 17th parallel in the same persuasive manner as the Seoul regime invoked the sanctity of the 38th parallel. The political settlement at Geneva in 1954 provided a formula for the nullification (rather than one for the maintenance) of the division. In Viet Nam, Saigon's establishment, rather than the subsequent attempt at its removal, of a political frontier at the 17th parallel represented the coercive challenge to world order.[55]

[53] E.g. Arnold S. Feldman, "Violence and Volatility: The Likelihood of Revolution," in Harry Eckstein, ed., *Internal War*, New York, Free Press, 1964, pp. 111-29.

[54] It can be persuasively argued, I think, that Formosa is wrongly conceived of as an integral part of China. Therefore, China is not "a divided country" at all, but there are two countries each of which is entitled to sovereign status. For a complete argument to this effect see L. Chen and Harold

D. Lasswell, *Formosa, China and the United Nations: Formosa's Place in the World Community*.

[55] See Bernard B. Fall, *The Two Viet-Nams*, 2nd rev. edn., New York, Praeger, 1967, pp. 231-32; the effort to build up the military strength of the Saigon regime was coupled with its refusal to allow the election provision of the Geneva settlement to be carried out. To defend the 17th parallel as if it were an international boundary was

In this spirit it is worth reexamining Professor Moore's central policy test in the Viet Nam setting—namely, the prohibition by international law of coercion as a strategy of major change. On one level such a policy is an essential ingredient of minimum world order in the nuclear age. But peace cannot be divorced from minimum expectations of fair play on related matters. The Geneva Conference confirmed the results of a long anticolonial war won at great cost to Vietnamese society by the armies of the Ho Chi Minh.[56] The achievement of national independence is a goal of such importance in the Afro-Asian world that it clearly takes precedence for these countries over generalized prohibitions on force or rules about nonintervention.[57] The Geneva Accords are not just an international agreement about which a dispute arose, but a formalized acknowledgment of a political outcome that it is reasonable to suppose could have been attained legitimately by the Vietminh in 1954 through military means.[58] In effect, the Accords were a political bargain struck by the French as an alternative to continuing the appalling destruction of lives and property. To cast aside this political bargain is to undermine severely the security of solemn international agreements and to put in jeopardy collective procedures for pacific settlement.[59]

My conclusion, then, is that Professor Moore has not persuasively demonstrated that the use of coercion across the 17th parallel by North Viet Nam should have been regarded as coercion across an international boundary. I wish to argue only that it was reasonable for Hanoi, given the stakes and outcome of the first Indochina war, to regard Saigon's intransigence on the issue of elections as a material breach of the Accords, allowing it to act on the basis of the *status quo*

---

itself tantamount to an illegal effort at splitting a state into two parts, an effort frequently productive of severe civil strife. It is only necessary to recall the American Civil War or the post-1960 efforts of Katanga to split off from the Congo.

[56] See *Hammer, op.cit. supra,* note 31.

[57] For example, the African states overtly proclaim their intention to resort to force against the countries of Southern Africa to end colonialism and racism. The legal status of this claim is considered in Falk, "The New States and International Order," 118 *Recueil des Cours* (forthcoming).

[58] After Dien Bien Phu the only way to prevent a total Vietminh victory would have been a massive United States military intervention that included combat troops; as it was, even Anthony Eden points out that the French received at least nine times as much foreign support from the

United States as the Vietminh did from China. Anthony Eden, *Full Circle,* London, Cassell, 1960, pp. 126-27.

[59] The refusal of the United States to take the Geneva Accords of 1954 more seriously as the terms of settlement may help partly to account for the reluctance of Hanoi to negotiate with the United States. Of course, there are independent reasons to suppose that the United States may not be sincere about its various offers to negotiate an end to the Viet Nam War. See Theodore Draper, "Vietnam: How Not to Negotiate," *New York Review of Books,* May 4, 1967, p. 17; Draper's criticism of the Government is so impressive because of his earlier support of the United States anti-Castro foreign policy. Theodore Draper, *Castroism, Theory and Practice,* New York, Praeger, 1965. Cf. Kahin and Lewis, pp. 207-37.

ante 1954: in my terms choosing this option would result in an example of Type III conflict, a situation of internal conflict for control of all of Viet Nam in which outside participation on behalf of either faction is "intervention," at least in the sense of interfering with the process of self-determination.[60]

Despite its plausibility from the perspective of law, there are three problems raised by this interpretation:

(1) Hanoi has not really contended that the action of Saigon nullifies the Geneva Accords; on the contrary, Hanoi continues to urge implementation and compliance;

(2) South Viet Nam has existed as a separate political entity for more than twelve years and has been accorded diplomatic recognition by many foreign governments; the consequence is a condition of statehood with all of the normal defensive prerogatives;

(3) During the last five years third powers have become increasingly involved on both sides in the Viet Nam War; South Korea, Thailand, Australia, New Zealand, the Philippines, the Soviet Union, and China are the principal third-party participants as of April 1967.

As I have indicated at the outset of this section, the war in Viet Nam now belongs in Type II; the functions of clarifying the argument that it was originally an example of Type III and that the United States should have left it that way are to indicate the reasonable basis of a settlement and to emphasize the unilateral role of the United States in shifting the war to an internationally more serious category of conflict.[61]

II. The Rationale Restated in Support of a Type II Classification of the Viet Nam War

To classify the Viet Nam War as a Type II conflict implies considering the war as a variety of civil strife in which two domestic factions, each of which receives substantial assistance from foreign states, are struggling for control of a sovereign state. I maintain that international law then requires that belligerent conduct remain within the territorial limits of South Viet Nam. The United States Government officially

---

[60] Quincy Wright has been a consistent advocate of this position. See Quincy Wright, "Legal Aspects of the Viet-Nam Situation," 60 *American Journal of International Law* 750 (1966); Wright, "United States Intervention in the Lebanon," 53 *American Journal of International Law* 112 (1959).

[61] As a conflict moves from Type III toward Type II it tends to become more dangerous to international peace and se-

curity; as it proceeds from Type II to Type I it tends to become even more dangerous other things being equal. Therefore, the United States role in transforming the conflict from Type II to Type I without seriously attempting a Type IV classification is to follow a path destructive of world order in relation to the civil strife-revolution phenomena occurring throughout the Afro-Asian world.

repudiates this interpretation of the war and insists that the violent conflict is properly viewed as "an armed attack" by North Viet Nam upon South Viet Nam. South Viet Nam is thus entitled to act in self-defense, including, to the extent necessary, the commission of acts of war in North Viet Nam. In my terms, the United States Government has inappropriately characterized "the facts" as vindicating a Type I classification.[62]

Professor Moore agrees with the Government that the war in Viet Nam belongs in Type I, but he goes further by arguing that even if the facts warrant a Type II classification there are no legal restrictions that necessarily confine the war to territorial boundaries and that, in the context of Viet Nam, the air and sea strikes against North Vietnamese territory have been legally reasonable. There are thus two broad sets of questions to which Professor Moore and I give different answers:

(1) Is North Viet Nam "intervening" in "civil strife" going on in South Viet Nam or is North Viet Nam "attacking" South Viet Nam? Who decides, by what criteria, and subject to what conditions?

(2) If North Viet Nam is regarded as merely "intervening" in civil strife, does international law prohibit South Viet Nam and states allied with her to commit war acts against the territory of North Viet Nam?

As Professor Moore effectively argues, South Viet Nam's *de facto* sovereignty makes it important to analyze the legal rights of the Saigon regime on the assumption that South Viet Nam is a sovereign state, as entitled as any other to act in self-defense and to receive military assistance. Moore's interpretation of North Viet Nam's role depends on two sets of assertions; neither of which I accept as to fact or law:

(1) The nature of North Viet Nam's military assistance to the N.L.F. and the political objectives motivating it constitute "an armed attack" upon South Viet Nam;

(2) The United States assistance to the Saigon regime, including bombing North Viet Nam, is a reasonable and lawful exercise of the right of self-defense.

My argument as formulated in the preceding chapter is that the conflict in South Viet Nam closely resembles other instances of prolonged civil strife in which substantial intervention by foreign countries on behalf of both the insurgent and the incumbent faction has taken place.

---

62 The objective of establishing two categories of international conflict, Type I and Type II, is to underline the importance in policy and in law to distinguish between the Korea-type situation and the Viet Nam-type situation. Analytic categories are ideal types; there is no comparable clarity in real-world situations. Nevertheless, the ambiguities and antagonistic misperceptions that are likely to accompany a conflict of the Viet Nam variety make it very important for states to limit their involvement to the boundaries of the society wherein the violence is located.

I regard two assertions as legally determinative of the argument being made by Professor Moore:

(1) Covert assistance, even of a substantial nature, to an insurgent faction does not constitute an armed attack;

(2) Counterintervention on behalf of an incumbent faction may not extend the conflict beyond its existing territorial boundaries.

This reasoning seemed directly applicable to the situation in Viet Nam with the consequence that the extension of the war to the territory of North Viet Nam by the United States is deemed to be a violation of international law.

Professor Moore, if I understand him correctly, argues:

(1) My Type II paradigm confuses what the rules of international law ought to be with what the rules actually are.

(2) The weight of legal authority supports Saigon's discretion to treat North Viet Nam's aid to the N.L.F. as an armed attack and thereby authorizes defensive measures undertaken against North Vietnamese territory.

(3) Bombing North Viet Nam has been a reasonable defensive measure for the United States to undertake on behalf of South Viet Nam in view of the facts of attack and the law authorizing a proportionate response to it.

(4) The policy interests at stake are more consistent with such discretion than with the territorial limitations embodied in the Type II paradigm. Thus Professor Moore concluded there is "greater reason [than not] to believe both as a matter of the is and the ought that the bombing of the North is a permissible defensive response."

THE DISTINCTION BETWEEN "IS" AND "OUGHT"
IN THE CONTEXT OF VIET NAM:
THE DOCTRINAL LEVEL OF DISCOURSE

I find it peculiar that Professor Moore argues, on the one hand, that the ambiguity of the legal and factual setting in Viet Nam makes it essential to assess the respective rights and duties of the parties by reference to the world order policies at stake, and on the other that my major line of legal analysis confuses what the law ought to be with what the law is. It is peculiar that Professor Moore should rely on Hans Kelsen, an arch-positivist to support a critique that is explicitly couched in terms of the sociological jurisprudence of Myres McDougal, especially when Kelsen is invoked to show what is meant by the phrase "armed attack" as it appears in Article 51 of the Charter. Of course, Kelsen stresses the dichotomy between the "is" and the "ought," but it is this stress that seems quite contrary to Moore's assertion, one that I share, that international law is above all a process whereby actors clarify through their conduct the world order policies that each deems decisive in a particular context. For sake of clarity of discussion I shall try, despite this jurisprudential ambivalence that I detect in Professor Moore's critique, to respond directly to his analysis.

DOES TYPE II EMBODY A PREFERENCE ABOUT WHAT INTERNATIONAL LAW OUGHT TO BE?

Type II acknowledges the indeterminacy of international law with respect to intervention and counterintervention. There is no weight of legal authority that can be crystallized in terms of rules commanding universal, or even widespread respect. In fact, respectable and responsible international jurists disagree as to whether international law:

(1) allows discrimination in favor of the incumbent;[63]

(2) requires impartiality as between the incumbent and the insurgent;[64]

(3) allows discrimination in favor of the just side.[65]

In face of this indeterminacy it seems useful to acknowledge the extent of sovereign discretion as to participating in a foreign civil war. International law does not provide authoritative rules of restraint, or stated more accurately, it provides contradictory rules of restraint of approximately equal standing. To invoke international law in this international setting, then, is to argue about desirable policy or to communicate in

[63] E.g. Professor Moore, *op.cit. supra*, note 1, pp. 1080-88 and James L. Garner, "Questions of International Law in the Spanish Civil War," 31 *American Journal of International Law* 66 (1937); see also E. Borchard, "'Neutrality' and Civil Wars," 31 *American Journal of International Law* 304 (1937).

[64] E.g. Quincy Wright, *op.cit. supra*, note 60, and William E. Hall, *International Law*, 8th edn., London, Oxford University Press, 1924, p. 347.

[65] This position has been enunciated in its classical form by Emmerich de Vattel, *The Law of Nations*, Washington, Carnegie Institution of Washington, 1916, Bk. II, § 56, p. 131. Although positive international law promotes either discrimination in favor of the incumbent or impartiality, the practice of states increasingly vindicates giving help to the side deemed "just." From the perspective of world order it is crucial to develop community procedures to identify which side is "just." Such procedures seem to work for those situations in which the principal rival states have apparently converging interests, as with the unresolved problems of bringing independence and racial equality to Rhodesia, South West Africa, Angola, Mozambique, and South Africa. But where rival principal states disagree, as when civil strife between "radical" and "conservative" elites occur in the developing countries, then the determination of which side is "just" is likely to generate competitive interventions if the contradictory perceptions are acted upon. The Communist ideas of support for wars of national liberation are in conflict with American thinking on the legitimacy of helping any anti-Communist regime sustain itself against Communist opposition. In a world of antagonistic ideologies it is dangerous to maintain complete discretion on the national level to identify which faction is "just"; but, equally, in a world of insistent legislative demands it is dangerous to preclude discrimination in favor of an insurgency that is deemed "just" by the overwhelming consensus of international society. One approach for cold war issues and another for Southern African issues seems imperative at this point.

precise form what a particular state intends to claim; international law does not, however, postulate rules of order the transgression of which is illegal.

One of the authorities relied upon by Moore, Ian Brownlie, an international lawyer in the strict positivist sense, gives the following support to insisting upon the applicability of territorial restriction in a Type II situation:

> When foreign assistance is given to the rebels, aid to the government threatened is now generally assumed to be legal. Whether this is permitted in relation to minor disturbances caused by foreign propaganda or other forms of interference is an open question. It is also uncertain as to whether the foreign assistance must be a decisive element in the imminent and serious threat to the existing government or whether it is sufficient if foreign assistance is a contributory cause. Finally, *foreign assistance to the government will be confined to measures on the territory of the requesting state unless the foreign aid to the rebels amounts in fact and law to an "armed attack."* (emphasis supplied)[66]

It is worth noticing that Brownlie attributes uncertainty to the positive law in this area, but more immediately, it is important to take account of his reliance upon territoriality as a limiting criterion. Brownlie reinforces the quoted passage in the course of his discussion of claims to use force in self-defense against alleged aggression:

> It is suggested that so far as possible defensive measures should be confined to the territory of the defending state and the hostile forces themselves unless there is clear evidence of a major invasion across a frontier which calls for extensive military operations which may not be confined merely to protecting the frontier line. The precise difficulty in the case of indirect aggression is to avoid major breaches of the peace of wide territorial extent arising from defensive measures based on vague evidence of foreign complicity.[67]

[66] Ian Brownlie, *International Law and the Use of Force by States*, London, Oxford University Press, 1963, p. 327. Roger Pinto, "Les Règles du Droit International Concernant la Guerre Civile," 114 *Recueil des Cours* 451-553, esp. 544-48 (1965).

[67] Brownlie, p. 373. "Indirect aggression and the incursions of armed bands can be countered by measures of defense which do not involve military operations across frontiers." *Id.*, p. 279. A recent Western visitor to North Viet Nam confirms the distinction between intervention in the South and bombing of the North as vital to the North Vietnamese perception of themselves as victims of United States aggression:

"Their [North Viet Nam] position is that the bombing of the North is a separate act of aggression from fighting in the South. While they might understand and tolerate, although disapprove, American intervention in the South on behalf of the Saigon government, they regard the bombing of the North as an unconscionable act of aggression against a sovereign nation." Harry Ashmore, *op. cit. supra*, note 21, p. 17.

It seems reasonable to regard Brownlie's discussion as a generalization of past state practice that reflects international law. My Type II boundary rule places an outer limit on the discretion of the sovereign state and is precisely the kind of quasi-objective limit that is so crucial for the maintenance of world order.

It is correct, as Professor Moore argues, that if the insurgent faction is the "agent" of the outside state then it is permissible for the victim state to respond at the source by regarding the apparent insurgency as an armed attack. But such a response requires a real demonstration of instigation and control, as distinct from either a mere allegation or evidence of some assistance to a faction that appears to possess an independent character and objectives.

International law is not really indefinite on this subject. A state is not permitted to use sustained military force against a foreign country unless the justification is overwhelmingly clear.[68] It is difficult to establish unilaterally that covert uses of force by an external enemy can ever constitute an ample justification. It is difficult to distinguish a pretext from a justification, especially as the status of assistance to either side in an ongoing civil war seems legally equivalent. That is, one side may discriminate in favor of the incumbent, whereas the other side may discriminate in favor of "the just" faction, and both possess an equal legal basis.[69] In such a situation any serious concern with the policies of conflict minimization would insist, at least, that neither side has the discretion to extend the war to foreign territory.

The dynamics of internal war are such that both sides must, as the war progresses, almost certainly seek increasing external support to

[68] Action and reaction sequences involving "incidents" have not been regulated in any very clear and definite way by international law. States interact by claim and counterclaim and the degree of legality is very largely dependent on the general impression of the reasonableness of the action undertaken by the contending states. The Gulf of Tonkin incident was a characteristic illustration of this process. The legality of the United States response depends primarily on (a) the reality of the provocation and (b) the proportionality of the response. For useful background as to practice, policy, and law in this kind of setting of sporadic violence see Fritz Grob, *The Relativity of War and Peace: A Study in Law, History and Politics*, New Haven, Yale University Press, 1949.

[69] This flexibility of international law is confirmed by the discretion states possess to accord or withhold recognition from a partially successful insurgency. Ti-Chiang Chen, *The International Law of Recognition*, London, Stevens and Sons, 1951. It is not necessary for recognition to be accorded in an express or formal manner. *De facto* recognition arising out of intercourse between the third-party state and the antigovernment faction is sufficient provided the facts of the civil war justify the inference of dual sovereignty; i.e. each faction governs a portion of the society and this situation is likely to continue for a considerable period of time. As Lauterpacht concludes, "It is not contrary to international law to recognize the insurgents as a government exercising *de facto* authority over the territory under its control." Hersch Lauterpacht, *Recognition in International Law*, Cambridge, Cambridge University Press, 1947, p. 294. See generally *id.*, pp. 279-94.

maintain their position in the struggle; if the scene of the internal war is a minor country then it is increasingly likely that both factions will become dependent for their political leadership upon a larger external ally.[70] Insurgent dependence on external support is not by itself proof of an aggressive design on the part of the supporter state. This dependence on an external ally is normally only an expression of the changing ratios of influence between the benefactor and recipient of military assistance on both sides as the conflict progresses to higher magnitudes. It would be detrimental to world order to treat such ratios as equivalent to an armed attack by one state on another and prior to the war in Viet Nam there had been neither serious juridical support nor diplomatic practice that would justify treating assistance to an insurgent as an armed attack. In fact, for world order purposes, bombing North Viet Nam has to be appraised as if it were seeking to establish a new legal precedent upon which other states could and should subsequently rely.[71]

Professor Moore regards as "mysterious" my assertion that bombing North Viet Nam is simultaneously both: (1) a violation of international law and; (2) a law-creating precedent. It may be mysterious, but it is a mystery embedded in the international legal process. As a consequence of the absence of a legislature in international society, the assertion of a claim by a state to act in a certain way, if supported by an appeal to the policies and rules of law and if effectively asserted in practice, is both a violation of law as measured by prior expectations about what was permissible in a given situation and a precedent that can be subsequently invoked to legitimate future conduct of a similar sort. This can be stated more concretely by asking about whether *prior* to the war in Viet Nam a response against the territory of the state assisting an insurgent faction was regarded to be as permissible as it might be in

[70] The process by which an internal war is internationalized is well-depicted in George Modelski, "The International Relations of Internal War," in James N. Rosenau, ed., *International Aspects of Civil Strife*, Princeton, Princeton University Press, 1964, pp. 14-44.

[71] The international law applicable to Type II situations is subject to "legislative" modification by principal states asserting new claims in an effective fashion and defending their assertion by an appeal to international law. It would be very difficult for the United States to oppose the legal argument it has developed to support its claim to bomb North Viet Nam. In this respect, my criticism of the Meeker legal rationale for "self-defense" in Viet Nam is more that it constitutes bad "legislation" than that it is "a violation." But cf. Meeker, *op.cit. supra*, note 23. Often a precedent established for one context can be successfully invoked for different objectives in a series of subsequent contexts. This general process is very ably depicted in connection with the activities of the International Labor Organization by Ernst Haas. See Ernst Haas, *Beyond the Nation-State*, Stanford, Stanford University Press, 1964, esp. pp. 381-425 (describing precedent-creation in a cold war context later being invoked in anticolonial and antiracist contexts with regard to "freedom of association").

some *subsequent* war of the Viet Nam variety.[72] Certainly, the precedent of Viet Nam will provide valuable support for any victim state that attacks foreign territory on the ground that it was substantially assisting the insurgent. Other international settings in which a legally dubious claim was converted by its successful assertion into a legally authoritative precedent can be mentioned—for instance, testing nuclear weapons on the high seas, orbiting reconnaissance satellites, and imposing criminal responsibility upon individuals who lead their country in an aggressive war. Professor Moore once again appears hesitant to accept the full jurisprudential implications of the McDougalian orientation that he advocates: if there is a process of law-creation at work in international society, then the distinction between a violation and a law-creating precedent is one of perspective and prediction, but not logic.[73]

IS NORTH VIET NAM'S ASSISTANCE TO THE N.L.F. "AN ARMED ATTACK?" THE FACTUAL LEVEL OF DISCOURSE

Only if North Viet Nam's assistance to the N.L.F. can be considered an armed attack, is proportionate self-defense available to Saigon and its allies.

Professor Moore argues that North Viet Nam is guilty of an armed attack on South Viet Nam for the following principal reasons:

(1) A substantial body of scholarly opinion holds that Hanoi actually *initiated*, as well as *assisted*, the insurgency;

(2) Hanoi exercises control over the activities of the N.L.F.;

(3) Hanoi's principal objective is to reunify Viet Nam under its control; therefore, its assistance is, in effect, a project for the territorial expansion of North Viet Nam at the expense of South Viet Nam.

---

[72] The United States has not even restricted bombing to certain specific objectives related directly to the Vietcong war effort—for instance, the specific interdiction of supplies and infiltrators or destruction of staging areas. President Johnson explicitly includes punishment as one of three principal objectives of bombing North Viet Nam: "We sought to impose on North Viet Nam a cost for violating its international agreements." "President Reviews U.S. Position on Bombing of North Viet-Nam," *U.S. State Department Bulletin*, LVI, 1967, pp. 514, 515. For a description of the impact of bombing on North Viet Nam see Harrison E. Salisbury, *Behind the Lines—Hanoi, December 23–January 7*, New York, Harper and Row, 1967.

[73] This process is summarized in part by the maxim *ex factis jus oritur*; without legislative organs and without a general conference procedure, the growth of international law reflects the process by which claims and counterclaims interact, especially if principal states are participants.

It is, of course, possible to distinguish an arbitrary recommendation of a particular author as to preferred regulatory schemes from a reasoned application of preexisting community legal policies to a controversial fact situation. In the former case one is dealing with *a criticism* of the legal order, whereas in the latter one is concerned with *an application of law*, albeit an application that interprets obligations in light of policy preference.

These issues concern the quality, quantity, and phasing of Hanoi's role. Reasonable men disagree about the facts. Many observers, especially in the United States, regard the resolution of these factual questions as critical to their assessment of whether the United States has responded in a lawful manner. For purposes of my own analysis I would argue that *even if* the facts are accepted in the form that Professor Moore presents them the conflict in Viet Nam is appropriately treated as Type II. I would additionally argue, however, that Professor Moore's construction of the facts relies on the reporting of biased observers. Furthermore, I would contend that it is inappropriate to appraise Hanoi's connection with the N.L.F. without taking into account Washington's connection with the Saigon regime, especially after the insurgency had succeeded in establishing itself as the government for many areas of South Viet Nam.

Construing the Controverted Facts. The ambiguity of the facts in a situation in which civil strife has been allegedly abetted by external assistance is one reason why it is important to regulate the scope of conflict by objective limits. It is obviously easy for any interested state to manipulate the evidence to vindicate any response. The gradual emergence of a serious struggle for the control of South Viet Nam gave the Saigon regime and the United States an adequate opportunity to establish the facts by impartial procedures and to have recourse to international institutions to vindicate the legal inferences of "aggression," and later, "armed attack," that were drawn from the facts. It is important to realize that the United States made very little effort to secure wider community support for its preferred course of action in the decade after the Geneva settlement of 1954.[74]

Furthermore, recourse to self-defense was not prompted by any sudden necessity. It was decided upon in February 1965, with considerable deliberateness after consideration over a period of months, if not years.[75] In this circumstance, the burden of justification seems to fall heavily on the United States for the following reasons:

(1) the essential ambiguity of the alleged aggression, especially in view of the refusal of the Saigon regime to implement the election provisions and its suppression of all political opposition;

(2) the nonrecourse to the organs of the United Nations, despite the time available and the refusal to adopt the war-terminating suggestions of the Secretary General;[76]

---

[74] *Consultative Council*, pp. 71-76.
[75] See the original official explanations for bombing North Viet Nam in *Background Information*, pp. 148-52, and the more recent explanation in the *U.S. State* *Department Bulletin, op.cit. supra*, note 72.
[76] Cf. *supra*, p. 243 *with* text of Goldberg's Letter to the Secretary General on December 19, 1966, *New York Times*, December 20, 1966, p. 6, col. 4, and ex-

(3) the absence of a clear showing of necessity and justification required in contemporary international law to validate the exercise of the right of self-defense;

(4) the consistent previous international practice of confining civil strife, even in cases where the insurgent faction was aided and abetted by outside powers, to territorial limits;

(5) the locus of conflict being outside the immediate security sphere of the United States, thereby distinguishing the protective role exhibited by United States diplomacy in Latin America.[77]

These factors in the Viet Nam context are mentioned to indicate the legal background. Such a background seems to require, at minimum, a clear demonstration that the facts are as the United States contends. The so-called white papers issued by the State Department[78] are considered to be too one-sided even for Professor Moore. Instead he relies heavily upon Douglas Pike, author of a detailed study entitled *Viet Cong*, written at the M.I.T. Center for International Studies, during a one-year leave of absence from his role as an official of the United States Information Agency;[79] Mr. Pike had spent the preceding six years serving in Viet Nam, during which period the research was done. One need not be an editor of *Ramparts* to note that M.I.T.'s Center has long been subsidized by the CIA and has given consistent guidance and support to United States foreign policy, especially with regard to the containment of Communism; a list of Center publications indicates a consistent pro-Administration outlook. Mr. Pike's analysis certainly deserves careful reading, and is to some degree endorsed by Bernard Fall's interpretations, but the danger of bias should be noted and his

---

cerpts from U Thant's introduction to the annual report on the work of the United Nations, September 19, 1966, p. 18, col. 5.

[77] There are broad deferences accorded to principal sovereign states to prevent hostile political changes in countries located within a traditional sphere of influence; these interferences, although vigorously controversial, do not generally endanger international peace and security because a principal state is reluctant to use force in a rival sphere of influence. Such geopolitical toleration is not intended to serve as a juridical vindication for unilateral interventionary practices that have been solemnly renounced. For a legal critique of intervention carried on within a sphere of influence see Chapter VI; this analysis of the Bay of Pigs applies *a fortiori* to the 1965 intervention in the Dominican Republic.

[78] *U.S. Department of State, A Threat to the Peace: North Viet-Nam's Effort to Conquer South Viet-Nam*, 1961; *U.S. Department of State, Aggression from the North: The Record of North Viet-Nam's Campaign to Conquer South Viet-Nam*, 1965, (reprinted in *U.S. State Department Bulletin*, LII, 1965, pp. 404-27).

[79] Douglas Pike, *Viet Cong: The Organization and Techniques of the National Liberation Front of South Vietnam*, Cambridge, Massachusetts Institute of Technology Press, 1966 (hereinafter cited as Pike); see also the apparent deception in an earlier attempt to show that Hanoi dominated the N.L.F., the author's CIA affiliation was disguised by presenting him as "a student of political theory and Asian affairs . . . former officer in U.S. Aid Mission in Saigon; author of 'Aesthetics and the Problem of Meaning.'" George A. Carver, Jr., "The Faceless Vietcong," *Foreign Affairs*, XLIV (1966), 347-72, at 347.

conclusions should be carefully tested against those reached by neutral observers.[80] In responding to Professor Moore, I would argue that by relying as heavily on Mr. Pike (without taking serious account of the significantly different interpretations of Jean Lacouture, George Kahin and John Lewis, and Bernard Fall) he bases his conclusions of fact on *ex parte* presentations which, due to an appearance of academic impartiality, are more misleading than "the white papers" he dismissed as "one-sided."[81]

Space permits me to give only two illustrations of why, aside from his vested vocational outlook, I find it difficult to regard Mr. Pike as a trustworthy guide to the facts in Viet Nam. The Preface ends with this rather emotional statement of Pike's personal commitment to the United States role in Viet Nam:

> The plight of the Vietnamese people is not an abstraction to me, and I have no patience with those who treat it as such. Victory by the Communists would mean consigning thousands of Vietnamese, many of them of course my friends, to death, prison, or permanent exile. . . . My heart goes out to the Vietnamese people—who have been sold out again and again, whose long history could be written in terms of betrayal and who, based on this long and bitter experience, can only expect that eventually America too will sell them out. If America betrays the Vietnamese people by abandoning them, she betrays her own heritage.[82]

What is striking about this passage is its identification of "the Vietnamese people" with the American support of the Saigon regime. Does not Mr. Pike think that if Marshal Ky prevails "thousands of Vietnamese" would be consigned "to death, prison, or permanent exile?"[83] This is what happened to the anti-Diem opposition in the South after 1954 (and, incidentally, to the anti-Ho opposition in the North), and it is a

[80] Among other unintended conclusions that emerge from Pike's study is the clear sense that the National Liberation Front possesses the organizational efficiency, cohesion, and talent to govern South Viet Nam in a manner never achieved by the Saigon regime. From the perspective of international order the capacity to govern is certainly an element in claiming political legitimacy. A second unintended conclusion is the extent to which Hanoi's increasing influence upon the N.L.F. has been a direct consequence of the American entry into combat operations. This increase in influence has, according to Mr. Pike, temporarily at least submerged real differences in outlook and objectives between the N.L.F. and Hanoi—differences that belie the more general hypothesis that the N.L.F. is a creation and creature of Hanoi's conjuring.

[81] See, e.g. Max F. Millikan's Foreword where he stresses the academic and disinterested character of the Center for International Studies and its sponsorship of Mr. Pike's inquiry. Pike, pp. v-vi.

[82] *Id.*, pp. xi-xii.

[83] Cf. R. W. Apple, Jr., *New York Times*, May 17, 1967, p. 3, col. 2, describing the activities of Miss Cao Ngoc Phuong in organizing a non-Communist, Buddhist opposition to the Saigon regime's war policy and the harassment to which she has been subjected by Premier Ky's police officials while trying to carry on her activities.

[296]

common, if tragic, sequel to a bitter civil war. To associate the prospect of such oppression exclusively with an N.L.F. victory, as Pike does, is to endorse the most naïve and sentimental American propaganda. Also Pike's passage indicates the emotional character of his commitment to "the American mission," a commitment that is unqualified by any reference to the doubtful claims to rulership possessed by the present Saigon leadership.[84]

When Pike explains the creation of the N.L.F. his bias appears in the form of the following undocumented conjecture: "The creation of the N.L.F. was an accomplishment of such skill, precision, and refinement that when one thinks of who the master planner must be, only one name comes to mind: Vietnam's organizational genius, Ho Chi Minh."[85] Even Pike suggests that prior to the emergence of the N.L.F. in 1960 there had been sustained resistance to the Diem government by "Communists, the religious sects, and other groups."[86] The point is that even a biased accounting of the facts is compelled to take account of the pre-Communist and non-Communist role in the early years of the insurgency.[87]

[84] Consider, for instance, the inconsistency between the claims of a democratic society in South Viet Nam and the Constitution approved by the Constituent Assembly in 1967. See, e.g. Article 5: "1. The Republic of Viet-Nam opposes communism in every form. 2. Every activity designed to propagandize or carry out communism is prohibited"; Article 81(2): "The Supreme Court is empowered to decide on the dissolution of a political party whose policy and activities oppose the republican regime." For text of the Constitution see *Congressional Record*, June 6, 1967, S7733-S7737. For a full account of the terror in South Viet Nam that commenced in 1954, see 2 Buttinger, pp. 893-916.

[85] Pike, p. 76.

[86] *Id.*, p. 75. This non-Communist resistance to Saigon has also been emphasized by Bernard Fall's accounts of the early phases of the insurgency. And as recently as May 1967, Miss Cao Ngoc Phuong, who according to R. W. Apple, Jr., of the *New York Times*, "is regarded as a heroine by peace-oriented intellectuals in South Vietnam," is quoted as saying: "Many of my friends seem to have joined the Vietcong. We are losing the elite of our country. These people know the National Liberation Front is closely allied with the Communists and we don't like Communism. But they see no future in this [the Ky] Government." *New York Times*, May 17, 1967, p. 3, col. 2.

[87] 2 Buttinger, pp. 972-92 contains a very balanced account (but one written from an anti-Communist perspective) of the origins of the second Indochina war during the Diem regime. Buttinger writes that "The Diem Government itself created the conditions that pushed the population to the brink of open rebellion, and this convinced the Communist leadership that the South could be conquered by force," *id.*, p. 977. Buttinger believes the "concerted effort to overthrow the Diem regime and its successor by force, was organized by the Communists, and while it would have made little headway without wide popular support, neither would it have had its amazing success without guidance and assistance from the North.

"But the Saigon-Washington version of these events, which had been reduced to the flat assertion that 'the Vietnam war is the result of external aggression' strays even farther from historical truth. Neither the strenuous efforts of Saigon nor those of Washington have produced evidence that anti-Diem terror and guerrilla warfare started as a result of infiltration of combatants and weapons from the North. No significant infiltration occurred before 1960, and very little during the next three years." *Id.*, pp. 981-82. Even according to the North as substantial a role as Buttinger does, great doubt is still cast on the American inference of "external aggression," without which Professor Moore's entire legal edifice is without proper foundation.

But if one turns to disinterested observers the situation looks significantly less supportive of the official American factual account. Jean Lacouture[88] wrote in May 1966:

> In the beginning most people in the National Liberation Front (N.L.F.) were not Communists, although more are becoming Communist day by day. . . . Until 1963, at least, the Communists were a minority in the N.L.F., and if they found it necessary one year before to create the People's Revolutionary Party (P.R.P.) within the heart of the N.L.F., it was precisely to bolster their inadequate influence.[89]

Lacouture also shows that the evidence of Hanoi's influence on the N.L.F. is very tenuous as a consequence of differences in the style and content of its textual pronouncements relevant to the war.[90]

It would appear, then, that impartial interpretations of the role of Hanoi in aiding the N.L.F. do not significantly support Professor Moore's factual inferences.[91] At best, the factual situation in Viet Nam is ambiguous with respect to the relations between North Viet Nam and the N.L.F.[92] Each side resolves the ambiguity to suit the image of the war that it seeks to rely upon. I am convinced that the facts, although ambiguous in some particulars, do not support *equally* convincing interpretations by the supporters of Saigon and by the supporters of Hanoi; I am convinced that the weight of the evidence and the burden of impartial commentary lends far closer support to Hanoi's version of "the facts" than it does to Saigon's version. But, for sake of analysis, let's assume that the ambiguity supports equally convincing, if mutually inconsistent, accounts of the role of Hanoi in the creation, control, and outlook of the N.L.F. Even so, neither legal precedent, nor legal commentary, nor sound policy analysis supports the United States contention, as of February 1965, that North Viet Nam had com-

---

[88] Jean Lacouture is a distinguished correspondent for *Le Monde* who has written extensively on Viet Nam for more than a decade, and holds a strongly anti-Communist position.

[89] Jean Lacouture, "The 'Face' of the Viet Cong," *War/Peace Report*, May 1966, p. 7 (written as a reply to Mr. Carver's article in *Foreign Affairs, op.cit. supra,* note 79); cf. Kahin and Lewis, pp. 109-16, esp. p. 109: "When the deadline for the promised election passed in July 1956, Hanoi Radio continued to counsel moderation and peaceful tactics to its Southern-based supporters.

"For the next two years revolts against Diem emanated primarily from non-

Vietminh quarters."

[90] Jean Lacouture, "The 'Face' of the Viet Cong," *War/Peace Report*, May 1966, p. 8.

[91] Kahin and Lewis, pp. 110-16.

[92] It is not only *the facts* as such, but *interpretation* of the character of the Vietcong depends on the orientation of the interpreter toward such related matters in the Viet Nam setting as Afro-Asian nationalism, the Saigon regime, the effects of American involvement, and the kind of society that would evolve from the various alternative lines of development open to South Viet Nam (including reunification with the North).

mitted "an armed attack." Such a claim to strike back virtually eliminates all legal restraint upon the discretion of a state or its allies to transform an internal war into an international war. As such, it repudiates the entire effort of twentieth century international law to fetter discretionary recourse to force by a sovereign state. In addition, in a situation of ambiguity the burden of asserting the right to use military power against the territory of a foreign country should be placed upon the claimant state. This burden is especially difficult to sustain when the claim to use force is generalized rather than being justified as a proportionate response to some specific provocation or being directed at some specific external target relevant to the internal war, such as a sanctuary or infiltration route. The United States has increasingly claimed for itself the right to bomb whatever it deems appropriate without restraint as to time, target, or magnitude.

Oppression by Saigon as a Causative Agent. Professor Moore's contextual account is strangely devoid of any reference to the effects of Premier Ngo Dinh Diem's regime of terror in the 1956-57 period in South Viet Nam. Bernard Fall, among others, points out that the uprising of peasants against Saigon arose as a consequence of Diem's policies that preexisted the formation of the Vietcong and was accomplished without any interference on the part of Hanoi.[93] It is difficult to establish causal connections in the Viet Nam setting, but any account of how the violence started in South Viet Nam should call attention to the priority in time, as well as to the oppressiveness and social backwardness of the Diem regime.

It seems worth considering the account given by Joseph Buttinger, an ardent anti-Communist and the most knowledgeable narrator of the relevant historical period (World War II to the assassination of Diem in 1963).[94] Buttinger calls "the manhunt against the Vietminh [the coalition of Vietnamese forces that had fought against French colonialism] an almost incomprehensible violation of common sense, and one of the major contributions to the success of the later Communist-led insurrection."[95] In addition to spreading terror throughout South Viet Nam there were "an unending series of sermons about the evils of Communism, delivered in compulsory meetings by officials whom the peasants had every reason to despise."[96] The victims of Diem's oppression included many non-Communists; "efficiency took the form of brutality and a total disregard for the difference between determined

[93] Bernard B. Fall, *The Two Viet- Nams,* 1st edn., New York, Praeger, 1963, p. 272: "the countryside largely went Communist in 1958-60," i.e. before the Vietcong came into existence. (Quoted in 2 Buttinger, p. 977.)
[94] 2 Buttinger, pp. 974-81.
[95] *Id.,* p. 975.
[96] *Ibid.*

foes and potential friends."[97] Death, preceded by torture, was the form of governmental action in this pre-Vietcong period in the South when there was only an apprehension about a Communist-led insurrection, but no action. Buttinger gives an explanation of why Diem's regime of terror did not provoke official American protest that exposes the root of the Viet Nam tragedy: "The American public, which a little later was told of the many Diem officials murdered by the so-called Vietcong, learned nothing at all about these earlier events, not so much because of Saigon's censorship but rather because of *the West's reluctance openly to condemn crimes committed in the name of anti-Communism.*"[98] It is this ideological biasing of perception that has led the United States Government and its supporters to believe in the rationalization of the war in Viet Nam as defense against aggression. To give Diem and his successors the kind of backing that we have given them can only be explained as part of a global crusade against the spread of Communist influence.[99]

The Relevance of United States Aid to the Incumbent Regime. The inference of "armed attack" should include an examination of the overall relevant context. But Professor Moore ignores altogether the relevance of the United States connection with the Saigon regime to an appraisal of Hanoi's role. The assistance to the N.L.F. given by Hanoi takes on a very different character if interpreted as neutralizing the assistance given by the United States to the other side in an ongoing civil struggle.[100] International law does not prohibit discrimination in favor of an insurgent, especially one that has already enjoyed a degree of success, who is deemed to be "just," nor does it prohibit counterinterventionary efforts designed to offset intervention on behalf of the incum-

97 *Id.*, p. 976.
98 *Ibid.*
99 This understanding of the American commitment must have prompted U Thant in the introduction to the annual report on the work of the United Nations in 1966 to say—"I see nothing but danger in the idea, so assiduously fostered outside Vietnam, that the conflict is a kind of holy war between two powerful political ideologies." *New York Times*, September 19, 1966, p. 18, col. 5. Stillman and Pfaff write in a similar vein in the course of a major analysis of U.S. foreign policy: "Our dominating impulse in Vietnam is ideological; the conventional political and strategic justifications for the American involvement in Vietnam seem peripheral, and even doubtful." Edmund Stillman and William Pfaff, *Power and Impotence*, New York, Random House, 1966, p. 171.
100 Consider the relevance of these words of John Stuart Mill: "But the case of a people struggling against a foreign yoke, or *against a native tyranny upheld by foreign arms*, illustrates the reasons for non-intervention in an opposite way; for in this case the reasons themselves do not exist. . . . To assist a people thus kept down, is not to disturb the balance of forces on which the permanent maintenance of freedom in a country depends, but to redress that balance when it is already unfairly and violently disturbed. . . . Intervention to enforce non-intervention is always rightful, always moral, if not always prudent." (Emphasis supplied) J. S. Mill, *Essays on Politics and Culture*, G. Himmelfarb, ed., New York, Anchor Books, 1962, p. 412.

bent.[101] The policies of self-determination at stake are best served by an attitude of impartiality. The coercive apparatus of the modern state is able to suppress even very widely based popular uprisings; the evolution of social control increasingly favors the government in a domestic struggle. The advantages of the domestic government are accentuated by its *normal* intercourse with foreign states, including its option to continue to receive foreign aid. If peaceful domestic opposition is disallowed and a coercive government is aided by a powerful external ally, then the sole possibility of approximating the ideas of self-determination is to accord equivalent rights to insurgent or anti-incumbent groups that solicit aid from foreign countries.

If the insurgency succeeds in establishing itself as the *de facto* government of a substantial portion of the territory in controversy, then foreign states are legally as entitled to deal with the insurgent faction as with the constituted government. Such discretion, expressed in traditional international law by the shifting of insurgent status from "rebellion" to "insurgency" to "belligerency," embodies a sound compromise between according respect to the constituted government as the source of domestic stability and avoiding interferences with the way in which contending groups in a national society work out a domestic balance of forces. This reasoning is applicable to the situation in South Viet Nam. As of 1961, at the latest, the National Liberation Front was in effective control of a substantial portion of South Viet Nam and often was exercising its authority in areas under its control with more success than was the constituted regime in Saigon.[102] At such a stage in civil strife international law fully allows third parties to treat the society in question as exhibiting a condition of *dual sovereignty*. In these circumstances North Viet Nam assistance to the N.L.F. enjoys the same legal status as does United States assistance to the Saigon regime.[103]

---

101 See notes 62-64 *supra* and p. 289.

102 Cf., e.g. Wilfred G. Burchett, *Vietnam: Inside Story of the Guerrilla War*, New York, International Publishers, 1965. No friend of the N.L.F., Bernard Fall nevertheless writes that "on the local level, American sources have privately stated matter-of-factly that the local NLF administration clearly outperformed the GVN's on every count until the heavy bombardments of 1965-66 made orderly government impossible. It was an established fact that in most areas the NLF did proceed with local elections that were by and large unfettered—Communist control would exist in the form of a *can-bo* (a cadre) detached to the village chief for his paperwork—and produced more effective and more popularly supported local government than the country had enjoyed since its loss of independence in the 1860's." Bernard B. Fall, *The Two Viet-Nams*, 2nd rev. edn., New York, Praeger, 1967, p. 365.

103 See generally Ann Van Wynen Thomas and A. J. Thomas, Jr., *Non-Intervention: The Law and Its Import in the Americas*, Dallas, Southern Methodist University Press, 1956, pp. 215-21; Falk, "The International Regulation of Internal Violence in the Developing Countries," *Proceedings, the American Society of International Law, 1966*, p. 58; for the reality and extent of N.L.F. control as of mid-1965 see Bernard B. Fall, *The Two Viet-Nams*, 2nd rev. edn., New York, Praeger, 1967.

Such an interpretation bears centrally on any contention that North Viet Nam committed an armed attack on South Viet Nam subsequent to whatever critical date is chosen to affirm substantial *de facto* sovereignty by the N.L.F.[104] The argument of the State Department, then, that the level of support given to the N.L.F. up through 1965 establishes "aggression" of such magnitude as to be "an armed attack" is unresponsive to the basic legal issues at stake. Even accepting as accurate the conclusion that "by the end of 1964, North Viet Nam might well have moved over 40,000 armed and unarmed guerrillas into South Viet Nam" there is no consideration given to the critical fact that as of 1962 the N.L.F. enjoyed enough *de facto* sovereignty in South Viet Nam to allow North Viet Nam to furnish military assistance on the same legal premises as relied upon by the United States vis-à-vis Saigon.[105] The whole legal tradition of third-party relationships to contending factions in a civil war is to distinguish the degrees to which a revolutionary struggle has succeeded in establishing itself as a partial "government." Neither the State Department nor Professor Moore take this essential contextual factor into account to any extent in characterizing North Viet Nam's role as "an armed attack."

Given a post-1962 assumption of *de facto* dual sovereignty in South Viet Nam, third powers are entitled to neutralize and offset external assistance to the other side. Certainly, then, military assistance by North Viet Nam to the N.L.F. seems proportionate to military assistance by the United States to the Saigon regime. Even more certainly, it is unreasonable to characterize North Viet Nam's role after 1962 as "an armed attack" and the United States' role as "lawful assistance." It is also relevant to note that no American official contended that the pre-1962 role of North Viet Nam deserved to be regarded as "an armed attack"; even during the debates on the American claims of "reprisal" arising out of the Gulf of Tonkin incident in August 1964,

---

[104] See especially the basis of argument in the State Department's Memorandum of Law in its opening section vindicating recourse to collective self-defense because of a prior armed attack. *Consultative Council*, pp. 113-14. There is obviously no "armed attack" if the foreign assistance is being given lawfully to one governmental unit in a situation of civil strife in which the adversary unit is receiving a much larger quantity of foreign assistance.

[105] That is, the notion of neutrality was supposed to guide third powers in the event of an ongoing civil war. See, e.g. Thomas and Thomas, *op.cit. supra*, note 103, p. 219: "A neutral power is always at liberty to decide whether it will permit or will prohibit aid to the disrupted state; its main duty as a neutral is that it must treat both sides equally." An obvious corollary of this norm is that when a neutral favors one side, then this advantage can be offset by discrimination in favor of the other side. Depending on the phasing of intervention with the existence of a conflict pronounced enough to qualify as a civil war, both the United States and North Viet Nam could reasonably perceive their roles to be one of offsetting or neutralizing the intervention or non-neutrality of the other side. Cf. White, *op.cit. supra*, note 3.

there was no intimation that North Viet Nam's role in South Viet Nam was of the extraordinary character justifying recourse to "self-defense." It seems clear and significant to conclude that the post-1965 contention of "armed attack" besides being unconvincing on its merits is also an example of arguing *post hoc, ergo propter hoc.*

In the months immediately after the Geneva Conference in 1954 it was widely believed that the Diem regime would collapse from its own dead weight because of its unpopularity and inefficiency. The United States gave substantial economic and indirect military support to the Saigon government from the beginning of its existence. This support included training, guiding, and paying the main units of Saigon's military establishment.[106] The United States also played an increasingly significant role in influencing the composition and outlook of Saigon's government, so significant that by the time serious civil strife broke out there was hardly any prospect of resolution being reached by the domestic balance of forces.

As the American military participation on the side of Saigon grew more overt and massive it became evident that it was Washington and not Saigon that was the main adversary of the N.L.F.[107] As Hanoi acted to offset this American military presence in South Viet Nam it was naturally drawn into ever more substantial and overt military participation on the side of the N.L.F.[108] And certainly since 1963 United States control of Saigon's war effort and war aims appears to be much more explicit and decisive than does Hanoi's control over the N.L.F.'s war effort and war aims. Given the ratio of external participation on the two sides of the Viet Nam War it seems contrary both to the perceptions of common sense and to the dictates of international law to regard North Viet Nam as guilty of an armed attack. The total context suggests that the phasing and extent of the United States participation in the war has had a much greater impact upon its course than has the North Vietnamese participation, and that neither side enjoys a privileged legal status so far as the principles of either self-defense or non-intervention are concerned, at least once it became clear that the insurgent challenge was a serious and prolonged one. In fact, the legal status of Hanoi's role in assisting the insurgency is according to conventional approaches of international law dependent upon the extent to

---

[106] Kahin and Lewis, pp. 77-80; *The Mansfield Report,* p. 20.

[107] Increasingly, it became clear that the United States, and not South Viet Nam, was determining the course of the war and the conditions for its settlement.

[108] But can one imagine a conference of the N.L.F. allies summoned under the auspices of North Viet Nam in the manner of the 1965-66 conferences at Honolulu, Manila, and Guam? For comparative statistics on foreign involvement in the war in Viet Nam see Kahin and Lewis, p. 186; Bernard B. Fall, *The Two Viet-Nams,* 2nd rev. edn., New York, Praeger, 1967, p. 358.

which it is reasonable to regard the insurgent faction as a countergovernment in effective political control over portions of the contested territory.[109] If Professor Moore stresses the *de facto* sovereignty of South Viet Nam (regardless of the terms at Geneva), then it seems essential to acknowledge all relevant *de facto* circumstances including those that benefit the legal contentions of North Viet Nam. In the first Mansfield Report it was acknowledged that "By 1961 it was apparent that the prospects for a total collapse in South Viet Nam had begun to come dangerously close."[110]

In the context of Viet Nam, however, the normal legal situation is even less favorable to the incumbent regime than it might otherwise be. Chapter III of the Cease-Fire Agreement contains a series of provisions that disallows the incumbent regime its normal freedom to receive military assistance.[111] Article 4 of the Final Declaration "takes note of the clauses in the agreement on the cessation of hostilities in Viet Nam prohibiting the introduction into Viet Nam of foreign troops and military personnel as well as all kinds of arms and munitions."[112] Therefore, it is arguable that without the authorization of the International Control Commission it was illegal to give any direct military assistance to the Saigon regime; it is also arguable that the United States immediately fostered the violation of the spirit of the Geneva Accords by the extension of SEATO to cover South Viet Nam and by the extension of economic aid of such a character that freed Saigon to develop and modernize its military capability as directed by a growing number of United States military advisers. It is difficult to read the Geneva Accords without receiving the strong impression that one of the principal purposes was to prohibit post-1954 Great Power intervention in Vietnamese affairs, and given the United States attempt to mobilize support for a Great Power intervention as an alternative to the Geneva settlement it is difficult to avoid the conclusion that the provisions on foreign military intervention were directed, above all, at the United States.

Professor Moore suggests that the belligerent objective of North Viet Nam is reunification under Hanoi's control, and he contends that this objective is the functional equivalent of territorial conquest. Such reasoning leads Moore to conclude that Hanoi's assistance to the N.L.F. is more suitably treated as equivalent to North Korea's attack on South Korea than it is to Germany's aid to the Franco insurgency during the

109 Cf. note 102 *supra* and accompanying text.
110 *The Mansfield Report*, p. 21.
111 Articles 16-18; for convenient text of Final Declaration, *Consultative Council*, pp. 148-50. *Further Documents Relating to the Discussion of Indochina at the Geneva Conference* (Misc. No. 20) Cmnd. No. 9239, 1954.
112 Convenient text of Final Declaration, *Consultative Council*, p. 148.

Spanish Civil War. I find Professor Moore's conclusion on this point, also, to rest upon a selective interpretation of the relevant context for the following reasons:

(1) Hanoi's pursuit of unification by limited, low-order coercion needs to be understood in light of the outcome of the first Indochina war and the terms of the Geneva settlement; from the perspective of law North Viet Nam should be accorded a reciprocal discretion in interpreting post-1954 events as is claimed for South Viet Nam;

(2) The evidence advanced by Professor Moore to show that North Viet Nam is seeking reunification is largely hypothetical and speculative;

(3) Both Hanoi and the N.L.F. disavow reunification as an objective of their war effort.[113]

On this basis it seems unconvincing to equate North Korea's sudden and massive overt attack upon South Korea with North Viet Nam's slow build-up of support for the N.L.F. through covert assistance to an insurgent effort against a hostile neighboring regime allied with a hostile superpower. The ill-fated support of the United States for the Bay of Pigs venture in 1961 was not so long ago.[114] We went to considerable lengths to disguise our sponsorship of the Cuban exiles intent on overthrowing Castro. Why? Precisely because different world order consequences attach to covert rather than to overt sponsorship of insurrectionary activity in a foreign country.[115] And what of the role of the CIA in the overthrow of an allegedly pro-Communist regime in Guatemala in 1954?[116] I mention these examples of covert interference not to defend this pattern of practice, but to suggest that when the United States has been an active party in support of insurrection a great effort has been made to keep its role as covert as possible for as long as possible. Likewise it was the overtness of our interference with domestic events in the Dominican Republic in 1965 that provoked such intense criticism of our action; it was probably less interventionary than the covert role in Guatemala.[117] Thus it is not accurate to analogize the covert pursuit of an interventionary policy in a foreign society with its overt pursuit in terms either of its perceived or actual world order con-

[113] *Both* sides evidently avow peaceful reunification. South Viet Nam goes so far as to incorporate the following two provisions into its new Constitution: Article 1(1): "Viet-Nam is a territorially indivisible, unified and independent republic." Article 107: "Article 1 of the constitution and this Article may not be amended or deleted." May not North Viet Nam espouse a comparable objective? See generally, Theodore Draper, "Vietnam: How Not to Negotiate," *New York Review of Books*, May 4, 1967, p. 17.

[114] See Chapter VI.
[115] See *supra*, pp. 287-92.
[116] David Wise and Thomas Ross, *The Invisible Government*, New York, Random House, 1964. For a relevant account of Guatemala events, see David Horowitz, *From Yalta to Vietnam*, New York, Penguin Books, 1965, pp. 160-61.
[117] For an account critical of the United States intervention in the Dominican Republic, see Senator J. William Fulbright, *The Arrogance of Power*, New York, Random House, 1966.

sequences, even assuming for the sake of argument that the two modes of interference are equally effective. And therefore, and this is critical for my approach, a unilateral, defensive extraterritorial response to covert coercion cannot possibly acquire the same legitimacy as would such a response if made to overt coercion. For these reasons I find it inappropriate to rely upon the Korea analogy; the Spanish Civil War I continue to regard as a helpful precedent because there was no counter-intervention undertaken against the territory of intervening states despite substantial foreign assistance to the insurgent faction.

TYPE II GEOGRAPHICAL RESTRICTIONS UPON
"DEFENSIVE" MEASURES PROMOTE WORLD ORDER:
THE NORMATIVE LEVEL OF DISCOURSE

Professor Moore argues that the restrictions imposed upon the incumbent regime in a Type II situation are arbitrary and that in a particular situation defensive measures against the territory of a state supporting an insurgent *ought* to be permitted. I would agree with Professor Moore that in a *particular* war it can be argued that extraterritorial military measures may minimize the extent and duration of destruction. Relevant rules of restraint, however, must be devised with a generality of instances in mind. In the context of a Viet Nam-type war I would maintain that Type II restrictions are, *in general*, desirable. First of all, the appreciation of whether a measure is "defensive" or "offensive" cannot be reliably achieved by interested parties. Second, to the extent that extraterritorial "defensive" measures are justified by the specific characteristics of foreign support, then a precise claim to use extraterritorial force should be explained in terms of particular military necessities. For example, an air strike directed against extraterritorial insurgent sanctuaries would be more easily justifiable in the context of normal Type II restraints if these sanctuaries bore a significant specific relationship to the conduct of the war. But bombing North Viet Nam has not been justified in terms of specific, limited military objectives requiring exceptional action; in fact, the American rationale for bombing North Viet Nam has been changed from time to time. At every stage of the war, however, the scope and intensity of the bombing action appear to have been disproportionate to the military justification. In addition, independent, non-Communist world public opinion almost universally condemns the continuation of bombing by the United States, and the Secretary General of the United Nations has repeatedly called upon the United States to stop bombing on a unilateral and unconditional basis. Hanoi, too, has insisted that the unconditional termination of bombing is the essential precondition for peace talks. The

United States effort to negotiate a reciprocal deescalation by North Viet Nam in exchange for a halt in bombing overlooks both the general attitude in opposition of the bombing and the inequality in bargaining power that exists between the greatest military colossus in world history and a small, war-torn and unmodernized state.

Third, the frequency of patterns of intervention and counterintervention in civil strife throughout international society underlines the danger of spreading violence beyond its original national locus. Greece and Turkey in Cyprus and the United Arab Republic and Saudi Arabia in The Yemen are two examples of civil struggles during the 1960's that could grow much worse if the external sponsor of the incumbent regime felt entitled and did, in fact, attack the territory of the insurgent's external sponsor.[118] It does not require much knowledge of fire-fighting to conclude that confining the spatial scope of a fire is one way to restrict its damaging impact.

If the coercion is sustained and substantial then the prospects of dealing with it by community procedures are improved. Because of the ambiguity of the facts and the tendency to interpret them in a self-justifying fashion in the Viet Nam setting it is important to restrict responses to the limits of Type II unless a sufficient consensus can be mobilized to shift the conflict into the Type IV category. If it qualifies as a Type IV conflict then the organized international community authorizes the response that is deemed appropriate. *Community authorization* takes the place of overtness as the key factor vindicating a defensive response against foreign territory. I have already indicated why covert forms of action are so difficult to construe, especially in a mixed-up political setting. It follows from this assessment that the resources of world order should be built up to facilitate the authoritative community identification of covert coercion as "aggression." For this reason it would be desirable to establish border-control, fact-finding machinery and peace observation groups in those sectors of the world containing target societies that are highly vulnerable to covert coercion. The objective of these devices is to make covert forms of coercion more *visible* to impartial observers, facilitating a consensus, legitimating a decisive defense response, and discouraging recourse to such coercion as a means to resolve international disputes.

My overall approach to Viet Nam-type conflicts has been altered in

---

[118] In fact, one would imagine a serious regional war emerging if either side transgressed the limits that I argue are embodied in a Type II conflict. Only the mutual forbearance of both sides, despite their recriminations about each other's aggression, keeps the conflict at its present level. It is only because the United States is a superpower and North Viet Nam a minor state that the war in Viet Nam has not escalated to much higher levels; it is the power differential that encouraged the United States to transgress Type II restrictions in the spirit of relative prudence.

response to Professor Moore's criticisms in several important respects:

(1) The creation of Type IV to establish an analytic contrast with Types I to III so as to permit "self-defense" in the Viet Nam-type setting provided a suitable prior community authorization has been given.[119]

(2) The realization that aggressive designs can be effectively carried out at present by covert forms of international coercion and that it would be desirable to discourage such coercion by making it more *visible*; the eventual world order goal would be to treat *covert* coercion as we now treat *overt* coercion. The effect would be to make Type II conflicts more easily transferable into the Type IV category or more susceptible to Type I treatment. However, in international society as now constituted it seems clearly preferable to deny the victim state unilateral discretion to treat what it perceives to be "aggression" by covert means as justifying its recourse to "self-defense."[120] In a sense this legal conclusion merely restates the adverse judgment rendered by the international community on several occasions when Israel has had recourse to *overt* military force in retaliation for damage that it has suffered from *semi-covert* coercion. The rejection of Israel's claim is impressive because Israel has a much more convincing security rationale than does South Viet Nam for striking back overtly and because the Arab states surrounding Israel are avowedly committed to its destruction.[121] One may argue against the fairness of such constraints upon Israel's discretion in these circumstances, but it is essentially an extra-legal appeal as the organs of the United Nations have the procedural capacity to authorize or prohibit specific uses of force and it is the exercise of this capacity that most clearly distinguishes what is "legal" from what is "illegal" with regard to the use of force in international society. Legality depends more upon the *identity* of the authorizing decision-maker than upon the *facts of the coercion*. With respect to Viet Nam, if a principal organ of the United Nations authorized the bombing of North Viet Nam by the United States then it would be legal (unless an argument could be successfully made that the decision was "unconstitutional").[122]

---

[119] A defensive alliance, such as SEATO, only multilateralizes decisions to use force to a very slight degree; "the community" must be defined in wide enough terms to include principal divergent elements.

[120] This denial is especially justifiable since (a) legitimate defensive interests can be upheld within the terms of Type II, and special exceptions thereto; and (b) a shift to Type I tends both to increase the obstruction of international peace and to increase the role of military power differentials in achieving a settlement of an international dispute.

[121] Israel's responses have seemed to conform much more closely to the requirements of proportionality than has the United States–South Viet Nam response, even if United States allegations of coercion are taken at face value.

[122] To be legal in the last analysis is to be authorized by the appropriate decision-maker; one can seek to correct "the mistake" attributed to the decision-maker, but the capacity to confer legality persists so long as the legal order is a valid one.

Professor Moore also usefully singles out "divided" country problems for separate treatments. He is correct in pointing out that world order is especially endangered by attempts to alter coercively the *status quo* prevailing in a divided country. In this respect the tragic consequences in Viet Nam can be understood as foredestined as soon as Saigon, with the backing of the United States, acted to locate Viet Nam in the divided country category.[123] The uncertainty as to whether Viet Nam is properly classified as "divided" in Professor Moore's sense involves an interpretation of the Geneva Accords. The classification of Viet Nam as a divided country also appears to have been imprudent in view of the logistic difficulties of securing South Viet Nam against attack and in view of the inability to evolve a tolerable regime in Saigon that could provide South Viet Nam with effective government without a huge American military and economic commitment.[124] Even without a hostile North Viet Nam embittered by a sense of being cheated by the non-implementation of the Geneva Accords, there is reason to suspect that without American backing the Saigon regime would have been unable to govern South Viet Nam with any success. Predictions of imminent collapse were widespread until the American military presence assumed major proportions in 1965.[125] In addition, there was only minimal and grudging alliance support, much less community support, for regarding South Viet Nam as an inviolable sovereign entity of the same sort as West Germany or South Korea, or even Formosa. For these reasons I do not find it convincing, independent of the issue of ambiguous facts, to analogize Viet Nam to other divided country problems.

III. Comments on Professor Moore's Policy Inquiry vis-à-vis Type III Conflict

Professor Moore's perceptive discussion of the considerations that bear on the international management of intrastate conflict deserves careful study. His stress in the setting of Type III upon the policies of self-determination and minimum world public order points up the difficulty that results from the sort of overgeneralization that is implicit in the kind of categorization of international conflict situations that I have proposed. I accept his criticism that my original formulation of

[123] The seeds of conflict seem to have been sown by the contradictory interpretations of what was "settled" at Geneva in 1954 with regard to the terms and timing of reunification; although there is room for some misunderstanding, my orientation is heavily influenced by regarding Hanoi's interpretation of the settlement as far more reasonable than Saigon's or Washington's.

[124] See the critique advanced by Edmund Stillman and William Pfaff, *Power and Impotence*, New York, Random House, 1966, pp. 169-74. The costs of the Viet Nam War are enormous both with respect to the pursuit of international security goals and with regard to domestic welfare goals.

[125] Kahin and Lewis, pp. 66-87.

Type III rules is "simplistic" if applied mechanically to a large variety of greatly varying international contexts. A complete response to Professor Moore's critique cannot be undertaken within the compass of this chapter, but will be attempted on another occasion.[126] I will restrict myself here to a few general comments on Professor Moore's approach to suggest wherein my policy emphasis differs from his with regard to the regulation of third-party participation in intrastate conflict.

Let me say in my own intellectual defense that the division of international conflict situations into three broad categories (now four)[127] was intended primarily to facilitate and organize thought about the management of all forms of international violence through a preliminary sorting out of relevant contexts and by explicating the decisive legal consequences of each. Once this preliminary task of classification has been accomplished then it is appropriate to question whether there need to be more specific subcategories and whether rules stating exceptions should not also be included.[128] On this level then, my response to Professor Moore is to accept his criticism, but to suggest that the attempt to categorize international conflict appears to add greater focus to policy inquiry than is possible by either an *ad hoc* response to a specific conflict (Viet Nam) or by a generalized description of the policies bearing most heavily on the legal regulation of recourse to international violence.

On a more fundamental level of policy Professor Moore, as the result of a very sophisticated analysis, appears to conclude that given the conditions of the modern world it is more desirable to endorse an approach to civil strife that authorizes discrimination in favor of the incumbent faction, especially in cold war settings, and prohibits assistance to the insurgent faction.

I am persuaded by Professor Moore's analysis to modify my original formulations to a certain extent. A neutral role of impartiality does not preclude the continuation of (or even the moderate increase in) the level of assistance furnished a constituted government prior to the outbreak of civil strife. There are, however, restraints upon the scope and form

---

126 For instance, Types I-IV should be appropriately subdivided to take account of recurrent contexts that can be grouped together within each broader category. Thus in Type III there is a difference between the legislative contexts relevant to uprisings in the five countries of southern Africa, the humanitarian context of the slaughter that followed the generals' counter-coup in Indonesia (1965-66), the anarchy that has been threatened from time to time in the Congo and Nigeria from prolonged civil strife, and the hege-

monial context that exists when one superpower has claimed over time special geopolitical prerogatives, acquiesced in by other states, in relation to a region.

127 See text accompanying note 30 *supra* for explanation.

128 Cf. the development of international law governing the use of the oceans as depicted by Myres S. McDougal and William T. Burke, *The Public Order of the Oceans*, New Haven, Yale University Press, 1962.

of discriminatory external participation.[129] For one thing, foreign assistance should not include direct participation in combat operations. For another, it should not attempt to bear more than a fairly small percentage, certainly under 50 per cent, of the increased military requirements created by the domestic uprising. And finally, the external assistance should not be conditioned upon increased influence in the process of decision-making within the recipient country. In the event that the restraints sketched above are ignored, then the conflict is shifted from Type III into the Type II category, the shift itself reflecting "the violation" committed by a third-party state. If the restraints are respected with respect to aid furnished to the incumbent, then substantial aid to instigate or sustain an insurgency is a violation of Type III restraints that shifts the conflict into the Type II category as a consequence of the legal conduct of the third party.

In the event, however, that the uprising succeeds in establishing control over a substantial portion of the area and population of the country, then a condition of *de facto* dual sovereignty exists such that third parties can furnish assistance to the insurgent on the same basis as to the incumbent. If substantial assistance is accorded to one or both sides subsequent to *de facto* dual sovereignty the conflict is necessarily shifted into Type II, but there is no violation of international law committed by third powers. The internal situation generated a shift from Type III to Type II, as distinct from a shift coming about through interventionary roles by foreign states on either side of a Type III conflict.

If the United States had chosen to give military assistance to the Batista regime in its struggle against the Castro insurgency in Cuba, then this would be permissible under the scheme outlined in the prior paragraph unless the United States entered Cuba in the last stages of the war by using its independent military capability to foreclose the outcome that would have resulted from the domestic balance of forces. The Soviet intervention in Hungary (1956) definitely succeeded in reversing the outcome of a domestic struggle, and was appropriately condemned by the political organs of the United Nations; the United States intervention in the Dominican Republic in 1965 designed to displace the incumbent regime was given presumably an even more objectionable form of decisive external assistance as it was directed against the incumbent faction.[130]

129 For a creative effort at emphasizing limits on the character of intervention rather than upon its occurrence see Tom Farer, "Intervention in Civil Wars: A Modest Proposal," 67 *Columbia Law Review* 266 (1967).

130 For a sympathetic account of the legal basis of the Dominican intervention, see Thomas and Thomas, *op.cit. supra,* note 103.

Professor Moore is also correct to suggest that in cold war contexts rules supporting the stability of existing regimes are probably desirable. It may be helpful to restrict pure Type III analysis to the Afro-Asian world wherein the geopolitical context is of a different order. In effect, Professor Moore is pointing out that the rival superpowers—the United States and the Soviet Union—provide their own form of conflict management within those segments of international society regarded as belonging to their respective spheres of influence or adhering to their respective security communities. In this regard it may be helpful to consider that concentric security zones surround each superpower and affect the actual treatment of Type III conflicts to a considerable degree:

I. *Primary Security Zone*: The United States, the Soviet Union, and possibly mainland China and the principal states of Western Europe, as sovereign states in relation to their own national security;

II. *Secondary Security Zones*: Groups of countries that are traditionally subject to the influence of one superpower or the other and whose security interests ultimately depend on the protection of one or the other superpower;[131]

III. *Tertiary Security Zones*: The Afro-Asian world of recently independent states in which policies of nonalignment and nonintervention are predominant.

These security zones describe the geopolitical condition in the world as of 1967. It is a complex world order issue to interrelate these political realities with the role of law in establishing common standards of restraint and interaction. It is generally true that in the Secondary Security Zones the dominant actor is able to exercise control over the outcome of Type III conflicts, although Hungary in 1956 and the Dominican Republic in 1965 were governed by interventions that did not accord generally with permissible uses of military power, at least as understood by general community expectations.[132] Viet Nam has become such a sustained and major war because the United States has converted a Type III conflict into a Type I conflict without the legitimizing benefit of an overt armed attack and without the geopolitical tolerance accorded to superpower diplomacy that is confined within its own Secondary Zone. Thereafter the extralegal categorization of security zones may help to identify those situations in which external military assistance

---

131 E.g. Latin America, East Europe; one might argue that the problems in Asian affairs arise out of China's attempt to establish a Secondary Security Zone on its periphery and the United States resistance to this attempt.

132 I.e. there is a geopolitical level of practice that exists in a state of tension with a moral-legal level of commitment; both levels converge in the policy-making process relevant to international decisions.

that is carried beyond a certain threshold is likely to trigger a major off-setting military action by a principal adversary. It is now commonplace to note that the most severe forms of international violence since World War II have been the result of competing superpower interferences in the Tertiary Security Zone, especially in those circumstances, such as Viet Nam, where it is unclear whether the territory in dispute belongs in the Secondary Zone, and if so on which side, or in the Tertiary Zone.

Professor Moore's discussion is strangely devoid of any reference to the role of international institutions or to the relevance of the will of the organized international community with respect to the relative merits of contending factions in a Type III situation.[133] It seems to me that many of the problems that Professor Moore points out, that arise in discriminating between various Type III contexts can be resolved by according regional and global international institutions the competence to identify which faction is entitled to benefit from external assistance.[134] Thus in the context of Southern Africa the decisive expression of the will of the international community would appear to legitimize discrimination in favor of the insurgent faction in the event that a Type III situation should arise endorsed in the African context by the Organization of African Unity.[135] Types I to III are residual categories that exist only when there is no consensus formally reached by a competent international institution.

A residual rule of impartiality does seem to minimize the role of both extranational and domestic violence in situations where no international consensus exists. The absence of consensus is itself indicative of a potentiality for major conflicts, disclosing seriously opposed interpretations of the appropriate external attitude toward the intrastate conflict. Therefore, in a Type III situation it would seem generally desirable to promote adherence to Hall's view that neither incumbent nor insurgent should be the beneficiary of discrimination.[136] What level of support for the incumbent constitutes "discrimination" and at what point a civil disturbance is properly regarded as belonging in Type III are complex determinations of fact and law for which no definite answer can here be provided.

Professor Moore, in my judgment, underrates once again the detri-

133 Cf. Falk, "The New States and International Legal Order," 118 *Recueil des Cours* (forthcoming).

134 On the jurisprudential basis see Falk, "On the Quasi-Legislative Competence of the General Assembly," 60 *American Journal of International Law* 782 (1966).

135 For some consideration of the difficulties that attend regional authorization of the use of force see Chapter IV.

136 On the assumption, of course, of some *de facto* control and some substantial prospect of eventual success, and subject to the geopolitical qualifications of the three-zone analysis.

mental consequences of affirming the discretion of sovereign states to project their military power into foreign political conflicts. It is true that covert forms of coercion can subject a society to an "attack" that jeopardizes its political independence and territorial sovereignty, but it is also true that "the defense" of that society may involve its destruction and manipulation. To allow discrimination in favor of the incumbent to increase without limit in a situation of civil strife is to defeat altogether the ideals of self-determination without promoting the kind of world order premised upon the ordering capacities of territorially based sovereign states. To insulate Type III conflicts it is as important to restrict discrimination in favor of the incumbent as it is to improve the process of detecting covert assistance to the insurgent by making it more visible. To do one without the other is to invite Viet Nam-type confrontations throughout the Tertiary Security Zone. I would espouse a foreign policy of Cosmopolitan Isolationism as most suited to the attainment of world order in the Tertiary Security Zone: national military power should be brought to bear, if at all, only after formal authorization by the organized international community.[137] In my revised system of categorization, then, external assistance beyond *status quo* levels is permissible only if the intrastate conflict can be shifted from Type III to Type IV.

IV. The State Department Brief: A Further Comment

Professor Moore explains that the State Department Memorandum of Law was written mainly to deal with the public debate initiated by a widely circulated (and now redrafted) brief of the Lawyers Committee on American Policy Towards Viet Nam.[138] As such, it should not be appraised as the full statement of the Government's position. This is undoubtedly true, but it is nevertheless disappointing that when the Department's Legal Adviser enters the public debate he does so in such an unconvincing manner. Certainly it does not clarify the discussion to overclarify the facts or to make complex legal questions appear self-evident. A citizens' white paper in opposition to Government policy is primarily a call for an impartial accounting. It is intentionally and appropriately one-sided; especially in the security area it is impossible to proffer criticism in effective form unless the issues are somewhat overstated.[139] It is true, as Professor Moore writes, that the Lawyers Com-

137 I have developed this viewpoint in an essay to appear in *Adept*, a literary journal published in Houston, Texas.

138 *Consultative Council*, pp. 19-111.

139 Citizens do not have access to classified information, national news coverage is slanted toward affirming foreign policy in periods of crisis, and only clear conclusions will receive attention in press or government; the more balanced scholarly critique will be ignored except, perhaps, by other scholars, but it will not influence the public debate.

mittee's first Memorandum emphasized many of the "wrong" issues or stated the "right" issues in the "wrong" way, but it did provoke the Government after a decade of involvement in Viet Nam to make its first serious effort to reconcile United States foreign policy in Viet Nam with our proclaimed commitment to a law-ordered international society. That serious effort was impaired, in my judgment, by defining the issues and maintaining the adversary spirit of the Lawyers Committee document. In a second round of public debate the Lawyers Committee has prepared under the auspices of a Consultative Council composed of academicians a reply to the Government's Memorandum. This reply does focus more directly on the world order issues at stake and does provide the Government with a new intellectual context within which to respond. It is a sign of health for a democratic polity to engage in this sort of dialogue during the course of a major war; it may be almost unprecedented for citizens to call their own government to account by an appeal to the constraints and institutional procedures of international law. The outcome of this dialogue, as well as its more scholarly analogues, may well shape our perceptions of the requirements of world order so as either to endorse or inhibit American involvements in a series of Viet Nam-type wars in the decades ahead.

V. On the Constitutionality of
Violating International Law

Professor Moore suggests that there is no legal authority to support a view that the executive has a constitutional obligation to obey international law. What is more, he accuses me of advancing a "somewhat monistic argument." I acknowledge my guilt. It appears to me that the Constitution embodies the legal framework within which the government is entitled to act. The condemnation of aggressive war and endorsement by the United States of the Principles of the Nuremberg Judgment seem to make adherence to international law a matter of constitutional necessity. True, there is no established legal doctrine to this effect, but the question is open enough that it seems reasonable to contend that this is the way the Constitution ought to be authoritatively construed. As in domestic affairs, so in foreign affairs, we should remember that it is a Constitution we are expounding; as the organic law of the society it must be constantly readapted to the needs of the nation and its citizenry. No need is more paramount at the present time than to develop a constitutional tradition of restraint upon the executive's virtually discretionary power to commit the nation to war of any scope and duration. To insist on constitutional sources of legal restraint is a part of the wider global need to erode the prerogatives of the sovereign state in the area of war and peace. So long as international society remains decentralized the most effective legal restraints are likely to be self-restraints, those that are applied from *within* rather than from *without* the sovereign state. For this reason we cannot neglect the constitutional dimension of an allegedly illegal participation by the United States in the Viet Nam War, and for this reason it seems appropriate for domestic courts to pronounce upon, rather than to evade, such legal challenges as have been presented in the selective service context.[140]

VI. *A Comment on Professor Moore's Conclusion*

Professor Moore concludes his article by affirming "that the conflict cannot be meaningfully generalized in black and white terms" and yet proceeds to do so. He acknowledges that "If because of Viet Nam Americans must ask themselves hard questions about the use of national power and the proper goals of foreign policy, the North Vietnamese must ask themselves equally hard questions about the use of force as an instrument of major international change." These two sets of questions as formulated by Professor Moore are not equally hard, nor are they, it is well to add, impartial in tone or content. As expressed throughout Professor Moore's article the United States failure in his view, may at most involve errors of judgment and lapses of prudence, whereas North Viet Nam's failure consists of committing the most serious possible international delinquency—waging a war of aggression. Such a construction of the adversary positions greatly falsifies, in my judgment, the true situation. An objective interpretation of the war, as sympathetic with the United States contentions as the facts seem to permit, would acknowledge that the conflict in Viet Nam is one in which both sides sincerely, and even reasonably, perceive the other side as the aggressor. Most disinterested interpretations would, in all probability, tend to regard the United States as the sole aggressor, at least with regard to carrying the war into North Vietnamese territory.

The way in which responsibility for the war is distributed is vitally connected with what sorts of steps taken by which side are reasonable preconditions to achieve a negotiated settlement. In this regard when Professor Moore invokes U Thant to support the conclusion that "the Viet Nam war [is] basically a political problem that can only be solved by a political settlement" it seems only reasonable to add that the Secretary General has laid most of the blame upon the United States for prolonging and intensifying the war. In fact, U Thant's precondi-

---

[140] See the important dissenting opinion of Mr. Justice Douglas in the decision by the Supreme Court to deny a petition for a writ of certiorari in Mitchell v. U.S., 35 *U.S.L.W.*, 3330, 1967.

tions for a negotiated settlement include the prior termination of war acts by the United States against North Vietnamese territory.

A second point of disagreement: Professor Moore writes as if the United States and North Viet Nam are in a position of bargaining parity. Such a predisposition not only overlooks the enormous disparity in scale between the two countries, but also overlooks the fact that the United States is fighting the war at a safe distance from its own society, whereas the destructive impact of the conflict is now focused directly upon the North Vietnamese homeland. This bargaining inequality is directly relevant to Professor Moore's comments about the "hard line from Hanoi." To advise the United States that it "must continue to emphasize a negotiated settlement" is to write as if no credibility gap existed as to the sincerity and diligence of prior American peace efforts. Such a statement also ignores the extent to which the American emphasis on negotiations has been expressed more through threatened and actual escalations than by realistic offers to end the war on some basis that preserves Hanoi's stake in the outcome to the same extent as it preserves Washington's stake.

It is not possible here to consider the basis for a negotiated settlement. I share Professor Moore's emphasis upon a search for compromise in Viet Nam and for a way eventually to give effect to the principle of self-determination for the forsaken Vietnamese population. There are, however, very serious problems with a negotiated settlement that explain, perhaps, why neither side can envision any middle ground between surrender and victory. Among these serious problems the following can be mentioned:

(1) A coalition government in South Viet Nam seems unworkable that either (a) excludes both Premier Ky and the N.L.F., (b) includes Premier Ky but excludes the N.L.F., (c) includes the N.L.F. but excludes Premier Ky, or (d) includes both Premier Ky and the N.L.F. These four alternative patterns exhaust the logical possibilities, and yet no one of them seems to be a plausible basis for a stable South Viet Nam if the war is ended without prior victory by either side.

(2) The negotiating dialogue has stressed bargaining between North Viet Nam and the United States without any close attention being accorded to the more immediately concerned adversaries, namely the N.L.F. and Saigon. There is no strong basis to believe either that the two external actors can completely impose their will upon the two internal factions or that the two external actors espouse views identical with those held by the two internal factors. Therefore, bargaining toward peace should be broadened at least conceptually to examine the positions and leverage of all four major participants in the Viet

Nam conflict. An obstacle to this position is the United States insistence, contrary to widespread neutral and expert interpretation, that the N.L.F. has no identity separate from Hanoi.

(3) The administration of a peaceful settlement in South Viet Nam must find a way to define what constitutes foreign military intervention. These conceptions are hard to define and even harder to administer effectively. Is an ethnic "Southerner" an infiltrator when he returns unarmed from North to South Viet Nam? By what criteria? Can the regime in Saigon purchase or receive military equipment from outside states as it wishes? Can the government in Hanoi? What criteria can be developed to limit foreign participation in a post-cease-fire environment in Viet Nam? Can a means be found to apply these criteria on a nonpolitical basis? The Geneva machinery of 1954, with its International Control Commission, operates on a troika principle (Poland, Canada, and India) with each rival ideological orientation holding a veto. Would either side be willing to eliminate its own veto or to allow a veto to its adversary? If not, can a mutually acceptable basis for impartial administration be agreed upon?

These are some of the tough questions that beset the search for a negotiated settlement. Their answer is obviously worth seeking. A solution may rely upon substituting an all-Asian presence, possibly under Japanese initiative, for the Western presence that has dominated Vietnamese society since the nineteenth century (except for the equally tragic interlude during World War II).

VII. A Concluding Unscientific Postscript

The extralegal setting of the United States involvement in Viet Nam is essential if a serious attempt is to be made to rethink the foreign policy premises that have led to this long and painful involvement. If it is correct that we have been led into a costly and unjust war in Viet Nam by ignoring our real interests in world affairs, then it is important to explain how this came about. In the context of a discussion of the relevance of international law the main contention is that a fair-minded attention to the restraints and procedures of the international legal order would have served and continue to serve the interests of the United States to a far greater extent than do policies arrived at by calculating short-term national advantage purely in terms of maximizing national power, wealth, and prestige. In Viet Nam, the American attempt to control the political outcome to accord with its geopolitical preferences (regardless of world order consequences) requires an altogether disproportionate commitment even if one approves of the objective sought.

Such a disproportionality suggests that our policy-making process is not being rationally focused upon our "real national interests" in world affairs. This lack of focus seems to arise from a sort of rigidity that comes from endorsing an ideological interpretation of contemporary international conflict. This endorsement takes precedence over world order considerations in American foreign policy and is likely to lead us into future Viet Nams unless it is repudiated. Ideological opposition to Communism and Communist influence as the main premise for military commitment is more dangerous than discredited foreign policies based on the pursuit of wealth and power. At least the policies of conquest left the victor with tangible gains and the prospect of tangible gain allowed for a rational calculation of the proportionality of means and ends. But in the circumstances of a Viet Nam, precisely because the putative gains are intangible—even sacrificial—there is no way to conclude that it costs too much. To question this reasoning it is necessary to be explicit about its relevance. Therefore, to convey my own sense about bringing United States foreign policy into a closer appreciation of its real interests, including a greater deference to the constraints and procedures of international law, it seems useful to carry the legal analysis beyond the boundaries of law and world order. Hence, this unscientific postscript that is at once an explication of the wider orientation of United States foreign policy and a plea for its reorientation.

The United States Government contends that it has no selfish motives in Viet Nam. As President Johnson explained: "We're not trying to wipe out North Vietnam. We're not trying to change their government. We're not trying to establish permanent bases in South Vietnam. And we're not trying to gain one inch of new territory for America."[141] This absence of selfish motives does not establish the beneficial quality of the American involvement in Viet Nam. The United States pursues its military course in Viet Nam because it is determined to defeat a Communist-led insurgency that sprang up years ago in South Viet Nam as a consequence of many domestic and international factors, only one of which was encouragement from and support by North Viet Nam. The United States acts *as if* the war in South Viet Nam was a consequence solely of aggression from the North.

In actuality, the war in South Viet Nam is being waged in a complex post-colonial setting wherein pressures for national self-assertion interact with ideological movements. Many Vietnamese are concerned with attaining their nationhood unencumbered by foreign domination. The United States is opposing revolutionary nationalism, as well as Com-

141 President Johnson's Address to the American Alumni Council, *New York*   *Times*, July 13, 1966, p. 2, col. 3.

munism, in South Viet Nam. And the United States is fighting on behalf of a native regime dominated by a reactionary military elite; Premier Ky was a mercenary pilot for the French in both the Algerian war of independence and the first Indochina war and identifies himself with the politics of military dictatorship.

To wage war for or against an idea is no less destructive than to embark upon conquest for territory or for treasure. Over a century ago John Stuart Mill warned about the use of military power in the service of an idea: "We have heard something lately about being willing to go to war for an idea. To go to war for an idea, if the war is aggressive, not defensive, is as criminal as to go to war for territory or revenue."[142]

Ideological motivation may indeed be intense. Its roots are often hidden in the past. We embarked upon a program to resist Communism in 1947 with the formulation of the Truman Doctrine.[143] Such a program, at that time, was closely and sensibly related to certain geopolitical realities. The Soviet Union was ruled by a military dictator and it maintained tight control over Communist states and parties elsewhere. Western Europe was still weak from World War II. The colonial system was in its early stages of disintegration. Global Communism was a reality to be resisted and feared, although the Communist adversary was cautious, itself badly stunned and damaged by World War II. Since 1947 many changes have taken place, not least of which is the development of nuclear weapons and their deployment in a posture of mutual deterrence. The Soviet Union has followed an increasingly conservative foreign policy and its domestic society has been the scene of progressive liberalization. The Communist group of states has fallen into conflict, and many rather disjoined national varieties of Communism have emerged. Communism is today often a species of nationalism, not internationalism. Western Europe has recovered fully. Its main states are prosperous and stable.

Despite these changes in the international setting the United States has not significantly altered its dogmatic opposition to Communism. In Viet Nam President Johnson is carrying forward the basic policies of prior Administrations.[144] These policies center upon the assumption that

[142] J. S. Mill, *Essays on Politics and Culture*, G. Himmelfarb, ed., New York, Anchor Books, 1962, p. 405.

[143] For a persuasive comprehensive analysis of the evolution of the United States foreign policy response to Communism, see D. Horowitz, *From Yalta to Vietnam*, New York, Penguin Books, 1965.

[144] "There is an American consensus on foreign affairs, and the Johnson Administration may legitimately argue that its programs carry out in action what the country demands in principle. . . . Mr. Johnson escalated the war in Vietnam, but so did Mr. Kennedy when he altered the American commitment in that country from one of assistance and counsel to the South Vietnamese government to direct, if still limited, military engagement with the Vietnamese insurgents. So did Mr. Eisenhower 'escalate,' or more properly inaugurate, the American involvement

it is always adverse to United States interests to allow a society to become identified as "Communist." To call a movement "Communist" that can also draw upon the revolutionary nationalism of a society, as both the Vietcong and Hanoi can, is to overlook one real base of political potency. Viet Nam, unlike other Asian states, is a country where Communist leadership under Ho Chi Minh has for several decades commanded almost all of the forces of anticolonialism and nationalism. To resist these elements is to become allied with reactionary elements in the society. Unaided, these reactionary elements would have no prospect of prevailing over a popularly based nationalist movement, whether or not it is Communist led. To defeat such a nationalist movement, if at all, presupposes an enormous foreign effort on behalf of the reactionary faction, an effort of the sort the United States has been making on behalf of successive military regimes in Saigon. The result for South Viet Nam is, at best, a dependence that entails a new subservience to an alien Western power. Certainly the United States has introduced more military might into Viet Nam than the French ever used to dominate the country during the colonial period. To have allowed a Vietcong victory and a possible subsequent reunification of Viet Nam under Hanoi's auspices would have merely ratified the process of self-determination internal to Viet Nam that evolved since the early efforts against the French. Such a nationalist solution even if Communist in form would not have posed any serious danger to Western interests and certainly not to direct United States security interests. Viet Nam has a long tradition of fearing and resisting Chinese domination, and there is every reason to suppose that this tradition would persist in a Communist era. The non-Communist neighbors of Viet Nam have, with the possible exception of Laos, stable governments and strong capabilities to maintain internal security.

The United States has made an utterly unconvincing appeal to principles of world order; it purports to be resisting aggression in South Viet Nam. Such a contention is without any firm factual base, but its allegation in a circumstance of ambiguity allows the United States Government to maintain its war effort without admitting its true motivation, thereby confusing its supporters and angering its opponents. As Ralph K. White, an American psychologist who has made an unemotional study of the basis for perceiving aggression in Viet Nam writes: "There has been no aggression on either side—at least not in the sense of a

---

when, in 1954, he stepped into the role the exhausted French abandoned and chose to sponsor and sustain a noncommunist government in Saigon that would prevent the country's unification under the communist Viet Minh movement which had led the war to expel the French." E. Stillman and W. Pfaff, *op.cit. supra*, note 99, p. 4.

cold-blooded, Hitler-like act of conquest. The analogies of Hitler's march into Prague, Stalin's takeover of Eastern Europe, and the North Korean attack on South Korea are false analogies." White also documents his conclusion that "aggression by us seems as obvious to them as aggression by them seems to us."[145]

One trouble with fighting for an idea is that there is no way to measure how much sacrifice its defense is worth. An absolutism sets in. The image of the enemy that justifies his destruction is held secure against prudence, reason, and morality. Only clear inferences of Communism, of aggression, and of good intentions vindicate the death and destruction inflicted upon Viet Nam. The United States can maintain these clear inferences only by denying reality or by testing reality in the same primitive way that the Aztecs justified their belief that the corn on which their civilization depended would not grow unless there were human sacrifices. "The fact that the corn did grow was probably considered solid evidence for such a view; and in those years when the harvest was bad, it was doubtless argued that the gods were angry because the sacrifices had been insufficient. A little greater military effort would result, a few more hearts would be torn from their quivering bodies, and the following year it was highly probable that the harvest would be better and the image consequently confirmed."[146] Kenneth Boulding regards primitive reasoning of this kind as the way we sustain our commitment in South Viet Nam—that is "by appeals to analogy, self-evidence, and to the principle that if at first you don't succeed try more of the same until you do."[147] We are entrapped in a dangerous, self-destructive myth in Viet Nam, the elimination of which can only be sought after the relief of peace, if then. Now we can only justify the sacrifices we have already made by increasing them to the point where we hope its objective will be reached, regardless of the cost to ourselves and to Viet Nam.

Finally there is "the credibility gap." Not only is the inference of aggression needed to enable the use of a rhetoric of legitimacy in describing the American efforts in Viet Nam, but the objective of these efforts is disguised. We proclaim over and over again our search for a negotiated settlement, the insincerity of which Professor Moore endorses, and yet we accompany this search by ever-higher escalation and by preconditions that by mid-1967 must be interpreted to entail surrender by the adversary. President Johnson writes to Ho Chi Minh that he is "prepared to order a cessation of bombing against your country and

[145] Ralph White, "Misperception of Aggression in Vietnam," *Journal of International Affairs*, XXI (1967), 123, 125.
[146] Kenneth Boulding, "The Learning and Reality-Testing Process in the International System," *Journal of International Affairs*, XXI (1967), 1.
[147] *Id.*, p. 2.

the further augmentation of United States forces in South Viet Nam as soon as I am assured that infiltration into South Viet Nam by land and by sea has stopped."[148] How could the Vietcong maintain itself at this stage without supplies and equipment from the North? The effect of Johnson's proposal is to suggest that United States military effort in the South cannot be matched by Northern aid to the N.L.F.: it is to compel the other side to act as if it had been the aggressor. Ho Chi Minh's rejection of such an effort had to be expected. Only a combined disposition by Hanoi and N.L.F. to call off the insurgency would seem acceptable, only a victory for American power and a defeat for its adversary made militarily possible, if at all, because we are *not* fighting against Communism, but only against the relatively beleaguered small Communist state of North Viet Nam.

This note in conclusion is an attempt to provide a political setting for the world order claims that the United States has made on behalf of its action in Viet Nam. Without a sense of this setting any appraisal of the legal issues at stake is ultimately without its proper context. Since it is "we" who are perceiving the aggression in Viet Nam it is essential to know why our understanding of the war is not shared by people elsewhere. Only after making an ideological jailbreak and thereafter rediscovering our real values and our interests at home and abroad can we avoid future Viet Nams. I am convinced that we will look back upon the war in Viet Nam as the greatest tragedy ever in American foreign policy, as a deviation from American political traditions that will appear comprehensible in retrospect only because, in Mill's phrase, we were "willing to go to war for an idea."

1967

[148] For the texts of President Johnson's letter (dated February 2, 1967) and President Ho Chi Minh's reply (dated February 15, 1967), see *New York Times*, March 22, 1966, p. 10, col. 2.

IX. Operation Stanleyville: A Lesson in Third World Politics

AMONG THE most crucial political phenomena of our time are regionalism, revolution, and racist interpretations of international behavior. The conduct of American foreign policy reveals an insufficient awareness of these phenomena, and especially of their interconnection with such national goals as the containment of Communism and the evolution of a stable and just system of world order based on cooperative participation by all groups of states, including the recently independent nations in Africa and Asia. To raise this issue in sharp perspective, let us consider the American role in the Stanleyville Operation of 1964, a touchstone event that exhibited a symbolic coalescence of regionalism, revolution, and racism and an equally symbolic failure of the United States to act and talk responsibly, either as measured by the requirements of national interest or by those of world order.

The experience of the Congo since 1960 epitomizes the traumas of post-independence in Africa. The bloodshed and chaos, the revival of intertribal barbarism and rivalry, and the apparent inability to establish a calmly progressive government exist in some degree almost everywhere in Africa, but these tendencies were exhibited in extreme form in the Congo between 1960 and the end of 1964.

Increasing United States support for the regime of Moise Tshombe, after his unexpected appointment as Prime Minister of the Congo on July 9, 1964, was a significant factor in the victory of the central government over the Gbenye rebellion in subsequent months.[1] This involvement of the United States seemed to arise from short-term cold war calculations rather than from any sympathy with Tshombe's regime. We explained our help for Tshombe by pointing to the apparent swing of the rebels toward Communism, and we accorded considerable weight to the fact that the rebels received equipment, guidance, and sanctuary from the anti-Tshombe neighbors of the Congo, who in turn seemed to be carrying out the policies of Ghana, Algeria, and the United Arab Republic. United States spokesmen have also been quick to point out that the rebels received both Soviet and Chinese military equipment and advice. Such a train of events is widely held in Washington to justify the countervailing posture, namely, support for Tshombe. Yet such a response seems to exaggerate the degree to which

---

[1] Tshombe was replaced as Prime Minister in October 1965 by General Joseph D. Mobutu. In March 1967 Mr. Tshombe was tried *in absentia* on charges of high treason and sentenced to death. This chapter was originally written in the middle of 1965.

it makes sense to translate African political conflicts into the calculus of global conflict at the strategic level. The future of relations between black Africa and the West depends upon an increase in Western sensitivity to several aspects of the African political scene other than the cold war. The character and importance of these additional aspects were dramatically disclosed by the hostile reaction in much of black Africa to the Western rescue of civilians held hostage at Stanleyville in 1964. For this reason it seems worthwhile to appraise the Stanleyville Operation as the basis for a critique of United States foreign policy in the Congo, and by inference, throughout all of Africa.[2]

In November of 1964 a battalion of Belgian paratroopers was flown in American transport planes from Ascension Island, a British possession, to rescue 1,700 civilian hostages being held and threatened by Mr. Gbenye's rebels in the Stanleyville region of the Congo. The United States and Belgium reported these activities to the President of the Security Council, and a group of angered African states (joined by Yugoslavia and Afghanistan) asked for an urgent meeting of the Security Council to consider the Stanleyville Operation, which it alleged to be "an intervention in African affairs, a flagrant violation of the Charter of the United Nations and a threat to the peace and security of the African continent."

Throughout December of 1964 a long and acrimonious debate in the Security Council ensued, giving vivid expression to the hostility, resentment, and distrust felt by many African states toward the United States and Europe. The formal outcome of the debate, it is true, was only a mild resolution that made no reference to Stanleyville more specific than "deploring the recent events in the Democratic Republic of the Congo," and thereby left the various sides at liberty to interpret as they saw fit which recent events were being deplored. But the significance of the debate and its political effects were far more profound than could be suggested by the language of the resolution.

The discussion of Stanleyville in the United Nations discloses a new radicalism on the part of many African states that carries with it a willingness to blame and condemn the West. Such a condemnation reveals a political tendency which, if allowed to mount, might eventually bring most of Africa within Communist spheres of influence, not out of any ideological preference, but in angry reaction to Western policies that are particularly offensive to the African sensibility. This danger has been abetted, perhaps unwittingly, but also perhaps decisively,

---

[2] For a similar assessment see Kenneth W. Grundy, "The Stanleyville Rescue: American Policy in the Congo," *The Yale Review* (Winter 1967), 242-55.

by the official policies adopted by the United States to deal with the Congo crises of the past few years.

Looking back, one wonders with dismay why the angry African reactions to Stanleyville surprised United States officials. It seems rather obvious that the use of military force in the Congo by the United States and Belgium at the behest of Tshombe for any purpose whatsoever would be deeply resented by much of Africa, and would provide the Sino-Soviet group with an easy pretext for increasing their claims to influence and participate in African affairs. This does not mean that the United States should have refused to join in the rescue, but it should have taken greater account of African sensitivities. And after the undertaking, the United States might have avoided further identification with Tshombe's cause. Let us examine now why so many African states were bound to reject our claim that the Stanleyville Operation was a rescue mission undertaken for purely humanitarian purposes, and, as such, beyond the realm of legitimate political criticism.

Regionalism

Perhaps we can acquire some sense of perspective on the Congo situation by considering what is, admittedly, a loose-fitting analogy. In 1823, acting in a post-colonial atmosphere to protect the gains from its war of national liberation, the United States took the first step toward asserting special regional prerogatives by proclaiming the Monroe Doctrine. Although the original objective by the United States was to oppose European plans for helping Spain regain control over her lost colonies in the Western Hemisphere, increasingly during the nineteenth century we asserted our own hegemony over the continent.

Thus the Latin American republics, having freed themselves from their colonial masters, were confronted with a new, more subtle form of imperialist control. Late in the nineteenth century and throughout the twentieth, these countries have struggled to realize full national autonomy. Acknowledging the justice of these claims over the past thirty years, the United States has helped create the Organization of American States. The original postulate of regional autonomy incorporated into the Monroe Doctrine is retained, but responsibility for its fulfillment is now shifted, in form at least, from the United States to the OAS. Certainly events in 1965 connected with the American intervention in the Dominican uprising make it plain that there are dramatic limits to the willingness by the United States to forego unilateral use of force in deference to regional security procedures. These limits were already evident to many in 1954 as a consequence of the role played by the United States in overthrowing the Arbenz regime in Guatemala.

It is true that the United States uses the nominal competence of the OAS as a device to shield essentially unilateral intervention in Latin America from scrutiny by the political organs of the United Nations. Thus, however ironic, it may be the case that the presence of the OAS facilitates rather than inhibits the tradition of U.S. hegemony in Latin America, and that the policies of nonintervention can only now be promoted if the Latin American republics either destroy the OAS or eliminate the participation of the United States.

However, the reliance by the United States upon the legitimizing role of the OAS, however insincere in the context of Latin America, does create an international precedent with many unintended consequences, principal among which is to undercut our opposition to comparable claims of regional autonomy being asserted elsewhere in the world, and especially on the continent of Africa. Perhaps brief attention to recent Cuban-American relations can make concrete the process whereby the unreality of regionalism in the Western Hemisphere nevertheless leads to the standard-setting reality of regionalism in Africa, and more generally, to increasing legitimacy for the principle even when it is invoked in support of coercion toward the members of a region.

Throughout our conflict with Cuba during the past five years, we have contended that Castro's complaints about aggression are of no concern to the United Nations or to individual states outside of the Western Hemisphere. At the time of the Bay of Pigs and then during the missile crisis, we acted to preserve the intraregional character of the conflict. When we prevented the emplacement of Soviet missiles in Cuba, we relied upon the regional authorization of the OAS to back up our claim to stop missile-carrying ships bound for Cuba on the high seas. The constituted government of Cuba had entered a bilateral defense arrangement with the Soviet Union, and yet the United States held that the regional objection took precedence over the normal sovereign right to exclusive control over defense arrangements. It is certainly true that the OAS was a mere conduit through which to process a claim asserted essentially by the United States. But significantly, the United States felt that the legitimacy and political acceptability of the claim was greatly enhanced as a consequence of receiving the imprimatur of the OAS.

Similarly, at Punta del Este, in the spring of 1962, the United States led a successful drive to exclude Castro's Cuba from participation in the inter-American system on the ground that Marxism-Leninism is incompatible with the ideals of the hemisphere. Here again, under the auspices of the OAS, the United States supported coercive measures against the Cuban regime on the basis of a regional consensus. Now let us ask ourselves: Is Castro more distasteful to the Western Hemisphere than Tshombe is to black Africa?

Since the United States, for reasons of its own, has championed regional authority in the Western Hemisphere, it might well be asked what about Africa, where a genuine sense of regional identification exists and where no single country is yet, despite some ambitious candidates, in a position to dominate the region? Many African countries go so far as to authorize their governments by constitutional provision to transfer national sovereignty to regional political institutions should they emerge. In addition, Africa is battling against the remnants of colonialism and is extremely sensitive to the reassertion of foreign control in various guises. Therefore, would a Monroe Doctrine for Africa be such an unreasonable claim for the Organization of African Unity to make? And was not part of the African reaction to the Stanleyville Operation an expression of extreme sensitivity to any signs of neocolonialist control being established over African affairs in the future?

Two main generalizations emerge from the analogy. First, United States support for regionalism in the Western Hemisphere has strengthened the claim of the OAU to exercise exclusive competence over events in the Congo, even to the exclusion of the United Nations and certainly to the exclusion of states that are not members of the region. The endorsement of such regional competence does pose some serious constitutional challenges that the international system has yet to meet. How, for example, does one balance the claims of a regional dissenter like Tshombe or Castro against the prevailing political views expressed in the official organ of the regional community? The resolution of this issue has great importance for the future of world order. Can the OAU, for instance, prohibit Tshombe from receiving military aid from states outside the region? United States attempts to isolate Castro have established a precedent in favor of taking seriously the paramount nature of regional claims in matters of regional security. The issue is complicated. Israel, South Africa, and possibly Formosa are additional examples of states that are victims of regional pressure. Regional institutions have an important subsidiary role to play in the maintenance of world order, but what are the limits of their capacity to coerce?

And second, the refusal to abide by a regional consensus is likely to engender severe political consequences, regardless of "the balance of power." The Stanleyville Operation set off a series of countermeasures including specific offers of military aid to the rebels by such leading African states as Algeria and the United Arab Republic. This, in turn, allowed greater Soviet and Chinese participation in African affairs.

The Soviet Union could agree to implement regional goals simply by offering to replace the military equipment shipped by African states to the Congo rebels, that is, by responding to an invitation. The case for mutual nonintervention was shattered at Stanleyville. Intervention became explicit, and the objections of the more moderate were cast aside. Here again Cuba is illustrative. Despite the permission of the Castro government, the Soviet attempt to bring missiles into Cuba over the objection of the OAS generated powerful political reactions that were able to nullify the Soviet claim.

Regional capability to respond is not always measurable purely in terms of military power but may consist of political maneuvers that have a formidable impact on events. For example, the acceptance of Soviet or Chinese support, the tolerance of small-scale military operations of sufficient magnitude to influence political outcomes in countries experiencing civil strife, or the delivery of a series of insulting speeches in the United Nations may each be effective political responses. We are badly deceived if we think that the ease with which the Congo rescue operation was completed reveals the potential for continuing military control by the West over events in Africa. In fact, our demonstration of military superiority may have been what goaded some Africans to take such grave offense. The cold war and the subtleties of involvement in an ongoing civil war combine to make the traditional forms of military superiority far less relevant than was once the case, and certainly one reason for this is that regional actors may be able to summon various kinds of political forces to offset their military impotence.

While an analogy can instruct, it can also deceive. There are many significant differences between the OAS and the OAU and between current conditions in Latin America and those in Africa. Within Africa there are struggles for intracontinental spheres of influence. Many of the new African states are not viable, nor able to maintain domestic order. It is not clear that effective action by the OAU could have resulted in an alternative to Stanleyville. Precisely because the colonial past cannot be altogether eliminated, extrahemispheric states retain important kinds of involvement in the new countries of Africa, including especially the lingering presence of their nationals. The case for intervention is not altogether capricious since the alternative may be to allow one's countrymen to be slaughtered without cause. In such a situation, to respond to the invitation of the constituted government to undertake only a rescue mission does not seem so unreasonable, especially if, as here, the rescuers leave when the rescue is completed. At the time of the Stanleyville Operation there existed no tradition of regional autonomy for Africa in any sense comparable to that which had been built up for over a century in the Western Hemisphere. The political expectations were different. In fact, it may well be that looking back upon Stanleyville several decades hence it will appear to have been the occasion when new expectations of regional autonomy for Africa were first given serious expression.

Revolution

Tshombe seemed temporarily able to turn the tide of the Congo civil war by employing more than 400 white mercenary soldiers mainly recruited in Rhodesia and South Africa, who organized and directed the government's military operations, and by receiving significant amounts of military equipment from foreign countries, including most visibly the United States. Whatever the reluctance of officials in Washington to support Tshombe's ascent to power, appearances would lead even the most reasonable observer to conclude that the United States wanted to stabilize the situation by helping the central government win the civil war that Tshombe had inherited from Adoula.

But can we expect the African statesmen to be reasonable men of detached judgment in the face of such appearances? To them Tshombe was the leading symbol of the most awful memories of the colonial period and, as well, a frightening portent of what independence might become if allowed to degenerate. He had been allied closely with both the economics and politics of Belgian colonialism in Katanga, benefiting personally from both at the sacrifice of the dignity and welfare of his people. In addition Tshombe had shown himself capable of tribal genocide and was widely supposed guilty of great political treachery in arranging the murder of Lumumba, who, despite his faults, symbolized African reassertion and hopes for the future. In fact, Lumumba has been the only Congolese leader so far to receive any degree of widespread popular backing in Africa. Tshombe also was an honored guest of Sir Roy Welensky, the racist head of Rhodesia, and relied upon white mercenaries to wage his military struggles, first in Katanga and later in the whole of the Congo. As Kenneth Grundy concludes Tshombe's "image as a stooge for the white racists of Africa becomes difficult to deny."[3]

This is all part of the background of Stanleyville. For let us not forget that one of the most salient features of the operation was that when the Belgian paratroopers landed, Stanleyville was the rebel capital and the center of their operations, but that when they left, it was firmly in the hands of Tshombe's mercenary-led armed forces. Let us

[3] *Id.*, p. 246.

even accept at face value the claim by Ambassador Stevenson in his letter to the Security Council that "the sole aim of my government has been and is to assist in the rescue of innocent civilians endangered by rebel activities in violation of international law," or his later contention in the Security Council debate that "the action taken by the United States and by Belgium was purely and simply a rescue mission, authorized in advance by the legally constituted Government of the Congo." Even if we perceived events in this way, could we expect it from others?

The facts are difficult to set straight. Tshombe's military columns were apparently advancing upon Stanleyville and were expected to reach the outskirts of the city on the day of the parachute drop. Our timing of the drop, it was said, coincided with the last available time to carry out the rescue, in view of the threats of the rebel leaders to massacre the civilian hostages as soon as Tshombe's forces entered Stanleyville. The landing of the paratroopers apparently scared the rebels away, resulting in Tshombe's entry into the city without battle. The outcome of the two-day effort by the United States and Belgium was to improve Tshombe's prospects in the civil war. This operation undoubtedly led to more foreign intervention on the side of the rebels, but it also apparently led to a greater involvement of the United States on the side of Tshombe. Certainly Tshombe's victory in the civil war was consistent with those earlier policies of the West, especially the United States, toward Elisabethville that led to the original shipment of arms and aid, including aircraft, and "made available" on contract the services of anti-Castro exile pilots to fly them.

My analysis endeavors here to show that the *appearances* of the Stanleyville Operation made it seem as though the U.S. was trying to intervene in an ongoing revolution. If we reverse the situation again and speculate about our responses in the event that a civil war breaks out in Cuba under Castro, would we overlook Soviet aid to the Castro forces? Would we feel that international law required us to observe the scene as spectators, concerned but paralyzed, as shiploads of Soviet military "advisers" arrived on the scene to take charge of battlefield operations against the anti-Castro forces? Would we not, in such a situation, view with suspicion—if not urgent alarm—a Soviet operation designed to rescue a gaggle of Soviet and East European political specialists who had been captured and whose lives were being bargained for concessions by Castro? Would we recite long speeches about our helplessness to oppose, much less to give aid, to the revolutionary cause because we believe that the constituted government, however abhorrent, should be allowed to prevail in a situation of civil strife? We do not seem so inhibited when we proclaim Captive Nations Week each year and pass Congressional resolutions calling upon the oppressed peoples of East Europe to rise up against their governments. Can we maintain seriously that Gomulka or Kadar or even Ulbricht are regarded as worse by us than the Tshombe regime by the majority of African states?

In the Congo context, the United States seems to be arguing that in a civil war it is always proper to continue help for the constituted or incumbent government. Such a posture belies our own revolutionary origins and the dominant line of policy throughout our diplomatic history. The United States has often stood for nonintervention in civil strife and the equal claims for external support of incumbent and rebel factions. In international law this approach is confined by the status of belligerency that is supposed to apply as soon as an insurrectionary challenge has established itself in firm administrative control over a significant portion of the state where the civil war is taking place. Once belligerency exists or is proclaimed, outside states are expected to treat both sides equally and maintain a posture of neutrality. In fact, except where cold war issues are prominent, our policy has been to subordinate our preferences in a civil war to our interest in avoiding an acceleration of its scale. In the cold war arenas, however, the facts and claims often warrant intervention as a response to prior acts of indirect aggression and subversion by Communist-inspired rebel movements. Thus our support for the incumbent is a response to prior interventions and takes the form of seeking to neutralize their impact upon domestic events; although, as the American role in South Viet Nam increasingly suggests, our response in favor of the incumbent seems out of all proportion to the interventions on the side of the insurgent —or so it appears to most uninvolved observers.

But notice that in the Congo our claims and the facts are somewhat different. However confused the Congo situation, it certainly seems impossible to dispose of the uprising against Tshombe on the basis of cold war slogans. In fact, our tendency to do so only infuriates the Africans by its suggestion that there are no genuine grievances against Tshombe. It is true that the rebels have received sanctuary and aid from friendly neighbors, who in turn have allowed some Soviet and Chinese equipment and influence to enter the Congo. But no simple label can be attached. Our consul in Stanleyville, Michael P.E. Hoyt, was among those held as a hostage and beaten during his captivity—not an experience likely to engender sympathy for the rebels. Yet when released, after recounting the frightening events he endured, Hoyt refrained from attacking the political objectives of the rebel movement. He is reported to have said, "It's definitely an African and a Congolese movement but all very confused." Hoyt added that the rebels claim to be socialists "but not communist." "There is no real dogma," he observed, "and there are many reasons to make them fight."

There are many issues caught up in the Congo civil war and in the attitude of the outside world toward it. A range of options exists. Since the Congo was given independence in 1960, the United States has given fairly consistent support to the claims of the central government to exercise unified control over the entire country. This policy has become unpopular in most of Africa since Tshombe took control. It has led the more radical African and North African states to give the rebels support in the hope that the rebels will gain control of the country or at least disrupt Tshombe's efforts. When the United States gives support to Tshombe, then it creates a *prima facie* justification for other African nations to help the opposition. This engenders a form of escalation peculiar to civil wars: interventions provoke corresponding counter interventions designed to offset the original acts. In this regard, the Stanleyville Operation was viewed by the friends of the rebels as a large step up the escalation ladder on the part of the friends of Tshombe; it called almost predictably for an equally large off-setting step. These states do not have the military power or political poise needed for a direct confrontation. Therefore, the countermeasures consisted of angry oratory in the United Nations, a series of promises to help the rebels, and an apparently increased indulgence of Soviet and Chinese participation in African affairs.

The main point is that the intertwining of the civil war and the humanitarian rescue was inevitable as soon as the latter was dependent upon a spectacular military presence by the United States and Belgium —soldiers descending from the skies. This image was strengthened by the strategic and symbolic importance of Stanleyville for the rebels and by the fact that somehow Tshombe acquired firm control of Stanleyville in the wake of the mission. We may have been innocent about these incidental consequences, but it was a disastrous innocence because it disclosed an almost fatal ignorance about the contemporary realities of world politics.

Racism

The delegates from the more radical states of black Africa introduced various racial issues into the debate on the Stanleyville Operation. Mr. Ganao, Foreign Minister of Brazzaville Congo, put the racial issue at the center of controversy. As his delegation saw it, the problem was the "aggression of the Americans, the Belgians, and the British against black populations." He attacked the humanitarian claims:

"In the name of which humanity did these people speak? They had massacred scores of thousands of innocent blacks on the pretext of saving the lives of an insignificant number of whites. To them, only the whites were important." Similarly intense accusations, unsupported by evidence, were made by delegates from Mali, Guinea, and Ghana.

In addition, the issue of reciprocity was forcefully introduced into the debate at several points. For instance, Mr. Batsio, the Foreign Minister of Ghana, asked whether the United States was any more entitled to intervene in the Congo than Ghana would be "to intervene in the southern states of the United States to protect the lives of Afro-Americans who were from time to time tortured and murdered for asserting their legitimate rights." In the background of the debate was, as well, the connection between racism and the colonial system and the resentment of black Africans about the failure of the West to help them get rid of the remaining colonies in Africa that combine the evils of racist rule with those of the colonial system. One senses from the debate that the Africans were infuriated by the appropriation of the word "humanitarian" by the Belgians and the Americans in view of what they had allowed to happen in the past and tolerated in the present.

Mr. Stevenson was obviously shaken and offended by the vigor and persistence of these attacks. He responded by saying that "racial hatred, racial strife, has cursed the world for too long. I make no defense of the sins of the white race in this respect. But the antidote for white racism is not black racism." His main argument was that there was nothing racist in the Stanleyville Operation, that our mission was designed only to save the lives of the hostages, that black hostages as well as white hostages were rescued, and that the Africans who spoke of racism were merely setting the stage for their own efforts to intervene on the side of the rebels and to distract the Council from chastising the rebels for their barbaric conduct.

My impression is that Mr. Stevenson's response was justified in most respects, although his heroic attempt to disentangle the rescue mission from the colonial past and the rebellious present is not altogether convincing. The fact remains that the United States cannot use military force in the Congo, unless authorized to do so by either the OAU or the UN, without engendering fury on the part of the more radical African governments. Whether this fury is grounded on fancy or not, it will enhance the influence of Communist countries on the African continent. For we must always remember that the Soviets and especially the Chinese come to Africa free from the stigma of having a racist or colonialist past. The European powers were the inventors and leaders of the colonial system; the United States, besides extending control over

Latin America by imperialist techniques, held blacks in slavery for nearly a century and still makes them victims of pervasive and painful, if declining, discrimination and persecution. Given the perspective of the new states of Africa, their emotional repudiation of our claims to render mercy at Stanleyville seem more understandable, if not any more accurate. The racist perception cannot be eradicated by our solemn denials, nor can the adverse political consequences be avoided. It is necessary to appreciate the complexity of the social and political ferment in Africa; a cold war mentality is obsolete in such a setting, distorting perceptions by exaggerating the importance and durability of whatever geopolitical allegiances are held by individuals or groups competing for leadership in African countries.

1967

X. On Legislative Intervention by the United Nations in the Internal Affairs of Sovereign States.[1]

THE GROWTH of legal order is but one aspect of the ongoing experience of human civilization. As Erich Kahler has said, "The historical process entails a gradual shift to broader units, and at the same time to higher levels of consciousness."[2] This chapter looks at this process as it pertains to the gradual shift of authority and power from the nation to the United Nations. Not only is there an emergence of a broader unit, but, as well, a higher level of consciousness. For today we begin to perceive our self-interest as more dependent upon the welfare of mankind than upon the success of any particular nationality.

But old habits of loyalty and traditional residences of power give way unwillingly to new wider claims. The defenders of the nation remain ardent and numerous, possess power, wield authority, and quickly solicit the enthusiasm of newly independent peoples. These defenders imperil the survival of man and his achievements of mind and spirit in an age when nuclear war threatens havoc and catastrophe. It remains doubtful whether the world can be transformed to a safer level of organization before it destroys itself in the course of this painful process of transition.

I

The traditional international order rested upon the primacy of the nation. Basic doctrines of sovereignty, territorial jurisdiction, equality of states, independence, nonintervention, and recognition each acknowledge this primacy. Yet it is a truism of the age that the nation no longer provides an adequate ordering unit for international relations. There is an urgent need for wider structures of authority supported by broader political values. This need informs our inquiry into the role of the United Nations in the life of domestic communities.

The orthodox view of the United Nations restricts its active role as a coercive agent to situations of violence which threaten or breach

[1] This chapter is closely linked in its reasoning to an article written in collaboration with Saul H. Mendlovitz, "Towards a Warless World: One Legal Formula to Achieve Transition," 73 *Yale Law Journal* 399 (1964).

I would also like to call attention to an excellent essay that expresses a parallel approach to the connections between inter-vention and social change: Manfred Halpern, "The Morality and Politics of Intervention," in James N. Rosenau, ed., *International Aspects of Civil Strife*, Princeton, Princeton University Press, 1964, pp. 249-88.

[2] Erich Kahler, "Culture and Evolution," *Centennial Review*, v (1961), 239, 258.

international peace. The presence of the United Nations in the Congo between 1960 and 1964 suggests, as did the earlier presence in Lebanon during 1958, that the distinctions between domestic and international violence and between pre-violence and violence are often virtually impossible to make in any widely acceptable form. It is clear that outbreaks or risks of internal violence increase the prospects of international warfare and can be treated as appropriate occasions for United Nations intervention. The insularity of the bloody language riots in India in the year following its independence contrast with the radiating impacts of civil strife in the Congo after its independence. Serious doubt remains as to both the Charter competence and the organizational willingness of the United Nations to protect the interest of the world in restraining the radiating impacts of a serious internal war.

Interventionary diplomacy is not the only threat to world peace arising from domestic arenas of conflict. Peace can also be endangered by certain repressive social policies which, if allowed to remain unaltered, will produce serious outbreaks of domestic violence. This prospect prompts the central contention of this chapter—that the United Nations should be authorized on a selective basis to coerce domestic social changes. This process of authorization will be referred to as "legislative intervention." Actually this proposed authorization is a narrow competence although it is somewhat incompatible with many popular conceptions of the proper limits for United Nations action. Nevertheless, I would contend that a limited legislative use of the United Nations can find its basis in the Charter, especially in light of the way certain provisions have been interpreted and applied on prior occasions. Legislative intervention is nothing more than a formalization and an extension of United Nations practice, an extension that has become imperative as a result of the delicate balance of forces that now keeps peace between the major states in the world. A sense of perspective about the character of legislative intervention is achieved by first considering the subject of intervention in general.

Intervention in internal affairs is a prominent characteristic of contemporary international conflict. On a single day newspapers report a new military buildup on American territory of Castro exiles planning a second invasion of Cuba and the construction of a supply road into Laos by Peking China to support the revolutionary cause of the Pathet Lao.[3] At the same time, internal war rages in South Viet Nam, sustained by rather clandestine support from North Viet Nam and countered by strident American military support for the Saigon regime; both

[3] *New York Times*, April 19, 1962, pp. 1, 5, 15.

activities are carried on in violation of the 1954 Geneva Accords.[4] Interventionary policy accounts for the most intense forms of violent conflict present in the world today.

The point is not to condemn these interventions, but to suggest that a foreign policy that depends upon unilateral military intervention by one nation in the affairs of another usually violates clear norms of international law, especially in the Western Hemisphere, where the standard of nonintervention has been worked out in a sequence of international agreements—solemnized as valid treaties. The willingness of the United States to adopt illegal interventionary tactics, under the pressure of the cold war, jeopardizes our moral commitment to a foreign policy of law-abidance, a commitment abstractly reiterated by our statesmen from many rostrums. More serious even than this hypocrisy is the fact that the stability of world politics requires the evolution of a reliable international legal order. This goal cannot be reached without the leadership of nonrevolutionary societies, especially the United States. For only a demonstration of the reality of a lawful alternative to power politics could tempt revolutionary nations to the point where they, too, might begin to perceive that the advantages of stability in a nuclear age outweigh the opportunities for expansion in an unstable world. For minimum order and security depend finally upon the joint willingness of all nuclear powers to establish a regime that is entrusted with the institutional management of force in world affairs; we need such a regime to overcome the dangers that arise from an obsolete reliance upon the tension between force and counterforce, the system of unstable equilibrium that continues to operate as the dominant ordering instrument of world politics.

Legislative intervention as a legitimate exercise of community power is intended to serve as a partial substitute for national intervention. The idea is to get certain domestic problems solved by the United Nations before they provoke domestic violence, the occasion that now so often induces rival national interventions. If we can eliminate the occasions upon which nations find it advantageous to use force—various interventions and indirect aggressions[5]—then the balance begins to tilt more heavily in favor of doing what must be done to cut the risks of nuclear

---

[4] See Chapters VII and VIII for full development of these themes. Cf. legalistic rhetoric of Soviet attack on the early indirect forms of United States intervention in South Viet Nam, *New York Times*, March 18, 1962, p. 30.

[5] If it is possible to discourage these residual uses of aggressive force in world politics, then the argument for community management of force grows correspondingly stronger. For if it is imprudent to seek expansion by indirect use of force, by interventionary tactics, then the risks of nuclear war by miscalculation, accident, catalytic agent, and escalation assume apparent dominance. This, in turn, helps to converge the perspectives of national interest and international peace.

war. Already the dangers of war discourage most recourse to direct aggression. The strength of the community mobilizes to resist expansion across international frontiers by armed attack. No nation, no matter how aggressive its objectives, can today adopt international war as a rational policy to achieve expansion. In complementary fashion, legislative intervention by the United Nations seeks to undermine the rationality of striving for national or ideological expansion through intervention in the internal affairs of foreign states.

This proposal may seem to involve some qualification of traditional notions of sovereignty. For the world community acting through the United Nations is accorded certain overseeing competences that appear to contradict the autonomy of the domestic order. But in fact, the domestic order has never enjoyed autonomy in any strict sense. It is now commonplace to accept the interdependence of economic, cultural, and military affairs. In fact, nations have always had a vital concern with what goes on elsewhere, even if "elsewhere" is a foreign state. Sovereignty only confers a primary competence upon a nation; it is not, and never was, an exclusive competence. Intervention in some form is an unavoidable concomitant of national existence. Pasquale Fiore's ideal international legal order acknowledged extranational concern and competence by coupling a *duty* of collective intervention with a *duty* of nonintervention.[6] Similarly, when the United States renounced its interventionary claims which had grown so enormous in the afterglow of the Monroe Doctrine, it properly insisted that Latin America accept collective responsibilities for certain threatening domestic events in the hemisphere. The renunciation of intervention does not substitute a policy of nonintervention; it involves the development of some form of collective intervention. This is not, however, a Hobson's choice, for the degree of effective centralization achieved by a legal order with respect to coercion is a decisive criterion of its quality as law. Up to a certain point, it is not only centralization but the level and quality of institutionalization that gives the appearance of just law to action undertaken on behalf of the affected community. A contrast between the *ad hoc* collective interventions of the Holy Alliance and the collective interventions of a juridical entity, like the Organization of American States, illustrates the relevance of institutionalization. Legislative intervention aims to combine the virtues of centralization with those of institutionalization.

Despite the confusion arising from the vagueness and multivariant reference of "intervention," its use as a term remains worthwhile to

---

[6] Pasquale Fiore, *International Law Codified and Its Legal Sanction or the Legal Organization of the Society of States,* 5th edn., trans. E. M. Borchard, New York, Baker, Voohris, 1918, pp. 265-72.

throw light upon the effort of international law to allocate authority and power among units acting in international affairs; as we have said, the doctrine of nonintervention exists alongside notions of sovereignty, equality of states, territorial supremacy, self-determination, and rights of independence as a fundamental conception in the traditional system of international law. In a classical context, "nonintervention" expressed the duty that is correlative to the right to administer people, things, and events within national boundaries. This use of the term aptly calls attention to the norms of reciprocity that regulate a decentralized international order. In particular it reminds us that the principal actors are nations that are supposed to respect one another's sovereignty. However, "intervention" was not only used to describe self-serving interference; it also referred to action taken by one state to compel another state to maintain internal order or to satisfy international obligations. Diplomatic protection of aliens abroad led to extensive interventionary practice designed to uphold the legal rights of the nationals of the intervening power. In this way intervention could be made to serve as a sanction; intervention, so conceived, illustrated the dependence of law in a primitive community upon various techniques of self-help. Much of the bewilderment that accompanied notions of intervention arises from this contradictory heritage. For intervention was used both to allege a wrongful intrusion of one state into the affairs of another and to defend a sanctioning enterprise that was conducted by one state on behalf of the general community interest in law enforcement.[7] This helps to account for the curious fact that writers on international law appear to disagree as to whether intervention is legal or illegal.[8]

The legal status of intervention reflects the character of the prevailing international system. The arbitrariness of self-justifying intervention was challenged by smaller nations that demanded an increased adherence to the principles of sovereign equality. The success of this challenge is disclosed by the fact that no one seriously contends today that intervention by one nation in the affairs of another is authorized, as such, by the international legal order.[9] However, as the alternative to intervention is not nonintervention, but some form of collective intervention,[10] our inquiry is not at an end. In fact, it is about to begin. A contemporary

[7] See Charles G. Fenwick, "Intervention: Individual and Collective," 39 *American Journal of International Law* 645 (1945).
[8] The most sustained defense of the legality of intervention is provided by Ellery C. Stowell, *Intervention in International Law*, Washington, J. Byrne, 1921.
[9] There is, however, a developing tolerance for symmetrical counterintervention.

That is, if A intervenes on behalf of faction X in state B, then C is entitled to intervene on behalf of faction Y to neutralize the effect of A's illegal intervention.
[10] Of course, the distinction between unilateral and collective intervention overgeneralizes for emphasis. The preference for collective intervention is an indication of emphasis. It does not purport to be a new standard of law.

appraisal of intervention must take into account the appropriate role in world affairs of a variety of nonnational actors who increasingly exercise significant authority and power.

We are becoming familiar with the transnational importance of the United Nations, the Organization of American States, the Soviet bloc, the Communist party, Radio Free Europe, the World Bank, the European Economic Community. These actors participate in world affairs in many ways, influencing especially the transformation of international law to meet the needs of the modern world. The activities of these nonnational actors alter the context within which classical notions of intervention and nonintervention evolved. It is essential to reformulate the relations between national community and world with due regard to these altered conditions. It is in this spirit that it seems useful to explore the implications of entrusting the United Nations with a limited right of legislative intervention. It is, of course, essential to appreciate that the facts of interdependence contradict the possibility, as well as the aspiration or the allegation of duty, of adherence to a policy of absolute nonintervention. The power to intervene, whether used or not, is what influences domestic outcomes in another state in an "interventionary" manner. The choice, then, concerns the *form* of intervention. Paradoxically enough, "nonintervention" is one form of intervention.

The relative legitimacy of an intervention, as active intrusion in the domestic affairs of a foreign state (as opposed to passive intrusion—"nonintervention"), is partly determined by the nature of the intervening actor. The quality of law is enhanced by centralizing decisions involving the application of coercion. Centralized decision-making gives value to widening the political basis of intervention beyond national boundaries to take account of regional and worldwide attitudes and institutions. This preference for authorization, on as broad a basis as possible, does not deny that a given interventionary policy, no matter how collectivized by the relevant community, may on occasion subject the target state to abusive and arbitrary claims. Improved procedures for the official application of coercion can reduce, but not eliminate, injustice. In criminal trials, for instance, rules of evidence and due process cut the risks of unjust conviction. It is no argument against prevailing methods of handling the prosecution of crime to establish the occasional conviction of an innocent man. In realms of contingency, we strive for the most beneficial alternative among several imperfect ones.

It may sharpen this perspective of choice to describe several prominent types of intervention. First, there is the classical form of unilateral intervention by which one nation intervenes in the internal affairs of another. The Soviet intervention in Hungary in 1956 is illustrative, as is the bulk of United States practice under the Monroe Doctrine. Second, there is counterintervention as when state A intervenes in the affairs of B to preempt or offset interference by state C. The present United States interventions in Laos and South Viet Nam are defended as protection against imminent and actual Communist interventions. Third, there is collective intervention as when a number of states join to coerce the will of the target state. The intervention in 1827 by France, England, and Russia on behalf of the Greek insurgency against Turkish rule is an instance of this. Fourth, there is regional intervention as when a group of states forms a juridical entity which then imposes the regional will upon a dissenting member of the group. The action of the Organization of American States against Cuba after 1961 is an obvious illustration, but the interventions in the nineteenth century by the Holy Alliance on behalf of dynastic legitimacy also fit, although more dubiously, into this category. And fifth, there is universal intervention under the aegis of the United Nations. The Congo operation presents, perhaps, the clearest instance that we presently possess of this type of intervention.

I would argue that each of these five types of intervention generates its own distinctive structure of normative restraint and tolerance. There is no single set of legal rules that is properly applicable to all interventional phenomena. My central argument is based, in fact, upon the relative legality of United Nations interventions to achieve results that would be illegal if sought by unilateral or national interventions. In this respect one can locate the Soviet intervention of 1956 in Hungary, the OAS intervention of 1962 in Cuba, and the UN intervention of 1960 in the Congo along a spectrum of ascending legality. However, it should be understood that the generality of the actor's base of authority is not the only determinant of legitimacy. For legitimacy also depends upon whether the intervention is based on prior principles that express patterns of general community consent or merely reflect an *ad hoc* political majority of the moment. In this sense the earlier declarations of Caracas (1954) and San José (1960) alleging the incompatibility of Communism with hemispheric values make the action taken at Punte del Este in 1962 appear less arbitrary. However, it is true that the dominance and insistence of the United States at the conference undermines, to some extent, the reality of community judgment. This tends to make the intervention look like a disguised version of the earlier practices of paternalistic intervention that the United States undertook throughout Latin America.

A definition of intervention may add some clarity to the discussion. With a full awareness of the difficulties of borderline application and the vagueness of the central variables, I offer the following definition of intervention: *"Intervention" refers to conduct with an external animus that credibly intends to achieve a fundamental alteration of the state of affairs in the target nation.* Although any international actor may initiate intervention, only a state may be the victim of it. As William Burke shows well in his excellent treatment of minor coercion,[11] it is important to distinguish between the facts alleged to constitute intervention and the legal determination of these facts as intervention. Does a documented assertion that United States military aid to South Viet Nam constitutes "intervention" make it "intervention" in a legal sense? This kind of question illustrates the importance of identifying the decision-makers authorized to interpret and apply the norms of intervention. This is a critical inquiry for any legal order, but it is especially so in the international legal order. The decentralized character of international relations often makes the authoritative decision-maker hard to locate, if not actually indeterminate.[12] For instance, in view of the United Nations rejection of Cuba's competence to complain in any higher forum about the illegality of the sanctions voted at Punta del Este, how can we assess the legality of the OAS action? Such a line of analysis, if pursued insistently, tends to identify "law" with the decisions of those entitled by the legal system to render them, and refers always to a "higher" authority capable of appraising the contested decision.[13]

II

Sir Frederick Maitland describes the rise of the Court of Chancery of fourteenth-century England as "an exceedingly curious episode." He observes that "the whole nation seems to enter into one large conspiracy to evade laws which it has not the courage to reform. The Chancellor, the Judges, and the Parliament seem all to be in the conspiracy." But as Sir Frederick goes on so shrewdly to observe, this was not really a conspiracy at all, but a gradual and subliminal transformation of the legal order on a case-to-case basis by honest men intent on justice in a series of particular controversies that happened to come before the Chancellor. Maitland also suggests that "somehow or other England, after a fashion all her own, had stumbled into a scheme for the recon-

[11] See William T. Burke, "The Legal Regulation of Minor International Coercion: A Framework of Inquiry," in Roland J. Stanger, ed., *Essays on Intervention*, Columbus, Ohio State University Press, 1964, pp. 88-89.

[12] It is the importance of this inquiry that makes study of the "Nottebohm" judgment of the International Court of Justice so suggestive. See *International Court of Justice Reports*, 1955, p. 4 (Judgment on the merits).

[13] Domestic analogies are instructive. For instance, the United States has developed a theory of judicial review to vindicate its search for authoritative decisions on the issue of constitutionality, whereas Great Britain relies upon a theory of parliamentary supremacy to achieve a parallel result.

ciliation of permanence with progress."[14] It seems, of course, that this example strays rather perversely from my topic, but I refer to Maitland's account of the rise of equity jurisprudence in order to highlight the problems of peaceful change that exist for *any* legal order, even though my interest is in the problem of peaceful change only as it exists for the international order. The more crafty purpose of using this analogy is to invoke the dignity of Maitland and the conservatism of England to soften the reaction to what may appear, at first, like a heretical solution for the problem of peaceful change in the international environment.

The crux of the problem can be put as a familiar question: How can we reconcile permanence with progress in international affairs?[15] The acuteness of the crisis that prompts the question is a rapid obsolescence of the traditional mechanism for change (war) and the absence of an adequate institution entrusted with responsibility for change (legislature). It is in this setting that I urge consideration of my proposal to endow the United Nations with a restricted legislative competence to intervene in domestic affairs. This competence would authorize United Nations intervention whenever civil strife threatens world peace or whenever gross abuses of fundamental human rights take place. It should be stressed that formal authorization is different from a set of recommendations. Authorization is concerned with the empowering of the United Nations to act, not with action itself. Prudential considerations of feasibility may often preclude the pursuit of an interventionary policy otherwise authorized. Thus, for instance, the power of the Soviet Union properly inhibited United Nations participation in the 1956 uprisings in Eastern Europe. Dangers of military escalation make it imperative that any advocacy of a policy of coercion appraise impacts upon the state of equilibrium within the entire international system, as well as the probable impacts upon the subsystem within which action is taken. It is crucial here to keep in mind the standard-setting, precedent-establishing quality of conduct in a social order in which power is broadly distributed; reciprocal adherence to standards and judicious self-restraint, rather than police procedures, are the principal ordering devices. Thus, for instance, a United States decision to share nuclear weapons technology authorizes symmetrical conduct by the Soviet Union.

14 F. W. Maitland and Francis C. Montague, *A Sketch of English Legal History*, New York; G. P. Putnam's Sons, 1915, p. 127. Chapter V, "Growth of Statute and Common Law and Rise of the Court of Chancery, 1307-1600," written by Maitland.

15 For good general inquiries see Charles De Visscher, *Theory and Reality in Public International Law*, Princeton, Princeton University Press, 1957, pp. 308-24; B.V.A. Röling, *International Law in an Expanded World*, Djambatan, Amsterdam, 1960.

An argument for legislative intervention is radical, at least on its surface, as it proposes that organs of the United Nations extend their competence from intersocietal conflict to embrace, as well, certain specified occasions of nonviolent intrasocietal conflict. Such a position appears to run contrary to ideas of national sovereignty and domestic jurisdiction that many observers regard as the firm basis of the United Nations. It is, of course, true that the Charter asserts that the United Nations "is based on the principle of sovereign equality" (Article 2[1]) and that "nothing contained in the present Charter shall authorize the United Nations to intervene in matters which are essentially within the domestic jurisdiction of any state" (Article 2[7]).

Despite these norms of deference to national societies, it seems clear that the Charter includes contrary assumptions of community responsibility that are sufficient to meet the needs of a developing international order. My argument for legislative competence accords precedence to the successful discharge of the affirmative responsibilities given by member nations to the United Nations. In this connection, it is important to regard the Charter as the organic law of a primitive world community. Perhaps it is helpful to imitate the imaginative response of John Marshall to the United States Constitution during its period of early development. Such a response engenders an attitude that perceives law not as a fixed matrix, but as a dynamic dimension of social change. The international order presently needs to use law in this flexible way if it is to adapt the old system to the new demands.

This gives an orientation. For the legislative use of the United Nations is an aspect of the larger problem of facilitating changes in the international system in a manner that transforms rather than destroys the prevailing standards of order. The aspirations of the modernizing nations in Africa, Asia, and Latin America and the revolutionary nations belonging to the Sino-Soviet bloc challenge deeply the authority of the traditional system of international law as it was developed by a few powerful Christian states of Western Europe who preached capitalist ethics and practiced imperialism. On a political level this challenge fans the flames of domestic discord throughout the world, giving grievance groups strong external backing. Cold war rivalry generates patterns of intervention and counterintervention to offset attempts by the ideological enemy to extend its sphere of political influence. The result is a familiar series of costly internal wars, divided national polities, and recurrent crises in the international relations of the nuclear superstates. The presence of nuclear weapons does give all states some incentive, although a variable one, to find a way to achieve fundamental domestic transitions by peaceful means, or failing this, by the minimum use of violence. This incentive appears to support cooperative action on a supranational level, at least with respect to those social changes that generate a strong consensus among the states. The possibilities for political integration in today's world depend as much upon the discernment of consensus as upon the resolution of conflict.

Efforts to encourage the hermetic solution of domestic conflict will not assure adequate outcomes, even assuming, as is doubtful, the capacity to seal off domestic politics from external intrusions. For one thing, reactionary elites, with an apparatus of repression at their disposal, can often deny progressive movements opportunities to reach their goals by peaceful or constitutional means. This prospect of repression provides protest groups with a choice between an abandonment of the protest and resort to extralegal means, usually involving violence. Fundamental social reorderings of power rarely take place, except perhaps in highly industrialized societies with long democratic traditions, without a period of sustained insurgency and rebellion, often culminating in bitter civil strife. Oppressive regimes can usually frustrate the objectives of domestic rebellion even when the rebels have the overwhelming support of the population. To counteract this, insurgent groups solicit intervention from sympathetic external sources. In current world politics this patterning of conflict tends to draw an internal war into the midst of the cold war, especially if the domestic arena of conflict is an uncommitted nation.[16] Of course, this process is abetted by the sense of revolutionary mission within the Sino-Soviet bloc. This combination of domestic frustration and revolutionary ideology produces an atmosphere that is very conducive to intervention. Cold war rivalry, however, encourages counterintervention and preventive intervention. Intervention and counterintervention increase the magnitude and intensity of internal conflict, yet often yield an indecisive outcome, leaving the basis for unrest present in the post-internal-war society. Frequently, to prevent escalation, the opposing interveners agree upon a stalemate, imposing the solution upon the domestic society which is the actual arena of violence. The internal wars of Asia that have led to the interventionary participation of rival cold war blocs in the years since World War II adhere to this pattern with intimidating fidelity. It is urged that we consider the feasibility of United Nations intervention as a beneficial alternative to the destructive and indecisive quality of symmetrical intervention by nuclear rivals.

[16] There is a tendency to remain aloof from a civil war that takes place in a society closely allied with either nuclear superpower. Thus the United States did not intervene in Hungary in 1956, nor did the Soviet Union intervene in Guatemala in 1954 nor in Cuba prior to the victory of Castro in 1959. The high risks of escalation evidently inhibit interventions in this set of instances. See generally Georg Schwarzenberger, "Hegemonial Intervention," *The Year Book of World Affairs*, London, Steven and Sons, 1955, pp. 236-65.

One can assert the preliminary legitimacy of United Nations intervention merely by suggesting the very obvious threat to international peace that exists whenever nuclear nations invest their prestige and power in the outcome of an internal war. Wherever action is necessary to eliminate such risks, the United Nations seems authorized, if not obliged, to take action.

However, there is a broader base upon which to rest United Nations intervention. For wherever the objectives of domestic insurgency express fundamental preferences of the world community, then the outcome of internal war automatically becomes a matter of international concern. To reach the 1962 Evian Accords, the Algerian war, fulfilling the anti-colonial will of the Moslem plurality of 9:1, required 250,000 lives and $20,000,000,000.[17] And yet such an outcome, despite the persistence of extremist terror, appears to have been inevitable from the outset. Thus it would appear beneficial to have used the coordinated power of the world community to achieve the inevitable outcome with greater decisiveness and less bloodshed. Of course, enormous problems of technique arise whenever political rivals embark on a cooperative venture. Often the common basis for action dissolves, replaced by antagonistic views of the appropriate way to structure the outcome. Nevertheless, the costs of restraint appear higher in many instances. The Congo operation suggests the benefits and dangers of relying upon an apparent community consensus to manage the outcome of domestic strife.

Despite the difficulties of sustaining an initial consensus, it seems advantageous to increase United Nations responsibility for speeding certain processes of social change. The benefit is to find short cuts to social progress that enhance the dignity of mankind and avoid the necessity to rely upon a prolonged transition marked by costly violence. The domestic situations in Angola and South Africa will predictably generate widespread violence to overcome colonial domination and institutional racism. Both violent protest movements will reach their objectives. But there exists an area of creative adaptation that presents a range of choices which point the way toward the outcome, and, hence, control the quality of the outcome itself. There are all sorts of ways to end colonial domination with more or less benefit to the domestic community and to the stability of world order. Why should the world community, almost universally opposed to colonialism and racism, remain an aloof spectator while the process of tension, conflict, and violent resolution works itself out? The repudiation of the incumbent policies is not just a matter of domestic protest; it is an expression of the overwhelming consensus that exists in the international community. The oppressed

17 *New York Times,* March 19, 1962, p. 13.

domestic groups assert their claims as a result of an awareness of their situation and its alternatives that almost always comes from contact with ideas and situations that exist outside the domestic order. Internal wars are deeply embedded in supranational social and political processes. The alternative to United Nations intervention is likely to be a cold war settlement of internal strife. This raises the risks of escalation and increases the costs of human suffering to intolerable levels.

For these reasons this chapter supports United Nations intervention as a legislative act of the world community, seeking, principally, to promote world stability and fundamental human rights. Practice already discloses this legislative competence. The participation of the United Nations in the Congo is an assertion of world community insistence upon internal order in circumstances threatening world peace, even though processes of self-determination are sacrificed. United Nations resolutions of censure condemning Portugal's administration of Angola express world community support for insurgent objectives, even though notions of domestic legitimacy are thereby undercut. Discussions and condemnations of the treatment of nonwhites in the Republic of South Africa express the opposition of the world community to political structures of racial domination even though the territorial supremacy of the incumbent regime is thereby challenged. In general, world community policies in these areas are already given precedence over traditional deferences to national sovereignty. Anticolonialism and antiracism are becoming legislative norms governing United Nations conduct. This assumption of competence on the part of the organization has not been seriously questioned in recent practices of the United Nations (except, of course, by the targets or victims and their friends). Controversy and formidable obstacles arise whenever implementation of this legislative competence uncovers cold war rivalry. In general, Western democracies advocate persuasive interference while revolutionary and excolonial nations prefer coercive interference, but each assumes the legitimacy of interference. Thus the legitimacy of United Nations legislative intervention seems increasingly established by the overwhelming support of member nations for a series of *ad hoc* ventures. We recall the relevance of Maitland's account of the rise of equity to suggest that there might appear to be a conspiracy by the membership of the United Nations to violate its own restraining norms. But here, too, it is only an apparent conspiracy arising from a case-to-case response by the organization to the desperate need of the world community to stabilize serious threats to nuclear peace and the presence of a vital consensus to carry out the Charter mandate to promote fundamental human rights. That is, legislative competence results from a series of gradual accretions which begin to form new standards of legitimacy. This process of agglutinative reform gives flexibility to what would otherwise become a rigid regime governed by an outmoded organic law.

Even from a strictly juridical perspective the basis for expanding United Nations participation in domestic affairs seems quite convincing. For the domestic jurisdiction exception is made explicitly subject to the overriding responsibility of the United Nations to maintain peace. The cold war and the development of nuclear weapons and electronic guidance systems make it necessary to anticipate threats to the peace at a stage prior to resort to international violence. Internal wars and obsolete domestic repressions are two political contexts in which it is quite possible to initiate an escalation cycle that ends in nuclear war. Thus the present condition of unstable equilibrium between nuclear antagonists links the advocacy of United Nations intervention to the maintenance of peace between nations. This provides the interpretative basis for construing the limitations imposed on the United Nations by Article 2(7). Crucial phrases like "to intervene in matters," "essentially within," and "domestic jurisdiction" acquire the gloss imposed by these altered minimum prerequisites of world peace.

Two important qualifications should be considered at this point. First, and this is too complicated to do more than acknowledge, advocacy of UN intervention is accompanied by serious reservations about the role and reliability of the United Nations as a lawmaking and law-applying institution. My position is simply that UN legislative intervention is the best available alternative to serve the community interests of the world in a time when national rivals stand poised to destroy one another (and a lot of others) in a nuclear war. It is not very good, but it is better than anything else that we have—better by far than continuing to tolerate internal wars fought as proxy wars between intervening nuclear powers.

The second qualification of my thesis arises from the special character of the United Nations as a political institution. The United Nations possesses scant autonomous power. Its decisions require the backing of its members, and especially the support of the powerful states. Effective action cannot be taken against a superpower except, perhaps, if it clearly violates the prime norm of the contemporary legal system by making a significant armed attack across a national boundary. Thus legislative intervention requires a consensus within the Organization that transcends the fissures of the cold war. We find such a consensus operative with respect to the initial authorization of the Congo operation and with regard to the existing situation in Angola and South Africa. It is essential that the United Nations achieve the status of a community organization, and resist the inclination to become a political weapon in the cold war. The United States, especially in the early years of the United Nations, with easy majorities at its disposal, used the Organization rather irresponsibly to act as a holy alliance against the Soviet bloc. The treatment of the China issue, especially the retention of Formosa on the Security Council, continues, it is felt, to underrate the national value to the United States of having the United Nations achieve the identity of a world community organization, acting to fulfill universal interests to the extent that they exist, however limited they may now appear to be.[18]

The appropriate institution for partisan supranational action is to be found on the regional level. Here the stabilizing value of political homogeneity for a group of closely related states favors a political use of regional organizations even though this may involve, on occasion, a betrayal of the ideal of national self-determination. It is the rationale of solidarity that seems most strongly to support the 1962 action taken against Castro's Cuba at Punta del Este which resulted in the exclusion of the present Cuban government from the inter-American system on the ground that adherence to Marxism-Leninism was incompatible with the politics of the hemisphere. In effect, the Soviet suppressions of the uprisings in East Germany, Poland, and Hungary similarly, although more brutally, expressed a *regional* intolerance of the principle of peaceful coexistence. It is unfortunate in many respects to compel dissenting national communities to conform to regional political preferences, but it may be indispensable for the maintenance of minimum conditions of international stability. As such, a reciprocal tolerance implicitly develops to accept intrabloc interventions, especially if authorized by a regional organization, to prevent a fundamental defection from existing bloc affiliation.[19] This rule of the game—in effect, a norm acknowledging spheres of influence—does not presently apply to nonaligned nations *inter sese*, although it is quite possible that adherence to the politics of nonalignment may also emerge soon as a regulative norm for this increasingly important group of nations.[20]

This discussion of regional intervention intends to reinforce the significance of coexistence within the United Nations, especially with re-

[18] There is a need to give attention to the discernment of areas of global consensus and its implications for world order. This inquiry would complement concern with conflict resolution.

[19] The refusal of the United Nations in 1961-62 to consider seriously Cuba's com-plaints about regional coercion provides interesting confirmation.

[20] That is, nonaligned states may come to take interventionary measures to prevent a state from shifting its affiliation from neutralist identification to cold war partisanship.

spect to legislative activity. The decentralized distribution of power, nuclear bipolarity, diversity of social and economic philosophy restrict effective coercion by the United Nations to areas within which there exists an almost universal consensus, and certainly agreement about basic legislative objectives on the part of the major cold war rivals. From this perspective even the Soviet championship of the troika principle seems less irresponsible. However, the reasonableness of troika-type restraint if applied to areas of legislative policy would become unreasonable if principles applicable to internal violence are extended to occasions of actual or threatened international violence. For the United Nations cannot permit itself to allow the cold war to take precedence over the need to mobilize community resources against potential violators of the international peace. The nonaligned nations deserve considerable credit for their resistance to troika, as it required them to subordinate their belief in coexistence and active neutralism to the demands for a nonpolitical response to situations involving force.

Internal wars often present intermediate situations partly calling forth rules of limitation appropriate to the role of the United Nations in the light of the cold war and partly counseling the unified intervention of the world community. In general, if the conflict can be internationalized prior to cold war involvement, then the United Nations can act effectively to stabilize the domestic society and keep the cold war out of the civil conflict. If cold war interventions already have significantly taken place, then the United Nations cannot restore order without choosing sides; a consequence of such a choice is to antagonize deeply the nations supporting the faction repressed by the United Nations. The Congo operation became problematic partly because the non-cold war domestic conflict acquired a cold war quality in the course of United Nations intervention. However, entry by the United Nations at a pre-cold war phase solicited wide community support for a Congo settlement as an alternative to unrestricted internal war. One contrasts the situation in the Congo with the possible control by the United Nations of the internal wars presently raging in Laos and South Viet Nam. UN intervention in these internal wars would need to stabilize the domestic scene by giving exclusive governmental authority to a single elite. Such an effort would require a choice between the warring elites, thus allying the United Nations with one cold war bloc against the other in a conflict situation that has been already fully articulated on the level of international ideological rivalry.

If UN intervention is requested by the legitimately constituted government prior to a state of full-fledged insurgency, then there is some reason to argue in behalf of a community response. This was the situation in Lebanon in 1958, where United Nations presence was a compromise alternative to American military intervention to bolster the shaky Chamoun regime. Here, as with the Congo, the United Nations was able to stabilize a threatening domestic situation, even when it was a part of the cold war, because it entered before the threshold of violence had been decisively crossed.

Coercive forms of intervention by the United Nations against a legitimate government, given the continuing strength of the principle of nationalism and the comparative weakness of the Organization, depend on the formation of a consensus that unites the superpowers in the pursuit of common interventionary goals. The advantages of overcoming colonialism or racism by world community standards and pressures, rather than by protracted civil war, commend the adoption of a more radical approach to legislative intervention by the United Nations. This would appear to be a stabilizing way to compel constituted governments to abandon their insistence upon adhering to highly objectionable policies and practices. An expanding competence for legislative intervention would help to create the kind of political stability that might eventually induce revolutionary nations to renounce recourse to indirect aggression and subversion. The attainment of such stability is also an essential aspect of the quest to create a social and political climate that is favorable for disarmament negotiations. As such, it expresses our responsibility to use all available means to achieve the urgent, but hazardous, transition to a warless world. The argument for legislative intervention presupposes that the activity of the United Nations will be designed to promote the values that we proclaim, requiring some acceleration of normal processes of social change in domestic societies, but change that is almost inevitable in the light of certain overwhelming historical pressures, as those that mount against colonialism or institutional racism.

This chapter concludes with another reference to Maitland's analysis of equity jurisprudence. In his masterful summing up Maitland reports that although the legal innovations of the Star Chamber and Chancery Court *were* severe threats to the political liberties of Englishmen, nevertheless, "if we look abroad [to Continental Europe] we shall find good reason for thinking that but for these institutions our old-fashioned national law, unable out of its own resources to meet the requirements of the new age, would have utterly broken down, and the 'ungodly jumble' would have made way for Roman jurisprudence and despotism."[21] So it may be that historians looking back on the second half

21 Maitland and Montague, *op.cit. supra*, note 14, pp. 127-28.

of the twentieth century will conclude that but for the ungodly jumble of legislative intervention by the United Nations the traditional system of international law and order would have been buried in oblivion far beneath the ruins wrought by some great nuclear conflagration.

1962

XI. On Regulating International Propaganda: A Plea for Moderate Aims

THE Draft Declaration on Rights and Duties of States is a fatuous document not because it purports to restrict sovereign discretion, but because the norms of restriction are so abstract and overgeneralized as to be detached from the realities of international order.[1] Article 1 prescribes that "Every State has the right to independence and hence to exercise freely, without dictation by any other State, all its legal powers, including the choice of its own form of government." Article 3 prescribes that "Every State has the duty to refrain from intervention in the internal or external affairs of any other State." Article 4 prescribes that "Every State has the duty to refrain from fomenting civil strife in the territory of another State, and to prevent the organization within its territory of activities calculated to foment such civil strife." These legal principles are broad endorsements of the Westphalia system of organizing international society in which the sovereignty of the nation-state is the prime organizing conception. Any attempt to implement the Westphalia system by specific restraints on the behavior of states is bound to fail. International politics are inevitably interventionary so long as international conflict persists among states of significantly unequal power and so long as no adequate centralized machinery for its effective regulation can be brought into being. Given this decentralized structure, the effort of international law to regulate mutually destructive forms of conflict is most likely to enjoy success by emphasizing the formulation of and promoting the adherence to "rules of the game"; these rules arise from an underlying supposition (1) that conflict is a persistent attribute of the international system, and (2) that reliance upon coercion below certain thresholds of intensity and magnitude to attain a successful resolution of conflict is unavoidable in the present international system.[2] Certain forms of hostile propaganda help to resolve international conflict by coercive competition without endangering the basic peace and security of the world, and deserve to be tolerated in the interests of world order; other forms of propaganda are detri-

[1] For convenient text of Draft Declaration see Louis B. Sohn, ed., *Basic Documents of the United Nations*, Brooklyn, Foundation Press, 1956, pp. 26-27.

[2] For a useful conceptualization of the problem of specifying the threshold separating the upper limit of permissible coercion from the lower limit of impermissible coercion, see William T. Burke, "The Legal Regulation of Minor International Coercion: A Framework of Inquiry," in Roland J. Stanger, ed., *Essays on Intervention*, Columbus, Ohio State University Press, 1964, pp. 87-125. My approach to the regulation of international propaganda is based upon seeking to identify the circumstances under which it is beneficial to classify propaganda on the impermissible side of the threshold and those when it is not. I argue that it is not desirable to characterize *all* international propaganda of a hostile variety as impermissible.

[354]

mental. It is the objective of this chapter to develop some tentative guidelines relevant to drawing the distinction just mentioned in a rational way, given the values and policies at stake.

Prior proposals to regulate international propaganda have been overgeneralized. They have failed to condition the regulatory claim by reference to either the *relatively decentralized* structure of international society or to the rather *diverse* patterns of international conflict. The consequence is the drafting of proposals that possess a legalistic quality in the sense that abstract rules and procedures are recommended without any detailed awareness of their impacts on international behavior. One supposes that such proposals, like the Draft Declaration, would not be implemented in any way that would seriously infringe upon a state's freedom of action. Hence, the enactment of the proposal would add to the corpus of international legal doctrine without altering prevailing patterns of international practice. The approach herein adopted is the reverse, to alter the behavior of states without any accretion to the former doctrines of international law.

I. An Inventory of Adverse Considerations

Propaganda is most generally defined as the use of symbols to influence audiences.[3] Propaganda so defined is too elusive to be susceptible to regulation, if only because its character is too vague and its quality too neutral. As has been often pointed out, propaganda may be put to beneficial or detrimental use. Are there any reliable criteria by which to identify propaganda that is sufficiently detrimental to be classed as impermissible? Among substantive criteria that have been suggested are the truthfulness of the content and the legality of the action proposed; thus any propaganda that is false or advocates illegal conduct should be prohibited. Some further restriction of the regulatory task would follow from the suggestion that international regulation be limited to propaganda activities under government auspices, in which the message is transmitted across an international frontier. Private dissemination of international propaganda would thus be unregulated except to the extent that it was restricted as a matter of national policy. In the liberal democracies national discretion is itself subject to the constitutional protections accorded free speech.

Various procedures for centralizing the identification of impermissible propaganda have been proposed. The objective of such centralization is to overcome self-serving interpretations of the permissibility of propa-

[3] For a representative sampling of definitions see L. John Martin, *International Propaganda*, Minneapolis, University of Minnesota Press, 1958, pp. 10-20.

ganda that would be likely in the event that regulation was based upon self-enforcement at the national level.

At the present time efforts to regulate international propaganda concentrate upon three main clusters of communication conceived to be impermissible because of their detrimental effects upon the peace and order of international society:

(1) War-mongering—the incitement to war and uses of force in international relations.

(2) Subversive intervention—the incitement of audiences to take illegal action against their own government.

(3) Defamation—the vilification of foreign governments and of their political leaders.[4]

It is the position of this chapter to oppose the use of international law to regulate international propaganda at the present time, except in very selective instances. Such an argument is advanced despite an awareness that propaganda may be used to incite violence and raise tensions in international relations and that the technology of propaganda increasingly threatens to manipulate human beings in dangerous directions that may not even reflect their conscious values.[5]

The argument stresses several distinct considerations. First of all, the prohibition of international propaganda must be related to the overall universe of propaganda. If this is done it will appear that the most coercive forms of propaganda are not connected with the manipulation of foreign audiences, but with the manipulation of domestic public opinion. Even in nation-states with long traditions of respect for democratic values, there is an increasing tendency to use propaganda techniques to generate support from the domestic public for controversial policies of government, including especially support for military undertakings carried out in foreign countries. International law makes no general claim to be able to regulate the relationship between a domestic government and its own population, nor do the main advocates of regulation propose such general coverage. The advocates of international regulation of propaganda are, by and large, concerned with transmissions across national boundaries. To isolate this form of propaganda from the overall context of hostile propaganda seems to be an endeavor which, even if successful, will not contribute to world peace in any significant manner. The more likely consequence of such partial regula-

---

[4] For delimitation of each of these three categories and helpful clarification of the legal issue relevant to each see John B. Whitton and Arthur Larson, *Propaganda—Toward Disarmament in the War of Words*, Dobbs Ferry, New York, Oceana Publi-cations, 1963, pp. 62-132.

[5] A comprehensive analysis of the dangers posed by improved techniques of propaganda is found in Jacques Ellul, *Propaganda*, New York, Knopf, 1964.

tion is to assure that national governments achieve proportionately more exclusive control over the transmission of propaganda to their own population. Such a development would merely intensify the sorts of international misunderstandings that arise from trends toward the nationalization of truth; as well, such insulation would have a tendency to strengthen the overall role of national sovereignties in international society.

Second, the ideological dimension of contemporary international society prevents the formation of the sort of consensus that would be necessary to draw a distinction between permissible and impermissible forms of international propaganda. There is general agreement that "information" as distinct from "propaganda" should be permitted, if not encouraged. Often the advocates of prohibitions focused on the right of recipient states to jam foreign broadcasts or to punish nationals for listening to them. It is, however, notoriously difficult in an era of ideological controversy to distinguish between impermissible propaganda and permissible information. There is no criterion of "truth" or "fact" generally available, as the content of the controversial message is typically a partisan interpretation of truth or fact, an interpretation following from adverse political values and contradictory goals of foreign policy. In the face of this essential ambiguity as to what is "false," it is naïve and futile to expect either self-regulation by sending states or an agreed international formula to curtail national discretion to transmit propaganda. This point, although generally valid, admittedly can be carried too far. There are some incendiary distortions of fact that could be identified as such—for example, an allegation of germ warfare—and there is some ground for supposing that a regulatory apparatus, including perhaps a right of reply, might deter such falsehoods or, at least, moderate their impact.

Third, given the diversity of domestic systems of government, there is no agreement among nations about the proper dividing line between communications for which the state has a responsibility and those for which it has not; with respect to international propaganda, antidemocratic societies refuse to acknowledge a private sphere, whereas in contrast, the liberal democracies underacknowledge the public control exerted over activities in the private sphere.

Fourth, as a result of decentralized sanctioning processes that operate in the international legal order, it is virtually impossible to regulate the behavior of nations unless the boundaries of impermissible conduct can be specified in fairly objective terms; as such boundaries are impossible to provide in relation to international propaganda, the prospect is that any regulating scheme would be arbitrarily interpreted and applied, if effective at all.

Fifth, the resolution of international conflict, especially in the nuclear age, depends to some degree upon the toleration of the less destructive forms of coercive competition in order to curtail recourse to more destructive forms. Intervention in internal affairs, of which international propaganda is one mode, is the characteristic form of coercive competition in the present era of international relations.[6] The organized international community lacks both the will and the capability to regulate such patterns of intervention, especially by the Great Powers. Thus the assertion of regulatory claims would produce ineffective international law in the event that international propaganda was dealt with in isolation from the overall context of intervention. The declaratory prohibition of hostile propaganda would not alter patterns of behavior unless there was some machinery made available to implement the prohibition.

Sixth, given the coercive policies of totalitarian and semitotalitarian regimes, it is probably, on balance, desirable to allow emigré elites and hostile governments to transmit international propaganda, subject only to self-regulation voluntarily imposed at the national level. International propaganda of this variety may on occasion dangerously intensify hostility in international relations and, even worse, encourage premature uprisings against oppressive governments. There is reason to believe, however, that the flow of international communication produces pressures for social and political change, which, although difficult to assess, may have a subtle moderating impact upon oppressive policies of foreign governments.[7]

Seventh, if the objective of propaganda is to condemn conduct that is viewed by a consensus approaching unanimity as threatening to the peace and order of international society, then propaganda that would otherwise be considered impermissible can operate as a legislative force in world affairs. In view of the absence of an international legislative organ, there is a need to find legislative substitutes that help the will of the international community to prevail over the absolute prerogatives of sovereignty claimed by dissenter states. The demands for social and political change in the countries of Southern Africa illustrate a context within which a legislative role is being appropriately entrusted to international propaganda.[8]

---

[6] I have developed this position elsewhere: see Chapter VIII, pp. 309-14.

[7] Such a generalization is hazardous and imprecise, at best. International propaganda directed at certain oppressive regimes may merely harden their oppressive policies, thereby intensifying the malady that it intends to alleviate.

[8] See, in this regard, Lewis Nkosi, "Propaganda in the South African Struggle," in

In addition to developing support for these assertions, some consideration is given to the major line of argument advanced by those who favor the regulation of international propaganda. In the course of this effort, certain restricted forms of international regulation—largely self-executed on the national level—will be acknowledged as desirable and feasible, despite my opposition to any general scheme of regulation. To examine the areas susceptible to constructive regulation, it is necessary to reformulate the case for regulating international propaganda in more specific terms than has been heretofore traditional in the literature on the subject; especially, this reformulation requires that we distinguish between the overall regulation of international propaganda by reference to the content of the message and the more restricted regulation of international propaganda in the interests of upholding prior rules of law prohibiting recourse to violence in situations in which, first, the advocacy of international violence is made and, second, such advocacy has not been converted into "a sanction" through formal procedures by which violence may be authorized to carry out an international mandate. It may clarify this distinction between illegal force and legalized force to cite the call by the Arab countries for the destruction of Israel as an example of illegal force, and the call by the United Nations or its members to use force to hasten decolonization or to bring about the termination of apartheid in Southern Africa as an example of legalized force. The Arab plea is an international wrong, one component of a pattern of conduct violative of Article 2(4) of the Charter to the extent that it consists of a threat to use force, whereas the plea by the United Nations may be considered to be an international sanction. This distinction admittedly evades the very real problem as to whether there are constitutional procedures available by which to test whether a particular authorization of violence by organs of the United Nations is itself compatible with the Charter and with general international law.

II. Policy Considerations Relevant to Appraising the Case for International Regulation

There are several distinct, although overlapping, policy considerations that bear upon the decision whether and in what forms to regulate international propaganda. These policies do not point unvaryingly in one direction or the other, but require balancing.

1. *World Peace.* The basic impulse to regulate propaganda arises from the alleged impact of hostile propaganda upon peaceful relations among and within states. In effect, the claim of those favoring regu-

---

John A. Davis and James K. Baker, eds., *Southern Africa in Transition*, New York, Praeger, 1966, pp. 229-43.

lation is that hostile propaganda leads to political violence and aggravates international relations through its tendency to vilify its targets. Hostile propaganda functions as the ideological dimension of international conflict.

2. *Nonintervention.* Hostile propaganda across national boundaries interferes to some extent with the exclusive claims of the domestic regime to exercise governmental control. The interventionary impact of international propaganda is clearly at variance with the traditional conceptions of international legal order resting upon mutual respect for the legitimacy of the constituted government and expressed in normative terms by such doctrines as nonintervention, territorial and domestic jurisdiction, sovereign immunity, and sovereign equality.

3. *Freedom of Speech.* The regulation of international propaganda, if transmitted by nongovernmental broadcasters, may collide with the right of free speech. There is no internationally protected right of free speech or any obligation imposed by international law upon domestic governments to accord individuals rights of free speech. It is also argued that the truth should be respected in the course of international communication and upheld by an international right of reply granted to governments that believe themselves to have been the victims of misleading, false, or unfair propaganda. Leading states have very different conceptions of the scope of the right of free speech.

4. *Social Change.* International propaganda may function as a legislative instrumentality on occasion, especially to the extent that it registers a demand for social and political change that is endorsed by an overwhelming majority of the membership of the international community. As such, international propaganda can be alleged to operate as a sanction or as an authorized form of coercion.

5. *International Stability.* The adjustment of international relations to reduce the prospects of calamity requires the elimination of destructive forms of international conflict, and this implies the maintenance of channels for the expression of less destructive forms of international conflict. Above all, in this period of international history, the objective of war prevention takes precedence in the efforts to regulate the course of international relations. Propaganda as a weapon for the conduct of international conflict bears an indefinite relation to war prevention. On the one side we have concern with peaceful relations, but on the other we have the need to tolerate the less destructive forms of international conflict to the uncertain extent that this toleration can be shown to inhibit recourse to more destructive forms. In an interdependent world beset by strategic conflict and by ideological controversy as to the proper form of domestic government, it would be artificial and

impossible to eliminate ideological rivalries by international fiat. Such rivalries may erupt into political violence, but their promotion through hostile propaganda seems to accord with the structure of international society at the present juncture, and their prohibition would tend to be ignored by major governments.

III. The Conditioning Context: Patterns of International Conflict

The regulation of international propaganda is conditioned by the character of international conflict. The more specific relevance of this conditioning can be made clearer by distinguishing three standard types of conflict now prevalent in international society. These types operate as models of analysis and their use may serve to show that many prior proposals for the regulation of international propaganda have suffered from overgeneralization. These models can in turn be correlated with a policy-oriented analysis of the relative utilities and disutilities of specific varieties of regulation.[9]

TYPE I. PRIMARY LEVELS OF CONFLICT

International society continues to be dominated by the bipolar rivalry between the Soviet Union and the United States.[10] These superpowers uphold the security and exercise partial hegemony over portions of international society outside of their national boundaries. Each superpower relies for its security ultimately upon its capacity to inflict unacceptable damage upon the other if provoked beyond a certain point. The destructiveness of nuclear warfare for both sides creates the basis for peaceful coexistence. Marginal risks of nuclear war arising from a sequence of unanticipated consequences create a strong common interest in adopting measures to reduce the risks of nuclear war, especially if these measures do not inhibit the pursuit of other goals in international life, such as the expansion of the sector over which national political influence exists.

Also, the immediate spheres of superpower concern are virtually impenetrable to its chief adversary. There is no present prospect of successful Western intervention in Eastern Europe or Soviet intervention in Western Europe. At the same time, the maintenance of high tension levels makes it difficult to improve the safety of the international system. Hostile propaganda, in relation to cold war conflict, freezes the *status*

9 These models of conflict are based upon the identity of the parties and upon the arena of violence rather than merely upon the pattern of violence as are the models used in Chapters VII and VIII.

10 For useful depiction of the continuing bipolar domination of international society see Kenneth N. Waltz, "The Stability of the Bipolar World," in Falk and Saul Mendlovitz, eds., *The Strategy of World Order*, New York, World Law Fund, 1966, I, pp. 186-214.

quo, accents distrust, and gives priority to national security through military strength.

The cause of international peace would be served by a *de facto* elimination of this sort of propaganda at the primary levels of international conflict. Such a specific objective is not suitable for any form of regulatory apparatus agreed upon through the negotiation of a treaty. What is called for is the voluntary demobilization of the domestic public with regard to its espousal of positions of ideological militancy, and this requires a defusing of hostility at home as well as a friendlier tone in transmissions abroad. More significant is the acceptance of the *status quo* at the main points of primary confrontation. International broadcasting could cease being an instrument of conflict and, instead, encourage a trend toward bipolar cooperation based on common interests and mutual respect for established spheres.[11]

No formal apparatus is needed to carry out this redirection of broadcasting energy. The elimination of hostile propaganda could proceed on the basis of mutual example, perhaps acknowledged as explicit strategy in quiet diplomacy between the two countries.[12] To make such a strategy overt might well be inadvisable and imprudent, implicitly advertising, as it would, that henceforth permissible and fruitful forms of primary struggle would be restricted to the areas of Latin America, Asia, and Africa, areas chosen as the battlegrounds where the war for world ascendancy could be waged without great risk to the principal adversaries.

TYPE II: SECONDARY LEVELS OF CONFLICT

There are certain international conflicts that dominate regional politics but are largely independent of the cold war. These conflicts threaten to produce international violence, and their intensity is abetted by hostile propaganda. The conflicts between Israel and its Arab neighbors, between South Africa and the black African states, and between Indonesia and Malaysia (1963-1966) offer illustrations. Warfare is quite possible in a form that will draw the Great Powers in as allies opposed to one another, but the Great Powers are not the immediate antagonists.

Propaganda in this setting either calls for a holy war against the target state, defames the leadership of a foreign government, or calls for an uprising against a foreign government. Middle Eastern govern-

---

[11] This is the central thesis of President Johnson's interview appearing in the Russian-language magazine *Amerika,* which is published by the United States Information Agency, and distributed in the Soviet Union by an official Soviet agency, Soyuzpechat. For text see *New York Times,* September 28, 1966, p. 1.

[12] Such an arrangement has been used with a certain success in the effort to control the stockpiling of fissionable material of weapons-grade by the Soviet Union and the United States.

ments have made particular use of hostile propaganda as an instrument of militant foreign policy.

In this setting there is a basis for the *ad hoc* assertion of regulatory authority in the event that an international consensus can be mobilized. Hostile propaganda directed at South Africa or Rhodesia is compatible with global support for coercive measures designed to alter the policies of these regimes. Hostile propaganda can be a *sanction* or an international wrong, or neither, in this setting. It is neither if there is no consensus for or against the transmission of the hostile propaganda. That is, hostile propaganda is permissible in the absence of a consensus against it.

TYPE III: TERTIARY LEVELS OF CONFLICT

These international conflicts are internal to single states, but are arenas of intervention by the Great Powers. Because of the dangers of war described in connection with Type I, the conflicts in Type III tend to be outside established spheres of superpower influence and are located in "the third world."[13] Competitive intervention by economic and ideological means constitutes a prime characteristic of world politics at this stage. Propaganda plays a crucial role in advancing the policies of ideological intervention. With respect to conflict in the third world, there is not likely to be an international consensus available in relation to specific instances of civil strife of the sort that might serve as a basis for *ad hoc* authorization or condemnation administered on a supranational level (Type II). At the same time the common interests among the Great Powers are not strong enough to support ideological de-escalation through the voluntary regulation of propaganda at the national level (Type I). As a consequence, it seems hopeless and even undesirable to attempt to regulate propaganda vis-à-vis Type III conflicts. For this class of conflicts the effort at international regulation should concentrate on preventing overt military interventions of the kind that have devastated Viet Nam since 1954. Nonmilitary intervention, whether by means of foreign aid or subversive propaganda, seems not to be susceptible to international regulation, partly because the conflict situation is not dangerous enough to the intervenors and partly because the incentives to intervene may often appear high. As such, struggles for influence in third world countries accord with prevailing "rules of the game" operative in international affairs.

The objective of this overschematic presentation of the main pat-

[13] For a general account of this sector of international political life see P. Worsley, *The Third World,* London, Weidenfeld, 1964, and Cecil V. Crabb, *The Elephants and the Grass—A Study of Nonalignment,* New York, Praeger, 1965.

terns of international conflict is to carry forward the argument that the *form* of international regulation must be clarified in relation to the extralegal international setting. Such a clarification indicates that certain forms of regulation are undesirable and infeasible, whereas other forms are desirable and feasible. The identification of desirable and feasible forms can be facilitated with respect to international propaganda by distinguishing between the main types of international conflict. In actuality, no additional rule of international law is needed to achieve desirable regulatory objectives. To the extent that hostile propaganda should be made subject to international regulation, this should be done by applying the existing rule prohibiting the threat to use force to resolve an international dispute as contained in Article 2(4) of the Charter. Such an approach to regulation emphasizes the need for authoritative action at the international level whenever the object of regulation is as ambiguous as propaganda. At worst, propaganda is a form of indirect aggression and its identification as such involves all the problems of subjective interpretation that prevent the formulation of clear rules of prohibition. Thus at the present stage of relative decentralization in international society it is essential that authoritative interpretation of vague legal rules—such as the prohibition upon a threat to use force or upon intervention—be based upon the formally declared finding of an overwhelming consensus of states, and taking the form of a resolution of the General Assembly.

Additional regulation of hostile propaganda may be desirable but it is unlikely to be attainable through either an international agreement ("treaty") or the expression of an *ad hoc* consensus. To the extent that common interests are mutually served by reducing the flow of hostile propaganda in both directions, it might be possible and beneficial to proceed by means of graduated and reciprocal initiatives. It is this sort of evolution that might help restore harmony to the relations between the Soviet Union and the United States. Thus the further clarification of the national interest in expanding the extent of international cooperation among rival states might operate as a functional equivalent to direct regulation of hostile propaganda, relying on self-interested action voluntarily *and* reciprocally undertaken at the national level.

IV. A Question of Principle: On the Need for Legislative Change in International Society

Propaganda plays a legislative role in international society generating pressure for social change. Perhaps the most widespread support for the pursuit of legislative objectives by means of hostile propaganda exists in relation to the racial and colonial practices of the regimes in control of the states in Southern Africa.[14] Given the capacity of modern governments to suppress political opposition, and given the absence of any supranationally organized legislative organ, there are serious reasons to favor allowing certain forms of propaganda, even those that advocate war against a foreign government, seek to provoke domestic uprisings, or defame the political leadership in control of foreign societies.

The elimination of violence from international life is not an absolute value, nor is it separable from other questions at issue in international society. From the perspective of the African states south of the Sahara, the rectification of the racial and colonial situation in Southern Africa takes precedence over the cause of war prevention. If war prevention demands a reduced capability to achieve their foreign policy goals with highest priority, then war prevention as a policy goal is in direct conflict with the elimination of racial discrimination and colonialism as policy goals, and a choice must be made. It is the refusal to confront the necessity for making this kind of choice that accounts for part of my criticism of prior advocates of the regulation of propaganda, and, in turn, for a critical attitude toward all efforts to promote world order by overgeneralized commandments and prohibitions that are insufficiently correlated with the interests of states active in world affairs.

V. A Tentative Sense of Direction

The status of international propaganda is both troublesome and interesting because it seems to be related to mutually destructive conflict and to be intricately intertwined with the legislative programs of revisionist actors. Is there any way to reconcile the restraint of mutually destructive propaganda with the toleration of propaganda incidental to the realization of legislative objectives? Given the horizontal or decentralized structure of international society in the nuclear age, there is no very strong prospect of promoting legislative changes opposed by one or more major nuclear power. The failure of the United States to support the anti-Soviet uprising in Hungary in 1956 is suggestive of the nuclear veto imposed upon the international advocacy of legislative policies. Pre-1956 American propaganda had created some impression that the United States would use its military power to assure the success of any substantial anti-Communist uprising in Eastern Europe, but in the situation of choice, the dangers of war with the Soviet Union took precedence. As a consequence, many heroic individuals may have been deceived by misconstruing hostile propaganda. The United States

14 I have outlined a legal argument in this setting: see Chapter X, pp. 347-52.

has been more prudent since 1956 about the impressions it creates through hostile propaganda. Minimum mutual toleration seems to be the basis of international relations between the superpowers *inter se*, and each shares with the other an interest in avoiding the provocation of its adversary. In such circumstances there has been in recent years a significant *de facto* reduction in the transmission of subversive, warmongering, or defamatory propaganda between the Soviet Union and the United States. The content of the propaganda has rather been confined to criticism, perhaps extended to denunciation in periods of international tension.

At one end of the consensual spectrum, then, is the operation of a nuclear veto, whereas at the other end is virtual unanimity about the direction of social change in Southern Africa. There is agreement broad enough to include both the United States and the Soviet Union that the regimes of Rhodesia, South Africa, Angola, and Mozambique need to alter their policies drastically and that this alteration can come about only through the change of regime. As the regimes in control disallow domestic political opposition, the only prospect for change is by an externally abetted internal revolt, or by force exerted from outside by a group of states or by international institutions. Propaganda is one component of "force" that is especially significant, given the inability of the African states to organize any kind of external military operation. Under these circumstances there exists an overwhelming international consensus favoring a legislative solution and no way to register effectively the results of the consensus. At a minimum the transmission of propaganda must be reconciled with the international legal order. Otherwise the Westphalia system offers a rationale for oppressive domestic regimes repudiated by the international community rather than a framework supportive of common interests in peace.

The new states themselves have failed to articulate their double interest in nonintervention as a basic rule of international conduct and in a highly interventionary legislative solution for Southern Africa. As a consequence, their simultaneous advocacy of both policy objectives, corresponding to the actuality of their dual interests, appears confused and opportunistic. The importance of reinforcing norms of nonintervention during the period of nation-building in Africa and Asia is obvious, but no more so than is the drive to finish off colonialism and its racist byproduct in Southern Africa. This analysis has belabored this point to illustrate the approach taken in this chapter to the problem of regulating international propaganda which is properly viewed as one aspect of the overall problem of regulating intervention in the internal affairs of foreign states. The essence of the approach is to relate the prospects for regulating to (1) the perceived interests of the major participants in international society and to (2) the basic decentralized structure of international society. As a consequence, the authority of law must reflect the perceived interests of the influential group of Afro-Asian states. In the context of intervention, then, there is legislative exception to the generalized prohibition expressed by Articles 1, 2, 3, and 4 of the Draft Declaration on Rights and Duties of States. The conditions for granting a legislative exception are only met when the will of the international community is substantially united by a consensus that includes two-thirds of all states and the absence of opposition by either the United States or the Soviet Union. In effect, the argument assumes that the will of the international community as expressed in a suitable fashion operates as the basic source of law in international affairs.[15] The partial validity of this contention has been accepted by at least three dissenting judges in the recent decision of the International Court of Justice in *The South West Africa Cases*.[16]

It is possible to summarize the jurisprudential underpinnings of the argument by saying that the Westphalia system for coordinating sovereign states has been qualified by a legislative exception—namely, that a requisite consensus of the international community can formulate demands for action and claims to act that take *legal* precedence over the will of the sovereign state. The quality of this consensus is as yet indefinite but it would seem to require overwhelming support that includes the two nuclear superpowers. On the basis of this background it now seems possible to approach more realistically proposals to regulate international propaganda. International propaganda that is disseminated to promote a legislative objective that has been endorsed by a requisite consensus is *ipso facto* legal, even if the objective of the propaganda is to provoke its audience to take action otherwise illegal.

In conclusion, several propositions emerge:

(1) No general scheme of international regulation appears feasible or desirable at the present time as a consequence of political decentralization and ideological controversy;

(2) Hostile propaganda presently discharges certain legislative tasks in the international system;

---

[15] For a survey of the traditional considerations see Clive Parry, *The Sources and Evidences of International Law,* Dobbs Ferry, New York, Oceana Publications, 1965; for an argument that the will of the international community is a basic source of international law see C. Wilfred Jenks, *Law, Freedom and Welfare,* Dobbs Ferry, New York, Oceana Publications, 1963, pp. 83-101.

[16] Cf. the dissenting opinions of Judges Tanaka (Japan), Nervo (Mexico), and Mbanefo (Nigeria), *The South West Africa Cases,* June 18, 1966, *International Court of Justice Reports* [1966], pp. 248-324, 441-73, 482-505.

(3) Hostile propaganda directed at the third world may restrict Great Power conflict to mutually tolerable limits;

(4) International propaganda is a less serious instrument for human manipulation than is national propaganda and, to some extent, impairs the total control over media of communication exerted by national governments in relation to their own population;

(5) *De facto* reductions of hostile propaganda by informal arrangements may be useful if both sides wish to defuse inflamed international relationships on some mutual basis.

1967

PART THREE

NUCLEAR WEAPONS

Introduction

THE IMPACT of nuclear weapons technology on the conduct of international relations is certainly the most dramatic and distinctive challenge to national security that is posed in our time. The awesome prospect of a nuclear war has encouraged the governments of the Great Powers, even those with expansionist goals, to conduct their foreign affairs with unprecedented prudence. The elaborate technology needed to sustain a major nuclear weapons industry has resulted in creating a hierarchy of sovereign states in which the main tiers of actors consist of nuclear superpowers, secondary nuclear powers, nuclear-capable powers, and nonnuclear powers. As nuclear weapons appear decisive in relation to an adversary that possesses neither nuclear weapons nor is reliably protected by a nuclear power, the nuclear stratification of international society seems to be an inevitable challenge to notions of sovereign equality upon which the formal organization of international society continues largely to be based. Of course, differentials in military power have always created a tension between "legal" equality and "political" inequality, but the clarity of the distinction between nuclear and nonnuclear states appears to create such significant differences in international status as to be worthy of careful, serious account.

Intimations of the destructiveness of nuclear weapons were dramatically, if only very partially, disclosed at Hiroshima and Nagasaki. The special horror associated with using such weapons against human targets has generated movements throughout the world "to ban the bomb" and have stimulated the search for and endorsement of drastic disarmament by most governments in the world.

The existence of nuclear weapons also appears to discourage reliance upon large-scale and overt uses of military power by nuclear powers in conflict with one another. The mutual destructiveness of a third world war fought with nuclear weapons creates a common interest in its avoidance that takes precedence over almost any competing consideration. As such, it may be reasonable to conclude that nuclear weapons technology has been an indispensable instrument in the struggle to sustain the peace in the period since World War II, a period of intense ideological and political rivalry that generated the kind of hostility between Communist and non-Communist worlds that has often led to international wars in the past. The gradual normalization of Soviet-American relations may reflect the essential futility of sustaining a posture of conflict in an international setting that does not allow either side to imagine victory for itself.

If it appears that the prospects of international violence on the scale of the two world wars is reduced to a significant degree by nuclear weapons, then their removal presents more complex issues of policy and choice than has been generally supposed by those who propose reform. It is necessary to consider and dispose of the issue of whether an attempt to deny legitimacy to nuclear weapons might not appear to encourage nonnuclear uses of military force of considerable magnitude. The awesome prospect of World War III fought with nuclear weapons should not blind us to the human suffering and physical destruction arising from the pre-nuclear weapons technology of World Wars I and II.

Nuclear weapons, then, improve the prospects for "peace" amid intense conflict by their capacity to inflict mutually unacceptable damage. Can such a peace be maintained? Are there tendencies in the international system, such as the acquisition of nuclear weapons by an increased number of states, including several that lack stable political leadership, which undermine the basis for nuclear peace that has existed since 1945? Are there feasible alternative courses of action whereby a more enduring foundation for international peace can be established?

Part of the nuclear challenge is a moral one. By pointing out that the central condition of peace is the maintenance of a credible threat to destroy the fabric of an enemy society, the ideals of the unity of mankind, ideals however breached in practice, that have permeated the moral consciousness of all of the great civilizations that survive to influence the modern world, are thus decisively compromised. Such a moral implication can either generate a cynical attitude toward any humanism of global proportions or it can lead to a repudiation of the present basis of peace and security—holding hostage large numbers of innocent people. This moral terrain, perhaps only more blatant than what had served as the basis for national security in the pre-nuclear age, is part of the extralegal background relevant to appreciating the role of nuclear weapons in the world today.

Chapter XII puts these themes in a legal focus by analyzing the decision of a Japanese domestic court in the *Shimoda* case, a legal controversy arising out of claims for compensation being pressed by some survivors of the atomic attacks on Hiroshima and Nagasaki. The *Shimoda* case is one of the first legal documents of the nuclear age. As well, the domestic setting of the litigation highlights the role played by national institutions in the evolution of law in international society, a decentralized social system.

Chapter XIII surveys the prospects for minimizing the negative impact of nuclear weapons by means short of a system-change. In general, certain adjustments are considered that might enhance the safety of international society, but which can be brought into being without altering the control over military power exercised by sovereign states. Finally, Chapter XIV argues in favor of a proposal prohibiting the use of nuclear weapons except in reprisal against a prior nuclear attack. Such an argument arises from a combination of prudential and policy considerations, and resolves, admittedly without benefit of objective evidence, the dilemma posed by the threat to use nuclear weapons constituting the keystone of peace in the modern world. To make choices in a situation of uncertainty as to the weight of comparative risks is an unavoidable and tragic aspect of the human condition. It is unavoidable because to propose nothing is also a choice involving an uncertain risk. At least by proposing action it is possible to work toward an international society that is compatible with one's preferences, normative as well as prudential.

XII. The Shimoda Case: A Legal Appraisal of the Atomic Attacks upon Hiroshima and Nagasaki

IN MAY OF 1955 five individuals instituted a legal action against the Japanese Government to recover damages for injuries allegedly sustained as a consequence of the atomic bombings of Hiroshima and Nagasaki in the closing days of World War II. On December 7, 1963, the twenty-second anniversary of the surprise attack by Japan upon Pearl Harbor, the District Court of Tokyo delivered its lengthy decision in the case. The decision has been translated into English and reprinted in full in *The Japanese Annual of International Law for 1964*.[1] This enables an accounting of this singular attempt by a court of law to wrestle with the special legal problems arising from recourse to atomic warfare.

Disposing of arguments that these atomic attacks were justified by "military necessity," the Japanese court reached the principal conclusion that the United States had violated international law by dropping atom bombs on Hiroshima and Nagasaki. It also concluded, however, that these claimants had no legal basis for recovering damages from the Japanese Government. Both sides in the litigation refrained from exercising their right of appeal to a higher Japanese court. Apparently, the five plaintiffs, although disappointed by the rejection of their claim for compensation, were satisfied enough by the finding of the court that the attacks themselves were illegal to let the litigation lapse, and the defendant Japanese Government, although evidently unpersuaded by the finding that the attacks were illegal, was willing to forego an appeal in view of the rejection by the court of the damage claim.[2]

The *Shimoda* case seems eminently worthy of attention by international lawyers for a series of reasons. First, it is the one and only attempt by a court to assess the legality of atomic, and, by extension, nuclear weapons. The decision thus offers a focus for a more general inquiry into the continuing relevance of the laws of war to the conduct of warfare in the nuclear age.[3] Second, the case is an illustration of an attempt by a court in a country defeated in war to appraise the legality of a major belligerent policy pursued by the victor. Third, the

[1] Pp. 212-52, cited hereinafter by page reference digested in 58 *American Journal of International Law* 1016 (1964).

[2] This explanation has been given to me by Yuichi Takano, Professor of International Law, in the course of a correspondence about the case. Professor Takano served as one of three experts on international law appointed by the court in the *Shimoda* case.

[3] The need for a revival of interest in the international law of war has been stressed by several authors, but by none more insistently than Josef Kunz. See, in particular, his "The Chaotic Status of the Laws of War and the Urgent Necessity for their Revision," 45 *American Journal of International Law* 37 (1951).

Japanese locus of the litigation gives us an unusual example of an Asian court taking for granted the validity and applicability of a body of international law developed by Western countries, although Japan, it should be noted, is not a newly independent Asian country, nor one that has generally joined with ex-colonial Afro-Asian states in the attack upon traditional international law. Fourth, the decision grapples with the problem of determining the extent to which individuals may assert legal rights on their own behalf for causes of action arising out of violations of international law. Fifth, the decision discusses the extent to which principles of sovereign immunity continue to bar claims by individuals against governments. Sixth, the decision considers the legal effect of a waiver in a peace treaty of the claims of nationals against a foreign country. Seventh, the court confronts a rather difficult question of choice of laws because of the need to decide whether the existence of the right of recovery is to be determined by Japanese or by United States law. And eighth, the whole nature of the undertaking by this Japanese court raises the problem of identifying the appropriate role for a domestic court in this kind of an international law case. As such it provides a new setting within which to continue the discussion of some of the more general questions present in the *Sabbatino* controversy.[4] This range of issues is part of the explanation for commending the *Shimoda* case for study by international lawyers. However, it is not possible here to deal equally with all of these points of interest. It is my intention to emphasize only that portion of *Shimoda* concerned with the legality of atomic warfare, although these other elements of the decision will be described as part of the effort to give the reader a complete narration of the case in the first part of this chapter.[5]

I. A Narration of the Judgment in the Shimoda Case

In narrating the *Shimoda* case I shall adhere rather closely to the plan of organization used in the decision itself. Thus I will begin by summarizing the contentions of the opposing litigants and follow this with a description of the reasoning used by the Tokyo District Court to reach its various legal conclusions.

The Argument of the Five Plaintiffs. The plaintiffs sought recovery for the injuries that they had sustained either to their person or to mem-

[4] Banco Nacional de Cuba v. Sabbatino, 376 U.S. 398, 1964; for some depiction of these issues see Falk, "The Complexity of Sabbatino," 58 *American Journal of International Law* 935 (1964).

[5] At present, the only available English translation of the opinion is to be found in *The Japanese Annual* (1964). This publication is often difficult to obtain. The full text of the decision is also reprinted in Falk and Saul H. Mendlovitz, eds., *The Strategy of World Order*, New York, World Law Fund, 1966, I, pp. 314-54. Besides, the reported version of *Shimoda* contains many passages that are rather obscure. It is on this basis that such a long explication of the case is offered here.

bers of their immediate families.[6] The amounts sought were in four cases 200,000 yen and in one, that of Shimoda, 300,000 yen, plus 5 per cent measured from the initiation of the suit on May 24, 1955.[7] The costs of the litigation, regardless of outcome, were to be borne by the plaintiffs.

The plaintiffs begin by describing the atomic attacks and their effects upon the cities of Hiroshima and Nagasaki. The description is detailed and emotional. For example, "People in rags of hanging skin wandered about and lamented aloud among dead bodies. It was an extremely sad sight beyond the description of a burning hell, and beyond all imagination of anything heretofore known in human history" (p. 214). The relevance of this description is to establish the claim that the atomic bomb caused such indiscriminate suffering and such unusually severe and grotesque pain as to violate rules governing the permissible limits of warfare.

In fact, the plaintiffs contend that the use of atomic bombs against these Japanese cities violated both conventional and customary international law. To avoid duplication of discussion, a detailed consideration of these contentions must await the description of the court's reasoning. In main, the claims were based upon the series of formal international acts prohibiting recourse to poisonous gas, restricting rights of aerial bombardment, buttressed by the more general condemnation of terror tactics that inflict indiscriminate injury and unnecessary suffering upon civilians. The principal argument is that the atomic attacks are covered by these preatomic legal instruments either directly or *mutatis mutandis*, and furthermore, that even if it is found that positive international law does not directly condemn these atomic bombings, these rules indirectly or rather "their spirit must be said to have the effect of natural law or logical international law" (p. 216), and by this process support a finding of illegality.

It was also pointed out that the destructive power of these atomic bombs was such that it caused indiscriminate casualties, without distinguishing between combatant and noncombatant, within the area of a circle having a radius of four kilometers as measured from the epicenter of the blast, and furthermore, that this effect was known to those who ordered its use. The pain caused, it is alleged, is far more severe

6 The description of the injuries is itself a very dramatic aspect of the *Shimoda* opinion and serves to make it one of the prime documents of war in the atomic age. Each of the plaintiffs is a survivor of the attacks and suffers from a variety of grotesque disabilities. As well, the family of each claimant was either completely wiped out or maimed; this, too, is described in detail. I have tried to assess the nonlegal importance of the case in a short article, "The Claimants of Hiroshima," *The Nation* (February 15, 1965), 157-61.

7 The exchange rate is about 360 yen for one United States dollar. The recoveries sought, then, were for rather modest amounts.

than that resulting from weapons that had been previously outlawed as agents of extreme suffering for the victim, such as poison gas or dum-dum bullets. The argument is also made by the plaintiff that, since Japan was obviously on the brink of defeat and had no war potential left, the only purpose of the attacks was "as a terrorizing measure intended to make officials and people of Japan lose their fighting spirit" (p. 217). The plaintiffs also point to the diplomatic protest based on international law issued by the Japanese Government immediately after the attacks (August 10, 1945). Finally, they suggest that if a weapon is permissible until explicitly prohibited, then a belligerent is entitled to act as "A Merchant of Death, or a Politician of Death" (p. 217).

The next link in the chain of accusation is to allege that what is illegal in international law is also illegal under municipal or domestic law. The plaintiffs also allege that to claim damages a suit could, in theory, be filed in a District Court of the United States against former President Truman and the United States, the parties they charge as responsible for the atomic attacks. And, if this is hypothesized, then the conflict rules of the court in the United States would apply and would determine that the controversy should be governed by Japanese law, as Japan was the place where both the illegal acts and the injury occurred. The statement in the opinion is not very clear at this point, but the claim being made is that the United States is the real defendant and that, if the case is looked upon in that way, the controversy is governed by international law as it is received by Japanese municipal law. When this is done, then the claim is made by the complainants that under Japanese law the state is responsible for the illegal acts of its officials and that the officials who acted are likewise responsible. The strategy of the complaint is evidently to circumvent the defenses that the presentation of the claim is barred because the acts complained about are nonreviewable acts of state or that the defendants are immune from suit as a consequence of the doctrine of sovereign immunity. Here also, the presentation of the plaintiff seems unclear, and appears limited to brushing aside these defenses on the ground that such technicalities cannot possibly apply to a calamity on the scale of an atomic attack.

The next step, and a difficult one for the plaintiff, is to show a basis for recovery by these private individuals. The problem is so formidable because of the governing notion that states are alone entitled to pursue claims arising out of violations of international law, and that individuals have, as a consequence, no cause of action or standing to complain about a violation of international law. The plaintiffs point to Article 19(a) of the Peace Treaty by which "Japan waives all claims of Japan and its nationals against the Allied Powers and their nationals arising out of the war or out of action taken because of the existence of the war," as presupposing the existence of claims against the victors by individual Japanese. If there was nothing to claim, the complaint reasons, then there was no need to waive. And, further, the allegation is made that these rights of individuals are directly available to them and did not depend for assertion upon their adoption by the government of the claimant. The argument here grows a bit abstract and fragmentary, but it seems that the plaintiffs want to suggest that if the victor is able to bar claims by individuals arising in the defeated country through the device of a waiver clause in the Peace Treaty, then there is no constraint whatsoever upon the belligerent policies of the side that wins the war.

The complaint also tries to demonstrate why a Japanese domestic court is the only appropriate forum for the litigation. The plaintiffs argue that the waiver in Article 19(a), because treaties are the supreme law of the land, would be effective to bar the presentation of the claim in a United States court, so that their only remedy is to proceed in Japan. The statement goes on, somewhat gratuitously, to say that, even if the plaintiffs did institute the action in the United States, they could not "easily obtain the cooperation of lawyers or the support of public opinion," adding that even in Japan "it is extremely difficult to find cooperators" (p. 220).

The final step of the argument in the complaint is to show that the Government of Japan wrongfully waived the claims of its nationals, and as a consequence, is responsible for the losses thereby inflicted. This position depends on a complicated process of analysis. First, the assertion is made that the inclusion of Article 19(a) in the Peace Treaty was an illegal exercise of public power under Japanese law and that Article 1 of the State Compensation Law of Japan makes the Japanese Government responsible for losses suffered by Japanese nationals if these losses result from illegal exercises of public power.[8] Second, the United States must have given certain benefits to Japan in exchange for this waiver provision, especially as it applied to responsibility for the atomic attacks. This means, in effect, that the Japanese Government was enriched as a result of the expropriation of private property (the causes of action of claimants like these plaintiffs) without paying just

---

8 Art. 1: (1) If an official or servant of the state or a public body intentionally or negligently commits an unlawful act and injures another in the course of performing his duties, the state or public body is liable to make compensation therefore. (2) In the case of the preceding paragraph, if there has been intent or gross negligence, the state or the public body may claim compensation from the official or servant involved. *Kokka Baisho Ho,* Law No. 125, October 27, 1947.

compensation as required by Article 29 of the Japanese Constitution.[9] Furthermore, even if the plaintiffs do not benefit directly from this clause in the Constitution, nevertheless the waiver imposes on the Japanese Government a legal obligation to compensate. The reasoning of the complaint here is not made entirely plain. The obligation of the government does not depend, as the defense contends, upon a specific law of expropriation, but arises from any governmental act that effectively expropriates and from the basic values of respect for private property and for human rights that are protected generally throughout the Japanese Constitution. The plaintiffs also suggest that the obligation to compensate arises from the illegal acts giving rise to the injury, and thus does not depend upon the discretion of the state to enact legislation for the relief of war victims. Here, the argument seeks to maintain that compensation is a nondiscretionary legal question, and not a political question as the defense contends.

It is on this basis that the responsibility of the Japanese Government is alleged to exist. The main steps in the argument are as follows, to recapitulate:

(1) The use of the atomic bomb by the United States violated international law.

(2) A violation of international law is necessarily a violation of municipal law.

(3) The municipal law of Japan governs the controversy before the court.

(4) Individuals are entitled on their own behalf to assert claims for injuries arising from violations of international law.

(5) The waiver in Article 19(a) of the Peace Treaty bars claiming directly against the United States Government.

(6) The Japanese Government violated the constitutional and vested rights of these claimants by agreeing to the waiver provision and is legally responsible for satisfying the claims wrongfully waived.

The Defense of the Japanese Government. To avoid repetition, the position of the defense will be stated as briefly as possible. This does not imply that the arguments are not well made, but only, as might be expected, that the defense devotes much of its presentation to denying the legal conclusions alleged by the plaintiffs. The objective of this section, it should be recalled, is to indicate the structure of the argument between the litigants as a background for an analysis of the decision itself.

---

[9] Art. 29: (1) The right to own or to hold property is inviolable. (2) Property rights shall be defined by law, in conformity with the public welfare. (3) Private property may be taken for public use upon just compensation therefore. *Nihon Koku Kempo,* November 3, 1947.

The defense concedes, of course, the facts of the atomic attacks, although it submits that the casualties were considerably lower than the plaintiffs contend. On the main issue of legality, the Japanese Government contends that the atomic bombs were new inventions and hence not covered by either the customary or the conventional rules of the international law of war. Since the use of atomic bombs was not expressly forbidden by international law, there is no legal basis upon which to object to their use by a belligerent.

But the Japanese Government concedes that the legality of use may be determined by the more general principles of international law governing belligerent conduct. But this source of limitation is not very relevant, it turns out, for the defense argues that, "From the viewpoint of international law, war is originally the condition in which a country is allowed to exercise all means deemed necessary to cause the enemy to surrender" (p. 225). In fact, the defense goes so far in the direction of *Kriegsraison* as to assert that, "Since the Middle Ages, belligerents, in international law, have been permitted to choose the means of injuring the enemy in order to attain the special purpose of war, subject to certain conditions imposed by international customary law and treaties adapted to the times" (pp. 225-26). This seems to suggest that if there is no explicit prohibition of a weapon, then there is no added inhibition placed in the way of a belligerent by international law.[10]

The defense goes on, after pausing to express its regret about the large number of casualties at Hiroshima and Nagasaki, to vindicate the atomic bombings because they tended to hasten the end of the war, and thereby reduce the net number of casualties on both sides and achieve the belligerent objective of unconditional surrender. It is significant that the Japanese Government is willing to associate itself, even for purposes of defense in this action for compensation, with the official justification of the use of atomic weapons that has been offered by the United States.[11] The defense goes so far as to say: "with the atomic bombing of Hiroshima and Nagasaki, *as a direct result*, Japan ceased further resistance and accepted the Potsdam Declaration" (p. 226).[12] The Japanese Government takes note of the diplomatic

[10] The range of issues considered in *Shimoda* is very well anticipated in two articles by William V. O'Brien. See "The Meaning of Military Necessity in International Law," 1 *Yearbook of World Polity* 109 (1957); and "Legitimate Military Necessity in Nuclear War," 2 *ibid.* 35 (1960), (this second article is hereinafter cited as O'Brien).

[11] Henry Stimson, "The Decision to Use the Atomic Bomb," *Bulletin of Atomic Scientists*, III (1947), 37; Harry S Truman, *Memoirs—Year of Decisions*, Garden City, Doubleday, 1955, Vol. 1, pp. 419-20.

[12] The documents connected with the Japanese surrender, including the Potsdam Proclamation, not Declaration, are conveniently collected. Robert J. C. Butow, *Japan's Decision to Surrender*, Stanford, Stanford University Press, 1959, pp. 241-50.

protest registered by Japan at the time of the atomic attacks,[13] but discounts its relevance, by observing that, "taking an objective view, apart from the position of a belligerent," it is not possible "to draw the same conclusion today" as to the illegality of the atomic bombing (p. 226).

Even if international law covers the atomic bombing, there is no cause of action, the defense contends, created in municipal law. The law of war is a matter of state-to-state relations and there is no expectation that individuals injured by a violation of the laws of war can recover directly or indirectly from the guilty government. The defense then considers the outcome of this litigation if it is treated as though it is brought against the United States in an American domestic court. And as courts in the United States refrain from questioning the legality of belligerent acts undertaken by the Executive to carry on a war, they would refuse to examine the legality of the use of atomic bombs against Japan. The defense suggests that this judicial restraint in the United States "necessarily results from the theory called Act of State" (p. 227).[14] At the time of the attacks, furthermore, sovereign immunity would bar, under the municipal law of the United States, claims of this sort being brought against either the United States Government or the public official responsible for the alleged wrongdoing. And finally, there is a somewhat abrupt assertion that "it is not possible to establish a tort under Japanese law by applying the conflict of law rules of the United States" (p. 227). This evidently refers back to the plaintiff's argument that, since the illegal acts took place in Japan, the conflict rules in effect in the United States would lead the law of Japan to apply, and, by reference to Japanese law, public officials are responsible to individuals for the wrongs that they do in their official capacity. But, says the defense, the *lex fori* would bar reference to foreign law if the claim itself was not admissible because of the immunity of

[13] The Japanese Government filed a diplomatic protest against the bombing of Hiroshima by submitting a formal note to the United States by way of the Swiss Government on August 10, 1945. The principal grounds relied upon in the protest were that the atomic bomb caused indiscriminate suffering and produced unnecessary pain, and, as such, violated the principles set forth in the Annex to the Hague Convention respecting the Laws and Customs of War on Land, Arts. 22 and 23(e) of the Regulations respecting the Laws and Customs of War on Land. This appeal to law was supplemented by a general appeal to elementary standards of civilization prohibiting recourse to methods of warfare that cause civilians great damage, and damage such immune objects as hospitals, shrines, temples, and schools. In fact, the diplomatic note calls the atomic bombing "a new offense against the civilization of mankind."

[14] This usage of "act of state" suggests that United States courts will not question the validity of official acts performed by their own Executive. In actual fact in American practice, the term "act of state" is only used in litigation that questions validity of an official act of a foreign government. However, *Shimoda* is correct in terms of results, if not in terms of doctrinal explanation. For a leading United States case dealing with internal deference, see United States v. Curtiss-Wright Export Co., 299 U.S. 304, 1936; cf. also Hooper v. United States, 22 Ct. Cl. 408, 1887, *infra*, note 51.

the government and its officials. This means that, if the action is thought of, as it must be (because it is the United States that dropped the bombs, that did the alleged wrong),[15] as instituted in the United States, then one never reaches the choice-of-law stage because the claim is barred at the prior stage at which the non-susceptibility of the defendant to suit requires the court to dismiss.[16]

The Japanese Government also denies the standing of the claimants to institute action on their own behalf. The defense subscribes to the traditional theory that it is the government on behalf of national victims, and only the government, that has the capacity, in the absence of a treaty conferring capacity on individuals, to assert claims against a foreign state. And in line with this approach, the defense argues that the government asserts the claim "as its own right" and determines "by its own authority" how to distribute the funds recovered because of an injury to its nationals (p. 228). The defense also argues that, even if somehow one assumes that the plaintiffs possessed an abstract legal right, there exists no procedure by which it can be realized. For, the defense submits, it is essential to engage, first, in international diplomatic negotiations and then, if negotiations fail, to proceed to the International Court of Justice.[17] The plaintiffs are in a position to do neither and, therefore, one must view the Peace Treaty as extinguishing their abstract claim (representing, presumably, the results of diplomatic negotiation), even if their legal rights be granted *arguendo* an independent existence prior to that.

On the issue of waiver, the defense suggests that only the claims of Japan as a state were waived by Article 19(a) and that whatever claims were possessed by Japanese nationals in their individual capacity survived intact. The defense points to the absence of an extinction clause (as is included in the Peace Treaty with Italy) in the Peace Treaty with Japan as indicating an intent to exclude the independent claims of individuals from the waiver provision, and even if one construes the waiver as intending to embrace those claims, it is ineffective to do so, as "it amounts to no more than a statement that Japan waived what could not be waived, and the citizens' own claims are not extinguished

---

15 But recall that the plaintiff does advance the theory that the wrongful waiver in Art. 19(a) of the Peace Treaty makes Japan an independent wrongdoer.

16 The plaintiff's submission on this point is quite obscure, as reported. See numbered par. 4 on p. 227, and my interpretation, pp. 395-96.

17 This view by the defense of the procedure for pursuing international claims seems rather rigid, especially as far as the need for recourse to the International Court of Justice is concerned. There are many other decision-makers used in international society for the settlement of international claims. See generally Richard B. Lillich and Gordon A. Christenson, *International Claims: Their Preparation and Presentation*, Syracuse, Syracuse University Press, 1962.

by the statement" (p. 229).[18] The defense, of course, wants to avoid legal responsibility for a wrongful waiver of its citizens' claim. The argument is complicated and somewhat hard to follow in the form in which it is reported. The defense evidently wants to assert a series of alternative contentions: that there were no legal rights possessed by the plaintiff, but that even if there were legal rights, they were extinguished by the Peace Treaty, and that even if this has the effect of violating Japanese municipal law, there is no illegality or responsibility on the part of the government.

The defense argues that

> If a defeated country cannot conclude a peace treaty, because the peace treaty would be contrary to the prohibition clause of the constitution of the defeated country, or because the legal procedures in the constitution cannot be taken, a defeated country could never conclude peace and consequently it would be required to continue the war as long as the capacity of conduct of war remains (p. 229).

This rather extreme formulation might be best understood as a rather misleading way to contend that the capacity to negotiate peace must take precedence over other normal legal obligations of the Japanese Government and these normal legal obligations must, in turn, be relaxed so as to conform with the exercise of this extraordinary power to negotiate a peace treaty.

The Japanese Government also argues that if, despite these contentions, the waiver in Article 19(a) is construed as a violation of Article 29 of the Japanese Constitution, then there is still no basis for recovery, as the Constitution "does not directly grant the people a concrete claim for compensation" (p. 230). The effect of Article 29 may be to render a law void that takes property without compensating, but it does not by itself confer a right of recovery in the event that the property is actually taken. Apparently, although that is not spelled out, implementing legislation would be needed, according to the defense, to support a claim for recovery.

In concluding its presentation, the defense describes itself as "unstinting in its deep sympathy" with the survivors of the atomic attacks,

---

[18] The defense appears to be making an inconsistent contention in relation to the waiver issue. On the one hand, it wants to maintain that the waiver extinguished whatever rights the plaintiffs might have possessed. On the other, it wants to establish that there were no rights to waive so that the Japanese Government cannot be held accountable for a wrongful exercise of governmental power by agreeing to the waiver. The position is not truly inconsistent, however, as the defense wants, if possible, to show that the waiver issue is irrelevant because there was nothing to waive. However, if the court disagrees, then the defense wants to rely upon the waiver to extinguish the plaintiff's cause of action, even though this risks a finding of responsibility as a result of a wrongful waiver.

but points out that "the way of consolation for these people must be balanced with the consolation for other general war victims, and by taking into due consideration the actual circumstances of finance of the State, etc." (p. 230). These matters of social justice are asserted to be matters of politics, not law, and must therefore, be left for settlement to the wisdom of the legislature; they are not resolvable by exercise of the adjudicative powers of the courts. And until the legislature sees fit to act, the Japanese Government, as such, cannot be said to have an obligation to compensate.

The statement of the defense ends with an admission of ignorance about the circumstances and extent of the damages actually suffered by these plaintiffs, neither admitting nor denying the claims posited.

The Judgment of the Tokyo District Court. The portion of the proceedings that I identify as "the judgment" is indicated in the translated excerpt by a single word in boldface type: REASONS. The court begins with a recital of background material. First, the attacks of August 1945, on Hiroshima and Nagasaki are described in some detail. The casualties are reported in accord with the more conservative figures submitted by the defense.[19] Second, a brief account of atomic energy is given to establish the basis for considering that these weapons possess tremendous and unprecedented destructive force. Third, a rather extended presentation is made of the varied effects and scope of destruction that are to be expected for atomic bombs having the explosive power of those used in Japan.[20] The most prominent of these effects is the bombshell blast proceeding from the fireball that is created by exploding an atomic bomb in the air and that results in "a wave of air (wave from bombardment) of high temperature and high pressure" that "spreads in all directions quickly" and "destroys buildings and other structures as if an earthquake or typhoon occurred" (p. 232). For Nagasaki this blast effect meant that "houses within 1.4 miles of the epicenter collapsed, those within 1.6 miles suffered rather heavy damage, and even those at the point of 1.7 miles had their roofs and walls damaged." The bombshell blast causes heat rays as a secondary effect: "These heat rays include ultraviolet rays as well as visible rays and ultrared rays. The heat rays reach the earth at the same speed as

[19] There is a considerable difference in the casualties reported. The plaintiffs list 260,000 killed at Hiroshima, 73,884 at Nagasaki; similar discrepancies exist for the figures on wounded at each place, the plaintiff contending 156,000 at Hiroshima, 76,796 at Nagasaki, and the defendant 51,408 at Hiroshima, 41,847 at Nagasaki.
[20] The bombs used against Japan had an explosive power approximating 20,000 tons of TNT (20 kilotons), whereas current nuclear warheads in standard weapons systems have an explosive power varying between 1,000,000 and 10,000,000 tons of TNT (1-10 megatons), and some of the nuclear devices that have been tested have an explosive capacity of over 50 megatons. The ratio between the atomic bombs used in World War II and a 50-megaton device is 1:2,500.

light, set fire to inflammable things on earth, burn the skin, and cause man's death according to the conditions" (p. 232). The court concludes that 20 per cent to 30 per cent of the deaths at Hiroshima and Nagasaki were caused by heat rays and that at Nagasaki burns were recorded as far away as 2.5 miles from the epicenter, and finally "the most peculiar effect comes from the first stage of nuclear radial rays and residual radioactivity" (p. 233). These radial rays cause death, disease, and severe injury both at the time of the blast and long afterwards. The court is obviously impressed by the added horror that stems from this atomic effect that spreads the suffering through time and space for an unknown duration and scope and with uncertain consequence. All in all, the opinion concludes that even "a small-scale bomb" like those used against Japan has a "power of destruction" and "terror" that are "so remarkable" as to mean that the atomic bomb "cannot for a moment be compared with bombs of the past" (p. 233). The opinion ends its survey of the effects of atomic bombs with this sentence: "We must say that the atomic bomb is a really cruel weapon" (p. 234).

It is on this basis that the court turns to examine the allegation that these atomic attacks violated international law. At the outset the court narrows the issue before it in a very significant way by observing that

> There is no doubt that, whether or not an atomic bomb having such a character and effect is a weapon which is permitted in international law as a so-called nuclear weapon, is an important and very difficult question in international law. In this case, however, the point at issue is whether the acts of atomic bombing of Hiroshima and Nagasaki by the United States are regarded as illegal by positive international law at that time. Therefore, it is enough to consider this point only (p. 234).

On the one hand, this delineation of the issue cannot be emphasized enough; on the other, the analysis adopted by the court to reach its conclusions goes beyond the facts of the attacks in World War II to disclose the unanimous view of the Tokyo District Court on the relevance of international law to the use of atomic or nuclear weapons against any heavily populated center. But certainly in a strict legal sense it is important to govern one's perception of the case in accord with the restrictive conception set forth by the Japanese court. And in this regard, it is well to emphasize that the opinion does not attempt to deal with the legality of atomic weapons as such, but only with the legality of their use against Hiroshima and Nagasaki. This accords with the best traditions of judicial craftsmanship; namely, the narrowing of the dispositive issue to the greatest extent possible. But even here there is an inevitable ambiguity arising from the fact that most of the legal authority found relevant by the court was developed to proscribe or restrict the use of weapons with certain characteristics (e.g. poisons, dum-dum bullets, bacteria) rather than to regulate their use against certain kinds of targets. Thus if the authority is relevant, then its implication, by common sense, extends to the status of atomic or nuclear weapons as such, that is, to the very issue that the court sets aside. These comments are interposed so as to suggest the complexity attending any interpretation of "the holding" in the *Shimoda* case.[21]

The court starts out by listing the documents comprising that portion of the international law of war deemed relevant to assessing the attacks on Hiroshima and Nagasaki. These documents consist of declarations of international conferences, widely ratified multilateral treaties, and a draft convention. Their subject matter includes specific prohibitions of explosives under 400 grams, dum-dum bullets, projectiles launched from balloons, submarines, poison gases, and bacteriological methods of warfare, and such general sets of regulations as the comprehensive codes governing land warfare adopted at The Hague and the Draft Rules of Air Warfare.[22] The court does not differentiate among these sources of legal authority to any very great extent, and certainly does not make any very sharp distinction between binding treaty obligations and declaratory standards never even intended for formal ratification. It acknowledges the distinction with respect to its discussion of the relevance of the Draft Rules of Air Warfare (1923) by suggesting "The Draft Rules of Air Warfare cannot directly be called positive law, since they have not yet become effective as a treaty." But the opinion goes on, without offering documentation, to aver that "international jurists regard the Draft Rules as authoritative" and that some coun-

[21] Throughout this discussion "atomic" and "nuclear" weapons will be treated alike for purposes of legal analysis. Also, some comments will be made to clarify obscure passages in the decision. The translated version of the decision will be treated as "authoritative" even when it results in awkward and incorrect English. The *Shimoda* opinion contains almost no formal documentation.

[22] The following legal materials are mentioned by the court as relevant to its deliberations: St. Petersburg Declaration, 1868, 1 *American Journal of International Law* Supp. 95 (1907); Hague Convention on the Law and Customs of Land Warfare and Annex of Regulations, 1899, Declaration on Expanding Bullets, 1899, *ibid.* 129, 155; Hague Convention on the Law and Customs of Land Warfare, 1907, 2 *American Journal of International Law* Supp. 90 (1908); Declaration Prohibiting Aerial Bombardment, 1907, *ibid.* 216; Treaty of Five Countries Concerning Submarines and Poisonous Gases, 1922, 16 *American Journal of International Law* Supp. 57 (1922); Draft Rules of Air Warfare, 1923, 32 *ibid.* 12 (1938); Protocol Prohibiting the Use in War of Asphyxiating, Poisonous or Other Gases, and of Bacteriological Methods of Warfare, 1925, 25 *ibid.* 94 (1931). These various legal documents are all to be found in the relevant volumes of Hudson, *International Legislation,* and in *The Hague Conventions and Declarations of 1899 and 1907,* 2nd edn., Scott, 1915.

tries even use them to guide the conduct of their armed forces (pp. 237-38). On these grounds the court is able to treat these Draft Rules as constituting customary international law. Such an inference is jurisprudentially significant in view of the absence of formal consent to these rules; but it is also significant that even the consistent pattern of nonadherence to the standards prescribed by the Draft Rules as governing aerial bombardment fails to shake the confidence of the court in the validity of these standards.[23] The invocation of these Draft Rules also illustrates the facility with which a domestic court can transform declaratory standards into binding legal obligations.[24] The *Shimoda* case suggests that the formal status of a legal standard may not be very critical to its role as an authoritative basis for decision.[25] This issue warrants emphasis because it suggests so clearly the method adopted by this court to apply international law.

Having recited the regulatory standards that are most applicable to the case, the court expresses what is manifest, that these legal standards developed prior to the development of the atomic bomb and cannot be understood as directly prohibiting its use. The opinion reaffirms the old consensual dictum that what is not forbidden states is permitted in the context of a new weapon: "Of course, it is right that the use of a new weapon is legal, as long as international law does not prohibit it" (p. 235). But a prohibition need not be direct or express to be applicable. By interpreting the spirit of existing rules or by extending their coverage through analogical reasoning it is possible to say that a new development is embraced within the earlier prohibition. Furthermore, wider principles of international law underlie the specific rules, and, if the use of the new weapon violates these principles, it violates international law without requiring any specific rule.[26] Thus a court is free to conclude that atomic warfare violates international law, at

[23] Most authors consider the relevant legal norms to be lapsed as a consequence of persistent violation, even if they are granted a hypothetical existence. See, in particular, Myres S. McDougal and Florentino P. Feliciano, *Law and Minimum World Public Order*, New Haven, Yale University Press, 1961, pp. 640-59 (hereinafter cited as McDougal-Feliciano); for comprehensive analysis of the relations between air war and international law see James M. Spaight, *Air Power and War Rights*, 3rd edn., New York, Longmans, Green, 1947.

[24] For a discussion of this process of evolving binding legal standards at the national level from non-binding declarations at the international level, see Egon Schwelb, *Human Rights and the International Community*, Chicago, Quadrangle Books, 1964.

[25] Such a question is at the root of two recent studies of the lawmaking activities of the political organs of the United Nations. Rosalyn Higgins, *The Development of International Law Through the Political Organs of the United Nations*, London, Oxford University Press, 1963; Oscar Schachter, "The Relation of Law, Politics and Action in the United Nations," 109 *Hague Academy Recueil des Cours* 165 (1963), II.

[26] These principles include the requirement of necessity attached to a military justification and a concept of proportionality with respect to the ratio between military and nonmilitary destruction. See McDougal-Feliciano, esp. pp. 59-96, 529-671; O'Brien, pp. 35-63.

least under certain circumstances, even in the absence of an express prohibition.[27]

The opinion takes up at this point the cynical-realist contention that it is "nonsensical" to prohibit a weapon capable of inflicting serious injury on an enemy, as history shows that it will be used in any event (pp. 235-36). The court admits that international practice has often legitimated weapons whose initial appearance occasioned objection and a sense of outrage, but asserts "this is not always true" (p. 236); for example, the decision points out that the prohibitions of dum-dum bullets and poison gas were largely successful in eliminating these weapons from use in war. On this basis the conclusion is reached that "therefore, *we cannot regard a weapon as legal only because it is a new weapon and it is still right that a new weapon must be exposed to the examination of positive international law*" (p. 236).[28]

At this stage the court turns to consider the teachings of positive international law relevant to atomic bombing. It first takes account of the traditional distinction between the right to bomb indiscriminately a defended city and the obligation to bomb only military objectives in a city that is undefended. These standards were incorporated in the Hague Regulations.[29] This distinction is relied upon and elaborated in the Draft Rules of Air Warfare. These rules, specifically invoked by the court, restrict the right of aerial bombardment to military objectives as these objectives are enumerated in Article 24(2): "military forces; military works; military establishments or depots; factories constituting important and well-known centers engaged in the manufacture of arms, ammunition, or distinctively military supplies, lines of communication or transportation used for military purposes."[30] Article 24(3) goes on to declare that "the bombardment of cities, towns, villages, dwellings, or buildings not in the immediate neighborhood of the operations of land forces is prohibited"; whereas Article 24(4) allows aerial bombardment if the populated region is near to the operations of land forces

[27] Cf. helpful discussion in Robert C. Tucker, *The Law of War and Neutrality at Sea,* Vol. 50, *International Law Studies,* Naval War College, 1955, pp. 54-55 (hereinafter cited as Tucker); cf. Georg Schwarzenberger, *The Legality of Nuclear Weapons,* London, Stevens and Sons, 1958, pp. 25-49; see also Hersch Lauterpacht, "The Problem of the Revision of the Law of War," 29 *British Year Book of International Law* (1952), p. 360.

[28] It should be observed that there has apparently never been evidence that a belligerent has refrained from using a weapon that might give it a decisive advantage out of deference to a legal prohibition. See, e.g. O'Brien, p. 92; cf. also Richard

R. Baxter, "The Role of Law in Modern War," *Proceedings, the American Society of International Law, 1953,* p. 90 (hereinafter cited as Baxter); and see general exposition of this viewpoint in Bernard Brodie, *Strategy in the Missile Age,* Princeton, Princeton University Press, 1959.

[29] The opinion invokes Art. 25 of the Hague Regulations on the Law of Land Warfare, 1907, and Arts. 1 and 2 of the Hague Convention concerning Naval Bombardment, 1907, 2 *American Journal of International Law* Supp. 147 (1908).

[30] The court also quotes Art. 24(1). The text of the Hague Rules of Aerial Warfare is in 32 *American Journal of International Law* Supp. 12 (1938).

and "there exists a reasonable presumption that the military concentration is sufficiently important to justify such bombardment, having regard to the danger thus caused to the civilian population." The court also quotes Article 22 that forbids "aerial bombardment for the purpose of terrorizing the civilian population, of destroying or damaging private property not of military character, or of injuring non-combatants . . ." (these articles are all quoted on p. 237). The *Shimoda* court concludes rather loosely that these Draft Rules "prohibit useless aerial bombardment and provide for the principle of the military objective first of all" (p. 237). It is at this point that the opinion tries to argue in favor of the authoritative character of these nonbinding rules.[31]

Furthermore, the opinion holds that the rules governing land warfare "analogically apply since the aerial bombardment is made on land" (p. 238). Turning then back to the Hague Rules of Land Warfare, the court suggests that a defended city (this is, one legally susceptible to indiscriminate bombing) is "a city resisting any possible occupation by land forces" (p. 238). That is, the defended city must be reasonably close to the battlefield. Even if the city is defended, the court says, indiscriminate bombing is legal only if it is restricted to an attack upon military objectives, although the opinion concedes that it is inevitable that such an attack will do some damage to noncombatants and to non-military objectives. But what is forbidden, according to the court's reading of customary international law, is an aerial bombardment of an undefended city that is either "directed at a non-military objective" or "without distinction between military objectives and non-military objectives (the so-called blind aerial bombardment)" (p. 238). On this basis, the court recalls that "even such small-scale atomic bombs" as used against Japan release "energy equivalent to a 20,000 TNT bomb" and that this "brings almost the same result as complete destruction of a middle-size city, to say nothing of indiscrimination of military objective and non-military objective" (p. 239). And so the court reasons that "*the act of atomic bombing an undefended city . . . should be regarded in the same light as a blind aerial bombardment; and it must be said to be a hostile act contrary to international law of the day*" (original in italics, p. 239). From here it is a short step, immediately taken by the court, to conclude that Hiroshima and Nagasaki were undefended cities that suffered the equivalent of blind aerial bombardments in violation of international law. This conclusion is reached, even though the court concedes that there were some military objectives in both cities and that the atomic bombs may have been dropped for the sole purpose of destroying these military objectives.[32]

[31] See pp. 385-87.
[32] The relevant language is italicized by the court: ". . . *even if the aerial bombardment has only a military objective as*

After pronouncing the illegality of the atomic attack the court pauses to consider whether the concept and practice of total war, especially as it developed in World War II, do not invalidate the underlying principles restricting bombardment to military objectives. The court affirms the survival of the older principles of limitation upon belligerent policy and points to the continuing inviolability of such objects as "schools, churches, temples, shrines, hospitals, and private houses" (p. 239), as evidence that nonmilitary objectives remain protected in modern war. Instead, total war is understood only to extend the concept of war to include the economic processes underlying the war effort, but not to authorize any policy of total obliteration. The court, it must be said, seems somewhat confused on this set of issues. For it enumerates "food, trade" and "human factors like population, manpower, etc." as being within the narrower concept of total war to which it subscribes (p. 240). But it is evident that if people are military objectives, then the attacks on Hiroshima and Nagasaki are legitimate within its own terms. In fairness, although it is nowhere said very explicitly, the court's opinion probably intends only to authorize attacks on those people who are contributing rather directly to the war effort, not to people in general. Even this restrictive interpretation is not very satisfactory, however, if activities relating to food and trade are considered to be part of the war effort. It seems evident that once any concessions of this sort are made in the direction of total war, then it is quite difficult to retain the distinction between military and nonmilitary objectives, and without this distinction the central basis of legal condemnation—the indiscriminate character of an atomic attack—is undercut.

The court goes on to say that this reasoning with respect to atomic attacks does not imply that strategic area bombing is a violation of international law, even if the idea of an area or zone is broader than that of military objective. The opinion points out that where military objectives are concentrated, defenses heavy, and camouflage effective, then by bombing a zone "the proportion of the destruction of non-military objective is small in comparison with the large military interests and necessity" (p. 240). But the court stops short of upholding area bombing, saying only that "it cannot say that there is no room for regarding it legal."[33] The *Shimoda* court seems eager here to emphasize

---

the target of its attack, it is proper to understand that an aerial bombardment with an atomic bomb on both cities of Hiroshima and Nagasaki was an illegal act of hostility as the indiscriminate aerial bombardment on undefended cities" (p. 239).

[33] Consistent with the mode of analysis adopted by the court, see Sections II and III in this chapter, it would not be necessary to condemn or exonerate strategic area bombing *as a whole,* but only to pass judgment upon its *various specific occasions of employment.*

the narrow scope of the holding and to avoid resting the opinion on Hiroshima and Nagasaki upon legal reasoning that would also necessarily condemn the nonatomic belligerent policy adopted on both sides throughout World War II.[34] The opinion concludes that the area principle, even if accepted as broadening the scope of a permissible attack on an undefended city, does not alter the legal status of the attacks upon Hiroshima and Nagasaki, as neither city was one in which military objectives were concentrated.

In addition to the law regulating aerial bombardment, there are quite separate grounds, however, the court asserts, for regarding the attacks upon these two Japanese cities as illegal. The court accepts as a principle of international law the duty to refrain from using means of warfare that cause unnecessary suffering, a principle it derives from the "just war" tradition and its expression in the St. Petersburg Declaration of 1868. At the same time the opinion acknowledges that humanitarian considerations must always be balanced against military ones to discover the limits of legitimate warfare. Thus, it is not possible to base a prohibition on the use of atomic bombs directly and uncritically upon the prohibition put upon projectiles under 400 grams in the St. Petersburg Declaration. For these latter weapons did not offer any military advantage comparable to that derived from the atomic bomb. But the court views as more relevant in this regard the prohibitions placed upon poison gas. The language in Article 23(a) of the Hague Regulations respecting Land Warfare, the Declaration prohibiting the use of projectiles the sole object of which is the diffusion of asphyxiating or deleterious gases (1899), and the Geneva Protocol of 1925 prohibiting "the use in war of asphyxiating, poisonous and other gases, and bacteriological weapons" are deemed relevant by the *Shimoda* court.[35] Apparently, although this is not explicit, the prohibition of poison gases is so relevant because, as with atomic weapons, gas is a significant weapon. Note that, as has already been mentioned, the fact that neither Japan nor the United States ratified the Geneva Protocol is not deemed to detract from its authority.[36] The court suggests that "there is not an established theory among international jurists

---

[34] Cf. on this James M. Spaight, who upholds the legality of strategic area bombing and challenges the legality of the atomic attacks in *Air Power and War Rights*, 3rd edn., New York, Longmans, Green, 1947, pp. 265-81 with McDougal-Feliciano, pp. 665-66, who regard the strategic area bombing and the atomic attacks as having the same legal footing.

[35] For texts, see documentary sources given in note 22 *supra*.

[36] For reliance upon the relevance of preatomic international law, especially by analogy to the prohibition of poison gas, see Nagendra Singh, *Nuclear Weapons and International Law*, New York, Praeger, 1959, pp. 147-73; Schwarzenberger, *op.cit. supra*, note 27, pp. 26-38; for skepticism, see McDougal-Feliciano, pp. 659-68; Tucker, pp. 50-55; O'Brien, pp. 88-94; Julius Stone, *Legal Controls of International Conflict*, New York, Rinehart, 1954, pp. 547-48.

in connection with the difference of poison, poison-gas, bacterium, etc. from atomic bombs" (p. 241). The court then argues that the decisive consideration is whether the weapon causes unnecessary suffering and is cruel in its effects. This depends, it would appear from the analysis, although again this is not spelled out, upon the proportionality of the relationship between military and nonmilitary destruction. Apparently it is on this basis that the court concludes that "it is doubtful whether atomic bombing really had an appropriate military effect at that time and whether it was necessary" (p. 241). And to call attention to the peculiarly cruel effects of the atomic bomb, the opinion refers to radiation sickness that continues to afflict its victims eighteen years after the attack, that is, in 1963. With this, the court formulates one of its several italicized holdings: *"It is not too much to say that the pain brought by the atomic bombs is severer than that from poison and poison-gas, and we can say that the act of dropping such a cruel bomb is contrary to the fundamental principle of the laws of war that unnecessary pain must not be given"* (pp. 241-42). It must be observed that the opinion makes no effort here to examine whether, in fact, the attacks upon Hiroshima and Nagasaki hastened the end of the war and saved lives on both sides.[37] Even if the court had considered these claims relevant and had been persuaded of their accuracy, it might still have concluded as it did by denying the right to seek unconditional surrender by a means that tends to arouse terror, and especially when these means are used to destroy populated cities that contain relatively few, and those insignificant, military targets.

The principal holding of the court is, of course, that the attacks with atomic bombs upon Hiroshima and Nagasaki on August 6 and 9 of 1945 were in violation of international law. In essence, the court concluded that no argument of military necessity was persuasive in the context of atomic attacks on cities inhabited by large numbers of people, especially if the cities in question were not of notable military importance. The principal reasons given were as follows:

(1) International law forbids an indiscriminate or blind attack upon an undefended city; Hiroshima and Nagasaki were undefended; therefore, the attacks were illegal.

(2) International law only permits, if at all, indiscriminate bombing of a defended city if it is justified by military necessity; no mili-

---

[37] The defendant asserted this as part of its argument for the legality of the atomic attacks. One commentator in the United States went so far as to conjecture that these attacks "saved the very national existence of Japan. It may have been a blessing in disguise to the Japanese nation: the Divine Wind that saved Japan from national hari-kiri." Ellery C. Stowell, "The Laws of War and the Atomic Bomb," 39 *American Journal of International Law* 784 (1945).

tary necessity of sufficient magnitude could be demonstrated here; therefore, the attacks were illegal.[38]

(3) International law as it has specifically developed to govern aerial bombardment might be stretched to permit zone or area bombing of an enemy city in which military objectives were concentrated; there was no concentration of military objectives in either Hiroshima or Nagasaki; therefore, no legal basis exists for contending that the atomic attacks might be allowable by analogy to zone bombing, because even the latter is legal, if at all, only if directed against an area containing a concentration of military targets.

(4) International law prohibits the use of weapons and belligerent means that produce unnecessary and cruel forms of suffering as illustrated by the prohibition of lethal poisons and bacteria; the atomic bomb causes suffering far more severe and extensive than the prohibited weapons; therefore, it is illegal to use the atomic bomb to realize belligerent objectives:[39]

(a) that is, the duty to refrain from causing unnecessary suffering is a principle of international law by which all belligerent activity is tested, whether specifically regulated or not;

(b) that is, specific prohibitions embody a wider principle and this principle extends to new weapons' developments not foreseen at the time when the specific prohibition was agreed upon.

Having reached these conclusions favorable to the plaintiffs, the opinion goes on to examine whether a Japanese court is able to award compensation to these individuals injured at Hiroshima and Nagasaki. The main issues in this part of the case are as follows:

(1) Assuming that there was an injury caused by a violation of international law, is there also a violation of domestic law that can be relied upon by a domestic court as the basis for recovery?

[38] This second rationale is important because it liberates, to some extent, the *Shimoda* decision from the archaic distinction between a defended and an undefended city. See Spaight, *op.cit. supra*, note 23, p. 261: "Not for a generation or more has the accepted criterion of a place's liability been its being fortified or not. Under the Land War Rules of The Hague, 1907, Art. 25, such liability depends on its being *defended*; being defended and being fortified are, of course, not necessarily synonymous. But even the criterion of defence has in its turn become outmoded. A town's immunity rests today on its containing no military objectives. . . . " But see retention of distinction in Art. 621(d) of the current United States manual, *Law of Naval Warfare*, 1955.

[39] There are two contentions here: first, the principles underlying specific rules may be extended to prohibit activity unregulated by specific rules—the principles serve as a sufficient legal criterion by themselves; second, prior specific rules incorporate and exhibit principles, and the rules may be extended to cover analogous situations.

(2) Are the municipal aspects of the case governed by Japanese or United States law?

(3) Can Japan be made responsible for waiving the international claims of its nationals?

(4) Can the United States be made responsible either in a Japanese court or by hypothesizing the outcome in an American court?

The court summarily concludes that, despite the absence of a specific provision in the Imperial Constitution of Japan (in force at the time of the atomic attacks), it was generally understood that a violation of international law, whether customary or treaty, was also a violation of Japanese municipal law. The same legal result, the opinion finds, occurs in the United States, and there treaty law has the benefit of an explicit constitutional provision, Article VI, paragraph 2.[40] Therefore, a violation of international law is *ipso facto* a violation of the domestic law of both Japan and the United States. But, as the opinion notes, the violation of municipal law is of no relevance unless these plaintiffs have the standing to present a claim and the court before which it is brought is competent to adjudicate such a suit on the merits.

The court affirms that when a belligerent injures another belligerent by an illegal act then it is liable to pay damages. But the liability is possessed by the United States and it is discharged by paying Japan. The only proper defendant is the United States and not, as the plaintiffs alternatively contended, the public official who ordered the illegal acts, President Truman. But is there a legal claim possessed by the injured individuals as well as the injured state? The opinion does not endorse the pure form of the traditional view that states, and only states, have the standing to pursue claims arising from violations of international law. The language used in the opinion is not entirely clear, but the court seems to affirm the potential capacity of the individuals to enforce international law. At the same time, the court denies that this capacity always, or even generally, exists in present-day international law. On the contrary, the individual only possesses a legal capacity to proceed on his own when the capacity has been specifically conferred in an international agreement.[41] In the italicized formulation of the court: "*It is still proper to understand that individuals are not the subject of rights in international law, unless it is concretely recognized by treaties*" (p. 245).

The court also discusses the relevance of the legal capacity of a state to assert a legal claim against another state in behalf of a national in-

[40] Art. VI, par. 2, reads in the relevant clause: "and all Treaties made, or which shall be made, under the Authority of the United States, shall be the supreme Law of the Land. . . ."

[41] The court gives some examples of treaties that have conferred procedural capacity upon individuals on p. 244.

jured by a violation of international law (the so-called right of diplomatic protection). The plaintiffs contend that individuals have a legal right to insist upon diplomatic protection. The court denies this, affirming the orthodox position that a plaintiff state has full discretion whether to proceed or not, and if it decides not to, its national has neither a claim against its own government nor a secondary or residual right to proceed against the alleged wrongdoer state. That is, a national is completely dependent on the willingness of his government to assert a claim for his benefit in a situation of the kind presented by the injuries done at Hiroshima and Nagasaki. In international law the government recovering on such a claim is not required to give the amount rewarded to the injured individuals. The role of this argument in the case is not made entirely plain. The court seems to be saying that on an international level state-to-state relations govern both the presentation of the suit and the rights of recovery, and that, therefore, these injured individuals have no independent legal rights.

The court goes on to inquire whether it is possible for these claimants to recover on the basis of a national cause of action in the domestic courts of either Japan or the United States.[42] Recovery on the basis of the wrongs alleged is impossible in a Japanese court, the opinion reasons, because Japan, in common with other countries and in deference to international law, does not allow a foreign country to be a defendant in its courts.[43] The same result follows in the United States as a consequence of the national adoption of the sovereign immunity doctrine allowing the government to be made a defendant only when it has given its consent. At the time of the illegal acts, there was no right to sue the United States Government in United States courts. Even if one gives the plaintiffs the benefit of the Federal Tort Claims Act, enacted after 1945 but before the suit commenced, it would not authorize this claim because it stipulates exceptions for the discretionary duties of administrative organs and for claims based on the hostile acts of land and sea forces or arising in a foreign country.[44] For these reasons claims

[42] Having considered the availability of an *international* claim, the Tokyo court goes on to inquire whether these claimants might not be able to bring a *national* claim based upon international law in the domestic courts of one or the other country. It is in this context that doctrines of sovereign immunity and act of state bar adjudication.

[43] The *Shimoda* opinion reasons this way apparently (it is not made explicit) because the court considers that the case, in one sense, is being tried *as if* it were brought against the United States; for without the waiver clause Japan would clearly not be a

permissible defendant. Therefore, it is necessary to see whether the plaintiffs would have had a claim in the absence of a waiver so as to determine if anything of value was waived. It is in this respect that it is relevant to assess whether the plaintiff could have proceeded against the United States in either United States or Japanese domestic courts.

[44] Cf. Federal Tort Claims Act, 28 U.S.C. § 2680; see Note, "The Discretionary Function Exception of the Federal Tort Claims Act," 66 *Harvard Law Review* 488 (1953).

of the *Shimoda* variety are not allowable in the domestic courts of the United States.

The remaining important issues arise from the waiver of Japan's claims against the United States in Article 19(a) of the Peace Treaty between the Allied Powers and Japan.[45] The court assumes that the waiver did embrace whatever claims were possessed by Japan and its nationals as a consequence of the illegal bombings of Hiroshima and Nagasaki. The claims of Japan that were waived consisted of its rights to assert diplomatic protection, and this, in the court's view, is "an inherent right of the state," the waiver of which would give the plaintiffs nothing to complain about under any circumstances.[46] What is more intricate is the effective waiver of the potential claims of these individuals in their own capacity. It should be remembered that, independently of the waiver, the court expressed the view that there were no causes of action available for individuals to pursue; in the view of the court, then, there was nothing to waive. But, following the canon of completeness of legal reasoning, the court goes on to investigate the proper scope of the waiver as if it mattered. It finds that a government does, by the authority given it under municipal law, have the competence to waive effectively the international claims of its nationals. And the decision concludes that, in fact, Article 19(a) waived "*the claims of Japanese nationals in the municipal laws of Japan and of the Allied Powers, against the Allied Powers and their nationals*" (original in italics, p. 249). This is the natural meaning of Article 19(a), the unanimous view of the three experts appointed by the court and the position taken by Kumao Nishimura, writing as Director of the Treaties Bureau in the Ministry of External Affairs, in an official article-by-article explanation of the Japanese Peace Treaty.[47]

The court also deals with a subtle subsidiary argument of the plaintiffs that the Japanese Peace Treaty must have created rights of Japanese nationals in order to be able to waive them; that is, if no rights existed there was nothing to waive, and there would be then no content for this part of Article 19(a). Therefore the waiver must be taken to admit the legal rights of these claimants to proceed directly under international law. The court denies this, observing that what was

[45] Art. 19(a): "Japan waives all claims of Japan and its nationals against the Allied Powers and their nationals arising out of the war or out of actions taken because of the existence of a state of war, and waives all claims arising from the presence, operations or actions of forces or authorities of any of the Allied Powers in Japanese Territory prior to the coming into force of the present Treaty."

[46] There is nothing to complain about because there is nothing lost. Without the waiver the plaintiff would have had no rights arising out of the law governing diplomatic protection.

[47] See p. 249; cf. also note 43 *supra*.

waived were the claims of Japanese nationals under the municipal laws of Japan and the Allied Powers.[48]

Is the Japanese Government legally responsible to these plaintiffs for the waiver? Was it a wrongful waiver? First the court points out that *"the claims of international law were not the object of waiver"* (p. 249) in Article 19(a), there were none;[49] and second, that even those claims that were waived could not, even in the absence of waiver, be pursued in the municipal system of either Japan or the United States as a consequence of sovereign immunity. On this basis it is easy for the court to conclude *"that the plaintiffs had no rights to lose, and accordingly there is no reason for asserting the defendant's legal responsibility therefor"* (p. 250).[50]

The opinion ends with a statement expressing compassion for the victims of atomic attack and looking forward to the abolition of war. The court even ventures to comment upon the nonlegal obligations of the Government of Japan to those who suffer from war damage. In its closing paragraph the opinion goes so far as to say: "The defendant State [Japan] caused many Nationals to die, injured them, and drove them to a precarious life by the war which it opened on its own authority and responsibility" (p. 250). The opinion also refers to the "Law respecting medical Treatment and the like for Sufferers of the Atomic Bomb" as providing relevant assistance, but on such a small scale that "it cannot possibly be sufficient for the relief and rescue of the sufferers of the atomic bomb" (p. 250). "Needless to say," the opinion states, "the defendant state should take sufficient measures" (p. 250). However, this is not something that can be done by a court, but is "a duty which the Diet or legislature or the Cabinet or the Executive must perform." Besides, it is desirable not only to give relief to these complainants but also to the "general sufferers of the atomic bombs; and there lies the *raison d'être* of the legislature and the administration" (p. 250). Responding rather caustically to the argument of the Japanese Government emphasizing the limits of its financial capability, the decision observes that "It cannot possibly be understood that the above is financially impossible in Japan, which has achieved a high degree of economic growth

---

[48] This conclusion reflects the view that the international (state-to-state) claims were not "claims of Japanese nationals" within the meaning of Art. 19(a).

[49] This seems confusing. When the court refers to "the claims of international law" in this setting, it means the state-to-state claims, but not the claims that might, but for sovereign immunity, be brought in a domestic court on the basis of international law.

[50] Here, again, some additional comment may avoid confusion. The court construes the waiver as directed at the possibility of claims brought in domestic courts, but considers these potential claims as not giving rise to "rights" because they were foreclosed *ab initio* by the bar of sovereign immunity operative in both the United States and Japan.

after the war. We cannot see this suit without regretting the political poverty" (p. 250).[51] This is a rather unusual and direct plea for legislative action by a lower court, although so far as I have been able to ascertain, without result.[52]

The decision ends by dismissing the plaintiffs' claims on the merits, and is signed by the three judges that composed the Tokyo District Court for this case.

II. The Shimoda Case as a Legal Precedent

At best, the process by which authoritative standards of law emerge in international society is a complicated one. This complexity is especially apparent for a subject matter that is at once so tinged with human emotion and so centrally connected with the power of the dominant nation-states as is the appropriate legal policy for the governance of nuclear weapons. Comment on *Shimoda* as a legal precedent must be understood as taking place against a background where the whole enterprise of law and order is in issue, where the passions of national sovereignty seem to command so much more allegiance than do appeals in behalf of world order.

At this stage it is, in addition, premature to discuss the relevance of *Shimoda* to an evolving international law of war applicable to the conditions of nuclear warfare. Despite, however, these grounds for caution some tentative remarks seem appropriate. Clearly, for instance, it is wrong to suppose that *Shimoda* by itself gives any answer to such hard questions as whether it is "legal" to resort to nuclear weapons for purposes of self-defense against a nonnuclear armed attack. But given the absence of applicable legal standards, the effort by *Shimoda* to apply the prenuclear international law of war to the use of atomic bombs is certainly significant in some respects. For *Shimoda*, at least, is illustrative of how a court might go about appraising a challenged use of nuclear weapons in the future, disclosing some of the kinds of considerations that might be relevant to a legal appraisal. Can we, however, go beyond this and say that, in any sense, legal standards, no matter how restricted, emerged from the holdings in *Shimoda*? Among the limitations of *Shimoda* as a legal precedent is the fact that its holdings are drawn narrowly and that the adjudicating tribunal is a lower court without any particular experience in handling international law

[51] Cf. analogous argument in the French Spoliation Cases, where individuals contended that the United States Government was liable for the satisfaction of claims waived by treaty. See Hooper v. United States, 22 Ct. Cl. 408, 1887. Subsequently, Congress accepted the merit of these contentions and granted relief by statute, just as the court urges in *Shimoda*. I am grateful to Professor Quincy Wright for calling my attention to this analogy.

[52] This conclusion is based upon my correspondence with Professor Yuichi Takano.

cases. These handicaps are offset to some degree by the fact that the *Shimoda* opinion is likely to strike readers as a thorough and impartial analysis of the legal issue raised in the case. Its value as legal authority is further enhanced by the fact that the court's reasoning was heavily influenced by the three reports submitted by experts appointed to advise the court. Each of these experts was a distinguished Japanese professor of international law, fully competent to analyze the legal problems at issue. The agreement among these experts and the court's acceptance of their guidance certainly seem relevant to an appraisal of the authoritativeness of *Shimoda*.

At the same time, it might be easy to detach the case from political reality and exaggerate its importance. By itself, *Shimoda* is unlikely to be taken into account by those entrusted with the formation of military policy in the leading nuclear powers. One wonders whether even legal advisers to these governments will consider *Shimoda* relevant to their advising functions. But *Shimoda* may be a factor fostering the creation of a world climate of opinion as to conditions justifying use of nuclear weapons that may exert influence upon governmental policy-making processes in the future.[53] The extent of this impact will depend, to some degree, upon what "becomes" of *Shimoda*, how and to what extent it is perceived as a significant source of policy guidance by those with the capacity to shape world opinion in this area.

The subtle and imperceptible influence of attitudes toward legitimacy upon national security policy is difficult to pin down, but nonetheless a potent political reality. It makes little difference whether the United States is formally bound or not by the prohibitions upon the use of poison gas; the vigor of the inhibition arises from the widespread repudiation of poison gas as legitimate, a repudiation so widespread that, if ignored, will undermine support at home and with allies for national policies. Deference to legal standards cannot be fully measured by their technical status as binding or not; the *Shimoda* case itself makes clear that the general acceptance of the standards in the world community is more *legally* relevant than whether they have been introduced into a convention that is binding upon the defendant state.[54]

Shimoda is also important as a formal juridical event that will certainly be asserted as relevant to similar juridical events in the future should they ever occur. Just as the *Eichmann* case was decisively shaped by the Nuremberg Judgment, so, but possibly to a lesser extent, will

[53] There seems to be some ground for thinking that world public opinion played a role in creating a climate favorable for the negotiation of the Partial Nuclear Test Ban Treaty of 1963.

[54] See pp. 385-87 for discussion of use by the Tokyo District Court of legal documents almost irrespective of their formal status as binding or not.

any subsequent legal appraisal of the use of nuclear weapons be conditioned by *Shimoda*. One side or the other in a legal controversy will undoubtedly find it helpful to their presentation and those given authority to decide will almost certainly take it into explicit account. *Shimoda* also has a potential relevance to current efforts to outlaw nuclear weapons or to prohibit their first use. This matter will be discussed shortly in Section IV.

Shimoda deals with a problematic area in the law of war—the regulation of the means used to wage warfare, and more specifically, the attempt by law to stigmatize certain weapons as impermissible. As Richard Baxter has written: "regulation of the use of weapons is the most difficult problem which the law of war faces and is the type of problem with which it deals least effectively."[55] Baxter explains that "International law has probably proved to be relatively ineffective in dealing with weapons because a state which has once determined that it must resort to the use of force cannot be persuaded that the law forbids the use of the most effective instruments of force which it has at its disposal."[56] In fact, Baxter goes so far in articulating the rationale used by those who favor the abandonment of this portion of the international law of war as to say: "There is so little distinction between the use of force in international relations and the use of weapons through which force is exercised that the two problems are actually one. If the devastation of modern war is to be avoided, it must be accomplished through measures which forbid the unlawful use of force and provide the international community with means of preventing and suppressing it."[57] The *Shimoda* court expressly and significantly rejects this line of reasoning by saying that international law does not acknowledge the doctrine of "total war," but places strict limits upon what it is permissible for the belligerent to do in order to win. And one of the limits concerns the kinds of weapons that are permissible and another concerns the kinds of targets that are permissible. As we have emphasized, the holding is limited to saying that the use of this kind of weapon against this kind of target is impermissible. It is, of course, still quite appropriate for Baxter to regard this as an unpromising area of the international law of war, although such a contention seems to discount the central assumption underlying the idea of mutual deterrence at the strategic level, especially as it is expected to operate in the relations between the

55 Baxter, p. 90.
56 *Id.* p. 91; cf. O'Brien on the role of natural law as a source of constraint that should always take precedence over pragmatic considerations, pp. 100-13; however, note that O'Brien interprets natural law in such a way that "a duty of success, particularly against a Communist attack" (p. 113) figures prominently in the process of identifying the limits of legitimate military necessity.
57 Baxter, pp. 94-95.

United States and the Soviet Union. In effect, there exists a prohibition upon recourse to nuclear weapons backed up by the sanction of threatened retaliation and by the shared objective of avoiding mutual devastation.

But suppose that a given prohibition in the law of war is ineffective in the sense of being frequently violated. To what extent should a court or commentator take considerations of effectiveness into account when pronouncing upon the past or prospective legality of challenged conduct? And it suggests, as well, the further problem as to whether patterns of practice that disregard fundamental legal policies should be understood as a repudiation of the policy rather than as a violation of the law.[58] This consideration is relevant to an interpretation of the argument that strategic area bombing using high explosives during World War II was no worse than the atomic attacks, and if the latter are illegal, then so are the former, despite their prevalence.[59] The *Shimoda* court, as we have seen, refuses to pronounce directly upon the legality of strategic area bombing but expressly rejects the implication that its widespread practice has made inapplicable or void the traditional legal limits upon the bombardment of inhabited cities.[60]

It is also possible to argue that any weapon can be used in war unless its use is expressly prohibited or regulated by an international convention.[61] This is an application of an approach to obligations in international law that received its purest statement in the majority opinion in the *Lotus* case.[62] Under this reasoning a state is permitted to do whatever is not expressly forbidden by some rule of international law to which it has given its tacit or explicit consent. This is apparently the official position of the United States with respect to the legal status of nuclear weapons, at least as it is expressed in the field manuals issued for the armed services by the Government. For example, Article 613 of the Law of Naval Warfare: "There is at present no rule of international law expressly prohibiting states from the use of nuclear weapons in warfare. In the absence of express prohibition, the use of such weapons against enemy combatants and other military objec-

---

[58] Relevant to an assessment of the connection between effectiveness and validity in international law are Robert C. Tucker, "The Principle of Effectiveness in International Law," in George Arthur Lipsky, ed., *Law and Politics in the World Community*, Berkeley, University of California Press, 1953, pp. 31-48; in the context of the legal regulation of nuclear weapons, see Schwarzenberger, *op.cit. supra*, note 27, pp. 57-59.

[59] On the legality of strategic area bombing, see sources cited in note 34; for a useful analysis of strategic bombing in World War II, see Brodie, *op.cit. supra*, note 28, pp. 107-44.

[60] See discussion pp. 388-91.

[61] See sources cited in note 27 *supra*.

[62] *The Lotus Case*, 1927, *Permanent Court of International Justice*, Ser. A, No. 10.

tives is permitted."[63] The *Shimoda* court cannot be said to constitute directly contradictory authority, although it does to some extent undercut the premise of Article 613 by assimilating atomic weapons into the prohibitions covering poison gas, and by its conclusion that the use of these weapons at least against inhabited cities, which are not places where military objectives are concentrated, amounts to illegal bombing because it is indiscriminate and because it produces terror and unnecessary suffering. But, again, it is important to realize that *Shimoda* is not concerned with the legality of weapons *as such*, but with a specific historic occasion of their use. Because of this restricted concern it is impossible to disentangle which portions of the rationale pertain to the properties of the weapon and which to the target chosen and the historical circumstances (especially, Japan on the brink of defeat) of its use. Certainly it is correct to say, however, that the *Shimoda* court seems opposed to a literal, perhaps an overly restrictive, reading of the *Lotus* opinion or Article 613; according to the opinion, there is no need for an express prohibition to support a finding of illegal use.[64] *Shimoda* expressly refuses to consider a weapon to be automatically legal just because it is new and not the subject of an express prohibition; even a new weapon may be regulated either by analogy to earlier prohibitions of other weapons or by reference to such guiding principles as those underlying the idea of military necessity.

Shimoda views military necessity in a fairly orthodox way. It refuses to exonerate the bombings because they may have hastened the Japanese decision to surrender and thereby achieved a net saving of lives, even of Japanese civilian lives, although these arguments were presented to the court by the defense and are frequently offered in the West[65] as the principal justification because it depends on such a highly conjectural view of what might have happened in World War II had these atomic bombs not been dropped. If a court accepted evidence

---

[63] *Law of Naval Warfare*, 1955; cf. Par. 35 of the U.S. Army's *Law of Land Warfare*: "The use of explosive 'atomic weapons,' whether by air, sea or land forces, cannot as such be regarded as violative of international law in the absence of any customary rule of international law or international convention restricting their employment."

[64] Art. 613 contains a footnote that says that "the employment, however, of nuclear weapons is subject to the basic principles stated in Section 220 and Article 221." Art. 221 sets out the three basic principles of the law of war—military necessity, humanity, and chivalry—that limit the discretion of belligerents in all circumstances.

The footnote also refers the reader to another footnote that forbids the use of any weapon that causes unnecessary suffering or devastation not justified by military necessity. It also refers to Arts. 621 and 622, which limit the right of bombardment. In Art. 621(a), for instance, "the wanton destruction of cities, towns, or villages, or any devastation not justified by military necessity, is prohibited"; and Art. 621(c) states that "Bombardment for the sole purpose of terrorizing the civilian population is prohibited." Thus the footnote limitations upon Art. 613 might lead one to construe it to be compatible with the decision in *Shimoda*.

[65] See authorities cited in note 11 *supra*.

on both sides on the relationship between the acceptance by Japan of the Potsdam Proclamation and the atomic bombings, it would still have an issue that was so conjectural as to be virtually incapable of resolution; the causal sequence is too complex (there are too many intervening variables) to permit any fair averment that event X (Hiroshima-Nagasaki) either caused or did not cause event Y (Japan's surrender).[66] Western writers blandly assert the connection and go on to say, in vindication of the attacks, that lives on both sides were saved, because the casualties in the two cities were far lower than would have been the casualties in the event of an invasion of Japan.[67]

As the *Shimoda* court notes, such reasoning, if accepted, would tend to legitimate any belligerent act, however extreme and horrible.[68] Thus the Japanese court rejects the extreme view of a contextual approach to legal valuation that tends to account for any act by reference to an acceptable goal, the surrender of the enemy and the restoration of peace. The relatedness of all experience makes it possible for such an abstract approach to legitimatize virtually all conduct, but the acceptability of the argument would probably vary with the pragmatic consequences of the challenged acts, that is, with whether the belligerent policy succeeded or not. It would seem much easier to make a *prima facie* showing of "military" relevance if there is an eventual victory for the side whose policy is challenged. One danger of the contextual approach is that it degenerates into the rationalization of national conduct in legal rhetoric. Whatever our side does is "legal," whatever they do is "illegal." Such an approach tends to undermine the whole structure of reciprocity that underlies the duty to uphold the rules of international law. As soon as the motivation of conduct, as well as conduct itself, enters into the determination of what is legal, the conclusions of legal analysis are almost certainly likely to be self-serving and those with contradictory motivations can generate an equally convincing, albeit contradictory, set of legal conclusions. This process of legal analysis impairs the actual and potential ordering role of international law in stabilizing relations between rival states pursuing incompatible objectives, and yet sharing a common interest in maintaining peaceful rela-

[66] For some assessment of the impact of the atomic bombing upon Japan's decision to surrender, see Brodie, *op.cit. supra,* note 28, pp. 138-52, and Robert J. C. Butow, *Japan's Decision to Surrender,* Stanford, Stanford University Press, 1954.

[67] For the claim that lives were saved see Henry Stimson, "The Decision to Use the Atomic Bomb," *Bulletin of Atomic Scientists,* III (1947), 37; Stowell, *loc.cit. supra,* note 37.

[68] To accept the approach of the "radical contextualists" is to move international law into virtual harmony with the practice and theory of "total war." The only limitation is that the belligerent policy be undertaken in the good faith expectation that it will somehow weaken the enemy, and thereby contribute to the war effort. And since the enemy's morale is a relevant target for military attack, any tactic, however terroristic, is legitimate.

tions, a common interest that might take increasing precedence over the goals of conflict in view of the mutual commitment to avoid nuclear warfare.

The *Shimoda* case does not delimit the context to include the remote political goals of the atomic attack, but rather restricts the context to the facts of the attack, the effects of the weapons, and the character of the target area.

This structure of analysis in *Shimoda* is supported by four principal types of legal authority used somewhat interchangeably. First, the positive legal *rules* contained in conventional and customary international law are cited as support. Second, the broader *principles* or *policies* underlying these rules are used both to assess the legality of conduct not expressly covered by the rules and to interpret the proper scope of the existing rules.[69] Third, the court makes general references to the views of international jurists as a basis for its own conclusions. And fourth, and perhaps most significantly, the opinion contains several references to the conclusions reached by one or more of the three experts in the international law of war that were appointed by the court to prepare separate reports on the various points of law raised by the controversy; these reports dealt with the application of the first three sources of law to the issues in *Shimoda* but, given the eminence of the experts and the apparent lack of experience on the part of the court, it does not seem far-fetched to regard these reports as providing the court with authoritative guidance in the case.[70]

III. The Shimoda *Case and Dominant Modes of Thinking in the International Law of War*

There is also a need to gain clarity about the mode of legal analysis appropriate for a discussion of nuclear warfare. *Shimoda* gives us a concrete occasion to consider how it is best to assess the legal status of nuclear weapons in view of the unlikelihood of achieving either clear or effective standards governing their use. In general, there are two dominant modes of thinking found in that part of the international law of war that is concerned with the regulation of instruments of warfare.[71]

---

[69] O'Brien deals with the connection between rules and principles very well in his articles on military necessity, *loc.cit. supra,* note 10. For a useful treatment of the relationship between different kinds of legal norms see Schachter, *loc.cit. supra,* note 25; see, in general, Roscoe Pound, "Hierarchy of Sources and Forms in Different Systems of Law," 7 *Tulane Law Review* 475 (1933).

[70] The three experts who submitted opinions to the court were Professors Kaoru Yasui, Shigejiro Tabata, and Yuichi Takano.

[71] It should be understood that these two modes of thought are *ideal types* useful to illustrate a basic conflict of emphasis in the relevant legal literature. Almost no writer is a *pure* example of one or the other type, although most lean toward one or the other pole.

The first mode, most familiar in connection with poison gas, is to deal with *the intrinsic legal character* of the weapon, either outlawing or permitting it. The second mode, often said to be residual to the first, assesses legality exclusively by reference to *the context in which the weapon is used* and by reference to certain general principles that are said to limit the conduct of warfare in all circumstances. The *Shimoda* opinion is an amalgam of both modes, as the reasoning relies both upon the intrinsic prohibitions applicable to the use of poison gas and to the contextual principles of the law of war forbidding unnecessary destruction and suffering and, more controversially, requiring belligerent operations to be concentrated against military objectives.

Arguments about the wisdom of defining aggression and about the most suitable form of definition similarly illustrate the contrast between intrinsic and contextual modes of legal analysis. As well, the related and highly inflamed debates about the interpretation of Article 2(4) and 51 of the Charter of the United Nations also represent a clash of these two modes.[72] Throughout contemporary discussions of the relevance of international law to the use of force by nation-states there is this conflict between these competing modes of thought. By making the conflict explicit and by sketching some implications of each, it may be possible to move the argument beyond polemics and make it into a more serious discussion of alternative conceptions of world order. In most general terms, those that emphasize the intrinsic mode incline toward a supranational conception of world order, whereas those that emphasize the contextual mode incline toward an international conception of world order.[73]

The *Shimoda* case looks at the legal character of atomic weapons in the context of their use against Hiroshima and Nagasaki, although it does not exclude an intrinsic pronouncement on the issue of legality. This contrasts with most of the early writing on the subject that endeavored to "demonstrate" the intrinsic illegality of these weapons.[74] It also contrasts with those writers, most prominently McDougal-Feliciano, Julius Stone, and William V. O'Brien, who advocate the contextual approach with great ardor but in much broader terms than *Shimoda*,

[72] Cf. Julius Stone, *Aggression and World Order,* Berkeley, University of California Press, 1958, with Louis B. Sohn, "The Definition of Aggression," 45 *Virginia Law Review* 697 (1959); and Louis Henkin, "Force, Intervention and Neutrality in Contemporary International Law," with Myres S. McDougal's "Comments" in criticism, *Proceedings, the American Society of International Law, 1963,* pp. 147, 163.

[73] For a sharp comparison of these two models of international order, see Klaus Knorr, "Supranational versus International Models of General and Complete Disarmament," in Richard J. Barnet and Falk, eds., *Security in Disarmament,* Princeton, Princeton University Press, 1965, pp. 384-410.

[74] Some examples: Singh, *op.cit. supra,* note 36; Schwarzenberger, *op.cit. supra,* note 27; Spaight, *op.cit. supra,* note 23.

suggesting the relevance of remote political and military goals to a legal analysis of contested acts.[75]

In its extreme form the intrinsic mode of thinking encourages the analyst to conclude that nuclear weapons are either permitted or are prohibited and to offer authoritative guidance to those who act on behalf of nation-states in world affairs as to the requirements of international law.

Few jurists who rely upon the intrinsic mode do so in pure form, especially in analyzing the legal status of nuclear weapons. Rather the more typical inclination is to admit an inability to pronounce one way or the other at this point, and concentrate on offering some tentative guidelines for some aspects of a legal analysis. For instance in the latest edition of Lauterpacht-Oppenheim, distinguished users of the intrinsic mode, Lauterpacht suggests that, if nuclear weapons are used against military objectives and cause little or no collateral civilian damage, then the legality of their use is easier to maintain. This standard treatise also mentions reprisals against prior use as possibly legal and also considers the special case for using nuclear weapons "against an enemy who violates rules of war on a scale so vast as to put himself altogether outside the orbit of considerations of humanity and compassion."[76] The example selected for this latter possibility is the argument for using atomic bombs, had they existed, against Nazi Germany to deter its commission of genocide against innocent civilians. Lauterpacht-Oppenheim also venture the view that the use of atomic bombs to prevent an aggressor from achieving world domination might have a special status, even if the use is considered to be one that would normally constitute a violation of international law. The passage goes on to say that the act would remain a violation, as international law applies "even in relation to an aggressor in an unlawful war," but concludes cryptically that, nevertheless, there is "no decisive reason for assuming that, in the extreme contingency of the nature described above

[75] In the discussion that follows there is an important distinction to be noted between the use of context by *Shimoda* and its use by writers such as Myres McDougal and Julius Stone. The *Shimoda* decision relies upon contextual thinking to suggest that "the facts" as well as the properties of a weapon must be examined to determine whether the use of a weapon on a given occasion is legal or illegal, and thereby to resist the temptation to decide whether atomic weapons, as such, are legal or not. McDougal and Stone, on the other hand, rely upon contextual thinking to take into account considerations of justice and policy, to determine whether the underlying use of force constitutes "aggression" or "self-defense." It is mainly in this latter sense of context that "the contextual approach" seems especially vulnerable to criticism as encouraging a subjective appreciation of the content of legal rights and duties. For citation to McDougal-Feliciano and Stone see *op.cit. supra*, note 36.

I wish to thank Professor Leo Gross for pointing out to me the need for clarification on this basic matter.

[76] Hersch Lauterpacht-L. Oppenheim, *International Law*, 7th edn., 1952, II, pp. 347-51.

[defense against world domination], that particular principle would or could be scrupulously adhered to."[77] This quotation serves to disclose the strain placed upon legal approaches based on intrinsic modes that seek to prescribe standards and yet allow for reasonable expectations about probable courses of behavior. It is commonplace to assume that a state confronted by a choice between subjugation and victory will do whatever is likely to promote victory, just as a man confronted by a choice between starvation and theft is likely to steal. All law, not just international law, is ineffective in extreme situations. If one, however, conceives the extreme to be the general or typical situation in warfare, as does Baxter with regard to the use of militarily significant weapons, then it becomes sensible to point out the deception and futility of legal regulation. In contrast, if one feels that there are marginal occasions on which the decision to use weapons depends to some extent, at least, on their legal status, then regulation may be a contribution to world order, even if one is aware that the legal prohibition cannot be expected to restrain use in extreme situations, that is, in those situations where breaking the law might make a decisive difference in the outcome of the war.[78]

The competing mode of analysis stresses the context of use. It refrains, as *Shimoda* refrained, from reaching the conclusion that nuclear weapons are either *necessarily* legal or illegal.

In the McDougal-Feliciano instance of the contextual approach, the crucial indication of illegality would be "disproportionate and unnecessary destruction of values."[79] With reference to nuclear weapons these authors do note such special characteristics of nuclear weapons as the prolonged period over which lethal damage takes place, the occurrence of genetic injury, and the possibility of effects upon nonparticipating countries. For this reason it may require "a showing of much more stringent necessity and much larger military advantage" to sustain the legality of a challenged use of nuclear weapons.[80] But these authors, consistently with their whole approach, refuse to pass any judgments on the intrinsic legal character of nuclear weapons. Everything depends on context.

The contextual approach used by McDougal-Feliciano should also be related to their development of a policy-oriented jurisprudence.[81] *Shimoda* tries to exclude policy factors from its legal analysis and ar-

[77] *Ibid.*, p. 351, n. 2.
[78] How important is the marginal occasion for this subject matter? It is difficult to carry a response beyond intuitive inclinations connected with the fear of nuclear war as distinct from the fear of other

calamities that might be supposed to arise from a renunciation of nuclear weapons.
[79] McDougal-Feliciano, p. 663.
[80] *Ibid.*, p. 667.
[81] See Preface, pp. vii-xi.

rive at a conclusion on the law that would be persuasive regardless of policy preferences. McDougal-Feliciano regard international law as a process by which authoritative decisions are reached. They recommend a contextual approach to decision-makers and spell out in systematic detail the factors that are to be taken into account if a reasonable effort is to be made to maximize the community policies at stake. The judge (or other official faced with the need to construe the law) is asked to make a finding of net policy effects arising out of the pattern of conduct challenged as illegal. As McDougal has so often maintained, the expectations of the community concerning what is legal is one crucial policy factor to be taken into account. Therefore, legal precedent is not discounted nor is it made necessarily determinative.

The chief advocates of the contextual approach for assessing the permissibility of using nuclear weapons are rather indefinite about how to go about identifying the limits of permissibility. McDougal-Feliciano and O'Brien, both conscious of their allegiance to Western interests in the global struggle for influence that has gone on between the nuclear superpowers since the end of World War II, are very reluctant to foreclose legal recourse to nuclear weapons by pronouncing limiting conditions in advance.[82] Writing under the impression that the United States was at the time superior in the field of nuclear armaments and inferior in conventional armaments—an impression whose accuracy is most difficult to assess—these authors favor taking account of political objectives (defeat of totalitarian powers, human dignity, etc.) as well as military ones, in the assessment of the legality of conduct, especially when the question at issue is a dispute about whether a given use of force constituted "aggression" or "self-defense." In their analysis of whether international law permits recourse to particular weapons under a given set of belligerent circumstances, McDougal and Feliciano argue that legality must be assessed by balancing considerations of "military necessity" against those of "humanitarianism"; such a process of balancing does not make the legal status of the use of atomic weapons turn on whether the user is "totalitarian" or not. The difficulty with their approach is of another sort, namely, that it accords virtually unfettered discretion to the national decision-maker's perception of what it is permissible to do in the course of war. There are almost always plausible reasons of military necessity to justify war acts and it is not very possible to review such a process of balancing, except in outrageous cases; as no quasi-objective standards exist by which to

[82] Illustrations of the candor with which these authors take cold war considerations into account are available. Myres S. McDougal and Norbert A. Schlei, "The Hydrogen Bomb Tests in Perspective: Lawful Measures for Security," 64 *Yale Law Journal* 648 (1955); O'Brien, pp. 35-38, 105-13.

assess how much military necessity must be present to vindicate a certain foreseeable quantum of human suffering, the effect is to remove legal control from the normal conduct of war. McDougal and Feliciano appear to legitimatize the use by the United States of atomic bombs against Japan, although they do so without any of the close analysis of context prescribed.[83]

The advantage of this broad contextual mode of analysis with its stress on balancing opposing considerations is to get away from the static view of the relevance of law to behavior. Furthermore, their approach can incorporate considerations of effectiveness as a contextual factor rather than as a determinative element in law.[84] McDougal-Feliciano place appropriate emphasis on what is reasonable, given the expectations of the community about permissible limits of conduct. It would appear that their approach would benefit from a somewhat stricter definition of context and from somewhat less reluctance to classify certain acts or instruments of conduct as intrinsically illegal. McDougal-Feliciano are apparently unwilling to curtail the subjectivism of their contextual approach, a subjectivism made acute by nationalism and by the exceptionally decentralized character of international society during a major war; these authors are unwilling to lay down certain minimum rules of the game that apply independently of circumstance. Instead, in the setting of war, they insist that all legal assessments must be made by weighing the facts of a context in light of the overarching polarity created by considerations of military necessity on the one hand, and by considerations of humanity on the other. This is one way, of course, to accommodate the pressures that lead states to do whatever is necessary to win, regardless of what the law says they should do, and it may be argued in support, that such an accommodation removes any lingering illusions about the capacities of law to shape belligerent conduct. McDougal and Feliciano, in effect, restrict the role of law to orienting a decision-maker toward taking explicit account of such wider concerns as the minimization of war damage.

An appraisal of the two modes of thought depends somewhat on what one understands to be the major purpose of the law of war. The intrinsic approach, if restrictive, will tend to be ignored by those making policy during war, whereas, if permissive or opportunistic, it will tend to make law irrelevant. On the other hand, it gives the appearance of objectivity when used to look back upon challenged activity so as to judge legal responsibility; as well, its clarity of ref-

---

[83] McDougal-Feliciano content themselves with a "longish" and equivocal comment in footnote 421, pp. 660-61, and O'Brien skirts an inquiry on pp. 103-04.
[84] Compare Baxter's views, p. 612.

erence makes it possible to understand the distinction between what is legal and what is not.

In contrast, a contextual analysis that gives a policy-maker flexibility to pursue realistic belligerent policies may allow the constraining influence of normative considerations to play a role in shaping action. Law does not seem utopian or irrelevant, but rather offers a prudent way to take some account of considerations favoring restraint, avoidance of suffering, and so on. The polarity between what is legal and what is militarily effective is eliminated and both dimensions are given relevance along with many other considerations. On the other hand, the judgmental act is complicated because the nature of what is legal is connected so closely with controversial ideas about what is politically desirable. As such, it tends to appear as a vindication of power and a rationalization of victory, as it is normally the successful side that sits in judgment of the loser or at least posits the controlling standard of what is politically desirable. *Shimoda* is so interesting because it is an exception, although one that makes its legal appraisal independent of any consideration of what was politically desirable; in fact, in its concluding remarks it concedes the heavy burden of Japan's responsibility for World War II.[85]

IV. The Legal Status of Nuclear Weapons Today

As Section III has argued, the resolution of the issue of legality is affected, in the first instance, by whether one accepts that mode of juristic thinking that deals with *intrinsic character or context of use.*

If the approach of intrinsic character is taken, it is possible to follow the U.S. service manuals and say that nuclear weapons are as legal as other weapons, in the absence of an express prohibition. It is also possible, however, to invoke the action of the General Assembly in 1961, especially Resolution 1653 (XVI), to illustrate the view that nuclear weapons are intrinsically illegal. Operative Section I of the Resolution puts the position strongly by declaring that:

(a) The use of nuclear and thermo-nuclear weapons is contrary to the spirit, letter and aims of the United Nations and, as such, a direct violation of the Charter of the United Nations;

(b) The use of nuclear and thermo-nuclear weapons would exceed even the scope of war and cause indiscriminate suffering and destruction to mankind and civilization and, as such, is con-

---

[85] As the opinion puts it: "The defendant State caused many nationals to die, injured them, and drove them to a precarious life by the war which it opened on its own authority and responsibility" (p. 250).

trary to the rules of international law and to the laws of humanity;

(c) The use of nuclear and thermo-nuclear weapons is a war directed not against an enemy or enemies alone but also against mankind in general, since the peoples of the world not involved in such a war will be subjected to all the evils generated by the use of such weapons.

(d) Any State using nuclear and thermo-nuclear weapons is to be considered as violating the Charter of the United Nations, as acting contrary to the laws of humanity and as committing a crime against mankind and civilization; . . .[86]

It is additionally possible to say that nuclear weapons are intrinsically illegal, either by validating and extending the prohibition on poison gas,[87] or by saying that the principles underlying the law of war outlaw weapons with the properties of nuclear weapons. Even under this approach, as Lauterpacht-Oppenheim show, exceptions for reprisal against an evil enemy may make the use of nuclear weapons legal under certain conditions. It is also possible, recalling Baxter's argument, to treat as lapsed for ineffectiveness, despite the action taken by the General Assembly on the opposite assumption, that portion of the international law of war purporting to regulate decisive weapons.

On the other hand, the approach by way of context necessarily refrains from either a blanket prohibition or endorsement of the legality of nuclear weapons. Their legality depends on whether, as used, they cause damage disproportionate to the military effect and whether their use is reasonably related to the pursuit of a legitimate belligerent objective. Those tending to widen the context to include the overall war effort and those tending to define belligerent objective as including the realization of peace on an acceptable political and moral basis seem to have a more flexible and manipulative view of when the use of nuclear weapons is legal than do those contextualists who limit what is relevant to the ratio between military and nonmilitary destruction at the scene of the nuclear attack. The *Shimoda* case illustrates this more conservative use of context.

How does one construe these somewhat conflicting lines of legal authority and methods of argumentation? Resolution 1653 (XVI) is expressive of a certain level of international consensus in favor of the prohibition of nuclear weapons under all circumstances. There is no agreement about how to assess the legal weight of resolutions by the

---

[86] U.N. General Assembly Res. 1653, XVI, adopted by a vote of 55-20-26, roll call. For full text of this Resolution and voting alignment see Appendix C, pp. 590-91.

[87] See authorities cited in note 36 *supra.*

General Assembly either as independent legal authority or as evidence of a relevant consensus expressive of the will of the international community.[88] The *Shimoda* case tends to reinforce the Assembly judgment, although its terms are limited to the facts of Hiroshima and Nagasaki; given the increased power of nuclear weaponry and the emphasis of the court on the properties of the earlier atomic devices and their analogy to gas, it would seem reasonable to regard *Shimoda* as supportive of a virtually unconditional prohibition of the use of nuclear weapons.

On the other hand, there is no prospect of implementing this consensus favoring prohibition by effective responses in the event of noncompliance. And, unlike poison gas, the national security policies of several leading states are intimately dependent upon their capability and willingness to use nuclear weapons. Short of nuclear disarmament, something not presently foreseeable, there is little prospect that legal restraints, as distinct from fear of retaliation, will have any influence upon a decision to use nuclear weapons, although contextual factors related to suffering and unnecessary damage are likely to inhibit all but the most callous belligerent. We are returned then to the central dilemma posed so clearly by Baxter's explanation of the ineffectiveness of that portion of the law of war that purports to regulate the use of weapons that a belligerent might come to regard as decisive.

The legal status of nuclear weapons, then, is very inconclusive. It depends greatly on the perspective one selects as dominant. There is fairly convincing evidence of a gathering consensus expressive of the will of the international community and certainly not irrelevant to the creation of binding legal obligations.[89] And there is on the other hand the awareness that the prospect of effectiveness is an integral element in the concept of law, and serves the key functions in international society of avoiding deception by, or sentimental reliance upon, norms that are detached from political realities. Those who advocate the adoption of a "No-First-Use Proposal" for nuclear weapons as an arms control measure are trying to shape the political realities so that they

[88] On weight to be given General Assembly resolutions see Gabriella Lande, "The Changing Effectiveness of General Assembly Resolutions," *Proceedings, the American Society of International Law, 1964,* p. 162; Krzysztof Skubiszewski, "The General Assembly of the United Nations and Its Power to Influence National Action," *ibid.,* p. 153; in general, on the role of consensus in the formation of legal standards, see C. Wilfred Jenks, "The Will of the World Community as the Basis of Obligation in International Law," in *Law, Welfare, and Freedom,* London, Stevens and Sons, 1963, pp. 83-100, and Falk, "The Adequacy of Contemporary Theories of International Law—Gaps in Legal Thinking," 50 *Virginia Law Review* 231, 243-48 (1964).

[89] See especially Final Act of 1964 Cairo Conference of Non-Aligned Countries.

come to support the international consensus.[90] For, to convince themselves and others that a no-first-use policy has been seriously adopted,
it is necessary for participating states to adapt defense policies in such
a way that security interests can be upheld without having to threaten
or use nuclear weapons.

V. Conclusion

However understood, *Shimoda* is a dramatic legal document. It warrants study and its analysis supports a widespread inquiry into the relevance of international law to the regulation of nuclear war. We need
not renounce our skepticism about the capacity of international law
to regulate war in reaching the conclusion that this most serious of
subjects might benefit from serious study. And looking back at Hiroshima and Nagasaki is one of the better ways of trying to look ahead
and gain insight into the various impacts of nuclear weaponry upon the
developing international law of war.

1965

[90] For discussion of various aspects of this approach, see Robert C. Tucker, Klaus Knorr, Richard A. Falk, and Hedley Bull, "Proposal for No First Use of Nuclear Weapons: Pros and Cons," Policy Memorandum No. 28, Center of International Studies, Princeton University, 1963.

XIII. Minimizing the Use of Nuclear Weapons

IS IT POSSIBLE to reform the international system without drastically altering its character? More specifically, is it feasible and desirable to reform the international system by taking steps to minimize the use of nuclear weapons? If so, what steps? These questions identify the concern of this chapter.

The notion of reform is somewhat ambiguous. Several conceptions of reform coexist in the context of thought about world order. The idea of a reformist approach to world order can be usefully compared with the revolutionary approach outlined in Chapter I. First, a series of reforms can be undertaken to build up confidence in the prospects for system-change. Reform, then, is a transition strategy designed to create principally a climate of attitude hospitable to drastic modifications in present arrangements for the management of military power—drastic in the sense of entailing either the partial transfer of control over military power to international institutions or the reduction of national military capabilities to a scale appropriate only for internal security. Reform, then, is a prelude to drastic revision, contributing essentially the psychological prerequisites.

A second, rather subordinate, somewhat vague conception of reform sees it as a permanent dynamic energy in international society, capable of an indefinite series of improvements in world order over time. If the interval is extended long enough, then the most drastic changes may be brought about. The general view of reform is that of a gradualist process—priding itself on the limits of realistic expectation—by which small changes are made. This orientation toward world order issues is popular in the United States, fitting in with an *ad hoc* approach to foreign policy-making, a reverence for the common law tradition, a philosophical heritage built upon pragmatism, and a political tradition of compromise and negotiation.[1]

[1] If such a gradualist strategy is seriously espoused as an approach to system-change, it may well be more "utopian" than the more radical approach advocated from a revolutionary perspective. To the extent that an elite is aware of its own vested interests and supporting values and beliefs, it will oppose all changes, however "gradual," that go beyond maintaining the existing order of things. Such opposition is currently very prominent in the United States, arising out of official responses to protests against the war in Viet Nam. Underlying the phenomena of protest—the marches and demonstrations, the questioning of the motives of one's own govern-

ment, the burning of draft cards, and the refusal to serve in the military forces—is a symbolic and salient rejection by part of the membership of society of the entire ethos associated with national sovereignty, citizenship, patriotism—an ethos summed up in the expression "my country, right or wrong." The action taken by the government to punish dissenters in various ways is an ethical reflex by those in control of the apparatus of the state, seeking to maintain control over individual action and to coerce allegiance and submission. The punitive measures have included the accelerated drafting of young men who take part in antigovernment demonstra-

The third conception of reform resembles the second, except that it is more conservative, confining change to system-maintaining acts. The pure gradualist envisages drastic reform through time, whereas the marginal reformer seeks only to safeguard the existing system of order.

It is evident that the reformist perspective bears no clear relation to the substantive problem at issue—minimizing the use of nuclear weapons. In each instance of proposed change, the consequences, objectives, and perceptions must be appraised for their probable effects on the risk of use. It is, of course, problematic whether any given change in international society—say, the Limited Test Ban Treaty—constituted a "reform," that is, an improvement in the stability and justice of the international system.

The important contrast between the reformist and the revolutionary outlook is that the reformer is skeptical about the feasibility and/or desirability of drastic revisions in the structure of international law within the foreseeable future. It is this posture of thought that dominates the thinking and practice both of decision-making elites and of their supporting publics. The object of analysis is to consider what can be done to minimize the use of nuclear weapons given this decision-making orientation. From our earlier analysis of this orientation we know that strict constraints limit freedom to alter what is presently being done. However, such a perspective on the problem enables the nuclear issue to be grasped more on its own and it does permit an inventory of the existing policies.

Let it be clear that the foreign policy of all nuclear powers, including China, seems to be based upon giving a high priority to the avoidance of nuclear war. Chinese foreign policy seems to be cautious when it comes to risking large-scale military involvement; this caution seems far more descriptive of Chinese policies than does the bellicose language used to goad the world revolution of Communism into being. Such a shared commitment is not equivalent in any sense to a renunciation of nuclear weapons or even indicative of a willingness to stockpile these weapons for purposes of nuclear reprisal only (the sort of willingness that largely applies to the use of lethal biological and chemical weapons). Nuclear weapons are "used" as active ingredients of what Kenneth Boulding aptly characterizes as "a threat system" of international order.[2] That is, these weapons introduce the fear of escalation into internal war, and are relied upon to inhibit re-

---

tions, the withdrawal of passports from dissenters who travel without authorization to the territory of "the enemy" (in this instance, North Viet Nam), and the actions taken to discourage criticism of the government war effort by drafted soldiers.

[2] "The Role of Law in the Learning of Peace," *Proceedings, the American Society of International Law, 1963*, pp. 92-103.

course to armed attacks in the main arenas of strategic contention. The removal of these implied threats in a fashion as credible as is their current presence might be expected to exercise considerable influence on risk-taking with regard to subnuclear violence. The apparent sanctity of the European territorial *status quo* is certainly one product of the reciprocal credibility of nuclear capability.

If we now look at what is done to minimize the use of nuclear weapons there are a variety of approaches taken. First of all, the whole notion of mutual deterrence is premised upon the neutralizing influence of an exchange of credible threats to inflict unacceptable damage on any enemy that has struck first with nuclear weapons. The United States also considers that it has achieved some Type II Deterrence as a consequence of its nuclear superiority (making credible a nuclear response, at least in Europe, to a nonnuclear military provocation of serious magnitude).[3] With some proliferation the existence of nuclear weapons might be used to reinforce the policy of avoiding their employment by making a strongly implemented pledge to defend with nuclear weapons any victim of nuclear attack. Such a policy if credibly embraced might discourage military adventuring of the sort susceptible to escalation toward the nuclear threshold.

At the same time that recourse to military expansion is inhibited by the fear of a nuclear response, it is part of the policy of minimization to find nonnuclear responses to provocation.[4] If, in other words, our

---

[3] For definitions of Type I and Type II deterrence see Herman Kahn, *Thinking About the Unthinkable*, New York, Horizon Press, 1962, pp. 110-17.

[4] There is an intricate web of considerations created by the uncertain relations between nuclear weapons and foreign policy. Short of very reliable accounts of decision-making and calculations of risk that have taken place in governmental circles, it is highly conjectural to speculate about this relationship. The issues can be posed, but their resolution tends again to be expressive of life-style rather than to be the outcome of an objective analytic procedure. Suppose one considers the People's Republic of China in 1967. To what extent has decision-making in Peking been influenced by the danger that their provocative action will produce a nuclear response? If the United States and the Soviet Union endorsed a no-first-use-proposal would China rely more fully upon military power to pursue expansionist policies? To what extent would an answer to this question depend on the existence of credible nonnuclear military capabilities on the part of China's military rivals?

It can be argued that if the danger of nuclear war is reduced by a perceptible degree then the scope for military adventurism is significantly increased. The reason for this increase is that part of the deterrent impact of nuclear weapons arises from the fear of escalation, that is, of exciting a causal spiral ending in a holocaust. To the extent that the fear of escalation is withdrawn from relevance, it may seem more plausible to probe by military means, withdrawing if necessary, but being less concerned that a small confrontation, whether won or lost, might lead to nuclear war. If potential military aggressors would be likely to take greater risks were the problem of escalation to be solved, then it would be necessary to weigh the uncertain gains of reducing the danger of World War III against the uncertain losses of making certain forms of subnuclear aggression more feasible. In this weighing process the relative claims of preventing aggression and of avoiding general war are posited as opposing one another. This opposition may also be unreal in either direction. If aggression does increase, then a reaction may take place that would make

rivals challenge security interests, as in the Far East, our first line of defense is by way of guerrilla and conventional capabilities, even if this form of military engagement sacrifices to some extent the possibility of quick and decisive victory. The refusal to use nuclear weapons in Korea and now in South Viet Nam partly bears witness to the assertion that the United States will give up some prospect of military advantage to maintain the policy of minimization. To sustain this policy, it is probably desirable to support contingency planning that envisions a defense capability equipped to uphold as many security interests as possible without a reliance on nuclear weapons.[5]

The quality of participation by the superpowers in the arms race also suggests an element of restraint. Some tacit expression is given to the common interest in a stable and balanced deterrent. As well, there is some evidence that the attainment of a decisive advantage might actually be self-destructive, inclining an apprehensive rival to preemptive strategies of threat and strike, thereby making international crises even more dangerous than at present. No apparent great effort is made by either side to gain a decisive military edge at the strategic level over its adversary, although a degree of unresolved anxiety has been recently created by the implications of a decision by either the Soviet Union or the United States to deploy different types of ballistic defense to improve the stability of its nuclear deterrent.

Connected with this mode of constraint is the foreclosing of certain arms development that might undercut the stability of the present balance. Notable examples of this expression of the policy of minimization include the agreement of the United States and the Soviet Union to cosponsor a resolution prohibiting the orbiting of weapons of mass

---

World War III more likely than it had been prior to the denuclearization of international politics. If, however, the denuclearization is not followed by aggression, but by more harmonious relations, then the atmosphere may be conducive to various undertakings, such as drastic disarmament and the creation of a world police force, which would reduce the risks of both limited aggression and unlimited warfare.

The difficulty here is that the analysis may clarify the choices, but it does not help us to choose. Causal connections are far too hypothetical, and relative risks cannot be reliably compared. How does one choose in the face of this contingency? However action occurs it will imply a choice, so that the reality of contingency cannot avoid the need for conclusions and policies. Further discussion of these issues

is to be found in Chapter I.
  [5] The word "reliance" is necessarily ambiguous. The present reliance is upon an uncertain threat to make actual use, or on the danger that if matters get out of control nuclear weapons may be used. To eliminate this sort of "reliance" altogether is almost impossible, but it can be reduced by finding substitutes to attain security objectives. An aggressor or provoker or, for that matter, any belligerent must, nevertheless, recognize that "the other side" may if pressed use nuclear weapons if it has access to them, and that the danger of escalation cannot be altogether eliminated so long as nuclear weapons exist or can be brought back into existence. T. C. Schelling analyzes these issues with characteristic clarity in "The Role of Deterrence in Total Disarmament," *Foreign Affairs* XL (April 1962) 392-406.

destruction in outer space and the concerted efforts of the United States, to find agreed alternatives to heavy investments in either ballistic defense systems or a civil defense program.[6] There is an increasing understanding of the interactive character of the arms race, that is, of the need to measure the impact of specific developments upon the probable behavior of one's opponent. A commitment to the avoidance of nuclear war may include a willingness to forego certain steps that, when viewed from the perspective of a given national society, seem to augment relative strength. Military preparedness, then, takes into increasing account the need to reassure rivals of peaceful intentions at the strategic level and to display a military posture of an essentially "defensive" nature.[7] Thus the arms race—perhaps the prime symbol of despair for those whose life-style counsels a system-change as the sole expedient in the nuclear age—is ironically also an arena wherein important, if somewhat disguised, expression is given to the policies of minimization.

Less disguised, and for this very reason perhaps less capable of being significant, are the explicit measures of arms control. The so-called hot line, a telecommunications link between the Kremlin and the White House, is illustrative of the acknowledgment by the chief nuclear rivals that it is important to have a means to verify intentions and clarify ambiguous events in periods of international crisis. It is part of the overall effort to improve the safety of the existing system and to avoid the outbreak of nuclear war by accident, miscalculation, catalytic agency, or unauthorized use. The elaborate national scheme of command and control to govern decisions to use nuclear weapons is indicative of a policy of minimization, unilaterally implemented and independent of any expectation of reciprocity. And such symbolic gestures as the bilateral reduction of stockpiles of fissionable materials by voluntary action on the part of the Soviet Union and the United States manifest further the desire to keep the system—at least so far as the

---

[6] See, generally, Louis Morton, "The Anti-Ballistic Missile: Some Political and Strategic Considerations," *Virginia Quarterly Review* XLII (1965), 28-42; see also on the asymmetry of the United States and Soviet decisions with regard to ABM systems, Freeman Dyson, "Defense Against Ballistic Missiles," in Falk and Saul Mendlovitz, eds., *The Strategy of World Order*, New York, World Law Fund, 1966, IV, pp. 48-58.

[7] Of course, the decisions to restrain the pace of the arms race and to reassure the other side are influenced by many additional, more self-interested calculations. Each side wants to achieve maximum stability and maximum relative strength in exchange for a minimum absolute and relative burden. Decisions to discourage the deployment of antimissile defense systems are heavily influenced in the United States by considerations of cost-effectiveness, and by the further consideration that the ratio of offense to defense, given the military posture of the United States and the Soviet Union, provides the United States with a strategic military justification for its cautious position on missile defense.

danger of nuclear war is concerned—under at least the present level of control.

Such a spirit is also belatedly manifest in the context of concern about the further proliferation of nuclear capabilities, although this concern might have been both more impressive and more constructive had it appeared sooner. As it now appears, the United States and the Soviet Union carried the development of their own capability to the maximum and only then acknowledged some need to foreclose proliferation. That is, the need was acknowledged only when its satisfaction involved no element of self-sacrifice for the senior members of the nuclear group. The Limited Test Ban, the main gesture in the direction of antiproliferation, came at a time when the potentialities for further testing were viewed as quite trivial.[8] The agreement could hardly be expected to inhibit such states as France and China, which had been making a great economic and psychological effort to bring themselves across the nuclear threshold. Even with respect to such secondary interests as international trade and the appeasement of allies, it is evident that for the United States, at least, the politics of antiproliferation are given a fairly low priority—even if they do receive dramatic affirmation from time to time. It is, of course, highly speculative to assert a direct correlation between the number of nuclear powers and the risks of nuclear war. The attitude toward this correlation is again expressive of a lifestyle as much as of reasoning from evidence. After all, we have almost no relevant experience, and our reliance upon analogies is neither rigorous nor persuasive. In general, those who incline toward a system-changing orientation view proliferation with alarm, whereas those who view the cold war as protracted and central tend to view proliferation with virtual indifference.

Obviously certain forms of proliferation are more disturbing than others—even if one takes a war-prevention perspective rather than a foreign-policy perspective. If nuclear weapons are acquired by states without much experience in international affairs and with a reckless tradition of foreign policy-making, then the prospects for minimization are more diminished than they are if the new nuclear powers are con-

---

[8] There is some disagreement concerning this conclusion evident in the extended hearings preceding the vote in the Senate on the Limited Nuclear Test Ban Treaty. See Nuclear Test Ban Treaty, Hearings before the Committee on Foreign Relations, U.S. Senate, Executive M, 88th Cong., 1st Sess., August 1963; Military Aspects and Implications of Nuclear Test Ban Proposals and Related Matters, Parts I and II, Hearings before the Preparedness Investigating Subcommittee of the Armed Services Committee, U.S. Senate, 88th Cong., 1st Sess., May, June, August 1963. Also subsequent to ratification there has been some indication that the development of missile-defense technology would proceed more rapidly and reliably on the basis of atmospheric testing. So at least in retrospect there may have been some self-sacrifice in military terms made by the United States and the Soviet Union.

servative states with a *status-quo* orientation. The whole speculation is rendered almost hopelessly complex by the plausible assumption that under certain conditions proliferation would appear to benefit rather than harm the hopes for minimization. For instance, it is at least arguable that if either Israel or the United Arab Republic were to acquire nuclear weapons, it would be better for both to have them. In general, however, antiproliferation seems consonant with minimization—one can fall back upon the common-sense, although not truly accurate, statistical reasoning of assuming that an increasing number of nuclear powers produces a roughly proportional increase in the risk of use.

The longer-term prospects of minimization in the existing system depend heavily upon the serious establishment of a tradition of nonuse, backed up by an authoritative legal prohibition and by compensatory defense planning. The General Assembly of the United Nations has been actively fostering this tradition, most dramatically in Resolution 1653 (XVI), which went so far as to declare the use of nuclear weapons an international crime (presumably of the sort that would potentially entail individual responsibility as that affixed at Nuremberg). The United States, France, and the United Kingdom were among the twenty states that voted against this resolution; the Soviet Union voted in favor as did fifty-five other states, more than the two-thirds majority relevant to General Assembly action on an important question.[9] The organized international community has itself made a formal commitment to endorse a tradition of nonuse.

In addition, the decision of the Tokyo District Court in the *Shimoda* case warrants mention.[10] In this opinion a Japanese court in a calm and persuasive manner arrived at the conclusion that the atomic attacks against Hiroshima and Nagasaki violated international law. Although the court expressly refrained from finding atomic weapons illegal as such, the legal conclusion that their use against these inhabited cities was illegal would seem to extend to a prohibition against their use against anything other than a purely military target. At least the decision seems to support the argument that traditional principles of international law governing the conduct of warfare reinforce, if they do not altogether require, a tradition of nonuse.[11]

[9] For text of Resolution 1653 (XVI), see Appendix C, pp. 590-91. For a discussion of the legal status of Resolutions passed by more than two-thirds of the General Assembly, see Rosalyn Higgins, *The Development of International Law Through the Political Organs of the United Nations*, London, Oxford University Press, 1963, pp. 1-10.

[10] For a full consideration of the *Shi-moda* case see Chapter XII. The renewed reference here to *Shimoda*, as well as to Resolution 1653 (XVI) is to show the relevance of these developments to the overall effort to minimize the use of nuclear weapons.

[11] The scholarly literature is quite divided on whether the use of nuclear weapons is legal under existing international law. For representative discussions see

The acceptance by the United States of a status for nuclear weapons comparable to that for poison gas would itself be a gesture of dramatic deference to world opinion on how to solve the issue of minimization, and would signal some ability to work for world order from a perspective other than that identified with bargaining and strategy. It is not a step that the United States is likely to take in the foreseeable future. Just because it would be a dramatic gesture it would mobilize the inertial energies at work in the existing domestic arrangement of power, influence, and belief. To revert to the argument of Chapter I, a withdrawal of legitimacy from nuclear weapons would be symbolic of (even if in actuality irrelevant to) a transition from an international life-style to a supranational one, and as such will not be likely to occur except under the combined impact of trauma and educational preparation. Even without the formal acknowledgment by the United States of the obligation to refrain from using nuclear weapons first, it would appear that further international action in support of such a tradition of nonuse will help mold ethical judgments of attentive publics and their elites and might operate as a deterrent to the marginal user of nuclear weapons.

Of course, the prospects for minimization in a sense are a function of the overall prospects for peace. Therefore, part of the endeavor at minimization is to strengthen peacekeeping and crisis management, as well as to build up a body of universally accepted rules of international conduct. By these indirect methods, the ability of the international system to restore equilibrium is increased and the spiraling of conflict toward the nuclear threshold is inhibited.

There is a tendency to assume that all is lost once the nuclear threshold has been crossed and therefore to restrict the analysis of policies of minimization to the avoidance of any use whatsoever of nuclear weapons. This is clearly unfortunate, and overlooks the ironic probability that policies of minimization might be expected to exert a much greater influence, especially if thought through and accepted in advance, after the nuclear threshold is crossed than before. Once nuclear weapons have been used, the life-style of the prevailing elites committed to system-maintenance has an enormous stake in giving a maximum effect to policies of minimization. The occurrence of a major nuclear war would either produce a collapse of the existing system or

Georg Schwarzenberger, *The Legality of Nuclear Weapons*, London, Stevens and Sons, 1958; Nagendra Singh, *Nuclear Weapons and International Law*, New York, Praeger, 1959; William V. O'Brien, "Legitimate Military Necessity in Nuclear War," 2 *Yearbook of World Polity*, 35-120 (1960); Myres S. McDougal and Florentino P. Feliciano, *Law and Minimum World Public Order*, New Haven, Yale University Press, 1961, pp. 640-59.

generate strong pressures for its change. Those in control would have a strong interest in most situations in avoiding these outcomes, although one can imagine scenarios where the objective "victory" took precedence over the policies of minimization. For example, suppose Communist China "provoked" the United States to initiate or respond to the use of nuclear weapons in the decade ahead, a period in which China appears certain to be growing more powerful and perhaps also more aggressive.

It does seem to be the case that the formulation of limiting doctrines and approaches might promote minimization, or rather, that the absence of such a sense of limits might lead decision-makers, in the event nuclear weapons should ever be used, to conceive of their options in more absolutist terms of all-or-nothing. An awareness of the range of nuclear responses would at least present to the policy-maker possibilities for minimization in the context of use, and inhibit the simplification of the process of action and reaction which seems to dominate the popular mind to such an extent that almost no distinction is made between the severity of different types of nuclear war. The prevailing popular view, especially outside the United States, is that any nuclear war would almost certainly be all-out. Of course, some of those most concerned about the nature of the nuclear danger consider this popular fear to be worth nurturing as "a white lie," reasoning that if the lie is believed then the prospects for avoidance are strengthened. That is, the qualitative inhibition upon risk-taking associated with the fear of nuclear war is diluted to the extent that sophisticated limiting notions gain acceptance and make the prospect of nuclear war no more serious than the prospect of other wars endured in the course of international history. Again the relevance of life-style seems overwhelming. Those who accept a system-maintaining outlook tend to exhibit a strong vested intellectual interest in finding justification to conduct international conflict for traditional national objectives, and underscore the continuing utility of national uses of military power even if part of this utility rests upon the credible threat to use nuclear weapons first. Those who adopt a system-changing outlook exhibit almost as strong a vested intellectual interest in arguing the need to give up the traditional pursuit of national objectives in world affairs in response to the danger of nuclear war and to oppose national uses of military power except for purposes of strict self-defense and under the authority of the United Nations. That is, part of the affirmative case for a system-change is the sense of urgency that arises if one perceives *any* use of nuclear weapons as catastrophic, and as generating a general nuclear exchange. Such an anticipation is unreasonable, but if its acceptance inhibits risk-taking or contributes to the "preparation" relevant to a system-change then it may still be beneficial. I think that this reasoning leads the antiwar system-changing perspective generally to avoid the analysis of secondary precautions once the nuclear threshold has been crossed—that is, what happens in the event of a military use of nuclear weapons.

But supposing that we put aside the objections to this inquiry. A preliminary point is that there could be minimizing policies manifest in the initiating use—limitations as to target, magnitude, civilian damage, fallout, and so on. There is a dramatic difference between using a nuclear weapon of kiloton scale to seal off a mountain pass or to sink an invading fleet and using a nuclear weapon of several megatons to attack large and defenseless inhabited cities. That is, minimizing considerations also apply to the decision to employ nuclear weapons and cross the threshold, and necessarily affect the character of the response. In general, a specific claim designed to uphold the *status quo*, clearly communicated to the adversary, is likely to discourage an overresponse or a widening of the conflict. It was this claiming strategy that was employed so successfully by the United States in the missile crisis of 1962, and that exhibited a process of decision and action pertinent to the minimization of all varieties of coercion, but especially applicable to the most intense variety of coercion, namely, nuclear coercion. If the initiating state communicates its objective clearly and employs the minimum force necessary to achieve it and has been provoked by visibly aggressive conduct by the target state, then the political structure for a minimizing response has been established. But let us be clear about the inevitable ambiguity of crisis communication. It is not easy to identify what is aggressive and what defensive, especially in an atmosphere of recrimination and tension. Why was it more "offensive" for the Soviet Union to emplace missiles in Cuba than for the United States to do so in Turkey?

But let us suppose that the initiating user of nuclear weapons lacks an adequate provocation and does not communicate a limited claim of the restorative variety. Suppose the Soviet Union in the midst of a future Berlin crisis drops a nuclear bomb on West Berlin. What considerations might, nevertheless, express the minimizing viewpoint in executing a response? First of all, it is important to restrict the context of dispute in both domestic and international arenas of controversy and explanation, and to resist the inclination to respond as if the other side had issued a general declaration of war.[12] Second, even if the other side

---

[12] On this see Richard J. Barnet, "Violations of Disarmament Agreements," in Richard J. Barnet and Falk, *Security in Disarmament*, Princeton, Princeton University Press, 1965, pp. 157-77; cf. Roger Fisher, "Enforcement of Disarmament: The Problem of the Response," *Proceedings, the American Society of International Law 1962*, pp. 1-12, and discussion, pp. 12-18.

seems to be clearly the aggressor, it is crucial to restrict defensive objectives to a restoration of the *status quo ante*, and thereby to reject
the more traditional notion that once a state has been unjustly attacked there is no reasonable limit to the use of defensive force short
of the enemy's unconditional surrender.[13] And third, it is important to
choose a nonescalatory proportional response, communicating to the
world community as well as to the adversary the proportionality of
intentions, and to maintain a willingness to negotiate an immediate
cease-fire and to bargain toward a solution of the conflict that erupted
beyond control.

Such a logic of minimization *after* use depends upon a fundamental
rationality that is somewhat at odds with the hypothetical occasion. A
first use of nuclear weapons, except when the scenario is exceptional
or the use is very restricted, is itself likely to represent a breaking of
the bonds of reason such that reason in response will neither seem
prudent nor prove effective. Putting the relevance of irrationality in extreme form, how does one respond to the nuclear power governed by
a psychopath? Perhaps, here too contingency planning has small prospect of limiting the catastrophe to modest proportions. Perhaps
thought can be given to techniques for the assassination of the enemy's leader or its elite rather than to recourse to a characteristic na-
tion-to-nation response. The aggressive agent might be the target of
response, the action being justified by the production of evidence.
Communication—its precision and reliability—seems to be the crucial
adjunct to a minimizing approach in any setting.

1966

[13] See Robert W. Tucker, *The Just War:
A Study in Contemporary American Doc-* *trine,* Baltimore, Johns Hopkins University
Press, 1960.

XIV. Thoughts in Support of a No-First-Use Proposal

PROPONENTS of a no-first-use proposal generally emphasize the distinctive dangers posed by the existence of nuclear weapons, the most serious of which is the possibility of their use in international conflict. An objective of a no-first-use proposal is to make less likely the introduction of nuclear weapons into armed conflict between states. In so doing, this policy seeks primarily to encourage the perception of these weapons as illegitimate instruments of conflict, and thus to promote a concept of defense planning that satisfies security interests without relying upon nuclear weapons, save in the instance when the enemy uses them first. Several of the bases for favoring a no-first-use proposal have been set forth with admirable clarity by Professor Robert C. Tucker.[1] I should like, however, to discuss some further considerations that, when added to those discussed by Tucker, account for my interest in such a proposal either as a unilateral measure or as a negotiated international agreement with one or more foreign states.

A no-first-use policy is only a partial substitute for those more fundamental changes in the international environment that some analysts now believe to be a necessary, although unattainable, adaptation to the existence of nuclear weapons, such as the development of a stable peace system requiring comprehensive disarmament and substantial world government. A rational adjustment to the mutual destructiveness of warfare in the contemporary world needs these radical developments, and yet they cannot be brought about until the state system is significantly weakened—a far from immediate prospect. Such a development presupposes the formation of new loyalty patterns and the abandonment of persistent habits of inter-state conflict. Although signs of some movement toward a universal political consciousness are visible, there exists no significant political disposition to abandon the state and its unilateral prerogatives, either in isolation or in alliance, as the basic unit of power and authority, entrusted with the promotion and the protection of human values in world affairs. As long as the state maintains this dominance, it is unlikely that nations can be persuaded to eliminate nuclear weapons altogether from their defense arsenals. A less ambitious and yet worthwhile improvement in the chances of maintaining nuclear peace could result, however, from the serious adoption of a no-first-use posture, position, and commitment.

History records numerous efforts to proscribe the use of certain weap-

[1] Cf. "No First Use of Nuclear Weapons: A Proposal," in "Proposal for No First Use of Nuclear Weapons: Pros and Cons," Robert C. Tucker, Klaus Knorr, Richard A. Falk, and Hedley Bull, Policy Memorandum No. 28, Center of International Studies, Princeton University, 1963, pp. 1-20.

[425]

ons that were considered at the time of their development to be especially destructive. These efforts largely failed, although the attempts to ban gas and germ warfare have enjoyed at least limited success. A study of the reasons why such prohibitions have been disregarded is instructive. The usual explanation—a reference to the primacy of "military necessity"—is too abstract to identify specific pressures or to explain notable exceptions. It is doubtful that the United States would have introduced atomic bombs into World War II under the claim of military necessity if their status as weapons had been previously declared, with some formality, to be illegitimate. Would we, for instance, have been willing to attain an equivalent impact upon the course of World War II (assuming the same quantum of damage) by the use of poison gas against Hiroshima and Nagasaki? I ask this question to suggest that the status of a weapon does appear to have some bearing upon the decision to use it. The argument in favor of a no-first-use position need not sustain the burden of arguing that it will prevent an initiating recourse to nuclear weapons under *all* circumstances. It is sufficient to show the creation of a significant inhibition in some crucial situations. No rule that is worth formulating anticipates absolute compliance.

The precedent created by the use of atomic bombs at the end of World War II is, I think, relevant in another respect: in augmenting the argument that the advent of nuclear weapons introduces a qualitative change in the status of war in international politics. In this regard, the depth of the response by the Japanese to their defeat in World War II, although no doubt partly a matter of the reassertion of national, cultural, and social values, is one consequence of the material and spiritual scars left by Hiroshima and Nagasaki. The constitutional prohibition against war and military establishments, the continuing potency of Japanese pacifism and neutralism, and the annual commemorations of Hiroshima all suggest that Japan, as a victim of this kind of war (a war that must now be understood as a miniscule prototype) has a special understanding of war different from that of other countries that have been ravaged and defeated.

Also relevant are the condemnations of nuclear weapons made in the United Nations. Resolution 1653 (XVI) adopted by the General Assembly in 1961 declares that the use of nuclear weapons would violate the United Nations Charter.[2] This resolution is tantamount to an insistence upon a no-first-use policy. It is usual, however, to discount altogether the hostility of Afro-Asian nations to nuclear weapons as irresponsible criticism coming from uninformed sources. This seems to be

[2] For a discussion of Resolution 1653 (XVI) see Chapter XIII, pp. 590-91. For the text of the Resolution see Appendix C.

a supercilious and complacent response by the West, even though it is inaccurate on one level, that of responsible judgment about alternatives. Detachment, even alienation from power, often produces irresponsible positions (as has frequently been observed by commentators in powerful states), but it may also produce a juster sense of proportion, a more discriminating and objective priority scale. We accept this as conventional wisdom in the context of dispute-settlement and judicial administration; it hardly occurs to anyone that the partisan would make a better judge than the impartial observer.[3] In similar fashion, I would urge that we should not be quite so quick to repudiate the priority scale recommended by the nonnuclear states or quite so confident about the priorities of the nuclear states. Neutral attitudes about the illegitimacy of nuclear weapons deserve attention, although it is admittedly unrealistic to accord them any operational relevance.

The occasion seems propitious for a reexamination of the assumptions that underlie the claim to rely upon nuclear self-defense, whether this reliance takes the form of threat or act. A willingness to reconsider the limits of self-defense is part of the intellectual climate that should prevail during an investigation of a no-first-use proposal. Just how absolute is the state system? Is it worth authorizing unlimited responses to attacks upon its existence? One way to conceive of a no-first-use proposal is in the form of a denial of the right to make use of nuclear weapons as instruments of self-defense, even if there is no effective alternative, against any kind of attack except a nuclear attack. It is also worth recalling the frequency with which nations and groups of nations have engaged in a course of action that appears, *in retrospect*, to have been tragically self-destructive. An insistence on unilateral rights of nuclear self-defense presupposes, I would maintain, a commitment that can be defended with ingenuity and reason today but that relies upon a style of argument that will be looked back upon, in the event of a major nuclear war, with incredulity and scorn.

[3] It is said that there are no nonpartisan states in international politics, that the aversion to nuclear weapons represents an attempt by nonnuclear powers to make up for their military insignificance, and that only states with a direct interest in the outcome of political controversies are in a position to make a rational calculation of the utility and disutility of a controversial policy. Such an attitude is partly accurate, partly simplistic. There are a multitude of factors that combine to produce a political viewpoint. Access to power, although an important one, is not the necessarily dominant factor and it is certainly not the only one. States with vital interests at stake have frequently adopted disastrous courses of action that appeared as such at the time to third states. The mixed motives of nonnuclear states include, I think it fair to say, an intense commitment to the avoidance of nuclear war of all forms, especially a major nuclear war. States with insignificant power may have a better understanding of the limits of national power in the nuclear age than stalemated nuclear states who also possess insignificant usable power, but are slower to shed illusions about the adequacy of national power because of the enormous potential for destruction at their disposal.

Some rather elementary technical observations about a no-first-use proposal seem pertinent. First of all, there are many relevant contexts for analysis. A no-first-use proposal may be considered as an attempt to construct a rule that will bind only the existing members of the nuclear club or to construct a rule that will operate as a constituent of universal order—an adjunct to the Charter norms governing the use of force. However, it may also be useful to consider a no-first-use proposal as a means to stabilize a variety of bilateral contexts or as a possible unilateral measure. As a unilateral measure, a no-first-use position may make sense for a state that would benefit from a clarification of its intentions; it may be also morally beneficial for a state able to uphold its security interests without relying upon nuclear weapons. No-first-use standards are subject to somewhat differing analyses, depending upon whether unilateral, bilateral, multilateral, or universal forms of the proposal are being considered.

A proposal of no first use need not be understood as consisting only of a declaration of intent. It is true that its adoption could be facilitated by the absence of any need to devise compliance machinery. This potential simplicity is perhaps subject to some qualification. If the proposal is envisaged in the form of an agreement, then it would be at least plausible to contemplate a variety of demands for the inclusion of provisions that establish a common procedure of implementation: for instance, a constitutional or Charter amendment, a legislative enactment, an oft-repeated pledge of executive intent, a specified readjustment of respective defense systems that accord most fully with adherence to a no-first-use posture, or an indoctrination of the public and of military officers that encourages a continuing and a serious adoption. If an implementation procedure is added to the mere declaration of intent, then it is evident that formidable problems of negotiation and compliance are likely to arise. The adoption of simultaneous unilateral measures circumvents some of these obstacles, since each participant does by way of implementation only what it wishes, although informality would deprive a no-first-use standard of some support for its claim to establish a new rule of order. Obviously, there is a wide difference between the adoption of a unilateral measure (especially if, as is probable, it were hedged about by qualifications) and the acceptance of a negotiated regime that added a variety of confidence-building requirements to a declaration of intent. A standard of this sort derives its effectiveness from the interactive processes of action and reaction on the part of major states. If a variety of steps are taken to implement a pledge, it then becomes a more reliable basis for reciprocating action by others in the system.

However, the difficulty in securing agreement on implementation standards need not nullify the campaign to veer United States policy away from its present dependence upon initiating use of nuclear weapons, most obviously upon tactical nuclear weapons in Europe. The renunciation of "germ warfare" rests upon declarations of intent, reinforced by moral revulsion; the effect is to create certain new expectations about permissible methods of military combat. In a variety of circumstances, these largely self-imposed restraints are challenged, or even overcome, by measures of expediency, often called "military necessity." Nevertheless, the advance acceptance of a limit, even if unaccompanied by sanctions or compliance machinery, acts as a marginal deterrent, helps to vindicate a punitive response, and perhaps even mobilizes a community response in favor of the victim. This is the status today of norms prohibiting aggression across international frontiers. The existence of these norms is itself a factor in the formation of a response and should enter into the calculations of a rational aggressor. The community responses to aggression in Suez and Korea are likely to influence potential aggressors to choose methods other than armed attack across a recognized international frontier. Thus, the mere act of drawing a line between what is permissible and what is prohibited, provided that the line corresponds with community values and is easily visible, may improve the quality of social order. Such a conclusion is based upon a more general analysis of the character of order in a decentralized social system, relying heavily upon objective limits that are visible to and traditional among all actors without elaborate interpretation. It can be suggested, therefore, that even a declaratory prohibition on the first use of nuclear weapons is a considerable gain with regard to the stability of the system as a whole, but not necessarily of a particular actor. Therefore, if it improves the relative strength of aggressive actors then this adverse consequence should certainly be taken into account. Nevertheless, it is important to distinguish between the advocacy and adoption of a declaration and the construction of a regime of order—that is, a declaration plus an appropriate system of implementation.

A no-first-use proposal that is considered in its declaratory form has certain important disarmament consequences. Even if the proposal takes the form of a negotiated international agreement, there is no need to design an elaborate system of inspection and control. A gross violation, as such, is immediately identifiable. The security system of states would be based upon the availability of an adequate response to a violation. It is thus possible to conceive of a rather simple international agreement. However, any effort to clarify the concept of "use" (supposing it to include the notion of "threat") would present major problems of definition and negotiation: is it a "threat" if nuclear weapons are redeployed with the evident objective of influencing the political behavior of other states, or if one side doubles the production of nuclear weapons? If "threat" is excluded from the concept of "use," some main objectives of the proposal are sacrificed: namely, the elimination of missile-rattling in periods of international crisis, and the strengthening of the threshold between nuclear and nonnuclear weapons. This whole problem disappears, of course, in the event that the proposal is advocated as a unilateral measure, for then the state that acts unilaterally can adopt whatever description of "use" it deems necessary.

It is not simple to clarify the concept of "use" beyond the crude image of detonation. If, as Professor Tucker suggests, the idea of "use" must be extended to include "threats," then the specification of a standard or the identification of a violation is very difficult to achieve without the creation of international machinery that is entrusted with the job of determining violations by deciding what patterns of words or acts amount to a "threat." Moreover, if a violation in the form of a "threat" is found to have taken place, what kind of responses short of abrogation or counterthreat can be developed? This difficulty suggests the more general response problem of making provision for a proportionate response. In the context of a no-first-use proposal, it must be emphasized that a violation of the rule of the agreement does not liberate the other side from all other rules. American notions of self-defense have been subjected to persuasive criticisms because limitless claims are deemed to be justifiable after (or in view of the fact that) the aggressor has violated the prime norm. It would be undesirable to regard a first use of nuclear weapons in violation of a declaration or agreement as entitling the victim to make unlimited subsequent uses. Only a proportionate response should be authorized. This is part of a general policy to construct secondary, tertiary, and quartanary rules of order in the event that primary, secondary, and tertiary rules are broken. We want as many firebreaks as possible in a highly inflammable forest so as to minimize the extent of damage in the event that a fire does break out, even though our primary effort is fire prevention.

Unlike the test ban negotiations, the dominant issues raised by a no-first-use proposal would foster an illuminating public debate. The arguments for and against the adoption of a no-first-use proposal would clarify the nature and implication of existing United States defense commitments and strategies. This kind of debate would also assist the

more educated portions of the public to form conclusions, or at least
to develop opinions about value priorities. This is almost impossible
today. The public consideration of a ban on nuclear testing—the only
major disarmament issue that has yet entered the realm of public debate—is hindered by the complex technical questions that surround
the problems of detection and reliability and the need for highly classified information in order to evaluate the prospects and needs for military research and development. A debate on no first use would have
considerable pedagogical value regardless of how it was resolved. This
is not a trivial gain, especially for a democratic society. All too often
in the recent past, the issues of war and peace have seemed so complex
that the public has dealt with them emotionally, apathetically, or not
at all. Part of the confusion arises, I think, because Communist-led
peace movements have blurred the distinction between the cold war
and the quest for peace. The recommendations of the Stockholm
Peace Proclamation, for example, approximate a no-first-use proposal,
and yet any association with the document has come to be considered
a sign of "disloyalty." Many people confuse Communist participation,
perhaps even sponsorship, with the merits of the substantive plan. Other
responsible people are perplexed by why it is "disloyal" to be in favor
of prohibiting the use of nuclear weapons and hence, bewildered, they
shun the subject altogether as unfit for normal civic awareness. Discussion of a no-first-use proposal might enable a more responsible public consideration of a whole class of disarmament issues. The society
as a whole must take a stand on policies that commit the United States
to the nuclear defense of Western Europe. This is a question of priorities; it is an issue that cannot be properly entrusted forever to resolutions by experts without severing the operation of our government from
its justifying premises.

Prolonged ignorance generates moral numbness. The nature of contemporary war requires the formation of a new morality of rights, duties, and limits. There is such a thing as moral obsolescence. Informed
advocacy of or opposition to a no-first-use proposal presupposes an
interpretation of the interplay of dominant military, political, and moral
commitments. For this reason, wholly aside from the substantive case
that can be made on its behalf, it deserves attention as a disarmament
measure.

Yet another aspect of argument is relevant. Certain tendencies in
international affairs presently incline the system toward eventual catastrophe unless they are both curtailed and reversed. The most dangerous
tendency concerns the interaction of things and attitudes. The development and spread of things—technology—seems subject to little hu-

man intervention; expansion seems irreversible, although perhaps the rate can be tempered. Such a realization generates gloomy predictions about the spread and the further refinement of nuclear weapons as well as additional weapons of mass destruction. The second variable, human attitudes, although also resistant to dramatic changes of direction, seems to be somewhat more responsive. The most optimistic aim of no-first-use proposals is, as Professor Tucker avers, an attempt to effectuate a gradual reversal of the major states' attitudes toward nuclear weapons. If successful, the formation of new attitudes might lead to all sorts of adaptations to the dangers of nuclear weapons, including loyalty to new kinds of social units as well as the emergence of new parameters for human conflict. This assertion is not meant as a prediction. Rather, it is a plea to check certain negative tendencies in the existing system at a vulnerable place. A no-first-use policy provides a good instrument for such a strategy. No past system of international reconciliation and threat has been able to avert an eventual breakdown. There is no reason to suppose that nuclear deterrence is qualitatively superior to other deterrence systems that have been developed throughout the history of international relations. However, the cost of a major failure by deterrence to maintain nuclear peace is so high that it makes imperative a search for ways to remove the capability for nuclear warfare from the system. A no-first-use proposal might contribute to the safety of the existing security system and, at the same time, foster a transition to a new system of international relations in which national military capabilities were drastically reduced. Despite these potentialities, a no-first-use position does not promise much right away, nor does it ask states to give up any tangible instruments of power or to cease the protection of their existing network of interests.[4]

A proposal to prohibit a first use of nuclear weapons raises a series of crucial and complicated problems of military defense and alliance cohesion that would have an impact on United States foreign policy. Can the United States defend Europe without nuclear weapons? Can the United States deter Soviet provocation in Europe and elsewhere without keeping open the possibility of a nuclear response? Would NATO collapse in the event that a no-first-use position is adopted?

[4] It asks states to say something and to take certain internal steps to make credible these words of intention. This may have a considerable impact on certain security interests in Europe. The United States would, for example, have to renounce its option to rely upon a nuclear defense against a conventional attack. In this sense the loss of freedom of action amounts to a serious diminution of power, especially if the declaration of intent is credible. But it is loss of discretion, not involving a visible destruction or transfer of capability to some supranational agency of control. For this reason it does not symbolize the decline of national sovereignty as strongly as do many other disarmament measures.

Can the United States protect India and contain China over the next decades without the threat of nuclear weapons in response to conventional military attacks?

There is no substantial evidence available that indicates a Soviet intention, even in the absence of nuclear weapons, to seek a military conquest of Europe except, perhaps, as a part of a general war with the United States or the West. The specter of a mass Soviet attack on Europe has dominated our strategic imagination without disclosing direct evidence that supports the reality of the danger. Until quite recently, it has blinded us to other dangers and to the more imminent security threats that exist at the subconventional and guerrilla levels of military operations.

Any remarks about the effect of a no-first-use declaration upon the political and military risk-taking of other states is exceedingly conjectural. It would depend, among other things, upon the degree to which the declaration could be relied upon; a common-sense logic suggests that the greater the implementation, the greater the prospects of adherence. If we assume that the prospects of adherence despite pressure and provocation are quite good, is an expanding or aggressive nation likely to assume added risks—that is, risks that are tenable because a no-first-use declaration has been made? Such a concern assumes an almost univocal direction of foreign policy with political expansion as the supreme goal. A major argument in support of no first use is that it might help slightly to change the perceptions and attitudes of foreign elites and their publics. This is part of a broader strategy toward the reorientation of perceptions of national self-interest. The process of analysis that would lead to an adoption of a no-first-use position would be, in most cases, conducive to the formation of peace-minded and world community attitudes.

Actually, the fear of an accelerated military risk-taking subsequent to the adoption of a no-first-use proposal seems misplaced. It assumes a subtle calculation of responses that is almost impossible to envision, much less to perform, as well as a mechanical process of causation.

Insubstantial evidence exists to support the belief that the threat of a nuclear response is essential to, or even effective as, a deterrent of Soviet and Chinese expansionist policies. There is little evidence that the present danger of a nuclear war spiraling out of a local subnuclear war is perceived as a reason for restraint. For one thing, the tactics of Communist advance, at least for the present, do not depend upon intense provocation.[5] Therefore, a threat of nuclear response,

5 The 1962 attempt by the Soviet Union to deploy missiles in Cuba stands forth as an apparent exception. But the Soviets' willingness to withdraw their missiles suggests, in part at least, an unwillingness to carry provocations close to the nuclear

even if made, is scarcely credible. Furthermore, there is no indication that the United States needs to rely upon activating such fears in order to maintain its security interests, except to defend itself and its allies against a nuclear attack. Europe may not agree and thus may demand a more formidable response to a threat of Soviet conventional attack. This may lead, it is admitted, to the noninclusion of Europe in a no-first-use system and to the development of an independent European nuclear deterrent.[6] A continental capability, as distinct from a series of national capabilities in Europe, may interfere with the prospects of universality for a no-first-use rule, but it will clarify the differences between the security interests of Europe and the United States. A more stable alliance could develop from the separation of common and opposed interests than will be possible as long as there is only a facade of Euro-American identity of interests.

These matters cannot be gone into further here. It may be worthwhile to point out that, even if the United States adoption of a no-first-use proposal is sufficiently important to generate an independent European defense system, this is not *necessarily* undesirable. Among other considerations of importance to arms control would be the effect of European nuclear independence upon the disposition to use nuclear weapons first. Although Europe might avoid making a no-first-use declaration, her position of nuclear inferiority would inhibit any inclination to initiate a nuclear exchange. In certain respects, Europe would be less able to rely upon a nuclear defense system than it is today, precisely because of the total or partial withdrawal of the United States. In fact, an independent European nuclear force would, by virtue of its inferiority, be limited to minimum deterrence strategies. This inferiority might conceivably expose Europe to various subtle forms of aggression. Such an exposure is one of the political risks of a no-first-use proposal, but it does not seem so great as to outweigh the gains in stability and transformation.

It should be kept in mind that a declaratory measure of no first use aims only to deter the marginal decision to resort to nuclear weapons.

---

threshold. Also the deployment itself appeared to be more an attempt to strengthen the Soviet deterrent than a part of an aggressive military design. Is there reason to suppose that the Soviet response to the United States ultimatum would have been different if a no-first-use declaration had been in force? Certainly the Soviet Union's retreat can be explained in terms of its military inferiority in the potential battlefield area (i.e. Cuba and the Atlantic Ocean); this inferiority had nothing much to do with whether states had pledged themselves not to use nuclear weapons first.

[6] Europe as actor, not as arena; that is, the Soviet Union and the United States would be bound by the renunciation in the event of European combat, but the states of Europe will refuse to renounce their first-use prerogatives.

As a consequence we do not acquire much protection against a determined aggressor or a desperate defender. Of course not, because no normative restraint can *by itself* significantly influence decision-making in extreme situations. The assumption of the marginal risk of a nuclear response bears such an indefinite relationship to the existence or absence of a no-first-use proposal that it is hard to regard this as a serious argument in opposition. The risk-taker, whether concerned about maintaining a nuclear defense against a conventional attack or about the escalation of a local war, is unlikely to be able to know (even if, as is unlikely, the problem comes to be perceived in this way) how to assess the impact of the self-restraining declaration against the use of nuclear weapons upon another state in a period of crisis. There is no evidence available to indicate that the prohibitions upon gas and germs have ever encouraged the assumption of additional military risks. Clearly the relevance of nuclear weapons to war today is deeply integrated with military planning. This has never been true for chemical and biological poisons. Nevertheless, it remains difficult to suppose that the military temperament, always suspicious of disarmament moves, would trust the willingness of a state to comply with a no-first-use declaration in adverse conditions. At least, it is difficult to envision the assumption of new military risks on this basis.

This does not mean that the declaration is worthless. As has been stated, a no-first-use declaration clarifies strategic positions and moral commitments; it opens up a debate that might eventually modify public attitudes toward war and peace and toward the development of a new world order; and it seeks to challenge the inertia of the international system—an inertia that has never maintained permanent peace nor has for very long evaded a crisis culminating in a costly and brutal breakdown. The prospect of these benefits makes a no-first-use proposal an attractive disarmament proposal at this time, especially because negotiations can begin with a statement by Premier Khrushchev —almost standard Soviet rhetoric—that amounts to a unilateral no-first-use declaration: "We are maintaining our rockets armed with the most powerful thermonuclear weapons in constant combat readiness, *but the Soviet Union will never be the first to set these weapons in motion and unleash a world war.*"[7] A similar statement of intention has accompanied each major nuclear test explosion of mainland China, up through June of 1967.

1965

[7] *New York Times*, July 20, 1963, p. 2 (emphasis supplied).

PART FOUR

A DISARMING WORLD

Introduction

MANAGING international violence in the existing international system has been the traditional domain of international lawyers. But concern with the dangers and nature of war and the costs of peace in the nuclear age has led jurists and even statesmen increasingly to contemplate with favor alternate international systems in which sovereign states would lose their almost unrestricted control over the use of military power. This loss of control can come about in a number of ways, but the one most frequently considered has been the drastic disarming of states and the concomitant building up of an international police force operating under supranational auspices.

There is no immediate prospect of substantial disarmament. The familiar difficulties connected with negotiating such a disarmament agreement, difficulties associated with mutual suspicion and a concern that the disarmament process might weaken some states more than others, create situations in which a state might capitalize on its relative increase in military strength at the expense of other disarming states. More fundamental even than these seemingly intractable problems of achieving mutually acceptable formulas for bringing about disarmament and supervising compliance with agreed terms, are the problems of shifting the political consciousness of governments and their populations away from a reliance on the security functions of the sovereign state. This reliance has been built up over the centuries to such a degree that it does not seem likely to alter except possibly under the impact of further large-scale warfare. A part of this reliance on the sovereign state arises from an uncertainty about the alternative forms of security that could be expected to emerge in a disarming and disarmed world. It thus appears appropriate to consider whether it would be possible to achieve comparable or greater security for vital interests in a disarming world. Military power is now used to guard the weak states of the world against certain forms of coercion. If this military power is reduced and eventually either eliminated altogether or transferred to the control of international institutions, then it might appear that the security of the weaker states would be gravely compromised by disarmament, as well as the geopolitical position of those powerful states interested in upholding the approximate prevailing international *status quo*. Such an anticipation of the impact of disarmament assumes that a revisionist (or expansionist or aggressor) state is, under modern conditions as explored in Part II, able to take advantage of the revolutionary situations found in foreign societies on the basis of a far smaller and less overt military input than is needed by the conservative state that is trying to prevent civil strife or to neutralize an intervention in favor of an antiregime faction. As interventionary diplomacy is the crucial arena of current conflict among sovereign states, any serious commitment to disarm must probably assure rival states that their geopolitical position will not be worsened by disarmament, as well as of course assuring all states that their national security in the strict sense will not decline. Most of the existing literature on disarmament is devoted only to security in this latter, narrow sense, whereas the study undertaken in Chapter XV examines, especially from the perspective of the United States, security in the broader, geopolitical sense. Chapter XV was written in the political setting surrounding the United States draft proposals for a general and complete disarmament treaty in 1962. As such, looking back upon it from the vantage point of 1968 there is an acceptance in the chapter, that now appears to me peculiar, of the logic of the cold war as developed from the Western perspective and an exaggerated assumption that the problems of world order were almost all reducible to the struggle between the United States and the Soviet Union. This bipolarism of the early 1960's has been increasingly displaced by a polycentric interpretation of international conflict.

XV. The Control of International Violence in a Disarming World

THIS CHAPTER analyzes the connection between drastic disarmament and international security. Special emphasis is placed upon the security of sovereign states vulnerable to intervention. The Great Powers were quite successful in maintaining peace and security in the Afro-Asian world during the colonial period. The attainment of national independence for the countries of Africa and Asia since World War II has not been accompanied by the achievement of national security. Relatively selective and invisible covert means of coercion can be applied to manipulate the policies and politics of these states. Some measure of security for some of these states has been provided by alliances with the military backing of the United States and ex-colonial states.

The underlying question posed in this chapter is whether drastic disarmament will make it easier for the government of a highly motivated expanding state to undermine the public order of states within the Afro-Asian world. This question also engenders inquiry into whether specific countermeasures cannot be built into the disarmament process to reduce the incentives of potential aggressors and, thereby, the dangers to the independence of potential victims of aggression. The whole process is further complicated by the fact that many Afro-Asian societies are highly likely to experience civil strife regardless of whether or not disarmament takes place. Therefore, it is difficult to isolate the distinctive impacts of disarmament carried to various depths upon the security of these states. Nevertheless, it appears worthwhile to explore these issues as part of the effort to consider in detail the real security risks of disarmament and then proceed to create, if possible, the means to cope with these risks.

To confront this class of problems is to begin the long intellectual and psycho-political process needed to evolve toward a world capable of disarming. Such an intellectual orientation on my part implies a belief that drastic disarmament is not presently feasible. To give a measure of concreteness, the Proposals of the United States of April 18, 1962 (as amended) consisting of an Outline of Basic Provisions of a Treaty on General and Complete Disarmament that were presented to the Eighteen-Nation Disarmament Committee at Geneva are used as models of what sort of formal framework is contemplated as suitable to a disarming world. (See Appendix B for text.)

I. Statement of the Problem: A General Introduction

Indirect aggression takes place whenever a nation makes substantial use of coercive tactics (other than the outright threat or use of military force) to influence the major policies or political structure of another sovereign state. The ordinary objective is either to help a non-incumbent elite gain preeminent power or to intimidate the incumbent elite. The aggressor normally seeks a fundamental erosion of the political independence and orientation of the target state. It is thus proper to identify indirect aggression on a spectrum of influence as sharply distinct from the routine attempts to use national power to influence the policies of foreign states in an interdependent world. There are no clear boundaries between permissible levels of influence and objectionable levels that are to be treated as a form of aggression; the problems of identification may be increased if groups in the domestic society welcome or even solicit the aggressor's presence. The Soviet Union and China have been guilty of indirect aggression in the period since World War II; on a more limited scale other revisionist states such as the United Arab Republic and Ghana have committed indirect aggression. Nazi Germany, by clever use of Fifth-Column tactics, made successful and economical use of indirect aggression to achieve political expansion. Indirect aggression is usually practiced by an expanding national system and it is often justified by a radical ideology that is extremely hostile to the leading conservative international actors. This mode of expansion is not just a twentieth-century pattern. Witness, for instance, the reaction of the European monarchies to the American and French Revolutions during the first half of the nineteenth century.

Subversion is the implementation of the aggressive design by covert and illegal activities carried on in the target state. The normal strategy is to undermine the authority of the government by provoking and abetting defiance by dissident elements.[1] The eventual objective is to overthrow or infiltrate the existing regime and replace it or fundamentally reshape its orientation.

It is obvious that indirect aggression and subversion play a prominent part in the cold war. This suggests the importance of comprehending as well as we can how this prominence will change, if at all, in a variety of arms control and disarmament environments.

There is a facile readiness to assume that problems of regulating indirect aggression and subversion will grow more severe in a disarming world. For this reason it is commonly regarded as essential to build control machinery into a disarmament arrangement. This study will ap-

[1] "Subversion—the clandestine attempt to undermine a regime or a society beyond one's own borders—is not new but the Russians have perfected and expanded it; the Russian word *provokatsia* embraces not merely the exploitation of a situation for subversive ends but also the deliberate fabrication of the situation." Peter Calvocoressi, *World Order and New States*, New York, Praeger, 1962, p. 6.

praise this supposition. Such an appraisal needs to examine the entire regulatory problem and consider the availability of effective methods of control. It is a preliminary study, in the sense that adequate appraisal requires a country by country analysis that relates the degree of national vulnerability to the risks and incentives that inhibit or encourage the indirect aggressor-subvertor. However, at this stage, it seems helpful to complicate our perception of the problem so that we will be less content to accept an over-simple view of the relevant requirements of national interest. In this respect the history of United States understanding of the relation between inspection and disarmament provides a useful analogue.[2] It is part of the general experience that our understanding of the problems of disarmament is greatly improved by sustained contemplation and research; one consequence is that unqualified generalizations are discovered to be misleading. It is evident, for instance, that we will require a series of vivid national scenarios before we can confidently assess the impact of various kinds of disarmament upon the prevalence of indirect aggression and subversion. Existing understanding is so sparce that general postulates of correlation are almost meaningless. However, it is possible and illuminating to develop gradually a general method for perceiving these problems. This development will enable the identification of recurrent variables. A general framework might also encourage a more systematic and less impressionistic approach toward this subject-matter by building toward better and better evidenced generalizations.

It is quite probable that if the control of indirect aggression and subversion is allowed to remain a part of the United States negotiating position it will become a formidable obstacle to agreement with the Soviet Union on arms control and disarmament measures. This prospect does not argue for its removal, but it does suggest that it is important for us to know why it is necessary to inject this troublesome demand into a negotiating process that is already beset by many difficulties.

In these introductory pages an attempt is made to describe briefly the plausible reasons that have prompted the United States to request treaty inclusion. These reasons are both alternative and overlapping explanations. As always, the adoption of policy here, as elsewhere, requires some comparison of the risks and costs that attend various alternatives. How much are we willing to compromise a national position on the proper treatment of indirect aggression so as to improve the over-

---

2 This progression may be perceived by comparing the sophistication of the Woods Hole Summer Study treatment of the inspection issue, *Verification and Response in Disarmament Agreements,* Summary Report, Annex Volumes I and II, The Institute for Defense Analyses, November 1962, with earlier discussions of the same subject matter.

all prospects for reaching a general disarmament agreement with the Soviet Union? How do the risks of the arms race compare with the risks of a disarming world?

The April 18th disarmament proposals of the United States require that parties to the treaty agree to refrain from indirect aggression and subversion throughout the life of the treaty.[3] The naked *pledge* of Stage I is to be *implemented* by rules and arrangements adopted under the auspices of the International Disarmament Organization (IDO) during Stages II and III.[4] It is thus necessary to assess the significance of indirect aggression and subversion in a disarming world. This suggests the need to take account, among other matters, of apparently inconsistent objectives: the discouragement of indirect aggression and subversion and the facilitation of peaceful change. An inquiry of this sort assumes that it is undesirable to establish a rigid political environment as a concomitant of the acceptance of general disarmament commitments. Stability in a disarming world, as in an armed one, must be based upon equilibrium mechanisms that balance the benefits of preserving existing forms of social order against the demands and pressures for social change. Thus it is assumed that we are seeking in a disarming world a situation in which national communities are less vulnerable to external penetration and yet not so invulnerable as to be able to resist indefinitely pressures for changes in the existing social, political, and economic distribution of power, especially when these changes are necessary to realize a widely shared conception of fundamental rights.

There is, however, an ambiguity that is deeply embedded in the subject matter of this study. As such, it deserves identification at the outset. It dominates and beclouds any consideration of indirect aggression

---

[3] For the text of the April 18th Proposals, officially called Outline of Basic Provisions of a Treaty on General and Complete Disarmament in a Peaceful World, As Submitted by the United States of America to the Eighteen-Nation Disarmament Committee at Geneva on April 18, 1962, amended on August 6 and 8, 1962 and on August 14, 1963, see Appendix B. For the text of the analogous Soviet proposals of March 15, 1962 see *Documents on Disarmament 1962*, Washington, Government Printing Office, Vol. I, pp. 103-27. A revised Soviet set of Proposals was submitted to the Eighteen-Nation Disarmament Committee on September 22, 1962; the text is in Vol. II, pp. 913-38. These revised proposals were amended on February 4, 1964 to some slight extent, see *Documents on Disarmament 1964*, p. 22.

[4] The *pledge* is the formal commitment to refrain; its *implementation* involves the adoption of methods to assure that conduct corresponds as closely as possible to the pledge. It is the familiar problem of closing the gap between "the law in the books" and "the law in action." Throughout this chapter the distinction should be kept in mind for the negotiation of a rule of conduct is quite different from the effective control of conduct, especially when the rule attempts to prohibit behavior that is previously approved of or tolerated by a substantial part of the community. For some members of the Soviet bloc the effective restraint of "indirect aggression" is probably as distasteful a course of action as is a legal decision requiring racial integration to members of the white oligarchy of a Southern state.

and subversion, and it is especially troublesome in the context of disarmament negotiations. The depth of the ambiguity may be attributed, in part, to the failure to give much detailed attention to the following question.[5] Just what does the United States expect to achieve by asking the Soviet Union to accept these treaty provisions dealing with indirect aggression and subversion? There are, as will be indicated briefly, several plausible, yet distinct objectives, the acceptance or rejection of which is exceedingly important not only for a better understanding of the problem and for the development of the appropriate position papers, but for an appraisal of the likelihood, nature, and seriousness of Russian resistance. At the root of this problem is a central disagreement between revolutionary and *status quo* societies about the use of coercion to promote social and political changes in foreign societies.[6] This disagreement is over issues of wider scope than the cold war. The various attitudes of nations towards the quantum and type of coercion that can be properly used to compel the Republic of South Africa to end apartheid politics illustrate the range and diversity of outlook. The United States, although less so than most of Western Europe, opposes at this stage any coercion against South Africa, whether undertaken by the United Nations or by some other combination of actors, that is more drastic than censure. The Afro-Asian states and the Sino-Soviet bloc appear ready to advocate as much external pressure as can be generated to compel South Africa to eradicate as quickly and as basically as possible the racist basis of its government.[7]

This illustration highlights, I think, a serious conflict that is temporarily hidden by the abstractness of the negotiating request that the participants in a general disarmament arrangement agree to renounce indirect aggression and subversion. This conflict will come to light, it is felt, as soon as the United States makes it clear how it proposes to *implement* the pledge. The pledge standing by itself is not seriously incompatible with the Soviet Union's own proposals for world order that have always included a comprehensive definition of aggression which

[5] There are no detailed accounts of the significance of indirect aggression for world politics and international order. Three shorter treatments help to identify and contour the problems: Calvocoressi, *op.cit. supra*, note 1; Samuel P. Huntington, "Patterns of Violence in World Politics," in Huntington, ed., *Changing Patterns of Military Politics*, New York, Free Press, 1962, pp. 17-50; George Modelski, "The International Relations of Internal War," in James N. Rosenau, ed., *International Aspects of Civil Strife*, Princeton, Princeton University Press, 1964, pp. 14-44.

[6] The character of this disagreement is developed in Falk, "Revolutionary Nations, and the Quality of International Legal Order," in Morton A. Kaplan, ed., *The Revolution in World Politics*, New York, Wiley, 1962, pp. 310-31.

[7] Despite this shared enthusiasm, secondary objectives of the two groups of states are generally quite different: the Afro-Asian states are usually interested primarily in obtaining control of the government for a black neutralist elite, whereas the Soviet bloc seeks to bring an elite with a radical social and international ideology to power.

extends to catch the more flagrant forms of indirect aggression and sub-version.[8] The incompatibility arises rather from the difference between the way in which the Soviet Union and the United States interpret the rules of the game applicable to different forms of participation in the internal affairs of foreign states.[9]

The United States emphasizes its discretion to provide incumbent governments everywhere with military and nonmilitary assistance, in-cluding the participating presence of United States military personnel in substantial numbers.[10] The Soviet Union condemns this pattern of participation as neocolonialism, although it practices it wherever it is in secure control (e.g. Hungary, 1956), and as imperialist aggression, for it is claimed often to inhibit the seizure of power by groups with a wider base of popular support within the society. In contrast, the Soviet Union evidently considers that it can help any insurgent cause in a non-Communist society, vindicating these practices as support for just wars of national liberation. It is precisely these "just wars," so far as their outcome is influenced by Communist participation, that the United States has in mind as instances of indirect aggression and subversion; one thinks particularly of the internal wars in Southeast Asia and the agitational activities of the Communist movement elsewhere in the world. And it is in precisely these situations that the West and the Sino-Soviet system experience their most violent confrontations. The West plays a usual, although not an invariable (viz. Iran, Guatemala) role, as protector of the *status quo*. So far as this undertaking involves the frustration of Communist penetration—from without (indirect aggres-sion) and from within (subversion)—United States global strategy

[8] Cf. Soviet draft definitions of aggres-sion which have been submitted on several occasions to international organizations since 1933. For instance, the Soviet draft resolution submitted to the 1956 Special Committee on the Question of Defining Ag-gression contains the following second principal paragraph: "2. That state shall be declared to have committed an act of in-direct aggression which: (a) encourages subversive activity against another State (acts of terrorism, diversionary acts, etc.); (b) promotes the fomenting of civil war within another State; (c) promotes an internal upheaval in another State or a change of policy in favour of the ag-gressor." (A/AC.77/L/4).

[9] There is also considerable insincerity evident when one compares the definition proposed by the USSR with its ideology, doctrine, and practices.

For a fuller discussion of these issues see Section IV.

For a useful statement of the Soviet position—what it condemns and what it vindicates—see *International Law,* a text-book for use in law schools prepared by joint authorship under the auspices of the Soviet Institute of State and Law, pp. 401-05. For Western responses see Albert Gore, "Principles of International Law Concern-ing Friendly Relations Among States," *U.S. State Department Bulletin,* XLVII, 1962, pp. 972-79; Edward McWhinney, "Peaceful Co-Existence and Soviet-Western Interna-tional Law," 56 *American Journal of International Law* 951-70 (1962).

[10] There have been many domestic criti-cisms of United States interventionary practices in recent years. One of the most persuasive of these has been the book of Edmund Stillman and William Pfaff, *Power and Impotence,* New York, Random House, 1966.

[446]

would receive side benefits from the adoption of any effective measures to implement the pledged renunciation of indirect aggression and subversion. It cannot be emphasized too strongly or too often that it is not the pledge, but its implementation, that seems to be stating a radical demand for the reform of Soviet conduct in world affairs.[11] If the Soviet Union goes along with the serious implementation of the pledge it appears to be a definite relinquishment of its role as an *active* agent of revolutionary social change,[12] at least if it perceives, as is almost certain, the significance of the undertaking; it might still be able to pursue a role as passive agent through example and ideology. If such an interpretation is plausible, then it is well to appreciate its potential role in the negotiation and success of disarmament.

One set of possibilities would be that the United States entered disarmament with the understanding that the pledge would be implemented. However, unless major attention is given to assuring the success of the implementation procedure in Stage I it would be very easy for the Soviet Union to block implementation by frustrating the parliamentary machinery. As matters now stand the parties to the treaty are obliged in Stage I to "study methods of assuring states against indirect aggression or subversion"; in Stage II participating states are expected to "agree to arrangements necessary to assure states against indirect aggression and subversion." What if there is a refusal or inability to agree? What if the study in Stage I uncovers, as must be anticipated, an irreconcilable conflict over the adoption of methods to implement the naked pledge? How does the fulfillment of these provisions relate to the duty to comply with the hardware provisions or to proceed to subsequent stages of disarmament? Who decides?

Another set of possibilities, perhaps more likely, but not much less troublesome, is the prospect of achieving compromises on issues of implementation. Perhaps the Soviet Union would go along with the formulation of an authoritative definition to guide actors and facilitate an IDO or UN response, but it may refuse to coordinate this degree of verbal agreement with border control and delimitation, international "presences," and various tolerances for preemptive and neutralizing interventions by national, regional, and universal actors.[13] What should be the minimum and optimum United States requirements for imple-

[11] Cf. *supra*, note 8; the USSR has appeared to be far more willing to make the pledge in formal terms than has the United States.

[12] This is compatible with the softer version of "peaceful coexistence" developed by Premier N. S. Khrushchev in an article that appeared in *Foreign Affairs*: "On Peaceful Coexistence," xxxviii (October 1959), 1-18.

[13] There must be an improved procedure for equity jurisprudence and legislative intervention in an international system that wants to do away with force as an instrument of radical social change.

mentation? Certainly it may be the case, as has been frequently argued,[14] that a definition of prohibited activity without the institutions and sanctions to enforce it impartially, is worse than nothing at all. Present patterns of bilateral participation in internal strife frequently include an important and relevant characteristic: the United States must act much more overtly than the Soviet Union to achieve even a neutralizing effect. This means, of course, that interdictions based on acts might more readily interfere with the effort of the United States to defend the independence of societies vulnerable to indirect aggression and subversion than with the Soviet Union's politics of expansion. This apparent Soviet advantage from a mutual agreement to forego intervention is a central irony and it suggests some of the hazards that arise from attempts to regulate foreign participation in domestic societies—the central focus of indirect aggression and subversion. Some Western commentators argue that this conclusion is accentuated by the tendency of the United States to adhere rather scrupulously to legal obligations that are specifically undertaken, whereas the Soviet Union tends to be more opportunistic—by doctrine and practice—about the duty to obey applicable rules of law.[15] It is well, then, to contemplate that efforts to implement the pledge to renounce indirect aggression and subversion might be objectionable not only because they promise to place major obstacles on the path that might otherwise lead more quickly to disarmament, but more dramatically, because they might result in giving the Communists a more, rather than a less, favorable environment within which to expand their political base of power and influence.

If the difficulties just discussed were surmounted by examining *purposes* rather than *practices*, then presumably the United States, as concerned primarily with the prevention of additional Communist encroachment, would benefit from a regime of law that was designed to resist aggression. For it would become permissible to help the incumbent retain power (this support would not ordinarily involve an aggressive undertaking) and impermissible to instigate and assist insurgent groups. This discrimination in favor of constituted regimes runs the danger, even if acceptable, of inhibiting changes of intolerable social and political conditions, including, for example, those of East Europe or South Africa. Besides, such a legal position rests upon a pervasive behavioral asymmetry. It becomes not *what is done*, but the *purpose*

---

[14] E.g. see statement of James O. Murdock, United States delegate to the Inter-American Juridical Committee on this issue in *Instrument Relating to Violations of the Principle of Nonintervention,* Pan American Union, CIJ-51, 1959, pp. 19-29.

[15] Cf. Leon Lipson, "Outer Space and International Law," RAND Paper P-1434, 1958.

for which it is done that distinguishes the legal from the illegal.[16] It is significant that an emphasis on motive or purpose is rarely relied upon to determine guilt in domestic criminal law; however, an appraisal of the purpose generally influences the quantum of punishment.[17] Besides shifting the area of contention to an identification of what purposes are forbidden, there would develop a strong tendency to introduce partisan politics into the operations of whatever agency is established to determine whether a violation has actually taken place. For when an administering agency, here presumably the IDO, must vindicate its decision by reference to intentions rather than to acts, it moves away from a system of law based on objective standards and toward a law system that is molded by the forces of subjective appreciation. This shift does not appear to be a suitable approach for the international legal community to adopt as it is already quite beset by distrust, tension, and conflict. The need for maximum objectivity seems paramount if the system is ever to generate the confidence of antagonistic actors.

It is hoped that the preceding comments make clear that it is important to know *why* and *how* to include the subject of indirect aggression and subversion in a general disarmament agreement. To highlight the available range of choice we indicate a number of the possible answers that can be given to the question—*why should the United States ask the Soviet Union to implement a pledge to renounce indirect aggression and subversion as part of the disarmament process*? (Of course, one nontrivial response is that it is unnecessary, or even undesirable, to implement the pledge, or even to ask for it.) We will now discuss several significant objectives, distinct, but overlapping:

(1) An effective renunciation of indirect aggression and subversion would go a long way toward establishing the United States conception of world order, including especially its view of friendly relations between nations with different economic, political, and social systems. An implemented pledge is one way to frustrate Sino-Soviet dynamism that has been incorporated into a spuriously named doctrine of "peaceful coexistence," a doctrine adopted, in part, to disguise expansionist politics in a nuclear age. Such an American negotiating demand, in the context of disarmament, can be construed either as a condition precedent to signature and ratification or as an element of stability that is neces-

---

[16] Advocacy of this kind of asymmetry is stated forcefully by Maynard Smith in a short article, "After the Crisis," appearing in *Worldview*, VI (1963), 5-7. One feels that there is a failure to distinguish the perspective of the strategist or national policy-maker from that of the designer of legal order.

[17] Cases involving mercy killing often involve the conflict between sympathy with the motives of the defendant and the importance of sustaining rules based upon the behavior of the accused.

sary if the disarmament process is to succeed in keeping peace and order. If considered part of the process, then the United States is asking for a pledge in Stage I and serving notice that the pledge must be implemented effectively by Stage II. Either interpretation evidently ties a United States willingness to disarm significantly to a Soviet commitment to give up its active leadership of world revolution, and this must probably be taken to include the withdrawal of support and guidance for national Communist parties. How else could the pledge become an effective inhibition upon Communist tactics?

(2) The pledge provides participating nations with a flexible way to withdraw from negotiations of disarmament itself. For it is always easy to allege a violation of this kind or to make the demands for implementing methods unacceptable to the other side. It is in this sense that the issue of indirect aggression and subversion could come to be a Gordian knot with a strength equal to that of inspection controversies.[18] This prospect is especially plausible if nations retain the discretion both to characterize conduct of the other side as "indirect aggression and subversion" and to determine their own response; this potential for manipulation corresponds to the status of indirect aggression and subversion in the present world except that there is no treaty to invoke and no disarmament proposal or process to disrupt or to threaten.

(3) The inclusion may emphasize the dependence of disarmament upon a political foundation that is expected to dilute progressively the intensity of global patterns of conflict. Any major shift in the relative strength of the cold war blocs would probably end the prospects for further disarmament; for example, if India joined the Communist bloc or if East Europe left it. The pledge as a provision of the agreement makes this eventuality explicit. Any major shift in cold war affiliation would probably involve internal strife and external contact of such a character that the side adversely affected by the change would have some basis to attribute the loss to indirect aggression and subversion. Putting it in our negotiating position serves notice of the relevance of world politics to the success of disarmament, as it compels an awareness of the relation between disarmament and an improving political environment, as well as to spread the realization that disarmament creates risks of rearmament, risks that may under certain circumstances exceed the dangers of the present uncurtailed arms race. For instance, any political loss in a disarming world would almost certainly be explained

[18] A recent investigation of disarmament negotiations centers upon the insistence of each side upon holding "a joker" to block the consummation of an agreement: John W. Spanier and Joseph L. Nogee, *The Politics of Disarmament: A Study in Soviet-American Gamesmanship,* New York, Praeger, 1962.

by critics of disarmament as a consequence of disarmament; this might influence domestic politics in such a way as to increase the dangers of immoderate government and the influence of patrioteering pressure groups such as the John Birch Society or some future equivalent. It may be well to protect ourselves against these dangers by making a special effort to improve our control in a disarming world over the kind of activity that has so often served as the means for Communist expansion.

(4) The pledge and its implementation seek to overcome the *added* vulnerability of national societies to the tactics of indirect aggression and subversion in a disarming world. For disarmament *seems* to involve an improvement of Soviet opportunities that coincides with the impairment of American deterrent and defense capabilities, at least if the issue is the capacity to influence the outcome of domestic political struggles. This inference is one way to interpret the aspects of the military, geopolitical, organizational, and psychological situations that are favorable to Communist expansion in a disarming world.[19] Thus the implementation of the pledge by such methods as border control, demilitarized zones, supranational presences, and the like would serve to equalize the competitive position of cold war rivals in a disarming world. The demand is, in effect, that the Soviet Union take steps to give up the prospect of strategic political gains that would otherwise accrue to it as a side benefit of disarmament.

(5) Finally, such a pledge may operate as a request to clarify the ground rules in a disarming world and to identify the areas of prime disagreement that are likely to breed antagonism and crises during the course of disarmament. The negotiating period will serve to remind actors that the cold war is not likely to end as soon as we cross a disarmament threshold. Such a function of the provisions dealing with indirect aggression and subversion is quite different from that envisioned in objective (1) where the initiation of the disarmament process is made to hinge upon a prior agreement to create methods that will effectively terminate the most troublesome aspects of Soviet sponsorship of political protest movements in foreign societies. In (5) the main objective may be to establish a bargaining position or, perhaps, to clarify for oneself and one's allies what is and what is not expected to follow from the initial decision to disarm. This means that the negotiating request for treaty inclusion is subject to compromise, trade-off, or possibly even partial or complete withdrawal—especially as regards setting up the machinery that would be needed to implement the commitment to

[19] This hypothesis is examined in some detail in Section III of this chapter.

implement the Stage I pledge. That is, in the April 18th Proposals, there are three main steps envisioned: first, the pledge; second, agreement within the IDO on methods to implement it; and third, putting those methods into effective operation.

II. Fundamental Issues

1. It is important to realize that indirect aggression and subversion are not legacies of disarmament, but on the contrary exist as severe problems prior to any substantial form of negotiated disarmament. When legal control of various degrees is placed upon national discretion to build defense systems, then presumably the problems posed by indirect aggression and subversion change. But how? Significant disarmament involves such a basic change in the system of international relations that it can be expected to alter everything else. To acquire usable understanding we must try to discern how the changed international environment might plausibly affect the frequency, intensity, and success of the varieties of political action that interest us: namely, indirect aggression and subversion. It is, first of all, a matter of assessing whether various arms control and disarmament measures will increase, decrease, or leave unchanged the opportunities for initiating or defending against the kind of expansionist politics we have in mind when we refer to "the problem of indirect aggression and subversion." The impact cannot be described precisely. For one thing, it depends heavily upon the intentions of the potential indirect aggressor-subvertor and the resolve to defend of the target state and its principal allies. Such variables do not usefully generate predictive propositions. There is no way to explicate the subjective side of a nation's will to power or survival. Domestic crises, shifts in leadership, new perceptions of national interest make a projection of present attitudes, so far as even they can be known, unreliable and the anticipation of new attitudes far too conjectural. It is almost impossible to predict persuasively how the Soviet Union will behave in a disarming world, whether the process begins in 1975, 2000, or 2050. For a prediction depends upon the priorities accorded by the effective leadership of the USSR to such considerations as expansion, nuclear peace, disarmament, China, the West, higher living standards at home, ideological commitments. It is helpful, therefore, to refrain from trying to make elegantly simple statements about the behavior of political rivals in the altered environment brought about by disarmament. Is it then necessary to prepare for the worst in order to defend United States interests in a disarming world? An answer requires an act of judgment about the relative merits of disarmament and other approaches to national security. It is possible to guide this

judgment somewhat by suggesting the kinds of problems that may exist in a disarming world. Certainly in this sense it is useful to examine indirect aggression and subversion as one area of disarmament risks.

2. It is strongly recommended that general conclusions be built up on the basis of a series of specific observations. There is a temptation to overgeneralize the *distinctive* problems that can be associated with indirect aggression and subversion in a disarming world. This chapter contends that an understanding of these forms of international coercion should be appraised with respect to the specific characteristics of the anticipated impacts of various arms control and disarmament schemes at various time periods upon the basic patterns of world politics. How else can we begin to isolate what is truly distinctive? The concern is with how patterns of indirect aggression and subversion affect disarmament risks, not indirect aggression and subversion in general.

The position taken here is that the distinctive elements cannot be grasped by asking such questions as "How will disarmament affect the ability of the United States to control Communist subversion?" Rather one must narrow inquiry to a more restricted range of questions—"How is a regional disarmament plan for Europe that includes a 100-mile demilitarized swathe likely to affect the capacities during the 1970's of various nations in Western Europe to maintain internal security in periods of crisis?" or "What might happen to Turkish domestic and foreign politics in 1970 if United States military installations were removed?" "How would it change the present tactics or the opportunities of Turkish radicalism?" "What role would Moscow and Peking play in making these changes?" A discussion on this level of inquiry helps to uncover special problems of contingency planning. Although it is not possible to predict the precise course of events, it is usefully possible to anticipate plausible contingencies and thereby identify some of the special problems of response that arise in the course of reducing military strength. A convenient way to correlate the response problems with the level of military strength is to distinguish between Stages I, II, and III as they are portrayed in the April 18th Proposals. However, there is a need for an understanding of the same problems in a context of evaluation that employs a wider variety of arms control and disarmament models.

3. No. 2 recommends the use of case studies and scenarios as a way to vivify plausible subversion and indirect aggression contingencies in a disarming world. Such specifications enable suitable account to be taken of regional, national, and cultural variables in the course of outlining the risks and opportunities presented by the different types of critical situations that one might suppose would arise in the course of disarmament. Of

course, the anticipation of contingencies should be offset by the difficulty of imagining how the initiation of a disarmament process, at least if the process is designed to reach general and complete disarmament, will change the behavior, goals, and perceptions of principal actors. One central characteristic of a system change, such as is implied by qualitative disarmament, is that its general quality cannot be reliably anticipated; this uncertainty is itself one source of the pressures that can be expected to be mounted against disarmament. The general problem is well illustrated by the perplexities that attend a contemplation of indirect aggression and subversion.

4. An oversimplification states a basic difficulty. It is a difficulty that colors all speculative studies of problems in a disarming world: minor disarmament seems to have a negligible impact upon world politics, whereas major disarmament has such a fundamental impact as to be virtually unimaginable. This observation discloses limits that apply to the subject matter of this chapter. For any kind of partial measure or quantitative disarmament (no changes in basic strategic patterns of defense and response) there does not seem to be any firm effect upon indirect aggression and subversion. In contrast, a qualitative disarmament process proposes such a radical and organic revision of world politics as to make it almost impossible to anticipate usefully the revised security requirements that concern defense against indirect aggression and subversion. Disarmament measures would inhabit this radically altered environment.

5. There are two sets of disarmament risks that can be usefully distinguished: military risks and political risks. An illustration suggests the reality of the distinction. A Southeast Asian nation is beset by a Communist-oriented insurgency; the incumbent government requests military support from the United States of the kind now being given to South Viet Nam. It is a *military* problem to determine what kinds of support are militarily effective and whether our defense establishment permits the extension of such support at various stages of disarmament, given the prior claims of defense requirements for other security interests (e.g. the defense of Western Europe). It is a *political* problem to realize that the affiliation of a nation with the Sino-Soviet bloc in a disarming world will be attributed by domestic critics of disarmament to disarmament whether or not substantial evidence of a connection exists.

6. This political perspective suggests that requirements for the regulation of indirect aggression and subversion might be considerably higher in a disarming world not because there is an increasing vulnerability of target societies or an increasing willingness to exploit opportunities, but because of patterns of probable domestic political response

within the United States. Several propositions follow from this: first, a shift of political orientation from the West to the Sino-Soviet bloc would be attributed by significant, and perhaps dominant, domestic groups to the reduced military effectiveness of the United States in a disarming world; second, the disarmament process might be slowed down, abrogated, or reversed by such domestic criticism; third, the prospect of this response is affected, but not determined by, Communist behavior. Thus, a domestic revolution in an uncommitted nation, even without external support of significant proportions, would be widely perceived in the United States as an instance of Sino-Soviet perfidy if it ended by putting in control a government near the Castroist end of the political spectrum. The character of this political problem is interestingly, if disturbingly, independent of the realities of either the causal connection between disarmament and the success of the insurgency or between external or internal Communist support for the revolution and its success. The American perception of Castroism is very instructive in these respects, suggesting that it is the terminal orientation, and not the facts of conflict, that generate the authoritative popular interpretation of political revolution. One implication, then, of this line of thinking is that we need to look at the probabilities for radical social revolutions in general—independent of Communist objectives—in order to understand the possibly destabilizing effects of indirect aggression and subversion on disarmament. For the point made here, and it seems worth emphasizing by repetition, is that whether or not the Sino-Soviet powers actually help revolutionary causes abroad the American response is likely to blame and interpret the outcome upon indirect aggression and subversion. Therefore, the problem is broader than a matter of Sino-Soviet good faith, it involves also an understanding of how the United States is likely to explain any kind of adverse political change in a disarming world.

Perhaps, then, it is just as important to understand the dynamics of political conflict in critical societies that are presently outside the Communist orbit as it is to examine patterns of subversion and indirect aggression as objective phenomena in the cold war. Otherwise it is probable that we may mistake the nature of U.S. security requirements. What might turn out to be necessary is the improvement of many nations' internal security systems and the expansion and deepening of programs for social reform. If it is radical discontent and not the shipment of arms across borders or the training of guerrillas that is most likely to produce the kind of political outcomes that will be treated as the result of indirect aggression and subversion, then precautionary action must take due account of this. Of course, there is a substantial connection between the expansion of a revolutionary system like Communism and the capture of protest movements in conflicted societies, but it is well to realize that even if there was no Soviet exploitation of the link, the problem of indirect aggression and subversion would not disappear; it is a more complicated problem than the pacification of the Communist system.

7. The successful study of indirect aggression and subversion must combine several principles. First of all, the facts of diversity must be respected by identifying the relevant differences between regions, and within regions between nations. We have a sufficiently different set of problems in Southeast Asia, in Latin America, in Western Europe, in the Middle East, to make it a mistake to lump them together in an analysis of the problem or in offering recommendations for a solution. As well, we have different problems for various nations in Latin America depending upon many factors such as internal security capability, rate of economic development, strength of the Communist Party, degree of popular disaffection, tradition of violent protest, and so on. Case studies are needed to supplement the effort of this study to depict a general method of approach. One conclusion does emerge clearly, however: the problem of indirect aggression and subversion is not one problem but a series of problems depending upon the particular way in which these regional, national, and cultural variables interact; thus what is needed for the United States is not *a* solution but *a series* of solutions.[20] This multifaceted diversity counsels against all approaches that promise unified legal control of indirect aggression and subversion whether by definitional prohibition or by institutional control.

8. Comprehension of this diversity does not preclude legal control.

[20] There may, however, be groups of similar solutions. The relevant image is a tree with branches of more or less width, rather than a row of dissimilar flowers. A diagram suggests the connectedness, and yet preserves the diversity, of our presentation:

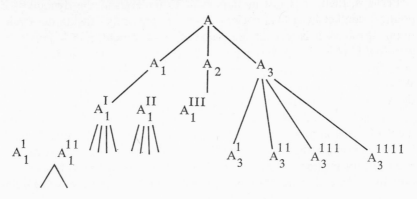

It merely influences the design for an appropriate legal regime in the direction of maximum flexibility. A major requirement is to have a variety of responses available from which to choose a particular one that is effective and yet not too destabilizing. Flexibility probably requires the retention of national discretion rather than its early transfer to the agency (IDO) administering the disarmament process. It does not preclude giving duplicatory or supplementary competence to the IDO. Such a conclusion produces a response apparatus for a disarming world that resembles what we have now. Security interests are expected to be primarily maintained by national responses, adapted to the changing international environment as the disarmament process proceeds. Therefore, it is not essential to weave much assurance into a treaty that the IDO will have adequate methods available to it to control indirect aggression and subversion. It is not that control is unimportant for the success of disarmament, but that it is too political in its character to be reliably susceptible to centralized control until the tensions characteristic for the cold war were no longer descriptive of the relations between the nuclear superpowers. This recognition would unburden both the negotiating process and the present expectations of Stage I implementation.

9. An insistence upon a comprehensive implementation of the pledge in Stage I suggests the need to clarify the political conditions that the United States seeks to attach to a major disarmament bargain; this means that disarmament must be considered in relation to other foreign policy objectives. Are we seeking to make the Soviet Union (and the Communist bloc) give up expansionist policies, maintain them on a predisarmament level, or reduce them in a progressive manner as disarmament itself proceeds? It is very important to keep these alternatives in contact with a discussion of the impact of disarmament upon the problems of indirect aggression and subversion. For we would need a different set of rules and implementing procedures for each set of assumptions made about the character of American foreign policy objectives. This aspect of indirect aggression is rather unexplored, especially in the context of contemplating an acceptable transition to a disarming world.

10. This need to clarify United States objectives suggests the complementary problem of assessing Soviet foreign policy objectives in a disarming world. Here, one is confronted by many difficulties caused by an emotional interpretation of Soviet behavior as a consequence of cold war tensions and hostilities and by the closed nature of Soviet society which increases the normal difficulties of assessing national motivations and objec-

tives.[21] It does seem possible, however, to make some suggestions for the improvement of the quality of discussion. We should not become obsessed with any single technique for an understanding of Soviet foreign policy objectives. This means, for one thing, that we should acknowledge the limits of our understanding and the processes of change which may alter the current Soviet priorities. To the extent that a coherent image of Soviet objectives is attainable it should be sought by combining a concern with Soviet ideological predispositions, doctrinal commitments, political capabilities, and actual behavior. It is not sufficient, although it may be helpful, to construct Soviet objectives on the basis of the 21 Conditions of Admission to the 3rd Communist International (as Approved by the Second Congress of the 3rd International at Moscow in 1920) or to rely fully upon the so-called New Communist Manifesto declared by the meeting of representatives of eighty-one Communist parties meeting in Moscow during November and December of 1960, or even the many statements of revolutionary strategy in the writings of Marx and Lenin.[22] It is also necessary to appreciate the significance of Communist nonparticipation in the Algerian civil war, Soviet withdrawal from Northern Iran, and Soviet willingness to accept a neutral Austria. We must seek, then, to assess Soviet intentions by independent examination of Soviet ideology, doctrine, and behavior, taking further account of regional and national variation based upon the noncomparability of opportunities and incentives for indirect aggression and subversion. Here, too, we must strive to put this analysis in the context of Soviet disarmament policy, particularizing, as before, inquiry in relation to the characteristics and impacts of various detailed proposals. It is strongly urged that we cannot understand the problems of indirect aggression and subversion so long as we insist upon a monolithic view of Soviet policy objectives in a disarming world. This, then, is a further part of the task of improving our knowledge by narrowing the scope of inquiry in such a way as to yield a *series* of Soviet or Communist objectives rather than offer a single all-embracing conclusion.

There are two subsidiary problems that concern the assessment of Communist objectives. First, Soviet withdrawal from the active leader-

[21] Cf. e.g. Robert Strausz-Hupé and associates, *Protracted Conflict*, New York, Harper and Brothers, 1959; *Soviet Conduct in World Affairs*, a selection of readings compiled by Alexander Dallin, New York, Columbia University Press, 1960; George Modelski, "The Communist International System," Research Monograph No. 9, Center of International Studies, Princeton University, December 1, 1960; with Erich Fromm, *May Man Prevail?*, New York, Anchor Books, 1961.

[22] For convenient compilation of recent Communist formulations, see *The New Communist Manifesto and Related Documents*, Dan N. Jacobs, ed., New York, Harper Torchbooks, 1962.

ship of the international Communist movement may merely have the effect of shifting authority to Peking. Thus assurance of Soviet compliance with the pledge may not reduce commensurately the dangers of Communist expansion that seem to be brought about by indirect aggression and subversion. Confidence in a control arrangement must include adequate methods of response to Chinese, as well as Soviet initiative; the condition of intra-bloc politics makes it less likely now, than a decade earlier, that the USSR can enforce its commitments and preferences on other bloc members. National Communist movements are likely to solicit support from wherever in the international Communist movement it is available.

The changing character of world Communism suggests a cognate problem. The degree to which either Moscow or Peking can or seeks to control the activity of many national Communist parties is uncertain. Thus the tactics of these parties may be increasingly a consequence of an independent calculation of the prospects of successful insurgency. This independence means that Communism may function in many environments as a domestic political force, but because of well-established habits of political perceptions in the West (cf. Section II, No. 5), domestic Communist activity, and certainly its success, will be perceived and attributed both to indirect aggression and subversion and to disarmament. Thus an assessment of Sino-Soviet or even bloc intentions is not enough. It is also necessary to think about the degree of independence of national Communist movements and their recourse to and participation in violent insurgencies.

It is also true that national revolutions that end with a Sino-Soviet orientation shift the international balance of power in the Communist direction, regardless of the explanation for this shift. And it may be that the political independence of nations depends more, not less, on the retention of equivalent power by the West in a disarming world. Thus, it is correct to consider any major adherence to the Communist bloc as incompatible with the U.S. commitment to disarmament as the best way to safeguard security interests that combine the quest for peace with the need to resist totalitarian encroachment.

11. There is also the problem posed by the necessary attempt to anticipate the perception and reality of emerging asymmetries that seem relevant to disarmament policy. Does disarmament, *as such*, enlarge, contract, or leave unaffected the opportunities for domestic Communist parties? To what extent? Which ones? Why? Or does Stage II and III disarmament reduce the will and capacity of the West and the United States to neutralize various Communist attempts at indirect aggression and subversion? Or, in contrast, does the atmosphere of a dis-

arming world cut some of the opportunities and incentives for indirect aggression and subversion? Where? Why? Does the geopolitical situation of the Sino-Soviet land mass give special advantages in a disarming world? Where? Why? To what extent? *In other words, how does disarmament of various types at different stages of completion change, if at all, the political and social terrain upon which patterns of indirect aggression and subversion take place?* And in what respect are these changes asymmetrical from the perspective of the cold war rivalry? If important asymmetries appear to emerge then in correlation with the considerations discussed in previous sections, it would probably be desirable to introduce offsetting controls into the disarmament structure. Thus, if American policy demanded that the status of these problems remain about what it is presently, and if the Soviets gained some special advantages by the initiation of the disarmament process, then it would be a requirement of an acceptable (to the United States) arrangement to neutralize these advantages by appropriate provisions in the control machinery. For instance, various techniques of border control might help to neutralize Sino-Soviet geopolitical advantage, if this appeared to be more usable in the political environment of the envisioned type of disarmament.

There is also a series of problems connected with the impacts of disarmament upon domestic revolutionary activity. Latin American dissident groups might step up revolutionary activity because *they considered* that disarmament would lessen the likelihood of a hostile American intervention, whether or not this was accurate or abetted by domestic or international Communist directives or support.[23] This is a part of the interpretative issue presented whenever it is necessary to decide whether or not to consider all revolutionary activity with leftist objectives as part of the indirect aggression and subversion problem. Is internal response or external support the critical variable for purposes of classification? Is the national security of the United States similarly jeopardized by any significant increase in the Communist bloc? Does the proscription of indirect aggression and subversion seek primarily to establish rules of international conduct or to protect national security during disarmament from deleterious changes in the political *status quo*? Is the character of foreign participation in a domestic revolution susceptible to IDO identification according to preestablished principles or should the United States insist on the discretion to make and act upon an *ad hoc* formulation of a national response? Answers to these ques-

---

[23] A suggestive essay on one aspect of the subject of this paragraph, with special reference to Latin America, has been written as a graduate seminar paper at Princeton University: Harold A. Feiveson and Charles N. Myers, "Indirect Aggression during the Initial Stages of Disarmament," January 19, 1963.

tions depend on policy and stability considerations that cannot be usefully weighted in this study (see Section IV, No. 35 for some effort to deal with these issues).

12. Problems of indirect aggression and subversion are part of a horizon of concern that is wider than the dynamics of "the confrontation" of the Soviet Union and the United States. Other nations may have strong incentives and opportunities to practice indirect aggression and subversion. One thinks, of course, of Peking China and Castro's Cuba, but it is also important to take account of Western temptations to undermine, at least by means of hostile propaganda, the control of Communist governments in East Europe, of the interest of African states in the subversion of incumbent governments in Rhodesia or the Republic of South Africa, and of various attempts by Middle Eastern nations to change the political orientation of hostile nations in their region. That is, indirect aggression and subversion are not just an aspect of Soviet-American relations, nor are they just modes of coercion brought into being by the cold war. In contrast, these problems are a pervasive aspect of the revolutionary quality of world politics, only one dimension of which is represented by the cold war. Thus it is important to be clear about what scope of control it is necessary to achieve in order to make various stages or types of disarmament work. Especially in Stage III, secondary indirect aggressor-subvertors may be in a position to generate dangerous forms of instability. Thus even if the cold war withers away as disarmament proceeds, it may still be crucial to build gradually a system of IDO and supranational responses to perceived or actual patterns of indirect aggression and subversion. For such purposes national responses by the United States may be insufficient or positively dysfunctional. The Congo operation already illustrates an occasion on which a supranational response promotes the national interest of the United States better than could a national response. If cold war discord began to diminish, it would be useful to have order-establishing responses available that minimized suspicions about a revived quest for political dominance in world politics. Presumably, the chief objective of the United States would be the protection of victims of aggression, not the establishment of increasing hegemony in a disarming world. This objective could often be reached better by restricting as narrowly as possible all national uses of coercion. Restraint would help, at the same time, to build up confidence and dependence upon the role of international institutions as the prime managers of international force in the advanced stages of disarmament.

13. If the objective of general and complete disarmament or Stage III disarmament is seriously envisioned, then it poses certain distinctive

problems for the design of control over indirect aggression and subversion. It would be necessary to imagine the status of these problems in a vastly different international atmosphere. For it seems highly unrealistic to contemplate Stage III disarmament in a world of conflict and hostility (cf. Annex C at the end of this chapter). Thus it seems that during the latter stages of disarmament the problems of indirect aggression and subversion must, as a political precondition to the decision to disarm below the level of a minimum nuclear deterrent, disappear from the international scene, at least so far as the relations between the major powers are concerned. But it is rather difficult to determine the extent to which this disappearance should be institutionalized in the administering machinery of disarmament. In fact, such analysis depends upon so many conjectures about the altered state of the world as to be almost valueless for guidance today. Some benefit may derive, however, from making evident the degree to which difficulties of anticipation limit one's capacity to design a rational control system for the entire disarmament process from a perspective dominated by an arms race and the cold war. If disarmament succeeds at all in its early stages, part of that success will be reflected in the adoption of a new set of perspectives by the leading national actors in world affairs. And it is with these changed perspectives that one must then try to meet the problems posed by what we now identify as indirect aggression and subversion. It is a serious mistake of analysis to assume either that disarmament can proceed very far without changing the pattern of cold war politics or to suppose that disarmament cannot proceed at all until the active manifestations of the cold war disappear. These two kinds of assumptions, so often implicit in the literature of disarmament, seem inconsistent with a realistic appraisal. Instead, it is urged that disarmament would be an important variable transforming in indeterminate ways the international scene, and that neither this prospect of influence nor its radical indeterminacy should be left out of analysis.

14. Political stability is obviously related to the success of the disarmament process. Instability can be generated by either too little or too much control over the opportunities for domestic revolution. A premise of this study is that the United States cannot enter safely into comprehensive disarmament unless it retains discretion to make national responses to instances of indirect aggression and subversion, especially if these instances are, or are perceived to be, part of the cold war struggle for international dominance. However, it would probably, nevertheless, be undesirable and unstable if the initiation of disarmament meant the virtual end of any possibility for staging a successful domestic revolution. The absence of a supranational legislature gives to the forces

of domestic revolution a special role as an instrument for social change in the international system. If the possibility of revolution is eliminated, it may not only extend the life expectancy of intolerable regimes but it may, as well, keep revolutionary pressures under control only until late in the disarmament process when their explosive outburst might be disastrously destabilizing. Assuring the availability of minimum opportunities for peaceful change (i.e. all fundamental changes in relations within or between societies achieved without threat or recourse to international force; therefore, a successful domestic revolution is, from the viewpoint of the international system of order a type of peaceful change provided that other nations do not substantially participate in it) is here conceived as a stability requirement that should not be separated from the effort to find solutions for the problems of indirect aggression and subversion. At least, it may be possible to tolerate revolutionary change in national arenas that are not the scene of cold war competition. Insurgencies are quick, however, to realize their need for external support and their ability to receive it by introducing the relevance of the cold war. Even a rebellion like the Kurd uprising in Iraq in 1962 displayed this tendency, its leader cajoling the West by proposing to turn otherwise to the East. Therefore, there are delicate problems contained in this subject that can only be hinted at here.

The relevance of the subject of peaceful change to the problems of controlling indirect aggression and subversion in a disarming world is usually stated as an aspect of the relationship between order and justice in world politics. It is important to find substitutes for force to achieve necessary and desirable changes between and within national societies. It is both unstable and unjust to accompany the decision to disarm and the policy to resist indirect aggression and subversion with a regime for world order that strives to maintain the international and intranational *status quo*. In a disarming world it might become easier for oppressive domestic governments to retain their control. Domestic protest movements often depend for success, in their struggle against the incumbent governments, upon varying amounts of external help and encouragement (cf. Annex B at the end of this chapter). If the control of indirect aggression and subversion leads to the elimination of interventionary politics, then it is probably important to find substitute methods to help promote changes that fulfill world community value standards. Increases in the responsibility of regional and international organizations for the solution of social problems, for the upholding of fundamental human rights, and for the control of domestic strife seem therefore to be desirable. In fact, this position can be summarized as one which favors accompanying the control of indirect aggression and subversion with a gradual and progressive endowment of supranational institutions with a legislative competence (cf. Annex A at the end of this chapter).

It is important to separate the indigenous pressures for radical change that exist throughout the world from Communist strategies of gaining influence over the exertion of these pressures. Thus intrastate violence to achieve social change is not just a matter of cold war politics. However, the dangers of escalating local violence makes it desirable to internationalize control over the course of civil strife as quickly as possible; this acknowledges the difficulty of treating revolutions as matters of exclusive domestic jurisdiction whenever there is significant and protracted recourse to techniques of political violence by organized insurgent groups.

However, it should be appreciated that a system of international response that relies only upon the request of the legitimate (or incumbent) government would tend to vindicate and maintain all domestic governments, even if totalitarian or oppressive. However, a response that depended upon value judgments would introduce the cold war into the midst of the primary task, already incredibly sensitive, of upholding domestic order or at least of sealing domestic violence off from foreign participation. This dilemma is a difficulty that arises from any attempt to give supranational institutions a role in the control of domestic violence in a world riven by ideological controversy. As such, it suggests a series of limits based upon certain overarching areas of consensus— the wrongfulness of racial oppression or colonial administration—if the intervening institution has a world community membership, as does the United Nations. More extensive control may, however, be effectively asserted if regional organizations act on the basis of a regional consensus. Such a limited consensus enables the Organization of American States to agree upon sanctioning Castro's Cuba for the introduction into the hemisphere of an incompatible social order, that is, a social order based upon Marxism-Leninism. Frequently, agreement of this sort would not be attainable within the wider institutional framework of the United Nations. The tolerance of a regular authority of regional institutions to intervene coercively creates severe problems at the same time that it solves others. It may make a state its victim just because it does not get along with its regional members. Should Israel's destiny be entrusted to a regional consensus? Or that of Formosa or even the Republic of South Africa? The doctrine that authorizes regional coercion in the event of incompatibility with regional values, so useful as a way to mobilize a coercive response to Castro, is a precedent for a pattern of response that might turn out to be exceedingly troublesome.

[464]

Greater deference to the overseeing authority of the Security Council as claimed in Article 53(1) of the UN Charter, should be encouraged as a way to guard against regional excess.

The problems treated here in No. 14 cannot be solved by neat distinctions between domestic and international civil wars, regional and global organizations, insurgent and incumbent factions, or cold war and non-cold war struggles. It is essential to be aware of the series of problems connected with the maintenance of channels for peaceful change in a disarming world. Otherwise there is a danger that we associate political stability only with the adequacy of social control and thus overlook the cognate need for adequate mechanisms of social change. Indirect aggression and subversion are not discrete phenomena that can be torn from the fabric of international life. Their control must be viewed from the perspective of the international system, as well as from the viewpoint of the United States as a principal actor in the current form of system struggle—the cold war.

15. It is important to identify the functions of law in this process of adjusting the tension between stability and change in a disarming world. First, it is essential to avoid abstract doctrinal formulations that are not responsive to the diversity of empirical conditions. This argues for a flexible legal regime with a reliance upon a multiplicity of control techniques. Second, it is important to conceive of the task of law as extending beyond the formulation of rules, however applicable to the behavior. For effective law must combine the standards it sets for behavior with suitable procedures for interpretation and enforcement. That is, the rules and their implementation should be conceived of as part of a single process. It is little help to draft a set of rules unless one also thinks about techniques and problems of implementation. Our interest is with the actual restraint of behavior, not with the formulation of standards for behavior. Third, despite this focus upon implementation, it is desirable to appreciate the extent to which rules can provide actors with mutually acceptable standards for behavior in a decentralized community. It is very important in international affairs to recognize that law depends upon the coordination of equals based on perceptions of reciprocal self-interest. Thus it is essential to establish as clear standards as possible for the discernment of permissible behavior. Agreed upon rules reduce the prospect for contradictory national interpretations of applicable legal duties, it tends to help crystallize the response of world opinion to allegations of illegality, and it provides an administering institution like the IDO with advance guidance that might depoliticize its assignment and make its conclusions acceptable to the community and to the nations involved in the controversy. Decisions of an

institution have more respect if they involve the application of a prior rule than if they are an *ad hoc* response to a dispute between political rivals. The existence of legal standards serves to guide national bureaucracies towards an understanding of what is permitted and forbidden and provides some insulation against domestic pressures favoring interventionary policies. Fourth, the role of law is determined by the political and social environment. Legal order is a quasi-dependent variable. Law cannot introduce order by itself. However, legal technique can cooperate with other tendencies toward order to help with the process. This dependence of law, and especially international law, makes it useful to consider the problems of law in the context established by the constellation of social, political, economic, and military conditions. This need for contextual analysis seems very strong for a study concerned with indirect aggression and subversion and peaceful change in a disarming world. Fifth, the techniques of law help actors to clarify their common interest and perceive their hostile interest in advance of conflict. This function would be served if serious efforts were made in a disarmament treaty process to implement the pledge of our April 18th Proposals to refrain from indirect aggression and subversion.

16. The use of law to facilitate a response to indirect aggression and subversion is not restricted to what is put into the disarmament treaty itself. In the course of disarmament an increasing competence may be developed for the organs of the United Nations to control the outcome of internal conflicts that seem to threaten international peace. It will also remain legal during disarmament for a nation to respond to a request from an incumbent government for help that is needed to suppress a domestic insurgency. A disarmament treaty inhibits a highly articulated normative environment already populated by rules, procedures, and institutions that intend, among other objectives to frustrate the indirect aggressor-subvertor. There is no formal need for an *independent treaty capability* to deal with the maximum levels of indirect aggression and subversion. Treaty methods can be used, if found essential, to supplement nontreaty methods. Perhaps nontreaty methods are enough without encumbering the treaty. There is a useful way to focus the decision that must be made: What perceived threats from indirect aggression and subversion during disarmament could be met only if methods of control were provided by the treaty itself? More modestly, and realistically, one can ask "What contemplated benefits would accrue from any specific treaty inclusion?" This question recalls the discussion of objectives at the end of Section I. It is a matter of relating the distinctive risks of disarmament to the appropriate norms for an optimal disarmament apparatus. This is not an abstract quest. Risks

must be specified and norms accordingly developed and located some-where in the international system, and perhaps explicitly, although not necessarily, in the disarmament process itself.

17. The endeavor to control indirect aggression and subversion can be conceived of as an effort to identify and proscribe certain forms of impermissible coercion in world politics. The interdependence of do-mestic and global life, the antagonistic images of the proper organiza-tion of domestic society, and the currents of rivalry between nations and ideologies make it inevitable that some coercion will be applied to induce or prevent certain political changes from taking place. The extension or withdrawal of foreign aid, the granting or withholding of diplomatic recognition, the willingness or refusal to enter into trade and cultural relations, the communication of diplomatic counsel, resolutions calling for reform or of censure by international organizations illustrate the widespread and unavoidable presence of a coercive component in foreign relations. This coercive component cannot nor should it be eliminated from world politics. In contrast, a main task of the methods adopted to control indirect aggression and subversion is to assure the visibility of the intolerable forms of minor coercion that are intertwined with normal intercourse, intolerable because the goals and results are so nearly equivalent to the evils of aggressive war: brutality, alien domi-nation, and totalitarianism. If the "indirectness" of this aggression can be denied the advantages of covertness, then the resources and resolve of community support that are available to the victims of many aggres-sions are easier to mobilize into the means of developing an effective defense. This position rests upon a moral foundation. For indirect ag-gression and subversion remain usable instruments of violence in the nuclear age that can be resorted to by the worst kind of aggressor. The same motives that encourage the collective defense of a victim of an old-fashioned armed attack should encourage the defense of a victim of indirect aggression and subversion. We must be prepared to meet the demands of this morality throughout the course of disarmament. It would seem that nations would become more reluctant to use their own diminishing military capability for the defense of others, that interna-tional organizations would be unable to make authoritative findings of indirect aggression if the aggressor is himself an important member, and that it would be difficult for the organization to make an effective response to events as ambiguous and covert as patterns of indirect ag-gression and subversion often tend to be. For it is often the design or purpose of the indirect aggressor—more than the constituent acts of coercion—that render the coercion unacceptable. Among the more troublesome contingencies is whether disarmament itself generates a

form of political isolationism that increases the exposure of weaker nations to the machinations of a strong indirect aggressor-subvertor. It would be a disarmament irony if the major nations gained security by throwing their weapons away while the minor nations, with virtually no weapons to throw away, lost their security.

18. It is difficult to draw the line between permissible and impermissible coercion in any generally satisfactory manner. Part of the difficulty arises because it is the forbidden result—the extension of national control over a foreign society *by violent means*—rather than the constituent acts that excite primary concern. Thus an indirect aggressor-subvertor may choose coercive instruments from an arsenal that includes money, weapons, and words. Hostile propaganda, guerrilla training, munitions, asylum and border sanctuary, premature recognition, terrorism, and assassinations may all contribute to the aggressive design. The acts themselves are less indicative than the willingness to use all means to advance the aggressive design. As with criminal conspiracy, anything that contributes substantially to the objective becomes tainted and is drawn within the network of the crime. But the design is usually hidden from view. Its existence is difficult to assess, easy to fabricate. Therefore, the evil intentions and plans of the putative aggressor are the critical behavior element and are also the most difficult to demonstrate. The history of criminal conspiracy suggests that it is dangerous to stress or overlook this element of purpose. The same characteristic is true for efforts to design a response policy that will give adequate assurance of control over indirect aggression and subversion in the initial stages of disarmament.

19. Normative control over indirect aggression and subversion promotes the common policy of safeguarding nations against impermissible levels of external coercion. It is, however, inconsistent with policies that try to safeguard the autonomy of domestic political processes, policies that have been translated into such normative principles as nonintervention and self-determination. These norms are often difficult to reconcile in a specific situation. The United States is often considered to be guilty of unwarranted interference in internal affairs when it acts to defend a society from Communist indirect aggression and subversion. It is difficult to adhere simultaneously to all applicable norms. This is a consequence of the existence of incompatible policy commitments; it is not necessarily hypocrisy or lawlessness. The problem exists for all social orders,[24] but it is most disturbing in international affairs where

[24] Cf. Myres S. McDougal, "The Ethics of Applying Systems of Authority: The Balanced Opposites of a Legal System," in Harold D. Lasswell and Harlan Cleveland, eds., *The Ethic of Power*, New York, Harper and Brothers, 1962.

no regularly available authoritative decision-makers exist to make *ad hoc* reconciliations. It appears arbitrary and undermines respect for law when the reconciliation is fully self-determined. Conferral of some classificatory and interpretative functions on the IDO might help to alleviate this problem.

III. The Vulnerability of Nations to Indirect Aggression and Subversion during Disarmament

20. There are certain environmental factors that permit the successful use of indirect aggression and subversion in the world today. An understanding of these factors identifies the necessity for an insistence upon minimum control in a disarming world. In the nuclear age and during the cold war, military aggression, international violence, and the extension of the totalitarian sphere of influence have mainly resulted from a combination of subtle and covert coercive tactics that we combine for purposes of analysis in the gross concepts "indirect aggression" and "subversion." But it is important to perceive that these gross concepts are shorthand expressions for doctrines and practices of international coercion, of designed and feasible aggression, of political behavior unanimously condemned after World War II in the Resolutions passed by the United Nations to express approval for the Principles of the Nuremberg Judgment.[25] That is, "minor" coercion[26] may perpetrate "major" political evil. For this reason it is not possible to neglect the regulation of minor coercion in our understandable eagerness to do away with, through comprehensive disarmament, the instruments of major coercion. It is not plausible to suppose that the possible use of the instruments of major coercion to defend the victims of minor coercion restrains contemporary indirect aggressors? And that disarmament will both encourage a fuller exploitation of the opportunities for minor coercion and diminish the capacity and will of nations to defend themselves against it? Does disarmament make nations more or less vulnerable to aggression by minor coercion? Does it make some nations more vulnerable, others less vulnerable? Which ones? What can be done to lessen the increased vulnerability that does seem to result? Is the reduction of the dangers of nuclear war worth an increase in the opportunities (how much? where?) of the indirect aggressor-subvertor? The nature of national vulnerability to external coercion in a dis-

---

[25] Cf. formulation by the International Law Commission of *Principles of International Law Recognized in the Charter of Nürnberg Tribunal and in the Judgment of the Tribunal,* GAOR, V, Supp. 12, A/1316, pp. 11-14.

[26] A very good basis for understanding the role of law in the control of minor coercion is given by William T. Burke in "The Legal Regulation of Minor Coercion: A Framework of Inquiry," in *Essays on International Law and Intervention,* Columbus, Ohio State University Press, 1963.

arming world is the subject of this section. This involves, as well, some consideration of what steps are contemplated within and without the treaty process to reduce whatever vulnerability presently exists.[27] Perhaps the historical destiny of the era will bring increased vulnerability without any disarmament. For recourse to domestic revolution, instigated and supported by foreign states, may be primarily governed by considerations other than the dangers of nuclear war posed by the presence of an arms race for superiority in the instruments of major coercion. The capability to help victims of minor coercion may be unaffected or even improved by the gradual reduction of the perceived dangers of nuclear war. It may be also just as important to find out that disarmament risks, or many of them, appear to be virtually unconnected with the vulnerability of nations to indirect aggression and subversion as that they seem vitally connected.

A depiction of relevant aspects of the international political system, as it is now functioning, helps us to grasp the extent and significance of this connection between minor coercion (indirect aggression and subversion) and disarmament risks.

21. There is, despite rifts and tensions, a unity of Communist purpose and practice that continues to make it accurate to identify a Sino-Soviet "bloc." It may not, if Chinese disaffiliation proceeds much further, remain an accurate designation.[28] However, the term calls attention to a global political apparatus centered in Moscow that is available to co-ordinate and direct the activities of the many national Communist parties. There are limits, no doubt, to the extent of leadership and control that can be presently exercised. These limits are clearly manifest in the refusal of the Chinese, the Albanians, and now the Cubans[29] to renounce the use of revolutionary violence as a principal means for Communist expansion. There are a number of significant characteristics of the bloc nature of the Soviet system that are relevant to the use of minor coercion to spread the reign of Communism.

a. Revolutionary strategy. The Communist system is based upon the legitimacy of and necessity for revolutions against the prevailing social and legal orders in non-Communist societies. This central commitment undercuts the reasonableness of relying upon Communist commitments to respect the political, social, and legal *status quo*. It also provides Communist strategists with a moral basis upon which to justify the use of indirect aggression and subversion to facilitate the expan-

[27] A discussion of the principal methods available to prevent indirect aggression and subversion is reserved for Section IV.

[28] Cf. *Polycentricism, The New Factor in International Communism,* a collection of essays edited by Walter Laqueur and Leopold Labedz, New York, Praeger, 1962.

[29] Cf. diplomatic note and excerpts from Castro's speech in which the role of violence in the promotion of revolutionary goals is underscored, "U.S. Warns of Castro's Declaration of War on Hemisphere," *U.S. State Department Bulletin,* XLVIII, February 18, 1963, pp. 263-64.

sion of the Communist system. This contrasts with the moral ambivalence of Western attitudes toward the use of force to influence the outcome of domestic social conflicts taking place in foreign societies.

b. Party apparatus. The existence of well-organized Communist parties in all major national societies provides the Sino-Soviet bloc with ready means for the export and guidance of revolutionary activity in a rather subtle manner that often is not visible to an observer and hence does not appear to be an unwarranted interference in internal affairs. That is, Communist party activity looks like, and it may actually be, merely a part of the domestic political environment. The Soviet Union (and even China) may refrain from any substantial participation in the formation of policy on the national Communist level. It may even lend support, as it has done in the United Arab Republic, to a government that is vigorously suppressing radical discontent and the activities of domestic Communists. Nevertheless, highly organized national units of the Communist party give Moscow and/or Peking a stable of Trojan horses, often indispensable for the fulfillment of the objectives of an indirect aggressor-subverter. However, the splintering of the world Communist party, as of 1967, makes uncertain and variable the exertion of influence by leading Communist states upon the Communist party apparatus elsewhere. At present, a range from virtual autonomy to virtual dependence characterizes the relationships between the governments in Moscow or Peking and particular Communist movements; in fact, in many national party structures the split on the global level is reflected on the domestic level so that there is no longer an assurance of Communist unity even within a single state.

c. Wars of national liberation. This widely proclaimed doctrine seems to confirm the commitment by the Soviet bloc to the techniques of indirect aggression and subversion for the promotion of foreign political objectives. That is, sides are taken in foreign wars on the basis of revolutionary considerations interpreted in the Marxist-Leninist tradition. This criterion of participation is incompatible with the norms of neutrality posited by traditional international law and with the commitment to support United Nations action that is contained in the Charter. It also expresses an official Soviet awareness that intrastate violence is the crucial arena within which to carry on the battle of the cold war. The classification of a "war of national liberation" as "a just war" in the official Soviet textbook of international law is an explicit repudiation of Charter norms banishing the use of force from international affairs.[30] Soviet intentions, if they are in fact firm, are difficult to establish

[30] Cf. Chapter X by F. I. Kozhevnikov in the textbook, *International Law*, published for the Institute of State and Law, Academy of Sciences of the USSR, pp. 401-54.

by reference to public statements. There are several versions of "peaceful coexistence" extant that can be differentiated, in part, by the degree to which exported coercion is expected to contribute to the attainment of the goals of Soviet foreign policy.[31] This may reflect some uncertainty within the Soviet decision-making elite about the choice of methods, as well as illustrate a tendency of Communist political leaders to vary their formulation to suit the audience that is being primarily addressed. Whatever uncertainty exists with reference to Soviet intentions is absent from an interpretation of Chinese attitudes which make explicit their militant advocacy of the use of minor coercion to assure the success of revolutions in foreign societies.[32] Are China's patterns of international behavior relevant to the design of a disarmament treaty? This is a troublesome, abiding question. If the objective is to protect national societies from Communist encroachment facilitated by minor coercion, then the successful restraint of the Soviet Union would not necessarily decrease the vulnerability of nations so long as other Communist or revolutionary states were ready and able to help win so-called wars of national liberation. This point suggests that it is probably desirable to focus attention upon methods of control that protect a national community during disarmament against indirect aggression and subversion regardless of the animus and source of the coercion. It is no solution to find methods that give effective assurance, but only against Soviet behavior.

22. The United States and the West. It is important to grasp the comparative looseness of the United States "bloc"[33] leadership. The persistence of sovereign initiative is the basis of the Western alliance system, especially in Europe. This means that there is must less agreement about the use of force to defend societies against Communist indirect aggression and subversion or to employ such tactics in an offensive manner to help protests succeed in Communist-dominated societies. The lack of a party apparatus to promote a liberal democratic ideology

31 Cf. e.g. N. S. Khrushchev, "On Peaceful Coexistence," *Foreign Affairs*, xxxviii (October 1959), 1-18 with the "Declaration of Eighty-one Communist Parties," Moscow, 1960, reprinted in *The New Communist Manifesto and Related Documents*, ed., Dan N. Jacobs, New York, Harper Torchbooks, 1962.

32 Cf. critique of Chinese position by a leading Yugoslav theorist: Edvard Kardelj, *Socialism and War: A Survey of Chinese Criticism of the Policy of Coexistence*, London, Methuen, 1960.

33 "I confess that it is very frustrating to us, who have to bear the brunt of the Soviet cold war, not to be at the head of a nice solid bloc. You read in the papers sometimes about the 'Soviet bloc' and the 'Western bloc' and even the 'neutralist bloc.' Well, unfortunately there *is* a Soviet bloc, but the other 'blocs' are not blocs at all—they are shifting alinements which vary from one issue to another, for the very simple reason that each of the governments has that priceless jewel, the right to think for itself." Adlai E. Stevenson, "The U.S., a View of the Road Ahead," *U.S. State Department Bulletin*, xlv, October 9, 1961, No. 1163, pp. 597, 598-99.

throughout the world hampers the effort of the United States to be a covert participant in domestic politics abroad. As well, the United States is both deferential to norms prohibiting intervention and ambivalent about destabilizing social changes in nations presently allied with Western policies. In addition, the internal functioning of a democratic society is not conducive to prolonged secrecy about the use of force in international affairs. It places a strain upon the moral fibre of the society to have the President advocate a law-oriented approach to foreign affairs and practice an interventionary approach. It generates a cynical climate of domestic and international opinion that is itself incompatible with undertaking serious disarmament risks. The United States lacks both the justifying ideology and the bureaucratic structure for the efficient use of minor coercion to achieve foreign policy objectives in other states. The abortive sponsorship of the Bay of Pigs expedition discloses the grave internal and external difficulties of implementation, although the apparent successes in Guatemala and Iran discourage generalizations about either United States capabilities or intentions.

a. Self-determination. The United States tends to support principles that favor the right of a society to choose its own political destiny. This support generates tolerance toward revolutionary movements in foreign societies, at least so long as there is no perceived affiliation with Communism or large-scale Communist participation. This value consideration complicates any United States decision to help an antidemocratic incumbent suppress a radical insurgent. Thus either aloofness or participation excites strenuous domestic opposition. The policy consequence is to wield an uneasy compromise which is dissatisfying to everyone with a clear preference for either an interventionary or a noninterventionary foreign policy.

b. Nonintervention. Particularly in the Western Hemisphere, but more generally as well,[34] the United States has accepted formal commitments to refrain from coercive interference in the affairs of sovereign states, regardless of the pretext for such interference. To pursue interventionary policies, as we have done several times during the cold war, is to jeopardize the principle of respect for law, a principle which the United States itself champions as the essential precondition for transition to a peaceful world. However, the willingness of Communist nations to exploit domestic instabilities in order to gain control

---

[34] For history of noninterventionism see Ann Van Wynen Thomas and A. J. Thomas, Jr., *Non-Intervention: The Law and Its Import in the Americas*, Dallas, Southern Methodist University Press, 1956; Doris A. Graber, *Crisis Diplomacy*, Washington, Public Affairs Press, 1959; J. Lloyd Mecham, *The United States and Inter-American Security, 1889-1960*, Austin, University of Texas Press, 1960; O. Edmund Smith, *Yankee Diplomacy: U.S. Intervention in Argentina*, Dallas, Southern Methodist University Press, 1953.

over radical protest movements makes it impossible for the United States to uphold its determination to resist Communist encroachment and yet adhere to applicable legal obligations. This confusion of objectives tends to frustrate attempts to clarify the nature of our foreign policy. This ambivalence of attitude influences behavior. It deprives an interventionary counterresponse of its effectiveness and a noninterventionary deference to legal norms of its righteousness. The consequence is an uncertain posture that is not even supported by the ethical predispositions of many concerned sectors of domestic public opinion.

It would seem persuasive to reinterpret norms of nonintervention in light of the contemporary patterns of international conflict. These patterns exhibit widespread interventionary participation in internal wars as part of a global struggle for power. Nonadherence by Communist states in specific instances, and perhaps in general, should be regarded as relieving the United States from an obligation to comply. Otherwise an asymmetrical adherence to norms by the United States would increase the opportunities of the indirect aggressor and the vulnerabilities of the victim nation.[35]

c. Legitimacy. There is a United States disposition to help all non-Communist incumbent governments that request help to suppress domestic protest, especially if the protest has important perceived cold war implications.[36] It is thought that support for the legitimate government (in a constitutional sense of legitimacy which is distinct from the Communist ideological view of legitimacy as a class concept) is an acceptable form of intervention in internal affairs, even if it enables the defeat of a revolutionary faction that seeks and is able to acquire power without external support. This view, besides its inconsistency with the principle of self-determination, allows, by the logic of reciprocity, Soviet support to be given to incumbent totalitarian governments within their bloc.[37] That is, intervention resting upon a constitutional concept of legitimacy stabilizes the political control of governments that follow extreme antidemocratic policies. Once again it plunges the prevailing patterns of U.S. policy into a morass of ambivalence and uncertainty of commitment. It may also identify the United States with the forces of reaction and tradition in an age that is revolutionary as a matter of history more than as a reflection of Communist tactics. A mechanical deference to constitutional legitimacy may be too facile

---

[35] This argument is developed more fully in Chapter IV.

[36] A contrast between the United States response to Castro before and after it perceived the cold war consequences of the Cuban revolution illustrate the emphasis on perception in the text.

[37] The Western objection to the use of Soviet troops in Hungary in 1956 was based, in part, on its refusal to respect the incumbency of Nagy; in this sense, the Kadar elite were in the position of feeble insurgents who were hoisted to power by the strength of Soviet tanks.

a way to dismiss certain sets of domestic claims for a new social order and a radical program of social justice and economic development.

It is difficult to suppose that a world community would stabilize international relations by an unqualified endorsement of constitutional legitimacy or even of *de facto* control of government machinery as a basis for world order. Not *every* government confronted by an insurgency, aided and abetted by foreign support, is entitled to protection as a victim of indirect aggression. The incumbent must also, at least in most cases, satisfy certain minimum requirements of contemporary decency in the course of administering a domestic society to be considered eligible for defensive support from the organized community. The case of Goa is an instructive instance of a refusal by the United Nations to respond to a plea for defense against direct coercion. Even without the cold war, then, deference to constitutional legitimacy is no more than a starting-point in the process by which to determine whether the victim of minor coercion deserves to receive the protection of collective security. Surely it is implausible to suppose that the United States would support the use of the United Nations to repress an uprising in East Germany, even if the uprising was instigated and supported by foreign states in the Western alliance, say West Germany. There is thus no consensus available to support a rule of international order that gives automatic deference to the claims of the victim of minor coercion; compare the consensus that does seem to assure support, although not invariably (Goa), for victims of an aggression carried on across an international frontier.

d. Cold war. Here again the main problem seems to involve a reconciliation of the conduct necessary for the containment of Communism with the legal and moral norms that have been designed to protect domestic societies from indirect aggression and subversion. To some extent the difficulties arise because the prohibition placed upon intervention is seriously deficient for contemporary interdependence and patterns of revolutionary politics. The exercise of control in a disarming world must include some reassessment of the adequacy of the traditional rules of international law governing the relations between independent states. This endeavor would raise special problems involving the relation between constitutional liberties and hostile propaganda. There are domestic limits upon Western discretion to negotiate the regulation of activity that provokes political revolt from a foreign base of operations.

23. Nonaligned Nations. A large and influential group of nations has adopted a policy of avoiding a commitment to either side in the cold war. However, these nations have a strong interest in achieving disarmament to make the world safer and to free resources from military

expenditures. The nonaligned nations, although disagreeing about the proper resolution of many issues, have certain common dispositions about the use of force in world affairs. In general, there is wide sympathy for interventionary policies that attempt to undermine Western European domination whether perpetuated in the form of colonialism or neocolonialist control as exercised through a traditional native elite kept in nominal control of the domestic order. This Afro-Asian consensus enables Communist bloc members to use techniques of subversion and indirect aggression with either the tacit or outright approval of non-aligned nations. In fact, it is the ardent Communist championship of many of the goals of the nonaligned Afro-Asian nations that provides opportunities for Communist infiltration of domestic protest groups.

a. Anticolonialism. There is a widespread and emotional commitment among the nonaligned nations to a policy that seeks to eliminate colonial regimes as soon as possible *by any means* that promise effective results. The pursuit of anticolonial goals is strong enough to foster explicit policies of indirect aggression and subversion. In this respect the policies of many nonaligned states with respect to the use of force converges with Communist doctrine and practice under the doctrine of support for wars of national liberation more than with Western dispositions. It is also true that the states most likely to be vulnerable to minor coercion and internal disorder are among the most ardent advocates of an interventionary foreign policy. The failure to build up a strong disposition in favor of *de facto* incumbency is *one of the factors* that restricts the capacity of the world community organization to take as effective action against indirect aggression as it has managed to take against direct aggressors (Korea, Suez). This failure creates opportunities and accentuates vulnerabilities.

b. Antiracism. The same reasoning also applies to a non-European nation that is governed by a white minority that treats the majority culture as socially, economically, and politically inferior. The Republic of South Africa is an obvious target. Again the intensity of Afro-Asian hostility is so great that it will support any effective method of interference, no matter how coercive or disruptive. This has the effect of weakening normative support for the prohibitions against recourse to subversion and indirect aggression. It might almost be concluded that resort to coercion is perceived by national actors as an indispensable, and hence permissible ingredient of any policy designed to attain the dominant international objectives of the nonaligned group of states.

c. Active neutralism. Neutralist nations, although keenly sensitive to the dangers of general nuclear war are quite often vigorous advocates of the use of force, if necessary, to hasten the end of colonial administration, feudal autocracy, or post-colonial foreign hegemony.[38] Therefore, the principle of constitutional legitimacy is not, for them, appealing as a basis for restraint. This makes these nations unwilling to take steps to curtail the external possibilities for indirect aggression and subversion. There is nothing to indicate that the nonaligned nations perceive the connection between improving internal security in the uncommitted nations and the achievement and the success of disarmament negotiations. It is quite possible, although ironic, that the maximum contribution that can be expected that the nonaligned nations might make to the avoidance of nuclear war would be to strengthen their capability to maintain internal security. And there are some indications of a willingness to consider internal security to be a matter that is of serious concern and appropriate for regional cooperation.[39] There is a split observable between the common concern of Afro-Asian states with the maintenance of their own defenses against minor coercion and their equally shared willingness to undermine the internal security of their enemies. This dichotomy may be, at least temporarily, the only working basis available for international order. Such a double standard is not conducive to the development of orthodox legal control over minor coercion. For a legal regime would ordinarily require the general application of rules to all relevant instances. Political conditions are not now conducive to the development of such a regime.

    d. An international welfare system. A truly effective renunciation of international coercion may turn out to depend upon the development of a radical new basis for distributing the world's wealth that would infringe upon old habits of national sovereignty more than would disarmament itself.[40] Until this is done, however, the incentives to commit aggression remain very strong. Thus the elimination of minor coercion from a disarming world probably will require some coordinated attention to such deep-rooted social problems as poverty, disease, and overpopulation. A compulsory system of progressive taxation, designed to achieve a partial redistribution of wealth in the direction of parity may be the only solution that really works. Thus the problem of indirect aggression and subversion may be more crucially a consequence of the rich nation-poor nation conflict of interest than of the cold war. This

[38] Cf. e.g. *Declaration of the Heads of State or Government, Final Act*, Belgrade Conference of Nonaligned Nations, 1961; Asia-Africa Speaks from Bandung, 1955.
[39] Cf. e.g. *Seminar on Countering Communist Subversion*, South-East Asia Treaty Organization, Philippines, 1957; Special Consultative Committee on Security, Initial General Report, OEA/Ser. L/X/II.1,

Rev., May 2, 1962.
[40] B. V. A. Röling, *International Law in an Expanded World*, Djambatan, Amsterdam, 1960; Wolfgang Friedmann, "The Changing Dimensions of International Law," 62 *Columbia Law Review* 1147-62 (1962); *Id., Law in a Changing Society*, Berkeley, University of California Press, 1959.

seems especially plausible if one tries to envision the shape of the problem in Stage III when, almost by definition, the fundamental antagonisms between the great nations must have disappeared, as otherwise there would be no transition from Stage II.

e. Modernization process. The objective situation of many newly independent states is receptive to radical internal transformations of economic, social, and political structure. This creates a revolutionary situation that makes a society vulnerable to indirect aggression and subversion, applied through the agency of radical domestic groups. The cold war is an aggravating condition, but an expectation of domestic tranquillity would be unrealistic even without it, so long as there remained pressure for radical domestic changes.

24. Minor Coercion and the Nuclear Stalemate. One consequence of nuclear weaponry is to shift the dominant pattern of violence from interstate to intrastate arenas of conflict.[41] Force is now far less usable across national boundaries to promote the politics of expansion.[42] This prudence, designed to curtail escalation, has been acknowledged by Soviet doctrine and is characteristic of Soviet practice (despite its role in initiating the Korean War). This means that the bulk of military spending is devoted to weapons systems for which no use is contemplated,[43] for which, in fact, the occasion of use would be an occasion of national disaster. Comparatively little attention, especially until recently, has been given to the expansion of national influence and relative power that can be achieved by successfully supporting the winning faction in an internal war. Techniques of indirect aggression achieve a special prominence in a nuclear age as they provide aggressor states avenues for expansion that do not appear doomed to end in a nuclear conflagration. However, opportunities for such expansion reinforce Communist adherence to doctrines and expectations of world domination. It is crucial to diminish such opportunities and thereby eliminate the inclination of expanding nations to produce and capitalize upon domestic instability. Such a diminution would then make the advantages of a disarming world a matter of prudence for all nations, regardless of ideological bias.

[41] See especially the chapters on peaceful coexistence, modernization, and internal war contributed by the editor, Cyril E. Black, to a volume entitled *Communism and Revolution*, Princeton University Press, 1964; cf. also Samuel P. Huntington, "Instability at the Non-Strategic Level of Conflict," Study Memorandum No. 2, Institute for Defense Analyses, October 6, 1961.

[42] There are exceptions: Goa, Tibet. But these instances were also exceptional. In neither case did the victim have a clear claim to sovereign status, nor did the defensive claimants have unambiguous standing to defend.

[43] The word "use" is quite defective and misleading as it may or may not include "threats." In the present state of international relations, threats influence the behavior of the threatened, and in a functional sense at least, constitute a use of force.

a. Rational uses of force to achieve political expansion. Occasions continue to exist when it is reasonable for national officials to employ force or its threat to achieve political expansion without incurring any substantial risk of a nuclear counterblow. These occasions are created by precisely the opportunities for the successful use of the instruments of minor coercion that have been discussed in this chapter. The availability of this aggressive path blocks the disarmament route by making it apparent that force is still usable for political gain and, therefore, defensive force must be maintained to frustrate the potential aggressor. Thus the opportunities for indirect aggression and subversion are an obstacle to disarmament, and their reduction in a predisarmament environment would help to establish an international atmosphere for disarmament. A military capability that could deter minor coercion might do as much for the cause of world peace as the formidable capability now available to deter major coercion.

b. Dangers. Indirect aggression and subversion inhibit efforts to curtail the arms race or to initiate the disarmament process. Also, the attempts to defend societies from indirect aggression and subversion produce political violence and raise cold war tensions. Such violence, if protracted, invites offsetting interventions which raise tensions still further, create dangers of escalation, and generally impair the fragile stalemate provided by mutual deterrence.

c. Capabilities. The development of a United States military capacity to resist multiple forms of indirect aggression and subversion would help to close off this avenue of political expansion for Communism. As such, it would help to stabilize the political atmosphere. This might prevent crisis confrontations and make a breakdown of the system less probable; it would also make the United States more secure with respect to the containment of Communist power when contemplating the protection of its interests in a disarming world. As indicated in No. 23, even the successful regulation of external Communist participation in domestic affairs does not assure the United States that the sphere of Communist influence in the world will not be enlarged through the influence of purely indigenous happenings. If containment of Communism is the real objective, then control over the Sino-Soviet export of coercion may not be enough; at least, unless an asymmetry is tolerated that allows an interventionary defense of the incumbent and assures nonintervention on behalf of the insurgent.

25. Indirect Aggression and Subversion in a Disarming World. From what has been said, some control over indirect aggression and subversion is itself almost a presupposition of the ratification of comprehensive disarmament. If this control is achieved then the shape of the prob-

lems change. During Stages I and II there is no military need to impose greater restrictions than now exist.[44] That is, there is no greater military vulnerability, although there may be some temptation for the Sino-Soviet bloc to combine the stimulation of local Communist party activities with a willingness to engage in a rearmament race, thereby generating intense domestic conflict in major non-Communist nations. There are, however, considerable political requirements even in Stages I and II. Even if the amount of Communist expansion resulting from indirect aggression and subversion was no greater or even somewhat less than what presently exists, its success in a disarming world would probably be attributed to disarmament. That is, disarmament would be held responsible by domestic politicians and public opinion for whatever political successes are achieved by the Communists in a disarming world. It is thus most essential to protect the stability of the disarmament process by obtaining reasonable assurance that techniques of indirect aggression and subversion can be neutralized in the early stages of disarmament. For Stage III, it would appear necessary for indirect aggression and subversion to disappear altogether from international politics, at least in the context of relations between major powers. The decision to enter Stage III would presuppose a prior solution for the problems associated with what might properly be called the international dimension of internal security. This does not depend upon the absence of all hostility, but upon the capacity of the system to channel it into relatively harmless expressions of antagonism. As the experience of the United States as a federal system suggests, the continuation of interstate rivalry is compatible with the maintenance of peace and order within the system. In the few instances in which the use of force has been needed, it has been to impose a federal solution upon a dissident state or group of states and not to keep states from fighting with one another.

26. Problems of Peaceful Change in the Contemporary World. We seek to classify these problems in relation to the decision to disarm and to the regulation of indirect aggression and subversion. There is a difference between the role of indirect aggression and subversion in the politics of expansion as practiced by Hitler in pre-World War II Europe and by Stalin in post-World War II Europe, and its role to resolve a particular dispute between nations involving, let's say, a boundary dispute or rights to the flow of a river with its source in another state. A dispute between nations is profoundly different from participation in a dispute within a nation. These distinctions are basic to a

---

[44] However, political requirements exist. Confidence must be retained and strengthened, institutions and habits developed, if the transition step is to be taken and domestic support for disarmament sustained.

systematic approach to peaceful change in the contemporary world. As we are concerned with peaceful alternatives to force, it is relevant to develop more reliable and available machinery of pacific settlement. Such machinery diminishes the incentive to resort to subversion and indirect aggression and generally contributes to a more orderly and just international atmosphere by providing noncoercive methods to fulfill reasonable national aspirations. The main thing is to recognize that pressures for internal and external changes exist and will continue to exist, and that a preparation of the world for disarmament involves accommodating such pressures with a minimum occasion for and experience of violence. In addition, peaceful accommodation, as a matter of course, reduces the opportunity for external powers to exploit internal dissatisfactions in order to expand spheres of influence.

27. Problems of Peaceful Change in a Disarming and Disarmed World. In a sense, as has been suggested, the problems exist in relatively unchanged form through Stages I and II. However, as disarmament proceeds one would expect that crises and instability, now accepted as a regular part of international politics, would be perceived as less and less acceptable. And by Stage III the prospect of an international political crisis would have to disappear if states were to abandon their systems of national defense. One major way to satisfy this projected change in the perception of international crises would be to increase the possibilities for peaceful change in situations that have otherwise often generated international and intranational tension and violence in the history of world politics. Part of the reason for emphasizing "peaceful change" in a study primarily devoted to indirect aggression and disarmament is to make the firm point that more is needed by way of response than better internal security mechanisms.

IV. Methods of Control

28. Introduction. Section H, Paragraph 2(b) of Stage I of the April 18th Proposal instructs the subsidiary body of the International Disarmament Organization to "study the methods of assuring states against indirect aggression or subversion." This section tries to outline some of the considerations that would arise in the course of carrying out such an instruction. There are several overall comments that apply generally to the search for methods to control indirect aggression and subversion in a disarming world. These comments will be given prior to a series of discussions of specific methods.

First, the purposes served by the methods chosen to exercise control should be understood to be various, and not only the prevention of activity that threatens political independence. In particular, it should be appreciated that a major objective of control mechanisms, especially with respect to those societies most vulnerable to indirect aggression and subversion, is to make the prohibited activity assume cruder instruments to reach its ends. This makes the participation of the indirect aggressor more visible. It is unmasked. This encourages community detection and censure. It also mobilizes support for defensive measures. This mobilization of support is important because it tends to vindicate a coercive response and makes it more probable that an administering agency, such as the IDO, would report the conduct as a treaty violation. The prospect of detection itself presumably operates often as a deterrent, perhaps even as a major deterrent. Thus an authoritative delimitation of a boundary or "the presence" of an international control commission may not give much protection against a diligent violator to make his conduct invisible and thus beyond community criticism. Allegations would become more persuasive. At present, U.S. claims of Soviet participation in indirect aggression often sound unconvincing as there is so little participation visible, especially as contrasted with the overtness of whatever United States support is given the incumbent. The civil strife in South Viet Nam illustrates this asymmetry. For many observers it appears that the United States, and not the Soviet Union or its allies, is the prime intervenor in the domestic struggle for power.[45] Techniques that make Communist participation in the domestic affairs of foreign states more visible are, perhaps, the proper and reasonable focus for the regulation of minor coercion as an aggressive instrument. For techniques that provide assurance against the activity of a willful violator are cumbersome, if not impossible, to devise and negotiate, and if adopted, such preventive techniques, if they are ever negotiated, are likely to overstabilize international politics, making domestic revolution and radical protest all but impossible. On the other hand, an emphasis on visibleness of participation makes an intervening aggressor nation "show its hand"; this might be enough to protect protectable societies. It might also guard the disarmament process from irresponsible critics who would probably allege that any unfavorable change in the international political *status quo* is a result of and attributable to disarmament. The falseness of this kind of charge could be more plausibly established if methods are developed to bring into better view what is going on in the way of foreign par-

[45] For a presentation from the United States viewpoint, with supporting evidence see "A Threat to the Peace—North Viet-Nam's Effort to Conquer South Viet-Nam," Parts I and II, Department of State Publication 7308, 1961; a less one-sided perception of the civil strife is given, as might be expected, in the various interim reports of the International Commission for Supervision and Control in Vietnam, issued as a series of Command Papers by Her Majesty's Stationery Office, e.g. Cmnd. 9461, Vietnam No. 1, 1955.

ticipation in internal politics. And this greater *knowledge* may be all that is necessary or desirable to do in the way of *regulating* indirect aggression.

Second, and somewhat connected, the quest for methods of control in the context of disarmament should not be approached in a vacuum, as if effective methods for certain kinds of response did not already exist. Presumably, a disarmament treaty should not be burdened with collateral matters unless their inclusion is essential for the ratification and stability of the disarmament arrangements. This may require an assessment of the extent to which, if at all, United States responses in a predisarmament situation are interfered with by the facts and atmosphere of disarmament. It must also take account of the political demands for reassurance that will be made in the United States when the issue of disarmament is introduced seriously into domestic politics. How much extra reassurance is needed with respect to the capability to constrain indirect aggression and subversion during disarmament? Such a perspective emphasizes the need to satisfy political demands, as well as the security requirements generated by disarmament. The security requirements shift attention from matters of domestic resolve and courage to the dynamics of national vulnerability in a disarming world.

Do vulnerability, opportunities, and intentions to engage in indirect aggression and subversion remain the same, increase, or decrease during the period of disarmament? This kind of anticipation should be correlated as specifically as possible with national case studies. Treaty approaches can be complemented by other forms of response, such as helping states to improve their internal security capabilities, undertaken outside of the treaty framework and independent of disarmament.

Third, the objectives sought by the adoption of methods explicitly designed to assure states against indirect aggression and subversion might be attained more easily by the development of other peace-maintaining provisions that are already outlined in the April 18th Proposals; the demand for provisions that do not have an obvious strategic role might avoid a breakdown of negotiations and an intrusion of cold war tensions. For instance, the entrustment of an expanding United Nations Peace Observation Corps (Stage I, H, 6) with a wide variety of functions in regard to civil strife might prove to be a very effective deterrent of crass forms of indirect aggression and subversion. That is, without necessarily mentioning the controversial status of national Communist activities in a disarming world it may be possible to guard nations against that portion of Communist potency that derives from illicit forms of external support. The development of techniques for pacific settlement[46] and peace-keeping machinery is also capable of making crucial contributions to the control of indirect aggression and subversion.

Fourth, it should be suggested once again, that there is no all-embracing solution for the present and future problems lumped together in this study. No method is capable of giving *all* states high confidence of protection in *all* circumstances. The highest objective is to find a *series* of methods that are able to give *some* states *some* protection under *certain* circumstances. What seems to be needed is a maximum range of responses—the selection of and coordination between them would depend upon the *ad hoc* interpretation of each occasion. Some of these responses should be made available at the national, others at the regional, and still others at the universal (UN) level. There is a further decision that must be made: are available responses enough to protect U.S. interests during disarmament? Or must some control methods be added in case they should be needed? Must these additional responses be woven into the disarmament treaty? It is quite clear that the proper goal is to become familiar with a spectrum of existing and potential responses to determine how much is needed if a nation is to respond plausibly to a proven instance of indirect aggression and subversion.

Fifth, the sum of methods is designed to give adequate assurance. It should not purport to give perfect assurance, for, if taken seriously, that becomes another way of making the initiation of disarmament conditional upon a prior and favorable termination of the cold war. We suggest that undertaking disarmament is a matter of negotiating toward a level of tolerable risk by the design of a system that is able to generate a ratifying consensus in the United States Senate.

Of course, no extended account of these background considerations can be undertaken here. The function of this discussion is merely to set the context for the fuller consideration that is to be given to what might be done and what it is necessary and feasible to do about indirect aggression and subversion within the framework of a disarmament treaty. It is part of the argument made here that the subject matter of this chapter is one which has generated concern and a tormented response by the West even before the prospects for arms control and disarmament crossed the horizon as a possibility.

29. Relevant Provisions of the April 18th Proposals. There are a variety of provisions other than those explicitly mentioning the sub-

[46] Cf. George Modelski, "International Conference on the Settlement of the Laotian Question 1961-62," Working Paper No. 2, Department of International Relations, The Australian National University; *id.*, "International Settlement of Internal Wars" in James N. Rosenau, ed., *International Aspects of Civil Strife*, Princeton, Princeton University Press, 1964, pp. 122-53.

ject in the April 18th Proposals that might usefully be developed into effective methods to control recourse by states to indirect aggression and subversion. In Stage I, Section H sets forth several approaches. Paragraph 1 requires treaty participants to renounce, in the manner already required by Article 2(4) of the United Nations Charter, the use or threat of force "of any type—including nuclear, conventional, chemical or biological"; it would thus become a disarmament obligation, as well as a general rule of international law to repudiate violence as an instrument of foreign policy (except for purposes of individual or collective self-defense against an armed attack). It would also be quite plain that the use of minor coercion to reach aggressive ends would fall within the prohibition and place the violating party in a position of breach with regard to the disarmament agreement. The essential connection between peaceful behavior and the viability of disarmament (as a means to attain national security in the nuclear age) is here made explicit.

Paragraph 2(a), agrees to support an IDO study "of the codification and progressive development of rules of international conduct related to disarmament." It is hard to know what this suggestion was designed to achieve. Presumably, it confers on a "subsidiary body" of IDO broad discretionary authority to fashion whatever rules of conduct are needed to assure the stable functioning of disarmament. These rules might include reference to the rights and duties of states with respect to civil strife in a foreign state. If such rules could be agreed upon, together with appropriate implementing procedures, then a real contribution could be made to international order that bears directly upon the opportunities for indirect aggression and subversion. There is now a background uncertainty as to what states may do to promote a preferred outcome in a foreign civil war. This allows the aggressor to exploit the situation of strife to extend national influence and domination across international boundaries. Thus the development of rules of international conduct might be a fruitful way to add stability and legal order to world affairs without setting out self-consciously to deal directly with Sino-Soviet cold war behavior. In fact, it is quite compatible with the Soviet Union's own request for rules of peaceful coexistence. It should be understood here as elsewhere that rules may be worse than nothing at all unless accompanied by the provision of means adequate for their translation into action.

In part b of Paragraph 2, the subsidiary body of IDO is directed to study specifically and explicitly "methods of assuring states against indirect aggression or subversion." It may be that it would be easier to obtain a consensus by proceeding primarily under the neutral language of part a, although it should be noted that the Soviet Union was the first major state to call the attention of the international community to the dangers of indirect aggression by including it in their proposals for draft definitions of aggression. Of course, a definition has never been officially accepted, but there remains something ironic about the chief perpetrator of a wrongful activity stepping forward so often to propose its outlawry; this also warns us against basing legal order on words of prohibition. The hazards of reliance are especially prominent if we are endeavoring to safeguard disarmament.

Paragraph 3 concerns the development of peaceful settlement procedures. If disputes can be resolved by satisfactory peaceful means, then the pretexts for coercion are removed. Frequently, the tactics of indirect aggression combine an international basis of grievance with the application of minor coercion and the agitation of domestic protest. Compulsory recourse to pacific settlement imposes a requirement upon the conduct of international relations that is quite inconsistent with the practice of international aggression of any sort; it sets up inner tensions within the bureaucratic structure that discourage the excitement of foreign strife. For one thing, those national officials that are trying to resolve disputes successfully by peaceful means have an interest in the constraint of a more belligerent national posture; this is both a matter of effectiveness and of intragovernmental prestige and dominance. In any event, the substantial routinization of dispute-settlement goes a long way toward the establishment of a peace system, a system of global relations that has little tolerance, use, or need for international coercion, whether major or minor, as an instrument of national policy.

Paragraph 4 proposes to strengthen the capacity of the United Nations to maintain peace and security. This is to be implemented, in part, by making arrangements in Stage I for the establishment of a United Nations Peace Force. The Soviet March 15th proposal contains a parallel Stage I provision (Article 18), that is to be implemented by national contingents earmarked for UN use in accord with agreements concluded under Articles 42 and 43 of the Charter. The United States also proposes examining the feasibility of concluding agreements under Article 43, although it appears to have in mind a more genuinely supranational force as the outcome.

Such a UN capability would be useful for the control of internal conflict in which there is foreign participation or a substantial prospect thereof. The institutionalization of such a competence might reduce the political pressures that presently impair the undertaking and weaken the Organization when the UN forms an *ad hoc* military force and mission as it has done in Korea, Suez, and the Congo. In any event, the prospect of an effective UN response would constitute, it is supposed, a powerful deterrent, especially if combined with other methods designed to make it easier to identify foreign military participation in domestic insurgencies. Thus coordination with border control techniques might bring into being a very important response pattern.

Finally in Paragraph 6 treaty participants are asked "to support the establishment within the United Nations of a Peace Observation Corps" available for prompt despatch "to investigate any situation which might constitute a threat to or a breach of the peace." The idea is to have the Peace Observation Corps "stationed as appropriate in selected areas throughout the world." This is an extremely fruitful way to supplement national responses on behalf of victims of indirect aggression and subversion. For it provides information for authoritative identification of foreign insurrectionary participation, the prospect of which is itself a deterrent. The use of UN presences in the Middle East, especially, has enjoyed considerable success. It is a well-established way to bring about political stability with a minimum interference with sovereign prerogative.

Stage II continues the processes initiated in Stage I. It proposes arrangements for peaceful settlement, including the acceptance of the compulsory jurisdiction, without reservation, of the International Court of Justice. Such a treaty demand may be difficult, if not impossible, to satisfy if seriously meant, without adding much to the stability of the world. Methods to assure states against indirect aggression and subversion, the United Nations Peace Force, and the United Nations Peace Observation Corps are each envisioned as processes that are to be instituted and expanded during Stage II. Thus the expectation is that by the stage in disarmament at which national capacities might begin to alter significantly, there will be a formidable array of supranational methods available to discourage political expansion by coercion, whether by major or minor instruments, whether Communist originated or not.

Paragraph 5, Section G of Stage II also imposes a duty on "Parties" to enact disarmament obligations into domestic law, thereby coupling national implementation with supranational. This dramatizes the need for formal expressions of national commitments to all that is involved in the disarmament process, including especially the emerging set of duties that are needed for international life in a stable, warless world.

Section H in Stage III envisions a further strengthening of the pacific settlement procedures, rules of international conduct, and the UN Peace Force. It adds, without much elaboration, to the settlement provision a new mandate to take the steps "necessary to provide a basis for peaceful change in a disarmed world." This is the only explicit recognition that eventually the international system will require a legislative substitute for force as an instrument of change. Such a recognition should probably not be postponed in future proposals until Stage III. Adequate mechanisms for peaceful change, if broadly conceived to include certain domestic readjustments, reduce the vulnerability of nations to outside interference. It deals with the deepest sources of human discontent and thereby diminishes the willingness of domestic elements to solicit and accept foreign interventionary support.

It should be mentioned that the failure of substantial compliance with any of these peace-keeping provisions can be invoked as a reason for refusing transition to the next stage, therefore, the United States could condition the continuation of disarmament upon its satisfaction with Soviet compliance with that part of the agreement dealing with the maintenance of peace.

It should be appreciated here, as elsewhere, that it is useful to increase the range of choice that is available in a specific situation by generating overlapping methods to control indirect aggression and subversion. The April 18th Proposals approach the development of a peace system by parallel methods, creating thereby a foundation for a flexible response structure, one that encourages selection and combination of specific control methods.

30. Internal Security Systems. There is an increasing awareness that the control of Communist penetration is effectively achieved by an adequate internal security system. This adequacy includes quantitative and qualitative factors. Size, training, esprit, discipline, popular support, loyalty, leadership, tactics, and equipment are among the important determinants of adequacy. Latin American and Southeast Asian regional organizations have taken on an increasing role in educating their members about the challenges of subversion and the availability of methods of response.[47] These regional activities could presumably continue throughout disarmament, identifying and documenting occurrences of indirect aggression and subversion and perhaps gathering evidence of an impermissible connection between external nations and internal protest movements, and giving advice and help to incumbent governments seeking to maintain domestic order.

31. Social and Economic Reform. Opportunities for indirect aggression and subversion are often created by a repressive, incompetent, or aristocratic government that causes radical discontent in significant portions of the society and makes others unwilling to give the incumbent elite support in the event of a well-organized bid for power. Reform usually depends upon combining military reforms with social and eco-

[47] See studies cited in note 39 *supra*.

nomic measures that give a larger share of the population a higher stake in the survival of the incumbent and in the maintenance of domestic order.[48] This combination of military and nonmilitary methods enabled the incumbents to inflict decisive defeat upon strong Communist guerrilla movements in the Philippines and Malaya.[49] It is rarely enough to build up the internal security forces. The government must win over the population by giving hard evidence of its willingness and ability to make social reforms (greater equality of land tenure, improved education and health facilities, progressive taxation), foster economic development, and establish a relatively humane pattern of administration. Terroristic tactics and the denial of individual rights by the government may not according to specialists, disaffect the general population if terror is convincingly used as a temporary expedient rather than as endemic to the administration of the state.[50] As governments grow more aware of their capacity to deal with domestic insurgency there may be less need for special supranational protection. States may help the incumbent carry out this anti-insurgency program by giving large amounts of foreign aid. There is nothing incorrect about such aid, at least according to current conceptions of international relations, nor would it become wrong in a disarming world.[51] Just as the threat of a Communist takeover in Western Europe disappeared after political stability and economic health were restored, so the same pattern may gradually dry up the opportunities for indirect aggression and subversion in the newly developing parts of the world.

Internal security needs are partly a function of the degree of spontaneous domestic opposition. An unpopular repressive regime, other things being equal, requires a larger internal security establishment than does a popularly supported regime. This requirement itself creates difficult problems in a disarming world besides its obvious tendency to stabilize totalitarian control. It gives the most aggressive states a justification for having larger military establishments than their more peaceful neighbors. If one grants some correlation between internal repression and a policy of external coercion, then a generalized tolerance of security forces adequate for internal needs may be convertible into policies of external

---

[48] See Lucian W. Pye, "Lessons from the Malayan Struggle Against Communism," M.I.T. Center for International Studies, C/57-17; Symposium, "Unconventional Warfare," *The Annals*, Vol. 341, 1962, pp. 1-107; but see Guy J. Parker, "Notes on Non-Military Measures in Control of Insurgency," RAND Paper, P-2642, October 1962.

[49] Lucian W. Pye, *Guerrilla Communism in Malaya*, Princeton, Princeton University Press, 1956; Alan Scaff, *The Philippine Answer to Communism*, Stanford, Stanford University Press, 1955.

[50] Cf. Charles T. R. Bohannan, "Antiguerrilla Operations" in Symposium cited in note 48 *supra*, pp. 19-29.

[51] George Liska, *The New Statecraft: Foreign Aid in American Foreign Policy*, Chicago, University of Chicago Press, 1960, especially Chapter IV.

expansion and intimidation. The large standing armies of the Soviet Union and China are perhaps necessary for internal security. They are certainly useful also to influence the political disposition of their non-Communist neighbors. Finland and neutralist Asia illustrate the interaction.

Thus the very capacity that is encouraged to overcome various national vulnerabilities to indirect aggression has the contradictory consequence of giving relatively more military strength to the most dangerous states. This dilemma illustrates the paradoxical character of political action. We need to put competing policies in balanced focus. This is not a setting in which to choose one policy and neglect the other, or to detach the problem of internal security from the overall maintenance of international security.

32. Collective Defense Arrangements. Regional security organizations such as SEATO or the OAS claim competence to act in response to indirect aggression or subversion. For instance, Article 2 of the Southeast Asia Collective Defense Treaty declares that:

> In order more effectively to achieve the objectives of this Treaty the Parties, separately and jointly, by means of continuous and effective self-help and mutual aid will maintain and develop their capacity to resist armed attack and to prevent and *counter subversive activities directed from without* against their territorial integrity and political stability. (Emphasis supplied)[52]

Presumably such a competence would survive disarmament, although it is difficult to assess its usefulness as a response to various hypothetical instances of alleged indirect aggression and subversion. If other methods of control were effective enough to establish persuasively significant external participation by the indirect aggressor-subverter then the collective machinery of a regional organization would legitimize to the wider community of nations a neutralizing response far better than could a unilateral response on the national level, especially if undertaken by a nonregional actor. That is, from the perspective of legitimacy, collective intervention is, in general, preferable to unilateral intervention; it represents more of a community judgment and undertaking. It is less subject to criticism as a neocolonialist or egocentric adventure initiated for the satisfaction of purely national interests. There are instances when collective intervention is as bad, or worse, than unilateral forms; one can imagine a wrathful collective intervention of Israel by an

[52] The Southeast Asia Collective Defense Treaty Signed at Manila, September 8, 1954; cf. also Articles 6 and 8, Inter-American Treaty of Reciprocal Assistance, Signed at Rio de Janiero, Brazil, 1947.

alliance of Arab states that serves no constructive functions. The effectiveness of collective intervention as a method to defend against indirect aggression depends greatly upon the genuineness of the regional consensus and the extent to which a firm basis exists to support the charges of external support. Weak incumbent governments faced with internal protest movements are naturally inclined to allege indirect aggression so as to receive support. If such a pattern tends to stabilize the control of unpopular and oppressive governments, then it becomes an undesirable way to control the threats of indirect aggression and subversion.

Regional organizations do not always share the interpretation of civil strife that is accepted by the United States. There may be a genuine disagreement. There is also a tendency to resist the policy guidance, beyond a certain point, that United States tries to give. The membership of these regional organizations is often unwilling to execute blandly American foreign policy decisions.

This is no place to discuss the role of collective security machinery in a disarming world except to suggest that it does have a place in the spectrum of methods available to combat dangers of indirect aggression and subversion. It is hard to say how important this place will become, but it does exist as a substitute or supplement to whatever competence is contemplated for the IDO or other UN organs.

33. Control at the Source: National Rules Prohibiting the Export of Coercion. Major states in the world have written into their domestic legal system duties to prevent their territory from becoming a base for hostile expeditions against a foreign state. For example the United States Criminal Code contains the following provision:

§960 Expedition against friendly nations

Whoever, within the United States, knowingly begins or sets on foot or provides or prepares a means for or furnishes the money for, or takes part in, any military or naval expedition or enterprise to be carried on thence against the territory or dominion of any foreign prince or state, or of any colony, district, or people with whom the United States is at peace, shall be fined not more than $3000 or imprisoned not more than three years, or both.

This national provision is made a matter of national duty and individual governmental responsibility by prominent declaratory documents that have the status of emerging international legal obligations.[53] The obliga-

---

[53] 18 USCA § 960, 1948; the declaratory documents are the Draft Declaration on Rights and Duties of States and the Draft Code of Offenses Against the Peace and Security of Mankind. For convenient texts see Louis B. Sohn, ed., *Basic Documents of the United Nations*, Brooklyn, Foundation Press, 1956, pp. 26-27, 99-100.

tion to introduce domestic litigation on this subject to implement the pledge of a disarmament treaty could not be expected to have much impact on the policy of a totalitarian society, the leadership of which is not bound by its own law to any significant extent.[54]

The extent to which a nation is obliged under existing rules of international law to prevent its territory from being used by private individuals for subversive activities against other states is uncertain.[55] The aggrieved state in traditional international law has no means to obtain redress other than to protest the activity. The United Nations Charter with its emphasis on the development of friendly and peaceful relations should probably be interpreted as prohibiting the official toleration of private activities designed to subvert or instigate revolution in a foreign state. Such a conception, as Garcia-Mora points out, can be traced back at least as far as Vattel who observed that:

> The Nation, or the sovereign, must not allow its citizens to injure the subjects of another State, much less to offend that State itself; and this is not only because no sovereign should permit those under his rule to violate the precepts of the natural law, which forbids such acts, but also because Nations should mutually respect one another and avoid any offense, injury, or wrong, in a word, anything which might be harmful to others.[56]

Such an attitude toward international relations extends also, one would suppose, to a duty to prohibit the use of territory for the private or public transmission of hostile propaganda.[57] Certainly, activity within the reach of this statute would be useful to regulate and prohibit, to the extent possible, in a disarming world, although regulation in a democratic society encounters problems of interference with private activities, as well as the guarantees of free speech and the policy of encouraging the harassment of authoritarian regimes by the application of external pressures. At least it should be constitutionally possible to prohibit hostile acts against foreign states to the same extent that we prohibit seditious and subversive acts against our own government.[58] And the notion of insulation is somewhat artificial if one takes account

54 Cold war pressure also leads the United States to follow a course of action that is not consistent with applicable rules of international law. See Chapters VI-IX.
55 Hersch Lauterpacht, "Revolutionary Activities by Private Persons against Foreign States," 22 *American Journal of International Law* 105 (1928); Manuel R. Garcia-Mora, "International Responsibility for Subversive Activities and Hostile Propaganda by Private Persons Against Foreign

States," 35 *Indiana Law Journal* 306 (1960).
56 Emmerich de Vattel, *Droit des Gens*, Bk. II, Chap. VI, § 72, Fenwick trans. 1916, quoted by Garcia-Mora, p. 311.
57 Garcia-Mora, *op.cit. supra*, note 55, pp. 322-23.
58 For a celebrated decision that elicited a variety of interpretations of the relations between individual right and the social defense see U.S. v. Dennis, 341 U.S. 494, 1951.

of the availability of the United Nations as a forum to expose, censure, and act against abuses of fundamental human rights.

This formal discussion does not take account of the evidence of a widespread unwillingness of expanding nations to restrain subversive activities against foreign societies governed in a manner that is perceived by them to be objectionable. This is not just a matter of cold war hostility. The efforts of Middle Eastern states to subvert one another is familiar, and the availability of a sympathetic haven in foreign territory is an ingrained aspect of their international relations. Newspaper reports gave prominence to the establishment of military training bases for Angolan rebels on Congolese territory;[59] the overtness of this undertaking indicates the ease with which anticolonial aspirations overcome duties to maintain peaceful relations. Such an immune sanctuary for insurgent preparations and operations often has a crucial relevance to the outcome of an internal struggle for power. The successful counterinsurgency in Greece was partly a consequence of Tito's refusal, after his break with Stalin, to permit, Yugoslav territory to be used by Greek rebels.[60] For a military sanctuary in a contiguous foreign state makes it most difficult to extinguish a rebellion, almost regardless of how strong, popular, or progressive the incumbent regime happens to be.[61]

National control over subversive and revolutionary activity with a foreign target presents a conflict between a commitment to world order and the pursuit of a certain conception of national justice. For instance, Jaja Wachuku, Minister of Foreign Affairs in Nigeria, expressed what appears to be a prevailing Afro-Asian attitude when he said: "Nowhere in the world . . . will Nigeria countenance humiliations of people of African descent; and we will not consider any action on our part as interference in the internal affairs of another state."[62] This commitment overrides other considerations to an extent that makes it unreliable to expect much implementation of national control if it is once pledged—and even if it is once pledged and even if it is introduced into the domestic legal system. The same limitation of an almost absolute nature, exists with respect to the control of the use of the Soviet Union and China as directional and training bases for the international

[59] Cf. e.g. reports in the *New York Times*, August 21, 22, 1962, p. 1.

[60] The participation in the civil war of Greece's Northern neighbors is fully described in a pamphlet issued by the Greek Under-Secretariat for Press and Informations, *The Conspiracy Against Greece*, 1962.

[61] For a useful survey of factors relevant to the outcome of an internal war see Klaus Knorr, "Unconventional Warfare: Strategy and Tactics in Internal Strife," *The Annals* Vol. 341, 1962, pp. 53-64.

[62] Quoted by Edward A. Tiryakian, "African Political Development," *World Politics*, xiv (1962), 700-12, 704. Tiryakian, an African specialist, adds that "this is a statement that all independent African countries affirm, a statement of intention that applies most readily to South Africa and Portuguese Africa, but not inconceivably to the United States as well" (p. 704).

Communist movement. Thus if we include the transnational operations of Communism as part of the subject-matter of indirect aggression and subversion then it is not plausible to rely too heavily upon norms of self-regulation. Even here, however, cynical oversimplification may mislead us. It may be significant if national control in Communist countries would work toward the elimination of hostile propaganda and of participation in foreign insurgencies from the cold war; this possibility may be consistent with the milder formulations of peaceful coexistence, especially if mildness is encouraged rather than abandoned after disarmament commences.

Agreements by Communist states to implement national control may not be as meaningless as they would appear to be from a cynical perspective.[63] However, it would be foolish to expect the adoption of national control to restrain a nation that considers its vital interests to require recourse to indirect aggression and subversion. United States toleration of the activities of Castro exiles on domestic territory between 1960 and 1962 illustrates the domestic pressures that can emerge; even under such special circumstances, however, the existence of prohibitive rules acts as a constraining force that restricts how far exiles will be allowed to go.

The presence of national rules inhibits the behavior of officials since a government will be reluctant to encourage attitudes of disrespect for the authority of its own law. This would apply even in a totalitarian society, especially if, as is the case today in the Soviet Union, terror is abandoned as a central technique of social control. Domestic critics of a foreign policy that includes subversion and indirect aggression can argue from national law, thereby maintaining their position without apparent disloyalty to their nation as the prime source of authority and values.

It is relevant to recall here Section IV, No. 29 on the obligation of parties to the treaty to introduce disarmament duties, including presumably the pledge to refrain from indirect aggression and subversion, into national legislation in Stage II (G, 5) of the April 18th Proposals. This provision could be extended to require the national adoption of whatever implementing methods are agreed upon by the subsidiary body of the IDO (which is presently entrusted with the task).

34. *Therapeutic Intervention and Counterintervention as a Means of Collective Self-Defense Against Indirect Aggression.* Nonintervention is a basic conception of the traditional system of international law. Behavior properly classifiable as indirect aggression or subversion is pre-

---

63 The expectation of reciprocity may induce nations to regulate subversive activity emanating from their territory, especially if the aspiration for minimum order grows stronger.

sumably a violation of nonintervention norms. The factual interdependence of modern political life, the pervasiveness of the cold war, and the practice of major international actors makes strict adherence to a policy of nonintervention inadvisable and implausible. The limitations of adherence are especially apparent if the duty of nonintervention implies an obligation to refrain from participation in civil strife taking place in a foreign state. The nonintervention approach was decisively rejected by the Western democracies after the lessons taught by the Spanish Civil War had been learned.[64] If help is given to one side in a civil war then it is permissible to help the other side. Operative restrictions upon participation arise mainly from considerations of prudence, discouraging support by the United States of the East European insurgencies of 1956, rather than of law or morality.[65]

The strategy of counterintervention, then, is fully available as a method of response to indirect aggression and subversion. The extension of support for the incumbent regime—the legitimate government in a constitutional sense—is a virtually unchallenged area of discretionary action in international relations. The retention of some of this discretion on a national level in a disarming world would seem more valuable than treaty pledges and IDO powers. Without retained national discretion, the prospects for successful counterinsurgency would diminish greatly especially in Southeast Asia. A major role of the national competence to participate in counterinterventionary movements is often to present an alternative to action undertaken by an organized community of nations such as the United Nations or the Organization of American States. Support for supranational intervention seems to depend upon a perception that the less desirable alternative is rival national interventions; such a process was evident in Lebanon in 1958 and in the Congo in 1960. It is important to retain a residual national competence in a disarming world to discourage the efforts of those that would otherwise act to paralyze a supranational response.

It would seem to be the case that the United States military capability to respond to appeals for defense against a subverter or indirect aggressor would not diminish in the early stages of disarmament. This would be emphatically true if the United States allocates its defense budget in the predisarmament period to combine minimum deterrence with a maximum capability for diverse participation in internal war. If a percentage cut is made in weapons and force levels that is similar to the numbers used in the April 18th Proposals, then it becomes essential to plan now

64 See Chapters IV and V.

65 For perceptive analysis see Manfred Halpern, "The Morality and Politics of Intervention," in James N. Rosenau, ed., *International Aspects of Civil Strife*, Princeton, Princeton University Press, 1964, pp. 249-88.

for projected defense needs in a disarming world. From such a perspective security objectives would be promoted more by the capacity for military responses to intervention in internal affairs than by the wasting asset of strategic nuclear superiority.

Unilateral coercive conduct in the contemporary world is both dangerous and unpopular. It is essential, therefore, to improve the capacity of supranational institutions to assist victims of indirect aggression and subversion. Such a capacity should not be made available to suppress every domestic rebellion. The applicant for support should not receive it unless persuasive evidence of significant external participation or its prospect is produced. Otherwise the possibility of revolutionary change is foreclosed. In an authoritarian society this would prevent radical change altogether as other modes of change are already foreclosed. There is thus a need here to reconcile the claims of the insurgent with those of the incumbent by a demonstration of the reality of the government's accusation of actual or imminent substantial external participation.

The basic idea here is to suggest that it appears sensible to retain a residual competence and defense capability for counterintervention, and perhaps anticipatory intervention, in a disarming world. At the same time it is important to build up the counterintervention competence and capability of regional and universal organizations.

35. On the Definition of Indirect Aggression. The most orthodox proposal for the specific control of aggression, including its indirect varieties, has been to commend the formal adoption of an authoritative definition. Such a proposal has been sponsored since the earliest days of Soviet participation in the League of Nations by the USSR. It continues to be advocated by the Soviet bloc (and others) and resisted by the United States and its NATO allies. Because of the continuing importance of the debate, and its obvious applicability to the design of a disarmament process, a rather detailed discussion of the merits and demerits of a definition of indirect aggression is given here.

If we assume a disarmament treaty which includes a pledge to refrain from indirect aggression and subversion, a series of important questions are presented for our consideration. We consider, first, those questions that touch upon the value of defining or otherwise specifying the character of indirect aggression and subversion. Such an inquiry considers the technique of definition to be one of the "arrangements necessary to assure states against indirect aggression and subversion." (See April 18th Proposals, Stage II, G, 2, b.)

Is it beneficial to supply a definition or specification of the character of indirect aggression and subversion for the guidance of the parties, the IDO, or any other decision-making organ of the United Nations? If it is in some sense beneficial, should the definition be included in the treaty or separated, at least formally, from an agreement that is primarily about weapons reduction? Should a definition be conceived of as "a method" to curtail recourse to the prohibited activity? Or if we favor entrusting the parties, the IDO, or the UN with an interpretation of an unspecified and unspecifiable pledge, then what sort of standard is available to distinguish between a true and false allegation of indirect aggression and subversion? What are the relationships between "indirect aggression and subversion" and direct aggression? Why was the April 18th pledge restricted to indirect aggression and subversion? Does the importance of the pledge remain constant throughout the disarmament process? Or is there a pattern of fluctuation that relates to the stage of disarmament?

In the search for an understanding of the role of law in the control of indirect aggression and subversion in a disarming world no issue occasions more confusion than the benefits, detriments, and wisdom of including a definition of the prohibited activity in the basic instrument of agreement. For one thing, there is present a tendency, almost a habit, to intertwine the inconsistent requirements of foreign policy with a formula for the growth of world order, which confuses the perception of the issue. If, for instance, one compares the policy perspectives of the American representative in the various relevant UN auspices[66] with the world order orientation of Quincy Wright[67] or Louis Sohn,[68] then it becomes apparent their disagreements about the effect of a definition represent a fundamental incompatibility in viewpoint: the diplomat is trying to maintain freedom of action for the United States to cope with certain techniques of political expansion adopted by our national rivals in world affairs, whereas these two commentators are thinking about the optimum conditions for the successful discharge of peace-keeping functions by international institutions.

It is crucial to realize that the Soviet Union and the United States seem to disagree about the propriety of coercive participation in foreign internal wars and that this disagreement would undoubtedly give rise to radically opposed interpretations of what was permitted and prohibited by a renunciation of indirect aggression and subversion. How, for instance, does it relate to the Soviet commitment to support wars of

[66] Cf. e.g. 1956 Special Committee on the Question of Defining Aggression, Report, A/AC 77/L.13; 6th Committee, Mtgs. 278-295, DocA/2087, GAOR, 6th Sess., January 1952.

[67] Quincy Wright, "The Concept of Aggression in International Law," 29 *American Journal of International Law* 386 (1935); *id.*, "The Prevention of Aggression," 50 *American Journal of International Law* 514 (1956).

[68] Louis B. Sohn, "The Definition of Aggression" 45 *Virginia Law Review* 697 (1959).

national liberation? Such differing perspectives toward the use of force when violence is between rival domestic factions contrast with the consensus that joins the Soviet Union and the United States to a rather similar attitude toward the use of violence by one nation against another. This contrast suggests that it is both more difficult (because of the divergence) and more necessary (to establish a common core of meaning) to define or otherwise specify the character of *indirect aggression and subversion* than of the direct forms of *aggression*.

It should also be pointed out that the Communist nations interpret United States military aid to foreign governments, especially to reactionary regimes, as "indirect aggression." It is partly a matter of where one locates legitimacy in a domestic social system. The Soviet interpretation of history precludes an automatic assumption that the incumbent regime is legitimate and thus entitled to support.

A failure to specify may avoid a hazardous, perhaps impossible, negotiation. But it may also suppress a disagreement about the ground rules in a disarming world that is likely to wreck the disarmament process. The resolution of this dilemma depends partly upon whether the United States requires any *additional protection* during disarmament against the dangers of the behavior that *it* identifies as indirect aggression and subversion. This raises complex problems that involve an assessment of Communist intentions, capabilities, and strategies in different parts of the world once disarmament commences. This chapter tries only to suggest the *texture* of the overall problem; it makes no pretense to provide specific solutions, a task often better entrusted to policy-makers expert in risk-balancing judgments.

The perspectives of politics and world order are joined by some scholarly observers who try to premise the growth of law upon the realities of the political atmosphere. Such a contextual analysis persuades Julius Stone[69] to consider attempts at definition, in the area of international force, to be futile and dangerous. In contrast, Myres McDougal[70] and B.V.A. Röling[71] favor a sophisticated, selective, and limited reliance upon the definition of concepts dealing with coercion as one way to improve the quality of international order.

It seems useful to depict very briefly the general role of definitions in various contexts of legal order. Without this perspective it is difficult to examine the long history of failures to achieve a binding agreement about a definition of aggression. This, in turn, encourages a considera-

---

[69] Julius Stone, *Aggression and World Order*, Berkeley, University of California Press, 1958.
[70] Myres S. McDougal and Florentino P. Feliciano, *Law and Minimum World Public Order—The Legal Regulation of*

International Coercion, New Haven, Yale University Press, 1961, pp. 59-67, 143-60.
[71] B.V.A. Röling, "The Question of Defining Aggression," in *Symbolae Verzijl*, The Hague, Martinus Nijhoff, 1958, pp. 314-36.

tion of the nature of the search for a definition of indirect aggression and subversion and the special bearing of this search upon the construction of a comprehensive disarmament system such as is envisioned by the April 18th Proposals.

Let it be said at once that it is a far different venture to try to come up with some verbal formula that is satisfying to most nations in the world in the abstract and the development of a verbal formula that is to function as a part of an institutional arrangement such as would accompany disarmament. For in the latter situation the rules described by the definition are not expected to generate by themselves conforming behavioral standards. Their function is primarily to communicate general guidance to national officials and supranational administrators, with an expectation of interpretation and implementation in the light of unfolding patterns of experience and controversy. The prior enunciation of the character of forbidden behavior might also help to mobilize world public opinion and to facilitate adequate community responses in the event of violative behavior. The prestige of a nascent institution might be enhanced if it could invoke prior standards to support its sanctioning activity rather than if it must act upon the basis of *ad hoc* political determinations made by the administering agency of control. The conscience of the participants is also engaged once their task is the application of a prior standard to contested facts instead of the composition *de novo* of a judgment of the overall merits of contending claims in an atmosphere already fraught with tension and hostility. Some might expect an acceptable definition to depoliticize the operation of the IDO in crisis situations, thereby perhaps increasing the stability of the entire disarmament system, especially in its early stages of operation.

The controversy about definitions also seems to express a nonpolitical aspect of intellectual history that leads the United States and the Soviet Union to oppose one another, each with sincerity growing out of a long tradition. Russians have from the time of Czar Alexander and the Congress of Vienna promoted a definitional approach to the maintenance of international peace. In contrast, British and Americans, nurtured in the nominalism of the common law tradition, dislike what they regard as the pretense of generalization; one European scholar has recently called vivid attention to "the Anglo-Saxon horror of defining at all—it is said that in the British Empire defining amounted almost to high treason."[72] The importance of national style is illustrated rather extremely by the willingness of Frenchmen, and no one else, to devote book-length studies to analyses of the Preamble of the United Nations Charter; this is not sheer folly—it is just one part of French

[72] *Id.,* p. 331.

fidelity to the Cartesian insistence on the cardinal importance of getting first principles straight.

These references to national approach are not meant as a digression. For it seems useful to suggest the relevance of nonpolitical factors in the formation of national attitudes toward definition. It helps us to understand international negotiations if we can sort out elements of disagreement that arise from sources deeper than the cold war. There is a banal and deceptive tendency to reduce everything in the dynamics of contemporary international relations to the terms set by the dyadic relationship of the United States and the Soviet Union as principal rivals. A sense of historical proportion is helpful to overcome self-righteous habits of interpreting every Soviet position that we dislike as a sinister attempt to promote the Communist cause. It harms the quest for world order to oppose something just because the Soviet Union favors it. But there is a discernible tendency to react in just this fashion to a proposal to define aggression. We can ill afford to neglect astute analysis here, especially in view of the non-Communist advocacy of a definition by nations in Latin America and Asia.[73] On the other hand, we must not forget that the cold war centers, as has been said, upon opposed interpretations of activity that each side views as "indirect aggression and subversion" by the other. Of course this comment applies *a fortiori* to Soviet interpretations of United States negotiating positions.

A sense of national diversity also suggests that an insistence upon the correctness of a given national approach—say, that of the United States —illustrates a rather fruitless instance of self-righteous parochialism. In other words, the simple-minded advocacy or opposition to a definition of aggression is certainly a matter for national policy, but it may also carry forth a national habit of thought that is no longer beneficial.

a. Some remarks on the nature of legal definitions. H.L.A. Hart asks a helpful clarifying question: "What are rules and to what extent is law an affair of rules?"[74] For the attempt to define is often undertaken to clarify the extent of a legal obligation so that those subject to it or charged with its application may distinguish between permitted and forbidden conduct. Such a definition is, as Hart suggests, a kind of map in which "at one and the same time it may make explicit the latent principle which guides our use of a word, and may exhibit relationships between the phenomena to which we apply the word and other phenomena."[75] We become clearer, or at least come to realize our unclarity, about what it is that we want people to refrain from doing. J. L. Austin put this quest for definitions in focus by saying that we "are look-

[73] Sohn, *op.cit. supra*, note 68, p. 698.
[74] Cf. H.L.A. Hart, *The Concept of Law*,

Oxford, Clarendon Press, 1961, p. 13.
[75] *Id.*, p. 14.

ing not merely at words . . . but also at realities we use words to talk about. We are using a sharpened awareness of words to sharpen our perception of the phenomena."[76]

Hart cautions that this variety of definition "is not always available nor, when it is available, always illuminating."[77] Beneficial availability depends upon whether the phenomena being differentiated by the definition fit into a larger family of things that can be referred to for the sake of comparison and contrast. In our context, this requires us to determine how indirect aggression and subversion relate to other forms of coercion, intervention, influence, interdependence and sympathy in the relations of one nation to the internal affairs in another.

Once a definition of a legal rule is achieved it will not then have an indisputable meaning in all instances for all observers. To suppose that it will misconceives the unavoidable indeterminacy in every rule-applying act. Hart does think that all legal rules have "a central core of undisputed meaning"; however, it is also the case that "all rules have a penumbra of uncertainty where the judge must choose between alternatives."[78] This view of legal rules contrasts with the ultra-legal realist position taken by Myres S. McDougal who regards indeterminacy to be an all-pervasive attribute of legal process. McDougal argues that there are always complementary rules available for the judge to choose between to support the preferred legal decision.[79] Thus, a definition, no matter how clear, can never govern the interpretation of a rule because the notion of interpretation is itself enmeshed in the complementarity of human response, necessarily allowing various interpretations of a given rule or the choice of the applicable rule from several inconsistent rules; and each conclusion is equally "correct" from the standpoint of logic.[80]

A final general consideration that it is useful to bear in mind is that the process of definition itself may improve the analysis and perception of the problem that the rule is designed to deal with. R.W.M. Dias says that ". . . what is important is not the definitions, but the analysis on which they are based."[81] Thus "the completeness of the definition reflects the completeness of the definer's knowledge of the subject-matter."[82]

[76] *Id.*, p. 14 quotes J. L. Austin, "A Plea for Excuses" (57 *Proceedings of the Aristotelian Society*, 1956-57, p. 8).

[77] *Id.*, p. 14.

[78] *Id.*, p. 12.

[79] A clear statement can be found in McDougal, "The Ethics of Applying Systems of Authority: The Balanced Opposites of a Legal System," in Harold D. Lasswell and Harlan Cleveland, eds., *The Ethic of Power*, New York, Harper and Brothers, 1962, pp. 221-40.

[80] An interesting application of a policy-oriented interpretation of "clear rules" can be found in McDougal and Richard N. Gardner, "The Veto and the Charter: an Interpretation for Survival" in Myres S. McDougal and Associates, *Studies in World Public Order*, New Haven, Yale University Press, 1960, pp. 718-60.

[81] R.W.M. Dias, "Mechanism of Definition as Applied to International Law," 1954 *Cambridge Law Journal* 215-31, at 215.

[82] *Id.* at 217.

This point is often overlooked. The search for a definition itself discloses the inadequacies of our capacity to deal with a problem and thereby identifies genuine policy disputes, as well as areas of insufficient knowledge. The failure to agree about a definition may facilitate the communication of national concerns in the course of international negotiations, and thus convey to the other side the sincerity and reasonableness of certain treaty demands. For example, the failure to be able to define indirect aggression may help to justify recourse to alternative or complementary techniques: regional security systems, boundary delimitation procedures, border control, procedures of nonrecognition or deferred recognition for revolutionary regimes.

The nature, then, of the definitional enterprise depends upon a network of variables in addition to the peculiar difficulties of specifying phenomena that remain as indeterminate as does indirect aggression and subversion.

b. The quest for a definition of aggression.[83] The Briand-Kellogg Pact of 1928 (The Pact of Paris for the Renunciation of War as an Instrument of National Policy)[84] gave rise to the first sustained attempt to define aggression. For when war is renounced as an instrument of national policy it seems natural to implement the renunciation with a clear conception of what it is that nations have pledged themselves not to do. As the right of self-defense is retained by nations it is especially essential to try to determine which kinds of force survive as permissible instances (self-defense) and which constitute forbidden behavior (war). As war suggests a condition of belligerent relationship rather than the unilateral recourse by one nation to illegal conduct the notion of aggression has developed as a pivotal concept for the establishment of rights and duties.

But why a definition? And why so much agony about the benefits and burdens that attend the acceptance of a definition of aggression? Some ardent advocates of a definition seek to use it as a substitute for adequate institutions of enforcement and interpretation. The renunciation of war amounts to an illusory promise if states retain freedom to characterize their own use of force as "self-defense." A definition, especially if quite specific, purports to condition this discretion upon compliance with objective standards. It thereby provides a primitive substitute for authoritative decision-making by centralized institutions.

A variation of this position, advanced most clearly by Quincy

[83] This is most fully documented in the book by Stone, *op.cit. supra*, note 69; cf. also Ricardo J. Alfaro, "La cuestión de la definición de la Agresión," 59 *Revista de Derecho Internacional* 361 (Cuba, 1951); Sir Gerald Fitzmaurice, "The Definition of Aggression," 1 *International and Comparative Law Quarterly* 137 (1952).
[84] 94 League of Nations Treaty Series 57.

Wright,[85] regards a definition of aggression as an essential component of the collective security systems envisioned by the League and now by the United Nations. Primitive legal institutions need to invoke fixed standards of interpretation when making a decision affecting vital political interests of hostile states; a clear definition enhances the capacity of supranational institutions to make a decision when peace is threatened by the use of force and tends to achieve more respect for the procedure and decision on the part of community membership.

Opponents of a definition are very distrustful of the capacity of words to delineate acceptable limits on behavior in a community that is as disorganized and riven as is the contemporary world. The vagueness of the concepts of self-defense and aggression, when left in an undefined state, accords fully with the impracticability of imposing, or purporting to impose, premature limits upon national discretion. It isn't possible to generalize, according to this view, about acts of nations that involve the use of force. This was well stated by Payson Wild: "Those who have wrestled with the problem of defining an aggressor well know that he who formally violates the stipulated bond, may, after all, have justice on his side, and not merit condemnation. That is the danger of formal and arbitrary definitions of aggression: the technical violator may not be the 'real' one."[86] This assessment accords with the summary of the remarks made by the United States member of the 1956 Special Committee on the Question of Defining Aggression:

He pointed out the difficulty of putting into words something that was so dependent on circumstances, on the context as a whole, of a given situation as was the case with an act of aggression. . . . Since each threat of aggression varied in its history and its facts in an infinite number of ways, it taxed human ingenuity and wisdom beyond reasonable limits to evolve a framework which would anticipate events and provide useful guidance.[87]

These objections to a definition assert the insufficiency of deeds to indicate whether or not a given instance of force is permissible self-defense or forbidden aggression. That crucial distinction depends upon a subtle combination of circumstances, including an assessment of the intentions of the actors, that is lost if criteria of action are mechanically used to classify the legality of a contested use of force. Thus the 1956 attack by Israel, France, and Great Britain upon Egypt must be understood in light of Arab threats to destroy Israel, *fedayeen* border harass-

[85] Quincy Wright, "The Prevention of Aggression," 50 *American Journal of International Law* 515 (1956).
[86] Payson S. Wild, Jr., *Sanctions and Treaty Enforcement*, Cambridge, Harvard University Press, 1934, p. 18.
[87] 1956 Special Report, *op.cit. supra*, note 66, p. 12.

ment, illegal interferences with Israeli shipping, refusals to negotiate compensation for the Suez Canal, and a general pattern of lawless and unjust behavior by Nasser, as well as by reference to which side committed an "armed attack."[88] Such a view of aggression regards it as very detrimental to isolate a factor like priority of armed attack—as would supposedly be done if a definition were applied—to identify the aggressor.[89]

Confusion about the role and function of a definition is partly a consequence of the mixed objectives that are to be thus served. Is a definition an intrinsic instrument of world order or is it a part of the collective security mechanism of the United Nations? If we conceive of aggression in the Charter context, then is it necessary to consider the meaning of such cognate norms as are represented by notions of "armed attack" and "self-defense"?[90] Röling regards it as helpfully clarifying to specify the nature of "armed attack" but deceptive and unwise to define "aggression."[91] For once aggression is defined then it is exceedingly difficult to determine the way in which it relates to the restraints of Article 2(4) and 41 and the tolerances of individual and collective self-defense. That is, it is better to clarify Charter norms than to superimpose a new conception of prohibited coercion-like aggression that somehow parallels without supplanting the Charter notions of prohibited force. The problem of correlation is already present in the Charter to the extent that an "act of aggression," in Article 39 is not adapted to the language of Article 51.

It is not important to attempt here to clarify the relations between these overlapping norms, but it is important to see that a definition is made in a normative environment inhabited by relevant and interdependent norms. It may put the security system in a state of normative disequilibrium[92] if there is great attention given to what is prohibited (direct and indirect aggression) but little to what is permitted (self-defense). Thus it may be important to combine IDO responsibility for implementing the renunciaton of indirect aggression with supervision over so-called defensive measures.

[88] Stone, op.cit. supra, note 69, pp. 100-03.
[89] But see Sohn, op.cit. supra, note 68 for response.
[90] D. W. Bowett, Self-Defense in International Law, New York, Praeger, 1958; McDougal and Feliciano, op.cit. supra, note 70, pp. 121-260.
[91] Cf. Röling, op.cit. supra, note 71.
[92] That is, complementary norms develop to satisfy complementary policies of actors in a social order. If one norm is made paramount, then the policies to be served by complementary, perhaps inconsistent, norms are to that extent sacrificed. Exposition of any particular norm and the claims that it makes with respect to behavior often neglects modifications that should be introduced in light of the behavioral needs of complementary norms. Thus in our haste to prohibit aggression we should not lose sight of the policies underlying norms of self-defense and collective security.

Of course, part of the confusion arises because of the existence of a wide variety of types of definitions. The enumerative style of definition specifies a series of acts, any of which lead a use of force to be an instance of aggression. The formula style of definition consists of a general clause forbidding recourse to force except in cases of self-defense which is not much more specific than are the Charter prohibitions that now exist. And finally, there are various mixtures of enumerative definitions with general formulas, thereby combining the advantages of specificity with those of flexibility.[93] Most of the states in the world appear to favor some variant of the mixed definition. Objections to the use of a general formula as a mode of definition are that it is vague and superfluous, that it leaves the burden of proof upon the victim of attack, and that it does not provide national officials or international administrators with requisite guidance. The purely enumerative mode of definition, however, has been criticized on the grounds that it is inflexible, that it is contrary to the Charter system which creates a duty in Articles 24 and 39 for the Security Council to make *ad hoc* assessments of responsibility for uses of force on the basis of a broad grant of discretion, that it is necessarily incomplete and thereby tempts an aggressor to find loopholes that would make his coercive behavior formally immune from censure, that the constituent acts in the definition are themselves unclear without a second level of definitions, and that some prohibited acts may in certain circumstances not amount to aggressive conduct.

The mixed definition, providing specific illustrations but withholding specific judgment and authorizing either the expansion of the concept of aggression beyond the illustration or its suspension in the light of circumstances, has been criticized as a confused combination of contradictory styles of approach to legal control. For either a definition should be a real guide to behavior, as the enumerative variety purports to be, or it should reconfirm the need to judge the legal character of a particular use of force by reference to the particularities of circumstance and claim. To weld the two together is to provide neither stable limits nor to express the political character of a judgment of aggression in the present kind of world.

McDougal and Feliciano clarify this debate about the appropriate style of definition considerably. They observe that ". . . it is of course as futile to seek a reificatory, absolutist, and all-sufficing definition of aggression as of any other legal concept or word. But the impossibility of absolute precision does not necessarily render complete confusion

---

[93] McDougal and Feliciano have a useful discussion of the three types of definition, *op.cit. supra*, note 70, pp. 143-55.

desirable."[94] The objective of a definition is to clarify the variables that should influence any official seeking to appraise legality: "In this most fundamental problem of all, as in lesser problems, legal principles might be formulated which would serve the same function that other legal principles serve—that of bringing to the focus of attention of a decision-maker relevant factors in context which should rationally affect decision. From this perspective, the basic task is one of categorizing such variable contextual factors with respect to the distinction between permissible and non-permissible coercion."[95] The authors then go on to list such variables as priority in resort to substantial coercion, the purpose, the degree of disruptive consequences, the need by the target state to resort to defensive coercion to protect its territory and independence, the level of coercion and the degree to which the defending state confines itself to a proportionate response, the relative willingness of the states involved to accept community decision, the relation of the coercion to the defense of nontotalitarian values of freedom and abundance, and the consequences of accepting a decision by the authoritative decision-maker.[96] Each of these variables is itself a complex and subtle characteristic of international behavior, but it is probably true that an agreed schedule of variables might raise the level of debate about contested uses of force and assist conscientious national officials to determine when it is reasonable to resort to force. It is important to differentiate a configurative approach from the enumerative type of definition in which the prior commission of any pattern of prohibited activity identifies that actor as the aggressor, regardless of the reasonableness of such behavior in context.

In contrast to McDougal-Feliciano, there is a significant approach to definition best expressed by Louis Sohn and Quincy Wright which accepts some inflexibility as a part of the costs of improving the system of world order. The Sohn-Wright approach to aggression argues in favor of stable limits on national discretion. Their argument proceeds from the implicit premise that law to be effective must concern itself with forbidden acts, not with the subtle configuration of events that give rise to the acts. Thus maximum objectification is desirable. We find that criminal responsibility in domestic society rests upon the performance of forbidden deeds by the defendant rather than upon the reasonableness of doing what was forbidden on a particular occasion. The focus of law upon the isolated forbidden act produces the novelist's fascination with the tension between law (objective determination of guilt) and justice (configurative assessment of innocence). McDougal and

[94] *Id.*, p. 62; cf. formulation, pp. 152-53.   [96] *Id.*, pp. 63-65.
[95] *Id.*, pp. 62-63.

Feliciano express this literary criticism of "legality" in the rhetoric of social science when they observe that ". . . the most basic defect of the Soviet and other comparable definitions is an overemphasis on material acts of coercion and on a mechanistic conception of priority; concomitantly they fail to take into account other factors which rationally are equally relevant, factors such as the nature of the objectives of the initiating and responding participants and the character of intensity of the coercion applied."[97]

Law does not seek a procedure to achieve a subjective appreciation of a particular event. Rather it forbids recourse to certain conduct on the basis of a sweeping prohibition that restricts the horizon of relevance on purpose and thereby risks offense to our sense of justice. Nevertheless, the standards established by unambiguous prohibition are ordinarily more easily applicable by those called upon to identify a violation or to guide their own conduct in conformity with law. In this respect a definition of aggression, according with the policy, doctrine, and practice of major states to avoid international war, may contribute most to the stability of the international system by asserting a series of acts which, if performed, constitute "aggression."[98] This would help to clarify the limits of what nations could do to pursue their objectives, reduce the prospects for international violence arising from miscalculation, mobilize community responses around pre-established norms, and crystallize the commitments of community conscience.

Two main obstacles block a full commitment to further clarification of the conception of aggression. First, the definiteness of this conception distorts international relationships in the absence of an adequate collective security arrangement. If a nation is unable to receive fair treatment of its claims except by force then it is both unjust and unrealistic to impose an absolute prohibition upon techniques of coercive settlement. Second, the political characteristics of revolutionary warfare give prominence to certain strategic asymmetries that make it very difficult for the West to contain Communist expansion without the use of force in foreign territories. Communist access to domestic politics by means of Communist party control, skill with infiltration and guerrilla tactics, and geopolitical proximity can only be neutralized in some societies by the use of Western military personnel and supplies. This means that a definition of aggression would appear to favor the Soviet interpretation of what it is legal to do in world affairs in the contemporary world. There are two ways to comprehend

[97] *Id.*, p. 145.
[98] Cf. Annex E at the end of this chapter for underlying reasoning.

such a conclusion. First, that strategic asymmetries make it dysfunctional to define aggression as the real aggressor (Communism) seems likely to benefit from it. Second, that the only way that the West can neutralize Communist expansive energy is by recourse to what would be considered aggression if a reasonable definition existed. Thus it might be argued that Sino-Soviet patterns of coercive influence are so elusive and minor (although highly effective) as to escape the definition whereas the Western patterns are necessarily explicit and major and would be caught within the definitional web.[99]

Part of the objection to a definition is more subtly related to the role of the United States in world politics. It suggests that we need to keep available the discretion to use force to prevent detrimental shifts in alliance or affinity, *whether or not* these shifts are attributable to Communist influence or recourse to techniques of indirect aggression and subversion. That is, the defense of American national interests requires us to use or threaten force to preserve a certain position of power in the world and this requirement is not satisfied *merely* by the neutralization of Communist activity. American activities in the Middle East, for instance, Iran and Lebanon, are illustrative of coercive participation that could not be reasonably justified by the theory of counter, preventive, or therapeutic intervention. Thus a definition that is effective would interfere with this kind of effort to protect the position of the United States in a disarming world. It is not only that we cannot find rules that would reliably govern our rivals but that we do not want to find *ourselves* bound by such rules. This is a very important line of thinking that pertains to the subject matter of this entire study.

There are several special problems that arise when one turns from a broad consideration of aggression to the special subject of indirect aggression and subversion. Is indirect aggression a type of aggression or is it something quite separate? There are two extra difficulties that harass the attempt to define indirect aggression and subversion that are not present when one is concerned to define the more classical conception of aggression as the wrongful initiation of war by one state against another. First, specific allegations of indirect aggression often arise from cold war confrontations in which each side feels that it is appropriately using force in a domestic struggle. That is, the character of indirect aggression is beclouded by the dispute about the limits and forms of permissible involvement in the domestic affairs of foreign states. This involves the status of the doctrine of national wars of lib-

[99] "Minor" and "major" refers only to the instruments of coercion used to advance the aggressor cause. It does not mean to suggest that impact of minor coercion is minor.

eration versus the status of Western claims to do whatever it wants to do to help an incumbent government, no matter how unpopular or undemocratic, to remain in control of the society. It is not that we help every bad incumbent or that the Soviets help every bad insurgent, but that each side deems itself free to decide on how to shape its policy toward an internal war in a foreign society. This means that adequate protection against indirect aggression requires a solution of the central dispute about how force may be used in contemporary world politics. For what we identify as indirect aggression the Soviets tend to call a just war of national liberation and what we regard as legitimate help to a constituted government they tend to regard as imperialism and aggression against "the people." An agreement about the character of indirect aggression that would be necessary for its definition must somehow come to terms with this ideological dispute at the center of the cold war. This contrasts with the difficulties of defining aggression which arise despite a firm consensus that includes *all* major states and supports in theory and practice the prohibition of the use of explicit force across boundaries, especially if it is likely to lead to encounters between military forces of different nations in an arena of combat that extends beyond the boundaries of a single nation.

The second extra difficulty arises from the vagueness that surrounds the subject of indirect aggression and subversion. The constituent facts are not visible in objective events discernible in the same manner by most observers. When an army attacks across a border it is easy to grasp what is happening, although it might not be so simple to assess responsibility. But with indirect aggression and subversion everything depends upon the *interpretation* given to inherently ambiguous objective events. How, for instance, does one interpret the activities of a national domestic Communist party? Is it assumed to be acting as a tool of Moscow or Peking or must this be established by evidence of explicit activity like central party directives, financial and material support, training activity, and so on? The vagueness of the objective events is accentuated by the imprecise boundary separating what is permitted from what is forbidden. Is it all right to encourage a revolution abroad by incendiary radio broadcasts? Does it depend upon whether the broadcast is made under government auspices or by private initiative? Legal order is always problematic when the proper legal disposition is not evident in the majority of cases from the acts themselves with a minimum of resort to their interpretation. This is especially true when interpretative perspectives are hostile to one another and proceed from different moral and political premises. Thus the cold war controversy about what makes the projection of influence and assistance across frontiers "aggression" is an input that aggravates the hazards of specifying a concept as indeterminate as "indirect aggression and subversion" in order to create rules of behavior for a legal system.

It is interesting that during the long debates about the definition of aggression there was considerable disagreement about whether to stretch the concept to include indirect aggression and subversion. The Report of the Special Committee says that ". . . many representatives spoke against the specific inclusion of indirect aggression in the definition," because "the concept of aggression would be unduly stretched" and similarly opposed inclusion of subversion on the ground that it "would harm its [the definition of aggression's] practical applicability."[100] Nevertheless, the International Law Commission in a report on its third session declared itself to favor the inclusion of indirect aggression within a definition of aggression. The following significant language was used:

> It was felt that a definition of aggression should cover not only force used openly by one State against another, but also indirect forms of aggression such as the fomenting of civil strife by one State in another, the arming by a State of organized bands for offensive purposes directed against another State, and the sending of "volunteers" to engage in hostilities against another State.[101]

It should be observed that a discussion in the context of the United Nations debate about a definition of aggression is significantly different than a proposal to include a definition as part of the ground rules accompanying comprehensive disarmament. Disarmament itself implies a gradual restructuring of world politics that might require and make easier certain coordinate renunciations of sovereign discretion to self-interpret what constitutes permissible interference in foreign societies.

Also it is essential to keep the focus rational. The hazards and difficulties that attend defining indirect aggression and subversion must be measured against the hazards and difficulties of leaving it undefined. It is no refutation to disclose problems with one course of action until this course has been balanced against alternatives.

c. A definition of indirect aggression and subversion in an arms control and disarmament agreement. A report by the Secretary General of the United Nations in 1952 gives a useful summary of various attitudes towards the definition of indirect aggression.[102] It is interesting that the discussion opens by observing that "the concept of indirect aggression is comparatively recent, having been discussed and introduced into in-

---

100 1956 Special Report, *op.cit. supra*, note 66, p. 12.

101 A/1858, para. 47; see also resolution 380, V, adopted by the General Assembly on November 17, 1950.

102 "Question of Defining Aggression," Report of the Secretary General, A/2211, October 3, 1952.

ternational law during the life of the United Nations."[103] Although as is observed elsewhere (paragraph 415) the practices covered by this new concept are of ancient origin, an abiding attribute of the struggle for the extension of power in international affairs. The Secretary General's Report usefully formulates the essence of indirect aggression:

> The characteristic of indirect aggression appears to be that the aggressor State, without itself committing hostile acts as a State, operates through third parties who are either foreigners or nationals seemingly acting on their own initiative. Representatives who have referred to indirect aggression have sometimes mentioned it in general terms, and at other times have pointed to certain facts which, in their view, constitute indirect aggression.[104]

The Report considers intervention in the affairs of another state, subversive action, incitement to civil war, maintenance of a fifth column, and "ideological" aggression or propaganda to be the major ways to commit indirect aggression. In light of this, we consider now the subject in a disarmament context.

B.V.A. Röling's analysis of the general problem of defining aggression seems helpful. He asks that we be "realists" and understand that "norms of law to be effective need a minimum of favorable circumstance." Furthermore, we must realize that ". . . the creation of norms for human behavior is only one factor contributing towards 'normal' behavior. The other factor is the creation of the conditions under which respect for these norms can be maintained."[105] Thus we cannot hope that a definition of prohibited conduct will by itself restrain behavior. It is essential to couple the prohibition with programs designed to make it effective. For indirect aggression this means attention to internal security, economic development, technical assistance, border delimitation, fundamental human rights, supranational legislative competence and some socialization of wealth-producing and wealth-distributing processes. Healthy domestic societies cut down the opportunities for this form of aggressive expansion. Well-administered and defined borders tend to make clandestine participation in civil strife more difficult, thereby inhibiting the participation or making it easily identifiable as aggression. Thus the behavior is moved from the penumbral region where it is hard to classify to the central core of undisputed meaning. Emphasis on the core meaning helps greatly the administration of a definition as it permits an international institution like the IDO or some

---

[103] *Id.*, p. 55, para. 408.
[104] *Id.*, p. 56, para. 414.
[105] Quotations in this paragraph are all to be found in Röling, *op.cit. supra*, note 71, p. 326.

other administrator to treat allegations in as nonpolitical a fashion as possible.

It is first important to examine a series of objectives which might be served by drawing up rules of prohibition for eventual inclusion in the disarmament agreement.[106] First, such provision would manifest the intentions of major signatories to make the disarmament process rest explicitly upon the continuation of the approximate political *status quo* for the cold war bloc rivals. Thus any major shift in cold war allegiance, especially to the Sino-Soviet bloc, would be attributed, especially in the West to disarmament and the consequent softening of defensive posture. The effect of making a renunciation of indirect aggression and subversion an integral part of the disarmament agreement is to give an aggrieved nation an easy way out. For it is quite simple for either side to explain radical political reversals in the rhetoric of indirect aggression and subversion; to wit, the fancied United States role in the 1956 Hungarian uprising or the supposed Soviet role in Castro's 1960 triumph over Batista. It is quite realistic, especially in the early stages of disarmament, to expect any cold war victory or defeat that significantly alter the *status quo* to lead to a breakdown of disarmament. Treaty inclusion serves warning of this possibility and provides states with a fairly easy escape from disarmament.

Second, the rules drafted might compensate the West for present disadvantages arising from strategic asymmetries. That is, neutralization of Communist opportunities for expansion are treated as almost a precondition for a renunciation of the use of force in world affairs. Thus there is a trade-off of indirect aggression for a gradual elimination of Western military superiority with respect to major or strategic instruments of coercion. An integral definition makes this clearly part of the disarmament bargain.

Third, rules governing indirect aggression and subversion might serve to clarify the limits of permissible national behavior in a disarming world. This would reinforce the dependence of peace upon mutual self-restraint and underscore the extent to which the success of disarmament rests upon behavior in nonmilitary sectors of international relations. It might also protect the disarmament process from unintended disturbances. Thus the process of drafting rules of indirect aggression would sharpen the appreciation of limits on the part of signatories and might serve to guide the conduct of national officials in a disarming world.

Fourth, these rules might enable the IDO and other international in-

---

[106] Section I attempts to specify the objectives that might be served by including the control of indirect aggression and subversion within the disarmament treaty framework.

stitutions to carry out its supervisory functions in a more successful manner. It would matter whether the IDO was expected to verify a violation, to take action that would restore the *status quo*, or to assure continuing compliance with the rules. It would also matter whether the response to a violation was left within the scope of national discretion or was made, at least in Stage III, an occasion for IDO or other supranational enforcement action.

Fifth, the endeavor to draft such rules might make clear the essential incapacity to regulate minor forms of coercion (indirect aggression and subversion) by reference to overt acts. This discovery would require either an abandonment of the venture or the development of some way to assess aggressive intent. At least, it would explain why a definition was impracticable, thereby making configurative analysis and an American insistence on retained discretion less of a denial of law and of a disparagement of legal methods of objectification than it might otherwise appear to be. An appreciation of the difficulty of negotiating a definition would create an intellectual foundation for giving wide discretionary competence to the IDO, but it would also disclose how closely the phenomenon of indirect aggression is intertwined with political perspectives. For a configurative approach does tend to uphold the bias of the particular observer. Thus if rival nations are given the decision-making role it would tend to allow withdrawal from disarmament in the event of any major shift in the *status quo*, whereas if the IDO characterized the contested conduct it would probably reach inconclusive interpretations that would not authorize countervailing extreme national responses. However, an unverified allegation of indirect aggression would be much less persuasive as a responsible basis for abrogating a disarmament agreement. The requirement of verification would guard somewhat against the dangers of threatened or actual premature or unjustifiable abrogation. The way in which responses to violations of rules governing indirect aggression and subversion are treated relates to the wisdom and type of specification that is appropriate.

Sixth, patterns of indirect aggression and subversion are the most usable kinds of force to achieve political expansion in the world today. Their prohibition in a disarmament agreement thus means that disarmament is a process to achieve peaceful relations as well as an agreement to throw weapons away. This supranational competence to prohibit indirect aggression and subversion could then be developed as a gradual and explicit substitute for unilateral and alliance defense systems. Thus the IDO would protect states from these forms of coercion and take over part of the role of regional defense communities.[107]

[107] For a useful series of essays on the way these problems are currently being

Seventh, in a disarmament environment the arrangements for peace-keeping must be more carefully articulated and appropriate institutions must be given implementing competence. Thus specification of the nature of indirect aggression and subversion is not just a draft of abstract rules. The discouraging history of trying to define aggression, in the abstract, is not especially relevant to the attempt to specify the character of indirect aggression and subversion as an element of the disarmament context. It is an assignment given to a functioning agency of a partial form of international government—the IDO or the IDO in conjunction with other international institutions. Specification (or definition) thus mobilizes public opinion in support of an agreed set of ground rules and helps to reduce confusion about what is permissible in a disarming world.[108]

There are certain reasons for excluding a specification of indirect aggression and subversion from the disarmament agreement. First, its inclusion might make it much more difficult to reach agreement. The presence of asymmetries means that it would be very hard for cold war antagonists to agree about a common set of rules and implementing procedures. In this regard it is interesting to compare the attitude of the American member of the Special Committee with that of the Soviet member. The American, eager to discount the acceptance of Western hemisphere specifications of aggression such as are included in the Act of Chapultepec (1945) and the Rio Treaty of Reciprocal Resistance (1947) emphasized that "the signatories . . . belonged to the same geographical area and were united by many bonds, including a feeling of solidarity, which were not present to the same degree among the Members of the United Nations." This absence of solidarity it is argued, denies the consensus that would be needed to support a definition in the international community. Arguing from this same phenomenon of political dissensus, the Soviet delegate reasons that "a definition of aggression would be even more useful if it were accepted by States with widely divergent opinions."[109]

Second, it might make the early stages of disarmament more stable if its stipulations were kept separate from the persisting cold war competition for dominance in "gray areas" and throughout the newly developing world. Thus disarmament is nothing more nor less than the progressive

---

met in a critical part of the world see George Modelski, ed., *SEATO—Six Studies*, Melbourne, Australia, Cheshire, 1962.

[108] It is precisely this type of reasoning which leads Röling to favor a definition of "armed attack" but to oppose a definition

of "aggression" within the present Charter framework.

[109] Both statements are reported in the 1956 Special Report, *op.cit. supra*, note 66, p. 13.

elimination of weapons systems. Such a view of the disarmament process is inconsistent with both the latest Soviet and U.S. proposals.

Third, a specification of the character of indirect aggression and sub-version might operate to frustrate U.S. neutralizing tactics, especially in Asia, without correspondingly hampering Sino-Soviet politics of expansion. The vague prohibition in Stage I serves notice that any real disturbance of the cold war political *status quo* can be treated as a disarmament violation, but it needs to set forth implementing rules that would illegitimize the paramilitary support given by the United States to incumbent regimes fighting Communist-inspired insurgencies. To base the concept of indirect aggression and subversion purely upon action contrary to the incumbent would stabilize satellite control in East Europe. The continuing competence to help incumbents retain power in a disarming world might provide the United States with enough reassurance, especially if the disarmament agreement could preclude such gross forms of interference as arms shipments, insurgency training, and asylum arrangements.

Fourth, there is a need to exempt from the concept of indirect aggression certain forms of external activity designed to produce changes in foreign regimes in order to maintain some opportunities for social change and to permit the free expression of political ideas across borders. However, it is very difficult, then, to specify by reference only to overt acts what is forbidden. The indirectness of indirect aggression poses a peculiar difficulty. For with regard to the relationship between Moscow-Peking and national Communist parties there is something more coercive than the persuasive power of ideas. There is a formalized relationship of superordination and subordination that commits the recipients of verbal messages to acquiesce in their content. This makes the recipient an agent of the sender of messages rather than an audience that might or might not be convinced. This is what is meant by adherence to a party line; it makes the distinction between the international transmission of ideas and the external organization of civil war almost impossible to make by reference to acts alone. For when words are commands then they function as something more than ideas.[110]

It might be useful to try to adopt a gradually more elaborated conception of indirect aggression and subversion as the disarmament process proceeds. In Stage I the treaty proposes only that parties refrain from indirect aggression and subversion and that a subsidiary body of the IDO "study methods of assuring states" against this kind of coercion. This keeps the obligation vague, allowing the parties to characterize hostile or threatening development in world politics, and thereby take

110 This point was suggested to me by David K. Harbison.

offsetting action or treat the behavior as a disarmament violation. This level of commitment merely reaffirms existing obligations with almost no added centralization of interpretation or control. Also the IDO takes on no explicit responsibility to protect states nor even to supervise the process whereby a party to the treaty is vindicated of or condemned for a violation under Section H, Article 2, paragraph b. This disposition seems all right because the world would continue to be about the same in objective character during Stage I since the military cuts would not, if prudently selected, interfere with predisarmament military commitments. It would probably strengthen the IDO in its early operations if it could be spared much participation in conflicts involving allegations and counterallegations of indirect aggression and subversion.

However, if Stage II is reached then there is a responsibility given to the subsidiary body of the IDO, to adopt methods that are indicated by the study conducted during Stage I as needed "to assure states against indirect aggression and subversion." (G, 2, b) The April 18th Proposals leave open the question of whether or not a definition or specification of the prohibited activity is one of the "methods" of assuring states. Stage II disarmament restricts the military capacity of states to meet political challenges of secondary and tertiary priority. For this reason from the American viewpoint it is essential to find substitutes for Western military support in the Middle East and Asia. A specification of the cruder forms of indirect aggression might strengthen the capacity of the IDO to respond in the event of a dispute about whether, in the course of civil strife, indirect aggression had taken place. That is, a definition would proscribe certain modalities of coercion, leaving rival blocs some discretion to influence political outcomes in foreign society. The main effort in Stage II, however, would be to introduce into the political environment obstacles to indirect aggression and subversion by means of border control and delimitation, demilitarized zones, and improved systems of internal security.

Stage III of the April 18th Proposals merely provides for a continuation of "the codification and progressive development of rules of international conduct" provided in Stage II. Security requirements in Stage III require the IDO to have the clear competence to prevent unauthorized uses of significant coercion across frontiers. This should not mean the suppression of every insurgency that has maintained external contacts, but it should mean that an aggressive state or ideology does not find it advantageous to use covert forms of coercion to promote its system of government abroad. The vulnerability of states in Stage III requires an entirely new conception of peaceful relations among states. One supposes that the initiation of Stage III would depend upon the prior termination of the cold war; otherwise the requisite confidence to abandon deterrent weapons is most unlikely to exist. This confidence requirement probably also means that unless there is virtually no prospect of adverse political outcomes arising from what is now identified as indirect aggression and subversion it is unlikely that parties will make the transition from Stage II. In fact, it would seem clear that these problems must be brought under adequate control by the end of Stage II.

A further specification of indirect aggression and subversion in Stage III would depend greatly on circumstances disclosed during the course of disarmament. For one thing, it would depend upon whether unsatisfactory responses by the IDO and controversial behavior by states could be fairly attributed, at least in part, to confusion about what it was that was prohibited by the agreement to refrain from indirect aggression and subversion. It might be evident that these problems were dealt with outside the disarmament process quite satisfactorily during Stages I and II or that the IDO was paralyzed by the need to assess responsibility in terms of a specification adopted in Stage II. So many intervening variables exist that it hardly seems fruitful to speculate about the relative benefits of a vague or a precise specification of indirect aggression and subversion. The patterns of cold war or alternate struggles for power, the character of regional politics, the health of the world economy, and the success of other methods of control all bear upon whether it is helpful, harmful, or of little consequence to negotiate toward a maximal specification of indirect aggression and subversion.

36. Legislative Intervention by the United Nations.[111] A more radical nontreaty method is to entrust the United Nations with the competence to intervene in internal affairs in order to coerce a social or political change that has been demanded by formal action of an overwhelming consensus of states. In the face of genocide, constitutional racism, or colonialism properly authorized coercion by the organized community eliminates a major breeding ground otherwise open to the indirect aggressor-subvertor. Domestic discontent, reinforced by widespread international sympathy, establishes a situation in which optimum opportunities for intervention on the side of the insurgent exist. An early and effective victory for the revolutionary cause will often prevent the movement from falling beneath the sway of extremist adherents, whose role grows dominant as the conflict protracts. French Indochina, Cuba, and perhaps Algeria offer instructive examples of the extremist legacy of prolonged conflict, whereas India illustrates the pattern that normally has followed rapid settlement.

The use of the United Nations as an organ of minimum legislation

---

[111] For a fuller consideration than is attempted here see Chapter X.

requires, quite obviously, much more detailed consideration than can be given here. In form at least, it is consistent with the peace-keeping and peaceful change measures contemplated by the April 18th Proposals to strengthen progressively the capability of the United Nations to maintain peace, and as disarmament proceeds to weaken correspondingly the capability of national defense establishments to act externally. The United Nations Peace Force and Peace Observation Corps would often be needed to carry out a mandate of legislative intervention unless the target nation voluntarily complied. The addition of "peaceful change" to the provision for the development of better dispute settlement machinery could also be construed and elaborated as the assumption of authorizing a certain limited competence by the United Nations. It is important to understand that if opportunities for indirect aggression are removed, then coercive tactics become an ineffective way to seek political expansion. Opportunities for indirect aggression frequently arise from domestic inequities which alienate members of the society sufficiently so that they are willing to serve the interests of a foreign power in order to remove them. The supranational elimination of the grossest inequities disrupts that symbiotic link between domestic discontent and external ambition which is so characteristically present in serious instances of indirect aggression. This generalization applies especially to weak states.

37. Border Control. One of the most effective ways for a foreign state to commit indirect aggression is to make use of the immunity of its own territory. This permits, for example, rebel groups in a contiguous state to train, rest, and regroup in military centers that are not subject to enemy attack. Furthermore, it allows an insurgent to be given military supplies and backing without much overt indication of foreign participation. For more limited objectives, it makes it easy to send agents across the frontier on a mission of subversion, infiltration, or intimidation.

The openness or closedness of borders has been a significant element in several civil wars: Greece, Laos, South Viet Nam; it has played a role, as well, in the course of international strife; the openness partly provoking the Israeli attack of 1956 as a reprisal against the *fedayeen* raids; subsequently, the control of the Sinai border led to relative stability until the breakdown in May-June 1967. The course of violent conflict is often decisively altered by the extent to which friendly support is given by contiguous national units. If the restraint of covert participation by foreign states is an objective, then it makes sense to consider border control techniques to be a method of assuring states against indirect aggression without insuring them against genuinely domestic revolution. The requirements for effective border control vary with the objectives of control, the terrain, availability of roads, density of population, climate, and the state of relations between the contiguous states. Air surveillance, checkpoints, a demilitarized zone, and roving inspection teams are among the more obvious techniques to be used either individually or in combination. The design of a border control system, as with any other information gathering apparatus of control, depends on how much information is desired to identify with what degree of reliability the coercive use by one state of the boundary-line relationship to commit acts directed at the security and independence of a neighboring state; external support may either involve allowing rebels of the target state to use domestic territory as some sort of base for hostile relations or it may mean that the guilty state is illicitly sending things and people across the border to support the insurgent or subversive cause. It may often involve a combination of sanctuary and intrusion.

The pacification of civil strife situations that have been fomented and inflamed by foreign incitement and participation is a major means of restraining indirect aggression and subversion. Border control provides a significant way to achieve this restraint. When Yugoslavia closed its borders to Greece in 1947 the insurgent cause sagged badly. It seems worthwhile to look closely at the possibilities for improved border control as a way to protect national societies with a high vulnerability to minor coercion, especially if they are contiguous to hostile neighbors with an expansive ideology and capability. Border control can be brought into the treaty framework by the subsidiary body of the IDO, it can be approached independently by the United Nations, or it can be the outcome of bilateral, multilateral, or regional understandings. There is present a wide range of choice which is itself consistent with the overall plea of this study for a flexible response system.

38. Boundary Delimitation. This is relevant in two ways. First, an authoritatively delimited boundary is important for the success and stability of border control techniques. Second, boundary disputes are widespread and offer an aggressor a pretext, with a long pedigree, for the application of coercion; the real objective of the tensions excited by the boundary dispute may be to unleash domestic insurgents or to distract the energies and resources of a target government from its primary tasks of administration and economic development. The overall stability of the disarmament process will be promoted, it is felt, if considerable attention is given to the development of bilateral, regional, and global procedures for the authoritative delimitation of boundaries.[112]

112 Cf. authoritative description of problems and procedures in Stephen B. Jones, *Boundary-Making—A Handbook for Statesmen, Treaty Editors and Boundary Commissioners*, Washington, Carnegie Endowment for International Peace, 1945.

This may also be an area, see Section IV, No. 36, where it is proper to entrust international organizations with a limited legislative competence. This would accord with the recognition in Stage III of the April 18th Proposals that "peaceful change" as well as "peaceful settlement" is an essential ingredient of a peaceful world.

39. International Supervisory Control Commissions. As with border control, the use of control commissions is an important method for the improvement of the stability of an area or nation troubled by and vulnerable to indirect aggression. A control commission is not by itself normally a sufficient method to assure a society, that is otherwise vulnerable and harassed, against strife and minor coercion. However, if carefully designed and employed in conjunction with other methods, control commissions might deter significantly by providing a valuable source of authoritative information. As well, the use of a control commission as a grievance committee provokes investigations and disclosures which would make, one would suppose, factions *less* inclined to engage in prohibited activity.

Control commissions can be used to report on the fulfillment of an international settlement of an internal war. This has been the role entrusted to the control commissions in Laos, Cambodia, and Viet Nam by the 1954 Geneva Accords.[113] It is exceedingly difficult to assess the activities of these commissions. Obviously, as an independent peace-keeping force, a control commission is bound to be swept aside, as in Laos and South Viet Nam, by substantial decisions to wage full-scale civil wars. However, if there is an uncertain political balance, then the presence and activity of a control commission may inhibit efforts to disrupt a social order.

Of course, the ability of a commission to function effectively depends heavily on such matters as budget, cooperation of the host government, technical competence of its staff, political affiliation of the commissioners, voting formula, reporting procedure, jurisdictional competence, and interests of outside powers. Somehow, despite informal reports that the Polish member of the various Geneva commissions was uncooperative and tried to paralyze operations, the formal interim reports on Viet Nam, for instance, which are signed by the Indian, the Polish, and the Canadian commissioners contain quite severe indictments of the activities of both sides.

[113] An excellent source of basic information is contained in the interim reports of the control commission set up by the 1954 Geneva Accords and published in Great Britain as a series of Command papers: e.g. Cmnd 9458, 9445, 9461, 253, 9499; cf. also 9763, especially "Message from the two Co-Chairmen of the Geneva Conference on Indo-China to the International Supervisory Commission for Vietnam," 1956, p. 11.

Control commissions are flexible methods for sustaining political order. Many models can be envisioned for use under various circumstances, especially in connection with the implementation of a cold war agreement that stabilizes a point of hostile contact that had generated severe tensions and violence. It is necessary to have a control commission that is politically acceptable to the parties and yet able to carry out its assigned functions; it often turns out to be impossible to satisfy both criteria of acceptability. If there has been a basic decision on both sides to abide by a stabilizing regime, as in Korea, then control commissions, even with cold war commissioners, seem able to reinforce the disposition to comply even though, as again in Korea, individual provisions may be mutually violated. If no such mutual decision to uphold the basic agreement has been made, as was evidently the case in Laos and South Viet Nam, then a control commission is a rather futile addition to the political environment, especially if unaccompanied by other control methods.

If the commissioners, or a majority of them, were international civil servants rather than appointees of political rivals, then the impartiality would ordinarily increase the authoritativeness and usefulness of this method of control. However, the creation of a commission so composed presupposes a willingness of major states to accept nonpolitical solutions for areas of controversy within which vital political issues are decided. The difficulty here is similar to the reluctance of the great states to confer compulsory jurisdiction upon the International Court of Justice.

40. International Presences. It may decrease the vulnerability of a given society to indirect aggression and subversion if various kinds of "international presences" can be introduced into sovereign states. This can be conceived of as an alternative to therapeutic intervention by a nation. Lebanon is an instructive illustration of the choice between a national and a supranational presence in a nation beset by civil strife abetted by foreign participation.[114]

Obviously an "international presence" is a broader way to describe the kind of peace-keeping measure that is envisioned by the provision calling for the establishment of a United Nations Peace Observation Corps. The separate treatment is given for the sake of completeness, and also to point out that the use of presences may be, on occasion, more effectively carried out under auspices other than the IDO or some

---

[114] Cf. Chapter on Lebanon in Arthur L. Burns and Nina Heathcote, *Peace-Keeping by U.N. Forces—From Suez to* *the Congo*, New York, Praeger, 1963, pp. 6-22.

other organ of the United Nations; for example, regional organizations might sometimes be the more appropriate administering agencies. The idea of a presence as a stabilizing factor also overlaps with the use of control commissions.

In the course of disarmament, especially if it proceeds far enough to eliminate the alliance system and to diminish the willingness of big nations to make extranational responses to protect foreign societies from the indirect aggressor, it may be essential to rely upon a widespread system of presences, perhaps including definite military defense missions. This kind of security arrangement may turn out to be more important for sustaining confidence in disarmament than adequate inspection, especially when it comes to be recognized that certain kinds of significant violations are virtually uninspectable.

41. The Choice of Method. This section has indicated the main sectors on the response spectrum; these are the methods that are available to assure states against indirect aggression and subversion during disarmament. It is apparent that many choices exist and that methods may be combined into an effective response to meet a particular challenge in a bewildering variety of appropriate ways. Many of these methods are used to protect victims of indirect aggression and subversion in a predisarmament world. Will the problems of protection increase as disarmament proceeds? Which methods are most compatible with disarmament? Which methods would it be useful to bring into the treaty framework? At what stage? Which methods are most likely to antagonize treaty parties at the negotiating stage? This kind of question is abidingly relevant, but quite hard to answer in any generally useful form. It is evident that the Soviet Union likes definitions and is adverse to the development of a genuine supranational military capability. How should this influence our initial treaty proposals? Our bargaining strategy? Our fallback conditions and our minimum demands?

The April 18th Proposals contain a rich variety of methods: rules, peaceful settlement and change machinery, UN observation and control apparatus, as well as a broad undertaking to provide whatever methods are needed to handle the specific substantive hazard of indirect aggression and subversion. It would probably be useful to develop more detailed provisions as negotiating proposals and to increase our appreciation of what it is that we are advocating. The development of models would increase our own understanding of what is needed for what purpose. At present, there is a vague appreciation that something should probably be done about indirect aggression and subversion in the treaty but few seem to know quite what or quite how. One way to become more sophisticated is to use the sort of quantitative economic analysis of the implications of choice that has been so successful in increasing the rationality of defense planning; this increases our awareness of available options.

V. Principal Conclusions

42. It is essential for the United States to include plans for the regulation of indirect aggression and subversion within its disarmament policy. There are four reasons for this. First, the containment of Communism in a disarming world seems to depend upon the elimination of opportunities for and vulnerabilities to indirect aggression and subversion. Second, domestic confidence in a general disarmament process could not be reliably generated or sustained without reasonable provision for meeting the dangers posed by the tactics of indirect aggression and subversion. Third, any cold war reversals that took place during disarmament as a partial consequence of Communist coercive tactics would be attributed, whether correctly or not, to the weakening of United States resolve and capability, a weakening brought about principally by the commencement of disarmament. Fourth, there is a sense in which the process of disarmament is cumulative and irreversible, making it difficult to recover without generating severe instability any political losses suffered as a consequence of the breakdown of disarmament.

43. It is far easier to assert the political than the military relevance of disarmament to the regulation of indirect aggression and subversion. It is hard to comprehend how the defensive military capability of the United States with respect to minor aggressors will be seriously impaired early in disarmament. It is equally hard to comprehend how the United States would proceed to a point in disarmament at which its nonstrategic military capability was impaired unless the phenomena of indirect aggression had first virtually disappeared from big power world politics.

The political relevance of disarmament is, however, evident. First, as has already been mentioned, domestic critics of disarmament would attribute every cold war setback to the fact of disarmament, perhaps generating a militaristic or antidisarmament response. Second, national Communist groups may misinterpret the initiation of disarmament as restricting the capacity of the United States to lend military support to an anti-Communist government and so intensify their pursuit of radical objectives. Third, confidence in significant disarmament requires a gradual elimination of all large-scale violence from political life; otherwise, reluctance to proceed beyond the point of strategic invulnerability would probably prove to be insurmountable.

44. The relevance of indirect aggression to disarmament does not suggest that methods of control should be introduced in whole or in

part into the explicit framework of the disarmament treaty. It may mean increasing foreign aid by a factor of five, working toward the implementation of Article 43 of the United Nations Charter, encouraging boundary settlements, subsidizing improved internal security systems, or any several of the multitude of potential stabilizing measures. The real task is to create a stable international environment in which the opportunities for and incentives of recourse to political violence were perceptibly diminishing. The extent to which this endeavor to predispose the environment in favor of disarmament should be included in the treaty is difficult to judge. It does make sense to make clear, at least, that continuing participation in a disarmament arrangement does depend upon being satisfied that parties to the treaty have truly renounced recourse to coercion, of whatever variety, to achieve their international objectives. Because of the nuclear stalemate this assurance involves mainly nonrecourse to the techniques of indirect aggression and subversion.

45. Therefore, a minimum treaty inclusion might be a pledge to refrain from indirect aggression and subversion. This would establish authoritatively the relevance of the proscribed activity to disarmament without interfering with the flexibility of the national response system now in use to meet situations in which United States interests are jeopardized by political violence incited or supported by foreign states. Furthermore, the pledge would be consistent with the Soviet Union's own advocacy of an international definition of aggression (including its indirect forms) as a basis for peaceful world order. The extent to which the pledge should be spelled out in a definition is an important issue, but its importance has been exaggerated. Elaborate arguments can be made in favor of or in opposition to each major variety of definition, but the consequences for international behavior seem relatively slight no matter which side is correct.

46. The pledge to refrain from indirect aggression and subversion does not by itself give much assurance of compliance. In fact, no specification of legal rules gives much assurance unless steps are taken to provide adequate implementation. However, the pledge by itself, whether defined or not, does establish the relevance of indirect aggression to disarmament obligations; it also forewarns treaty participants and the world in general that the continuation of disarmament depends upon the progressive elimination of aggression from international life. This dependence is taken for granted with respect to the direct forms of aggression. A pledge makes the less obvious point that disarmament also depends on the absence of indirect varieties of aggression.

47. Effective control of behavior results less from the specification

of legal standards, than from their appropriate implementation. There are many procedures available for implementing prohibitions placed upon indirect aggression and subversion. A main objective of control is to make the participation of the indirect aggressor easier to identify by forcing it to become more visible. Border control identifies a violator as well as tries to restrain him. Effective control also depends on the particular conditions prevailing in the society that is the object of protection. It is possible to decrease indirect aggression either by decreasing domestic discontent, increasing internal security, or by regulating external participation. There is no overall control formula. Rather the specific vulnerability of a nation must serve as the primary regulatory focus.

48. The retention of a flexible system of national responses seems to give the United States the best obtainable protection against indirect aggression and subversion during disarmament, at least until late in Stage II. That means the retention of a degree of national discretion to take counter and preventive measures and its nonimpairment by disarmament restraints. During the same period, a parallel effort should be made to build a supranational peace system, by strengthening the peace-keeping machinery and competency of international organizations, especially the United Nations.

49. It is difficult to comprehend assuredly the relevance of national Communist parties to the regulation of indirect aggression in a disarming world. First, it is hard to determine the degree to which genuine central control resides in Moscow. Second, it is difficult to evaluate the challenge of Peking and certain indications of polycentrism within the bloc. Third, it is unclear whether national autonomy for Communist party operations is likely to grow in the future, and whether this growth will be retarded, unaffected, or discouraged by disarmament. A rise in national autonomy would not be an unmixed blessing for the West. It is true that transnational party loyalty and obedience gives the Soviet Union a trojan horse in almost every key society in the world, but it might also be true that Moscow, in the interests of stable disarmament, could, if its control was genuine, assure the renunciation of violent tactics by national Communist movements. Without such centralization in Moscow, decision-making authority for world Communist strategy might merely be transferred to the more militant Chinese. A second alternative would involve the national formation of Communist strategy based upon an assessment of domestic opportunities; this does cut the movement off from centralized control, but it may also lead to failures to restrain local violence so as to guard international stability. National Communist officials would presumably be less sensitive to the casual connec-

tions between revolutionary violence and the maintenance of nuclear peace than would the leaders of the party in the Soviet Union. Nothing short of the genuine disappearance of Communism as a political movement outside of the present Communist states would be fully satisfactory if the objective is to regulate recourse to domestic violence of which the outcome has major psychological and political significance for the international *status quo*.

50. It is uncertain what the United States seeks to achieve by making indirect aggression an explicit part of general disarmament negotiations. Is it a way to argue the basic disagreement with the Soviets about the use of force in world affairs which was uncovered in the 1961 Vienna meeting between President Kennedy and Premier Khrushchev? Is it a bargaining counter? A permanent roadblock? A minimum insistence upon asserting the connection between military and political issues in the disarmament context? Is it essential, marginal, or frivolous for the United States to couple the initiation of disarmament with some assurance that problems of indirect aggression and subversion will grow less serious? Many of these questions can only be answered by the adoption of an attitude toward the relationship between the cold war and disarmament. Must the cold war disappear prior to or early in disarmament, on terms that are favorable to the West? The relevance of these fundamental issues suggests a certain potential similarity between indirect aggression and the long controversy about the role and extent of inspection requirements.

51. A disarming world must not exclude opportunities for changing the international and domestic *status quo* in fundamental respects. These changes have in the past been brought about by violence. Therefore, disarmament requires the development of legislative substitutes for violence. All changes that were encouraged by violence less than a war between nations were considered to be instances of peaceful change. Indirect aggression and subversion functioned as major instruments of peaceful change in the traditional system of international relations, and continue to do so in the world today. Indonesia, Algeria, Laos, Cyprus, Yemen, and Israel owe their present political status to domestic political violence that depended upon external support. Angola, South West Africa, Rhodesia are likely to be arenas within which it is plausible to expect violent challenges directed at the *status quo* to combine internal and external coercive elements. To avoid this seems impossible. But perhaps, as the Congo operation (1960-1964) suggests, the dangers to world peace can be considerably reduced if the elements of external coercion can be lifted from the level of national competition to the level of supranational management.

52. There is an unavoidable element of internal inconsistency introduced by the simultaneous effort to widen and deepen the channels open for peaceful change and to eliminate the opportunities of the indirect aggressor-subverter. This troublesome reality arises whenever a social order tries to satisfy complementary policies by contradictory principles of order. An exclusive interest in the prevention of indirect aggression would also mean the insulation of intolerable political regimes. An exclusive effort to end intolerable political regimes would generate anarchy and wholesale recourse to international coercion. An uneasy acceptance of the complementariness of social systems of order is already a part of political subconsciousness in domestic societies; it will require some time before it is similarly assimilated into our basic understanding of the relationship between law and behavior in international society.

53. Stage III disarmament presupposes an international environment in which indirect aggression and subversion are no longer problems in the relations between major states. Of course, methods of regulating behavior can predispose actors to pursue their ends by noncoercive means, but it is unrealistic to envision regulatory substitutes for international trust and harmony, especially when concern is over the international use of minor coercion. Regulation is found to be too imperfect and vulnerability too pronounced for any serious effort to proceed to Stage III, or anywhere beyond a credible minimum deterrence posture, until leading national actors perceive each other in noncompetitive and friendly terms. The dangers of uninspectable military violations in Stage III reinforces what also seems quite evident from a sense of political dynamics.

54. A response system to deal with indirect aggression and subversion should not alter its structure with the commencement of disarmament. Either before or after disarmament the basic model for response is a graduated deterrence system incorporating national and supranational elements and effective enough to make a potential aggressor perceive as few opportunities as possible to employ minor coercion as a means to promote aggressive ends abroad.

55. Early in disarmament a strengthened version of the existing response system seems adequate to deal with indirect aggression and subversion. Deep in disarmament the existing response system, no matter how much it can be strengthened, is incapable of generating by itself confidence in the ability to frustrate the indirect aggressor; instead, it is necessary to have a transformed international environment in which major nations are no longer inclined to use force directly or indirectly to gain rival ends. That is, a new response system must be fashioned for Stage III disarmament, whereas nothing much needs to be done

with the existing system to meet envisionable needs in Stages I and II, except, perhaps, the need to prepare for Stage III.

Annex A. The Use of Supranational Institutions to Constrain Domestic Violence in a Disarming World

Domestic instability, especially if it includes violent conflict, is relevant to the maintenance of peaceful relations and to the regulation of indirect aggression and subversion; the typical indirect aggressor-subverter exploits domestic instability to promote his own aggressive and egocentric political objectives. Supranational institutions can usefully interpose themselves, on occasion, between domestic factions and prevent foreign participation in civil strife. This cuts down upon the opportunities and temptations of the indirect aggressor.[115] More radical than this, would be a move to support the gradual expansion of a legislative competence for the United Nations to engage in remedial interventions designed to solve domestic social problems before their presence provoked recourse to violence.[116] The alternative to national interventionary participation upon the encounter of rival ideologies in the cold war is the gradual toleration of community interventionary participation on a regional and universal level. The Congo operation, despite its many difficulties, indicates a community response to domestic violence that succeeded in keeping cold war participation at a minimum.

Once domestic violence takes place then it is often too late to gain control over the situation by action emanating from supranational sources. It is probable, for instance, that the domestic conflict has already been polarized in cold war terms, thereby precluding, or almost so, effective community action by any international institution which included states on both sides of the cold war.

These problems seem especially acute for a disarming world as there must be a growth in international organization and world community responsibility if the path toward the advanced stages of disarmament is to be cleared. If the objective of arms control and disarmament is modestly envisioned as the control of the arms race, and is not seriously intended to eliminate the weaponry of nuclear war, then the argument for supranational competence to respond to domestic violence rests primarily upon the need to reduce the dangers of escalation. Even if one can regard escalation dangers as slight—there being little evidence that nonstrategic encounters breed strategic violence—there are, nevertheless, important reasons to support supranationalizing competence over severer forms of domestic instability. It is part of the effort to displace the nation as the prime center of power in world affairs. The

---

115 See Chapter IV.
116 These views are put forward in more complete form in Chapter X.

use of supranational coercion also involves the gradual development of an international welfare system—when the Organization intervenes it must have a mission to perform that derives from a sense of what the public good requires. Certainly the Congo operation has illustrated this.

The generality of this endorsement of supranational interventionary powers should be qualified in several respects. First, the consent of the constituted government of the host state should be obtained unless an overwhelming consensus of the world community favors supranational intervention to rectify serious violations of the Charter. Second, the United States and the Soviet Union should usually agree on the broad ends to be served by the intervention, at least at the outset. Third, the nations comprising the region should ordinarily take the initiative in soliciting and administering the intervention. Fourth, a humanitarian rationale should be widely advocated as the primary justification for the use of supranational coercion.

Annex B. The Relevance of Revolutionary and
Neutralist Politics to the Maintenance of
International Order in a Disarming World

It seems important to take due account of the dominant national perspectives that oppose one another on matters of social change and interventionary support.[117] Sino-Soviet support for wars of national liberation and Middle Eastern-African support for certain domestic social changes within their cultural sphere provide a continuing justification for strategies of indirect aggression and subversion. To some extent these motivations are an intractable aspect of the problem of political conflict. However, so far as these national perspectives represent an emerging universal consensus, then it becomes desirable to act upon them in a cooperative manner at a stage prior to violence and polarization. This suggests the importance to United States policy of joining with revolutionary and neutralist nations in action against the vestiges of colonialism and the perseverance of white supremacy in the South of Africa. Obviously, at least from a pragmatic perspective, it is necessary to balance this preference against the resulting strains upon Atlantic solidarities.

Annex C. The Significance of Stage III or General
and Complete Disarmament for the Problems
of Political Instability

The third phase of disarmament cannot be brought about without a

117 This argument is presented in Falk, "Historical Tendencies, Modernizing and Revolutionary Nations, and the International Legal Order," 8 *Howard Law Journal*, 128-51 (1962).

prior elimination of cold war tensions and conflicts. Therefore, the problems of indirect aggression and subversion must disappear by the end of Stage II. This means that it is almost pointless to be concerned with the special control problems that might arise if patterns of indirect aggression and subversion persisted into Stage III since the existence of the problem is itself fundamentally incompatible with the trust that is demanded after Stage II.[118] If certain disarmament violations are virtually uninspectable—that is, no inspection system can provide much confidence in compliance—then inspection cannot operate as a substitute for trust. Trust itself must exist or the malicious violator will have reasonable prospects of success. The perception of malice is therefore incompatible with radical disarmament. A level of harmony at least comparable to contemporary Canadian-United States relations is a *precondition*. What has been said about inspection also applies to assurances about the effective prohibition of indirect aggression and subversion. As no regulatory body could be made adequate for Stage III, it is deceptive to formulate the problem as one of regulation rather than as a demand for a prior radical transformation of the international environment.

Annex D. The Usability of Conventional Forces and Weaponry in a Disarming World

If national control responses remain the primary way to resist Communist aggression and subversion, then Western conventional military capabilities assume a special significance.[119] As nuclear weapons would presumably remain unusable in a local war it becomes necessary to have the conventional forces and weapons available for counterintervention in the event of a prior intervention by way of indirect aggression and subversion. The quantitative problems of making sure that a sufficient defensive capability exists throughout the world is a major area in which disarmament may have serious military relevance in Stages I and II.

Annex E. The Obligation to Obey a Rule of International Law

Very little systematic attention has been given to the extent of the obligation to comply with applicable rules of international law in conditions of stress. The United States Constitution, supported by interpretations of the United States Supreme Court, acknowledges that rules con-

---

[118] A more complete treatment can be found in Falk, "The Limits of Inspection for Drastic Disarmament," in Falk and Richard J. Barnet, eds., *Security in Disarmament*, Princeton, Princeton University Press, 1965, pp. 226-39.

[119] A more complete treatment can be found in Falk, "Inspection, Trust, and Security during Disarmament," *ibid.*, pp. 37-49.

tained in ratified treaties have the status of "the supreme law of the land." Under what conditions, if any, can the President use his authority to suspend the duty to comply? It should be recalled that a reciprocal tolerance is involved: a discretion to noncomply is, then, itself precedential for other states in the international system.

Interpretative discretion allows a state almost an unrestricted capacity to reconcile its behavior with an applicable legal standard. If, however, the authority to interpret is conferred upon an impartial international institution, a state may find itself in a position of virtually unambiguous violation, outraged protestations of legality notwithstanding. Therefore, the critical control factor is less the prescriptive norm governing behavior, susceptible of service by self-interested manipulation of its meaning, than the locus of authority to interpret and apply the norm. Without the centralization of this authority there is no way to identify conclusively illegal behavior. It is a matter of national allegations and explanations without the existence of some supranational criterion of judgment.

There is also the relevant ethical question: when should a nation disobey international law? This parallels the inquiries that have always been made into the relationship that exists between domestic law and individual conscience.

February 1963

APPENDICES

Appendix A
The Legality of United States Participation in the Defense of Viet Nam

MEMORANDUM OF LAW, DEPARTMENT OF STATE, OFFICE OF THE LEGAL ADVISER, MARCH 8, 1965

I. The United States and South Viet Nam Have the Right Under International Law To Participate in the Collective Defense of South Viet Nam Against Armed Attack

In response to requests from the Government of South Viet Nam, the United States has been assisting that country in defending itself against armed attack from the Communist North. This attack has taken the forms of externally supported subversion, clandestine supply of arms, infiltration of armed personnel, and most recently the sending of regular units of the North Vietnamese army into the South.

International law has long recognized the right of individual and collective self-defense against armed attack. South Viet Nam and the United States are engaging in such collective defense consistently with international law and with United States obligations under the United Nations Charter.

A. SOUTH VIET NAM IS BEING SUBJECTED TO ARMED ATTACK BY COMMUNIST NORTH VIET NAM

The Geneva Accords of 1954 established a demarcation line between North Viet Nam and South Viet Nam. They provided for withdrawals of military forces into the respective zones north and south of this line. The Accords prohibited the use of either zone for the resumption of hostilities or to "further an aggressive policy."

During the five years following the Geneva Conference of 1954, the Hanoi regime developed a covert political-military organization in South Viet Nam based on Communist cadres it had ordered to stay in the South, contrary to the provisions of the Geneva Accords. The activities of this covert organization were directed toward the kidnapping and assassination of civilian officials—acts of terrorism that were perpetrated in increasing numbers.

In the three-year period from 1959 to 1961, the North Viet Nam regime infiltrated an estimated 10,000 men into the South. It is estimated that 13,000 additional personnel were infiltrated in 1962, and, by the end of 1964, North Viet Nam may well have moved over 40,000 armed and unarmed guerrillas into South Viet Nam.

The International Control Commission reported in 1962 the findings of its Legal Committee:

> . . . there is evidence to show that arms, armed and unarmed personnel, munitions and other supplies have been sent from the Zone in the North to the Zone in the South with the objective of supporting, organizing and carrying out hostile activities, including armed attacks, directed against the Armed Forces and Administration of the Zone in the South.

> . . . there is evidence that the PAVN [People's Army of Viet Nam] has allowed the Zone in the North to be used for inciting, encouraging and supporting hostile activities in the Zone in the South, aimed at the overthrow of the Administration in the South.

Beginning in 1964, the Communists apparently exhausted their reservoir of southerners who had gone North. Since then the greater number of men infiltrated into the South have been native-born North Vietnamese. Most recently, Hanoi has begun to infiltrate elements of the North Vietnamese army in increasingly larger numbers. Today, there is evidence that nine regiments of regular North Vietnamese forces are fighting in organized units in the South.

In the guerrilla war in Viet Nam, the external aggression from the North is the critical military element of the insurgency, although it is unacknowledged by North Viet Nam. In these circumstances, an "armed attack" is not as easily fixed by date and hour as in the case of traditional warfare. However, the infiltration of thousands of armed men clearly constitutes an "armed attack" under any reasonable definition. There may be some question as to the exact date at which North Viet Nam's aggression grew into an "armed attack," but there can be no doubt that it had occurred before February 1965.

B. INTERNATIONAL LAW RECOGNIZES THE RIGHT OF
INDIVIDUAL AND COLLECTIVE SELF-DEFENSE
AGAINST ARMED ATTACK

International law had traditionally recognized the right of self-defense against armed attack. This proposition has been asserted by writers on international law through the several centuries in which the modern law of nations has developed. The proposition has been acted on numerous times by governments throughout modern history. Today the principle of self-defense against armed attack is universally recognized and accepted.[1]

[1] See, e.g., Jessup, *A Modern Law of Nations* 163 ff. (1948); Oppenheim, *Inter-*

The Charter of the United Nations, concluded at the end of World War II, imposed an important limitation on the use of force by United Nations Members. Article 2, paragraph 4, provides:

> All members shall refrain in their international relations from the threat or use of force against the territorial integrity or political independence of any state, or in any other manner inconsistent with the Purposes of the United Nations.

In addition, the Charter embodied a system of international peacekeeping through the organs of the United Nations. Article 24 summarizes these structural arrangements in stating that the United Nations Members—

> confer on the Security Council primary responsibility for the maintenance of international peace and security, and agree that in carrying out its duties under this responsibility the Security Council acts on their behalf.

However, the Charter expressly states in Article 51 that the remaining provisions of the Charter—including the limitation of Article 2, paragraph 4, and the creation of United Nations machinery to keep the peace—in no way diminish the inherent right of self-defense against armed attack. Article 51 provides:

> Nothing in the present Charter shall impair the inherent right of individual or collective self-defense if an armed attack occurs against a Member of the United Nations, until the Security Council has taken the measures necessary to maintain international peace and security. Measures taken by Members in the exercise of this right of self-defense shall be immediately reported to the Security Council and shall not in any way affect the authority and responsibility of the Security Council under the present Charter to take at any time such action as it deems necessary in order to maintain or restore international peace and security.

Thus, Article 51 restates and preserves, for Member States in the situations covered by the Article, a long-recognized principle of international law. The Article is a "saving clause" designed to make clear that no other provision in the Charter shall be interpreted to impair the inherent right of self-defense referred to in Article 51.

Three principal objections have been raised against the availability of the right of individual and collective self-defense in the case of Viet

---

national Law 297 ff. (8th ed. Lauterpacht *in International Law* (1958).
1955). See generally Bowett, *Self-Defense*

Nam: (1) that this right applies only in the case of an armed attack on a United Nations Member; (2) that it does not apply in the case of South Viet Nam because the latter is not an independent sovereign state; and (3) that collective self-defense may be undertaken only by a regional organization operating under Chapter VIII of the United Nations Charter. These objections will now be considered in turn.

C. THE RIGHT OF INDIVIDUAL AND COLLECTIVE SELF-DEFENSE APPLIES IN THE CASE OF SOUTH VIET NAM WHETHER OR NOT THAT COUNTRY IS A MEMBER OF THE UNITED NATIONS

1. *South Viet Nam Enjoys the Right of Self-Defense.* The argument that the right of self-defense is available only to Members of the United Nations mistakes the nature of the right of self-defense and the relationship of the United Nations Charter to international law in this respect. As already shown, the right of self-defense against armed attack is an inherent right under international law. The right is not conferred by the Charter, and, indeed, Article 51 expressly recognizes that the right is inherent.

The Charter nowhere contains any provision designed to deprive non-Members of the right of self-defense against armed attack.[2] Article 2, paragraph 6, does charge the United Nations with responsibility for ensuring that non-Member States act in accordance with United Nations "Principles so far as may be necessary for the maintenance of international peace and security." Protection against aggression and self-defense against armed attack are important elements in the whole Charter scheme for the maintenance of international peace and security. To deprive non-Members of their inherent right of self-defense would not accord with the Principles of the Organization, but would instead be prejudicial to the maintenance of peace. Thus Article 2, paragraph 6—and, indeed, the rest of the Charter—should certainly not be construed to nullify or diminish the inherent defensive rights of non-Members.

2. *The United States Has the Right To Assist in the Defense of South Viet Nam Although the Latter Is Not a United Nations Member.* The cooperation of two or more international entities in the defense of

---

[2] While non-Members, such as South Viet Nam, have not formally undertaken the obligations of the United Nations Charter as their own treaty obligations, it should be recognized that much of the substantive law of the Charter has become part of the general law of nations through a very wide acceptance by nations the world over. This is particularly true of the Charter provisions bearing on the use of force. Moreover, in the case of South Viet Nam, the South Vietnamese Government has expressed its ability and willingness to abide by the Charter, in applying for United Nations membership. Thus it seems entirely appropriate to appraise the actions of South Viet Nam in relation to the legal standards set forth in the United Nations Charter.

one or both against armed attack is generally referred to as collective self-defense. United States participation in the defense of South Viet Nam at the latter's request is an example of collective self-defense.

The United States is entitled to exercise the right of individual or collective self-defense against armed attack, as that right exists in international law, subject only to treaty limitations and obligations undertaken by this country.

It has been urged that the United States has no right to participate in the collective defense of South Viet Nam because Article 51 of the United Nations Charter speaks only of the situation "if an armed attack occurs *against a Member of the United Nations*." This argument is without substance.

In the first place, Article 51 does not impose restrictions or cut down the otherwise available rights of United Nations Members. By its own terms, the Article preserves an inherent right. It is, therefore, necessary to look elsewhere in the Charter for any obligation of Members restricting their participation in collective defense of an entity that is not a United Nations Member.

Article 2, paragraph 4, is the principal provision of the Charter imposing limitations on the use of force by Members. It states that they—

> shall refrain in their international relations from the threat or use of force against the territorial integrity or political independence of any state, or in any other manner inconsistent with the Purposes of the United Nations.

Action taken in defense against armed attack cannot be characterized as falling within this proscription. The record of the San Francisco Conference makes clear that Article 2, paragraph 4, was not intended to restrict the right of self-defense against armed attack.[3]

One will search in vain for any other provision in the Charter that would preclude United States participation in the collective defense of a non-Member. The fact that Article 51 refers only to armed attack "against a Member of the United Nations" implies no intention to preclude Members from participating in the defense of non-Members. Any such result would have seriously detrimental consequences for international peace and security and would be inconsistent with the Purposes of the United Nations as they are set forth in Article 1 of the Charter.[4]

---

[3] See, *e.g.*, 6 *U.N. Conf. Int'l Org. Docs.* 459.

[4] In particular, the statement of the first Purpose:

"To maintain international peace and security, and to that end: to take effective collective measures for the prevention and removal of threats to the peace, and for the suppression of acts of aggression or other breaches of the peace, and to bring about by peaceful means, and in conformity with the principles of justice and international law, adjustment or settlement of international disputes or situations which might lead to a breach of the peace. . . ."

The right of Members to participate in the defense of non-Members is upheld by leading authorities on international law.[5]

D. THE RIGHT OF INDIVIDUAL AND COLLECTIVE SELF-DEFENSE APPLIES WHETHER OR NOT SOUTH VIET NAM IS REGARDED AS AN INDEPENDENT SOVEREIGN STATE

1. *South Viet Nam Enjoys the Right of Self-Defense.* It has been asserted that the conflict in Viet Nam is "civil strife" in which foreign intervention is forbidden. Those who make this assertion have gone so far as to compare Ho Chi Minh's actions in Viet Nam with the efforts of President Lincoln to preserve the Union during the American Civil War. Any such characterization is an entire fiction disregarding the actual situation in Viet Nam. The Hanoi regime is anything but the legitimate government of a unified country in which the South is rebelling against lawful national authority.

The Geneva Accords of 1954 provided for a division of Viet Nam into two zones at the 17th parallel. Although this line of demarcation was intended to be temporary, it was established by international agreement, which specifically forbade aggression by one zone against the other.

The Republic of Viet Nam in the South has been recognized as a separate international entity by approximately sixty governments the world over. It has been admitted as a member of a number of the specialized agencies of the United Nations. The United Nations General Assembly in 1957 voted to recommend South Viet Nam for membership in the Organization, and its admission was frustrated only by the veto of the Soviet Union in the Security Council.

In any event there is no warrant for the suggestion that one zone of a temporarily divided state—whether it be Germany, Korea, or Viet Nam—can be legally overrun by armed forces from the other zone, crossing the internationally recognized line of demarcation between the two. Any such doctrine would subvert the international agreement establishing the line of demarcation, and would pose grave dangers to international peace.

The action of the United Nations in the Korean conflict of 1950 clearly established the principle that there is no greater license for one zone of a temporarily divided state to attack the other zone than there is for one state to attack another state. South Viet Nam has the same right that South Korea had to defend itself and to organize collective

[5] Bowett, *Self-Defense in International Law* 193-95 (1958); Goodhart, *The North Atlantic Treaty of 1949*, 79 *Recueil des Cours* 183, 202-04 (1951, vol. II), quoted in Whiteman's *Digest of International Law* 1067-68 (1965); Kelsen, *The Law of the United Nations* 793 (1950); see Stone, *Aggression and World Order* 44 (1958).

defense against an armed attack from the North. A resolution of the Security Council dated June 25, 1950 noted "with grave concern the armed attack upon the Republic of Korea by forces from North Korea" and determined "that this action constitutes a breach of the peace."

2. *The United States Is Entitled To Participate in the Collective Defense of South Viet Nam Whether or Not the Latter Is Regarded as an Independent Sovereign State.* As stated earlier, South Viet Nam has been recognized as a separate international entity by approximately sixty governments. It has been admitted to membership in a number of the United Nations specialized agencies, and has been excluded from the United Nations Organization only by the Soviet veto.

There is nothing in the Charter to suggest that United Nations Members are precluded from participating in the defense of a recognized international entity against armed attack merely because the entity may lack some of the attributes of an independent sovereign state. Any such result would have a destructive effect on the stability of international engagements such as the Geneva Accords of 1954 and on internationally agreed lines of demarcation. Such a result, far from being in accord with the Charter and the Purposes of the United Nations, would undermine them and would create new dangers to international peace and security.

E. THE UNITED NATIONS CHARTER DOES NOT LIMIT THE RIGHT OF SELF-DEFENSE TO REGIONAL ORGANIZATIONS

Some have argued that collective self-defense may be undertaken only by a regional arrangement or agency operating under Chapter VIII of the United Nations Charter. Such an assertion ignores the structure of the Charter and the practice followed in the more than twenty years since the founding of the United Nations.

The basic proposition that rights of self-defense are not impaired by the Charter—as expressly stated in Article 51—is not conditioned by any Charter provision limiting the application of this proposition to collective defense by a regional arrangement or agency. The structure of the Charter reinforces this conclusion. Article 51 appears in Chapter VII of the Charter, entitled "Action With Respect to Threats to the Peace, Breaches of the Peace, and Acts of Aggression," whereas Chapter VIII, entitled "Regional Arrangements," begins with Article 52 and embraces the two following articles. The records of the San Francisco Conference show that Article 51 was deliberately placed in Chapter VII rather than Chapter VIII, "where it would only have a bearing on the regional system."[6]

6 17 *U.N. Conf. Int'l Org. Docs.* 288.

Under Article 51, the right of self-defense is available against any armed attack, whether or not the country attacked is a member of a regional arrangement and regardless of the source of the attack. Chapter VIII, on the other hand, deals with relations among members of a regional arrangement or agency, and authorizes regional action as appropriate for dealing with "local disputes." This distinction has been recognized ever since the founding of the United Nations in 1945.

For example, the North Atlantic Treaty has operated as a collective security arrangement, designed to take common measures in preparation against the eventuality of an armed attack for which collective defense under Article 51 would be required. Similarly, the Southeast Asia Treaty Organization was designed as a collective defense arrangement under Article 51. Secretary of State Dulles emphasized this in his testimony before the Senate Foreign Relations Committee in 1954.

By contrast, Article 1 of the Charter of Bogota (1948), establishing the Organization of American States, expressly declares that the Organization is a regional agency with the United Nations. Indeed, Chapter VIII of the United Nations Charter was included primarily to take account of the functioning of the Inter-American System.

In sum, there is no basis in the United Nations Charter for contending that the right of self-defense against armed attack is limited to collective defense by a regional organization.

F. THE UNITED STATES HAS FULFILLED ITS OBLIGATIONS TO THE UNITED NATIONS

A further argument has been made that the Members of the United Nations have conferred on United Nations organs—and, in particular, on the Security Council—exclusive power to act against aggression. Again, the express language of Article 51 contradicts that assertion. A victim of armed attack is not required to forgo individual or collective defense of its territory until such time as the United Nations organizes collective action and takes appropriate measures. To the contrary, Article 51 clearly states that the right of self-defense may be exercised "*until* the Security Council has taken the measures necessary to maintain international peace and security."[7]

As indicated earlier, Article 51 is not literally applicable to the Viet

---

[7] An argument has been made by some that the United States, by joining in the collective defense of South Viet Nam, has violated the peaceful settlement obligation of Article 33 in the Charter. This argument overlooks the obvious proposition that a victim of armed aggression is not required to sustain the attack undefended while efforts are made to find a political solution with the aggressor. Article 51 of the Charter illustrates this by making perfectly clear that the inherent right of self-defense is impaired by "Nothing in the present Charter," including the provisions of Article 33.

Nam situation since South Viet Nam is not a Member. However, reasoning by analogy from Article 51 and adopting its provisions as an appropriate guide for the conduct of Members in a case like Viet Nam, one can only conclude that United States actions are fully in accord with this country's obligations as a Member of the United Nations.

Article 51 requires that:

> Measures taken by Members in the exercise of this right of self-defense shall be immediately reported to the Security Council and shall not in any way affect the authority and responsibility of the Security Council under the present Charter to take at any time such action as it deems necessary in order to maintain or restore international peace and security.

The United States has reported to the Security Council on measures it has taken in countering the Communist aggression in Viet Nam. In August 1964 the United States asked the Council to consider the situation created by North Vietnamese attacks on United States destroyers in the Tonkin Gulf. The Council thereafter met to debate the question, but adopted no resolutions. Twice in February 1965 the United States sent additional reports to the Security Council on the conflict in Viet Nam and on the additional measures taken by the United States in the collective defense of South Viet Nam. In January 1966 the United States formally submitted the Viet Nam question to the Security Council for its consideration and introduced a draft resolution calling for discussions looking toward a peaceful settlement on the basis of the Geneva Accords.

At no time has the Council taken any action to restore peace and security in Southeast Asia. The Council has not expressed criticism of United States actions. Indeed, since the United States submission of January 1966, Members of the Council have been notably reluctant to proceed with any consideration of the Viet Nam question.

The conclusion is clear that the United States has in no way acted to interfere with United Nations consideration of the conflict in Viet Nam. On the contrary, the United States has requested United Nations consideration, and the Council has not seen fit to act.

G. INTERNATIONAL LAW DOES NOT REQUIRE A DECLARATION
OF WAR AS A CONDITION PRECEDENT TO TAKING
MEASURES OF SELF-DEFENSE AGAINST ARMED ATTACK

The existence or absence of a formal declaration of war is not a factor in determining whether an international use of force is lawful as a matter of international law. The United Nations Charter's restrictions focus on the manner and purpose of its use and not on any formalities of announcement.

It should also be noted that a formal declaration of war would not place any obligations on either side in the conflict by which that side would not be bound in any event. The rules of international law concerning the conduct of hostilities in an international armed conflict apply regardless of any declaration of war.

H. SUMMARY

The analysis set forth above shows that South Viet Nam has the right in present circumstances to defend itself against armed attack from the North and to organize a collective self-defense with the participation of others. In response to requests from South Viet Nam, the United States has been participating in that defense, both through military action within South Viet Nam and actions taken directly against the aggressor in North Viet Nam. This participation by the United States is in conformity with international law and is consistent with our obligations under the Charter of the United Nations.

II. The United States Has Undertaken Commitments To Assist South Viet Nam in Defending Itself Against Communist Aggression from the North

The United States has made commitments and given assurances, in various forms and at different times, to assist in the defense of South Viet Nam.

A. THE UNITED STATES GAVE UNDERTAKINGS AT THE END OF THE GENEVA CONFERENCE IN 1954

At the time of the signing of the Geneva Accords in 1954, President Eisenhower warned "that any renewal of Communist aggression would be viewed by us as a matter of grave concern," at the same time giving assurance that the United States would "not use force to disturb the settlement." And the formal declaration made by the United States Government at the conclusion of the Geneva Conference stated that the United States "would view any renewal of aggression in violation of the aforesaid agreements with grave concern and as seriously threatening international peace and security."

B. THE UNITED STATES UNDERTOOK AN INTERNATIONAL OBLIGATION TO DEFEND SOUTH VIET NAM IN THE SEATO TREATY

Later in 1954 the United States negotiated with a number of other countries and signed the Southeast Asia Collective Defense Treaty. The Treaty contains in the first paragraph of Article 4 the following provision:

Each Party recognizes that aggression by means of armed attack in the treaty area against any of the Parties or against any State or territory which the Parties by unanimous agreement may hereafter designate, would endanger its own peace and safety, and agrees that it will in that event act to meet the common danger in accordance with its constitutional processes. Measures taken under this paragraph shall be immediately reported to the Security Council of the United Nations.

Annexed to the Treaty was a Protocol stating that:

The parties to the Southeast Asia Collective Defense Treaty unanimously designate for the purpose of Article IV of the Treaty the States of Cambodia and Laos and the free territory under the jurisdiction of the State of Viet Nam.

Thus, the obligations of Article IV, paragraph 1, dealing with the eventuality of armed attack, have from the outset covered the territory of South Viet Nam. The facts as to the North Vietnamese armed attack against the South have been summarized earlier, in the discussion of the right of self-defense under international law and the Charter of the United Nations. The term "armed attack" has the same meaning in the SEATO Treaty as in the United Nations Charter.

Article IV, paragraph 1, places an obligation on each party to the SEATO Treaty to "act to meet the common danger in accordance with its constitutional processes" in the event of an armed attack. The Treaty does not require a collective determination that an armed attack has occurred in order that the obligation of Article IV, paragraph 1, become operative. Nor does the provision require collective decision on actions to be taken to meet the common danger. As Secretary Dulles pointed out when transmitting the Treaty to the President, the commitment in Article IV, paragraph 1, "leaves to the judgment of each country the type of action to be taken in the event an armed attack occurs."

The Treaty was intended to deter armed aggression in Southeast Asia. To that end it created not only a multilateral alliance but also a series of bilateral relationships. The obligations are placed squarely on "each Party" in the event of armed attack in the Treaty area—not upon "the Parties," a wording that might have implied a necessity for collective decision. The Treaty was intended to give the assurance of United States assistance to any Party or protocol state that might suffer a Communist armed attack, regardless of the views or actions of other parties. The fact that the obligations are individual, and may even to some extent differ among the parties to the Treaty, is demonstrated by the United States understanding, expressed at the time of signature, that its obligations under Article IV, paragraph 1, apply only in the event of *Communist* aggression, whereas the other parties to the Treaty were unwilling so to limit their obligations to each other.

Thus, the United States has a commitment under Article IV, paragraph 1, in the event of armed attack, independent of the decision or action of other treaty parties. A joint communiqué issued by Secretary Rusk and Foreign Minister Thanat Khoman of Thailand on March 6, 1962, reflected this understanding:

> The Secretary of State assured the Foreign Minister that in the event of such aggression, the United States intends to give full effect to its obligations under the Treaty to act to meet the common danger in accordance with its constitutional processes. The Secretary of State reaffirmed that this obligation of the United States does not depend on the prior agreement of all other Parties to the Treaty, since this Treaty obligation is individual as well as collective.

Most of the SEATO countries have stated that they agreed with this interpretation. None has registered objection to it.

When the Senate Committee on Foreign Relations reported on the Southeast Asia Collective Defense Treaty, it noted that the treaty area was further defined so that the "Free Territory of Viet Nam" was an area "which, if attacked, would fall under the protection of the instrument." In its conclusion the Committee stated:

> The Committee is not impervious to the risks which this treaty entails. It fully appreciates that acceptance of these additional obligations commits the United States to a course of action over a vast expanse of the Pacific. Yet these risks are consistent with our own highest interests.

The Senate gave its advice and consent to the Treaty by a vote of 82 to 1.

C. THE UNITED STATES HAS GIVEN ADDITIONAL ASSURANCES TO THE GOVERNMENT OF SOUTH VIET NAM

The United States has also given a series of additional assurances to the Government of South Viet Nam. As early as October 1954 President Eisenhower undertook to provide direct assistance to help make South Viet Nam "capable of resisting attempted subversion or aggression through military means." On May 11, 1957 President Eisenhower and President Ngo Dinh Diem of the Republic of Viet Nam issued a joint statement which called attention to "the large build-up of Vietnamese Communist military forces in North Viet Nam" and stated:

Noting that the Republic of Vietnam is covered by Article IV of the Southeast Asia Collective Defense Treaty, President Eisenhower and President Ngo Dinh Diem agreed that aggression or subversion threatening the political independence of the Republic of Vietnam would be considered as endangering peace and stability.

On August 2, 1961 President Kennedy declared that "the United States is determined that the Republic of Viet Nam shall not be lost to the Communists for lack of any support which the United States can render." On December 7 of that year President Diem appealed for additional support. In his reply of December 14, 1961 President Kennedy recalled the United States declaration made at the end of the Geneva Conference in 1954, and reaffirmed that the United States was "prepared to help the Republic of Viet Nam to protect its people and to preserve its independence." This assurance has been reaffirmed many times since.

III. Actions by the United States and South Viet Nam Are Justified Under the Geneva Accords of 1954

A. DESCRIPTION OF THE ACCORDS

The Geneva Accords of 1954[8] established the date and hour for a cease-fire in Viet Nam, drew a "provisional military demarcation line" with a demilitarized zone on both sides, and required an exchange of prisoners and the phased regroupment of Viet Minh Forces from the south to the north and of French Union Forces from the north to the south. The introduction into Viet Nam of troop reinforcements and new military equipment (except for replacement and repair) was prohibited. The armed forces of each party were required to respect the demilitarized zone and the territory of the other zone. The adherence of either zone to any military alliance, and the use of either zone for the resumption of hostilities or to "further an aggressive policy," were prohibited. The International Control Commission was established, com-

---

[8] These Accords were composed of a bilateral cease-fire agreement between the "Commander-in-Chief of the People's Army of Viet Nam" and the "Commander-in-Chief of the French Union Forces in Indo-China," together with a Final Declaration of the Conference, to which France adhered. However, it is to be noted that the South Vietnamese Government was not a signatory of the cease-fire agreement and did not adhere to the Final Declaration. South Viet Nam entered a series of reservations in a statement to the Conference. This statement was noted by the Conference, but by decision of the Conference Chairman it was not included or referred to in the Final Declaration.

posed of India, Canada and Poland, with India as Chairman. The task of the Commission was to supervise the proper execution of the provisions of the Cease-Fire Agreement. General elections that would result in reunification were required to be held in July 1956 under the supervision of the ICC.

B. NORTH VIET NAM VIOLATED THE ACCORDS FROM THE BEGINNING

From the very beginning, the North Vietnamese violated the 1954 Geneva Accords. Communist military forces and supplies were left in the South in violation of the Accords. Other Communist guerrillas were moved north for further training and then were infiltrated into the South in violation of the Accords.

C. THE INTRODUCTION OF UNITED STATES MILITARY PERSONNEL AND EQUIPMENT WAS JUSTIFIED

The Accords prohibited the reinforcement of foreign military forces in Viet Nam and the introduction of new military equipment, but they allowed replacement of existing military personnel and equipment. Prior to late 1961 South Viet Nam had received considerable military equipment and supplies from the United States, and the United States had gradually enlarged its Military Assistance Advisory Group to slightly less than 900 men. These actions were reported to the ICC and were justified as replacements for equipment in Viet Nam in 1954 and for French training and advisory personnel who had been withdrawn after 1954.

As the Communist aggression intensified during 1961, with increased infiltration and a marked stepping up of Communist terrorism in the South, the United States found it necessary in late 1961 to increase substantially the numbers of our military personnel and the amounts and types of equipment introduced by this country into South Viet Nam. These increases were justified by the international law principle that a material breach of an agreement by one party entitles the other at least to withhold compliance with an equivalent, corresponding, or related provision until the defaulting party is prepared to honor its obligations.[9]

[9] This principle of law and the circumstances in which it may be invoked are most fully discussed in the Fourth Report on the Law of Treaties by Sir Gerald Fitzmaurice, Articles 18, 20 (UN Doc. A/CN.4/120 [1959]), II Yearbook of the International Law Commission 37 (UN Doc. A/CN.4/SER.A/1959/Add. 1), and in the later Report by Sir Humphrey Waldock, Article 20 (UN Doc. A/CN.4/156 and Add.1-3 [1963]), II Yearbook of the International Law Commission 36 (UN Doc. A/CN.4/SER.A/1963/Add.1). Among the authorities cited by the Fourth Report for this proposition are: II Oppenheim, *International Law* 136, 137 (7th ed. Lauterpacht 1955); I Rousseau, *Principes généraux du droit international public* 365

In accordance with this principle, the systematic violation of the Geneva Accords by North Viet Nam justified South Viet Nam in suspending compliance with the provision controlling entry of foreign military personnel and military equipment.

D. SOUTH VIET NAM WAS JUSTIFIED IN REFUSING TO IMPLEMENT THE ELECTION PROVISIONS OF THE GENEVA ACCORDS

The Geneva Accords contemplated the reunification of the two parts of Viet Nam. They contained a provision for general elections to be held in July 1956 in order to obtain a "free expression of the national will." The Accords stated that "consultations will be held on this subject between the competent representative authorities of the two zones from 20 July 1955 onwards."

There may be some question whether South Viet Nam was bound by these election provisions. As indicated earlier, South Viet Nam did not sign the cease-fire agreement of 1954, nor did it adhere to the Final Declaration of the Geneva Conference. The South Vietnamese Government at that time gave notice of its objection in particular to the election provisions of the Accords.

However, even on the premise that these provisions were binding on South Viet Nam, the South Vietnamese Government's failure to engage in consultations in 1955, with a view to holding elections in 1956, involved no breach of obligation. The conditions in North Viet Nam during that period were such as to make impossible any free and meaningful expression of popular will.

Some of the facts about conditions in the North were admitted even by the Communist leadership in Hanoi. General Giap, currently Defense Minister of North Viet Nam, in addressing the Tenth Congress of the North Vietnamese Communist Party in October 1956, publicly acknowledged that the Communist leaders were running a police state where executions, terror and torture were commonplace. A nationwide election in these circumstances would have been a travesty. No one in the North would have dared to vote except as directed. With a substantial majority of the Vietnamese people living north of the 17th parallel, such an election would have meant turning the country over to the Communists without regard to the will of the people. The South Vietnamese

---

(1944): II Hyde, *International Law* 1660 et seq. (2d ed. 1947); II Guggenheim, *Traité de droit international public* 84, 85 (1935); Spiropoulos, *Traité théorique et pratique de droit international public* 289 (1933); Verdross, *Völkerrecht* 328 (1950); Hall, *Treatise* 21 (8th ed., Higgins 1924); 3 Accioly, *Tratado de Direito Internacional Publico* 82 (1956-57). See also draft articles 42 and 46 of the Law of Treaties by the International Law Commission, contained in the Report on the work of its Fifteenth Session (General Assembly, Official Records, 18th Session, Supplement No. 9[A/5809]).

Government realized these facts and quite properly took the position that consultations for elections in 1956 as contemplated by the Accords would be a useless formality.[10]

IV. The President Has Full Authority To Commit United States Forces in the Collective Defense of South Viet Nam

There can be no question in present circumstances of the President's authority to commit United States forces to the defense of South Viet Nam. The grant of authority to the President in Article II of the Constitution extends to the actions of the United States currently undertaken in Viet Nam. In fact, however, it is unnecessary to determine whether this grant standing alone is sufficient to authorize the actions taken in Viet Nam. These actions rest not only on the exercise of Presidential powers under Article II but on the SEATO Treaty—a treaty advised and consented to by the Senate—and on actions of the Congress, particularly the Joint Resolution of August 10, 1964. When these sources of authority are taken together—Article II of the Constitution, the SEATO Treaty, and actions by the Congress—there can be no question of the legality under domestic law of United States actions in Viet Nam.

A. THE PRESIDENT'S POWER UNDER ARTICLE II OF THE CONSTITUTION EXTENDS TO THE ACTIONS CURRENTLY UNDERTAKEN IN VIET NAM

Under the Constitution, the President, in addition to being Chief Executive, is Commander-in-Chief of the Army and Navy. He holds the prime responsibility for the conduct of United States foreign relations. These duties carry very broad powers, including the power to deploy American forces abroad and commit them to military operations when the President deems such action necessary to maintain the security and defense of the United States.

At the Federal Constitutional Convention in 1787, it was originally proposed that Congress have the power "to make war." There were objections that legislative proceedings were too slow for this power to be vested in Congress; it was suggested that the Senate might be a better repository. Madison and Gerry then moved to substitute "to declare war" for "to make war," "leaving to the Executive the power to

---

[10] In any event, if North Viet Nam considered there had been a breach of obligation by the South, its remedies lay in discussion with Saigon, perhaps in an appeal to the Co-Chairmen of the Geneva Conference, or in a reconvening of the Conference to consider the situation. Under international law, North Viet Nam had no right to use force outside its own zone in order to secure its political objectives.

repel sudden attacks." It was objected that this might make it too easy for the Executive to involve the nation in war, but the motion carried with but one dissenting vote.

In 1787 the world was a far larger place, and the framers probably had in mind attacks upon the United States. In the 20th century, the world has grown much smaller. An attack on a country far from our shores can impinge directly on the nation's security. In the SEATO Treaty, for example, it is formally declared that an armed attack against Viet Nam would endanger the peace and safety of the United States.

Since the Constitution was adopted there have been at least 125 instances in which the President has ordered the armed forces to take action or maintain positions abroad without obtaining prior Congressional authorization, starting with the "undeclared war" with France (1798-1800). For example, President Truman ordered 250,000 troops to Korea during the Korean War of the early 1950's. President Eisenhower dispatched 14,000 troops to Lebanon in 1958.

The Constitution leaves to the President the judgment to determine whether the circumstances of a particular armed attack are so urgent and the potential consequences so threatening to the security of the United States that he should act without formally consulting the Congress.

B. THE SOUTHEAST ASIA COLLECTIVE DEFENSE TREATY AUTHORIZES THE PRESIDENT'S ACTIONS

Under Article VI of the United States Constitution, "all Treaties made, or which shall be made, under the Authority of the United States, shall be the supreme Law of the Land." Article IV, paragraph 1 of the SEATO Treaty establishes as a matter of law that a Communist armed attack against South Viet Nam endangers the peace and safety of the United States. In this same provision the United States has undertaken a commitment in the SEATO Treaty to "act to meet the common danger in accordance with its constitutional processes" in the event of such an attack.

Under our Constitution it is the President who must decide when an armed attack has occurred. He has also the constitutional responsibility for determining what measures of defense are required when the peace and safety of the United States are endangered. If he considers that deployment of U.S. forces to South Viet Nam is required, and that military measures against the source of Communist aggression in North Viet Nam are necessary, he is constitutionally empowered to take those measures.

The SEATO Treaty specifies that each party will act "in accordance with its constitutional processes."

It has recently been argued that the use of land forces in Asia is not authorized under the Treaty because their use to deter armed attack was not contemplated at the time the Treaty was considered by the Senate. Secretary Dulles testified at that time that we did not intend to establish (1) a land army in Southeast Asia capable of deterring Communist aggression, or (2) an integrated headquarters and military organization like that of NATO; instead, the United States would rely on "mobile striking power" against the sources of aggression. However, the Treaty obligation in Article IV, paragraph 1, to meet the common danger in the event of armed aggression, is not limited to particular modes of military action. What constitutes an adequate deterrent or an appropriate response, in terms of military strategy, may change; but the essence of our commitment to act to meet the common danger, as necessary at the time of an armed aggression, remains. In 1954 the forecast of military judgment might have been against the use of substantial United States ground forces in Viet Nam. But that does not preclude the President from reaching a different military judgment in different circumstances, twelve years later.

C. THE JOINT RESOLUTION OF CONGRESS OF AUGUST 10, 1964 AUTHORIZES UNITED STATES PARTICIPATION IN THE COLLECTIVE DEFENSE OF SOUTH VIET NAM

As stated earlier, the legality of United States participation in the defense of South Viet Nam does not rest only on the constitutional power of the President under Article II—or indeed on that power taken in conjunction with the SEATO Treaty. In addition, the Congress has acted in unmistakable fashion to approve and authorize United States actions in Viet Nam.

Following the North Vietnamese attacks in the Gulf of Tonkin against United States destroyers, Congress adopted, by a Senate vote of 88-2 and a House vote of 416-0, a Joint Resolution containing a series of important declarations and provisions of law.

Section 1 resolved that "the Congress approves and supports the determination of the President, as Commander in Chief, to take all necessary measures to repel any armed attack against the forces of the United States and to prevent further aggression." Thus, the Congress gave its sanction to specific actions by the President to repel attacks against United States naval vessels in the Gulf of Tonkin and elsewhere in the western Pacific. Congress further approved the taking of "all necessary measures . . . to prevent further aggression." This authorization extended to those measures the President might consider necessary to ward off further attacks and to prevent further aggression by North Viet Nam in Southeast Asia.

The Joint Resolution then went on to provide in section 2:

> The United States regards as vital to its national interest and to world peace the maintenance of international peace and security in southeast Asia. Consonant with the Constitution of the United States and the Charter of the United Nations and in accordance with its obligations under the Southeast Asia Collective Defense Treaty, the United States is, therefore, prepared, as the President determines, to take all necessary steps, including the use of armed force, to assist any member or protocol state of the Southeast Asia Collective Defense Treaty requesting assistance in defense of its freedom.

Section 2 thus constitutes an authorization to the President, in his discretion, to act—using armed force if he determines that is required —to assist South Viet Nam at its request in defense of its freedom. The identification of South Viet Nam through the reference to "protocol state" in this section is unmistakable, and the grant of authority "as the President determines" is unequivocal.

It has been suggested that the legislative history of the Joint Resolution shows an intention to limit United States assistance to South Viet Nam to aid, advice, and training. This suggestion is based on an amendment offered from the floor by Senator Nelson which would have added the following to the text:

> The Congress also approves and supports the efforts of the President to bring the problem of peace in Southeast Asia to the Security Council of the United Nations, and the President's declaration that the United States, seeking no extension of the present military conflict, will respond to provocation in a manner that is "limited and fitting." Our continuing policy is to limit our role to the provision of aid, training assistance, and military advice, and it is the sense of Congress that, except when provoked to a greater response, we should continue to attempt to avoid a direct military involvement in the Southeast Asian conflict.[11]

Senator Fulbright, who had reported the Joint Resolution from the Foreign Relations Committee, spoke on the amendment as follows:

> Mr. Fulbright. It states fairly accurately what the President has said would be our policy, and what I stated my understanding was as to our policy; also what other Senators have stated. In other words, it

[11] 110 *Cong. Rec.* 18459 (Aug. 7, 1964).

states that our response should be appropriate and limited to the provocation, which the Senator states as "respond to provocation in a manner that is limited and fitting," and so forth. We do not wish any political or military bases there. We are not seeking to gain a colony. We seek to insure the capacity of these people to develop along the lines of their own desires, independent of domination by communism.

The Senator has put into his amendment a statement of policy that is unobjectionable. However, I cannot accept the amendment under the circumstances. I do not believe it is contrary to the joint resolution, but it is an enlargement. I am informed that the House is now voting on this resolution. The House joint resolution is about to be presented to us. I cannot accept the amendment and go to conference with it, and thus take responsibility for delaying matters.

I do not object to it as a statement of policy. I believe it is an accurate reflection of what I believe is the President's policy, judging from his own statements. That does not mean that as a practical matter I can accept the amendment. It would delay matters to do so. It would cause confusion and require a conference, and present us with all the other difficulties that are involved in this kind of legislative action. I regret that I cannot do it, even though I do not at all disagree with the amendment as a general statement of policy.[12]

Senator Nelson's amendment related the degree and kind of U.S. response in Viet Nam to "provocation" on the other side; the response should be "limited and fitting." The greater the provocation, the stronger are the measures that may be characterized as "limited and fitting." Bombing of North Vietnamese naval bases was a "limited and fitting" response to the attacks on U.S. destroyers in August 1964, and the subsequent actions taken by the United States and South Viet Nam have been an appropriate response to the increased war of aggression carried on by North Viet Nam since that date. Moreover, Senator Nelson's proposed amendment did not purport to be a restriction on authority available to the President but merely a statement concerning what should be the continuing policy of the United States.

Congressional realization of the scope of authority being conferred by the Joint Resolution is shown by the legislative history of the measure as a whole. The following exchange between Senators Cooper and Fulbright is illuminating:

Mr. Cooper. . . . The Senator will remember that the SEATO Treaty, in article IV, provides that in the event an armed attack is

[12] *Ibid.*

made upon a party to the Southeast Asia Collective Defense Treaty, or upon one of the protocol states such as South Vietnam, the parties to the treaty, one of whom is the United States, would then take such action as might be appropriate, after resorting to their constitutional processes. I assumed that would mean, in the case of the United States, that Congress would be asked to grant the authority to act.

Does the Senator consider that in enacting this resolution we are satisfying that requirement of article IV of the Southeast Asia Collective Defense Treaty? In other words, are we now giving the President advance authority to take whatever action he may deem necessary respecting South Vietnam and its defense, or with respect to the defense of any other country included in the treaty?

Mr. Fulbright. I think that is correct.

Mr. Cooper. Then, looking ahead, if the President decided that it was necessary to use such force as could lead into war, we will give that authority by this resolution?

Mr. Fulbright. That is the way I would interpret it. If a situation later developed in which we thought the approval should be withdrawn it could be withdrawn by concurrent resolution.[13]

The August 1964 Joint Resolution continues in force today. Section 2 of the Resolution provides that it shall expire "when the President shall determine that the peace and security of the area is reasonably assured by international conditions created by action of the United Nations or otherwise, except that it may be terminated earlier by concurrent resolution of the Congress." The President has made no such determination, nor has Congress terminated the Joint Resolution.[14]

[13] 110 *Cong. Rec.* 18409 (Aug. 6, 1964).
Senator Morse, who opposed the Joint Resolution, expressed the following view on August 6, 1964, concerning the scope of the proposed resolution:
"Another Senator thought, in the early part of the debate, that this course would not broaden the power of the President to engage in a land war if he decided that he wanted to apply the resolution in that way.
That Senator was taking great consolation in the then held belief that, if he voted for the resolution, it would give no authority to the President to send many troops into Asia. I am sure he was quite disappointed to finally learn, because it took a little time to get the matter cleared, that the resolution places no restriction on the President in that respect. If he is still in doubt, let him read the language on page 2, lines 3 to 6, and page 2, lines 11 to 17. The first reads:
'The Congress approves and supports the determination of the President, as Commander in Chief, to take all necessary measures to repel any armed attack against the forces of the United States and to prevent further aggression.'
It does not say he is limited in regard to the sending of ground forces. It does not limit that authority. That is why I have called it a predated declaration of war, in clear violation of article I, section 8 of the Constitution, which vests the power to declare war in the Congress, and not in the President.
What is proposed is to authorize the President of the United States, without a declaration of war, to commit acts of war."
110 *Cong. Rec.* 18426-27 (Aug. 6, 1964).
[14] On March 1, 1966, the Senate voted,

Instead, Congress in May 1965 approved an appropriation of $700 million to meet the expense of mounting military requirements in Viet Nam. (Public Law 89-18, 79 Stat. 109.) The President's message asking for this appropriation stated that this was "not a routine request. For each member of Congress who supports this request is also voting to persist in our efforts to halt Communist aggressions in South Viet Nam." The Appropriation Act constitutes a clear Congressional endorsement and approval of the actions taken by the President.

On March 1, 1966 the Congress continued to express its support of the President's policy by approving a $4.8 billion supplemental military authorization by votes of 392-4 and 93-2. An amendment that would have limited the President's authority to commit forces to Viet Nam was rejected in the Senate by a vote of 94-2.

D. NO DECLARATION OF WAR BY THE CONGRESS IS REQUIRED TO AUTHORIZE UNITED STATES PARTICIPATION IN THE COLLECTIVE DEFENSE OF SOUTH VIET NAM

No declaration of war is needed to authorize American actions in Viet Nam. As shown in the preceding sections, the President has ample authority to order the participation of United States armed forces in the defense of South Viet Nam.

Over a very long period in our history, practice and precedent have confirmed the constitutional authority to engage United States forces in hostilities without a declaration of war. This history extends from the undeclared war with France and the war against the Barbary Pirates, at the end of the 18th century, to the Korean War of 1950-53.

James Madison, one of the leading framers of the Constitution, and Presidents John Adams and Jefferson all construed the Constitution, in their official actions during the early years of the Republic, as authorizing the United States to employ its armed forces abroad in hostilities in the absence of any Congressional declaration of war. Their views and actions constitute highly persuasive evidence as to the meaning and effect of the Constitution. History has accepted the interpretation that was placed on the Constitution by the early Presidents and Congresses in regard to the lawfulness of hostilities without a declaration of war. The instances of such action in our history are numerous.

In the Korean conflict, where large-scale hostilities were conducted with an American troop participation of a quarter of a million men, no declaration of war was made by the Congress. The President acted on the basis of his constitutional responsibilities. While the Security

92-5, to table an amendment that would have repealed the Joint Resolution.

Council, under a treaty of this country—the United Nations Charter—recommended assistance to the Republic of Korea against the Communist armed attack, the United States had no treaty commitment at that time obligating us to join in the defense of South Korea. In the case of South Viet Nam we have the obligation of the SEATO Treaty and clear expressions of Congressional support. If the President could act in Korea without a declaration of war, *a fortiori* he is empowered to do so now in Viet Nam.

It may be suggested that a declaration of war is the only available constitutional process by which Congressional support can be made effective for the use of United States armed forces in combat abroad. But the Constitution does not insist on any rigid formalism. It gives Congress a choice of ways in which to exercise its powers. In the case of Viet Nam the Congress has supported the determination of the President by the Senate's approval of the SEATO Treaty, the adoption of the Joint Resolution of August 10, 1964, and the enactment of the necessary authorizations and appropriations.

V. *Conclusion*

South Viet Nam is being subjected to armed attack by Communist North Viet Nam, through the infiltration of armed personnel, military equipment and regular combat units. International law recognizes the right of individual and collective self-defense against armed attack. South Viet Nam, and the United States upon the request of South Viet Nam, are engaged in such collective defense of the South. Their actions are in conformity with international law and with the Charter of the United Nations. The fact that South Viet Nam has been precluded by Soviet veto from becoming a Member of the United Nations, and the fact that South Viet Nam is a zone of a temporarily divided state, in no way diminish the right of collective defense of South Viet Nam.

The United States has commitments to assist South Viet Nam in defending itself against Communist aggression from the North. The United States gave undertakings to this effect at the conclusion of the Geneva Conference in 1954. Later that year the United States undertook an international obligation in the SEATO Treaty to defend South Viet Nam against Communist armed aggression. And during the past decade the United States has given additional assurances to the South Vietnamese Government.

The Geneva Accords of 1954 provided for a cease-fire and regroupment of contending forces, a division of Viet Nam into two zones, and a prohibition on the use of either zone for the resumption of hostilities or to "further an aggressive policy." From the beginning, North Viet

Nam violated the Geneva Accords through a systematic effort to gain control of South Viet Nam by force. In the light of these progressive North Vietnamese violations, the introduction into South Viet Nam beginning in late 1961 of substantial United States military equipment and personnel, to assist in the defense of the South, was fully justified; substantial breach of an international agreement by one side permits the other side to suspend performance of corresponding obligations under the agreement. South Viet Nam was justified in refusing to implement the provisions of the Geneva Accords calling for reunification through free elections throughout Viet Nam since the Communist regime in North Viet Nam created conditions in the North that made free elections entirely impossible.

The President of the United States has full authority to commit United States forces in the collective defense of South Viet Nam. This authority stems from the Constitutional powers of the President. However, it is not necessary to rely on the Constitution alone as the source of the President's authority, since the SEATO Treaty—advised and consented to by the Senate and forming part of the law of the land—sets forth a United States commitment to defend South Viet Nam against armed attack, and since the Congress—in the Joint Resolution of August 10, 1964, and in authorization and appropriations acts for support of the U.S. military effort in Viet Nam—has given its approval and support to the President's actions. United States actions in Viet Nam, taken by the President and approved by the Congress, do not require any declaration of war, as shown by a long line of precedents for the use of United States armed forces abroad in the absence of any Congressional declaration of war.

The Treaty would contain three stages designed to achieve a permanent state of general and complete disarmament in a peaceful world. The Treaty would enter into force upon the signature and ratification of the United States of America, the Union of Soviet Socialist Republics and such other states as might be agreed. Stage II would begin when all militarily significant states had become Parties to the Treaty and other transition requirements had been satisfied. Stage III would begin when all states possessing armed forces and armaments had become Parties to the Treaty and other transition requirements had been satisfied. Disarmament, verification, and measures for keeping the peace would proceed progressively and proportionately beginning with the entry into force of the Treaty.

Appendix B
Outline of Basic Provisions of a Treaty on General and Complete Disarmament in a Peaceful World

*As submitted by the United States of America
to the Eighteen-Nation Disarmament Committee at
Geneva on April 18, 1962, amended on August 6
and 8, 1962 and on August 14, 1963**

In order to assist in the preparation of a treaty on general and complete disarmament in a peaceful world, the United States submits the following outline of basic provisions of such a treaty. The Preamble of such a treaty has already been the subject of negotiations and is therefore not submitted as part of this treaty outline.

A. Objectives

1. To ensure that (a) disarmament is general and complete and war is no longer an instrument for settling international problems, and (b) general and complete disarmament is accompanied by the establishment of reliable procedures for the settlement of disputes and by effective arrangements for the maintenance of peace in accordance with the principles of the Charter of the United Nations.

2. Taking into account paragraphs 3 and 4 below, to provide, with respect to the military establishment of every nation, for:

(a) Disbanding of armed forces, dismantling of military establishments, including bases, cessation of the production of armaments as well as their liquidation or conversion to peaceful uses;

(b) Elimination of all stockpiles of nuclear, chemical, biological and other weapons of mass destruction and cessation of the production of such weapons;

(c) Elimination of all means of delivery of weapons of mass destruction;

(d) Abolition of the organizations and institutions designed to organize the military efforts of states, cessation of military training, and closing of all military training institutions;

(e) Discontinuance of military expenditures.

3. To ensure that, at the completion of the program for general and complete disarmament, states would have at their disposal only those

---

* This document is the latest version, as of March 1, 1964, of the proposals of the   United States.

non-nuclear armaments, forces, facilities and establishments as are agreed to be necessary to maintain internal order and protect the personal security of citizens.

4. To ensure that during and after implementation of general and complete disarmament, states also would support and provide agreed manpower for a United Nations Peace Force to be equipped with agreed types of armaments necessary to ensure that the United Nations can effectively deter or suppress any threat or use of arms.

5. To establish and provide for the effective operation of an International Disarmament Organization within the framework of the United Nations for the purpose of ensuring that all obligations under the disarmament program would be honored and observed during and after implementation of general and complete disarmament; and to this end to ensure that the International Disarmament Organization and its inspectors would have unrestricted access without veto to all places as necessary for the purpose of effective verification.

B. Principles

The guiding principles during the achievement of these objectives are:

1. Disarmament would be implemented until it is completed by stages to be carried out within specified time limits.

2. Disarmament would be balanced so that at no stage of the implementation of the treaty could any state or group of states gain military advantage, and so that security would be ensured equally for all.

3. Compliance with all disarmament obligations would be effectively verified during and after their entry into force. Verification arrangements would be instituted progressively as necessary to ensure throughout the disarmament process that agreed levels of armaments and armed forces were not exceeded.

4. As national armaments are reduced, the United Nations would be progressively strengthened in order to improve its capacity to ensure international security and the peaceful settlement of differences as well as to facilitate the development of international cooperation in common tasks for the benefit of mankind.

5. Transition from one stage of disarmament to the next would take place upon decision that all measures in the preceding stage had been implemented and verified and that any additional arrangements required for measures in the next stage were ready to operate.

STAGE I

Stage I would begin upon the entry into force of the Treaty and would be completed within three years from that date.

[560]

During Stage I the Parties to the Treaty would undertake:

1. To reduce their armaments and armed forces and to carry out other agreed measures in the manner outlined below;

2. To establish the International Disarmament Organization upon the entry into force of the Treaty in order to ensure the verification in the agreed manner of the obligations undertaken; and

3. To strengthen arrangements for keeping the peace through the measures outlined below.

A. Armaments

1. REDUCTION OF ARMAMENTS

a. Specified Parties to the Treaty, as a first stage toward general and complete disarmament in a peaceful world, would reduce by thirty per cent the armaments in each category listed in subparagraph b. below. Each type of armament in the categories listed in subparagraph b. would be reduced by thirty per cent of the inventory existing at an agreed date.

b. All types of armaments within agreed categories would be subject to reduction in Stage I (the following list of categories, and of types within categories, is illustrative):

(1) Armed combat aircraft having an empty weight of 40,000 kilograms or greater; missiles having a range of 5,000 kilometers or greater, together with their related fixed launching pads; and submarine-launched missiles and air-to-surface missiles having a range of 300 kilometers or greater.

(Within this category, the United States, for example, would declare as types of armaments: the B-52 aircraft; Atlas missiles together with their related fixed launching pads; Titan missiles together with their related fixed launching pads; Polaris missiles; Hound Dog missiles; and each new type of armament, such as Minuteman missiles, which came within the category description, together with, where applicable, their related fixed launching pads. The declared inventory of types within the category by other Parties to the Treaty would be similarly detailed.)

(2) Armed combat aircraft having an empty weight of between 15,-000 kilograms and 40,000 kilograms and those missiles not included in category (1) having a range between 300 kilometers and 5,000 kilometers, together with any related fixed launching pads. (The Parties would declare their armaments by types within the category.)

(3) Armed combat aircraft having an empty weight of between 2,500 and 15,000 kilograms. (The Parties would declare their armaments by types within the category.)

(4) Surface-to-surface (including submarine-launched missiles) and

air-to-surface aerodynamic and ballistic missiles and free rockets having a range of between 10 kilometers and 300 kilometers, together with any related fixed launching pads. (The Parties would declare their armaments by types within the category.)

(5) Anti-missile missile systems, together with related fixed launching pads. (The Parties would declare their armaments by types within the category.)

(6) Surface-to-air missiles other than anti-missile missile systems, together with any related fixed launching pads. (The Parties would declare their armaments by types within the category.)

(7) Tanks. (The Parties would declare their armaments by types within the category.)

(8) Armoured cars and armoured personnel carriers. (The Parties would declare their armaments by types within the category.)

(9) All artillery, and mortars and rocket launchers having a caliber of 100 mm. or greater. (The Parties would declare their armaments by types within the category.)

(10) Combatant ships with standard displacement of 400 tons or greater of the following classes: Aircraft carriers, battleships, cruisers, destroyer types and submarines. (The Parties would declare their armaments by types within the category.)

2. METHOD OF REDUCTION

a. Those Parties to the Treaty which were subject to the reduction of armaments would submit to the International Disarmament Organization an appropriate declaration respecting inventories of their armaments existing at the agreed date.

b. The reduction would be accomplished in three steps, each consisting of one year. One-third of the reduction to be made during Stage I would be carried out during each step.

c. During the first part of each step, one-third of the armaments to be eliminated during Stage I would be placed in depots under supervision of the International Disarmament Organization. During the second part of each step, the deposited armaments would be destroyed or, where appropriate, converted to peaceful uses. The number and location of such depots and arrangements respecting their establishment and operation would be set forth in an annex to the Treaty.

d. In accordance with arrangements which would be set forth in a Treaty annex on verification, the International Disarmament Organization would verify the foregoing reduction and would provide assurance that retained armaments did not exceed agreed levels.

3. LIMITATION ON PRODUCTION OF ARMAMENTS AND ON RELATED ACTIVITIES

a. Production of all armaments listed in subparagraph b of paragraph 1 above would be limited to agreed allowances during Stage I and, by the beginning of Stage II, would be halted except for production within agreed limits of parts for maintenance of the agreed retained armaments.

b. The allowances would permit limited production of each type of armament listed in subparagraph b of paragraph 1 above. In all instances during the process of eliminating production of armaments, any armament produced within a type would be compensated for by an additional armament destroyed within that type to the end that the ten per cent reduction in numbers in each type in each step, and the resulting thirty per cent reduction in Stage I, would be achieved.

c. The testing and production of new types of armaments would be prohibited.

d. The expansion of facilities for the production of existing types of armaments and the construction or equipping of facilities for the production of new types of armaments would be prohibited.

e. The flight testing of missiles would be limited to agreed annual quotas.

f. In accordance with arrangements which would be set forth in the annex on verification, the International Disarmament Organization would verify the foregoing measures at declared locations and would provide assurance that activities subject to the foregoing measures were not conducted at undeclared locations.

4. ADDITIONAL MEASURES

The Parties to the Treaty would agree to examine unresolved questions relating to means of accomplishing in Stages II and III the reduction and eventual elimination of production and stockpiles of chemical and biological weapons of mass destruction. In light of this examination, the Parties to the Treaty would agree to arrangements concerning chemical and biological weapons of mass destruction.

B. Armed Forces

1. REDUCTION OF ARMED FORCES

Force levels for the United States of America and the Union of Soviet Socialist Republics would be reduced to 2.1 million each and for other specified Parties to the Treaty to agreed levels not exceeding 2.1 million each. All other Parties to the Treaty would, with agreed exceptions, reduce their force levels to 100,000 or one per cent of their population, whichever were higher, provided that in no case would the force levels of such other Parties to the Treaty exceed levels in existence upon the entry into force of the Treaty.

2. ARMED FORCES SUBJECT TO REDUCTION

Agreed force levels would include all full-time, uniformed personnel maintained by national governments in the following categories:

a. Career personnel of active armed forces and other personnel serving in the active armed forces on fixed engagements or contracts.

b. Conscripts performing their required period of full-time active duty as fixed by national law.

c. Personnel of militarily organized security forces and of other forces or organizations equipped and organized to perform a military mission.

3. METHOD OF REDUCTION OF ARMED FORCES

The reduction of force levels would be carried out in the following manner:

a. Those Parties to the Treaty which were subject to the foregoing reductions would submit to the International Disarmament Organization a declaration stating their force levels at the agreed date.

b. Force level reductions would be accomplished in three steps, each having a duration of one year. During each step force levels would be reduced by one-third of the difference between force levels existing at the agreed date and the levels to be reached at the end of Stage I.

c. In accordance with arrangements that would be set forth in the annex on verification, the International Disarmament Organization would verify the reduction of force levels and provide assurance that retained forces did not exceed agreed levels.

4. ADDITIONAL MEASURES

The Parties to the Treaty which were subject to the foregoing reductions would agree upon appropriate arrangements, including procedures for consultation, in order to ensure that civilian employment by military establishments would be in accordance with the objectives of the obligations respecting force levels.

C. Nuclear Weapons

1. PRODUCTION OF FISSIONABLE MATERIALS FOR NUCLEAR WEAPONS

a. The Parties to the Treaty would halt the production of fissionable materials for use in nuclear weapons.

b. This measure would be carried out in the following manner:

(1) The Parties to the Treaty would submit to the International Disarmament Organization a declaration listing by name, location and production capacity every facility under their jurisdiction capable of producing and processing fissionable materials at the agreed date.

(2) Production of fissionable materials for purposes other than use in nuclear weapons would be limited to agreed levels. The Parties to the Treaty would submit to the International Disarmament Organization periodic declarations stating the amounts and types of fissionable materials which were still being produced at each facility.

(3) In accordance with arrangements which would be set forth in the annex on verification, the International Disarmament Organization would verify the foregoing measures at declared facilities and would provide assurance that activities subject to the foregoing limitations were not conducted at undeclared facilities.

2. Transfer of Fissionable Material to Purposes Other than Use in Nuclear Weapons

a. Upon the cessation of production of fissionable materials for use in nuclear weapons, the United States of America and the Union of Soviet Socialist Republics would each transfer to purposes other than use in nuclear weapons agreed quantities of weapons grade U-235 from past production. The United States of America would transfer . . . . kilograms, and the Union of Soviet Socialist Republics would transfer . . . . kilograms of such weapons grade U-235. For this purpose, "weapons grade U-235" means the U-235 contained in metal of which at least 90 per cent of the weight is U-235.

b. To ensure that the transferred materials were not used in nuclear weapons, such materials would be placed under safeguards and inspection by the International Disarmament Organization, either in stockpiles or at the facilities in which they would be utilized for purposes other than use in nuclear weapons. Arrangements for such safeguards and inspection would be set forth in the annex on verification.

3. Transfer of Fissionable Materials Between States for Peaceful Uses of Nuclear Energy

a. Any transfer of fissionable materials between states would be for purposes other than for use in nuclear weapons and would be subject to a system of safeguards to ensure that such materials were not used in nuclear weapons.

b. The system of safeguards to be applied for this purpose would be developed in agreement with the International Atomic Energy Agency and would be set forth in an annex to the Treaty.

4. Non-Transfer of Nuclear Weapons

The Parties to the Treaty would agree to seek to prevent the creation of further national nuclear forces. To this end the Parties would agree that:

a. Any Party to the Treaty which had manufactured, or which at any time manufactures, a nuclear weapon would:

(1) Not transfer control over any nuclear weapons to a state which had not manufactured a nuclear weapon before an agreed date;

(2) Not assist any such state in manufacturing any nuclear weapons.

b. Any Party to the Treaty which had not manufactured a nuclear weapon before the agreed date would:

(1) Not acquire, or attempt to acquire, control over any nuclear weapons;

(2) Not manufacture, or attempt to manufacture, any nuclear weapons.

5. Nuclear Weapons Test Explosions

a. If an agreement prohibiting nuclear weapons test explosions and providing for effective international control had come into force prior to the entry into force of the Treaty, such agreement would become an annex to the Treaty, and all the Parties to the Treaty would be bound by the obligations specified in the agreement.

b. If, however, no such agreement had come into force prior to the entry into force of the Treaty, all nuclear weapons test explosions would be prohibited, and the procedures for effective international control would be set forth in an annex to the Treaty.

6. Additional Measures

The Parties to the Treaty would agree to examine remaining unresolved questions relating to the means of accomplishing in Stages II and III the reduction and eventual elimination of nuclear weapons stockpiles. In the light of this examination, the Parties to the Treaty would agree to arrangements concerning nuclear weapons stockpiles.

D. Outer Space

1. Prohibition of Weapons of Mass Destruction in Orbit

The Parties to the Treaty would agree not to place in orbit weapons capable of producing mass destruction.

2. Peaceful Cooperation in Space

The Parties to the Treaty would agree to support increased international cooperation in peaceful uses of outer space in the United Nations or through other appropriate arrangements.

3. NOTIFICATION AND PRE-LAUNCH INSPECTION

With respect to the launching of space vehicles and missiles:

a. Those Parties to the Treaty which conducted launchings of space vehicles or missiles would provide advance notification of such launchings to other Parties to the Treaty and to the International Disarmament Organization together with the track of the space vehicle or missile. Such advance notification would be provided on a timely basis to permit pre-launch inspection of the space vehicle or missile to be launched.

b. In accordance with arrangements which would be set forth in the annex on verification, the International Disarmament Organization would conduct pre-launch inspection of space vehicles and missiles and would establish and operate any arrangements necessary for detecting unreported launchings.

4. LIMITATIONS ON PRODUCTION AND ON RELATED ACTIVITIES

The production, stockpiling and testing of boosters for space vehicles would be subject to agreed limitations. Such activities would be monitored by the International Disarmament Organization in accordance with arrangements which would be set forth in the annex on verification.

E. Military Expenditures

1. REPORT ON EXPENDITURES

The Parties to the Treaty would submit to the International Disarmament Organization at the end of each step of each stage a report on their military expenditures. Such reports would include an itemization of military expenditures.

2. VERIFIABLE REDUCTION OF EXPENDITURES

The Parties to the Treaty would agree to examine questions related to the verifiable reduction of military expenditures. In the light of this examination, the Parties to the Treaty would consider appropriate arrangements respecting military expenditures.

F. Reduction of the Risk of War

In order to promote confidence and reduce the risk of war, the Parties to the Treaty would agree to the following measures:

1. Advance Notification of Military Movements and Manoeuvres

Specified Parties to the Treaty would give advance notification of major military movements and manoeuvres to other Parties to the Treaty and to the International Disarmament Organization. Specific arrangements relating to this commitment, including the scale of movements and manoeuvres to be reported and the information to be transmitted, would be agreed.

2. Observation Posts

Specified Parties to the Treaty would permit observation posts to be established at agreed locations, including major ports, railway centers, motor highways, river crossings, and air bases to report on concentrations and movements of military forces. The number of such posts could be progressively expanded in each successive step of Stage I. Specific arrangements relating to such observation posts, including the location and staffing of posts, the method of receiving and reporting information, and the schedule for installation of posts would be agreed.

3. Additional Observation Arrangements

The Parties to the Treaty would establish such additional observation arrangements as might be agreed. Such arrangements could be extended in an agreed manner during each step of Stage I.

4. Exchange of Military Missions

Specified Parties to the Treaty would undertake the exchange of military missions between states or groups of states in order to improve communications and understanding between them. Specific arrangements respecting such exchanges would be agreed.

5. Communications Between Heads of Government

Specified Parties to the Treaty would agree to the establishment of rapid and reliable communications among their heads of government and with the Secretary-General of the United Nations. Specific arrangements in this regard would be subject to agreement among the Parties concerned and between such Parties and the Secretary-General.

6. International Commission on Reduction of the Risk of War

The Parties to the Treaty would establish an International Commission on Reduction of the Risk of War as a subsidiary body of the International Disarmament Organization to examine and make recommendations regarding further measures that might be undertaken during Stage I or subsequent stages of disarmament to reduce the risk of war by accident, miscalculation, failure of communications, or surprise attack. Specific arrangements for such measures as might be agreed to by all or some of the Parties to the Treaty would be subject to agreement among the Parties concerned.

G. The International Disarmament Organization

1. ESTABLISHMENT OF THE INTERNATIONAL DISARMAMENT ORGANIZATION

The International Disarmament Organization would be established upon the entry into force of the Treaty and would function within the framework of the United Nations and in accordance with the terms and conditions of the Treaty.

2. COOPERATION OF THE PARTIES TO THE TREATY

The Parties to the Treaty would agree to cooperate promptly and fully with the International Disarmament Organization and to assist the International Disarmament Organization in the performance of its functions and in the execution of the decisions made by it in accordance with the provisions of the Treaty.

3. VERIFICATION FUNCTIONS OF THE INTERNATIONAL DISARMAMENT ORGANIZATION

The International Disarmament Organization would verify disarmament measures in accordance with the following principles which would be implemented through specific arrangements set forth in the annex on verification:

a. Measures providing for reduction of armaments would be verified by the International Disarmament Organization at agreed depots and would include verification of the destruction of armaments and, where appropriate, verification of the conversion of armaments to peaceful uses. Measures providing for reduction of armed forces would be verified by the International Disarmament Organization either at the agreed depots or other agreed locations.

b. Measures halting or limiting production, testing, and other specified activities would be verified by the International Disarmament Organization. Parties to the Treaty would declare the nature and location of all production and testing facilities and other specified activities. The International Disarmament Organization would have access to relevant facilities and activities wherever located in the territory of such Parties.

c. Assurance that agreed levels of armaments and armed forces were not exceeded and that activities limited or prohibited by the Treaty were not being conducted clandestinely would be provided by the International Disarmament Organization through agreed arrangements which would have the effect of providing that the extent of inspection during any step or stage would be related to the amount of disarmament being undertaken and to the degree of risk to the Parties to the Treaty of possible violations. This might be accomplished, for example, by an arrangement embodying such features as the following:

(1) All parts of the territory of those Parties to the Treaty to which this form of verification was applicable would be subject to selection for inspection from the beginning of Stage I as provided below.

(2) Parties to the Treaty would divide their territory into an agreed number of appropriate zones and at the beginning of each step of disarmament would submit to the International Disarmament Organization a declaration stating the total level of armaments, forces, and specified types of activities subject to verification within each zone. The exact location of armaments and forces within a zone would not be revealed prior to its selection for inspection.

(3) An agreed number of these zones would be progressively inspected by the International Disarmament Organization during Stage I according to an agreed time schedule. The zones to be inspected would be selected by procedures which would ensure their selection by Parties to the Treaty other than the Party whose territory was to be inspected or any Party associated with it. Upon selection of each zone, the Party to the Treaty whose territory was to be inspected would declare the exact location of armaments, forces and other agreed activities within the selected zone. During the verification process, arrangements would be made to provide assurance against undeclared movements of the objects of verification to or from the zone or zones being inspected. Both aerial and mobile ground inspection would be employed within the zone being inspected. In so far as agreed measures being verified were concerned, access within the zone would be free and unimpeded and verification would be carried out with the full cooperation of the state being inspected.

(4) Once a zone had been inspected it would remain open for further inspection while verification was being extended to additional zones.

(5) By the end of Stage III, when all disarmament measures had been completed, inspection would have been extended to all parts of the territory of Parties to the Treaty.

4. COMPOSITION OF THE INTERNATIONAL DISARMAMENT ORGANIZATION

a. The International Disarmament Organization would have:

(1) A General Conference of all the Parties to the Treaty;

(2) A Control Council consisting of representatives of all the major signatory powers as permanent members and certain other Parties to the Treaty on a rotating basis; and

(3) An Administrator who would administer the International Disarmament Organization under the direction of the Control Council and who would have the authority, staff, and finances adequate to ensure effective and impartial implementation of the functions of the International Disarmament Organization.

b. The General Conference and the Control Council would have power to establish such subsidiary bodies, including expert study groups, as either of them might deem necessary.

5. FUNCTIONS OF THE GENERAL CONFERENCE

The General Conference would have the following functions, among others which might be agreed:

a. Electing non-permanent members to the Control Council;

b. Approving certain accessions to the Treaty;

c. Appointing the Administrator upon recommendation of the Control Council;

d. Approving agreements between the International Disarmament Organization and the United Nations and other international organizations;

e. Approving the budget of the International Disarmament Organization;

f. Requesting and receiving reports from the Control Council and deciding upon matters referred to it by the Control Council;

g. Approving reports to be submitted to bodies of the United Nations;

h. Proposing matters for consideration by the Control Council;

i. Requesting the International Court of Justice to give advisory opinions on legal questions concerning the interpretation or application of the Treaty, subject to a general authorization of this power by the General Assembly of the United Nations;

j. Approving amendments to the Treaty for possible ratification by the Parties to the Treaty;

k. Considering matters of mutual interest pertaining to the Treaty or disarmament in general.

6. FUNCTIONS OF THE CONTROL COUNCIL

The Control Council would have the following functions, among others which might be agreed:

a. Recommending appointment of the Administrator;

b. Adopting rules for implementing the terms of the Treaty;

c. Establishing procedures and standards for the installation and operation of the verification arrangements, and maintaining supervision over such arrangements and the Administrator;

d. Establishing procedures for making available to the Parties to the Treaty data produced by verification arrangements;

e. Considering reports of the Administrator on the progress of disarmament measures and of their verification, and on the installation and operation of the verification arrangements;

f. Recommending to the Conference approval of the budget of the International Disarmament Organization;

g. Requesting the International Court of Justice to give advisory opinions on legal questions concerning the interpretation or application of the Treaty, subject to a general authorization of this power by the General Assembly of the United Nations;

h. Recommending to the Conference approval of certain accessions to the Treaty;

i. Considering matters of mutual interest pertaining to the Treaty or to disarmament in general.

7. FUNCTIONS OF THE ADMINISTRATOR

The Administrator would have the following functions, among others which might be agreed:

a. Administering the installation and operation of the verification arrangements, and serving as Chief Executive Officer of the International Disarmament Organization;

b. Making available to the Parties to the Treaty data produced by the verification arrangements;

c. Preparing the budget of the International Disarmament Organization;

d. Making reports to the Control Council on the progress of disarmament measures and of their verification, and on the installation and operation of the verification arrangements.

8. PRIVILEGES AND IMMUNITIES

The privileges and immunities which the Parties to the Treaty would grant to the International Disarmament Organization and its staff and to the representatives of the Parties to the International Disarmament Organization, and the legal capacity which the International Disarmament Organization should enjoy in the territory of each of the Parties to the Treaty would be specified in an annex to the Treaty.

9. RELATIONS WITH THE UNITED NATIONS AND OTHER
INTERNATIONAL ORGANIZATIONS

a. The International Disarmament Organization, being established within the framework of the United Nations, would conduct its activities in accordance with the purposes and principles of the United Nations. It would maintain close working arrangements with the United Nations, and the Administrator of the International Disarmament Organization would consult with the Secretary-General of the United Nations on matters of mutual interest.

b. The Control Council of the International Disarmament Organization would transmit to the United Nations annual and other reports on the activities of the International Disarmament Organization.

c. Principal organs of the United Nations could make recommendations to the International Disarmament Organization, which would consider them and report to the United Nations on action taken.

NOTE: The above outline does not cover all the possible details or aspects of relationships between the International Disarmament Organization and the United Nations.

*H. Measures to Strengthen Arrangements
for Keeping the Peace*

1. OBLIGATIONS CONCERNING THREAT OR USE OF FORCE

The Parties to the Treaty would undertake obligations to refrain, in their international relations, from the threat or use of force of any type —including nuclear, conventional, chemical or biological means of warfare—contrary to the purposes and principles of the United Nations Charter.

2. RULES OF INTERNATIONAL CONDUCT

a. The Parties to the Treaty would agree to support a study by a subsidiary body of the International Disarmament Organization of the codification and progressive development of rules of international conduct related to disarmament.

b. The Parties to the Treaty would refrain from indirect aggression and subversion. The subsidiary body provided for in subparagraph a. would also study methods of assuring states against indirect aggression or subversion.

3. PEACEFUL SETTLEMENT OF DISPUTES

a. The Parties to the Treaty would utilize all appropriate processes for the peaceful settlement of all disputes which might arise between them and any other state, whether or not a Party to the Treaty, including negotiation, inquiry, mediation, conciliation, arbitration, judicial settlement, resort to regional agencies or arrangements, submission to the Security Council or the General Assembly of the United Nations, or other peaceful means of their choice.

b. The Parties to the Treaty would agree that disputes concerning the interpretation or application of the Treaty which were not settled by negotiation or by the International Disarmament Organization would be subject to referral by any party to the dispute to the International Court of Justice, unless the parties concerned agreed on another mode of settlement.

c. The Parties to the Treaty would agree to support a study under the General Assembly of the United Nations of measures which should be undertaken to make existing arrangements for the peaceful settlement of international disputes, whether legal or political in nature, more effective; and to institute new procedures and arrangements where needed.

4. MAINTENANCE OF INTERNATIONAL PEACE AND SECURITY

The Parties to the Treaty would agree to support measures strengthening the structure, authority, and operation of the United Nations so as to improve its capability to maintain international peace and security.

5. UNITED NATIONS PEACE FORCE

The Parties to the Treaty would undertake to develop arrangements during Stage I for the establishment in Stage II of a United Nations Peace Force. To this end, the Parties to the Treaty would agree on the following measures within the United Nations:

a. Examination of the experience of the United Nations leading to a further strengthening of United Nations forces for keeping the peace;

b. Examination of the feasibility of concluding promptly the agreements envisaged in Article 43 of the United Nations Charter;

c. Conclusion of an agreement for the establishment of a United Nations Peace Force in Stage II, including definitions of its purpose, mission, composition and strength, disposition, command and control, training, logistical support, financing, equipment and armaments.

6. UNITED NATIONS PEACE OBSERVATION CORPS

The Parties to the Treaty would agree to support the establishment within the United Nations of a Peace Observation Corps, staffed with a standing cadre of observers who could be despatched promptly to investigate any situation which might constitute a threat to or a breach of the peace. Elements of the Peace Observation Corps could also be stationed as appropriate in selected areas throughout the world.

I. Transition

1. During the last three months of Stage I, the Control Council would review the situation respecting the following listed circumstances with a view to determining in the light of specified criteria, whether these circumstances existed at the end of Stage I:

a. All undertakings to be carried out in Stage I had been carried out.

b. All preparations required for Stage II had been made; and

c. All militarily significant states had become Parties to the Treaty.

2. Transition from Stage I to Stage II would take place at the end of Stage I or at the end of any periods of extension of Stage I, upon a determination, in the light of specified criteria, by affirmative vote of two-thirds of the members of the Control Council, including at least the United States and the Union of Soviet Socialist Republics, that the foregoing circumstances existed.

3. If, at the end of Stage I, one or more permanent members of the Control Council should declare that the foregoing circumstances did not exist, the agreed period of Stage I would, upon the request of such permanent member or members, be extended by a period or periods totalling no more than three months for the purpose of bringing about the foregoing circumstances.

4. Upon the expiration of such period or periods, the Control Council would again consider whether the foregoing circumstances did in fact exist and would vote upon transition in the manner specified in paragraph 2 above.

STAGE II

Stage II would begin upon the transition from Stage I and would be completed within three years from that date.

During Stage II, the Parties to the Treaty would undertake:

1. To continue all obligations undertaken during Stage I;

2. To reduce further the armaments and armed forces reduced during Stage I and to carry out additional measures of disarmament in the manner outlined below;

3. To ensure that the International Disarmament Organization would have the capacity to verify in the agreed manner the obligations undertaken during Stage II; and

4. To strengthen further the arrangements for keeping the peace through the establishment of a United Nations Peace Force and through the additional measures outlined below.

APPENDIX B

A. *Armaments*

1. REDUCTION OF ARMAMENTS

a. Those Parties to the Treaty which had during Stage I reduced their armaments in agreed categories by thirty per cent would during Stage II further reduce each type of armaments in the categories listed in Section A, subparagraph 1. b of Stage I by fifty per cent of the inventory existing at the end of Stage I.

b. Those Parties to the Treaty which had not been subject to measures for the reduction of armaments during Stage I would submit to the International Disarmament Organization an appropriate declaration respecting the inventories by types, within the categories listed in Stage I of their armaments existing at the beginning of Stage II. Such Parties to the Treaty would during Stage II reduce the inventory of each type of such armaments by sixty-five per cent in order that such Parties would accomplish the same total percentage of reduction by the end of Stage II as would be accomplished by those Parties to the Treaty which had reduced their armaments by thirty per cent in Stage I.

2. ADDITIONAL ARMAMENTS SUBJECT TO REDUCTION

a. The Parties to the Treaty would submit to the International Disarmament Organization a declaration respecting their inventories existing at the beginning of Stage II of the additional types of armaments in the categories listed in subparagraph b. below, and would during Stage II reduce the inventory of each type of such armaments by fifty per cent.

b. All types of armaments within further agreed categories would be subject to reduction in Stage II (the following list of categories is illustrative):

(1) Armed combat aircraft having an empty weight of up to 2,500 kilograms (declarations by types).

(2) Specified types of unarmed military aircraft (declarations by types).

(3) Missiles and free rockets having a range of less than 10 kilometers (declarations by types).

(4) Mortars and rocket launchers having a caliber of less than 100 mm. (declarations by types).

(5) Specified types of unarmoured personnel carriers and transport vehicles (declarations by types).

(6) Combatant ships with standard displacement of 400 tons or greater which had not been included among the armaments listed in Stage

I, and combatant ships with standard displacement of less than 400 tons (declarations by types).

(7) Specified types of non-combatant naval vessels (declarations by types).

(8) Specified types of small arms (declarations by types).

c. Specified categories of ammunition for armaments listed in Stage I, Section A, subparagraph 1. b, and subparagraph b. above would be reduced to levels consistent with the levels of armaments agreed for the end of Stage II.

3. METHOD OF REDUCTION

The foregoing measures would be carried out and would be verified by the International Disarmament Organization in a manner corresponding to that provided for in Stage I, Section A, paragraph 2.

4. LIMITATION ON PRODUCTION OF ARMAMENTS AND ON RELATED ACTIVITIES

a. The Parties to the Treaty would halt the production of armaments in the specified categories except for production, within agreed limits, of parts required for maintenance of the agreed retained armaments.

b. The production of ammunition in specified categories would be reduced to agreed levels consistent with the levels of armaments agreed for the end of Stage II.

c. The Parties to the Treaty would halt development and testing of new types of armaments. The flight testing of existing types of missiles would be limited to agreed annual quotas.

d. In accordance with arrangements which would be set forth in the annex on verification, the International Disarmament Organization would verify the foregoing measures at declared locations and would provide assurance that activities subject to the foregoing measures were not conducted at undeclared locations.

5. ADDITIONAL MEASURES

a. In the light of their examination during Stage I of the means of accomplishing the reduction and eventual elimination of production and stockpiles of chemical and biological weapons of mass destruction, the Parties to the Treaty would undertake the following measures respecting such weapons:

(1) The cessation of all production and field testing of chemical and biological weapons of mass destruction.

(2) The reduction, by agreed categories, of stockpiles of chemical

and biological weapons of mass destruction to levels fifty per cent below those existing at the beginning of Stage II.

(3) The dismantling or conversion to peaceful uses of all facilities engaged in the production or field testing of chemical and biological weapons of mass destruction.

b. The foregoing measures would be carried out in an agreed sequence and through arrangements which would be set forth in an annex to the Treaty.

c. In accordance with arrangements which would be set forth in the annex on verification the International Disarmament Organization would verify the foregoing measures and would provide assurance that retained levels of chemical and biological weapons did not exceed agreed levels and that activities subject to the foregoing limitations were not conducted at undeclared locations.

B. Armed Forces

1. REDUCTION OF ARMED FORCES

a. Those Parties to the Treaty which had been subject to measures providing for reduction of force levels during Stage I would further reduce their force levels on the following basis:

(1) Force levels of the United States of America and the Union of Soviet Socialist Republics would be reduced to levels fifty per cent below the levels agreed for the end of Stage I.

(2) Force levels of other Parties to the Treaty which had been subject to measures providing for the reduction of force levels during Stage I would be further reduced, on the basis of an agreed percentage, below the levels agreed for the end of Stage I to levels which would not in any case exceed the agreed level for the United States of America and the Union of Soviet Socialist Republics at the end of Stage II.

b. Those Parties to the Treaty which had not been subject to measures providing for the reduction of armed forces during Stage I would reduce their force levels to agreed levels consistent with those to be reached by other parties which had reduced their force levels during Stage I as well as Stage II. In no case would such agreed levels exceed the agreed level for the United States of America and the Union of Soviet Socialist Republics at the end of Stage II.

c. Agreed levels of armed forces would include all personnel in the categories set forth in Section B, paragraph 2 of Stage I.

2. METHOD OF REDUCTION

The further reduction of force levels would be carried out and would be verified by the International Disarmament Organization in a manner corresponding to that provided for in Section B, paragraph 3 of Stage I.

3. ADDITIONAL MEASURES

Agreed limitations consistent with retained force levels would be placed on compulsory military training, and on refresher training for reserve forces of the Parties to the Treaty.

C. Nuclear Weapons

1. REDUCTION OF NUCLEAR WEAPONS

In the light of their examination during Stage I of the means of accomplishing the reduction and eventual elimination of nuclear weapons stockpiles, the Parties to the Treaty would undertake to reduce in the following manner remaining nuclear weapons and fissionable materials for use in nuclear weapons:

a. The Parties to the Treaty would submit to the International Disarmament Organization a declaration stating the amounts, types and nature of utilization of all their fissionable materials.

b. The Parties to the Treaty would reduce the amounts and types of fissionable materials declared for use in nuclear weapons to minimum levels on the basis of agreed percentages. The foregoing reduction would be accomplished through the transfer of such materials to purposes other than use in nuclear weapons. The purpose for which such materials would be used would be determined by the state to which the materials belonged, provided that such materials were not used in nuclear weapons.

c. The Parties to the Treaty would destroy the non-nuclear components and assemblies of nuclear weapons from which fissionable materials had been removed to effect the foregoing reduction of fissionable materials for use in nuclear weapons.

d. Production or refabrication of nuclear weapons from any remaining fissionable materials would be subject to agreed limitations.

e. The foregoing measures would be carried out in an agreed sequence and through arrangements which would be set forth in an annex to the Treaty.

f. In accordance with arrangements that would be set forth in the verification annex to the Treaty, the International Disarmament Organization would verify the foregoing measures at declared locations and would provide assurance that activities subject to the foregoing limitations were not conducted at undeclared locations.

2. REGISTRATION OF NUCLEAR WEAPONS FOR VERIFICATION PURPOSES

To facilitate verification during Stage III that no nuclear weapons remained at the disposal of the Parties to the Treaty, those Parties to the Treaty which possessed nuclear weapons would, during the last six months of Stage II, register and serialize their remaining nuclear weapons and would register remaining fissionable materials for use in such weapons. Such registration and serialization would be carried out with the International Disarmament Organization in accordance with procedures which would be set forth in the annex on verification.

D. Military Bases and Facilities

1. REDUCTION OF MILITARY BASES AND FACILITIES

The Parties to the Treaty would dismantle or convert to peaceful uses agreed military bases and facilities, wherever they might be located.

2. METHOD OF REDUCTION

a. The list of military bases and facilities subject to the foregoing measures and the sequence and arrangements for dismantling or converting them to peaceful uses would be set forth in an annex to the Treaty.

b. In accordance with arrangements which would be set forth in the annex on verification, the International Disarmament Organization would verify the foregoing measures.

E. Reduction of the Risk of War

In the light of the examination by the International Commission on Reduction of the Risk of War during Stage I the Parties to the Treaty would undertake such additional arrangements as appeared desirable to promote confidence and reduce the risk of war. The Parties to the Treaty would also consider extending and improving the measures undertaken in Stage I for this purpose. The Commission would remain in existence to examine extensions, improvements or additional measures which might be undertaken during and after Stage II.

F. The International Disarmament Organization

The International Disarmament Organization would be strengthened in the manner necessary to ensure its capacity to verify the measures undertaken in Stage II through an extension of the arrangements based upon the principles set forth in Section G, paragraph 3 of Stage I.

G. Measures To Strengthen Arrangements for Keeping the Peace

1. PEACEFUL SETTLEMENT OF DISPUTES

a. In light of the study of peaceful settlement of disputes conducted during Stage I, the Parties to the Treaty would agree to such additional steps and arrangements as were necessary to assure the just and peaceful settlement of international disputes, whether legal or political in nature.

b. The Parties to the Treaty would undertake to accept without reservation, pursuant to Article 36, paragraph 1 of the Statute of the International Court of Justice, the compulsory jurisdiction of that Court to decide international legal disputes.

2. Rules of International Conduct

a. The Parties to the Treaty would continue their support of the study by the subsidiary body of the International Disarmament Organization initiated in Stage I to study the codification and progressive development of rules of international conduct related to disarmament. The Parties to the Treaty would agree to the establishment of procedures whereby rules recommended by the subsidiary body and approved by the Control Council would be circulated to all Parties to the Treaty and would become effective three months thereafter unless a majority of the Parties to the Treaty signified their disapproval, and whereby the Parties to the Treaty would be bound by rules which had become effective in this way unless, within a period of one year from the effective date, they formally notified the International Disarmament Organization that they did not consider themselves so bound. Using such procedures, the Parties to the Treaty would adopt such rules of international conduct related to disarmament as might be necessary to begin Stage III.

b. In the light of the study of indirect aggression and subversion conducted in Stage I, the Parties to the Treaty would agree to arrangements necessary to assure states against indirect aggression and subversion.

3. United Nations Peace Force

The United Nations Peace Force to be established as the result of the agreement reached during Stage I would come into being within the first year of Stage II and would be progressively strengthened during Stage II.

4. United Nations Peace Observation Corps

The Parties to the Treaty would conclude arrangements for the expansion of the activities of the United Nations Peace Observation Corps.

5. National Legislation

Those Parties to the Treaty which had not already done so would, in accordance with their constitutional processes, enact national legislation in support of the Treaty imposing legal obligations on individuals and organizations under their jurisdiction and providing appropriate penalties for noncompliance.

H. Transition

1. During the last three months of Stage II, the Control Council would review the situation respecting the following listed circumstances with a view to determining, in the light of specified criteria, whether these circumstances existed at the end of Stage II:

a. All undertakings to be carried out in Stage II had been carried out.

b. All preparations required for Stage III had been made; and

c. All states possessing armed forces and armaments had become Parties to the Treaty.

2. Transition from Stage II to Stage III would take place at the end of Stage II or at the end of any periods of extension of Stage II, upon a determination, in the light of specified criteria, by affirmative vote of two-thirds of the members of the Control Council, including at least the United States and the Union of Soviet Socialist Republics, that the foregoing circumstances existed.

3. If, at the end of Stage II, one or more permanent members of the Control Council should declare that the foregoing circumstances did not exist, the agreed period of Stage II would, upon the request of such permanent member or members, be extended by a period or periods totalling no more than three months for the purpose of bringing about the foregoing circumstances.

4. Upon the expiration of such period or periods, the Control Council would again consider whether the foregoing circumstances did in fact exist and would vote upon transition in the manner specified in paragraph 2 above.

STAGE III

Stage III would begin upon the transition from Stage II and would be completed within an agreed period of time as promptly as possible.

During Stage III, the Parties to the Treaty would undertake:

1. To continue all obligations undertaken during Stages I and II;

2. To complete the process of general and complete disarmament in the manner outlined below;

3. To ensure that the International Disarmament Organization would have the capacity to verify in the agreed manner the obligations undertaken during Stage III and of continuing verification subsequent to the completion of Stage III; and

4. To strengthen further the arrangements for keeping the peace during and following the achievement of general and complete disarmament through the additional measures outlined below.

A. Armaments

1. REDUCTION OF ARMAMENTS

Subject to agreed requirements for non-nuclear armaments of agreed types for national forces required to maintain internal order and protect the personal security of citizens, the Parties to the Treaty would eliminate all armaments remaining at their disposal at the end of Stage II.

2. METHOD OF REDUCTION

a. The foregoing measure would be carried out in an agreed sequence and through arrangements that would be set forth in an annex to the Treaty.

b. In accordance with arrangements that would be set forth in the annex on verification, the International Disarmament Organization would verify the foregoing measures and would provide assurance that retained armaments were of the agreed types and did not exceed agreed levels.

3. LIMITATIONS ON PRODUCTION OF ARMAMENTS AND ON RELATED ACTIVITIES

a. Subject to agreed arrangements in support of national forces required to maintain internal order and protect the personal security of citizens and subject to agreed arrangements in support of the United Nations Peace Force, the Parties to the Treaty would halt all applied research, development, production, and testing of armaments and would cause to be dismantled or converted to peaceful uses all facilities for such purposes.

b. The foregoing measures would be carried out in an agreed sequence and through arrangements which would be set forth in an annex to the Treaty.

c. In accordance with arrangements which would be set forth in the annex on verification, the International Disarmament Organization would verify the foregoing measures at declared locations and would provide assurance that activities subject to the foregoing measures were not conducted at undeclared locations.

B. Armed Forces

1. REDUCTION OF ARMED FORCES

To the end that upon completion of Stage II they would have at their disposal only those forces and organizational arrangements necessary for agreed forces to maintain internal order and protect the personal security of citizens and that they would be capable of providing agreed manpower for the United Nations Peace Force, the Parties to the Treaty would complete the reduction of their force levels, disband systems of reserve forces, cause to be disbanded organizational arrangements comprising and supporting their national military establishment, and terminate the employment of civilian personnel associated with the foregoing.

2. METHOD OF REDUCTION

a. The foregoing measures would be carried out in an agreed sequence through arrangements which would be set forth in an annex to the Treaty.

b. In accordance with arrangements which would be set forth in the annex on verification, the International Disarmament Organization would verify the foregoing measures and would provide assurance that the only forces and organizational arrangements retained or subsequently established were those necessary for agreed forces required to maintain internal order and to protect the personal security of citizens and those for providing agreed manpower for the United Nations Peace Force.

3. OTHER LIMITATIONS

The Parties to the Treaty would halt all military conscription and would undertake to annul legislation concerning national military establishments or military service inconsistent with the foregoing measures.

C. Nuclear Weapons

1. REDUCTION OF NUCLEAR WEAPONS

In light of the steps taken in Stages I and II to halt the production of fissionable material for use in nuclear weapons and to reduce nuclear weapons stockpiles, the Parties to the Treaty would eliminate all nuclear weapons remaining at their disposal, would cause to be dismantled or converted to peaceful use all facilities for production of such weapons, and would transfer all materials remaining at their disposal for use in such weapons to purposes other than use in such weapons.

2. METHOD OF REDUCTION

a. The foregoing measures would be carried out in an agreed sequence and through arrangements which would be set forth in an annex to the Treaty.

b. In accordance with arrangements which would be set forth in the annex on verification, the International Disarmament Organization would verify the foregoing measures and would provide assurance that no nuclear weapons or materials for use in such weapons remained at the disposal of the Parties to the Treaty and that no such weapons or materials were produced at undeclared facilities.

[584]

D. Military Bases and Facilities

1. REDUCTION OF MILITARY BASES AND FACILITIES

The Parties to the Treaty would dismantle or convert to peaceful uses the military bases and facilities remaining at their disposal, wherever they might be located, in an agreed sequence except for such agreed bases or facilities within the territory of the Parties to the Treaty for agreed forces required to maintain internal order and protect the personal security of citizens.

2. METHOD OF REDUCTION

a. The list of military bases and facilities subject to the foregoing measures and the sequence and arrangements for dismantling or converting them to peaceful uses during Stage III would be set forth in an annex to the Treaty.

b. In accordance with arrangements which would be set forth in the annex on verification, the International Disarmament Organization would verify the foregoing measures at declared locations and provide assurance that there were no undeclared military bases and facilities.

E. Research and Development of Military Significance

1. REPORTING REQUIREMENT

The Parties to the Treaty would undertake the following measures respecting research and development of military significance subsequent to Stage III:

a. The Parties to the Treaty would report to the International Disarmament Organization any basic scientific discovery and any technological invention having potential military significance.

b. The Control Council would establish such expert study groups as might be required to examine the potential military significance of such discoveries and inventions and, if necessary, to recommend appropriate measures for their control. In the light of such expert study, the Parties to the Treaty would, where necessary, establish agreed arrangements providing for verification by the International Disarmament Organization that such discoveries and inventions were not utilized for military purposes. Such arrangements would become an annex to the Treaty.

c. The Parties to the Treaty would agree to appropriate arrangements for protection of the ownership rights of all discoveries and inventions reported to the International Disarmament Organization in accordance with subparagraph a. above.

2. INTERNATIONAL CO-OPERATION

The Parties to the Treaty would agree to support full international co-operation in all fields of scientific research and development, and to engage in free exchange of scientific and technical information and free interchange of views among scientific and technical personnel.

F. Reduction of the Risk of War

1. IMPROVED MEASURES

In the light of the Stage II examination by the International Commission on Reduction of the Risk of War, the Parties to the Treaty would undertake such extensions and improvements of existing arrangements and such additional arrangements as appeared desirable to promote confidence and reduce the risk of war. The Commission would remain in existence to examine extensions, improvements or additional measures which might be taken during and after Stage III.

2. APPLICATION OF MEASURES TO CONTINUING FORCES

The Parties to the Treaty would apply to national forces required to maintain internal order and protect the personal security of citizens those applicable measures concerning the reduction of the risk of war that had been applied to national armed forces in Stage I and II.

G. International Disarmament Organization

The International Disarmament Organization would be strengthened in the manner necessary to ensure its capacity (1) to verify the measures undertaken in Stage III through an extension of arrangements based upon the principles set forth in Section G, paragraph 3 of Stage I so that by the end of Stage III, when all disarmament measures had been completed, inspection would have been extended to all parts of the territory of Parties to the Treaty; and (2) to provide continuing verification of disarmament after the completion of Stage III.

H. Measures To Strengthen Arrangements
For Keeping the Peace

1. PEACEFUL CHANGE AND SETTLEMENT OF DISPUTES

The Parties to the Treaty would undertake such additional steps and arrangements as were necessary to provide a basis for peaceful change in a disarmed world and to continue the just and peaceful settlement of all international disputes, whether legal or political in nature.

2. RULES OF INTERNATIONAL CONDUCT

The Parties to the Treaty would continue the codification and progressive development of rules of international conduct related to disarmament in the manner provided in Stage II and by any other agreed procedure.

3. UNITED NATIONS PEACE FORCE

The Parties to the Treaty would progressively strengthen the United Nations Peace Force established in Stage II until it had sufficient armed forces and armaments so that no state could challenge it.

I. Completion of Stage III

1. At the end of the time period agreed for Stage III, the Control Council would review the situation with a view to determining whether all undertakings to be carried out in Stage III had been carried out.

2. This determination would be made by affirmative vote of two-thirds of the members of the Control Council, including at least the United States and the Union of Soviet Socialist Republics. If an affirmative determination were made, Stage III would be deemed completed.

3. In the event that one or more of the permanent members of the Control Council should declare that such undertakings had not been carried out, the agreed period of Stage III would, upon the request of such permanent member or members, be extended for a period or periods totalling no more than three months for the purpose of completing any uncompleted undertakings. Upon the expiration of such period or periods, the Control Council would again consider whether such undertakings had been carried out and would vote upon the question in the manner specified in paragraph 2 above.

4. After the completion of Stage III, the obligations undertaken in Stages I, II and III would continue.

GENERAL PROVISIONS APPLICABLE
TO ALL STAGES

1. SUBSEQUENT MODIFICATIONS OR AMENDMENTS OF THE TREATY

The Parties to the Treaty would agree to specific procedures for considering amendments or modifications of the Treaty which were believed desirable by any Party to the Treaty in the light of experience in the early period of implementation of the Treaty. Such procedures would include provision for a conference on revision of the Treaty after a specified period of time.

2. INTERIM AGREEMENT

The Parties to the Treaty would undertake such specific arrangements, including the establishment of a Preparatory Commission, as were necessary between the signing and entry into force of the Treaty to ensure the initiation of Stage I immediately upon the entry into force of the Treaty, and to provide an interim forum for the exchange of views and information on topics relating to the Treaty and to the achievement of a permanent stage of general and complete disarmament in a peaceful world.

3. PARTIES TO THE TREATY, RATIFICATION, ACCESSION
AND ENTRY INTO FORCE OF THE TREATY

a. The Treaty would be open to signature and ratification, or accession by all members of the United Nations or its specialized agencies.

b. Any other state which desired to become a Party to the Treaty could accede to the Treaty with the approval of the Conference on recommendation of the Control Council.

c. The Treaty would come into force when it had been ratified by _____states, including the United States of America, the Union of Soviet Socialist Republics, and an agreed number of the following states:

. . . .

d. In order to assure the achievement of the fundamental purpose of a permanent state of general and complete disarmament in a peaceful world, the Treaty would specify that the accession of certain militarily significant states would be essential for the continued effectiveness of the Treaty or for the coming into force of particular measures or stages.

e. The Parties to the Treaty would undertake to exert every effort to induce other states or authorities to accede to the Treaty.

f. The Treaty would be subject to ratification or acceptance in accordance with constitutional processes.

g. A Depository Government would be agreed upon which would have all of the duties normally incumbent upon a Depository. Alternatively, the United Nations would be the Depository.

4. FINANCE

a. In order to meet the financial obligations of the International Disarmament Organization, the Parties to the Treaty would bear the International Disarmament Organization's expenses as provided in the budget approved by the General Conference and in accordance with a scale of apportionment approved by the General Conference.

b. The General Conference would exercise borrowing powers on behalf of the International Disarmament Organization.

5. AUTHENTIC TEXTS

The text of the Treaty would consist of equally authentic versions in English, French, Russian, Chinese and Spanish.

Appendix C

General Assembly Resolution 1653 (XVI): Declaration on the Prohibition of the Use of Nuclear and Thermonuclear Weapons, November 24, 1961[1]

The General Assembly,

Mindful of its responsibility under the Charter of the United Nations in the maintenance of international peace and security, as well as in the consideration of principles governing disarmament,

Gravely concerned that, while negotiations on disarmament have not so far achieved satisfactory results, the armaments race, particularly in the nuclear and thermo-nuclear fields, has reached a dangerous stage requiring all possible precautionary measures to protect humanity and civilization from the hazard of nuclear and thermo-nuclear catastrophe,

Recalling that the use of weapons of mass destruction, causing unnecessary human suffering, was in the past prohibited, as being contrary to the laws of humanity and to the principles of international law, by international declarations and binding agreements, such as the Declaration of St. Petersburg of 1868,[2] the Declaration of the Brussels Conference of 1874,[3] the Conventions of The Hague Peace Conferences of 1899 and 1907,[4] and the Geneva Protocol of 1925,[5] to which the majority of nations are still parties,

[1] A/RES/1653 (XVI), Nov. 28, 1961. The resolution as a whole was adopted by a vote of 55-20-26:
For: Afghanistan, Albania, Bulgaria, Burma, Byelorussian S.S.R., Cambodia, Cameroun, Central African Republic, Ceylon, Chad, Congo (Brazzaville), Congo (Léopoldville), Cuba, Cyprus, Czechoslovakia, Dahomey, Ethiopia, Gabon, Ghana, Guinea, Hungary, India, Indonesia, Iraq, Ivory Coast, Japan, Jordan, Lebanon, Liberia, Libya, Madagascar, Mali, Mauritania, Mexico, Mongolia, Morocco, Nepal, Niger, Nigeria, Poland, Rumania, Saudi Arabia, Senegal, Sierra Leone, Somalia, Sudan, Syria, Togo, Tunisia, Ukrainian S.S.R., U.S.S.R., U.A.R., Upper Volta, Yemen, Yugoslavia.
Against: Australia, Belgium, Canada, China, Costa Rica, France, Greece, Guatemala, Ireland, Italy, Luxembourg, Netherlands, New Zealand, Nicaragua, Portugal, South Africa, Spain, Turkey, U.K., U.S.
Abstaining: Argentina, Austria, Bolivia, Brazil, Chile, Colombia, Denmark, Ecuador, El Salvador, Finland, Haiti, Honduras, Iceland, Iran, Israel, Malaya, Norway, Pakistan, Panama, Paraguay, Peru, Philippines, Sweden, Thailand, Uruguay, Venezuela.
Rollcall votes were also taken on subpar. (a) of operative par. 1, operative par. 1 as a whole, and operative par. 2. These votes were identical with the final vote, except that Malaya voted in favor of subpar. (a) of operative par. 1 and operative par. 1 as a whole, and Costa Rica abstained; Japan, Mexico, and Ireland abstained on operative par. 2.
[2] *British and Foreign State Papers,* vol. 58, pp. 16-17.
[3] *Ibid.,* vol. 65, pp. 1081, 1110-1111.
[4] William M. Malloy, comp., *Treaties, International Acts, Protocols and Agreements Between the United States of America and Other Powers, 1776-1909,* vol. II, pp. 2042, 2052, 2269, 2285-2286.
[5] Senate Foreign Relations Committee, *Disarmament and Security: A Collection of Documents, 1919-55* (S. Com. print, 84th Cong., 2d sess.), pp. 169-170.

Considering that the use of nuclear and thermo-nuclear weapons would bring about indiscriminate suffering and destruction to mankind and civilization to an even greater extent than the use of those weapons declared by the aforementioned international declarations and agreements to be contrary to the laws of humanity and a crime under international law,

Believing that the use of weapons of mass destruction, such as nuclear and thermo-nuclear weapons, is a direct negation of the high ideals and objectives which the United Nations has been established to achieve through the protection of succeeding generations from the scourge of war and through the preservation and promotion of their cultures,

1. *Declares* that:

(*a*) The use of nuclear and thermo-nuclear weapons is contrary to the spirit, letter and aims of the United Nations and, as such, a direct violation of the Charter of the United Nations;

(*b*) The use of nuclear and thermo-nuclear weapons would exceed even the scope of war and cause indiscriminate suffering and destruction to mankind and civilization and, as such, is contrary to the rules of international law and to the laws of humanity;

(*c*) The use of nuclear and thermo-nuclear weapons is a war directed not against an enemy or enemies alone but also against mankind in general, since the peoples of the world not involved in such a war will be subjected to all the evils generated by the use of such weapons;

(*d*) Any State using nuclear and thermo-nuclear weapons is to be considered as violating the Charter of the United Nations, as acting contrary to the laws of humanity and as committing a crime against mankind and civilization;

2. *Requests* the Secretary-General to consult the Governments of Member States to ascertain their views on the possibility of convening a special conference for signing a convention on the prohibition of the use of nuclear and thermo-nuclear weapons for war purposes and to report on the results of such consultation to the General Assembly at its seventeenth session.

Index

action, vs. thought, 25
Act of Chapultepec, 514
actor perception, self-interest and, 82-83
actors, kinds of, and international law, 116-17; rights and duties of in international war, 129
Adams, John, 168, 556
Adams, John Quincy, 192
Additional Protocol Relative to Non-Intervention, Buenos Aires, 211-12
Adoula, Cyrille, 330
adversary process, legal system and, 136n
Africa, colonial system in, vii, 329, 347-48; Communist China and, 329; Monroe Doctrine for, 328; national identity in, 32; racism in, 23, 42, 289, 313, 333-34, 347-48, 362, 365-66, 445, 529; regional authority in, 328; Sino-Soviet bloc in, 326. *See also* South Africa
Afro-Asian world, polarities in, 103
aggression, atomic bomb and, 408; border control and, 518; cold war and, 442; by Communist China, 442; concept of, vii; covert coercion as, 307; dangers of, 339; and Declaration of Lima, 213; defense against, 37; definitions of, 63, 66, 92-93, 262, 502-03; disarmament and, 441, 452-53, 460, 467-68, 479; discretion in, 506; "indirect," 164, 469-81 (*see also* indirect aggression); intervention as, 226; legal doctrine and, 58-59; objectification of, 33, 506-07; pledges against, 449-51; self-defense and, 225, 290, 408, 502; by Soviet Union, 442, 449; subversion and, 443, 446-47, 452-53; in Vietnam War, 235, 262-64, 268, 294, 321-22
aggressor state, nonintervention and, 162, 167
airspace, legal rights in, 46
air warfare, rules of, 386-87
Alexander, Czar (Russia), 499
Alfaro, Ricardo J., 502n
Algeria, coup in, 227, 324; recognition of, 153
Algerian Provisional Government, 153
Algerian war, cost of, 347
alliances, polarity and, 59
American Society of International Law, 248
American Society of Newspaper Editors, 187
Angola, racism in, 289, 347
Antarctica Treaty, 40
anticolonial war, 145; disarmament and, 476; intervention and, 229
anti-Communist war, 145
anti-incumbent faction, 154
anti-insurgency program, disarmament and, 489

anti-intervention doctrine, 134. *See also* nonintervention
anti-mass-war position, 14
antitrust law enforcement, extraterritorial, 181-83
Apple, R. W., Jr., 296n, 297n
Arab-Israel war, 151, 362, 503
Arbenz (Jacob Arbenz Guzmán), regime of, Guatemala, 175, 185, 216, 327
armed attack, concept of, vii, 287, 290, 293-94, 299, 302
arms races, doom of civilization in, 19. *See also* disarmament
Aron, Raymond, 14n
Ashmore, Harry, 271n, 290n
Asia, colonial system in, vii; zero-sum concept in, 32n. *See also* Southeast Asia
asymmetry, disarmament and, 512; of rights and duties, 54
atomic bomb and bombing, basis for recovery in, 393-94; compared with gas warfare, 392; as "cruel" weapon, 385; disproportionate destruction of values by, 407; as "divine wind," 392n; fireball of, 384; first use of, 426; in Hiroshima and Nagasaki, 371-413; humanitarianism and, 408; illegality of, 389-90; impact on human experience, 20n; and Japanese surrender, 392, 403; legal characteristics of, 375, 389-90, 405; number killed by, 384n; vs. poison gas, 392, 426; psychological impact of in Japan, 14n, 20n; survivors of, 376; of undefended city, 389; world opinion and, 398-99. *See also* nuclear warfare; nuclear weapons
Attorney General, law and, 45
Austin, J. L., 115, 500-01
Austria, Hitler intervention in, 173
authority, centralization of, 139-40; legal system and, 47, 81; among sovereign states, 137; transfer of to supranational body, 112-14, 336, 414-24
awareness, quest for, 90n

Baker, James K., 359n
balance of terror, world order and, 23, 99
ballistic missile, as nuclear weapon, 417-18
Bao Dai, 280n
Barnett, Richard J., 14n, 33n, 100n, 267n, 405n, 423n, 530n
Batista, Juan, 133n, 139, 199, 217, 311, 512
Bator, Victor, 281
Baxter, Richard R., 388n, 400, 407, 409n, 412
Baylor University, 105
Bay of Pigs invasion, 184-223, 228, 239, 305, 327, 473. *See also* Cuban missile crisis

93; of killing, 96; legality and, 78; norm of, 84

rebellion, insurgency and, 120-21; in international law, 117-18

recognition, of belligerent or insurgent state, 136-38; U.S. policy on, 178-81

Red China, *see* Communist China

reform, perspectives on, 8-9; following revolutionary change, 37

regional organizations, 116

regional veto, of political system, 163

Reichenbach, Hans, 86n

Reischauer, Edwin O., 266n

Renaissance, law in, 58

research, in social science, 26

responsibility, national and individual, 66-67

Reston, James, 38n

Reuter, Paul, 159n

revolution, foreign intervention in, 69; reform and, 37; Soviet Union and, 447. *See also* internal war

rhetoric, security and, 29

Rhodesia, racial equality in, 289n; United Nations resolution on, 144

Rhyne, Charles S., 62n

Rice, William G., 267n

rigidity, in international relations, 17-18

Rio Treaty of Reciprocal Assistance, 177, 214, 514

risk, assessing of in nuclear peace, 16

Robertson, Walter, 265n

Roche, John P., 203n

Rock, Vincent, 32n

Röling, B. V. A., 344n, 477n, 498, 504, 511, 514n

Roman Catholic Church, as legal institution, 58

Roman law, 58

Romney, George, 266n

Roosevelt, Franklin D., 172-73, 198, 210

Roosevelt, Theodore, 206

Roosevelt Corollary, to Monroe Doctrine, 170-71, 197

Root, Elihu, 196

Rosenau, James N., 70n, 125n, 132n, 146n, 224n, 292n, 336n, 445n, 484n, 495n

Ross, Alf, 90n, 158n, 160n

Ross, Thomas, 232n, 305n

Rostow, Walt W., 276n

Rougier, Antoine, 109n

roulette, analogy of, 16n, 17n

Rousseau, Charles, 109n, 162n, 548n

Rovere, Richard, 201n

"rule of law," 184-90

Rules of Air Warfare, 386-88

Rules of Land Warfare, 386n, 389, 391, 402n. *See also* Laws of Naval Warfare

Rusk, Dean, 37, 226n, 248-51, 260, 546

Rusk Doctrine, 37, 251

Russell, Bertrand, 267n

Sabbatino controversy, 375

Sadoul, P., 109n

safety, law and, 45

Saigon regime, 230, 232-34; identified with "Vietnamese people," 296; irreversible support of, 251; need for U.S. backing, 309; vs. NLF, 276-77, 317-18 (*see also* National Liberation Front); political status of, 231; oppression by, 299-300; repudiation of Geneva agreement by, 238, 253-54; weakness of, 234. *See also* South Vietnam

St. Petersburg, Declaration of (1868), 65, 91, 391

Salisbury, Harrison E., 293n

San Jose Declaration, 215, 342

Santiago, Declaration of, 215

Sartre, Jean-Paul, 29n, 267n

Saudi Arabia, Yemen crisis and, 307

Scaff, Alan, 489n

Scelle, George, 81

Schachter, Oscar, 387n, 404n

Schelling, Thomas C., 94n, 135n, 417n

Schiffer, Walter, 25n, 60n

Schlei, Norbert A., 91, 408n

Schlesinger, Arthur M., Jr., 228n, 239n

Schurmann, Franz, 269n, 274n

Schwarzenberger, Georg, 65n, 184n, 346n, 388n, 391n, 401n, 405n, 421n

Schwelb, Egon, 387n

Scott, James Brown, 65n, 118n

Scott, Peter Dale, 269n, 274n

SEATO (Southeast Asia Treaty Organization), collective self-defense in, 250-51; disarmament and, 490; State Department Legal Memorandum and, 545-58; and Vietnam "commitment," 249-50, 257-59, 268n, 273n, 304, 308n

security, nuclear "shelters" and, 20-21; mass destruction as means toward, 23; reciprocity and, 54; rhetoric and, 29; and *status quo*, 166; strength and, 19, 24; temporary sense of following major wars, 18-19

security zones, classification of, 312-14

self-defense, aggression and, 225, 290, 408, 502; "armed attack" and, 251; atomic bomb and, 393n, 408; bombing of North Vietnam as, 292n; collective, 237, 240, 250-51; community welfare and, 84; concept of, viii, 76; in Cuban crisis, 204-05; defined, 502-03; force and, 54; identification of, 33; internal wars and, 140; intervention as, 148, 164-65; nuclear weapons and, 422, 427; permissible acts of, 262; in State Department Legal Memorandum, 540-42; in Vietnam War, 234, 237, 241n, 268, 303

self-destruction, through nuclear war, 11n, 427; will to, 20

self-determination, 309; Communism as, 177; impartiality toward, 301; insurgency and, 120; internal wars and, 140; inter-

Other books published for
The Center of International Studies
Princeton University

Gabriel A. Almond, *The Appeals of Communism*
Gabriel A. Almond and James S. Coleman, editors, *The Politics of the Developing Areas*
Gabriel A. Almond and Sidney Verba, *The Civic Culture: Political Attitudes and Democracy in Five Nations*
Richard J. Barnet and Richard A. Falk, *Security in Disarmament*
Henry Bienen, *Tanzania: Party Transformation and Economic Development*
Cyril E. Black and Thomas P. Thornton, editors, *Communism and Revolution: The Strategic Uses of Political Violence*
Robert J. C. Butow, *Tojo and the Coming of the War*
Miriam Camps, *Britain and the European Community, 1955-1963*
Bernard C. Cohen, *The Political Process and Foreign Policy: The Making of the Japanese Peace Settlement*
Bernard C. Cohen, *The Press and Foreign Policy*
Charles De Visscher, *Theory and Reality in Public International Law*, translated by P. E. Corbett
Frederick S. Dunn, *Peace-making and the Settlement with Japan*
Harry Eckstein, *Division and Cohesion in Democracy: a Study of Norway*
Robert Gilpin, Jr., *France in the Age of the Scientific State*
Richard F. Hamilton, *Affluence and the French Worker in the Fourth Republic*
Herman Kahn, *On Thermonuclear War*
W. W. Kaufmann, editor, *Military Policy and National Security*
Klaus Knorr, *On the Uses of Military Power in the Nuclear Age*
Klaus Knorr, *The War Potential of Nations*
Klaus Knorr, editor, *NATO and American Security*
Klaus Knorr and Sidney Verba, editors, *The International System: Theoretical Essays*
Peter Kunstadter, editor, *Southeast Asian Tribes, Minorities, and Nations*
Linda B. Miller, *World Order and Local Disorder*
Sidney J. Ploss, *Conflict and Decision-making in Soviet Russia*
Lucian W. Pye, *Guerrilla Communism in Malaya*
James N. Rosenau, editor, *International Aspects of Civil Strife*
James N. Rosenau, *National Leadership and Foreign Policy: A Case Study in the Mobilization of Public Support*
Rolf Sannwald and Jacques Stohler, *Economic Integration: Theoretical Assumptions and Consequences of European Unification.* Translated by Herman F. Karreman
Richard L. Sklar, *Nigerian Political Parties: Power in an Emergent African Nation*
Glenn H. Snyder, *Deterrence and Defense*
Harold and Margaret Sprout, *The Ecological Perspective on Human Affairs, With Special Reference to International Politics*
Thomas P. Thornton, *The Third World in Soviet Perspective: Studies by Soviet Writers on the Developing Areas*
Richard H. Ullman, *Britain and the Russian Civil War*
Sidney Verba, *Small Groups and Political Behavior: A Study of Leadership*
Karl von Vorys, *Political Development in Pakistan*
Myron Weiner, *Party Politics in India*
E. Victor Wolfenstein, *The Revolutionary Personality: Lenin, Trotsky, Gandhi*
Oran R. Young, *The Intermediaries: Third Parties in International Crises*